Enduring Voices

Document Sets to Accompany

The Enduring Vision

A History of the American People

Fourth Edition

Volume One: To 1877

by

Paul S. Boyer • Clifford E. Clark, Jr. • Joseph F. Kett
Neal Salisbury • Harvard Sitkoff • Nancy Woloch

James J. Lorence

University of Wisconsin
Marathon County

Houghton Mifflin Company
Boston   New York

Sponsoring Editor: Jeffrey Greene
Editorial Assistant: Shoma Aditya
Editorial Assistant: Heather Hubbard
Associate Production/Design Coordinator: Jodi O'Rourke
Senior Cover Design Coordinator: Deborah Azerrad Savona
Senior Manufacturing Coordinator: Marie Barnes
Senior Marketing Manager: Sandra McGuire
Cover Design: Sarah Melhado Bishins
Cover Image: John Lewis, Krimmel, Night Life in Philadelphia: an Oyster Barrow in Front of the
          Chestnut Street Theater (1793). The Metropolitan Museum of Art, Rogers Fund, 1942.

Printed in the U.S.A.

ISBN-13: 978-0-395-96084-4   ISBN-10: 0-395-96084-3

15 16 17 18 19 20-HES-09 08 07

PREFACE

Enduring Voices: Document Sets to Accompany The Enduring Vision: A History of the American People, Fourth Edition, has been prepared with the objectives of exploiting students' latent interest in history, stimulating critical thinking, and immersing students in the historian's process—evaluating the kinds of evidence from which the historian builds interpretations of past events and developments. By plunging into documentary analysis, students not only become familiar with the tools of the historian's trade but experience firsthand the excitement and satisfaction of "doing history" and of unlocking the "secrets" of the past in a systematic way.

Yet using documents can be complicated, and the history instructor must instill in students a healthy skepticism. As students engage in the analytical process, they will discover on their own, often with some unease, that it is an oversimplification to "let the documents speak for themselves." They will realize that multiple readings of the evidence are frequently possible. An equally important goal in using *Enduring Voices,* then, becomes sensitizing students to interpretive complexity—making them comfortable with uncertainty.

For every chapter of *The Enduring Vision, Enduring Voices* presents several sets of documents, each built around a "problem" closely related to a major theme in the corresponding textbook chapter. In all, over four hundred individual pieces of historical evidence—comprising traditional forms such as letters, petitions, speech excerpts, and testimony, as well as nontraditional evidence like patent applications and product advertisements—are represented in the two-volume *Enduring Voices* anthology. Each Document Set is introduced by a brief essay establishing background and textual linkage and spotlighting a central analytical question, and by a series of questions for students' consideration. The instructor is free to photocopy any and all Document Sets for classroom use with *The Enduring Vision;* Houghton Mifflin has obtained all the necessary permissions.

Other relevant aspects of the format and objectives of *Enduring Voices* include the following.

- *Each Document Set focuses on a limited body of evidence.* Instructors will want to select the specific issues that will be emphasized in their own classroom discussions.

- *Each set also provides maximum opportunity for instructors to set students free to make their own sense of the evidence.* It is assumed that instructors will encourage students to think creatively—to exercise historical imagination by taking the final intuitive leap. By engaging in the historian's process, the student should develop the ability to frame and test hypotheses and to arrive at informed conclusions.

- *Part and parcel of this process is the matter of defining basic terms such as* primary source *and* document. By incorporating nontraditional evidence, *Enduring Voices* aims to stimulate students to consider the nature of documentation itself. A broadened definition of admissible evidence should result.

In the last analysis, the Document Sets are based on the belief that history can be a discipline second to none in its potential appeal to students. It is my hope that *Enduring Voices* will demonstrate how stimulating and rewarding is the pursuit of historical knowledge. By providing small windows into the past, these documents confirm our oneness with the people of generations long gone. As students use the historical record to understand their world, they will themselves become part of a new and distinguished group, the society of educated people. Exposure to the historian's craft can ease the way.

ACKNOWLEDGMENTS

A comprehensive project such as *Enduring Voices: Document Sets to Accompany the Enduring Vision, Fourth Edition,* must necessarily reflect the ideas and insights of teacher-scholars throughout the historical profession. The preparation of this collection has been especially influenced by the creative work of William Bruce Wheeler, Susan D. Becker, James West Davidson, Mark Hamilton Lytle, Robert Kelley, John and Selma Appel, Dimitri Lazo, John E. O'Connor, Stanley Mallach, Verna Posever Curtis, and the editors of *Restoring Women to History: Materials for US I, II* (1984). Moreover, these materials are the product of countless discussions of teaching techniques with my colleagues in the University of Wisconsin's Department of History. Particular acknowledgment is due Professor Donald Dennis of the University of Wisconsin Center—Fond du Lac for his work on the first drafts of several early chapters. In preparing the revisions, I have benefited from the advice of Paul S. Boyer, Clifford E. Clark, Jr., Joseph F. Kett, Neal Salisbury, Harvard Sitkoff, and Nancy Woloch, the authors of *The Enduring Vision;* and from Michael L. Krenn and John L. Rector. The editors at D. C. Heath have eased the task of manuscript preparation. I am especially grateful to Pat Wakeley, Sylvia Mallory, Shoma Aditya, and Jeffrey Greene for their criticism and encouragement. Andrew Mergendahl provided cheerful assistance with source checking and other matters of detail. Any errors in judgment and execution are mine.

James J. Lorence

CONTENTS

CHAPTER 1

DOCUMENT SET 1
The World of Native Americans: Oral Tradition

The first chapter of your textbook provides a sweeping introduction to the diversity of Native American cultures that developed on the American continent long before the arrival of Europeans. The purpose of this document set is to highlight the variety and richness of those pre-Columbian societies, especially by analyzing the Native Americans' own accounts of the ways in which their world and societies came into being.

The most important channel through which we can access these Native American beliefs is the recollections handed down through the oral tradition. Story-telling plays an important role in all nonliterate societies, essential to the preservation of tribal history, identity, and culture. Although the materials in this document set were recorded after the arrival of Europeans, they reflect traditional native cultures that survived nearly intact long after the Europeans came to North America.

Note that these accounts were often transmitted through European chronicles. As a result, they were sometimes altered by those who recorded them, which means that Native American ideas and narratives have not always been preserved in their original form. Nonetheless, oral tradition remains one of the most effective tools available to historians and anthropologists seeking to understand Native American belief systems.

The documents offer insight into the various ways in which Native Americans, especially those in the eastern part of the continent, understood their world and their tribal histories. You can use these accounts to form your own opinion of the cultures that preceded what is inappropriately thought of as the "discovery" of a New World. Be aware of the highly developed cultures that were firmly established long before Columbus landed on San Salvador.

As you think about the Native American depictions of their world and its origins, watch for evidence that the traditional accounts may have been influenced by Europeans. Compare those accounts with the observations of Europeans who were trying to describe the Native American belief system. Think about the cultural attitudes and values that surface in the European version of traditional American religion. These Native American creation myths are reminders that most peoples and societies share a felt need to account for human existence, understand the world, and cope with social evolution. As you review the documents, look for those ideas and values which separated Europeans and Native Americans, as well as those which may have held potential for drawing them together.

Questions for Analysis

1. What was the most remarkable achievement of the Iroquois who created the confederation? How do the sources differ in their depiction of the confederation's origins? How does the oral tradition shed light on the background for the consolidation of Iroquois unity? What cultural values are evident in the legend of the confederation's genesis?

2. Search the documents for common themes in the Native American belief systems. What united the tribal groups?

3. What evidence do you find in the oral tradition that European culture influenced Native American beliefs about the creation?

4. What do the European accounts of the Native American creation myths and other religious ideas reveal about the cultural assumptions made by non-Indians? How did these European values and suppositions influence the future direction of cross-cultural relations?

5. What role did nature and natural phenomena play in Native American beliefs? How would you account for the presence of these factors in their world-view?

6. From your analysis of the documents, what would you say are the strengths and weaknesses of the oral tradition as historical source material? What can be learned about pre-Columbian life and thought among indigenous peoples from a close reading of the materials available?

1. The Indians of New Netherlands Account for the Creation, ca. 1650s

From the young Indians who frequent our settlements, and continue somewhat wild, we cannot derive any certain information of their belief on these matters; but we must have recourse to their aged men of understanding when we desire to know their belief on these important subjects.

It sometimes happens when we enter into a curious discourse with them that they ask us our opinions on the origin of man, and how they came to this country; and when we inform them in broken language of the creation of Adam, they cannot believe, or will not understand relative to their people and the negroes, on account of their great difference and the inequality of colour. According to their opinion the world was not created as described in the first and second chapters of the book of Genesis; but they say the world was before all mountains, men, and animals; that God then was with that beautiful woman, who now is with him, without knowing when or from whence they came; then was all water, or the water covered all; and they add that if there had been any eyes in being, there was nothing but water to be seen, and nothing else visible in every direction.

It happened at this period, they say, that the before mentioned beautiful woman or goddess gradually descended from heaven, even into the water, gross or corpulent like a woman who apparently would bring forth more than one child. Having gradually settled into the water, she did not go under it; but immediately at the place where she descended some land appeared under her, whereon she remained sitting. This land increased, and in time became greater and dry around the place where she sat; like one who is placed on a bar, whereon the water is three or four feet deep, which by the ebbing of the tide becomes dry land.

Thus they say and mean to be understood, it occurred with this descended goddess. And that the land became of greater extent around her, until its extent was unbounded to the sight, when vegetation appeared; and in time fruitful and unfruitful trees began to grow throughout the world as it now appears. Whether the world of which you speak originated at this time, we cannot say.

At this period of time, when those things had taken place and were accomplished, this great person was overtaken in labour and brought forth three distinct and different creatures. The first was like a deer as those now are, the second like a bear, and the third like a wolf in every respect. The woman suckled those animals to maturity, and remained a considerable time upon the earth, cohabiting with those several animals, and bringing forth at every birth more than one of a different species and appearance; from which have originated and proceeded all the human beings, animals and creatures, of every description and species, as the same now are and appear; being propagated according to nature, each in their peculiar order, as the same are in succession continued.

When all those subjects were brought to a state of perfection, and could continue, this common mother rejoiced greatly and ascended up to heaven, where she will continue to remain and dwell, enjoying pleasure, and subsist in goodness and love, which her upper Lord will afford her, for which she is particularly desirous, and God also loves her supremely above all things.

Here on the earth, in the meanwhile, the human species, and the animals after their kind, have multiplied and produced so many different creatures, and increased exceedingly, which every other thing that was created also does, as the same at present is seen. Therefore it is at this time that all mankind, wherever they be, are always born with the nature of one or the other of the aforesaid animals. They are timid and innocent like the deer; they are brave, revengeful, and just of hand, like the bear; or they are deceitful and bloodthirsty, like the wolves. Although their dispositions are apparently somewhat changed, this they attribute to the subtlety of men, who know how to conceal their wicked propensities.

This, they say, is all they have learned from their fathers on the subject of the Creation, which has been handed down to them, and which they believe to be true.

2. The Origins of Ottawa Society, as Related by Nicolas Perrot, ca. 1720

After the creation of the earth, all the other animals withdrew into the places which each kind found most suitable for obtaining therein their pasture or their prey. When the first ones died, the Great Hare caused the birth of man from their corpses, as also from those of the fishes which were found along the shores of the rivers which he had formed in creating the land. Accordingly, some of the savages derive their origin from a bear, others from a moose, and others similarly from various kinds of animals; and before they had intercourse with the Europeans they firmly believed this, persuaded that they had their being from those kinds of creatures whose origin was as above explained. Even today [ca. 1720] that notion passes among them for undoubted truth, and if there are any of them at this time who are weaned from believing this dream, it has been only by dint of laughing at them for so ridiculous a belief. You will hear them say that their villages each bear the name of the animal which has given its people their being— as that of the crane, or the bear, or of other animals. They imagine that they were created by other divinities than those which we recognize, because we have many inventions which they do not possess, as the art of writing, shooting with a gun, making gunpowder, muskets, and other things which are used by [civilized] mankind.

Those first men who formed the human race, being scattered in different parts of the land, found out that they had minds. They beheld here and there buffaloes, elks, and deer, all kinds of birds and animals, and many rivers abounding in fish. These first men, I say, whom hunger had weakened, inspired by the Great Hare with an intuitive idea, broke off a branch from a small tree, made a cord with the fibers of the nettle, scraped the bark from a piece of a bough with a sharp stone, and armed its end with another sharp stone, to serve them as an arrow; and thus they formed a bow [and arrows] with which they killed small birds. After that, they made *viretons* [crossbow arrows], in order to attack the large beasts; they skinned these, and tried to eat the flesh. But as they found only the fat savory, they tried to make fire, in order to cook their meat; and, trying to get it, they took for that purpose hard wood, but without success; and [finally] they used softer wood, which yielded them fire. The skins of the animals served for their covering. As hunting is not practicable in the winter on account of the deep snows, they invented a sort of racket [snowshoe], in order to walk on this with more ease; and they constructed canoes, in order to enable them to cross the rivers.

They relate also that these men, formed as I have told, while hunting found the footprints of an enormously tall man, followed by another that was smaller. They went on into his territory, following up this trail very heedfully, and saw in the distance a large cabin; when they reached it, they were astonished at seeing there the feet and legs of a man so tall that they could not descry his head; that inspired terror in them, and constrained them to retreat. This great colossus, having wakened, cast his eyes on a freshly-made track, and this induced him to step toward it; he immediately saw the man who had discovered him, whom fear had driven to hide himself in a thicket, where he was trembling with dread. The giant said to him, "My son, why art thou afraid? Reassure thyself; I am the Great Hare, he who has caused thee and many others to be born from the dead bodies of various animals. Now I will give thee a companion." Here are the words that he used in giving the man a wife: "Thou, man," said he, "shalt hunt, and make canoes, and do all things that a man must do; and thou, woman, shalt do the cooking for thy husband, make his shoes, dress the skins of animals, sew, and perform all the tasks that are proper for a woman." Such is the belief of these peoples in regard to the creation of man; it is based only upon the most ridiculous and extravagant notions—to which, however, they give credence as if they were incontestable truths, although shame hinders them from making these stories known.

3. The Dekanawida Myth and the Achievement of Iroquois Unity, ca. Sixteenth Century

North of the beautiful lake [Ontario] in the land of the Crooked Tongues, was a long winding bay and at a certain spot was the Huron town, Ka-ha-nah-yenh. Near by was the great hill, Ti-ro-nat-ha-ra-da-donh. In the village lived a good woman who had a virgin daughter. Now strangely this virgin conceived and her mother knew that she was about to bear a child. The daughter about this time went into a long sleep and dreamed that her child should be a son whom she should name Dekanawida. The messenger in the dream told her that he should become a great man and that he should go among the Flint people to live and that he should also go to the Many Hill Nation. . . .

The Ongwe-oweh had fought long and bravely. So long had they fought that they became lustful for war and many times Endeka-Gakwa, the Sun, came out of the east to find them fighting. It was thus because the Ongwe-oweh were so successful that they said the Sun loved war and gave them power.

All the Ongwe-oweh fought other nations sometimes together and sometimes singly and, ah-gi! ofttimes they fought among themselves. The nation of the Flint had little sympathy for the Nation of the Great Hill, and sometimes they raided one another's settlements. Thus did brothers and Ongwe-oweh fight. The nation of the Sunken Pole fought the Nation of the Flint and hated them, and the Nation of the Sunken Pole was Ongwe.

Because of bitter jealousy and love of bloodshed sometimes towns would send their young men against the young men of another town to practise them in fighting. . . .

In those same days the Onondagas had no peace. A man's life was valued as nothing. For any slight offence a man or woman was killed by his enemy and in this manner feuds started between families and clans. At night none dared leave their doorways lest they be struck down by an enemy's war club. Such was the condition when there was no Great Law.

South of the Onondaga town lived an evil-minded man. His lodge was in a swale and his nest was made of bulrushes. His body was distorted by seven crooks and his long tangled locks were adorned by writhing living serpents. Moreover, this monster was a devourer of raw meat, even of human flesh. He was also a master of wizardry and by his magic he destroyed men but he could not be destroyed. Adodarhoh was the name of the evil man.

Notwithstanding the evil character of Adodarhoh the people of Onondaga, the Nation of Many Hills, obeyed his commands. . . .

Dekanawida requested some of the Mohawk chiefs to call a council, so messengers were sent out among the people and the council was convened.

Dekanawida said, "I, with my co-worker, have a desire to now report what we have done on five successive midsummer days, of five successive years. We have obtained the consent of five nations. These are the Mohawks, the Oneidas, the Onondagas, the Cayugas and the Senecas. Our desire is to form a compact for a union of our nations. Our next step is to seek out Adodarhoh. It is he who has always set at naught all plans for the establishment of the Great Peace. We must seek his fire and look for his smoke." . . .

The council heard the message and decided to go to Onondaga at midsummer.

Then Dekanawida taught the people the Hymn of Peace and the other songs. He stood before the door of the longhouse and walked before it singing the new songs. Many came and learned them so that many were strong by the magic of them when it was time to carry the Great Peace to Onondaga.

When the time had come, Dekanawida summoned the chiefs and people together and chose one man to sing the songs before Adodarhoh. Soon then this singer led the company through the forest and he preceded all, singing the Peace songs as he walked. . . .

Then Dekanawida himself sang and walked before the door of Adodarhoh's house. When he finished his song he walked toward Adodarhoh and held out his hand to rub it on his body and to know its inherent strength and life. Then Adodarhoh was made straight and his mind became healthy.

When Adodarhoh was made strong in rightful powers and his body had been healed, Dekanawida addressed the three nations. He said, "We have now overcome a great obstacle. It has long stood in the way of peace. The mind of Adodarhoh is now made right and his crooked parts are made straight. Now indeed may we establish the Great Peace.

"Before we do firmly establish our union each nation must appoint a certain number of its wisest and purest men who shall be rulers, Rodiyaner. They shall be the advisers of the people and make the new rules that may be needful. These men shall be selected and confirmed by their female relations in whose lines the titles shall be hereditary. When these are named they shall be crowned, emblematically, with deer antlers." . . .

Each chief then delivered to Dekanawida a string of lake shell wampum a span in length as a pledge of truth.

Dekanawida then said: "Now, today in the presence of this great multitude I disrobe you and you are not now covered by your old names. I now give you names much greater." Then calling each chief to him he said: "I now place antlers on your head as an emblem of your power. Your old garments are torn off and better robes are given you. Now you are Rodiyaner, each of you. You will receive many scratches and the thickness of your skins shall be seven spans. You must be patient and henceforth work in unity. Never consider your own interests but work to benefit the people and for the generations not yet born. You have pledged yourselves to govern yourselves by the laws of the Great Peace. All your authority shall come from it." . . .

Then did Dekanawida repeat all the rules which he with Ayonhwatha had devised for the establishment of the Great Peace.

Then in the councils of all the Five Nations he repeated them and the Confederacy was established.

4. The Foundation of the Iroquois Confederacy, 1570, as Recounted in the Tuscarora Oral Tradition

When another day had expired, the council again met. Hiawatha entered the assembly with even more than ordinary attention, and every eye was fixed upon him, when he began to address the council in the following words:

"Friends and Brothers:—You being members of many tribes, you have come from a great distance; the voice of war has aroused you up; you are afraid [for] your homes, your wives and your children; you trembled for your safety. Believe me, I am with you. My heart beats with your hearts. We are one. We have one common object. We come to promote our common interest, and to determine how this can be best done.

"To oppose those hordes of northern tribes, singly and alone, would prove certain destruction. We can make no progress in that way. We must unite ourselves into one common band of brothers. We must have but one voice. Many voices makes confusion. We must have one fire, one pipe and one war club. This will give us strength. If our warriors are united they can defeat the enemy and drive them from our land; if we do this, we are safe.

"Onondaga, you are the people sitting under the shadow of the *Great Tree,* whose branches spread far and wide, and whose roots sink deep into the earth. You shall be the first nation, because you are warlike and mighty.

"Oneida, and you, the people who recline your bodies against the *Everlasting Stone,* that cannot be moved, shall be the second nation, because you always give good counsel.

"Seneca, and you, the people who have your habitation at the foot of the *Great Mountain,* and are overshadowed by its crags, shall be the third nation, because you are all greatly gifted in speech.

"Cayuga, you, whose dwelling is in the *Dark Forest,* and whose home is everywhere, shall be the fourth nation, because of your superior cunning in hunting.

"Mohawk, and you, the people who live in the open country, and possess much wisdom, shall be the fifth nation, because you understand better the art of raising corn and beans and making cabins.

"You five great and powerful nations, with your tribes, must unite and have one common interest, and no foe shall disturb or subdue you.

"And you of the different nations of the south, and you of the west, may place yourselves under our protection, and we will protect you. We earnestly desire the alliance and friendship of you all. . . .

"If we unite in one band the Great Spirit will smile upon us, and we shall be free, prosperous and happy; but if we shall remain as we are we shall incur his displeasure. We shall be enslaved, and perhaps annihilated forever.

"Brothers, these are the words of Hiawatha. Let them sink deep into your hearts. I have done."

A deep and impressive silence followed the delivery of this speech. On the following day the council again assembled to act on it. High wisdom recommended this deliberation.

The union of the tribes into one confederacy was discussed and unanimously adopted. To denote the character and intimacy of the union they employed the figure of a single council-house, or lodge, whose boundaries be co-extensive with their territories. Hence the name of Ako-no-shu-ne, who were called the Iroquois. . . .

Hiawatha, the guardian and founder of the league, having now accomplished the will of the Great Spirit, immediately prepared to make his final departure. Before the great council, which had adopted his advice just before dispersing, he arose, with a dignified air, and addressed them in the following manner:

"Friends and Brothers:—I have now fulfilled my mission here below; I have furnished you seeds and grains for your gardens; I have removed obstructions from your waters, and made the forest habitable by teaching you how to expel its monsters; I have given you fishing places and hunting grounds; I have instructed you in the making and using of war implements; I have taught you how to cultivate corn, and many other arts and gifts. I have been allowed by the Great Spirit to communicate to you. Last of all, I have aided you to form a league of friendship and union. If you preserve this, and admit no foreign element of power by the admission of other nations, you will always be free, numerous and happy. If other tribes and nations are admitted to your councils, they will sow the seed of jealousy and discord, and you will become few, feeble and enslaved.

"Friends and brothers, these are the last words you will hear from the lips of Hiawatha. The Great Creator of our bodies calls me to go; I have patiently awaited his summons; I am ready to go. Farewell."

As the voice of the wise man ceased, sweet strains of music from the air burst on the ears of the multitude. The whole sky appeared to be filled with melody; and while all eyes were directed to catch glimpses of the sights, and enjoy strains of the celestial music that filled the sky, Hiawatha was seen, seated in his snow-white canoe, amid the air, *rising, rising* with every choral chant that burst out. As he rose the sound of the music became more soft and faint, until he vanished.

Chapter 1: Document Set 1 References

1. The Indians of New Netherlands Account for the Creation, ca. 1650s
   Adriaen Van der Donck, *A Description of the New Netherlands*, Thomas F. O'Donnell, ed. (Syracuse, 1968), pp. 102–109.

2. The Origins of Ottawa Society, as Related by Nicolas Perrot, ca. 1720
   Nicolas Perrot, in Emma Helen Blair, ed. and trans., *The Indian Tribes of the Upper Mississippi Valley and Region of the Great Lakes* (Cleveland: The Arthur H. Clark Co., 1911), Vol. 1, pp. 37–40.

3. The Dekanawida Myth and the Achievement of Iroquois Unity, ca. Sixteenth Century
   Arthur C. Parker, "The Constitution of the Five Nations," *New York State Museum Bulletin*, Vol. 184 (1916), pp. 14, 16–17, 26, 27, 28–29.

4. The Foundation of the Iroquois Confederacy, 1570, as Recounted in the Tuscarora Oral Tradition
   Chief Elias Johnson, *Legends, Myths and Laws of the Iroquois, or Six Nations, and History of the Tuscarora Indians* (Lockport: Union Printing and Publishing Company, 1881), pp. 50–53.

CHAPTER 1

Native American Life: European Observations on Social Institutions and Ecological Change

The textbook's discussion of "family and community" in Native American societies reveals a clear division of labor along gender lines, one which met the needs of the cultures that produced it. However, the variety of roles assumed by women in Indian communities makes it difficult to generalize about the character of family relations. Despite the complexity of the Indians' social, economic, and political institutions, European observers often arrived at firm (and sometimes erroneous) conclusions about domestic relations among native peoples. The following documents examine selected aspects of the Native American community, with emphasis on the sexual division of labor and the ecological change that occurred as a result of European penetration.

As you review these materials, focus on evidence of ethnocentrism or bias in the European accounts of Native American life and institutions. Your task is to identify those distortions and determine why European observers often depicted indigenous peoples in a negative light. By carefully analyzing the documents and considering their authors' backgrounds, you should be able to evaluate these misrepresentations and explain why they appeared.

Your analysis of the documents should also take into consideration the fact that the earliest European explorers, missionaries, and settlers were able to observe the Native Americans in something close to their natural state. Because of their intense curiosity about the Indian way of life, these observers often recorded detailed descriptions of what they saw. Your job is to separate truth from the sometimes colored European perception of reality. It will soon become clear to you that the historical commentaries often contradict one another. You must approach them with objectivity to determine why this disparity existed.

Although European analyses of Indian culture vary, they tend to agree on the long-term effect of European encroachment on Native American society. They are also fairly consistent in describing the impact of the human element on the ecological balance that had prevailed in the pre-Columbian era. Most observers concluded that this balance was profoundly disrupted by the colonizers' acquisitiveness and preoccupation with economic development. Search the documents for evidence of these changes in the environment. Can you discern the European attitude toward these alterations?

In sum, your analysis should focus on European perceptions of an unfamiliar way of life and on the impact of expansion (especially British) on the indigenous peoples of America and their environment. Search for an explanation for these perceptions and assess the ultimate outcomes.

Questions for Analysis

1. In what ways did the backgrounds of European commentators influence their observations of the Native American way of life? How did cultural biases affect their objectivity? To what extent does the presence of bias limit or condition the value of these accounts as historical evidence?

2. How would you account for the European observers' conclusions with regard to the sexual division of labor within the Indian family? What assumptions did these commentators make with regard to the impact of Native American work practices on women? Were these assumptions valid? By what standards?

3. One common assumption made by Europeans was that Native American men were lazy. When the commentators observed Indian life and work patterns, what impressed them about male roles? What was the relationship between male occupations and the culture of which they were a part?

4. What elements in the European way of life were threatening to Native Americans? In the cultural exchange between Indians and whites, which party derived the greater benefit? Explain.

5. In what ways was the Indian way of life adapted to the natural environment? What do the documents reveal about the ecological impact of European encroachment? How was the ecological balance affected by European expansion? How did this disruption influence the human component of the ecologic system?

6. What light do the documents shed on the roles of Indian women outside the family and the economy? What is your assessment of female power in Iroquois society and civil government? How was power exercised?

1. Jesuit Observations on the "Enslavement" of Native American Women, 1633, 1710

[1633]

To obtain the necessaries of life they [the Indians of Acadia] endure cold and hunger in an extraordinary manner. During eight or ten days, if the necessity is imposed on them, they will follow the chase in fasting, and they hunt with the greatest ardor when the snow is deepest and the cold most severe. And yet these same Savages, the offspring, so to speak, of Boreas [The North Wind] and the ice, when once they have returned with their booty and installed themselves in their tents, become indolent and unwilling to perform any labor whatever, imposing this entirely upon the women. The latter, besides the onerous rôle of bearing and rearing the children, also transport the game from the place where it has fallen; they are the hewers of wood and drawers of water; they make and repair the household utensils; they prepare food; they skin the game and prepare the hides like fullers; they sew garments; they catch fish and gather shellfish for food; often they even hunt; they make the canoes, that is, skiffs of marvelous rapidity, out of bark; they set up the tents wherever and whenever they stop for the night—in short, the men concern themselves with nothing but the more laborious hunting and the waging of war. For this reason almost every one has several wives, and especially the Sagamores, since they cannot maintain their power and keep up the number of their dependents unless they have not only many children to inspire fear or conciliate favor, but also many slaves to perform patiently the menial tasks of every sort that are necessary. For their wives are regarded and treated as slaves.

[1710]

. . . Now, if you inquire concerning the customs and character of this people [Canadian Indians in general], I will reply that a part of them are nomads, wandering during the winter in the woods, whither the hope of better hunting calls them—in the summer, on the shores of the rivers, where they easily obtain their food by fishing; while others inhabit villages. They construct their huts by fixing poles in the ground; they cover the sides with bark, the roofs with hides, moss and branches. In the middle of the hut is the hearth, from which the smoke escapes through an opening at the peak of the roof. As the smoke passes out with difficulty, it usually fills the whole hut, so that strangers compelled to live in these cabins suffer injury and weakening of the eyes; the savages, a coarse race, and accustomed to these discomforts, ridicule this. The care of household affairs, and whatever work there may be in the family, are placed upon the women. They build and repair the wigwams, carry water and wood, and prepare the food; their duties and position are those of slaves, laborers and beasts of burden. The pursuits of hunting and war belong to the men. Thence arise the isolation and numerical weakness of the race. For the women, although naturally prolific, cannot, on account of their occupation in these labors, either bring forth fully-developed offspring, or properly nourish them after they have been brought forth; therefore they either suffer abortion, or forsake their newborn children, while engaged in carrying water, procuring wood and other tasks, so that scarcely one infant in thirty survives until youth. To this there is added their ignorance of medicine, because of which they seldom recover from illnesses which are at all severe.

2. Father Pierre de Charlevoix Describes the Female Role in Iroquois Governance, 1721

In the northern parts, and wherever the Algonquin tongue prevails, the dignity of chief is elective; and the whole ceremony of election and installation consists in some feasts, accompanied with dances and songs: the chief elect likewise never fails to make the panegyrick of his predecessor, and to invoke his genius. Amongst the Hurons, where this dignity is hereditary, the succession is continued through the women, so that at the death of a chief, it is not his own, but his sister's son who succeeds him; or, in default of which, his nearest relation in the female line. When the whole branch happens to be extinct, the noblest matron of the tribe or in the nation chuses the person she approves of most, and declares him chief. The person who is to govern must be come to years of maturity; and when the hereditary chief is not as yet arrived at this period, they appoint a regent, who has all the authority, but which he holds in name of the minor. These chiefs generally have no great marks of outward respect paid them, and if they are never disobeyed, it is because they know how to set bounds to their authority. It is true that they request or propose, rather than command; and never exceed the boundaries of that small share of authority with which they are vested. Thus it is properly reason which governs, and the government has so much the more influence, as obedience is founded in liberty; and that they are free from any apprehension of its degenerating into tyranny.

Nay more, each family has a right to chuse a counsellor of its own, and an assistant to the chief, who is to watch for their interest; and without whose consent the chief can undertake nothing. These counsellors are, above all things, to have an eye to the public treasury; and it is properly they who determine the uses it is to be put to. They are invested with this character in a general council, but they do not acquaint their allies with it, as they do at the elections and installations of their chief. Amongst the Huron nations, the women name the counsellors, and often chuse persons of their own sex.

This body of counsellors or assistants is the highest of all. . . .

The women have the chief authority amongst all the nations of the Huron language; if we except the Iroquois canton of Onneyouth [Oneida], in which it is in both sexes alternately. But if this be their lawful constitution, their practice is seldom agreeable to it. In fact, the men never tell the women any thing they would have to be kept secret; and rarely any affair of consequence is communicated to them, though all is done in their name, and the chiefs are no more than their lieutenants. . . . The real authority of the women is very small: I have been however assured, that they always deliberate first on whatever is proposed in council; and that they afterwards give the result of their deliberation to the chiefs, who make the report of it to the general council, composed of the elders; but in all probability this is done only for form's sake, and with the restrictions I have already mentioned. The warriors likewise consult together, on what relates to their particular province, but can conclude nothing of importance which concerns the nation or town; all being subject to the examination and controul of the council of elders, who judge in the last resource.

It must be acknowledged, that proceedings are carried on in these assemblies with a wisdom and a coolness, and a knowledge of affairs, and I may add generally with a probity, which would have done honour to the areopagus of Athens, or to the senate of Rome, in the most glorious days of those republics: the reason of this is, that nothing is resolved upon with precipitation; and that those violent passions, which have so much disgraced the politics even of Christians, have never prevailed amongst the Indians over the public good.

3. Sir William Johnson Confronts the Iroquois Women, 1758

May 5th [1758]. Sir William having no further accounts of the enemy's appearance, sent a scout of two Mohawks, two Canajoharies, and a white man, to go as far as Wood Creek and the Oneida Lake, in order to obtain the certainty of the alarm. About noon all the women of the chief men [the clan matrons or the chiefs' female deputies] of this castle [Onondaga] met at Sir William's lodging, and brought with them several of the sachems [clan chiefs], who acquainted Sir William that they had something to say to him in the name of their chief women.

Old Nickus (Brant) being appointed speaker, opened his discourse with condoling with Sir William for the losses his people had sustained, and then proceeded:—

Brother, we understand you intend to go to a meeting to Onondaga; we can't help speaking with this belt of wampum to you, and giving out sentiments on your intended journey. In the first place we think it quite contrary to the customs of any Governors or Superintendent of Indian affairs being called to Onondaga upon public business, as the council fire which burns there serves only for private consultations of the confederacy; and when matters are concluded and resolved upon there, the confederacy are to set out for the great fire place which is at your house, and there deliver their conclusion. In the next place we are almost convinced that the invitation is illegal, and not agreed upon or desired by the confederacy, but only the Oneidas—which gives us the more reason to be uneasy about your going, as it looks very suspicious. . . .

Brother, by this belt of wampum, we, the women, surround and hang about you like little children, who are crying at their parents' going from them, for fear of their never returning again to give them suck; and we earnestly beg you will give ear to our request, and desist from your journey. We flatter ourselves you will look upon this our speech, and take the same notice of it as all our men do, who, when they are addressed by the women, and desired to desist from any rash enterprise, they immediately give way, when, before, every body else tried to dissuade them from it, and could not prevail.

Gave the [wampum] Belt.

May 10th. This afternoon Sir William returned his answer to the speech of the chief women of this castle, made to him on the 5th instant, which is as follows:—

Dyattego, your tender and affectionate speech, made some days ago, I have considered, and thereupon have dispatched messengers to Oneida, in order to inquire how things stand there after what happened at the German Flatts, and whether my presence at the meeting would be still necessary. These messengers are returned, and I find by them that the sachems of Oneida likewise disapprove my proceeding any farther, for sundry reason they give in their reply. Wherefore I shall comply with your request to return, and heartily thank you for the great tenderness and love expressed for me in your speech.

Returned their Belt.

4. A Challenge to European Stereotypes of Native American Gender Relations, 1819

There are many persons who believe, from the labour that they see the Indian women perform, that they are in a manner treated as slaves. These labours, indeed, are hard, compared with the tasks that are imposed upon females in civilised society; but they are no more than their fair share, under every consideration and due allowance, of the hardships attendant on savage life. Therefore they are not only voluntar-

ily, but cheerfully submitted to; and as women are not obliged to live with their husbands any longer than suits their pleasure or convenience, it cannot be supposed that they would submit to be loaded with unjust or unequal burdens. . . .

When a marriage takes place, the duties and labours incumbent on each party are well known to both. It is understood that the husband is to build a house for them to dwell in, to find the necessary implements of husbandry, as axes, hoes, &c., to provide a canoe, and also dishes, bowls, and other necessary vessels for housekeeping. The woman generally has a kettle or two, and some other articles of kitchen furniture, which she brings with her. The husband, as master of the family, considers himself bound to support it by his bodily exertions, as hunting, trapping, &c; the woman, as his *help-mate,* takes upon herself the labours of the field, and is far from considering them as more important than those to which her husband is subjected, being well satisfied that with his gun and traps he can maintain a family in any place where game is to be found; nor do they think it any hardship imposed upon them; for they themselves say, that while their field labour employs them at most six weeks in the year, that of the men continues the whole year round. . . .

The work of the women is not hard or difficult. They are both able and willing to do it, and always perform it with cheerfulness. Mothers teach their daughters those duties which common sense would otherwise point out to them when grown up. Within doors, their labour is very trifling; there is seldom more than one pot or kettle to attend to. There is no scrubbing of the house, and but little to wash, and that not often. Their principal occupations are to cut and fetch in the fire wood, till the ground, sow and reap the grain, and pound the corn in mortars for their pottage, and to make bread which they bake in the ashes. When going on a journey, or to hunting camps with their husbands, if they have no horses, they carry a pack on their backs which often appears heavier than it really is; it generally consists of a blanket, a dressed deer skin for mocksens [moccasins], a few articles of kitchen furniture, as a kettle, bowl, or dish with spoons, and some bread, corn, salt, &c., for their nourishment. I have never known an Indian woman complain of the hardship of carrying this burden, which serves for their own comfort and support as well as of their husbands.

The tilling of the ground at home, getting of the fire wood, and pounding of corn in mortars, is frequently done by female parties, much in the manner of those husking, quilting, and other *frolics* (as they are called), which are so common in some parts of the United States [among the whites], particularly to the eastward. The labour is thus quickly and easily performed; . . .

When the harvest is in, which generally happens by the end of September, the women have little else to do than to prepare the daily victuals, and get fire wood, until the latter end of February or beginning of March, as the season is more or less backward, when they go to their sugar camps, where they extract sugar from the maple tree. The men having built or repaired their temporary cabin, and made all the troughs of various sizes, the women commence making sugar, while the men are looking out for meat, at this time generally fat bears, which are still in their winter quarters. When at home, they will occasionally assist their wives in gathering the sap, and watch the kettles in their absence, that the syrup may not boil over.

A man who wishes his wife to be with him while he is out hunting in the woods, needs only tell her, that on such a day they will go to such a place, where he will hunt for a length of time, and she will be sure to have provisions and every thing else that is necessary in complete readiness, and well packed up to carry to the spot; . . .

The husband generally leaves the skins and peltry which he has procured by hunting to the care of his wife, who sells or barters them away to the best advantage for such necessaries as are wanted in the family; not forgetting to supply her husband with what he stands in need of, who, when he receives it from her hands never fails to return her thanks in the kindest manner. If debts had been previously contracted, either by the woman, or by her and her husband jointly, or if a horse should be wanted, as much is laid aside as will be sufficient to pay the debts or purchase the horse.

5. Aspects of Native American Life

A. English Trade with Indians, as Seen by Theodor de Bry, 1634

B. Virginia Indians Burning Trees for Canoes, 1705

C. A Huron Woman at Work, Seventeenth
   Century

D. Iroquois Women in the Fields and Forests, 1724

E. Natchez Men at Work, Eighteenth Century

Chasse Générale au Bœuf mais a pièd.

6. Indian Agriculture and Nature's Balance, Seventeenth Century

It is their custom for every family to live on its fishing, hunting, and planting, since they have as much land as they need; for all the forests, meadows, and uncleared land are common property, and anyone is allowed to clear and sow as much as he will and can, and according to his needs; and this cleared land remains in his possession for as many years as he continues to cultivate and make use of it. After it is altogether abandoned by its owner, then anyone who wishes uses it, but not otherwise. Clearing is very troublesome for them, since they have no proper tools. They cut down the trees at the height of two or three feet from the ground, then they strip off all the branches, which they burn at the stump of the same trees in order to kill them, and in course of time they remove the roots. Then the women clean up the ground between the trees thoroughly, and at distances a pace apart dig round holes or pits. In each of these they sow nine or ten grains of maize, which they have first picked out, sorted, and soaked in water for a few days, and so they keep on until they have sown enough to provide food for two or three years, either for fear that some bad season may visit them or else in order to trade it to other nations for furs and other things they need; and every year they sow their corn thus in the same holes and spots, which they freshen with their little wooden spade, shaped like an ear with a handle at the end. The rest of the land is not tilled, but only cleansed of noxious weeds, so that it seems as if it were all paths, so careful are they to keep it quite clean.

7. A Narragansett Leader Complains of English Encroachment, 1642

[O]ur fathers had plenty of deer and skins, our plains were full of deer, as also our woods, and of turkies, and our coves full of fish and fowl. But these English having gotten our land, they with scythes cut down the grass, and with axes fell the trees; their cows and horses eat the grass, and their hogs spoil our clam banks, and we shall all be starved.

8. Mohegan Indians Describe Effects of White Settlement, 1789

The times are Exceedingly Alter'd, Yea the times have turn'd everything upside down, or rather we have Chang'd the good Times, Chiefly by the help of the White People, for in Times past, our Fore Fathers lived in Peace, Love, and great harmony, and had everything in Great plenty. . . . But alas, it is not so now, all our Fishing, Hunting and Fowling is entirely gone.

9. Father Sebastian Rasles Comments on the Hunting Practices of the Illinois, 1692

After three months in Quebec studying the Algonquin language, I embarked in a canoe to go to the Illinois Country, 1,200 miles distant. So long a voyage in those barbarous regions holds great risks and hardships. We had to cross vast lakes where storms are as frequent as on the ocean. . . .

As soon as spring came I embarked for the Illinois, and after 40 days I entered the River of the Illinois [probably via the portage at Chicago]. Following this river for 130 miles, I arrived at the first village of the Illinois, which contained 300 lodges and four or five fires.

The Illinois cover themselves about the waist, and leave the rest of the body naked. They tattoo all kinds of figures on their bodies in place of clothes. Only for visits to our church do they clothe themselves, during the summer in a dressed skin, and during the winter in a skin with fur on it. They put colored feathers on their heads, arranging garlands and crowns with great taste. They paint their faces with colors, mostly red. From their ears they hang small stones, some red, others blue, others white as alabaster. . . .

When not involved in games, feasts or dances, the men remain on their mats, sleeping or making bows, arrows and pipes. As for the women, they work like slaves. In summer they cultivate the earth and plant Indian corn. In winter they make mats, dress skins and provide everything necessary for their lodge.

Of all the nations in Canada, none live in such abundance as the Illinois. Their rivers are covered with swans, geese, ducks and teal. With every mile one sees a multitude of turkeys in flocks as large as 200. These turkeys are much larger than those in France. I weighed one at 36 pounds. Bear and deer are found in great numbers. Buffalo and elk are seen in vast herds. Each year the Illinois kill more than 2,000 buffalo. Four to five thousand buffalo can often be seen at once, grazing on the prairies. They have a hump on the back and a very large head. Their hair is curled and soft as wool. The meat is light, with a naturally salty taste. Even if eaten raw it does not cause indigestion. When the savages kill a buffalo that appears too lean, they take only the tongue and go in search of one that is fatter.

Arrows are the weapons the Illinois use most often in war and the hunt. These are pointed with stones sharpened in the shape of a snake's tongue. If no knife is at hand, they use arrow points to skin animals they have killed. They hardly ever miss their aim, and they can shoot a hundred arrows in the time it takes another to load his gun. They don't take the trouble to make fish nets, because of the abundance of animals. When they fancy to have fish, they stand upright in a canoe and shoot fish with an arrow.

The only way for an Illinois man to gain esteem is to be an able hunter or a good warrior.

Chapter 1:
Document Set 2 References

1. Jesuit Observations on the "Enslavement" of Native American Women, 1633, 1710
   Pierre Biard, 1633; Joseph Jouvency, 1710; in Reuben Gold Thwaites, *The Jesuit Relations and Allied Documents* (Cleveland, 1896–1901), Vol. 1, pp. 257, 259; Vol. 2, pp. 77, 79.

2. Father Pierre de Charlevoix Describes the Female Role in Iroquois Governance, 1721
   Pierre de Charlevoix, *Journal of a Voyage to North America* (London: 1761), Vol. 2, pp. 23–27.

3. Sir William Johnson Confronts the Iroquois Women, 1758.

James Sullivan *et al.*, eds., *The Papers of Sir William Johnson* (Albany: The University of the State of New York, 1921–1965), Vol. 13, pp. 111–113; Vol. 3, pp. 707–712.

4. A Challenge to European Stereotypes of Native American Gender Relations, 1819.
   Rev. John Heckenwelder, *History, Manners, and Customs of the Indian Nations Who Once Inhabited Pennsylvania and the Neighboring States*, rev. ed. by Rev. William Reichel (Philadelphia: Historical Society of Pennsylvania, 1876), pp. 154–158.

5. Aspects of Native American Life
   A. English Trade with Indians as Seen by Theodor de Bry, 1634. Theodor de Bry, *America Pars Decima*, Part 13 (Frankfort-am-Main, 1634).
   B. Virginia Indians Burning Trees for Canoes, 1705. Engraving, Simon Gribelin, in Robert Beverley, *The History and Present State of Virginia* (London, 1705), p. 62.
   C. A Huron Woman at Work, Seventeenth Century. Map, Giuseppi Bressani, Newberry Library, in Alvin M. Josephy, Jr., ed., *America in 1492: The World of Indian Peoples Before the Arrival of Columbus* (New York: Alfred A. Knopf, 1992), p. 132.
   D. Iroquois Women in the Fields and Forests, 1724. Father Joseph Francois Lafitau, *Moeurs des Sauvages Ameriquains*, 1724, in Josephy, p. 118.
   E. Natchez Men at Work, Eighteenth Century. Antoine Simon Le Page du Pratz, Newberry Library, in Josephy, p. 134.

6. Indian Agriculture and Nature's Balance, Seventeenth Century

Gabriel Sagard, *The Long Journey into the Country of the Hurons*, George M. Wrong, ed., 1939, in James Axtell, ed., *The Native American Peoples of the East* (West Haven: Pendulum Press, 1973), p. 61.

7. A Narragansett Leader Complains of English Encroachment, 1642
   "Leift Lion Gardner His Relation of the Pequot Warres," *Massachusetts Historical Society Collections*, 1st Ser., Vol. 3 (1833), pp. 154–155.

8. Mohegan Indians Describe Effects of White Settlement, 1789
   Harry Quaduaquid and Robert Ashpo to the Most Honourable Assembly of the State of Connecticut, May 14, 1789, quoted in Peter Matthiesen, *Wildlife in America* (1989), in Cronon, p. 107.

9. Father Sebastian Rasles Comments on the Hunting Practices of the Illinois, 1692
   Father Sebastian Rasles, in William I. Kip, ed., *The Early Jesuit Missions in North America* (New York: 1846), pp. 30–43.

Chapter 1:
Document Set 2 Credits

5. A. Photo Courtesy of the Edward E. Ayer Collection, The Newberry Library
   B. Colonial Williamsburg Foundation
   C. Photo Courtesy of the Edward E. Ayer Collection, The Newberry Library
   D. Photo Courtesy of the Edward E. Ayer Collection, The Newberry Library
   E. Photo Courtesy of the Edward E. Ayer Collection, The Newberry Library

CHAPTER 2

DOCUMENT SET 1

The Lost Colony: The 1590 Relief Expedition and the Fate of the Roanoke Colony

The English first tried to colonize the New World during the Elizabethan era when Sir Humphrey Gilbert and Sir Walter Raleigh sponsored North American expeditions. Gilbert's Newfoundland effort ended in 1583 when he died without having established a colony. Raleigh's Roanoke ventures in 1585 and 1587 resulted in colonies, but the settlements were not permanent. These explorations were not in vain, however, since they stimulated an interest in colonization that ensured the eventual creation of permanent English colonies in the New World.

Raleigh, upon the death of his half-brother Gilbert, took up Gilbert's patent to establish a colony and in 1585 sent one hundred men, including John White, a painter, and Thomas Harriot, a mathematician and historian, to study the land and prepare for a more complete settlement. The adventurers landed at Roanoke Island (just off the coast of present-day North Carolina) and survived there about a year. They explored, gathered information, and eventually reached the conclusion that the Chesapeake Bay area north of Roanoke should be the site of the next settlement. Difficulty getting adequate food, conflict with the Indians, and bad weather brought the exploratory effort to a premature end.

Less than a year later, in 1587, Raleigh sponsored another expedition. Better planned, it included well over one hundred men, women, and children under the governorship of John White, the artist who had explored Roanoke earlier. With instructions to establish a colony in the Chesapeake Bay area, the party arrived along the Virginia coast in the middle of July, stopping at Roanoke Island to check on fifteen men left there the previous year (they found no signs of survivors). Instead of proceeding to the Chesapeake, as instructed, the party remained at Roanoke and established a colony. About a month after arrival, White sailed for England to secure more supplies, with the intention of an immediate return; but the encroaching Spanish Armada (1588) and war with Spain prevented another voyage until 1590.

The documents include portions of John White's account of the 1590 relief expedition, detailing what he found when he again reached Roanoke. After reviewing your textbook's account of the Roanoke colony, examine the documents, noting the route taken and the experiences of White and others who made the voyage. Modern historians remain uncertain about the fate of the "lost colony." Do the documents provide any clues to the mystery?

Questions for Analysis

1. Using the documents as a guide, trace both the chronology and the route of John White's relief expedition in 1590 from Plymouth, England, to the Roanoke colony and back. How many days did it take White to reach Roanoke and return to Plymouth? Why did he return to England the way he did?

2. En route to Roanoke, the relief expedition was delayed several times. Why? Explain.

3. Discuss the experiences of White and the relief expedition in the Roanoke Island area. How did they proceed? What did they find? What did White assume about his fellow Virginia colonists?

4. How would you explain the fate of Raleigh's lost colony of Roanoke? Compare your textbook's account of the Roanoke colony with White's narrative. Speculate on an explanation for the outcome. Support your view with evidence drawn from White's account.

5. The efforts of neither Sir Humphrey Gilbert nor Sir Walter Raleigh in the 1580s resulted in a permanent English colony in the New World. Despite their failure, what historical significance did their efforts have, and what realities did the fate of the Roanoke colony illustrate? What relationship can you establish between the Roanoke experience and future British colonial efforts? What were the implications of Roanoke for the establishment of meaningful cross-cultural relations?

1. John White's Relief Expedition, 1590

The fifth voyage of *Master* John White into the West Indies and parts of America called Virginia, in the year 1590.

The 20 of March the three ships the Hopewell,[1] the John Evangelist,[2] and the Little John,[3] put to Sea from Plymouth[4] with two small Shallops. . . .

On Saturday the 4 [of April] we saw Alegranza, the East Ile of the Canaries. . . .

On Monday the 6 we saw Grand Canary, and the next day we landed and took in fresh water on the Southside thereof.

On the 9 we departed from Grand Canary, and framed our course for Dominica.

The last of April we saw Dominica, and the same night we came to an anchor on the Southside thereof. . . .

On the 14 [of May] we departed from Mona, and the next day after we came to an Island called Saona . . . lying on the Southside of Hispaniola near the East end: between these two Islands we lay off and on 4 or 5 days, hoping to take [attack] some of the Domingo fleet. . . .

The second of July Edward Spicer whom we left in England came to us at Cape Tyburon, accompanied with a small Pinnesse, whereof one *Master* Harps was Captain. And the same day we had sight of a fleet of 14 sail all of Santo Domingo, to whom we presently gave chase, but they upon the first sight of us fled, and separating themselves scattered here and there: Wherefore we were forced to divide our selves and so made after them until 12 of the clock at night. But then by reason of the darkness we lost sight of each other, yet in the end the Admiral and the Moonlight happened to be together the same night at the fetching up of the Viceadmiral of the Spanish fleet, against whom the next morning we fought and took him, with loss of one of our men and two hurt, and of theirs 4 slain and 6 hurt. But what was become of our Viceadmiral, our Pinnesse, and Prize, and two Frigates, in all this time, we were ignorant.

The 3 of July we spent about rifling, rummaging and fitting the Prize to be sailed with us.

The 6 of July we saw Jamayca which we left on our larboard, keeping Cuba in sight on our starboard. . . .

On Sunday the 26 of July plying to and fro between the Matanças and Havana, we were espied of three small Pinnesses of S. John de Ullua bound for Havana, which were exceeding richly laden. These 3 Pinnesses came very boldly up unto us, and so continued until they came within musket shot of us. And we supposed them to be Captain Harps pinnesse, and two small Frigates taken by Captain Harp: wherefore we showed our flag. But they presently upon the sight of it turned about & made all the sail they could from us toward the shore, & kept themselves in so shallow water, that we were not able to follow them, and therefore gave them over with expence of shot & powder to no purpose. But if we had not so rashly set out our flag, we might have taken them all three, for they would not have known us before they had been in our hands. This chase brought us so far to leeward as Havana: wherefore not finding any of our consorts at Matanças, we put over again to the cape of Florida, & from thence through the channel of Bahama. . . .

The 15 of August towards Evening we came to an anchor at Hatoras, in 36 degr. and one third, in five fathom water, three leagues from the shore. At our first coming to anchor on this shore we saw a great smoke rise in the Isle Roanoak near the place where I left our Colony in the year 1587, which smoke put us in good hope that some of the Colony were there expecting my return out of England.

The 16 and next morning our 2 boats went a shore, & Captain Cooke, & Cap*tain* Spicer, & their company with me, with intent to pass to the place at Roanoak where our countrymen were left. At our putting from the ship we commanded our Master gunner to make ready 2 Minions and a Falkon well loaded, and to shoot them off with reasonable space between every shot, to the end that their reports might be heard to the place where we hoped to find some of our people. This was accordingly performed, & our two boats put off unto the shore, in the Admirals boat we sounded all the way and found from our ship until we came within a mile of the shore nine, eight, and seven fathom: but before we were half way

---

[1] Alias the *Harry and John* of London, Abraham Cocke, captain, Robert Hutton, master, the admiral of the squadron.

[2] Of London, William Lane captain, a pinnace.

[3] Alias the *John* of London, Christopher Newport, captain, viceadmiral of the squadron. All three belonged to 'John Wat*tes* and Company of London merchants' and held letters of reprisal against the Spaniards from the Lord High Admiral.

[4] Leaving, it was alleged, their consort, the *Moonlight*, behind.

between our ships and the shore we saw another great smoke to the Southwest of Kindrikers mounts: we therefore thought good to go to that second smoke first: but it was much further from the harbor where we landed, then we supposed it to be, so that we were very sore tired before we came to the smoke. But that which grieved us more was that when we came to the smoke, we found no man nor sign that any had been there lately, nor yet any fresh water in all this way to drink. Being thus wearied with this journey we returned to the harbor where we left our boats, who in our absence had brought their cask a shore for fresh water, so we deferred our going to Roanoak until the next morning, and caused some of those sailors to dig in those sandy hills for fresh water which we found very sufficient. That night we returned aboard with our boats and our whole company in safety.

The next morning being the 17 of August, our boats and company were prepared again to go up to Roanoak, but Captain Spicer had then sent his boat ashore for fresh water, by means of which it was ten of the clock aforenoon before we put from our ships which were then come to an anchor within two miles of the shore. The Admirals boat was half way toward the shore, when Captain Spicer put off from his ship. The Admirals boat first passed the breech, but not without some danger of sinking, for we had a sea break into our boat which filled us half full of water, but by the will of God and careful steerage of Captain Cooke we came safe ashore, save only that our furniture, victuals match and powder were much wet and spoiled. For at this time the wind blew at Northeast and direct into the harbor so great a gale, that the Sea broke extremely on the bar, and the tide went very forcibly at the entrance. By that time our Admirals boat was hauled ashore, and most of our things taken out to dry, Captain Spicer came to the entrance of the breech with his mast standing up, and was half passed over, but by the rash and indiscreet steerage of Ralph Skinner his Masters mate, a very dangerous Sea broke into their boat and overset them quite, the men kept the boat some in it, and some hanging on it, but the next sea set the boat on ground, where it beat so, that some of them were forced to let go their hold, hoping to wade ashore, but the Sea still beat them down, so that they could neither stand nor swim, and the boat twice or thrice was turned the keel upward; whereon Captain Spicer and Skinner hung until they sunk, & seen no more. But four that could swim a little kept themselves in deeper water and were saved by Captain Cookes means, who so soon as he saw their oversetting, stripped himself, and four other that could

swim very well, & with all haste possible rowed unto them, & saved four. They were 11 in all, & 7 of the chiefest were drowned, whose names were Edward Spicer, Ralph Skinner, Edward Kelley, Thomas Bevis, Hance the Surgeon, Edward Kelborne, Robert Coleman. This mischance did so much discomfort the sailors, that they were all of one mind not to go any further to seek the planters. But in the end by the commandment & persuasion of me and Captain Cooke, they prepared the boats: and seeing the Captain and me so resolute, they seemed much more willing. Our boats and all things fitted again, we put off from Hatoras, being the number of 19 persons in both boats: but before we could get to the place, where our planters were left, it was so exceeding dark, that we overshot the place a quarter of a mile: there we espied towards the North end of the Island the light of a great fire through the woods, to the which we presently rowed: when we came right over against it, we let fall our Grapnel near the shore, & sounded with a trumpet a Call, & afterwards many familiar English tunes of Songs, and called to them friendly; but we had no answer, we therefore landed at day-break, and coming to the fire, we found the grass & sundry rotten trees burning about the place. From hence we went through the woods to that part of the Island directly over against Dasamongwepeuk, & from thence we returned by the water side, round about the Northpoint of the Island, until we came to the place where I left our Colony in the year 1586. In all this way we saw in the sand the print of the Savages feet of 2 or 3 sorts troaden that night, and as we entered up the sandy bank upon a tree, in the very brow thereof were curiously carved these fair Roman letters C R O: which letters presently we knew to signify the place, where I should find the planters seated, according to a secret token agreed upon between them & me at my last departure from them, which was, that in any ways they should not fail to write or carve on the trees or posts of the doors the name of the place where they should be seated; for at my coming away they were prepared to remove from Roanoak 50 miles into the main. Therefore at my departure from them in Anno 1587 I willed them, that if they should happen to be distressed in any of those places, that then they should carve over the letters or name, a Cross ✠ in this form, but we found no such sign of distress. And having well considered of this, we passed toward the place where they were left in sundry houses, but we found the houses taken down, and the place very strongly enclosed with a high palisade of great trees, with cordons and flankers very Fort-like, and one of the chief trees or posts at the right side of the entrance had the bark taken off, and 5. foot from the ground in fair Capital letters was graven CROATOAN without any cross or sign of distress; this done, we entered into the palisade, where we found many bars of Iron, two pigs of Lead, four iron fowlers, Iron sacker-shot, and such like heavy things, thrown here and there, almost overgrown with grass and weeds. From thence we went along by the water side, towards the point of the Creek to see if we could find any of their boats or Pinnesse, but we could perceive no sign of them, nor any of the last Falkons and small Ordinance which were left with them, at my departure from them. At our return from the Creek, some of our sailors meeting us, told us that they had found where many chests had been hidden, and long since digged up again and broken up, and much of the goods in them spoiled and scattered about, but nothing left, of such things as the Savages knew any use of, undefaced. Presently Captain Cooke and I went to the place, which was in the end of an old trench, made two years past by Captain Amadas: where we found five Chests, that had been carefully hidden of the Planters, and of the same chests three were my own, and about the place many of my things spoiled and broken, and my books torn from the covers, the frames of some of my pictures and Maps rotten and spoiled with rain, and my armour almost eaten through with rust; this could be no other but the deed of the Savages our enemies at Dasamong-wepeuk, who had watched the departure of our men to Croatoan; and as soone as they were departed, digged up every place where they suspected any thing to be buried: but although it much grieved me to see such spoile of my goods, yet on the other side I greatly joyed that I had safely found a certain token of their safe being at Croatoan, which is the place where Manteo was born, and the Savages of the Island our friends.

When we had seen in this place so much as we could, we returned to our Boats, and departed from the shore towards our Ships, with as much speed as we could: For the weather began to overcast, and very likely that a foul and stormy night would ensue. Therefore the same Evening with much danger and labour, we got our selves aboard, by which time the wind and seas were so greatly risen, that we doubted our Cables and Anchors would scarcely hold until Morning; wherefore the Captain caused the Boat to be manned with five lusty men, who could swim all well, and sent them to the little Island on the right hand of the Harbor, to bring aboard six of our men, who had filled our cask with fresh water: the Boat the same night returned aboard with our men, but all our Cask ready filled they left behind, impossible to be had aboard without danger of casting away both men and Boats; for this night proved very stormy and foul.

The next Morning it was agreed by the Captain and my self, with the Master and others, to weigh anchor, and go for the place at Croatoan, where our planters were: for that then the wind was good for that place, and also to leave that Cask with fresh water on shore in the Island until our return. So then they brought the cable to the Capston, but when the anchor was almost up, the Cable broke, by means whereof we lost another Anchor, wherewith we drove so fast into the shore, that we were forced to let fall a third Anchor; which came so fast home that the Ship was almost aground by Kenricks mounts: so that we were forced to let slip the Cable end for end. And if it had not chanced that we had fallen into a channel of deeper water, closer by the shore than we accompted of, we could never have gone clear of the point that lay to the Southwards of Kenricks mounts. Being thus clear of some dangers, and gotten into deeper waters, but not without some loss; for we had but one Cable and Anchor left us of four, and the weather grew to be fouler and fouler; our victuals scarce, and our cask and fresh water lost: it was therefore determined that we should go for Saint John or some other Island to the Southward for fresh water. And it was further proposed, that if we could any way supply our wants of victuals and other necessaries, either at Hispaniola, Saint John, or Trinidad, that then we should continue in the Indies all the Winter following, with hope to make 2 rich voyages of one, and at our return to visit our countrymen at Virginia. The captain and the whole company in the Admiral (with my earnest petitions) thereunto agreed, so that it rested only to know what the Master of the Moonlight our consort would do herein. But when we demanded them if they would accompany us in that new determination, they alleged that their weak and leaky Ship was not able to continue it; wherefore the same night we parted, leaving the Moonlight to go directly for England, and the Admiral set his course for Trinidad, which course we kept two days.

On the 28. the wind changed, and it was set on foul weather every way: but this storm brought the wind West and Northwest, and blew so forcibly, that we were able to bear no sail, but our forecourse half mast high, wherewith we ran upon the wind perforce, the due course for England, for that we were driven to change our first determination for Trinidad, and stood for the Islands of Azores, where we proposed to take in fresh water, and also there hoped to meet with some English men of where about those Islands, at whose hands we might obtain some supply of our wants. . . .

The 2. of October in the Morning we saw S. Michaels Island on our starboard quarter.

The 23. at 10. of the clock afore noon, we saw Ushant in Brittany.

On Saturday the 24. we came in safe, God be thanked, to an anchor at Plymouth.

2. The Roanoke Voyages, 1584–1590

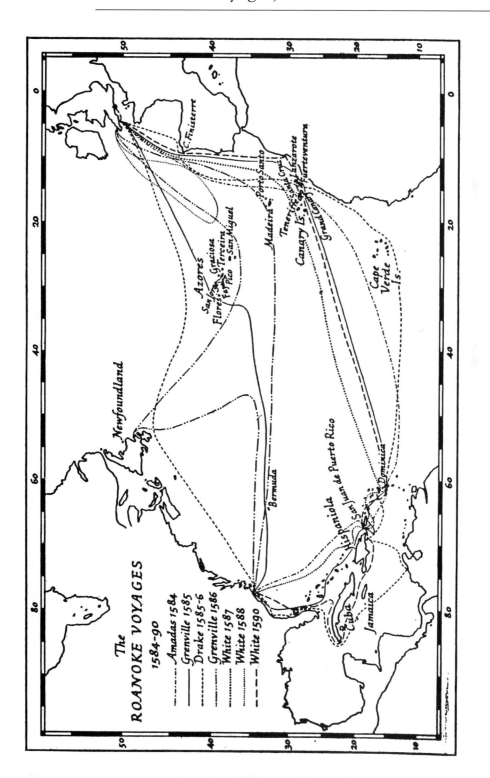

The
ROANOKE VOYAGES
1584-90

----- Amadas 1584
——— Grenville 1585
········· Drake 1585–6
———— Grenville 1586
-·-·- White 1587
——·——· White 1588
——— White 1590

Chapter 2:
Document Set 1 References

1. John White's Relief Expedition, 1590
   Richard Hakluyt, *Principal Navigations, Voyages of the English Nation*, III (1600), pp. 288–295.

2. The Roanoke Voyages, 1584–1590
   "The Roanoke Voyages, 1584–1590" (map), in David Beers Quinn, ed., *The Roanoke Voyages, 1584–1590, Documents to Illustrate the English Voyages to North America Under the Patent Granted to Walter Raleigh in 1584*, Vol. 1 (Lessingdruckerei Wiesbaden, Germany: Hakluyt Society, 1955; rep. Nendeln/Liechtenstein: Kraus Reprint Limited, 1967), inset.

CHAPTER 2

DOCUMENT SET 2

Trying Times at Jamestown: The Early Months of the First Permanent English Colony

A generation after the failure of Roanoke Island, the English established a permanent colony in the New World. The colony had a difficult beginning, barely surviving its early years. One hundred forty-four men commanded by Captain Christopher Newport departed England for Virginia in December 1606. One hundred four completed the crossing, reaching the Virginia capes in late April of the next year. A few weeks later, Jamestown was under way, the colonists having located fifty miles up the James River. In June, Captain Newport left for England to replenish supplies and secure more settlers. When he returned in January 1608, only 38 of the colonists were still living. In six short months, more than half had perished, and many of the survivors wanted to return home. *Why?*

The following documents, which recount the Jamestown experience during these early months, help answer the question. Included are selections from George Percy's *Observations* (1607) and John Smith's *General History* (1624). Both men made the initial trip to Jamestown, witnessed events during the critical months, and functioned as important leaders in the colony. Smith was a member of the governing council, presiding as president from September 1608 to September 1609. When the council was first created, however, he was excluded by other members; and in early 1608, Smith was nearly condemned to die by council members who alleged he was responsible for the death of two men. Although a controversial figure during the early years, many historians accept Smith's personal account of his own central role in the colony's survival. Smith justified dictatorial methods as necessary to obtain provisions from the Indians and to organize and motivate the colonists to work.

Percy faced similar problems as council president from September 1609 to May 1610, during the horrible "starving time" described in your textbook, a period when the population dwindled from some 500 to fewer than 100, and again from March to May of 1611. The writings of these two leaders are among the most important sources available concerning England's first permanent colony in the New World. Compare their observations with your textbook's account of Virginia's origins.

These documents reveal more than the details of the settlers' struggle for survival. They also provide information and insight into the early social and political history of Jamestown. As you study them, determine how the colony's inhabitants worked, lived, governed themselves, and adjusted to an alien environment. Be aware of Smith's and Percy's personal reasons for recounting the story of early Jamestown. Make a judgment about their reliability as sources of information on the true character of Virginia society. Finally, use these accounts as resources in developing an explanation for the acute hardship of the colony's early years.

Questions for Analysis

1. What provisions were made for governance in the Jamestown colony? What problems of governance emerged? How were they resolved?

2. Drawing on the evidence in the documents, explain why the Jamestown colonists had such a difficult time in the colony's first seven months. What problems in addition to leadership difficulties confronted them? How did they attempt to deal with these challenges?

3. How did John Smith and George Percy account for the Jamestown colony's survival, despite the problems? What is your evaluation of Smith and Percy as witnesses? Were they in agreement on the "facts"? Explain.

4. In what ways did the Native Americans and the colonists interact? Describe and account for the attitude of the colonists toward the Indians. Speculate on the Indians' attitude toward the colonists, using evidence from the documents to support your views. What were the implications of these contacts for the future?

5. What do the 1625 population statistics reveal about the quality of life in early Virginia? How do these data illuminate the facts of life in the first stage of colonization?

6. What was the significance of the importation of women after 1618? How did this innovation reflect the evolving goals of the London Company? What do the documents reveal about gender relations and the sexual division of labor in early Virginia?

1. George Percy's Observations on Jamestown's Early Months, 1607

The sixth of August [1607], there died *John Asbie*, of the bloody Flux.

The ninth day, died *George Flowre*, of the swelling.

The tenth day, died *William Bruster* Gentleman, of a wound given by the Savages, and was buried the eleventh day.

The fourteenth day, *Jerome Alikock* [*Ensign*], died of a wound. The same day, *Francis Midwinter* [died], [and] *Edward Moris* Corporal died suddenly.

The fifteenth day, there died *Edward Browne* and *Stephen Galthorpe*.

The sixteenth day, there died *Thomas Gower* Gentleman.

The seventeenth day, there died *Thomas Mounslic*.

The eighteenth day, there died *Robert Pennington*, and *John Martine* Gentlemen.

The nineteenth day, died *Drue Piggase* Gentleman.

The two and twentieth day of August [1607], there died Captain *Bartholomew Gosnold*, one of our Council: he was honorably buried, having all the Ordnance in the Fort shot off, with many volleys of small shot.

After Captain *Gosnol[d]s* death, the Council could hardly agree by the dissension of Captain *Kendall*; [who] afterwards was committed about heinous matters which was proved against him.

The four and twentieth day, died *Edward Harington* and *George Walker*; and were buried the same day.

The six and twentieth day, died *Kenelme Throgmortine*

The seven and twentieth day, died *William Roods*.

The eight and twentieth day, died *Thomas Stoodie*, Cape Merchant.

The fourth day of September [1607], died *Thomas Jacob* Sergeant.

The fifth day, there died *Beniamin Beast*.

Our men were destroyed with cruel diseases, as Swellings, Fluxes, Burning Fevers, and by wars; and some departed suddenly: but for the most part, they died of mere famine.

There were never *Englishmen* left in a foreign Country in such misery as we were in this new discovered *Virginia*. We watched every three nights, lying on the bare cold ground, what weather soever came; [and] warded all the next day: which brought our men to be most feeble wretches. Our food was but a small Can of Barly sod[den] in water, to five men a day. Our drink, cold water taken out of the River; which was, at a flood, very salt; at a low tide, full of slime and filth: which was the destruction of many of our men.

Thus we lived for the space of five months [*August 1607–8 Jan.* 1608] in this miserable distress, not having five able men to man our Bulwarks upon any occasion. If it had not pleased God to have put a terror in the Savages hearts, we had all perished by those wild and cruel Pagans, being in that weak estate as we were; our men night and day groaning in every corner of the Fort most pitiful to hear. If there were any conscience in men, it would make their hearts to bleed to hear the pitiful murmurings and out-cries of our sick men without relief, every night and day, for the space of six weeks [? *8 Aug.–19 Sept.* 1607]: some departing out of the World, many times three or four in a night; in the morning, their bodies [being] trailed out of their Cabins like Dogs, to be buried. In this sort, did I see the mortality of many of our people.

It pleased God, after a while, to send those people which were our mortal enemies, to relieve us with victuals, as Bread, Corn, Fish, and Flesh in great plenty; which was the setting up of our feeble men: otherwise we had all perished. Also we were frequented by many Kings in the Country, bringing us store of provision to our great comfort.

The eleventh day [*of September*, 1607], there was certain *Articles* laid against Master *Wingfield* which was then President: thereupon he was not only displaced out of his Presidentship, but also from being of the Council. Afterwards Captain *John Ratcliffe* was chosen President.

The eighteenth day [*of September*], died one *Ellis Kinistone*, which was starved [*frozen*] to death with cold. The same day at night, died one *Richard Simmons*.

The nineteenth day [*of September*], there died one *Thomas Mouton*.

2. John Smith's Impressions of the Jamestown Experience, 1607

Captain *Bartholomew Gosnoll*, one of the first movers of this plantation, having many years solicited many of his friends, but found small assistance; at last prevailed with some Gentlemen, as Captain *John Smith*, Master *Edward-maria Wingfield*, Master *Robert Hunt*, and divers [many] others, who depended a year upon his projects, but nothing could be effected, till by their great charge and industry, it came to be apprehended by certain of the Nobility, Gentry, and Merchants, so that his Majestie by his letters patents [10 *April* 1606], gave commission for establishing Councils, to direct here; and to govern, and to execute there. To effect this, was spent another year, and by that, three ships were provided, one of 100 Tons, another of 40. and a Pinnace of 20. The transportation of the company was committed to Captain *Christopher Newport*, a Mariner well practiced for the Western parts of *America*. But their orders for government were put in a box, not to be opened, nor the governors known until they arrived in *Virginia*.

On the 19 of December, 1606. we set sail from Blackwall, but by unprosperous winds, were kept six weeks in the sight of *England*; all which time, Master *Hunt* our Preacher, was so weak and sick, that few expected his recovery. . . .

The first land they made they called *Cape Henry*; where thirty of them recreating themselves on shore, were assaulted by five Savages, who hurt two of the English very dangerously.

That night was the box opened, and the orders read, in which *Bartholomew Gosnoll*, *John Smith*, *Edward Wingfield*, *Christopher Newport*, *John Rat[c]liffe*, *John Martin*, and *George Kendall*, were named to be the Council, and to choose a President amongst them for a year, who with the Council should govern. Matters of moment were to be examined by a Jury, but determined by the major part of the Council, in which the President had two voices.

Until the 13 of May [1607] they sought a place to plant in; then the Council was sworn, Master *Wingfield* was chosen President, and an Oration made, why Captain *Smith* was not admitted of the Council as the rest.

Now falleth every man to work, the Council contrive the Fort, the rest cut down trees to make place to pitch their Tents; some provide clapbord to reload the ships, some make gardens, some nets, &c. The Savages often visited us kindly. The Presidents overweening jealousy would admit no exercise at arms, or fortification but the boughs of trees cast together in the form of a half moon by the extraordinary pains and diligence of Captain *Kendall*.

Newport, *Smith*, and twenty others, were sent to discover the head of the river: by many small habitations they passed. . . . The people in all parts kindly entreated them, till being returned within twenty miles of *James* town, they gave just cause of jealousy: but had God not blessed the discoverers otherwise then those at the Fort, there had then been an end of that plantation; for at the Fort, where they arrived the next day, they found 17 men hurt, and a boy slaine by the Savages, and had it not chanced a cross bar shot from the Ships struck down a bough from a tree amongst them, that caused them to retire, our men had all been slaine, being securely all at work, and their arms in dry fats.

Hereupon the President was contented the Fort should be pallisaded, the ordnance mounted, his men armed and exercised: for many were the assaults, and ambuscades of the Savages, and our men by their disorderly straggling were often hurt, when the Savages by the nimbleness of their heels well escaped.

What toil we had, with so small a power to guard our workmen days, watch all night, resist our enemies, and effect our business, to reload the ships, cut down trees, and prepare the ground to plant our Corn, &c, I refer to the readers consideration.

Six weeks being spent in this manner, Captain *Newport* (who was hired only for our transportation) was to return with the ships.

Now Captain *Smith,* who all this time from their departure from the Canaries was restrained as a prisoner upon the scandalous suggestions of some of the chief (envying his repute) who feigned he intended to usurp the government, murder the Council, and make himself King, that his confederates were dispersed in all the three ships, and that many of his confederates that revealed it, would affirm it; for this he was committed as a prisoner.

Thirteen weeks [24 *Mar.*–10 *June* 1607], he remained thus suspected, and by that time the ships should return they pretended out of their commiserations, to refer him to the Council in *England* to receive a check, rather than by particulating his designs [to] make him so odious to the world, as to touch his life, or utterly overthrow his reputation. But he so much scorned their charity, and publicly defied the uttermost of their cruelty; he wisely prevented their policies, though he could not suppress their envies; yet so well he demeaned himself in this business, as all the company did see his innocence, and his adversaries malice, and those suborned to accuse him, accused his accusers of subornation; many untruths were alledged against him; but being so apparently disproved, begat a general hatred in the hearts of the company against such unjust Commanders, that the President [*Wingfield*] was adjudged to give him 200*l.*; so that all he had was seized upon, in part of satisfaction, which *Smith* presently returned to the Store for the general use of the *Colony.*

Many were the mischiefs that daily sprung from their ignorant (yet ambitious) spirits; but the good Doctrine and exhortation of our Preacher Master *Hunt* reconciled them, and caused Captain *Smith* to be admitted of the Council [20 *June, or rather on* 10 *June*].

The next day all received the Communion, the day following [*June* 22] the Savages voluntarily desired peace, and Captain *Newport* returned for *England* with news; leaving in *Virginia* 100. the 15 [*or rather* 22] of June 1607. . . .

Being thus left to our fortunes, it fortuned that within ten days scarce ten amongst us could either go, or well stand, such extreme weakness and sickness oppressed us. And thereat none need marvel, if they consider the cause and reason, which was this.

While the ships stayed, our allowance was somewhat bettered, by a daily proportion of Bisket, which the sailors would pilfer to sell, give, or exchange with us, for money, Sassefras, furs, or love. But when they departed, there remained neither tavern, beer house, nor place of relief, but the common Kettell. Had we been as free from all sins as gluttony, and drunkenness, we might have been canonized for Saints; But our President [*Wingfield*] would never have been admitted, for engrossing to his private [*i.e., his own use*], Oatmeale, Sacke, Oyle, *Aquavitæ*, Beef, Eggs, or what not, but the Kettell; that indeed he allowed equally to be distributed, and that was half a pint of wheat, and as much barley boiled with water for a man a day, and this having fried some 26. weeks [*Dec.* 1606–*June* 1607] in the ships hold, contained as many worms as grains; so that we might truly call it rather so much bran than corn, our drink was water, our lodgings Castles in the air.

With this lodging and diet, our extreme toil in bearing and planting Pallisades, so strained and bruised us, and our continual labor in the extremity of the heat had so weakened us, as were cause sufficient to have made us as miserable in our native Country, or any other place in the world.

From May, to September [1607], those that escaped, lived upon Sturgeon, and Sea-crabs, fifty in this time we buried, the rest seeing the Presidents projects to escape these miseries in our Pinnace by flight (who all this time had neither felt want nor sickness) so moved our dead spirits, as we deposed him [10 *Sept.* 1607]; and established *Ratcliffe* in his place, (*Gosnoll* being dead [22 *Aug.* 1607]) *Kendall* deposed [?*Sept* 1607]. *Smith* newly recovered, *Martin* and *Ratcliffe* was by his care preserved and relieved, and the most of the soldiers recovered with the skillful diligence of Master *Thomas Wotton* our Chirurgian general.

But now was all our provision spent, the Sturgeon gone, all helps abandoned, each hour expecting the fury of the Savages; when God the patron of all good endevors, in that desperate extremity so changed the hearts of the Savages, that they brought such plenty of their fruits, and provision, as no man wanted.

And now where some affirmed it was ill done of the Council to send forth men so badly provided, this incontradictable reason will show them plainly they are too ill advised to nourish such ill conceits; first, the fault of our going was our own, what could be thought fitting or necessary we had; but what we should find, or want, or where we should be, we were all ignorant, and supposing to make our passage in two months, with victual to live, and the advantage of the spring to work; we were at Sea five months, where we both spent our victual and lost the opportunity of the time and season to plant, by the unskilfull presumption of our ignorant transporters, that understood not at all, what they undertook.

Such actions have ever since the worlds beginning been subject to such accidents, and every thing of worth is found full of difficulties: but nothing so difficult as to establish a Common wealth so far remote from men and means, and where mens minds are so untoward as neither do well themselves, nor suffer others. But to proceed.

The new President [*Ratcliffe*], and *Martin*, being little beloved, of weak judgement in dangers, and less industry in peace, committed the managing of all things abroad to Captain *Smith*: who by his own example, good words, and fair promises, set some to mow, others to bind thatch, some to build houses, others to thatch them, himself always bearing the greatest task for his own share, so that in short time, he provided most of them lodgings, neglecting any for himself.

This done, seeing the Savages superfluity begin to decrease [he] (with some of his workmen) shipped himself [9 *Nov.* 1607] in the Shallop to search the Country for trade. . . .

Wingfield and *Kendall* living in disgrace, seeing all things at random in the absence of *Smith*, the company dislike of their Presidents weakness, and their small love to *Martins* never mending sickness, strengthened themselves with the sailors and other confederates, to regain their former credit and authority, or at least such means abord the Pinnace, (being fitted to sail as *Smith* had appointed for trade) to alter her course and to go for *England*.

Smith unexpectedly returning had the plot discovered to him, much trouble he had to prevent it, till with store of sakre and musket shot he forced them stay or sink in the river: which action cost the life of captain *Kendall*.

These brawls are so disgustfull, as some will say they were better forgotten, yet all men of good judgement will conclude, it were better their baseness should be manifest to the world, then the business bear the scorn and shame of their excused disorders.

The President [*Ratcliffe*] and captain *Archer* not long after intended also to have abandoned the country, which project also was curbed, and suppressed by *Smith*. . . .

And now the winter approaching, the rivers became so covered with swans, geese, ducks, and cranes, that we daily feasted with good bread, Virginia pease, pumpions, and putchamins, fish, fowle and diverse sorts of wild beasts as fast as we could eat them: so that none of our Tuftaffaty humorists desired to go for *England*.

But our *Comœdies* never endured long without a Tragedie. . . .

Now whether it had been better for Captain *Smith*, to have concluded with any of those several projects, to have abandoned the Country, with some ten or twelve of them, who were called the better sort, and have left Master *Hunt* our Preacher, Master *Anthony Gosnoll*, a most honest, worthy, and industrious Gentleman, Master *Thomas Wotton*, and some 27 others of his Countrymen to the fury of the Savages, famine, and all manner of mischiefs, and inconveniences, (for they were but forty in all to keep possession of this large Country;) or starve himself with them for company, for want of lodging: or but adventuring abroad to make them provision, or by his opposition to preserve the action, and save all their lives; I leave to the censure of all honest men to consider.

3. Virginia Population Characteristics, 1625

Ages Given for 750 Persons out of 1,210 Living in January and February, 1625 (Figures in parentheses are percentages)

Age	Male	Female	All
1–5	30	23	53
	(4.7)	(19.8)	(7.1)
6–9	5	9	14
	(0.8)	(7.8)	(1.9)
10–15	41	10	51
	(6.5)	(8.6)	(6.8)
16–19	81	4	85
	(12.8)	(3.4)	(11.3)
20–24	212	32	244
	(33.4)	(27.6)	(32.6)
25–29	106	14	120
	(16.7)	(12.1)	(16.0)
30–34	65	11	76
	(10.3)	(9.5)	(10.1)
35–39	41	5	46
	(6.5)	(4.3)	(6.1)
Over 39	53	8	61
	(8.4)	(6.9)	(8.1)
Total	634	116	750
	(100)	(100)	(100)

4. The London Company Instructs the Governor in Virginia, 1622

There come now over in this ship, and are immediately to follow in some others many hundreds of people, to whom as we here think ourselves bound to give the best encouragement for their going, there is no way left to increase the plantation, but by abundance of private undertakers; so we think you obliged to give all possible furtherance and assistance, for the good entertaining and well settling of them, that they may both thrive and prosper and others by their welfare be drawn after them. This is the way that we conceive most effectual for the engaging of this state, and securing of Virginia, for in the multitude of people is the strength of a kingdom. . . .

We send you in this ship one widow and eleven maids for wives for the people in Virginia: there hath been especial care had in the choice of them; for there hath not any one of them been received but upon good commendations. We pray you all therefore in general to take them into your care; and more especially we recommend that at their first landing they may be housed, lodged, and provided for of diet till they be married; for such was the haste of sending them away, as that straightened with time we had no means to put provisions aboard. And in case they cannot be presently married we desire they may be put to several households that have wives till they can be provided of husbands. There are nearly fifty more which are shortly to come, are sent by certain worthy gentlemen, who taking into their consideration that the plantation can never flourish till families be planted, and the respect of wives and children fix the people on the soil. Therefore have given this fair beginning: for the reimbursing of whose charges it is ordered that every man that marries them give 120 weight of the best leaf tobacco for each of them, and in case any of them die, that proportion must be advanced to it upon those that survive. That marriage be free according to the law of nature, yet would we not have these maids deceived and married to servants, but only to such free men or tenants as have means to maintain them. We pray you therefore to be fathers to them in this business, not enforcing them to marry against their wills; neither send we them to be servants, save in case of extremity, for we would have their condition so much bettered as multitudes may be allured thereby to come unto you. And you may assure such men as marry those women that the first servants sent over by the company shall be consigned to them; it being our intent to preserve families, and to prefer married men before single persons.

5. The Trappan'd Maiden: or, The Distressed Damsel, ca. Seventeenth Century

The Girl was cunningly Trappan'd, sent to Virginny from England, Where she doth Hardship undergo, there is no Cure it must be so:
    But if she lives to cross the Main, she vows she'll ne'r go there again.

    Tune of *Virginny*, or, *When that I was weary, weary, O.*

    Give ear unto a Maid, that lately was betray'd,
        And sent into Virginny, O:
    In brief I shall declare, what I have suffer'd there,
        When that I was weary, weary, weary, weary, O.

    [Since] that first I came to this Land of Fame,
        Which is called Virginny, O,
    The Axe and the Hoe have wrought my overthrow,
        When that I was weary, weary, weary, weary, O.

    Five years served I, under Master Guy,
        In the land of Virginny, O,
    Which made me for to know sorrow, grief and woe,
        When that I was weary, weary, weary, weary, O.

    When my Dame says "Go" then I must do so,
        In the land of Virginny, O;
    When she sits at Meat, then I have none to eat,
        When that I am weary, weary, weary, weary, O.

    The Cloath[e]s that I brought in, they are worn very thin,
        In the land of Virginny, O,
    Which makes me for to say, "Alas, and Well-a-day!"
        When that I am weary, weary, weary, weary, O.

    Instead of Beds of Ease, to lye down when I please,
        In the Land of Virginny, O;
    Upon a bed of straw, I lye down full of woe,
        When that I am weary, weary, weary, weary, O. . . .

    So soon as it is day, to work I must away,
        In the Land of Virginny, O;

Then my Dame she knocks, with her tinder-box,
When that I am weary, weary, weary, weary, O.

I have play'd my part both at Plow and Cart,
In the Land of Virginny, O;
Billets from the Wood upon my back they load,
When that I am weary, weary, weary, weary, O. . . . .

A thousand woes beside, that I do here abide,
In the Land of Virginny, O;
In misery I spend my time that hath no end,
When that I am weary, weary, weary, weary, O.

Then let Maids beware, all by my ill-fare,
In the Land of Virginny, O;
Be sure to stay at home, for if you do here come,
You all will be weary, weary, weary, weary, O.

But if it be my chance, Homewards to advance,
From the Land of Virginny, O;
If that I, once more, land on English Shore,
I'll no more be weary, weary, weary, weary, O.

Chapter 2:
Document Set 2 References

1. George Percy's Observations on Jamestown's Early Months, 1607
Samuel Purchas, ed., *Observations Gathered Out of a Discourse of the Plantation of the Southerne Colonie in Virginia by the English, 1606: Written by that Honorable Gentleman, Master George Percy* (from Samuel Purchas's *Pilgrimes*, iv, 1685–1690), in Edward Arber, ed., *Travels and Works of Captain John Smith: President of Virginia, and Admiral of New England, 1580–1631*, a New Edition, with a Biographical and Critical Introduction by A. G. Bradley, Part I (Edinburgh: John Grant, 1910), pp. lxxi-lxxiii.

2. John Smith's Impressions of the Jamestown Experience, 1607
John Smith, *The General Historie of Virginia, New England, and the Summer Isles* (1624), in Arber, pp. 385–389, 391–395, 402.

3. Virgina Population Characteristics, 1625
Patent Books, Virginia State Library, in Edmund S. Morgan, *American Slavery, American Freedom: The Ordeal of Colonial Virginia* (New York: W. W. Norton, 1975), Table 2, p. 408.

4. The London Company Instructs the Governor in Virginia, 1622
"Letter to the Governor and Council in Virginia," August 12, 1622, *Records of the Virginia Company of London*, ed. S. M. Kingsbury (Washington, D.C., 1933), in David J. Rothman and Sheila Rothman, eds., *Sources of the American Social Tradition* (New York: Basic Books, 1975), Vol. 1, pp. 16–17.

5. The Trappan'd Maiden: or, The Distressed Damsel, ca. Seventeenth Century
"The Trappan'd Maiden: or, the Distressed Damsel," *An American Garland: Being a Collection of Ballads Relating to America, 1563–1759*, ed. C. H. Firth (Oxford University Press, 1915), pp. 251–253.

Chapter 2:
Document Set 2 Credits

3. "Virginia Population Characteristics, 1625," reprinted from *American Slavery, American Freedom: The Ordeal of Colonial Virginia* by Edmund S. Morgan, by permission of W. W. Norton & Company, Inc.

CHAPTER 2

Varieties of Interaction: The Consequences of Cross-Cultural Contact in the New World

Chapter 2's central theme involves the explosive effect of the encounter between Old World and New World cultures that took place in sixteenth- and early-seventeenth-century America. In many respects, the Native American cultures described in Chapter I were disrupted by European incursions during the first century of interaction. It is equally true that an enormously significant biologic, economic, and intellectual exchange was the result of this clash of cultures. It is your task to use the documents as the basis for an assessment of this interaction and its ramifications for the future.

For many years scholars have dwelt on the undeniable brutality of the Spanish conquest of Mexico, Peru, and the Caribbean, which gave rise to a "Black Legend" with regard to Spain's role in sixteenth-century America. Be aware of the legend's origins in the ideological struggle between Catholic Spain and Protestant Europe, especially England. The result of this battle was a flood of anti-Spanish propaganda that emphasized the alleged inhumanity of the *conquistadores* who claimed large areas of the Americas and their resources for Spain. Use the textbook account of the conquest to shape your own view of the Black Legend as part of the larger story of cross-cultural relations. As you review the writings of the clerical critics, including Bartolomé de Las Casas and Bernardino de Sahagún, compare them with the accounts of Spain's Florida missions by Father Juan Rogel and some of the English chroniclers of American exploration. Try to arrive at your own interpretation of the motivations and activities of the Spanish in the Caribbean basin.

As you examine the evidence, you should also be aware of the multiplicity of white-Indian contacts that were taking place throughout the Americas. Search the documents for indications of the diverse motives, values, and assumptions of the Europeans who entered into a variety of working relationships with Native American peoples in widely scattered regions of North and South America. Think about the forces which drew together the parties to this encounter as well as the conflicts that separated them. Try to view these contacts from the viewpoints of both Europeans and Indians as you attempt to formulate a more complex generalization about the character of white-Indian relations than that implied by the Black Legend.

Your analysis should also probe the reasons for the adverse reaction to Spanish behavior in sixteenth-century America. Study the documents, including the visual representations of cross-cultural contacts, with an eye to the assumptions of the writers and artists who created them. Consider the impact of religious, political, and economic factors on the accounts of the New World that circulated in Europe. As you review the evidence, try to understand how these images of America and its indigenous inhabitants influenced future settlement and the development of cross-cultural relationships as the European presence became stronger.

Questions for Analysis

1. What is the meaning of the "Black Legend," and how did it originate? According to Las Casas, how did the Spanish treat Native Americans? To what extent are his accounts trustworthy? How do they compare with the report of Father Juan Rogel's efforts in Florida? Explain any discrepancies in the many accounts of Spanish activity in the New World.

2. To what extent did first contacts and relationships between the English and the Indians differ from those which prevailed in Mexico and the Caribbean at the time of the Spanish conquest? How would you account for these differences? Why are some accounts more reliable than others?

3. Examine the artistic renditions of sixteenth-century encounters between Europeans and Indians. What can be learned from these illustrations concerning the assumptions of both European and Native American artists with regard to the "other"? What does the work of European artists such as Theodor de Bry reveal about the values and assumptions of those who portrayed the Spanish conquest? How did these visual documents influence European expectations and ideas about the peoples of the New World?

4. What do the documents reveal about the Indians' reactions to their earliest contacts with Europeans? Why did Native Americans respond as they did? What were the results of their behavior for their own and future generations of Indians?

1. Bartolomé de Las Casas Indicts the *Conquistadores, 1542*

God has created all these numberless people to be quite the simplest, without malice or duplicity, most obedient, most faithful to their natural Lords, and to the Christians, whom they serve; the most humble, most patient, most peaceful, and calm, without strife nor tumults; not wrangling, nor querulous, as free from uproar, hate and desire of revenge, as any in the world.

They are likewise the most delicate people, weak and of feeble constitution, and less than any other can they bear fatigue, and they very easily die of whatsoever infirmity; so much so, that not even the sons of our Princes and of nobles, brought up in royal and gentle life, are more delicate than they; although there are among them such as are of the peasant class. They are also a very poor people, who of worldly goods possess little, nor wish to possess: and they are therefore neither proud, nor ambitious, nor avaricious. . . .

Among these gentle sheep, gifted by their Maker with the above qualities, the Spaniards entered as soon as they knew them, like wolves, tigers, and lions which had been starving for many days, and since forty years they have done nothing else; nor do they otherwise at the present day, than outrage, slay, afflict, torment, and destroy them with strange and new, and many kinds of cruelty, never before seen, nor heard of, nor read of. . . .

Of the Island of Hispaniola

The Christians, with their horses and swords and lances, began to slaughter and practise strange cruelty among them. They penetrated into the country and spared neither children nor the aged, nor pregnant women, nor those in child labour, all of whom they ran through the body and lacerated, as though they were assaulting so many lambs herded in their sheepfold.

They made bets as to who would slit a man in two, or cut off his head at one blow: or they opened up his bowels. They tore the babes from their mothers' breast by the feet, and dashed their heads against the rocks. Others they seized by the shoulders and threw into the rivers, laughing and joking, and when they fell into the water they exclaimed: "boil body of so and so!" They spitted the bodies of other babes, together with their mothers and all who were before them, on their swords.

They made a gallows just high enough for the feet to nearly touch the ground, and by thirteens, in honour and reverence of our Redeemer and the twelve Apostles, they put wood underneath and, with fire, they burned the Indians alive.

They wrapped the bodies of others entirely in dry straw, binding them in it and setting fire to it; and so they burned them. They cut off the hands of all they wished to take alive, made them carry them fastened on to them, and said: "Go and carry letters": that is; take the news to those who have fled to the mountains.

They generally killed the lords and nobles in the following way. They made wooden gridirons of stakes, bound them upon them, and made a slow fire beneath: thus the victims gave up the spirit by degrees, emitting cries of despair in their torture. . . .

Of New Spain

New Spain [Mexico] was discovered in the year 1517. And the discoverers gave serious offence to the Indians in that discovery, and committed several homicides. In the year 1518 men calling themselves Christians went there to ravage and to kill; although they say that they go to populate. And from the said year 1518, till the present day (and we are in 1542) all the iniquity, all the injustice, all the violence and tyranny that the Christians have practised in the Indies have reached the limit and overflowed: because they have entirely lost all fear of God and the King, they have forgotten themselves as well.

2. The Aztec View of the Conquest, ca. Sixteenth Century

Then [Cortés] said to Moctezuma: "Is this not thou? Art thou not he? Art thou Moctezuma?"

Moctezuma replied: "Indeed yes; I am he." . . .

And when Moctezuma's address which he directed to the Marquis [Cortés] was ended, Marina [Malinche, a native woman working for the Spanish] then interpreted it, she translated it to him. And when the Marquis had heard Moctezuma's words, he spoke to Marina; he spoke to them in a barbarous tongue; he said in his barbarous tongue:

"Let Moctezuma put his heart at ease; let him not be frightened. We love him much. Now our hearts are indeed satisfied, for we know him, we hear him. For a long time we have wished to see him, to look upon his face. And this we have seen. Already we have come to his home in Mexico. At his leisure he will hear our words."

Thereupon [the Spaniards] grasped [Moctezuma] by the hand. Already they went leading him by it. They caressed him with their hands to make their love known to him. . . .

And when they had gone to arrive in the palace, when they had gone to enter it, at once they firmly seized Moctezuma. They continually kept him closely under observation; they never let him from their sight. With him was Itzquauhtzin. But the others just came forth [unimpeded].

And when this had come to pass, then each of the guns shot off. As if in confusion there was going off to one side, there was scattering from one's sight, a jumping in all directions. It was as if one had lost one's breath; it was as if for the time there was stupefaction, as if one were affected by mushrooms, as if something unknown were shown one. Fear prevailed. It was as if everyone had swallowed his heart. Even before it had grown dark, there was terror, there was astonishment, there was apprehension, there was a stunning of the people. . . .

And when [the Spaniards] were well settled, they thereupon inquired of Moctezuma as to all the city's treasure—the devices, the shields. Much did they importune him; with great zeal they sought gold. And Moctezuma thereupon went leading the Spaniards. They went surrounding him, scattered about him; he went among them, he went in their lead; they went each holding him, each grasping him. And when they reached the storehouse, a place called Teocalco, thereupon were brought forth all the brilliant things; the quetzal feather head fan, the devices, the shields, the golden discs, the devils' necklaces, the golden nose crescents, the golden leg bands, the golden arm bands, the golden forehead bands.

Thereupon was detached the gold which was on the shields and which was on all the devices. And as all the gold was detached, at once they ignited, set fire to, applied fire to all the various precious things [which remained]. They all burned. And the gold the Spaniards formed into separate bars. . . .

And four days after they had been hurled from the [pyramid] temple, [the Spaniards] came to cast away [the bodies of] Moctezuma and Itzquauhtzin, who had died, at the water's edge at a place called Teoaloc. For at that place there was the image of a turtle carved of stone; the stone had an appearance like that of a turtle.

And when they were seen, when they were known to be Moctezuma and Itzquauhtzin, then they quickly took up Moctezuma in their arms. They carried him there to a place called Copulco. Thereupon they placed him on a pile of wood; thereupon they kindled it, they set fire to it. Thereupon the fire crackled, seeming to flare up, to send up many tongues of flame; many tongues of flame, many sprigs of flame seemed to arise. And Moctezuma's body seemed to lie sizzling, and it smelled foul as it burned. . . .

And everywhere on the roads the Spaniards robbed the people. They sought gold. They despised the green stone, the precious feathers, and the turquoise. [The gold] was everywhere in the bosoms, in the skirts of the poor women. And as for us who were men: it was everywhere in their breech clouts, in their mouths.

And [the Spaniards] seized, they selected the women—the pretty ones, those whose bodies were yellow: the yellow [light-skinned] ones. And some women, when they were to be taken from the people,

muddied their faces, and clothed themselves in old clothing, put rags on themselves as a shift. It was all only rags that they put on themselves.

And also some were selected from among us men—those who were strong, those soon grown to manhood, and those of whom later as young men they would make messengers, who would be their messengers, those known as *tlamacazque*. Of some they then burned [branded] the cheeks; of some they painted the cheeks; of some they painted the lips.

And when the shields were laid down, when we fell, it was in the year count Three House; and in the day count it was One Serpent.

3. A Jesuit Description of the Missionary Alternative to Violence, 1570

From Father Juan Rogel to Pedro Menendez

Havana, December 9, 1570

1. I would have wished to write Your Lordship much better news than that which I have to write you concerning that for which Your Lordship works with such holy zeal; but it seems that the Lord in his mysterious judgement permits that neither the wishes, the work, nor the large allowance paid by Your Lordship, nor our industry are enough. . . .

2. In setting up the house on Santa Elena, Father Vice-Provincial then ordered me to go to live in Orista, where I went with much delight, with the wish and the great expectations that I had that we ought to begin to reap some harvest. And at first when I dealt with those Indians, they seemed to me to have improved very much, seeing them clothed and with a much better way of life than those of Carlos [Father Rogel's first mission in La Florida]. I praised God, seeing each Indian, married to one woman only, understanding how to work his land and take care of his house and raise his children very carefully. Seeing them not contaminated with the generally accepted abominable sins, and not incestuous, not cruel, not thieves; seeing them dealing with one another with much truth and much peace and simplicity.

3. Finally, it seemed to me that we were sure of our catch, and that it would take me longer to learn

their language in order to explain to them the mysteries of our holy faith, than it would take them to receive it and become Christians. And thus I, together with the other three in my company, hastened to learn it, with such luck that in six months I spoke to them and preached to them in it. . . . But I saw that instead of improving, they were getting worse, making fun of that which was told them. . . .

7. Your Lordship sees here the course I have followed and the way I have dealt with the Indians and the meager results and the little readiness that I see in them for their conversion if God, our Lord, does not miraculously provide for it. The chief cause for this is that they scatter and are without any residential base for nine months out of the twelve each year. That even if, when they move from one place to another, they would stay together, there would be some hope, by going with them, of making some impression, hammering upon them like a constant drip of water on a hard rock. But each one goes his own way. And thus I have experienced the opposite of the principle Your Lordship feels so deeply about, that our faith must be spread in this land. What I find is quite the opposite, that in order to bear fruit among the blind and sad souls of this province, it is necessary, first to order how the Indians are to gather and live in villages and cultivate the land, gathering food for the whole year. And after they are thus very settled, enter the preaching. Because if this is not done, even if

priests go among them for 50 years, their efforts will not be more fruitful than what we have achieved these four years that we have gone among them, which is nothing, not even hope nor any appearance of it. And gathering them together in this manner, Your Lordship must understand, will take a great deal of work and a long time, to do it justly and as God, our Lord, orders it, not compelling them with armed force either. . . . And thus I conclude that if the Lord does not miraculously provide some means to us, incognito, as He may very well do, no human means present themselves to me, if not that which I have written, and for it there are these additional burdens.

4. Samuel de Champlain Establishes a Trade Relationship with the Indians, 1604

I directed our interpreter to say to our savages that they should cause Bessabez, Cabahis, and their companions to understand that Sieur de Monts [Champlain's patron] had sent me to see them, and also their country, and that he desired to preserve friendship with them and to reconcile them with their enemies, the Souriquois . . . , and moreover that he desired to inhabit their country and show them how to cultivate it, in order that they might not continue to lead so miserable a life as they were doing, and some other words on the same subject. This our savages interpreted to them, at which they signified their great satisfaction, saying that no greater good could come to them than to have our friendship, and that they desired to live in peace with their enemies, and that we should dwell in their land, in order that they might in the future more than ever before engage in hunting beavers, and give us a part of them in return for our providing them with things which they wanted. After he finished his discourse, I presented them with hatchets . . . , caps, knives, and other little knickknacks, when we separated from each other. All the rest of this day and the following night, until break of day, they did nothing but dance, sing, and make merry, after which we traded for a certain number of beavers. Then each party returned, Bessabez with his companions on the one side, and we on the other, highly pleased at having made the acquaintance of this people.

5. Sir Walter Raleigh Describes the English Approach to the Caribbean Indians, 1595

The Arawakan pilot with the rest, feared that we would have eaten them, or otherwise have put them to some cruel death (for the Spaniards, to the end that none of the people in the passage towards Guiana or in Guiana itself might come to talk with us, persuaded all the nations, that we were cannibals) but when the poor men and women had seen us, and that we gave them food, and to every one something or other, which was rare and strange to them, they began to conceive the deceit and purpose of the Spaniards, who indeed (as they confessed) took from them both their wives and daughters daily, and used them for the satisfying of their own lusts, especially such as they took in this manner by strength. But I protest before the Majesty of the living God, that I neither know nor believe, that any of our company one or other, by violence or otherwise, ever knew [sexually] any of their women, and yet we saw many hundreds, and had many in our power, and of those very young, and excellently favored, which came among us without deceit, stark naked.

Nothing got us more love among them than this usage: for I suffered not any man to take from any of the nations [natives] so much as a pineapple, or a potato root, without giving them payment, nor any man so much as to offer to touch any of their wives or daughters: which course so contrary to the Spaniards (who tyrannize over them in all things) drew them to admire her Majesty [Elizabeth I] whose commandment I told them it was, and also wonderfully to honor our nation.

But I confess it was a very impatient work to keep the baser sort from despoiling and stealing, when we came to their houses: which because in all I could not prevent, I caused my Indian interpreter at every place when we departed, to know of the loss or wrong done, and if ought were stolen or taken by violence, either the same was restored, and the perpetrator punished in their sight, or else was payed [sic] for to their uttermost demand.

6. The Plymouth Settlers Strike an Agreement with the Indians, 1620

All this while the Indians came skulking about them, and would sometimes show themselves aloof off, but when any approached near them, they would run away; and once they stole away their tools where they had been at work and were gone to dinner. But about the 16th of March, a certain Indian came boldly amongst them and spoke to them in broken English, which they could well understand but marveled at it. . . . His name was Samoset. He told them also of another Indian whose name was Squanto, a native of this place, who had been in England and could speak better English than himself.

Being, after some time of entertainment and gifts dismissed, a while after he came again, and five more with him, and they brought again all the tools that were stolen away before, and made way for the coming of their great Sachem, called Massasoit. Who, about four or five days after, came with the chief of his friends and other attendance, with the aforesaid Squanto. With whom, after friendly entertainment and some gifts given him, they made a peace with him (which hath now continued this 24 years) in these terms:

1. That neither he nor any of his should injure or do hurt to any of their people.

2. That if any of his did hurt to any of theirs, he should send the offender, that they might punish him.

3. That if anything were taken away from any of theirs, he should cause it to be restored; and they should do the like to his.

4. If any did unjustly war against him, they would aid him; if any did war against them, he should aid them.

5. He should send to his neighbours confederates to certify them of this, that they might not wrong them, but might be likewise comprised in the conditions of peace.

6. That when their men came to them, they should leave their bows and arrows behind them.

After these things he returned to his place called Sowams, some 40 miles from this place, but Squanto continued with them and was their interpreter and was a special instrument sent of God for their good beyond their expectation. He directed them how to set their corn, where to take fish, and to procure other commodities, and was also their pilot to bring them to unknown places for their profit, and never left them till he died.

7. William Wood's Impressions of New England Indians, 1639

To enter into a serious discourse concerning the natural conditions of these Indians might procure admiration from the people of any civilized nations, in regard of their civility and good natures. If a tree may be judged by his fruit, and dispositions calculated by exterior actions, then may it be concluded that these Indians are of affable, courteous, and well-disposed natures, ready to communicate the best of their wealth to the mutual good of one another; . . .

If it were possible to recount the courtesies they have showed the English since their first arrival in those parts, it would not only steady belief that they are a loving people, but also win the love of those that never saw them, and wipe off that needless fear that is too deeply rooted in the conceits of many who think them envious and of such rancorous and inhumane dispositions that they will one day make an end of their English inmates. . . . And whereas once there was a proffer of an universal league amongst all the Indians in those parts, to the intent that they might all join in one united force to extirpate the English, our Indians refused the motion, replying they had rather be servants to the English, of whom they were confident to receive no harm and from whom they had received so many favors and assured good testimonies of their love, than equals with them who would cut their throats upon the least offence and make them the shambles of their cruelty. Furthermore, if any roving ships be upon the coasts and chance to harbor either eastward, northward, or southward in any unusual port, they will give us certain intelligence of her burthen and forces, describing their men either by language or features, which is a great privilege and no small advantage. Many ways hath their advice and endeavor been advantageous unto us, they being our first instructors for the planting of their Indian corn, by teaching us to cull out the finest seed, to observe the fittest season, to keep distance for holes and fit measure for hills, to worm it and weed it, to prune it and dress it as occasion shall require. . . .

These people be of a kind and affable disposition, yet are they very wary with whom they strike hands in friendship. Nothing is more hateful to them than a churlish disposition, so likewise is dissimulation; he that speaks seldom and opportunely, being as good as his word, is the only man they love. The Spaniard they say is all one aramouse (viz., all one as a dog); the Frenchman hath a good tongue but a false heart; the Englishman all one speak, all one heart, wherefore they more approve of them than of any nation. Garrulity is much condemned of them, for they utter not many words, speak seldom, and then with such gravity as is pleasing to the ear. Such as understand them not desire yet to hear their emphatical expressions and lively action.

8. Images of the New World

A. Savagism Unleashed in the European Imagination, ca. Sixteenth Century

**B. An Indian Depiction of First Cultural
Contacts in Peru, ca. Sixteenth Century**

C. Native Images of the Spanish Landing in Mexico, Sixteenth Century

D. A Protestant View of the Spanish Conquest, 1590

E. Theodor de Bry's Vision of the
Conquerors and the Victims,
ca. Sixteenth Century

F. Slave Labor in New World Mines, ca. Sixteenth Century

Chapter 2:
Document Set 3 References

1. Bartolomé de Las Casas Indicts the *Conquistadores,* 1542
   Bartolomé de Las Casas, *Very Brief Account of the Destruction of the Indies,* trans. F. A. McNutt, *Bartolomé de Las Casas . . .* (Cleveland: The Arthur H. Clark Co., 1909), pp. 312–319, passim.

2. The Aztec View of the Conquest, ca. Sixteenth Century
   Bernardino de Sahagún, *Florentine Codex: General History of the Things of New Spain,* trans. A. J. O. Anderson and C. E. Dibble (Salt Lake City: School of American Research and University of Utah, 1950–1982), Book 12: *The Conquest of Mexico,* Chaps. 16, 17, and 23, pp. 44–66, passim.

3. A Jesuit Description of the Missionary Alternative to Violence, 1570
   Father Juan Rogel to Pedro Menendez, December 9, 1570, in David Hurst Thomas, ed., *Ethnology of the Indians of Spanish Florida* (New York: Garland Publishing, Inc., 1991), pp. 10–12.

4. Samuel de Champlain Establishes a Trade Relationship with the Indians, 1604
   Samuel de Champlain, Journal, 1604, in William L. Grant, ed., *The Voyages of Samuel de Champlain* (New York: 1907), pp. 49–50; 202–205.

5. Sir Walter Raleigh Describes the English Approach to the Caribbean Indians, 1595
   "The Voyage of Sir Walter Raleigh (1595) to Trinidad and Guiana," in Richard Hakluyt, *Voyages* (London: Everyman's Library, 1907, rep. 1962), Vol. 7, pp. 314–349, passim.

6. The Plymouth Settlers Strike an Agreement with the Indians, 1620
   William Bradford, *Of Plymouth Plantation, 1620–1647,* ed. Samuel Eliot Morison (New York: Alfred A. Knopf, 1952), pp. 79–81.

7. William Wood's Impressions of New England Indians, 1639
   William Wood, *New England's Prospect: A True, Lively, and Experimental Description of That Part of America, commonly called New England* (London: John Dawson, 1639), pp. 88–89, 91–92.

8. Images of the New World
   A. Savagism Unleashed in the European Imagination, ca. Sixteenth Century.
      Theodor de Bry, *Peregination in Americam* (Frankfort-am-Main: 1597), Newberry Library, in Marvin Lunenfeld, ed., *1492: Discovery, Invasion, Encounter: Sources and Interpretations* (Lexington, Mass.: D. C. Heath, 1991), p. 245.
   B. An Indian Depiction of First Cultural Contacts in Peru, ca. Sixteenth Century. Felipe Guaman Poma de Ayala (Wayman Puma), *El Premier Nueva Crónica y Buen Gobierno* (1583–1615), eds. J.V. Murra and Rolena Adorno, trans. J. L. Urioste (Mexico City: Siglo vientiuno editores, 1980); Original in Royal Library of Copenhagen, in Lunenfeld, p. 250.
   C. Indian Images of the Spanish Landing in Mexico, ca. Sixteenth Century. de Sahagún in Lunenfeld, p.168.
   D. A Protestant View of the Spanish Conquest, 1590. Theodor de Bry, *India Occidentalis,* Vol. 22, (Impression Francofurti, 1590), Newberry Library in Lunenfeld, p. 247.
   E. Theodor de Bry's Vision of the Conquerors and the Victims, ca. Sixteenth Century.
      Theodor de Bry, illustration, Historical Pictures Service, Chicago, in Robert V. Hine, *The American West: An Interpretive History* (Boston: Little, Brown and Company, 1973), p. 4.
   F. Slave Labor in the New World Mines, ca. Sixteenth Century. de Bry, *Peregrination in America,* in Lunenfeld, p. 251.

Chapter 2:
Document Set 3 Credits

8. A. Photo Courtesy of the Edward E. Ayer Collection, The Newberry Library
   B. The Royal Library (Det Kongelige Bibliotek), Copenhagen, Denmark
   C. Firenze, Biblioteca Medicean Laurenziana, Ms. Laur. Med. Palat. 220, c. 406. By courtesy of Ministero per i Beni e le Attività Culturali. Reproduction by any means is forbidden.
   D. Photo Courtesy of the Edward E. Ayer Collection, The Newberry Library
   E. Stock Montage
   F. Photo Courtesy of the Edward E. Ayer Collection, The Newberry Library

CHAPTER 3

DOCUMENT SET 1
The Clash of Cultures: The Pequot War

When the English established permanent settlements at Jamestown, Plymouth, and Boston, they did not occupy an empty continent. Already the Spanish were present, the French and Dutch were beginning to arrive, and Native Americans had been living on the land for centuries. Consequently, the seventeenth and eighteenth centuries witnessed extensive cultural conflict as the English, other Europeans, and Native Americans struggled for control of North America. The English colonists' initial wars focused on the Native Americans. The Pequot War of 1637, New England's first, illustrates the issues at stake in these early white–Indian confrontations.

In the middle 1630s, Massachusetts settlers began moving southwest to the Connecticut Valley. With the aid of several of the Massachusetts Bay gentry, John Winthrop, Jr., founded the town of Saybrook near the mouth of the Connecticut River in 1635. The same year Thomas Hooker, pastor of the Newton (Cambridge) Church, and his congregation, who were interested primarily in finding better farmland, received permission from the Massachusetts Court to establish plantations upstream on the Connecticut River. By 1636 the Hartford, Windsor, and Wethersfield plantations were also under way.

In 1634, the Pequots had signed a treaty with Massachusetts giving up claim to the Connecticut Valley. Among the Native Americans in the area, including Mohegans and Narragansetts, the aggressive Pequots were dominant. As Puritan colonists migrated in, their relations with the Pequots deteriorated, and reports of Indian raids against the encroaching whites increased. Consequently, Massachusetts sent troops under the command of John Endicott on a pacification mission, an encounter that soon escalated into open warfare.

The colonial military subdued the Pequots, who were virtually exterminated. Over 800 were killed, wounded, or captured, whereas the colonists suffered fewer than thirty casualties. The few surviving Pequots were either enslaved or driven from their land to be absorbed by other tribes. An uneasy truce between the remaining Indians and the whites ensued, lasting until King Philip's War in the 1670s.

What follows are excerpts from Major General John Mason's first-hand account of the Pequot War. Mason was then captain of the Connecticut militia and the leader of the attack on the Pequots' village at Mystic. After the war he was made major general of all Connecticut forces, and from 1660 until his retirement in 1670 he served as the Connecticut deputy governor. This account, not initially intended for print, was made public at the request of the Connecticut General Court and is based on Mason's recollections rather than on documents. As you study the account, be aware not only of the chronology of events during the war, but also of Mason's interpretation and presuppositions. Think about the significance of the confrontation for the future of white–Native American relations on the colonial frontier. As you do so, be sure to consider the environmental implications of Puritan expansion, which were reflected in the words of the Narragansett sachem, Miantonomi, in 1642.

Questions for Analysis

1. What does John Mason's account reveal about him and his intent in relating the narrative? Is the story presented objectively? Is objectivity possible for anyone writing as a historian?

2. What judgments did Mason make about the Pequots as a people? Are they justified by the evidence provided? What assumptions are made about the English colonists?

3. According to Mason, why did the English colonists attack the Pequots? What possible unstated reasons or unconscious motivations may have contributed to the decision to attack? In what way did the Puritans' religious convictions influence their opinions of the Indians? Under the circumstances might the English colonists have adopted a different strategy than the extermination of the Pequots?

4. What reasons did the Pequots have for fighting the English?

5. Compare and contrast your textbook's description of the Pequot War with Mason's observations, and identify factual or interpretive differences in the two accounts. What are the correct "facts"? Explain.

6. What was the significance of Puritan expansion for the ecological balance that had prevailed in New England prior to British settlement? What was the place of the Indian in the natural order, and how did contact with Europeans affect the interrelationships among living things?

1. Connecticut and Rhode Island, 1637

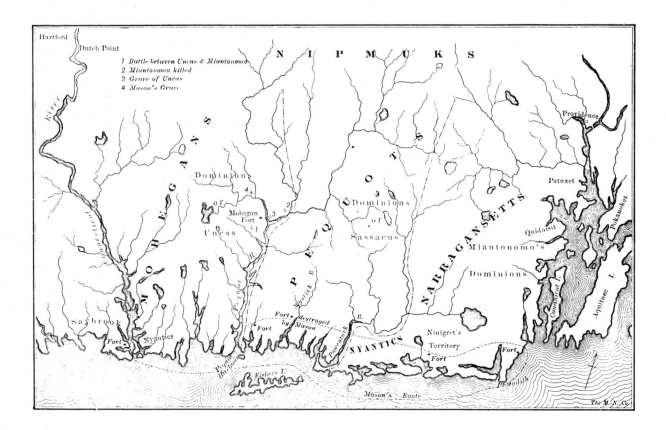

2. A Puritan Account of the Pequot War, 1637

To the Honorable the General Court of Connecticut. Honored Gentlemen, . . .

I shall endeavour in plainness and faithfulness impartially to declare the Matter, not taking the Crown from the Head of one and putting it upon another. There are several who have Wrote and also Printed at random on this Subject, greatly missing the Mark in many Things as I conceive. I shall not exempt my self from frailties, yet from material Faults I presume you may pronounce it not Guilty, and do assure you that if I should see or by any be convinced of an Error, I shall at once confess and amend it. . . .

Judge of me as you please; I shall not climb after Applause, nor do I much fear a Censure; there being many Testimonies to what I shall say. . . . I desire my Name may be sparingly mentioned: My principal Aim is that God may have his due praise. . . .

I shall therefore, God helping, endeavor not so much to stir up the Affections of Men, as to declare in Truth and Plainness the Actions and Doings of Men; I shall therefore set down Matter in order as they Began and were carried on and Issued; that so I may not deceive the Reader in confounding of Things, but the Discourse may be both Plain and Easy. . . .

Some Grounds of the War Against the Pequots

About the Year 1632 one Capt. Stone arrived in the Massachusetts in a Ship from Virginia; who shortly after was bound for Virginia in a small Bark with one Capt. Norton; who sailing into Connecticut River about two Leagues from the Entrance cast Anchor; there coming to them several Indians belonging to that Place whom the Pequots Tyrannized over, being a potent and warlike People, it being their Custom so to deal with their neighbor Indians; Capt. Stone having some occasion with the Dutch who lived at a trading House near twenty Leagues up the River, procured some of those Indians to go as Pilots with two of his Men to the Dutch: But being benighted before they could come to their desired Port, put the skiff in which they went, ashore, where the two Englishmen falling asleep, were both Murdered by their Indian Guides: There remaining with the [boat] about twelve of the aforesaid Indians; who had in all probability formerly plotted their bloody Design; and waiting an opportunity when some of the English were on Shore and Capt. Stone asleep in his Cabin, set upon them and cruelly Murdered every one of them, plundered what they pleased and sunk the [boat].

These Indians were not native Pequots, but had frequent recourse unto them, to whom they tendered some of those Goods, which were accepted by the Chief Sachem of the Pequots: Other of the said Goods were tendered to Nynigrett Sachem of Nayanticke, who also received them.

The Council of the Massachusetts being informed of their proceedings, sent to speak with the Pequots, and had some Treaties with them: But being unsatisfied therewith, sent forth Captain John Endicot Commander in Chief, with Captain Underhill, Captain Turner, and with them one hundred and twenty Men: who were firstly designed on a Service against a People living on Block Island, who were subject to the Narragansett Sachem; they having taken a [boat] of one Mr. John Oldham, Murdering him and all his Company: They were also to call the Pequots to an Account about the Murder of Capt. Stone; who arriving at Pequot had some Conference with them; but little effected; only one Indian slain and some Wigwams burnt. After which, the Pequots grew enraged against the English who inhabited Connecticut, being but a small Number, about two hundred and fifty, who were there newly arrived; as also about twenty Men at Saybrook, under the Command of Lieutenant Lyon Gardner, who was there settled by several Lords and Gentlemen in England. The Pequots falling violently upon them, slew many Men at Saybrook; keeping almost a constant siege upon the Place; so that the English were constrained to keep within their pallisaded Fort; being so hard Beset and sometimes Assaulted, that Capt. John Mason was sent by Connecticut Colony with twenty Men out of their small Numbers to secure the Place: But after his coming, there did not one Pequot appear in view for one Month Space, which was the time he there remained.

In the Interim certain Pequots about One Hundred going to a Place called Wethersfield on Connecticut; having formerly confederated with the Indians of that Place (as it was generally thought) lay in Ambush for the English; many of them going into a large Field adjoining to the Town to their Labor, were there set upon by the Indians: Nine of the English were killed outright, with some Horses, and two young Women taken Captives.

At their Return from Wethersfield, they came down the River of Connecticut (Capt. Mason being then at Saybrook Fort) in three Canoes with about one hundred Men, which River of necessity they must pass: We seeing them, concluded they had been acting some Mischief against us, made a Shot at them with a Piece of Ordnance, which beat off the Beak Head of one of their Canoes, wherein our two Captives were: it was at a very great distance: They then hastened, drew their Canoes over a narrow Beach with all speed and so got away.

Upon which the English were somewhat dejected: But immediately upon this, a Court was called and met in Hartford the First of May, 1637, who seriously considering their Condition, which did look very Sad, for those Pequots were a great People, being strongly fortified, cruel, warlike, munitioned, &c. and the English but an handful in comparison: But their outrageous Violence against the English, having Murdered about Thirty of them, their great Pride and Insolence, constant pursuit in their malicious Courses, with their engaging other Indians in their Quarrel against the English, who had never offered them the least Wrong; who had in all likelihood Espoused all the Indians in the Country in their Quarrel, had not God by more than an ordinary Providence prevented: These Things being duly considered, with the eminent Hazard and great Peril they were in; it pleased God so to stir up the Hearts of all Men in general, and the Court in special, that they concluded some Forces should forthwith be sent out against the Pequots; their Grounds being Just, and necessity enforcing them to engage in an offensive and defensive War; the Management of which War we are nextly to relate. . . .

An Epitome or Brief History of the Pequot War

In the Beginning of May 1637 there were sent out by Connecticut Colony Ninety Men under the Command of Capt. John Mason against the Pequots, with Onkos an Indian Sachem living at Mohegan,* who was newly revolted from the Pequots. . . .

Upon a Wednesday we arrived at Saybrook, where we lay Windbound until Friday; often consulting how and in what manner we should proceed in our Enterprise, being altogether ignorant of the Country. At length we concluded, God assisting us, for Narragansett, and so to March through their Country, which Bordered upon the Enemy; where lived a great People, it being about fifteen Leagues beyond Pequot. . . .

By Narragansett we should come upon 'their Backs, and possibly might surprise them un-awares, at worst we should be on firm Land as well as they.' All which proved very successful as the Sequel may evidently demonstrate. . . .

On Friday Morning we set Sail for Narragansett-Bay, and on Saturday towards Evening we arrived at our desired Port, there we kept the Sabbath.

On the Monday the Wind blew so hard at North-West that we could not go on Shore; as also on the Tuesday until Sun set; at which time Capt. Mason landed and Marched up to the Place of the Chief Sachem's Residence; who told the Sachem, 'That we had not an opportunity to acquaint him with our coming Armed in his Country sooner; yet not doubting but it would be well accepted by him, there being Love between himself and us; well knowing also that the Pequots and themselves were Enemies, and that he could not be unacquainted with those intolerable Wrongs and Injuries these Pequots had lately done unto the English; and that we were now come, God assisting, to Avenge our selves upon them; and that we did only desire free Passage through his Country.' Who returned us this Answer, 'That he did accept of our coming, and did also approve of our Design; only he thought our Numbers were too weak to deal with the Enemy, who were (as he said) very great Captains and Men skillful in War.' . . .

On the Wednesday Morning, we Marched from thence to a Place called Nayanticke, it being about eighteen or twenty miles distant, where another of those Narragansett Sachems lived in a Fort; it being a Frontier to the Pequots. . . .

There we quartered that Night, the Indians not offering to stir out all the while.

In the Morning there came to us several of Miantomo* his Men, who told us, they were come to assist us in our Expedition. . . .

On the Thursday about eight of the Clock in the Morning, we Marched thence towards Pequot, with about five hundred Indians . . . And having Marched about twelve Miles, we came to Pawcatuck River, at a Ford where our Indians told us the Pequots did usually Fish; there making [a stop], we stayed some small time: The Narragansett Indians manifesting great Fear, in so much that many of them returned. . . .

And after we had refreshed our selves with our mean Commons, we Marched about three Miles, and came to a Field which had lately been planted

---

*Onkos: usually called Uncas, the Great Sachem of the Moheags.

*Miantomo: He was usually called Miantonomi the Great Sachem of the Narragansett Indians.

with Indian Corn: There we made another stop, and called our Council, supposing we drew near to the Enemy: and being informed by the Indians that the Enemy had two Forts almost impregnable. . . .

We then Marching on in a silent Manner, the Indians that remained fell all into the Rear, who formerly kept the Van; (being possessed with great Fear) we continued our March till about one Hour in the Night: and coming to a little Swamp between two Hills, there we pitched our little Camp; much wearied with hard Travel, keeping great Silence, supposing we were very near the Fort; as our Indians informed us; which proved otherwise: The Rocks were our Pillows; yet Rest was pleasant: The Night proved Comfortable, being clear and Moon Light: We appointed our Guards and placed our Sentinels at some distance; who heard the Enemy Singing at the Fort, who continued that Strain until Midnight, with great Insulting and Rejoicing, as we were afterwards informed: They seeing our Pinnaces sail by them some Days before, concluded we were afraid of them and dare not come near them; the Burden of their Song tending to that purpose.

In the Morning, we awaking and seeing it very light, supposing it had been day, and so we might have lost our Opportunity, having proposed to make our Assault before Day; roused the Men with all expedition, and briefly commended ourselves and Design to God, thinking immediately to go to the Assault; the Indians showing us a Path, told us that it led directly to the Fort. . . . Then Capt. Underhill came up, who Marched in the Rear; and commending ourselves to God, divided our Men: There being two Entrances into the Fort, intending to enter both at once: Captain Mason leading up to that on the North East Side; who approaching within one Rod, heard a dog bark and an Indian crying Owanux! Owanux! which is Englishmen! Englishmen! We called up our Forces with all expedition, gave Fire upon them through the Palisade; the Indians being in a dead indeed their last Sleep: Then we wheeling off fell upon the main Entrance, which was blocked up with Bushes about Breast high, over which the Captain passed, intending to make good the Entrance, encouraging the rest to follow. Lieutenant Seeley endeavored to enter; but being somewhat [blocked], stepped back and pulled out the Bushes and so enterd, and with him about sixteen Men: We had formerly concluded to destroy them by the Sword and save the Plunder.

Whereupon Captain Mason seeing no Indians, enterd a Wigwam; where he was beset with many Indians, waiting all opportunities to lay Hands on him, but could not prevail. At length William Heydon [seeing] the Breach in the Wigwam, supposing some English might be there, enterd; but in his Entrance fell over a dead Indian; but speedily recovering himself, the Indians some fled, others crept under their Beds: The Captain going out of the Wigwam saw many Indians in the Lane or Street; he making towards them, they fled, were pursued to the End of the Lane, where they were met by Edward Pattison, Thomas Barber, with some others; where seven of them were Slain, as they said. The Captain facing about, Marched a slow Pace up the Lane he came down, perceiving himself very much out of Breath; and coming to the other End near the Place where he first enterd, saw two Soldiers standing close to the Pallisade with their Swords pointed to the Ground: The Captain told them that We should never kill them after that manner: The Captain also said, We must Burn them; and immediately stepping into the Wigwam where he had been before, brought out a Firebrand, and putting it into the Matts with which they were covered, set the Wigwams on Fire. Lieutenant Thomas Bull and Nicholas Omsted beholding, came up; and when it was thoroughly kindled, the Indians ran as Men most dreadfully Amazed.

And indeed such a dreadful Terror did the Almighty let fall upon their Spirits, that they would fly from us and run into the very Flames, where many of them perished. And when the Fort was thoroughly Fired, Command was given, that all should fall off and surround the Fort; which was readily attended by all; only one Arthur Smith being so wounded that he could not move out of the Place, who was happily seen by Lieutenant Bull, and by him rescued. . . .

Thus were they now at their Wits End, who not many Hours before exalted themselves in their great Pride, threatening and resolving the utter Ruin and Destruction of all the English, Exulting and Rejoicing with Songs and Dances: But God was above them, who laughed his Enemies and the Enemies of his People to Scorn, making them as a fiery Oven: Thus were the Stout Hearted spoiled, having slept their last Sleep, and none of their Men could find their Hands: Thus did the Lord judge among the Heathen, filling the Place with dead Bodies!

And here we may see the just Judgment of God, in sending even the very Night before this Assault, One hundred and fifty Men from their other Fort, to join with them of that Place, who were designed as some of themselves reported to go forth against the English, at that very Instant when his heavy Stroke came upon them where they perished with their Fellows. So that the Mischief they intended to us, came upon their own Plate: They were taken in their own snare, and we through Mercy escaped. And thus in little more than one Hour's space was their impregnable Fort with themselves utterly Destroyed, to the Number of six or seven Hundred, as some of themselves confessed. There were only seven taken captive, and about seven escaped.*

Of the English, there were two Slain outright, and about twenty Wounded: Some Fainted by reason of the sharpness of the Weather; it being a cool Morning, and the lack of such Comforts and Necessaries as were needful in such a Case. . . .

And was not the Finger of God in all this? . . . What shall I say: God was pleased to hide us in the Hollow of his Hand; I still remember a Speech of Mr. Hooker at our going aboard; That they should be Bread for us. And thus when the Lord turned the Captivity of his People, and turned the Wheel upon their Enemies; we were like Men in a Dream; then was our Mouth filled with Laughter, and our Tongues with Singing; thus we may say the Lord hath done great Things for us among the Heathen, for which we are glad. Praise ye the Lord!

I shall mention two or three special Providences that God was pleased to vouchsafe to Particular Men; . . . two Men, being one Man's Servants, namely, John Dier and Thomas Stiles, were both of them Shot in the Knots of their Handkerchiefs, being about their Necks, and received no Hurt. Lieutenant Seeley was Shot in the Eyebrow with a flat headed Arrow, the Point turning downwards: I pulled it out myself. Lieutenant Bull had an Arrow Shot into a hard piece of Cheese, having no other Defence: Which may verify the old Saying, A little Armor would serve if a Man knew where to place it. Many such Providences happened; some respecting myself; but since there is none that Witness to them, I shall [not] mention them.

---

*The place of the Fort being called Mistick, this Fight was called Mistick Fight: And Mr. Increase Mather, from a Manuscript he met with, tells us; It was on Friday, May 26. 1637, a memorable Day!

3. An Indian's Fears of Puritan Expansion, 1642

For so are we all Indians as the English are, and say brother to one another; so must we be one as they are, otherwise we shall all be gone shortly, for you know our fathers had plenty of deer and skins, our plains were full of deer, as also our woods, and of turkies, and our coves full of fish and fowl. But these English having gotten our land, they with scythes cut down the grass, and with axes fell the trees; their cows and horses eat the grass, and their hogs spoil our clam banks, and we shall all be starved.

Chapter 3:
Document Set 1 References

1. Connecticut and Rhode Island, 1637
   Connecticut and Rhode Island, in Charles Orr, ed., *History of the Pequot War: The Contemporary Accounts of Mason, Underhill, Vincent and Gardner* (Cleveland: The Helman-Taylor Co., 1897; rep., New York: AMS Press, 1980), frontispiece.

2. A Puritan Account of the Pequot War, 1637
   John Mason, *A Brief History of the Pequot War: Especially of the Memorable Taking of Their Fort at Mistick in Connecticut in 1637 [1656]* (Boston: S. Kneeland and T. Green, 1736), in Orr., pp. 11–12, 15–21, 23–31, 44–46.

3. An Indian's Fears of Puritan Expansion, 1642
   Miantonomi, Narragansett sachem, to the Montauk Indians of eastern Long Island, summer 1642, in Lion Gardner, "Leift Lion Gardner, his relation of the Pequot Warres," Massachusetts Historical Society, *Collections*, 3d Ser., 3(1833), p. 154.

Chapter 3:
Document Set 1 Credits

1. Map reproduced from *Life of John Mason*, by George E. Ellis, in *Library of American Biography*

DOCUMENT SET 2
Witchcraft at Salem: The Social and Cultural Context

One of the key developments outlined in your textbook was the extension of Puritan settlements in the mid-seventeenth century. As the New England towns grew, the congregational principle and the town system contributed to rising tensions over group autonomy and access to land and resources. One result of an orderly pattern of expansion was the mutual watchfulness described in your text. By encouraging centers of settlement, Massachusetts Bay authorities forced close interaction among settlers that, in turn, facilitated the preservation of community values.

By the 1670s, however, the enforcement of close control was breaking down as new communities emerged. Worse yet, many Puritans were distressed by an awareness that the Puritan mission, as defined by the founders, had failed. After the Restoration, the Puritans increasingly turned inward, afflicted by a sense that history had passed them by.

Some scholars view the outbreak of the witchcraft phenomenon in 1692 as a symptom of that sense of failure. The bizarre episode began when several adolescent girls exhibited hysterical behavior following a fortune-telling session with a West Indian slave. Their accusations of witchcraft drew a supportive and increasingly alarming response from adult relatives and friends, resulting in the involvement of the local minister, Samuel Parris, whose home had been the scene of the beginning of the outbreak. With his encouragement, the accusations escalated, trials were held, and more than twenty accused witches were executed.

Historians have explained this grisly affair in a variety of ways, stressing the rise of materialism, adolescent psychology, intergenerational tension, and religious fervor. More recently, scholars have focused attention on the social and economic conflicts present in Salem village and its larger neighbor, Salem town. Differences between rural Salem village and commercial Salem town surfaced, together with sharp conflicts over the pastorate and leadership of Samuel Parris. Similarly, tensions over the autonomy of the more distant settlements were evident in the social and religious alignments that were formed.

The following documents provide evidence to support a number of interpretive positions on the origins of this episode. As you examine the transcripts of the interrogation, the deposition and confession of accuser Ann Putnam, Samuel Parris's sermon, and the later findings of the Council of Elders, be alert to the social and psychological roots of the Salem crisis. Evaluate the written record in the light of statistical material detailing the generational and demographic bases for conflict. Finally, relate the social divisions and religious differences that emerge to your textbook's discussion of rising materialism and the failure of the New England Way.

Questions for Analysis

1. What do the maps and charts reveal about the identities of the parties to the conflict over the witchcraft issue in Salem? How do you account for the support for and opposition to the militant position taken by Samuel Parris?

2. What is the connection between the witchcraft episode of 1692 and the religious trends described in your textbook? What motives and concerns lay behind the Parris sermon? What threat did witches pose, according to Parris? How could they be identified? What was the social significance of their alleged presence?

3. What do the charts that identify accusers and accused by age group reveal about the origins of the witchcraft episode? What is the significance of family relationships in understanding the events in Salem? What does the statistical evidence suggest with regard to the accusers' possible motives?

4. What does the Salem situation in 1692 suggest about social classes and economic change in late-seventeenth-century New England? What was the significance of the economic differences between Salem village and Salem town? What evidence is provided by the documents to clarify the changes under way at this moment in Massachusetts history?

5. Do the documents shed light on the relations between the sexes in seventeenth-century New England? Examine Martha Corey's testimony. How would you explain her viewpoint?

6. Given the world-view, religious environment, and belief systems of the seventeenth century, to what extent does the serious attention devoted by the community to witchcraft accusations seem irrational? What was the meaning of the witchcraft episode to Puritan divines and political leaders?

1. Samuel Parris Sets a Tone, 1692

Christ Knows How Many Devils There Are (1692)

27 March 1691/92, Sacrament day.
Occasioned by dreadful Witchcraft broke out here a few weeks past, and one Member of this Church, and another of Salem, upon public examination by Civil Authority vehemently suspected for she-witches, and upon it committed.

John 6:70. "Have not I chosen you twelve, and one of you is a Devil." . . .

Doctrine: *Our Lord Jesus Christ knows how many Devils there are in his Church, and who they are.*

1. There are devils as well as saints in Christ's Church.
2. Christ knows how many of these devils there are.
3. Christ knows who these devils are.

Proposition 1: There are devils as well as saints in Christ's church. Here three things may be spoken to: (1) Show you what is meant here by *devils;* (2) That there are such devils in the church; (3) That there are also true saints in such churches.

(1). What is meant here by *devils?* "One of you is a devil." Answer: By *devil* is ordinarily meant any wicked angel or spirit. Sometimes it is put for the prince or head of the exil spirits, or fallen angels. Sometimes it is used for vile and wicked persons—the worst of such, who for their villainy and impiety do most resemble devils and wicked spirits. Thus Christ in our text calls Judas a devil: for his great likeness to the devil. "One of you is a devil": i.e., a devil for quality and disposition, not a devil for nature—for he was a man, etc.—but a devil for likeness and operation (John 8: 38, 41, 44—"Ye are of your father the devil.")

(2). There are such devils in the church. Not only sinners, but notorious sinners; sinners more like

to the devil than others. So here in Christ's little Church. (Text.) This also Christ teacheth us in the parable of the tares (Matth. 13:38), where Christ tells us that such are the children of the wicked one—i.e., of the devil. Reason: Because hypocrites are the very worst of men—*corruptio optimi est pessimi.* Hypocrites are the sons and heirs of the devil, the free-holders of hell—whereas other sinners are but tenants. When Satan repossesseth a soul, he becomes more vile and sinful (Luke 11: 24–26). As the jailer lays loads of iron on him that hath escaped. None are worse than those who have been good, and are naught; and might be good, but will be naught. . . .

Proposition 2: Christ knows how many of these devils there are in his churches. As in our text there was one among the twelve. And so in our churches God knows how many devils there are: whether one, two, three, or four in twelve—how many devils, how many saints. He that knows whom he has chosen (John 13: 18), he also knows who they are that have not chosen him, but prefer farms and merchandise above him and above his ordinances (2 Tim. 4: 10). . . .

Use 1. Let none then build their hopes of salvation merely upon this: that they are church members. This you and I may be, and yet devils for all that (Matth. 8: 11–12—"Many shall come from the east and west, and shall sit down, etc. And however we may pass here, a true difference shall be made shortly, etc.")

Use 2. Let none then be stumbled at religion, because too often there are devils found among the saints. You see, here was a true church, sincere converts and sound believers; and yet here was a devil among them.

Use 3. Terror to hypocrites who profess much love to Christ but indeed are in league with their lusts, which they prefer above Christ. Oh! remember that you are devils in Christ's account. Christ is lightly esteemed of you, and you are vilely accounted for by Christ. Oh! if there be any such among us, forbear to come this day to the Lord's table, lest Satan enter more powerfully into you—lest while the bread be between your teeth, the wrath of the Lord come pouring down upon you (Psalm 78: 30–31). . . .

Use 5. Examine we ourselves well, what we are—what we church members are. We are either saints or devils: the Scripture gives us no medium. The Apostle tells us we are to examine ourselves (2 Cor. 13: 5). Oh! it is a dreadful thing to be a devil, and yet to sit down at the Lord's table (1 Cor. 10: 21). Such incur the hottest of God's wrath (as follows—v. 22). Now, if we would not be devils, we must give ourselves wholly up to Christ, and not suffer the predominancy of one lust—and particularly that of covetousness, which is made so light of, and which so sorely prevails in these perilous times. Why, this one lust made Judas a devil (John 12: 6, Matth. 26: 15). And no

doubt it has made more devils than one. For a little pelf [money], men sell Christ to his enemies, and their souls to the devil. But there are certain sins that make us devils; see that we be not such:

1. A liar or murderer (John 8: 44)

2. A slanderer or an accuser of the godly

3. A tempter to sin

4. An opposer of godliness, as Elymos (Acts 13: 8 etc.)

5. Envious persons as witches

6. A drunkard (I Sam. 1: 15–16)

7. A proud person

2. Martha Corey's Testimony, 1692

"Mr. HATHORNE: You are now in the hands of authority. Tell me, now, why you hurt these persons.—I do not.

"Who doth?—Pray, give me leave to go to prayer.

"(This request was made sundry times.)

"We do not send for you to go to prayer; but tell me why you hurt these.—I am an innocent person. I never had to do with witchcraft since I was born. I am a gospel woman.

"Do not you see these complain of you?—The Lord open the eyes of the magistrates and ministers: the Lord show his power to discover the guilty.

"Tell us who hurts these children.—I do not know.

"If you be guilty of this fact, do you think you can hide it?—The Lord knows.

"Well, tell us what you know of this matter.—Why, I am a gospel woman; and do you think I can have to do with witchcraft too? . . .

"(CHILDREN: There is a man whispering in her ear.)

"HATHORNE continued: What did he say to you?—We must not believe all that these distracted children say.

"Cannot you tell what that man whispered?—I saw nobody.

"But did not you hear?—No.

"(Here was extreme agony of all the afflicted.)

"If you expect mercy of God, you must look for it in God's way, by confession. Do you think to find mercy by aggravating your sins?—A true thing.

"Look for it, then, in God's way.—So I do.

"Give glory to God and confess, then.—But I cannot confess.

"Do not you see how these afflicted do charge you?—We must not believe distracted persons. . . .

"You charge these children with distraction: it is a note of distraction when persons vary in a minute; but these fix upon you. This is not the manner of distraction.—When all are against me, what can I help it?

"Now tell me the truth, will you? Why did you say that the magistrates' and ministers' eyes were blinded, you would open them?

"(She laughed, and denied it.)

"Now tell us how we shall know who doth hurt these, if you do not?—Can an innocent person be guilty?

"Do you deny these words?—Yes.

"Tell us who hurts these. We came to be a terror to evil-doers. You say you would open our eyes, we are blind.—If you say I am a witch. . . .

"You say you are no witch. Maybe you mean you never covenanted with the Devil. Did you never deal with any familiar?—No, never.

"What bird was that the children spoke of?

"(Then witnesses spoke: What bird was it?)

"I know no bird.

"It may be you have engaged you will not confess; but God knows.—So he doth.

"Do you believe you shall go unpunished?—I have nothing to do with witchcraft. . . .

"Do not you believe there are witches in the country?—I do not know that there is any.

"Do not you know that Tituba confessed it?—I did not hear her speak.

"I find you will own nothing without several witnesses, and yet you will deny for all.

"(It was noted, when she bit her lip, several of the afflicted were bitten. When she was urged upon it that she bit her lip, saith she, What harm is there in it?)

"(Mr. NOYES: I believe it is apparent she practiseth witchcraft in the congregation: there is no need of images.)

"What do you say to all these things that are apparent?—If you will all go hang me, how can I help it? . . .

"What book is that you would have these children write in?—What book? Where should I have a book? I showed them none, nor have none, nor brought none.

"(The afflicted cried out there was a man whispering in her ears.)

"What book did you carry to Mary Walcot?—I carried none. . . .

"Who is your God?—The God that made me.

"What is his name?—Jehovah.

"Do you know any other name?—God Almighty.

"Doth *he* tell you, that you pray to, that *he* is God Almighty?—Who do I worship but the God that made [me]?

"How many gods are there?—One.

"How many persons?—Three. . . .

"Do not you see these children and women are rational and sober as their neighbors, when your hands are fastened?

"(Immediately they were seized with fits: and the standers-by said she was squeezing her fingers, her hands being eased by them that held them on purpose for trial.

"Quickly after, the marshal said, 'She hath bit her lip'; and immediately the afflicted were in an uproar.)

"[Tell] why you hurt these, or who doth?

"(She denieth any hand in it.)

"Why did you say, if you were a witch, you should have no pardon?—Because I am a woman."

3. Ann Putnam's Deposition, 1692

Who testified and said that on 20th of April, 1692 at evening she saw the Apparition of a minister at which she was grieviously frightened and cried out oh dreadful: dreadful here is a minister come, what are Ministers witches too: whence come you and What is your name for I will complain of you though you be a Minister: if you be a wizard. . . . and Immediately I was tortured by him being Racked and almost choked by him: and he tempted me to write in his book which I Refused with loud outcries and said I would not write in his book though he tore me all to pieces but told him that it was a dreadful thing: that he which was a Minister that should teach children to fear God should come to persuade poor creatures to give their souls to the devil; oh, dreadful, dreadful, tell me your name that I may know who you are; then again he tortured me and urged me to write in his book; which I refused and then presently he told me that his name was George Burroughs, and that he had had three wives: and that he had bewitched the Two first of them to death; and that he had killed Miss T. Lawson because she was so unwilling to go from the village, and also killed Mr Lawson's child because he went to the eastward with Sir Edmon and preached to the soldiers and that he had made Abigail Hobbs a witch and several witches more: and he has continued ever since; by times tempting me to write in his book and grievously torturing me by beating, pinching and almost choking me several times a day and he also told me that he was above a witch he was a conjuror.

4. Salem Village, 1692

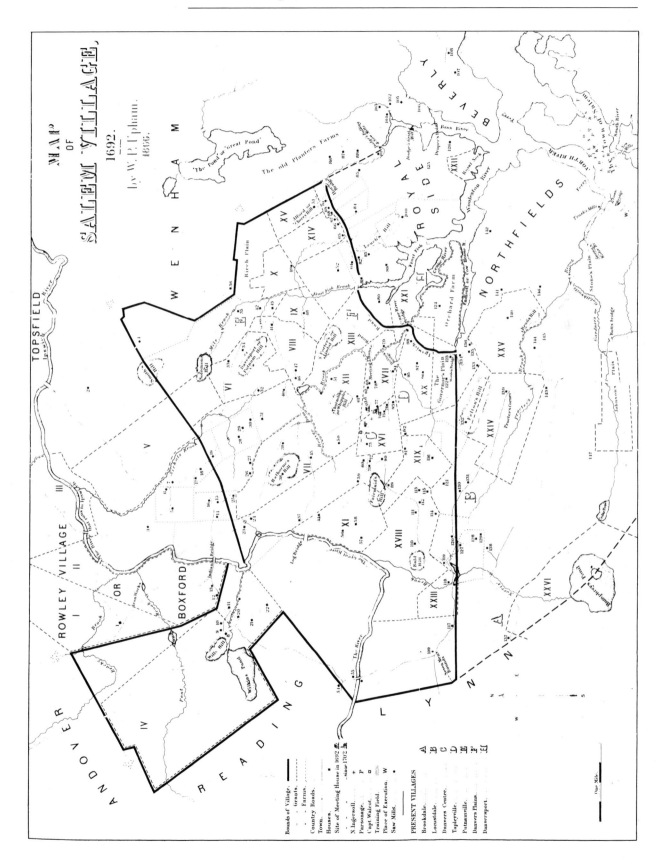

5. The Geography of Witchcraft in Salem Village, 1692

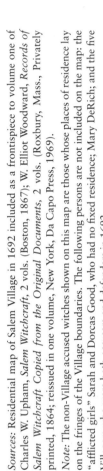

Sources: Residential map of Salem Village in 1692 included as a frontispiece to volume one of Charles W. Upham, *Salem Witchcraft*, 2 vols. (Boston, 1867); W. Elliot Woodward, *Records of Salem Witchcraft Copied from the Original Documents*, 2 vols. (Roxbury, Mass., Privately printed, 1864; reissued in one volume, New York, Da Capo Press, 1969).

Note: The non-Village accused witches shown on this map are those whose places of residence lay on the fringes of the Village boundaries. The following persons are not included on the map: the "afflicted girls" Sarah and Dorcas Good, who had no fixed residence; Mary DeRich; and the five Villagers who were both accusers and defenders in 1692.

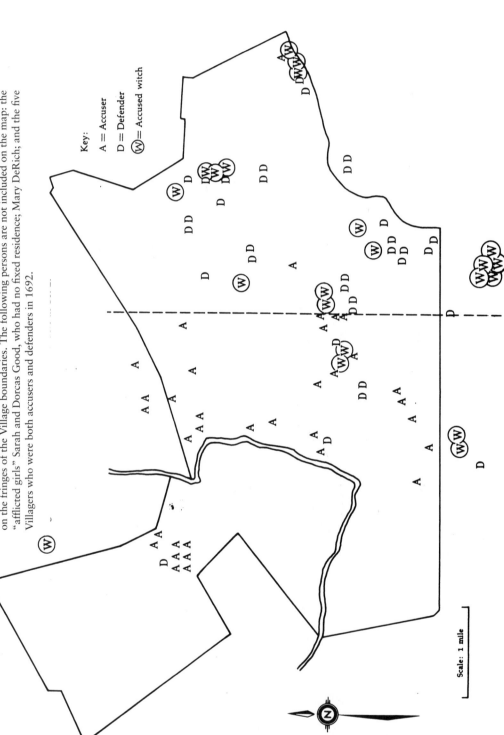

Key:

A = Accuser
D = Defender
(W) = Accused witch

Scale: 1 mile

6. Factionalism and Wealth in Salem Village, 1695

	Number of householders in each tax bracket		Percentage of householders in each tax bracket	
Amount of 1695–96 tax	Pro-Parris (average tax: 10.9 shillings)	Anti-Parris (average tax: 15.3 shillings)	Pro-Parris	Anti-Parris
Under 10 shillings	31	15	61	43
10–20 shillings	16	12	31	34
Over 20 shillings	4	8	8	23
Total	51	35	100	100

Sources: Tax list, Village Records, Dec. 13, 1695; pro-Parris and anti-Parris petitions as transcribed by Samuel Parris in the Village Church Records preceding the entry for June 2, 1695.

7. Ann Putnam's Confession, 1706

"I desire to be humbled before God for that sad and humbling providence that befell my father's family in the year about '92; that I, then being in my childhood, should, by such a providence of God, be made an instrument for the accusing of several persons of a grievous crime, whereby their lives were taken away from them, whom now I have just grounds and good reason to believe they were innocent persons; and that it was a great delusion of Satan that deceived me in that sad time, whereby I justly fear I have been instrumental, with others, though ignorantly and unwittingly, to bring upon myself and this land the guilt of innocent blood; though what was said or done by me against any person I can truly and uprightly say, before God and man, I did it not out of any anger, malice, or ill-will to any person, for I had no such thing against one of them; but what I did was ignorantly, being deluded by Satan. And particularly, as I was a chief instrument of accusing of Goodwife Nurse and her two sisters, I desire to lie in the dust, and to be humbled for it, in that I was a cause, with others, of so sad a calamity to them and their families; for which cause I desire to lie in the dust, and earnestly beg forgiveness of God, and from all those unto whom I have given just cause of sorrow and offence, whose relations were taken away or accused.

[Signed]

"This confession was read before the congregation, together with her relation, Aug. 25, 1706; and she acknowledged it.

"J. Green *Pastor.*"

8. Witchcraft in Salem: Analysis by Age and Sex, 1692

Accused Witches

Sex	Total
Male	42
Female	120
Total	162

Marital Status	Male	Female	Total
Single	8	29	37
Married	15	61	76
Widowed	1	20	21
Total	24	110	134

Age	Male	Female	Total
Under 20	6	18	24
21–30	3	7	10
31–40	3	8	11
41–50	6	18	24
51–60	5	23	28
61–70	4	8	12
Over 70	3	6	9
Total	30	88	118

Young Witches

Sex	Total
Male	5
Female	29
Total	34

Marital Status	Male	Female	Total
Single	5	23	28
Married	0	6	6
Widowed	0	0	0
Total	5	29	34

Age	Male	Female	Total
Under 11	0	1	1
11–15	1	7	8
16–20	1	13	14
21–25	0	1	1
26–30	0	1	1
Over 30	0	4	4
Total	2	27	29

Witnesses

Sex	Total
Male	63
Female	21
Total	84

Marital Status	Male	Female	Total
Single	11	3	14
Married	39	16	55
Widowed	3	1	4
Total	53	20	73

Age	Male	Female	Total
Under 20	3	2	5
21–30	13	4	17
31–40	14	6	20
41–50	18	7	25
51–60	11	1	12
61–70	2	1	3
Over 70	2	0	2
Total	63	21	84

9. The Conclusions of the Massachusetts Bay Elders, 1695

The elders and messengers of the churches—met in council at Salem Village, April 3, 1695, to consider and determine what is to be done for the composure of the present unhappy differences in that place,—after solemn invocation of God in Christ for this direction, do unanimously declare and advise as followeth:—

I. We judge that, albeit in the late and the dark time of the confusions, wherein Satan had obtained a more than ordinary liberty to be sifting of this plantation, there were sundry unwarrantable and uncomfortable steps taken by Mr. Samuel Parris, the pastor of the church in Salem Village, then under the hurrying distractions of amazing afflictions; yet the said Mr. Parris, by the good hand of God brought unto a better sense of things, hath so fully expressed it, that a Christian charity may and should receive satisfaction therewith.

II. Inasmuch as many Christian brethren in the church of Salem Village have been offended at Mr. Parris for his conduct in the time of the difficulties and calamities which have distressed them, we now advise them charitably to accept the satisfaction which he hath tendered in his Christian acknowledgments of the errors therein committed; yea, to endeavor, as far as 'tis possible, the fullest reconciliation of their minds unto communion with him, in the whole exercise of his ministry, and with the rest of the church (Matt. vi. 12–14; Luke xvii. 3; James v. 16). . . .

V. Having observed that there is in Salem Village a spirit full of contentions and animosities, too sadly verifying the blemish which hath heretofore lain upon them, and that some complaints brought against Mr. Parris have been either causeless and groundless, or unduly aggravated, we do, in the name and fear of the Lord, solemnly warn them to consider, whether, if they continue to devour one another, it will not be bitterness in the latter end; and beware lest the Lord be provoked thereby utterly to deprive them of those which they should account their precious and pleasant things, and abandon them to all the desolations of a people that sin away the mercies of the gospel (James iii. 16; Gal. v. 15; 2 Sam ii. 26; Isa. v. 4, 5, 6; Matt. xxi. 43).

VI. If the distempers in Salem Village should be (which God forbid!) so incurable, that Mr. Parris, after all, find that he cannot, with any comfort and service, continue in his present station, his removal from thence will not expose him unto any hard character with us, nor, we hope, with the rest of the people of God among whom we live (Matt. x. 14; Acts xxii. 18).

All which advice we follow with our prayers that the God of peace would bruise Satan under our feet. Now, the Lord of peace himself give you peace always by all means.

INCREASE MATHER, *Moderator.*

JOSEPH BRIDGHAM.
SAMUEL CHECKLEY.
WILLIAM TORREY.
JOSEPH BOYNTON.
RICHARD MIDDLECOT.
JOHN WALLEY.
JER: DUMMER.
NEHEMIAH JEWET.
EPHRAIM HUNT.
NATHLL. WILLIAMS.
SAMUEL PHILLIPS.
JAMES ALLEN.
SAMUEL TORREY.
SAMUEL WILLARD.
EDWARD PAYSON.
COTTON MATHER.

Chapter 2:
Document Set 2 References

1. Samuel Parris Sets a Tone, 1692
Samuel Parris, "Christ Knows How Many Devils There Are," March 27, 1692, in Paul S. Boyer and Stephen Nissenbaum, *Salem Village Witchcraft: A Documentary Record of Local Conflict in Colonial New England* (Belmont, CA: Wadsworth, 1972), pp. 129–130.

2. Martha Corey's Testimony, 1692
Samuel Parris, "The Examination of Martha Corey," March 21, 1692, in Charles W. Upham, *Salem Witchcraft: With an Account of Salem Village and a History of Opinions on Witchcraft and Kindred Subjects* (Boston, 1867; rep. Williamstown: Corner House, 1971), Vol. 2, pp. 43, 45–49.

3. Ann Putnam's Deposition, 1692

Ann Putnam, "Deposition," April 20, 1692, W. Elliot Woodward, *Records of Salem Witchcraft Copied from the Original Documents* (Roxbury: privately printed, 1864, in William Woods, ed., *A Casebook of Witchcraft* (New York: G. P. Putnam's Sons, 1974), pp. 203–204.

4. Salem Village, 1692
   "Map of Salem Village, 1692, by W. P. Upham," 1866, in Upham, Vol. 1, frontispiece.

5. The Geography of Witchcraft in Salem Village, 1692
   "The Geography of Witchcraft: Salem Village," 1692, in Paul Boyer and Stephen Nissenbaum, *Salem Possessed: The Social Origins of Witchcraft* (Cambridge: Harvard University Press, 1974), p. 34.

6. Factionalism and Wealth in Salem Village, 1695

"Factionalism and Wealth in Salem Village," 1695, in Boyer and Nissenbaum, *Salem Possessed,* p. 82.

7. Ann Putnam's Confession, 1706
   Ann Putnam, "The Confession of Ann Putnam, when she was received to Communion,"August 25, 1706, in Upham, Vol. 2, p. 510.

8. Witchcraft in Salem, Analysis by Age and Sex, 1692
   John Demos, "Underlying Themes in the Witchcraft of Seventeenth-Century New England," *American Historical Review,* Vol. 75 (June 1970), pp. 1315–1316.

9. The Conclusions of the Massachusetts Bay Elders, 1695
   Increase Mather et al., "Declarations, Records of the Salem Village Church," April 3, 1695, in Upham, Vol. 2, pp. 551–553.

Chapter 3:
Document Set 2 Credits

1. Text taken from Paul S. Boyer and Stephen Nissenbaum, *Salem Witchcraft: A Documentary Record of Local Conflict in Colonial New England,* Wadsworth Publishing, 1972, pp. 129-130. Used with permission of the authors.

5. "The Geography of Witchcraft: Salem Village, 1692" from *Salem Possessed: The Social Origins of Witchcraft* by Paul Boyer and Stephen Nissenbaum. Copyright © 1974 by the President and Fellows of Harvard College. Reprinted by permission of Harvard University Press.

6. "Factionalism and Wealth in Salem Village, 1695" from *Salem Possessed: The Social Origins of Witchcraft* by Paul Boyer and Stephen Nissenbaum. Copyright © 1974 by the President and Fellows of Harvard College. Reprinted by permission of Harvard University Press.

8. Three charts from "Underlying Themes in the Witchcraft of Seventeenth-Century New England" by John Demos, p. 1315, from *American Historical Review,* Vol. LXXV, Number 5, June 1970. Reprinted with permission of John Demos.

CHAPTER 3

Men and Women in a Developing Society: Rights and Responsibilities in New England and the Chesapeake

The textbook devotes substantial attention to gender relations and family life in both New England and the Chesapeake. The social and economic bases for these colonies were markedly different, and as a result, domestic relationships developed along divergent lines. The following documents will help you explore relationships between men and women in colonial America and gain insight into the roles, rights, and responsibilities assumed by women in both regions.

Any discussion of women in colonial America should begin with an examination of the home, family, and marriage relationships that formed the core of female experience in the seventeenth century. Central to this experience was childbearing, a function essential to the success of any colonial enterprise. Because women were vital to the future in this sense, they were able to claim certain rights as vested partners in the marriage relationship.

As the textbook notes, the family was the foundation of Puritan society. This reality was recorded in the body of legal rights claimed by Massachusetts women, who were able to insist on a portion of the family fortune or property ("thirds," according to the usage of the time). These entitlements mirrored the reality of women's investment in marriage, as well as the substantial risks undertaken in pregnancy and childbirth. Review the demographic data and the poem by Anne Bradstreet for evidence of the transitory nature of life in seventeenth-century New England, especially the unique burdens shouldered by women. (Be aware, however, as you review the statistics for Plymouth Colony in 1621, that that year was particularly harsh and not representative of the entire seventeenth-century experience.)

The documents also reveal an acute consciousness of mutual obligations within the Puritan family. These reciprocal responsibilities were inherent in covenant theology, which is based on the concept of contractual agreement. Search the documents for evidence of this reciprocity in the marriage relationship, and try to identify the outlines and structure of the family in New England.

As you apply these generalizations to the New England experience, compare family relationships and roles of women in that region with those which developed in the Chesapeake Bay area of Virginia and Maryland. Be especially aware of the dower rights enjoyed by Chesapeake widows, as revealed by the statistics on bequests of husbands to wives in St. Mary's County and Charles County in Maryland. Try to determine why the outcomes were so favorable to Maryland women.

The documents dealing with Chesapeake society also reflect the peculiar economic and social problems of that region. The excerpts from the Virginia legal code indicate that the social relationships created by a chronically labor-short economy forced the development of legal institutions reflecting that environment. Consider the significance of the Virginia legal structure for servant women who found themselves trapped in a social status somewhere between slavery and freedom.

The materials on the Chesapeake raise the question of women's economic and occupational status in an emerging plantation society. Try to use these documents to form an impression of that society and the class system that had begun to develop in an area dominated by staple-crop agriculture. Explain why women occupied the positions they did.

These documents provide you with a basis for comparison of two very different social systems. Use them to extract evidence of the characteristics unique to each region and to account for distinctions between them.

Questions for Analysis

1. What do the documents reveal about mortality rates in seventeenth-century New England? Compare these figures with the population data given for Virginia in Document Set 2-2. What are the implications of these data for an understanding of women's experiences?

2. Compare and contrast the rights claimed by women in New England and the Chesapeake. Which claims could women insist on most strongly? Why?

3. What is meant by the concept of "reciprocal obligations" inside the family unit? Do you find evidence that these obligations were respected? Explain.

4. How did the respective economies of New England and the Chesapeake affect the experiences of women? How did the social structure reflect the economic realities of colonial life? Were there hazards for normal social relationships in a developing society?

5. Compare the legal systems in New England and the Chesapeake as tools for the preservation of marriage. To what extent did they acknowledge the reality of potential marital discord? What solutions and/or legal remedies existed to deal with these problems? Why were they necessary, and how were they justified?

1. Massachusetts Defines the Rights of Women, 1641

The Body of Liberties of 1641

The Liberties of the Massachusetts Colony in New England, 1641

Liberties of Women

79. If any man at his death shall not leave his wife a competent portion of his estate, upon just complaint made to the General Court she shall be relieved.

80. Every married woman shall be free from bodily correction or stripes by her husband, unless it be in his own defence upon her assault. If there be any just cause of correction complaint shall be made to Authority assembled in some Court, from which only she shall receive it.

Liberties of Children

81. When parents die intestate, the Elder son shall have a double portion of his whole estate real and personal, unless the General Court upon just cause alledged shall judge otherwise.

82. When parents die intestate having no heirs males of their bodies their Daughters shall inherit as Copartners, unless the General Court upon just reason shall judge otherwise.

83. If any parents shall wilfully and unreasonably deny any child timely or convenient marriage, or shall exercise any unnatural severity towards them, such children shall have free liberty to complain to Authority for redress. . . .

94. Capital Laws

Deut. 13. 6, 10. Deut. 17. 2, 6. Ex. 22. 20.	1. If any man after legal conviction shall have or worship any other god, but the lord god, he shall be put to death.
Ex. 22. 18. Lev. 20. 27. Deut. 18. 10.	2. If any man or woman be a witch, (that is hath or consult with a familiar spirit,) They shall be put to death. . . .
Lev. 20. 15, 16.	7. If any man or woman shall lie with any beast or brute creature by Carnal Copulation, They shall surely be put to death. And the beast shall be slain, and buried and not eaten.
Lev. 20. 13	8. If any man lie with mankind as he lie with a woman, both of them have committed abomination, they both shall surely be put to death.
Lev. 20. 19 and 18. 20. Dut. 22. 23, 24.	9. If any person commits Adultery with a married or espoused wife, the Adulterer and Adulteress shall surely be put to death.

2. A Massachusetts Wife Ensures Her Economic Stake in Marriage, 1653

Articles of agreement, dated Apr. 30, 1653, between Joseph Jewett of Rowley, merchant, and Ann, late wife to Capt. Bozoon Allen, deceased . . . ; Joseph Jewett, in consideration of a marriage shortly to be solemnized between him and Ann, widow of said Allen, and with receipt of her thirds and 600li., the children's portions, agreed in case of his death to leave the 600li. to his wife, and also agreed that his wife might dispose of 100li. during her life to her children by said Allen; that the eldest son should be brought up to learning, kept at a good school, found in diet, apparel, and books until he should be fitted for the University, and to be there maintained; that the other children should be brought up to learning and be supported until the age of twenty-one or marriage; that said Anne might give away to any of her children, a feather bed, bolster and pillow, with a bedstead, covering, pair of blankets, pair of fine sheets, five pillowbeers, curtains and wrought vallance, livery cupboard and cupboard cloth of needle-work suitable for the vallance, two wrought cushions, two tables, one chair, two wrought stools, two trunks, two chests, two cases with glasses, one silver tankard, one silver bowl, six silver spoons, two gold rings, one silver dram cup, with the childbed linen in the trunk; that Joseph agreed to pay to Priscilla, the eldest daughter of said Anne 20li. over and above her portion; also that the mares which Captain Allen left, mentioned in the inventory, be allowed to run with their increase as the profit of that part of the double portion of John Allen until he came of age, and that said Joseph pay to John, Priscilla, Ann, Deborah, Isaac, and Bozoon Allen the portions their father left them in corn or cattle, when they become of age or are married, etc. Wit: Thomas Broughton, Thomas Buttolph, and Tho. Roberts. Acknowledged, 1: 8: 1653, before William Hibbins. Recorded, Feb. 3, 1653, by Edward Rawson, recorder. Copy made by Isa. Addington, cleric.

3. Gender Differences in Life Expectancy at Plymouth, ca. Seventeenth Century

Life Expectancy in Plymouth Colony

Age	Men	Women
21	69.2	62.4
30	70.0	64.7
40	71.2	69.7
50	73.7	73.4
60	76.3	76.8
70	79.9	80.7
80	85.1	86.7

Note: The figures in the left-hand column are the control points, that is, a 21-year-old man might expect to live to age 69.2, a 30-year-old to 70.0, and so forth. The sample on which this table is based comprises a total of 645 persons.

Deaths Arranged According to Age (Plymouth Colony)

Age Group	Men (percentages)	Women (percentages)
22–29	1.6	5.9
30–39	3.6	12.0
40–49	7.8	12.0
50–59	10.2	10.9
60–69	18.0	14.9
70–79	30.5	20.7
80–89	22.4	16.0
90 or over	5.9	7.6

Note: The figures in columns two and three represent the percentages of the men and women in the sample who died between the ages indicated in column one. The sample is the same as in the preceding table.

Mortality at Plymouth Plantation

	Total on First Boat	Number Died by End of 1621	Percent Died by End of 1621
Saints			
Men	17	8	47
Women	10	7	70
Children	14	3	21
Strangers			
Men	17	11	64
Women	9	7	77
Children	14	2	14
Servants			
Men	11	7	63.6
Women	1	0	0
Children	6	4	66.6
Hired hands, men	5	2	40
Total			
Men	50	26	52
Women	20	14	70
Children	34	9	26.4

Source: Compiled from biographic data in George Willson, *Saints and Strangers.*

4. Anne Bradstreet Reflects on Family Relationships, ca. 1650s

Before the Birth of One of Her Children

All things within this fading world hath end,
Adversity doth still our joys attend;
No ties so strong, no friends so dear and sweet,
But with death's parting blow is sure to meet.
The sentence past is most irrevocable,
A common thing, yet oh, inevitable.
How soon, my Dear, death may my steps attend,
How soon't may be thy lot to lose thy friend,
We both are ignorant, yet love bids me
These farewell lines to recommend to thee,
That when that knot's untied that made us one,
I may seem thine, who in effect am none.
And if I see not half my days that's due,
What nature would, God grant to yours and you;

The many faults that well you know I have
Let be interred in my oblivious grave;
If any worth or virtue were in me,
Let that live freshly in thy memory
And when thou feel'st no grief, as I no harms,
Yet love thy dead, who long lay in thine arms,
And when thy loss shall be repaid with gains
Look to my little babes, my dear remains.
And if thou love thyself, or loved'st me,
These O protect from stepdame's injury.
And if chance to thine eyes shall bring this verse,
With some sad sighs honor my absent hearse;
And kiss this paper for thy love's dear sake,
Who with salt tears this last farewell did take.

5. A Puritan Prescription for Marital Concord, 1712

Christians should endeavor to please and glorify God, in whatever capacity or relation they sustain.

Under this doctrine, my design is (by God's help) to say something about relative duties, particularly in families. I shall therefore endeavor to speak as briefly and plainly as I can about: (1) family prayer; (2) the duties of husbands and wives; (3) the duties of parents and children; (4) the duties of masters and servants. . . .

About the Duties of Husbands and Wives

Concerning the duties of this relation we may assert a few things. It is their duty to dwell together with one another. Surely they should dwell together; if one house cannot hold them, surely they are not affected to each other as they should be. They should have a very great and tender love and affection to one another. This is plainly commanded by God. This duty of love is mutual; it should be performed by each, to each of them. When, therefore, they quarrel or disagree, then they do the Devil's work; he is pleased at it, glad of it. But such contention provokes God; it dishonors Him; it is a vile example before inferiors in the family; it tends to prevent family prayer.

As to outward things. If the one is sick, troubled, or distressed, the other should manifest care, tender-

ness, pity, and compassion, and afford all possible relief and succor. They should likewise unite their prudent counsels and endeavors, comfortably to maintain themselves and the family under their joint care.

Husband and wife should be patient one toward another. If both are truly pious, yet neither of them is perfectly holy, in such cases a patient, forgiving, forbearing spirit is very needful. . . .

The husband's government ought to be gentle and easy, and the wife's obedience ready and cheerful. The husband is called the head of the woman. It belongs to the head to rule and govern. Wives are part of the house and family, and ought to be under the husband's government. Yet his government should not be with rigor, haughtiness, harshness, severity, but with the greatest love, gentleness, kindness, tenderness that may be. Though he governs her, he must not treat her as a servant, but as his own flesh; he must love her as himself.

Those husbands are much to blame who do not carry it lovingly and kindly to their wives. O man, if your wife is not so young, beautiful, healthy, well-tempered, and qualified as you would wish; if she did not bring a large estate to you, or cannot do so much for you, as some other women have done for their husbands; yet she is your wife, and the great God commands you to love her, not be bitter, but kind to her. What can be more plain and expressive than that?

Those wives are much to blame who do not carry it lovingly and obediently to their own husbands. O woman, if your husband is not as young, beautiful, healthy, so well-tempered, and qualified as you could wish; if he has not such abilities, riches, honors, as some others have; yet he is your husband, and the great God commands you to love, honor, and obey him. Yea, though possibly you have greater abilities of mind than he has, was of some high birth, and he of a more common birth, or did bring more estate, yet since he is your husband, God has made him your head, and set him above you, and made it your duty to love and revere him.

Parents should act wisely and prudently in the matching of their children. They should endeavor that they may marry someone who is most proper for them, most likely to bring blessings to them.

6. Maryland Husbands Fulfill Their Obligations to Widows, 1640–1710

Bequests of Husbands to Wives with Children, St. Mary's and Charles Counties, Maryland, 1640 to 1710

	N	All Estate		All or Dwelling Plantation for Life		All or Dwelling Plantation for Widowhood		All or Dwelling Plantation for Minority of Child		More than Dower in Other Form		Dower or Less or Unknown	
		N	%	N	%	N	%	N	%	N	%	N	%
1640s	3	1	33	33								2	67
1650s	16	1	6	2	13	1	6	1	6	4	25	7	44
1660s	45	8	18	8	18	2	4	3	7	9	20	15	33
1670s	61	4	7	21	34	2	3	3	5	13	21	18	30
1680s	52	5	10	19	37	2	4	2	4	11	21	13	25
1690s	69	1	1	31	45	7	10	2	3	10	14	18	26
1700s	62			20	32	6	10	2	3	14	23	20	32
Totals	308	20	6	101	33	20	6	13	4	61	20	93	30

Source: Wills, 1–XIV, Hall of Records, Annapolis, Md.

7. Virginia Law Acknowledges the Social Consequences of a Labor-Short Economy, 1705

An Act Concerning Servants and Slaves

How long servants shall serve.

I. *Be it enacted, by the governor, council, and burgesses, of this present general assembly, and it is hereby enacted, by the authority of the same,* That all servants brought into this country without indenture, if the said servants be christians, and of christian parentage, and above nineteen years of age, shall serve but five years; and if under nineteen years of age, 'till they shall become twenty-four years of age, and no longer. . . .

Women servants having bastards.

XVIII. And if any woman servant shall be delivered of a bastard child within the time of her service aforesaid, *Be it enacted, by the authority of aforesaid, and it is hereby enacted,* That in recompence of the loss and trouble occasioned her master or mistress thereby, she shall for every such offence, serve her said master or owner one whole year after her time by indenture, custom, and former order of court, shall be expired; or pay her said master or owner, one thousand pounds of tobacco; and the reputed father, if free, shall give security to the church-wardens of the parish where that child shall be, to maintain the child, and keep the parish indemnified; or be compelled thereto by order of the country court, upon the said church-wardens complaint: But if a servant, he shall make satisfaction to the parish, for keeping the said child, after his time by indenture, custom, or order of court, to his then present master or owner, shall be expired; or be compelled thereto, by order of the county court, upon complaint of the church-wardens of the said parish, for the time being. And if

Duty of reputed father.

Master getting his servant with child.

any woman servant shall be got with child by her master, neither the said master, nor his executors administrators, nor assigns, shall have any claim of service against her, for or by reason of such child; but she shall, when her time due to her said master, by indenture, custom or order of court, shall be expired, be sold by the church-wardens, for the time being, of the parish wherein such child shall be born, for one year, or pay one thousand pounds of tobacco; and the said one thousand pounds of tobacco, or whatever she shall be sold for, shall be employed, by the vestry, to the use of the said parish. And if any woman servant shall have a bastard child by a negro, or mulatto, over and above the years service due to her master or owner, she shall immediately, upon the expiration of her time to her then present master or owner, pay down to the church-wardens of the parish wherein such child shall be born, for the use of the said parish, fifteen pounds current money of Virginia, or be by them sold for five years, to the use aforesaid: And if a free christian white woman shall have such bastard child, by a negro, or mulatto, for every such offence, she shall, within one month after her delivery of such bastard child, pay to the church-wardens for the time being, of the parish wherein such child shall be born, for the use of the said parish fifteen pounds current money of Virginia, or be by them sold for five years to the use aforesaid: And in both the said cases, the church-wardens shall bind the said child to be a servant, until it shall be of thirty one years of age.

Women servants having bastards by negroes.

Or free women.

How long the child to be bound.

8. Divorce in Maryland, 1678

To the Honorable Thomas Notley, Esq., Lieutenant General and Chief Governor of Maryland

The Humble Petition of Robert Leshley Humbly Shows. That your Petitioner's wife being a woman of an Implacable turbulent Spirit has at several times unjustly & wrongfully made many complaints and Accusations against your Petitioner before several of his Lordships Justices of the peace of Calvert County but finding they took not the effect she hoped for, and that her Design of procuring a considerable part of your Petitioner's Estate to be allowed her for a maintenance with which she might live at her pleasure ... was wholly frustrated, she has since very falsely injuriously & maliciously accused your Petitioner of Buggery to the great scandal & irreparable prejudice [of his] credit and reputation. . . .

Wherefore your Petitioner humbly prays that your Honor will be graciously pleased to grant him a Warrant, that she may be brought before your Honor and her complaints & accusations heard and Examined. . . .

Upon hearing and Examination of the whole matter the Substance gathered from thence was that the Petitioner & his wife having had several Differences between them which could not be composed Did Declare that they were fully resolved never any more to live together, She Desiring an allowance proportionable to what she had at her Intermarriage with him. He Declared himself willing to allow her such a reasonable maintenance as the Governor and Council should think fit to award her with Due consideration had to his Capacity. . . . They both referred to the Discretion of the Governor and Council to order therein what to them should seem fair, they would submit to.

The Governor and Council having Duly and maturely considered the promises Did order.

By the Governor and Council

October 24, 1678

Whereas appeared before the Governor and Council this Day Robert Leshley of Calvert County & Elizabeth his wife, and Did both jointly and severally openly Declare that for several Differences between them both public and private they were fully resolved never to cohabit together again, and forasmuch as the said Elizabeth did Demand a reasonable maintenance to be allowed her by her Husband, which he readily consented to they both submitting themselves to the Discretion of the Governor and Council to apportion the same as to them should seem fair. It is Ordered.

That the said Robert Leshley pay or cause to be paid yearly and every year unto the said Elizabeth his wife for and During her natural life the just sum of two thousand pounds of tobacco for a maintenance and no more.

9. A Virginia Gentlewoman Crosses Class Lines, ca. 1730

The widow smiled graciously upon me, and entertain'd me very handsomely. Here I learnt all the tragical Story of her Daughter's humble Marriage with her Uncle's Overseer. Besides the [low station] of this mortal's Aspect, the Man has not one visible Qualification, except Impudence, to recommend him to a Female's Inclinations. But there is sometimes such a Charm in that Hibernian Endowment, that frail Woman cant withstand it, tho' it stand alone without any other Recommendation. Had she run away with a Gentleman or a pretty Fellow, there might have been some Excuse for her, tho' he were of inferior Fortune: but to stoop to a dirty Plebian, without any kind of merit, is the lowest Prostitution. I found the Family justly enraged at it; and tho' I had more good Nature than to join in her Condemnation, yet I cou'd devise no Excuse for so senseless a Prank as this young Gentlewoman had play'd.

Chapter 3:
Document Set 3 References

1. Massachusetts Defines the Rights of Women, 1641
   The Body of Liberties of 1641, in Edwin Powers, *Crime and Punishment in Early Massachusetts, 1620–1692* (Boston: Beacon Press, 1966), Appendix A.

2. A Massachusetts Wife Ensures Her Economic Stake in Marriage, 1653
   Records and Files of the Quarterly Court of Essex County, Massachusetts, Vol. 5, 1672–1674 (Salem, Mass.: Essex Institute, 1916), pp. 394–395.

3. Gender Differences in Life Expectancy at Plymouth, ca. Seventeenth Century
   John Demos, *A Little Commonwealth: Family Life in Plymouth Colony* (London: Oxford University Press, 1970), Appendix, Tables II and III; George Willson, *Saints and Strangers: Being the Lives of the Pilgrim Fathers and Their Families* (New York: Reynal and Hitchcock, 1945), comp. in Elizabeth Fox-Genovese *et al.,* eds., *Restoring Women to History: Materials for U.S. History* (Bloomington: Organization of American Historians, 1984), Vol. 1, p. 38.

4. Anne Bradstreet Reflects on Family Relationships, ca. 1650s
   Anne Bradstreet, "Before the Birth of One of Her Children," *Works of Anne Bradstreet,* ed. Jeannie Hensley (Cambridge: Harvard University Press, 1967).

5. A Puritan Prescription for Marital Concord, 1712
   Benjamin Wadsworth, *A Well-Ordered Family* (Boston, 1712), 2d ed., pp. 22–59, passim.

6. Maryland Husbands Fulfill Their Obligations to Widows, 1640–1710
   Lois Green Carr and Lorena Walsh, "The Planter's Wife: The Experience of White Women in Seventeenth Century Maryland," *William and Mary Quarterly,* Vol. 34 (1977), Table II.

7. Virginia Law Acknowledges the Social Consequences of a Labor-Short Economy, 1705
   William Waller Hening, *The Statutes at Large, Being a Collection of All the Laws of Virginia,* October 1705, Chap. 49, pp. 447, 452–453.

8. Divorce in Maryland, 1678
   William Hand Browne, ed., *Archives of Maryland: Proceedings of the Council of Maryland, 1671–1681* (Baltimore: Historical Society, 1896), Vol. 15, pp. 206–207.

9. A Virginia Gentlewoman Crosses Class Lines, ca. 1730
   William Byrd II, *A Progress to the Mines* (1732), in *The Westover Manuscripts,* ed. Edmund Ruffin (Petersburg, Va., 1841), in Howard W. Quint *et al.,* eds., *Main Problems in American History* (Chicago: Dorsey Press, 1987), 5th ed., p. 50.

CHAPTER 4

The Transatlantic Slave Trade: Human Degradation for Economic Advantage

During the eighteenth century, the British economy grew rapidly, owing in no small measure to the stimulus provided by an expanding colonial trade. A key component of the burgeoning commerce between England and America was the transatlantic slave trade, by which England supplied the labor-short colonial economy with the human resources to support plantation agriculture. Although, as your textbook notes, only 5 percent of the transplanted Africans reached the British North American colonies, the influx was nonetheless dramatic in the first half of the century. Equally significant was the role the slave trade played in capital formation as the tempo of England's economy quickened.

The following documents focus on this traffic's development and its impact on the British economy, African societies, and the lives of its unfortunate victims. As you examine the source material, try to understand why subjects of a Christian nation found it acceptable to engage in this commerce.

Your review of former slave trader John Newton's memoir and the excerpt from commercial promoter Malachy Postlethwayt's justification of the traffic should provide insight into the reasons the trade persisted. Concentrate especially on the economic argument and the problem of international commercial and industrial competition. At the same time, be aware of Newton's critique of the general economic rationale presented by supporters of the slave trade. His comments hint at the reasoning behind his own change in thinking with regard to England's toleration of this sordid practice.

One of the leading criticisms of the slave trade involved the physically devastating impact of the horrible "middle passage" on the blameless Africans who made up the human cargo in this branch of international commerce. As you review the recollections of the former slave Olaudah Equiano, watch for areas of agreement or disagreement with Newton's attack on the trade. Consider the results in terms of black psychological stability, family relationships, mortality rates, and general physical well-being.

Equally significant was the disruptive influence of the slave trade on the rich and complex cultures of West Africa, the homeland of most American bondsmen. The slave narratives contain evidence of both the jarring impact of the European commercial revolution on African society and the internal conflicts that set African kingdoms and peoples against one another. Your task is to search the documents for clues concerning the results of the slave trade, both for African cultures and for the slave culture that ultimately developed in North America. Try to determine why many aspects of African culture were obliterated in the New World while others survived.

Your analysis should produce an awareness of the deep origins of African-American culture, as well as insight into the unique forms taken by slave culture in the United States. Moreover, the documents will clarify the place occupied by the slave trade in the British commercial system. Use them to gain an understanding of the tension between economic needs and moral considerations within the rising British Empire of the eighteenth century.

Questions for Analysis

1. Trace the African roots of the men and women who shaped the development of slave culture in British North America. What do the documents reveal about the cultural practices and social/political organizations that prevailed in the African homeland? How did the transatlantic slave trade affect West African societies?

2. How do you think the assimilation and acculturation of African Americans compared with those of other eighteenth-century immigrants into America? What sort of slave culture emerged in British North America? In what ways did African culture survive in America? How would you account for these results?

3. What was the justification for the enslavement of Africans? What was the relationship between slavery and prejudice in the minds of the British?

4. What was the place of the slave trade in the overall Atlantic trade patterns of the eighteenth century? How did these patterns relate to the development of the British economy? What was the connection between economic advantage and the development of an intellectual rationale for slavery?

5. What reasons did critics put forth for ending the slave trade? Which interest groups in England and America were destined to mount a resistance against the traffic? What was Newton's background, and how did it influence his account of the trade?

1. A Child's Memory of Abduction in Africa, 1735

I was born at Dukandarra, in Guinea, about the year 1729. My father's name was Saungm Furro, Prince of the tribe of Dukandarra. . . .

. . . A certain relation of the king came and informed him, that the enemy who sent terms of accommodation to him and received tribute to their satisfaction, yet meditated an attack upon his subjects by surprise, and that probably they would commence their attack in less than one day, and concluded with advising him, as he was not prepared for war, to order a speedy retreat of his family and subjects. He complied with this advice.

The same night which was fixed upon to retreat, my father and his family set off about the break of day. The king and his two younger wives went in one company, and my mother and her children in another. We left our dwellings in succession, and my father's company went on first. We directed our course for a large shrub plain, some distance off, where we intended to conceal ourselves from the approaching enemy, until we could refresh ourselves a little. But we presently found that our retreat was not secure. . . . It alarmed both me and the women, who being unable to make any resistance, immediately betook ourselves to the tall thick reeds not far off, and left the old king to fight alone. For some time I beheld him from the reeds defending himself with great courage and firmness, till at last he was obliged to surrender himself into their hands.

They then came to us in the reeds, and the very first salute I had from them was a violent blow on the back part of the head with the fore part of a gun, and at the same time a grasp round the neck. I then had a rope put about my neck, as had all the women in the thicket with me, and was immediately led to my father, who was likewise pinioned and haltered for leading. In this condition we were all led to the camp. The women and myself being pretty submissive, had

tolerable treatment from the enemy, while my father was closely interrogated respecting his money which they knew he must have. But as he gave them no account of it, he was instantly cut and pounded on his body with great inhumanity, that he might be induced by the torture he suffered to make the discovery. All this availed not in the least to make him give up his money, but he despised all the tortures which they inflicted, until the continued exercise and increase of torment, obliged him to sink and expire. He thus died without informing his enemies where his money lay. I saw him while he was thus tortured to death. . . .

The army of the enemy was large, I should suppose consisting of about six thousand men. Their leader was called Baukurre. After destroying the old prince, they decamped and immediately marched towards the sea, lying to the west, taking with them myself and the women prisoners. . . .

The invaders then pinioned the prisoners of all ages and sexes indiscriminately, took their flocks and all their effects, and moved on their way towards the sea. On the march the prisoners were treated with clemency, on account of their being submissive and humble. Having come to the next tribe, the enemy laid siege and immediately took men, women, children, flocks, and all their valuable effects. They then went on to the next district which was contiguous to the sea, called in Africa, Anamaboo. The enemies' provisions were then almost spent, as well as their strength. The inhabitants knowing what conduct they had pursued, and what were their present intentions, improved the favorable opportunity, attacked them, and took enemy, prisoners, flocks and all their effects. I was then taken a second time. All of us were then put into the castle, and kept for market. On a certain time I and other prisoners were put on board a canoe, under our master, and rowed away to a vessel belonging to

Rhode Island, commanded by Captain Collingwood, and the mate Thomas Mumford. While we were going to the vessel, our master told us all to appear to the best possible advantage for sale. I was bought on board by one Robertson Mumford, steward of said vessel, for four gallons of rum, and a piece of calico, and called VENTURE, on account of his having purchased me with his own private venture. Thus I came by my name. All the slaves that were bought for that vessel's cargo, were two hundred and sixty.

2. Olaudah Equiano Recalls the Horrors of the Middle Passage, 1756

The first object which saluted my eyes when I arrived on the coast was the sea, and a slave ship, which was then riding at anchor, and waiting for its cargo. These filled me with astonishment, which was soon converted into terror, when I was carried on board. I was immediately handled, and tossed up, to see if I were sound, by some of the crew; and I was now persuaded that I had got into a world of bad spirits, and that they were going to kill me. Their complexions too differing so much from ours, their long hair, and the language they spoke (which was very different from any I had ever heard) united to confirm me in this belief. Indeed such were the horrors of my views and fears at the moment, that, if ten thousand worlds had been my own, I would have freely parted with them all to have exchanged my condition with that of the meanest slave in my own country. When I looked round the ship too and saw a large furnace or copper boiling, and a multitude of black people of every description chained together, every one of their countenances expressing dejection and sorrow, I no longer doubted of my fate; and, quite overpowered with horror and anguish, I fell motionless on the deck and fainted. When I recovered a little I found some black people about me, who I believed were some of those who had brought me on board, and had been receiving their pay; they talked to me in order to cheer me, but all in vain. . . . I now saw myself deprived of all chance of returning to my native country, or even the least glimpse of hope of gaining the shore, which I now considered as friendly; and I even wished for my former slavery in preference to my present situation, which was filled with horrors of every kind, still heightened by my ignorance of what I was to undergo. I was not long suffered to indulge my grief; I was soon put down under the decks, and there I received such a salutation in my nostrils as I had never experienced in my life: so that with the loathsomeness of the stench, and crying together, I became so sick and low that I was not able to eat, nor had I the least desire to taste any thing. I now wished for the last friend, death, to relieve me; but soon, to my grief, two of the white men offered me eatables; and, on my refusing to eat, one of them held me fast by the hands, and laid me across, I think the windlass, and tied my feet, while the other flogged me severely. I had never experienced any thing of this kind before: and, although not being used to the water, I naturally feared that element the first time I saw it, yet, nevertheless, could I have got over the nettings, I would have jumped over the side, but I could not; and, besides, the crew used to watch us very closely who were not chained down to the decks, lest we should leap into the water. . . . The stench of the hold while we were on the coast was so intolerably loathsome, that it was dangerous to remain there for any time, and some of us had been permitted to stay on the deck for the fresh air; but now that the whole ship's cargo were confined together, it became absolutely pestilential. The closeness of the place, and the heat of the climate, added to the number in the ship, which was so crowded that each had scarcely room to turn himself, almost suffocated us. This produced copious perspirations, so that the air soon became unfit for respiration, from a variety of loathsome smells, and brought on a sickness amongst the slaves, of which many died, thus falling victims to the improvident avarice, as I may call it, of their purchasers. This wretched situation was again aggravated by the galling of the chains, now become insupportable; and the filth of the necessary tubs, into which the children often fell, and were almost suffocated. The shrieks of the women, and the groans of the dying, rendered the whole a scene of horror almost inconceivable. . . . On a signal given, (as the beat of a drum) the buyers rush at once into the yard where the slaves are confined, and make choice of that parcel they like best. The noise and clamour with which this is attended, and the eagerness visible in the countenances of the buyers, serve not a little to increase the apprehension of terrified Africans, who may well be supposed to consider them as the ministers of that destruction to which they think themselves devoted. In this manner, without scruple, are relations and friends separated, most of them never to see each other again.

3. A Reformed Slave Trader Denounces the Traffic, 1788

The slave trade was always unjustifiable; but inattention and interest prevented, for a time, the evil from being perceived. It is otherwise at present; the mischiefs and evils connected with it have been, of late years, represented with such undeniable evidence, and are now so generally known, that I suppose there is hardly an objection can be made to the wish of thousands, perhaps of millions, for the suppression of this trade, but upon the ground of political expedience.

Though I were even sure that a principal branch of the public revenue depended upon the African trade (which I apprehend is far from being the case), if I had access and influence, I should think myself bound to say to Government, to Parliament, and to the nation, 'It is not lawful to put it into the treasury, because it is the price of blood' (Matt xxvii. 6). . . .

. . . I know of no method getting money, not even that of robbing for it upon the highway, which has so direct a tendency to efface the moral sense, to rob the heart of every gentle and humane disposition, and to harden it, like steel, against all impression of sensibility.

Usually, about two-thirds of a cargo of slaves are males. When a hundred and fifty or two hundred stout men, torn from their native land, many of whom never saw the sea, much less a ship, till a short space before they had embarked; who have, probably, the same natural prejudice against a white man, as we have against a black; and who often bring with them an apprehension they are bought to be eaten: I say, when thus circumstanced, it is not to be expected that they will tamely resign themselves to their situation. It is always taken for granted, that they will attempt to gain their liberty if possible. Accordingly, as we dare not trust them, we receive them on board, from the first as enemies; and, before their number exceeds, perhaps, ten or fifteen, they are all put in irons; in most ships, two and two together. And frequently, they are not thus confined, as they might most conveniently stand or move, the right hand and foot of one to the left of the other, but across; that is, the hand and foot of each on the same side, whether right or left, are fettered together: so that they cannot move either hand or foot, but with great caution, and with perfect consent. Thus they must sit, walk, and lie, for many months (sometimes for nine or ten), without any mitigation or relief, unless they are sick. . . .

When the women and girls are taken on board a ship, naked, trembling, terrified, perhaps almost exhausted with cold, fatigue, and hunger, they are often exposed to the wanton rudeness of white savages. The poor creatures cannot understand the language they hear, but the looks and manner of the speakers are sufficiently intelligible. In imagination, the prey is divided, upon the spot, and only reserved till opportunity offers. Where resistance or refusal, would be utterly in vain, even the solicitation of consent is seldom thought of. . . .

I judge, the principal source of the slave trade, is, the wars which prevail among the natives. Sometimes these wars break out between those who live near the sea. The English, and other Europeans, have been charged with fomenting them; I believe (so far as concerns the Windward coast) unjustly. That some would do it, if they could, I doubt not; but I do not think they can have opportunity. Nor is it needful they should interfere. Thousands, in our own country, wish for war, because they fatten upon its spoils. . . .

With our ships, the great object is, to be full. When the ship is there, it is thought desirable she should take as many as possible. The cargo of a vessel of a hundred tons, or little more, is calculated to purchase from two hundred and twenty to two hundred and fifty slaves. Their lodging rooms below the deck, which are three (for the men, the boys, and the women), besides a place for the sick, are sometimes more than five feet high, and sometimes less; and this height is divided towards the middle, for the slaves lie in two rows, one above the other, on each side of the ship, close to each other, like books upon a shelf. I have known them so close, that the shelf would not, easily, contain one more. And I have known a white man sent down, among the men, to lay them in these rows to the greatest advantage, so that as little space as possible might be lost.

Let it be observed, that the poor creatures, thus cramped for want of room, are likewise in irons, for the most part both hands and feet, and two together, which makes it difficult for them to turn or move, to attempt either to rise or to lie down, without hurting themselves, or each other. Nor is the motion of the ship, especially her heeling, or stoop on one side, when under sail, to be omitted; for this, as they lie athwart, or cross the ship, adds to the uncomfortableness of their lodging, especially to those who lie on the leeward or leaning side of the vessel.

Dire is the tossing, deep the groans.—

The heat and smell of these rooms, when the weather will not admit of the slaves being brought upon deck, and of having their rooms cleaned every day, would be almost insupportable to a person not accustomed to them. If the slaves and their rooms can be constantly aired, and they are not detained too long on board, perhaps there are not many die; but the contrary is often their lot. They are kept down, by the weather, to breathe a hot and corrupted air, sometimes for a week: this, added to the galling of their irons, and the despondency which seizes their spirits when thus confined, soon becomes fatal. And every morning, perhaps, more instances than one are found, of the living and the dead, like the captives of Mezentius, fastened together.

Epidemical fevers and fluxes, which fill the ship with noisome and noxious effluvia, often break out, and infect the seamen likewise, and thus the oppressors, and the oppressed, fall by the same stroke. I believe, nearly one-half of the slaves on board, have, sometimes, died; and that the loss of a third part, in these circumstances, is not unusual. . . .

When the slaves are landed for sale (for in the Leeward Islands they are usually sold on shore), it may happen, that after a long separation in different parts of the ship, when they are brought together in one place, some who are nearly related may recognize each other. If, upon such a meeting, pleasure should be felt, it can be but momentary. The sale disperses them wide, to different parts of the island, or to different islands. Husbands and wives, parents and children, brothers and sisters, must suddenly part again, probably to meet no more.

4. A British Defense of the Slave Trade on Economic Grounds, 1745

But is it not notorious to the whole World, that the Business of *Planting* in our *British Colonies,* as well as in the *French,* is carried on by the Labour of *Negroes,* imported thither from *Africa?* Are we not indebted to that valuable People, the *Africans,* for our *Sugars, Tobaccoes, Rice, Rum,* and all other *Plantation Produce?* And the greater the Number of *Negroes* imported into our *Colonies,* from *Africa,* will not the Exportation of *British* Manufacturers among the *Africans* be in Proportion; they being paid for in such Commodities only? The more likewise our Plantations abound in *Negroes,* will not more Land become cultivated, and both *better* and greater *Variety* of *Plantation Commodities* be produced? As those Trades are subservient to the Well Being and Prosperity of each other; so the more either flourishes or declines, the other must be necessarily affected; and the general Trade and Navigation of their *Mother Country* will be proportionately benefited or injured. May we not therefore say, with equal Truth, as the *French* do . . . that the general NAVIGATION of *Great Britain* owes all its *Encrease* and *Splendor* to the Commerce of its *American* and *African Colonies;* and that it cannot be maintained and enlarged otherwise than from the constant Prosperity of both those Branches, *whose Interests are mutual and inseparable?*

Whatever *other* Causes may have conspired to enable the *French* to beat us out of all the Markets in Europe in the *Sugar* and *Indigo Trades,* etc. the great and extraordinary Care they have taken to cherish and encourage their *African Company,* to the End that their *Plantation* might be cheaply and plentifully stocked with Negroe Husbandmen, is amply sufficient of itself to account for the Effect; for this Policy, they wisely judged, would enable them to produce those Commodities cheaper than we, who have suffered the

British Interest to decline in *Africa*, as that of the *French* has advanced; and when they could produce the Commodities cheaper, is it at all to be admired that they have undersold us at all the foreign Markets in *Europe,* and hereby got that most beneficial Part of our Trade into their own Hands?

As their great Care and our great Neglect of the *African Trade,* has for many Years past given *France* the Advantage over us in *Planting;* so while the same *Cause* continues, Is it not impossible, in the Nature of Things that the *Effect* should cease, and our Trade return to its former flourishing State? All other Measures as they hitherto have, so always will prove only *temporary Expedients,* not *effectual Restoratives:* They have none of them struck at the Root of the Evil; nor is it possible to work a thorough Cure any other way, but by enabling the *African Company* effectually to maintain and support *British* Rights and Privileges on the Coast of *Africa* against the Encroachments of the *French,* and all other Rivals; and in Consequence thereof, by stocking our own Plantations with greater Plenty of *Negroes,* and at *cheaper Rates* than our Rivals would, in such Case, be able to do. . . .

As *Negroe Labor* hitherto has, so that only can support our *British* Colonies, as it has done those of other Nations. It is *that* also will keep them in due Subserviency to the Interest of their *Mother Country;* for while our Plantations depend only on Planting by *Negroes,* and that of such Produce as interferes only with the Interests of our Rivals not of their *Mother Country,* our Colonies can never prove injurious to *British* Manufacturers, never become independent of these Kingdoms, but remain a perpetual Support to our *European* Interest, by preserving to us a Superiority of Trade and Naval Power.

5. Images of the Slave Trade and Slave Ownership

A. Slave Trades on the African Coast, ca. 1830s

B. Slave Advertisements, 1784

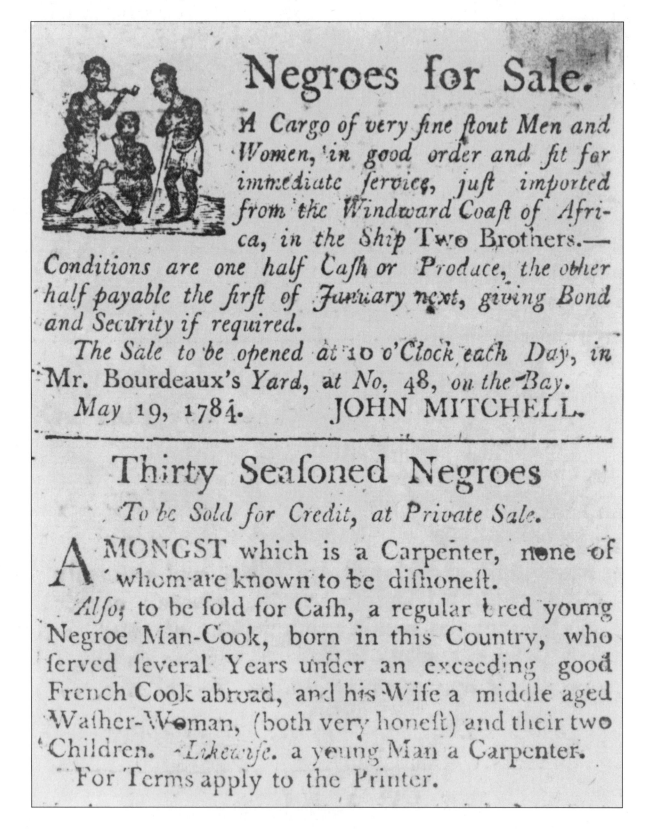

Negroes for Sale.

A Cargo of very fine stout Men and Women, in good order and fit for immediate service, just imported from the Windward Coast of Africa, in the Ship Two Brothers.— Conditions are one half *Cash or Produce,* the other half payable the first of *January next,* giving Bond and Security if required.

The Sale to be opened at 10 o'Clock each *Day,* in Mr. Bourdeaux's *Yard,* at No. 48, on the Bay. May 19, 1784.   JOHN MITCHELL.

Thirty Seasoned Negroes

To be Sold for Credit, at Private Sale.

AMONGST which is a Carpenter, none of whom are known to be dishonest.

Also, to be sold for Cash, a regular bred young Negroe Man-Cook, born in this Country, who served several Years under an exceeding good French Cook abroad, and his Wife a middle aged Washer-Woman, (both very honest) and their two Children. *Likewise.* a young Man a Carpenter. For Terms apply to the Printer.

C. Inspection and Sale of a Black Man,
ca. 1830

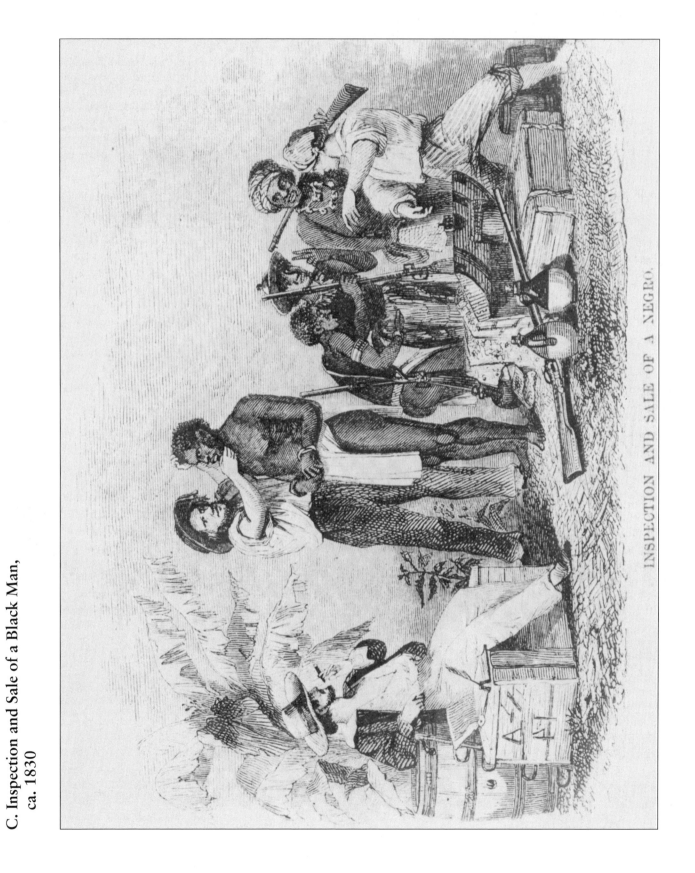

INSPECTION AND SALE OF A NEGRO.

Chapter 4:
Document Set 1 References

1. A Child's Memory of Abduction in Africa, 1735
   Venture Smith, *A Narrative of the Life and Adventures of Venture, A Native of Africa but Resident about Sixty Years in the United States of America* (New London, 1798). Reprinted in 1835 and published by a descendant, pp. 3–9.

2. Olaudah Equiano Recalls the Horrors of the Middle Passage, 1756
   Olaudah Equiano, *The Interesting Narrative of the Life of Olaudah Equiano or Gustavus Vasa, The African*, Vol. 1 (New York, 1791), pp. 49–62.

3. A Reformed Slave Trader Denounces the Traffic, 1788
   John Newton, *The Journal of a Slave Trader*, with Newton's *Thoughts upon the African Slave Trade*, eds. Bernard Martin and Mark Spurrell (London: Epworth Press, 1788), pp. 100, 103, 105, 108, 110–113.

4. A British Defense of the Slave Trade on Economic Grounds, 1745
   Malachy Postlethwayt, *The African Trade: The Great Pillar and Support of the British Plantation Trade in America, by a British Merchant*, 1745, David C. Douglas, ed., *English Historical Documents, 1714–1783* (London: Eyre and Spottiswoode, Ltd., 1957), pp. 824–825.

5. Images of the Slave Trade and Slave Ownership
   A. Slave Traders on the African Coast, ca. 1830s. Library of Congress.
   B. Slave Advertisements, 1784. Library of Congress.
   C. Inspection and Sale of a Black Man, ca. 1830. Library of Congress.

Chapter 4:
Document Set 1 Credits

5. A. Library of Congress
   B. Library of Congress
   C. Library of Congress

CHAPTER 4

DOCUMENT SET 2
Religious Enthusiasm and Revolution

The dramatic religious revivals known as the Great Awakening, amply described in your textbook, reverberated through the colonies in the eighteenth century. Although it spanned the period from the 1720s until the 1770s, the Awakening's most intense manifestation occurred in the 1740s when itinerant preacher George Whitefield often spoke to massive crowds (purportedly 30,000 on Boston Common in 1740). Whitefield and other itinerants used new, highly emotional rhetoric, spawning imitators who also spread the gospel. They typically preached at out-of-parish, open-air meetings and emphasized the need for new-birth conversion.

The Awakening was a "psychological earthquake" that "reshaped the human landscape." The masses experienced religious renewal while the established churches, splintered by dissent over the revivals, expressed fear and opposition, as did alarmed civil authorities. Missionary activity, religious conversions, and church attendance increased, and new churches, sects, and colleges were created, including Princeton, Columbia, Brown, Rutgers, and Dartmouth. Baptists became the Awakening's chief beneficiaries, whereas the Congregationalists and Presbyterians were torn apart by internal disagreements between proponents (New Lights) and opponents (Old Lights) of the revivals. Out of the rancor and schisms, the New Lights emerged dominant. Insistent on pure churches that limited membership to the regenerate (those who could testify to a new birth), they contributed to the growth of voluntarism and the separation of church and state in America.

The Awakening had important social and political effects, detailed in your textbook reading. The Protestant evangelical tradition, a powerful social force in nineteenth-century America, was established. Moreover, some historians argue that the Awakening contributed to a shift from a collectivist, organic social order to an individualistic, atomistic system, promoting among the nonelite a disregard for authority and social status. As you examine the evidence, think about the relationship between this popular preference for democracy and egalitarianism and the origins of the American Revolution.

The following documents include excerpts from the journals of George Whitefield and Charles Woodmason. Whitefield, an Anglican cleric and leading proponent of the Awakening, recounts his visit to Charleston in 1740, including a conversation with Alexander Garden, the Bishop of London's Commissary for South Carolina. Woodmason, an upper-class Anglican cleric and opponent of the New Lights, describes his experiences in the South Carolina backcountry in 1768. In reviewing the documents, note the contrasting views and attitudes of the two clergymen toward religious enthusiasm, and look for signs of social tension.

Finally, Sarah Osborn's account of her own conversion reveals the intensity of the religious experience characteristic of the Great Awakening. Examine her words for evidence of the emotional impact of evangelical religion, as well as its influence on converts.

Questions for Analysis

1. One characteristic of New Light ministers was a tendency to judge and criticize the established clergy. What evidence of this inclination do you find in the excerpt from Whitefield's journal? Even Woodmason acknowledged that there were problems with Anglican clergymen in South Carolina. What charges did he make against them? What other criticisms might have been made against Old Light ministers?

2. Woodmason committed himself to what seemed the thankless task of extending civilization and true, genuine Christianity to the backcountry. What evidence do the documents provide of the difficulties he experienced? How would you account for the resistance he faced?

3. Do the documents contain evidence to suggest that there was social conflict in eighteenth-century South Carolina? Explain. What factors in addition to religious disagreements may have been involved in the conflict?

4. Some historians believe that the Great Awakening was a stimulus to the American Revolution, in that it conditioned people to reject hierarchical authority, ignore social distinctions, and appreciate individualism and egalitarianism. In what ways do Whitefield's or Woodmason's journals support or disprove this thesis? Explain. What characteristics of the Awakening's enthusiastic New Light religion might have promoted these behavorial tendencies?

5. In what ways did evangelical religion influence the self-image and behavior of converts? What evidence do the documents provide concerning the place of religion in the lives of eighteenth-century Americans?

1. The Reverend George Whitefield in South Carolina, 1740

Friday, March 14. Arrived last night at *Charleston,* being called there to see my Brother, who lately came from *England,* and had brought me a Packet of Letters from my dear Friends. . . . Waited on the Commissary, with my Brother and other Companions, but met with a cool Reception. . . . He charged me with *Enthusiasm* and Pride, for speaking against the Generality of the Clergy, and desired I would make my Charge good. I told him, I thought I had already; but, as yet, I had scarce begun with them. He then asked me, Wherein were the Clergy so much to blame? I answered, they did not preach up *Justification by Faith alone;* and, upon talking with the Commissary, I found he was as ignorant of it as any of the rest. . . . He charged me with breaking the Canons and Ordination vow; And notwithstanding I told him I was ordained by Letters Dismissory from the Bishop of *London.* Yet in a great rage he told me, if I preached in any public church in that Province, he would suspend me. I replied, "I shall regard that as much as I would a Pope's Bull." . . . [I said to him,] "But if you will make an application to yourself, be pleased, Sir, to let me ask you one Question: have you delivered your Soul by exclaiming against the Assemblies and Balls here?" "What, Sir," says he, "must you come to catechise me? No, I have not exclaim'd against them; I think there is no Harm in them." "Then, Sir," said I, "I shall think it my Duty to exclaim against you." "Then, Sir," replied he, (*in a very great Rage*) "get you out of my House." Upon which I made my Bow, and, with my Friends took my leave, pitying the Commissary, who I really tho't was more noble than to give such Treatment. . . .

Saturday, March 15. Breakfasted, sung a Hymn, and had some religious Conversation on board my Brother's Ship. Preached in the *Baptist* Meeting-House, and was much pleased, when I heard afterwards, that from the same Pulpit, a Person not long ago, had preached, who denied the Doctrine of Original Sin, the Divinity and Righteousness of our dear Lord, and the Operations of God's blessed Spirit upon the Heart. I was led out to show the utter Inability of Man to save himself, and the absolute Necessity of his depending on the rich and sovereign Grace of God in Christ Jesus, in order to be restored to his primitive Dignity. Some, I observ'd, were put under concern, and most seem'd willing to know, whether those Things were so. In the Evening I preach'd again in the *Independent* Meeting-House, to a more attentive Auditory than ever; And had the Pleasure afterwards of Finding that a Gentlewoman, whose Family has been carried away for some time with Deistical Principles, began now to be unhinged, and to see that there was no Rest in such a Scheme, for a fallen Creature to rely on. . . .

Monday, March 17. Preach'd in the Morning at the *Independent* Meeting-House, and was more explicit than ever, in exclaiming against Balls and Assemblies, to which the People seem'd to hearken with much Attention.

Preached again in the Evening, and being excited thereto by some of the Inhabitants, spoke on Behalf of my poor Orphans. God was pleased to give it his Blessing, and I collected upwards of *Seventy Pounds Sterling* for them, the largest Collection I ever yet made on that Occasion. A further Earnest to me, that we shall yet see great things in *America,* and that God will carry on and finish the Work, begun in his Name at *Georgia.*

Tuesday, March 18. Preached twice again today, and took an affectionate Leave of, and gave Thanks to, my Hearers for their great Liberality. Many wept, and my own Heart yearn'd much towards them. For I believe a good Work is begun in many Souls. Generally every Day several came to me, telling me with weeping Eyes, how God had been pleas'd to convince them, by the Word preach'd, and how desirous they were of laying hold on, and having an Interest in the compleat and everlasting Righteousness of the Lord Jesus Christ. Numbers desired privately to converse with me. Many sent me little presents as Tokens of their Love, and earnestly entreated that I would come among them again. Invitations were given me from some of the adjacent Villages, and People daily came to Town more and more from their Plantations to hear the Word. . . . The Congregations grew larger on the Week Days, and many Things concurred to induce us to think that God intended to visit some in *Charlestown* with his Salvation.

2. The Reverend Charles Woodmason in the South Carolina Backcountry, 1768

'Tis these roving Teachers that stir up the Minds of the People against the Establish'd Church, and her Ministers—and make the Situation of any Gentleman extremely uneasy, vexatious, and disagreeable. I would sooner starve in England on a Curacy of 20£ p ann, than to live here on 200 Guineas, did not the Interests of Religion and the Church absolutely require it—Some few of these Itinerants have encountered me—I find them a Set of Rhapsodists—Enthusiasts—Bigots—Pedantic, illiterate, impudent Hypocrites—Straining at Gnats, and swallowing Camels, and making Religion a Cloak for Covetousness Detraction, Guile, Impostures and their particular Fabric of Things.

Among these Quakers and Presbyterians, are many concealed Papists—They are not tolerated in this Government—And in the Shape of New Light Preachers, I've met with many Jesuits. We have too here a Society of *Dunkards*—these resort to hear me when I am over at Jacksons Creek.

Among this Medley of Religious—True Genuine Christianity is not to be found. And the perverse persecuting Spirit of the Presbyterians, displays it Self much more here than in Scotland. It is dang'rous to live among, or near any of them—for if they cannot cheat, rob, defraud or injure You in Your Goods—they will belie, defame, lessen, blacken, disparage the most valuable Person breathing, not of their Communion in his Character, Good Name, or Reputation and Credit. They have almost worm'd out all the Church People—who cannot bear to live among such a Set of Vile unaccountable Wretches.

These Sects are eternally jarring among themselves—The Presbyterians hate the Baptists far more than they do the Episcopalians, and so of the Rest—But (as in England) they will unite altogether—in a Body to distress or injure the Church establish'd.

Hence it is, that when any Bills have been presented to the Legislature to promote the Interests of Religion, these Sectaries have found Means to have them overruled, for the leading Men of the House being all Lawyers, those People know how to grease Wheels to make them turn.

If Numbers were to be counted here, the Church People would have the Majority—But in Point of Interest, I judge that the Dissenters possess most Money—and thereby they can give a Bias to things at Pleasure.

The Grand Juries have presented as a Greivance, the Shame and Damage arising from such Itinerant Teachers being suffer'd to ramble about—They have even married People under my Eye in defiance of all Laws and Regulations—And I can get no Redress—I do all the Duty—take all the Pains. If there is a Shilling to be got by a Wedding or Funeral, these Impudent fellows will endeavour to pocket it: and are the most audacious of any Set of Mortals I ever met with. . . .

Such is the General State of Religion in these Parts delegated to me, and yet, when it is laid out into Parishes, and all Ferments subside, I query if I get a Parish or Settlement among them—for, so far from being thanked for my Labours, many, even of our Clergy, say, I do too much—My Activity displays their Indolence. None yet among them ever went out of his Parish, nay not even round his Parish to baptize—and I have seen in Charlestown, Children brought to the font to be baptized, and the Minister put them off till another Day, because he was going to Dinner, or Tea, or Company. If such cannot forgo a Meal for an Hour, how would they go without any Sustenance save Indian Meal and Water, or Bacon and Eggs for a Month, and that but once in 24 Hours? Or taste nothing better than Water for 6 Months together, and ride 200 Miles ev'ry Week, or Month?

I must freely say, that it has been owing to the Inattention and Indolence of the Clergy, that the Sectaries have gain'd so much Ground here. . . .

They have now got a Schoolmaster at this Place. An old Presbyterian fellow, or between that and a Quaker—They send their Children to him readily, and pay him, tho' they would not to me, who would have educated them Gratis. Such is their attachment to their Kirk:—Some call me a Jesuit—and the Liturgy the Mass—I have observ'd what Tricks they would have play'd on Christmas Day, to have disturbed the People. I will mention another.

Not long after, they hir'd a Band of rude fellows to come to Service who brought with them 57 Dogs (for I counted them) which in Time of Service they set fighting, and I was obliged to stop—In Time of Sermon they repeated it—and I was oblig'd to desist and dismiss the People. It is in vain to take up or commit these lawless Ruffians—for they have nothing, and the Charge of sending of them to Charlestown, would take me a Years Salary—We are without any Law, or Order. . . .

Another Time (in order to disapoint me of a Congregation, and to laugh at the People) they posted a Paper, signifying, That the King having discovered the Popish Designs of Mr. Woodmason and other Romish Priests in disguise, to bring in Popery and Slavery, had sent over Orders to suspend them all, and to order them to be sent over to England, so that there would be no more preaching for the future. This was believed by some of the Poor Ignorants, and kept them at home. . . .

What I could not effect by Force—or Reason—I have done by Sarcasm—for at the Time when they sent the fellows with their Dogs, one of the Dogs followed me down here—which I carried to the House of one of the principals—and told Him that I had 57 Presbyterians came that Day to Service, and that I had converted one of them, and brought Him home—I left the Dog with Him—This Joke has made them so extremely angry that they could cut my

Throat—But I've gained my Aim, having had no disturbance from them since. . . .

I am exactly in the same situation with the Clergy of the primitive Church, in midst of the Heathens, Arians, and Heretics—and endeavour like them to make my Life and Converse agreeable and unexceptionable (tho' its next to an impossibility) and to be all things to all Men that I may gain some; and yet I cannot please All. To engage the Dissenters I give an extempore prayer before Sermon, and sometimes an extempore Discourse—but this disgusts the Church People, and made severals with draw. . . .

The open profanation of the Lords Day in this Province is one of the most crying Sins in it—and is carried to a great height—Among the low Class, it is abus'd by Hunting fishing fowling, and Racing—By the Women in frolicing and Wantoness. By others in Drinking Bouts and Card Playing—Even in and about Charlestown, the Taverns have more Visitants than the Churches. . . .

Great Insolencies are now committed by those fellows who call themselves *Regulators*—They are [ever?] wanton in Wickedness and Impudence—And they triumph in their Licentiousness. Its said that above two thousand Presbyterians from North Carolina are coming down to join them—We have but 2 or 3 Magistrates who are Episcopalians in this Vast Back Country—And these they have threatened to Whip for issuing Writs against some of their Lawless Gang. They have actually whipped all the Constables and Sheriffs officers took and tore the Kings Writs—and Judges Writs. Silenced the Constables—Stopp'd payment of all Public Taxes—and We are now without Law, Gospel, Trade, or Money. Insulted by a Pack of vile, levelling common wealth Presbyterians In whom the Republican Spirit of 41 yet dwells, and who would very willingly put the Solemn League and Covenant now in force—Nay, their Teachers press it on them, and say that [it] is as binding on the Consciences of all the Kirk, as the Gospel it Self, for it is a Covenant enter'd into with God, from which they cannot recede. . . .

It will require much Time and Pains to New Model and form the Carriage and Manners, as well as Morals of these wild Peoples—Among this Congregation not one had a Bible or Common Prayer—or could join a Person or hardly repeat the Creed or Lords Prayer—Yet all of 'em had been educated in the Principles of our Church. So that I am obliged to read the Whole Service, omitting such Parts, as are Repetitious, and retaining those that will make the different Services somewhat Uniform—Hence it is, that I can but seldom use the Litany, because they know not the Responses.

It would be (as I once observ'd before) a Great Novelty to a Londoner to see one of these Congregations—The Men with only a thin Shirt and pair of Breeches or Trousers on—barelegged and barefooted—The Women bareheaded, barelegged and barefoot with only a thin Shift and under Petticoat—Yet I cannot break [them?] of this—for the heat of the Weather admits not of any [but] thin Cloathing—I can hardly bear the Weight of my Whig and Gown, during Service. The Young Women have a most uncommon Practise, which I cannot break them of. They draw their Shift as tight as possible to the Body, and pin it close, to shew the roundness of their Breasts, and slender Waists (for they are generally finely shaped) and draw their Petticoat close to their Hips to shew the fineness of their Limbs—so that they might as well be in Puri Naturalibus—Indeed Nakedness is not censurable or indecent here, and they expose themselves often quite Naked, without Ceremony—Rubbing themselves and their Hair with Bears Oil and tying it up behind in a Bunch like the Indians—being hardly one degree removed from

them—In few Years, I hope to bring about a Reformation, as I already have done in several Parts of the Country. . . .

Thus You have a Journal of two Years—In which have rode near Six thousand Miles, almost on one Horse. Wore my Self to a Skeleton and endured all the Extremities of Hunger, Thirst, Cold, and Heat. Have baptized near 1200 Children—Given 200 or more Discourses—Rais'd almost 30 Congregations—Set on foot the building of sundry Chapels Distributed Books, Medicines, Garden Seed, Turnip, Clover, Timothy Burnet, and other Grass Seeds—with Fish Hooks—Small working Tools and variety of Implements to set the Poor at Work, and promote Industry to the amount of at least One hundred Pounds Sterling: Roads are making—Boats building—Bridges framing, and other useful Works begun thro' my Means, as will not only be of public Utility, but make the Country side wear a New face, and the People become New Creatures. And I will venture to attest that these small, weak Endeavours of mine to serve the Community, has (or will) be of more Service to the Colony, than ever Mr. Whitfield's Orphan House was, or will be.

3. Sarah Osborn's Conversion, 1741

I thought I trusted in God; and used frequently, in time of trial, to go and pour out my complaints to him, thinking he was my only support. But I dare not now be positive, or really conclude, that I know what it was to put my trust in God; for my conduct after this seems so inconsistent with grace, that I dare not say I had one spark of it then; but rather think I was only under a common work of the Spirit: Though some times I think I had true grace, though very weak. . . . After this (O that with deep humility of soul, with sorrow and shame, I could speak of it) I relapsed again, and was full of vanity. I kept company with a young man, something against my parents' will. But that was owing to false reports raised of him; for at first they liked him. I made resolutions, that, after I was married, I would lead a new life, flattering myself that then I should not have the hinderances which I now had. I used bitterly to reflect upon myself, when I had given myself liberty to be merry; for though I appeared outwardly so, I had no real pleasure: but still put off repentance, or an entire breaking off from vanity, till

a more convenient season; and so resisted the Spirit of God. . . .

I met with many trials in my lying in, it being an extreme cold season. My child was born on Oct. 27, 1732. The next spring, my husband returned home; but went to sea again, and died abroad in November, 1733. I was then in my twentieth year. The news of my husband's death came to me on the first of the next April. . . . But God appeared wonderfully for my support. I saw his hand, and was enabled to submit with patience to his will. I daily looked round me, to see how much heavier the hand of God was laid on some others, than it was on me, where they were left with a large number of children, and much involved in debt. And I had but one to maintain; and, though poor, yet not involved. Others, I saw, as well as myself, had their friends snatched from them by sudden accidents. The consideration of these things, together with the thoughts of what I deserved, stilled me so, that though the loss of my companion, whom I dearly loved, was great; yet the veins of mercy, which I saw running through all my afflictions, were so great likewise, that, with Job, I could say, "The Lord gave, and the Lord hath taken away, and blessed be the name of the Lord."

. . . I grew slack again, and got into a cold, lifeless frame. As I grew better in bodily health, my soul grew sick. I daily laid up a stock for repentance. But, through rich grace, I was again convinced of my stupidity, and began to be more diligent in attending on the means of grace. But I found I could not profit by the word preached: Nothing reached my heart; all seemed but skin deep: And the more I went to meeting, the more I found it so. . . .

. . . After all this, I began to grow more conformed to the world. Things which, when I was thus lively, appeared insipid, and indeed odious to me, began to grow more tolerable, and by degrees in a measure pleasant. And depraved nature and Satan together pleaded for them thus, "That there was a time for all things; and singing and dancing now and then, with a particular friend, was an innocent diversion. Who did I see, besides myself, so precise and strict? Other christians allowed themselves in such things, who, I had reason to think, were far superior to me in grace; especially one with whom I was very intimate. Sure, if it was sin, she would not allow herself in it. . . .

Thus I sunk by degrees lower and lower, till I had at last almost lost all sense of my former experiences. I had only the bare remembrance of them, and they seemed like dreams or delusion; at some times. At others again, I had some revivals. . . . But I knew I was a dreadful backslider, and had dealt treacherously with God. . . .

In Sept. 1740, God in mercy sent his dear servant Whitefield here, which in some measure stirred me up. But when Mr. Tennent came soon after, it pleased God to bless his preaching so to me, that it roused me. But I was all the winter after exercised with dreadful doubts and fears about my state. I questioned the truth of all I had experienced, and feared I had never yet passed through the pangs of the new birth, or ever had one spark of grace.

. . . Then, and not till then, was I fully convinced what prodigal wasters of precious time such things were. And, through grace, I have abhorred them all ever since.

. . . After I was thus revived, my longings to be made useful in the world returned, and I earnestly pleaded with God that he would not suffer me to live any longer an unprofitable servant; but would point out some way, in which I might be useful: And that I might now be as exemplary for piety, as I had been for folly. And it pleased God so to order it, that I had room to hope my petitions were both heard, and in a measure answered. For soon after this a number of young women, who were awakened to a concern for their souls, came to me, and desired my advice and assistance, and proposed to join in a society, provided I would take the care of them. To which, I trust with a sense of my own unworthiness, I joyfully consented. . . .

About this time I had the offer of a second marriage, with one who appeared to be a real christian (and I could not think of being unequally yoked with one who was not such). I took the matter into serious consideration. . . . But after weighing all circumstances, as well as I could, in my mind, and earnest prayer, which God enabled me to continue in for some time, I concluded it was the will of God, that I should accept of the offer, and accordingly was married to Mr. Henry Osborn. . . .

[W]e fell into disagreeable and difficult worldly circumstances, with respect to living and paying the debts we owed. My greatest concern was with respect to the latter, lest we should not be able to do justice, and so wrong our creditors, and bring dishonor on God, and our profession. Under this pressure and distress, I was relieved and supported by the following words of Scripture, "Let your conversation be without covetousness, and be content with such things as ye have; for he hath said, I will never leave thee, nor forsake thee." I lived cheerfully, upon this promise, for a considerable time. And God ordered things so that our creditors were paid to their satisfaction.

I have often thought God has so ordered it throughout my days hitherto, that I should be in an afflicted, low condition, as to worldly circumstances, and inclined the hearts of others to relieve me in all my distresses, on purpose to suppress that pride of my nature, which doubtless would have been acted out greatly to his dishonor, had I enjoyed health, and had prosperity, so as to live independent of others. I will therefore think it best.

Chapter 4:
Document Set 2 References

1. The Reverend George Whitefield in South Carolina, 1740
   George Whitefield, *A Continuation of the Reverend Mr. Whitefield's Journal: From a Few Days After His Arrival in Georgia to His Second Return Thither from Pennsylvania* (Philadelphia: B. Franklin, 1740), pp. 14–21.

2. The Reverend Charles Woodmason in the South Carolina Backcountry, 1768
   Charles Woodmason, The Journal of the Rev. Charles Woodmason: "Journal of C. W. Clerk. Itinerant Minister in South Carolina 1766, 1767, 1768," in Richard J. Hooker, ed., *The Carolina Backcountry on the Eve of the Revolution: The Journal and Other Writings of Charles Woodmason, Anglican Itinerant* (Chapel Hill: University of North Carolina Press, 1953), pp. 42–47, 54–55, 61, 63.

3. Sarah Osborn's Conversion, 1741
   Samuel Hopkins, ed., *Memoirs of the Life of Mrs. Sarah Osborn* (Worcester, Mass.: Leonard Worcester, 1799), pp. 15–21, 39, 42–43, 45–46, 49–55.

Chapter 4:
Document Set 2 Credits

CHAPTER 4

DOCUMENT SET 3

Nature Observed: Changing Perceptions of the Landscape in the Seventeenth and Eighteenth Centuries

One of the key aspects of the eighteenth-century Enlightenment was the application of scientific principles to all aspects of intellectual inquiry. Your textbook observes that such pioneer scientists as Benjamin Franklin and Thomas Jefferson were determined that progress should be achieved through rigorous observation and rational thought. In a developing area like North America, it was perhaps natural that some of these scientific energies be expressed through the observation of flora, fauna, and the earth's physical features. The following documents focus on descriptions of the natural environment by seventeenth- and eighteenth-century observers. Examine the sources with an eye to nuances of difference in attitude toward nature and assumptions concerning the utility of its resources.

As you review the early descriptions by Francis Higginson and Edward Williams, consider their purposes in writing about New England and Virginia. Be aware of the natural features they chose to emphasize, and try to account for their decisions. As you examine these accounts of New World resources, decide which aspects of the environment were most impressive to colonial promoters.

By the late seventeenth century, an added dimension to travel accounts was a new concentration on scientific inquiry. John Lederer, the first European to explore the Appalachian Mountains, expressed substantial intellectual curiosity in his account of an expedition into the Virginia backcountry. Watch for the features emphasized in Lederer's remarks.

Compare these early observations with those of eighteenth-century naturalists such as Peter Kalm, William Bartram, and Thomas Jefferson. Note their deep interest in scientific detail and natural phenomena. Using your textbook as a resource, arrive at a definition of *rationalism*. Then review these documents for evidence of rational thought in the writers' reactions to nature. Examine Kalm's criticisms of American land-use patterns and their relationship to the predominant intellectual currents of the eighteenth century.

Once you have identified the Enlightenment influences in the documents, return to the sources for a fresh look at their content. Focus on the nonscientific dimension of these writings, particularly those of Bartram and Jefferson. Look for evidence of an emotional dimension to their otherwise rational observations of natural phenomena. Try to account for this apparently contradictory aspect of Enlightenment science.

Finally, think about the tension between nature's inspirational effect and its practical utility. Look for evidence that natural resources were to have a dual function as a source of solace for modern Americans and as fuel for the engine of economic progress. Think about the implications of this duality for the future of national development.

Questions for Analysis

1. Compare the seventeenth- and eighteenth-century accounts of natural phenomena. How would you explain the differences in the descriptions? How did the authors' backgrounds vary? What were their purposes?

2. What is meant by the term *rationalism*? How is it related to the Enlightenment mentality described in your textbook? In what ways do the documents reflect rationalism and Enlightenment thought?

3. What interests were shared by William Bartram, Peter Kalm, John Lederer, and Thomas Jefferson? What does the term *naturalist* mean? How did these observers reflect the assumptions and goals of the naturalist?

4. What is the connection between the criticisms of Kalm and the observations of Edward Williams and Francis Higginson? How do they relate to the future of land-use patterns in America? What consequences flowed from seventeenth-century assumptions?

5. How did the observations of Jefferson and Bartram reflect a dualistic or ambivalent perspective on nature and virgin resources? Define *romanticism*. To what extent do romantic ideas surface in these analyses of natural phenomena? How would you account for this apparent contradiction?

1. Francis Higginson Describes New England's Natural Endowments, 1630

Letting pass our voyage by sea, we will now begin our discourse on the shore of New England. . . .

For wood there is no better in the world I think, here being four sorts of oak differing both in the leaf, timber and colour, all excellent good. There is also good ash, elm, willow, birch, beech, sassafras, juniper cypress, cedar, spruce, pines, and fir that will yield abundance of turpentine, pitch, tar, masts and other materials for building both of ships and houses. Also here are store of sumac trees; they are good for dyeing and tanning of leather; likewise such trees yield a precious gum called white benjamin [benzoin] that they say is excellent for perfumes. . . .

For beasts there are some bears, and they say some lions also for they have been seen at Cape Anne. Also here are several sorts of deer, some whereof bring three or four young ones at once, which is not ordinary in England. Also wolves, foxes, beavers, otters, martens, great wildcats, and a great beast called a molke [moose] as big as an ox. I have seen the skins of all these beasts since I came to this plantation, excepting lions. Also here are great store of squirrels, some greater, and some smaller and lesser; there are some of the lesser sort, they tell me, that by a certain skill will fly from tree to tree though they stand far distant. . . .

New England has water enough, both salt and fresh, the greatest sea in the world, the Atlantic Sea, runs all along the coast thereof. There are abundance of islands along the shore, some full of wood and mast to feed swine; and others clear of wood, and fruitful to bear corn. Also we have store of excellent harbours for ships, as at Cape Anne, and at Massachusetts Bay, and at Salem, and at many other places; and they are the better because for strangers there is a very difficult and dangerous passage into them, but to such as are well acquainted with them, they are easy and safe enough. The abundance of seafish are almost beyond believing, and sure I should scarce have believed it except I had seen it with my own eyes. I saw great store of whales and grampus, and such abundance of mackerel that it would astonish one to behold; likewise codfish [in] abundance on the coast, and in their season are plentifully taken. There is a fish called a bass, a most sweet and wholesome fish as ever I did eat; it is altogether as good as our fresh salmon, and the season of their coming was begun when we came first to New England in June, and so continued about three months' space. Of this fish our fishers may take many hundreds together which I have seen lying on the shore to my admiration; yea their nets ordinarily take more than they are able to haul to land, and for want of boats and men they are constrained to let amany go after they have taken them, and yet sometimes they fill two boats at a time with them. And besides bass we take plenty of skate and thornbacks, and abundance of lobsters, and the least boy in the plantation may both catch and eat what he will of them. For my own part I was soon [full] with them, they were so great, and fat, and luscious. I have seen some myself that have weighed 16 pounds, but others have had many times so great lobsters as have weighed 25 pounds, as they assure me. . . .

Thus we see both land and sea abound with store of blessings for the comfortable sustenance of man's life in New England.

2. Edward Williams Promotes Virginia's Resources, 1630, 1650

[1630] It [Virginia] will give us the liberty of storing a great part of Europe with a larger plenty of incomparable better fish, then the Hollander hath found means to furnish it with, and will make us in no long tract of time, if industriously prosecuted, equal, if not transcend him in that his most beneficial staple.

It will be to this Commonwealth a standing and plentiful magazine of Wheat, Rice, Coleseed, Rapeseed, Flax, Cotton, Salt, Potashes, Sope-ashes, Sugars, Wines, Silke, Olives, and what ever single is the staple of other Nations, shall be found in this jointly collected.

It will furnish us with rich Furs, Buffs, Hides, Tallow, Beef, Park, &c. the growth and increase of Cattle in this Nation, receiving a grand interuption and stop, by killing commonly very hopeful young breed to furnish our markets, or store our shipping, . . . occasioned by want of ground to feed them, whereas those Provinces afford such a large proportion of rich ground, that neither the increase of this or the succeeding age can in any reasonable probability overfeed the [country].

That all these, and many inestimable benefits may have their rise, increase, and perfection from the South parts of Virginia, a country unquestionably our own, devolved to us by a just title, and discovered by John Cabot *at the English expenses, who found out and took seisure, together with the voluntary submission of the Natives to the English obedience of all that Continent from* Cape Florida *Northward, the excellent temper of the air, the large proportion of ground, the incredible richness of soil, the admirable abundance of Minerals, vegetables, medicinal drugs, timber, location, no less proper for all European commodities, then all those Staples which entitle* China, Persia, *and other the more opulent Provinces of the East to their wealth, reputation, and greatness . . . is agreed upon by all who have ever viewed the Country.*

[1650] The [location] and Climate of *Virginia* is the Subject of every Map, to which I shall refer the curiosity of those who desire more particular information.

Yet to show that Nature regards this Ornament of the new world with a more indulgent eye then she hath cast upon many other Countries, whatever *China, Persia, Japan, Cyprus, Candy, Sicily, Greece,* the South of *Italy, Spain,* and the opposite parts of *Africa,* to all which she is parallel, may boast of, will be produced in this happy Country. The same bounty of Summer, the same mild remission of Winter, with a more virgin and unexhausted soil being material ar-

guments to show that modesty and truth receive no diminution by the comparison.

Nor is the present wildness of it without a particular beauty, being all over a natural Grove of Oaks, Pines, Cedars, Cypress, Mulberry, Chestnut, Laurel, Sassafras, Cherry, Plumtrees, and Vines, all of so delectable an aspect, that the melancholyest eye in the World cannot look upon it without contentment, nor content himself without admiration. No shrubs or underwoods choke up your passage, and in its season your foot can hardly direct it self where it will not be died in the blood of large and delicious Strawberries: The Rivers which every way glide in deep and Navigable Channels, between the breasts of this . . . Country, and contribute to its conveniency beauty and fertility, labor with the multitude of their fishy inhabitants in greater variety of species, and of a more incomparable delicacy in tast and sweetness then whatever the European Sea can boast of: Sturgeon of ten feet, Drumms of six in length; Conger, Eels, Trout, Salmon, Bret, Mullet, Cod, Herrings, Perch, Lampreys, and whatever else can be desired to the satisfaction of the most voluptuous wishes.

Nor is the Land any less provided of native Flesh, Elks bigger then Oxen, whose hide is admirable soft, flesh excellent, and may be made, if kept domestic, as useful for draft and carriage, as Oxen. Deer in a numerous abundance, and delicate Venison, Racoons, Hares, Conyes, Beavers, Squirrel, Bears, all of a delightful nourishment for food, and their Furs rich, warm, and convenient for clothing and Merchandise.

That no part of this happy Country may be ungrateful to the Industrious, The air itself is often clouded with flights of Pigeons, Partriges, Blackbirds, Thrushes, Dottrels, Cranes, Herons, Swans, Geese, Brants, Ducks, Widgeons, [innumerable] wild Turkeys, which have been known to weigh fifty pound weight, ordinarily forty.

3. John Lederer Explores the Appalachian Mountains, 1670

On the twentieth of *August* 1670, Col. *Catlet* of *Virginia* and myself, with nine English Horse [mounted men], and five Indians on foot, departed from the house of one *Robert Talifer,* and that night reached the falls of *Rappahanock*-river, in Indian *Mantepeuck.*

The next day we passed it over where it divides into two branches North and South, keeping the main branch North of us.

The three and twentieth we found it so shallow, that it only wet our horses hoofs.

The four and twentieth we traveled through the *Savanna* among vast herds of Red and Fallow Deer which stood gazing at us; and a little after, we came to the Promontories of Spurs of the *Appalachian* mountains.

These *Savanna* are low grounds at the foot of the *Appalachians*, which all the Winter, Spring, and part of the Summer, lie under snow or water, when the snow is dissolved, which falls down from the Mountains commonly about the beginning of *June*; and then their verdure is wonderful pleasant to the eye, especially of such as having traveled through the shade of the vast Forest, come out of a melancholy darkness of a sudden, into a clear and open sky. To heighten the beauty of these parts, the first Springs of most of those great Rivers which run into the *Atlantic* Ocean, or *Cheseapeake* Bay, do here break out, and in various branches interlace the flowry [meadows], whose luxurious herbage invites numerous herds of Red Deer (for their unusual largeness improperly termed Elks by ignorant people) to feed. . . .

. . . They are certainly in a great error, who imagine that the Continent of North-*America* is but eight or ten days journey over from the *Atlantic* to the *Indian* Ocean: which all reasonable men must acknowledge, if they consider that Sir *Francis Drake* kept a West-North-west course from *Cape Mendocino* to *California*. Nevertheless, by what I gathered from the stranger Indians at *Akenatzy* of their Voyage by Sea to the very Mountains from a far distant Northwest Country, I am brought over to their opinion who think that the Indian Ocean does stretch an Arm or Bay from *California* into the Continent as far as the *Appalachian* Mountains, answerable to the Gulfs of *Florida* and *Mexico* on this side. Yet I am far from believing with some, that such great and Navigable Rivers are to be found on the other side [of] the *Appalachians* falling into the Indian Ocean, as those which run from them to the Eastward. My first reason is derived from the knowledge and experience we already have of South-*America*, whose *Andes* send the greatest Rivers in the world (as the *Amazon* and *Rio de la Plata*, &c.) into the *Atlantic*, but none at all into the *Pacific* Sea. Another Argument is, that all our Waterfowl which delight in Lakes and Rivers, as Swans, Geese, Ducks, &c. come over the Mountains from the Lake of *Canada*, when it is frozen over every Winter, to our fresh Rivers; which they would never do, could they find any on the other side of the *Appalachians*.

4. Peter Kalm Indicts Wastefulness in American Land Use, 1750

Agriculture was in a very bad state hereabouts. Formerly when a person had bought a piece of land, which perhaps had never been plowed since Creation, he cut down a part of the wood, tore up the roots, tilled the ground, sowed seed on it, and the first time he got an excellent crop.—But the same land after being cultivated for several years in succession, without being manured, finally loses its fertility of course. Its possessor then leaves it fallow and proceeds to another part of his land, which he treats in the same manner. Thus he goes on till he has changed a great part of his possessions into grain fields, and by that means deprived the ground of its fertility. He then returns to the first field, which now has pretty well recovered. This he tills again as long as it will afford him a good crop; but when its fertility is exhausted he leaves it fallow again and proceeds to the rest as before.

It being customary here to let the cattle go about the fields and in the woods both day and night, the people cannot collect much dung for manure. But by leaving the land fallow for several years a great quantity of weeds spring up in it, and get such strength that it requires a considerable time to extirpate them. This is the reason why the grain is always so mixed with the seed of weeds. The great richness of the soil which the first European colonists found here, and which had never been plowed before, has given rise to this neglect of agriculture, which is still observed by many of the inhabitants. But they do not consider that when the earth is quite exhausted a great space of time and an infinite deal of labor are necessary to bring it again into good condition, especially in these countries which are almost every summer scorched by the excessive heat and drought. . . .

. . . We can hardly be more hostile toward our woods in Sweden and Finland than they are here: their eyes are fixed upon the present gain, and they are blind to the future. Their cattle grow poorer daily in quality and size because of hunger, as I have before mentioned. On my travels in this country I observed several plants, which the horses and cows preferred to all others. They were wild in this country and likewise grew well on the driest and poorest ground, where no other plants would succeed. But the inhabitants did not know how to turn this to their advantage, owing to the little account made of Natural History, that science being here (as in other parts of the world) looked upon as a mere trifle, and the pastime of fools.

5. William Bartram Recounts an Alligators' Feast, 1791

It was by this time dusk, and the alligators had nearly ceased their roar, when I was again alarmed by a tumultuous noise that seemed to be in my harbor, and therefore engaged my immediate attention. Returning to my camp, I found it undisturbed, and then continued on to the extreme point of the promontory, where I saw a scene, new and surprising, which at first threw my senses into such a tumult, that it was some time before I could comprehend what was the matter; however, I soon accounted for the prodigious assemblage of crocodiles at this place, which exceeded every thing of the kind I had ever heard of.

How shall I express myself so as to convey an adequate idea of it to the reader, and at the same time avoid raising suspicions of my veracity? Should I say, that the river (in this place) from shore to shore, and perhaps near half a mile above and below me, appeared to be one solid bank of fish, of various kinds, pushing through this narrow pass of St. Juan's into the little lake, on their return down the river, and that the alligators were in such incredible numbers, and so close together from shore to shore, that it would have been easy to have walked across on their heads, had the animals been harmless? What expressions can sufficiently declare the shocking scene that for some minutes continued, whilst this mighty army of fish were forcing the pass? During this attempt, thousands, I may say hundreds of thousands, of them were caught and swallowed by the devouring alligators. I have seen an alligator take up out of the water several great fish at a time, and just squeeze them between his jaws, while the tails of the great trout flapped about his eyes and lips, ere he had swallowed them. The horrid noise of their closing jaws, their plunging amid the broken banks of fish, and rising with their prey some feet upright above the water, the floods of water and blood rushing out of their mouths, and the clouds of vapor issuing from their wide nostrils, were truly frightful. This scene continued at intervals during the night, as the fish came to the pass. After this sight, shocking and tremendous as it was, I found myself somewhat easier and more reconciled to my situation; being convinced that their extraordinary assemblage here was owing to the annual feast of fish; and that they were so well employed in their own element, that I had little occasion to fear their paying me a visit.

6. Thomas Jefferson's Impressions of Virginia's Natural Bridge, 1785

The *Natural Bridge,* the most sublime of nature's works, though not comprehended under the present head, must not [go unnoticed]. It is on the ascent of a hill, which seems to have been cloven through its length by some great convulsion. The fissure, just at the bridge, is, by some admeasurements, two hundred and seventy feet deep, by others only two hundred and five. It is about forty-five feet wide at the bottom and ninety feet at the top; this of course determines the length of the bridge, and its height from the water. Its breadth in the middle is about sixty feet, but more at the ends, and the thickness of the mass, at the summit of the arch, about forty feet. A part of this thickness is constituted by a coat of earth, which gives growth to many large trees. The residue, with the hill on both sides, is one solid rock of lime-stone. The arch approaches the semi-elliptical form; but the larger axis of the ellipsis, which would be the cord of the arch, is many times longer than the transverse. Though the sides of this bridge are provided in some parts with a parapet of fixed rocks, yet few men have resolution to walk to them, and look over into the abyss. You involuntarily fall on your hands and feet, creep to the parapet, and peep over it. Looking down from this height about a minute, gave me a violent head-ache. If the view from the top be painful and intolerable, that from below is delightful in an equal extreme. It is impossible for the emotions arising from the sublime to be felt beyond what they are here; so beautiful an arch, so elevated, so light, and springing as it were up to heaven! The rapture of the spectator is really indescribable! The fissure continuing narrow, deep, and straight, for a considerable distance above and below the bridge, opens a short but very pleasing view of the North mountain on one side and the Blue Ridge on the other, at the distance each of them of about five miles. This bridge is in the county of Rockbridge, to which it has given name, and affords a public and commodious passage over a valley which cannot be crossed elsewhere for a considerable distance. The stream passing under it is called Cedar-creek. It is a water of James' river, and sufficient in the driest seasons to turn a grist-mill, though its fountain is not more than two miles above.

Chapter 4:
Document Set 3 References

1. Francis Higginson Describes New England's Natural Endowments, 1630
   Francis Higginson, *New England's Plantation or a Short and True Description of the Commodities of that Country,* 1630, Massachusetts Historical Society, *Proceedings,* LXII, pp. 307–318.

2. Edward Williams Promotes Virginia's Resources, 1630, 1650
   Edward Williams, *Virginia Richly Valued* (London: Published by T. Harper for John Stephenson, 1650), in Peter Force, ed., *Tracts and Other Papers Relating Principally to the Origins, Settlement, and Progress of the Colonies in North America* (Washington, D.C., 1836–1846), in Robert McHenry and Charles Van Doren, eds., *A Documentary History of Conservation in America* (New York: Praeger Publishers, 1972), pp. 27, 89.

3. John Lederer Explores the Appalachian Mountains, 1670
   John Lederer, *The Discoveries of John Lederer,* trans., Sir William Talbot (London: Published by J. C. for Samuel Herick, 1672), pp. 20–24, in James Axtell, *America Perceived: A View from Abroad in the 17th Century* (New Haven: Pendulum Press, 1974), pp. 234, 236.

4. Peter Kalm Indicts Wastefulness in American Land Use, 1750
   Peter Kalm, *Travels in North America, etc. etc.,* trans. John R. Forster, Warrington (Engl.), 1770, in McHenry and Van Doren, pp. 168–169, 172.

5. William Bartram Recounts an Alligators' Feast, 1791
   William Bartram, *Travels Through North and South Carolina, Georgia, East and West Florida* (Philadelphia: James Johnson, 1791), Penguin Books edition, 1988, pp. 118–119.

6. Thomas Jefferson's Impressions of Virginia's Natural Bridge, 1785
   Thomas Jefferson, *Notes on the State of Virginia,* 1785 (New York: Harper & Row, 1964), pp. 21–22.

CHAPTER 5

DOCUMENT SET **1**

Crises and Responses: The Concept of Intercolonial Unity

The colonial legislatures, each jealously guarding its own powers, were slow to find common ground for resisting parliamentary authority. As your textbook indicates, even the reality of frontier insecurity was not enough to move the suspicious assemblies toward intercolonial cooperation when Benjamin Franklin advanced his ill-fated Albany Plan of Union in 1754. Over the next twenty years, however, Parliament's encroachment on cherished British liberties stimulated colonial cooperation in a series of ventures that climaxed in the disruption of the British Empire. Focusing on three crises, the following documents trace the development of greater intercolonial unity following the Seven Years' War. When you analyze the evidence, concentrate on the reasons colonial attitudes changed.

Confronted with a heightened Indian threat in 1754, delegates from seven colonies gathered at Albany to discuss the common danger. Although the conference produced mixed results, its plan for a colonial union represented the first serious effort to bridge differences among Englishmen in North America. Study the excerpts from the plan, together with Franklin's later assessment of its unrealized potential. Try to determine why the proposal was rejected by both the crown and the colonial legislatures.

Eleven years later, mutual suspicions were overcome as colonists coped with the consequences of Lord George Grenville's economic program. Review the Stamp Act's provisions with an eye to the relationship between the tax liabilities of British subjects in both England and North America (see your textbook for background and details). Then, as you examine the resolutions adopted by the Stamp Act Congress in October 1765, identify the issues, fears, and concerns that prompted the colonies to take concerted action in opposition to this particular revenue measure.

In this instance, political resistance, mob action, and British economic interests combined to bring about repeal of the stamp tax; more significant, however, was the Declaratory Act, which reasserted parliamentary legislative authority over the colonies. Reread your textbook's account of the escalating symbolic struggle over imperial and colonial prerogatives, a conflict that resulted in a significant step toward intercolonial union in 1774. By 1774, colonists had developed more sophisticated retaliatory techniques for dealing with parliamentary initiatives. Moreover, the concept of united resistance moved toward political collaboration when the Continental Congress was established. Analyze its Declaration of Rights and Grievances and the pledge made by the 1774 "Association" for evidence of a stronger tendency toward intercolonial unity.

These documents are linked by an underlying concern with the relationship among separate entities within the imperial structure. In your search for evidence of developing ties among the colonies, think about the principles of federalism.

Questions for Analysis

1. As you review the escalating tensions after 1763, identify the mechanisms employed by the colonial resistance to coordinate actions in the separate colonies. What do the documents reveal about the functions of the nonimportation agreements, the Stamp Act Congress, the Committees of Correspondence, the Continental Congress, and the Continental Association? How did these networks and gatherings contribute to the onset of rebellion against England?

2. What was the eighteenth-century meaning of the term *rights of Englishmen?* In what way do the documents reflect colonial insistence on those rights? Were colonial rights and obligations identical with those of British subjects living in England? Explain.

3. Approach the documents from an eighteenth-century British perspective. What were the key issues, and why did the British authorities react as they did to the Albany Plan, Stamp Act Congress, and Continental Congress? How did the imperial and colonial conceptions of the British Empire and the relationships between its constituent parts differ?

4. Search the documents for the use of terms such as *liberty, tyranny, republic, constitution, conspiracy, equality,* and *rights.* To what extent was colonial reliance on constitutional argument and political ideology sincere, and to what extent were matters of self-interest the dominant reasons for the insistence on colonial autonomy? What do your textbook's narrative and the documents reveal about the relationship among perceptions, expectations, and rhetoric as factors in the onset of rebellion?

5. Define the term *federalism.* In what way do the documents reflect federalist principles in embryonic form? Looking ahead to the late revolutionary period, discuss the relationship between the prerevolutionary concept of union and the revolutionary principle of confederation.

1. The Albany Plan of Union, 1754

It is proposed that humble application be made for an act of Parliament of Great Britain, by virtue of which one general government may be formed in America, including all the said colonies, within and under which government each colony may retain its present constitution, except in the particulars wherein a change may be directed by the said act, as hereafter follows.

[1.] That the said general government be administered by a President-General, to be appointed and supported by the crown; and a Grand Council, to be chosen by the representatives of the people of the several Colonies met in their respective assemblies.

[2.] That within ———— months after the passing such act, the House of Representatives that happen to be sitting within that time, or that shall be especially for that purpose convened, may and shall choose members for the Grand Council, in the following proportion, that is to say,

Massachusetts Bay	7
New Hampshire	2
Connecticut	5
Rhode Island	2
New York	4
New Jersey	3
Pennsylvania	6
Maryland	4
Virginia	7
North Carolina	4
South Carolina	4
	48...

[4.] That there shall be a new election of the members of the Grand Council every three years; and, on the death or resignation of any member, his place should be supplied by a new choice at the next sitting of the Assembly of the Colony he represented. . . .

[6.] That the Grand Council shall meet once in every year, and oftener if occasion require, ...

[7.] That the Grand Council have power to choose their speaker; and shall neither be dissolved, prorogued, nor continued sitting longer than six weeks at one time, without their own consent or the special command of the crown. . . .

[15.] That they raise and pay soldiers and build forts for the defence of any of the Colonies, and equip vessels of force to guard the coasts and protect the trade on the ocean, lakes, or great rivers; but they shall not impress men in any Colony, without the consent of the Legislature.

[16.] That for these purposes they have power to make laws, and lay and levy such general duties, imposts, or taxes, as to them shall appear most equal and just. . . .

[21.] That the laws made by them for the purposes aforesaid shall not be repugnant, but, as near as may be, agreeable to the laws of England, and shall be transmitted to the King in Council for approbation, as soon as may be after their passing; and if not disapproved within three years after presentation, to remain in force. . . .

[25.] That the particular military as well as civil establishments in each Colony remain in their present state, the general constitution notwithstanding; and that on sudden emergencies any Colony may defend itself, and lay the accounts of expense thence arising before the President-General and General Council, who may allow and order payment of the same, as far as they judge such accounts just and reasonable.

2. Benjamin Franklin's Recollection of the Albany Plan's Potential, 1789

On reflection it now seems probable, that if the foregoing Plan or some thing like it, had been adopted and carried into Execution, the subsequent Separation of the Colonies from the Mother Country might not so soon have happened, nor the Mischiefs suffered on both sides have occurred, perhaps during another Century. For the Colonies, if so united, would have really been, as they then thought themselves, sufficient to their own Defence, and being trusted with it, as by the Plan, an Army from Britain, for that purpose would have been unnecessary: The Pretences for framing the Stamp-Act would then not have existed, nor the other Projects for drawing a Revenue from America to Britain by Acts of Parliament, which were the Cause of the Breach, and attended with such terrible Expence of Blood and Treasure: so that the different Parts of the Empire might still have remained in Peace and Union. But the Fate of this Plan was singular. For tho' after many Days thorough Discussion of all its Parts in Congress it was unanimously agreed to, and Copies ordered to be sent to the Assembly of each Province for Concurrence, and one to the Ministry in England for the Approbation of the Crown. The Crown disapprov'd it, as having plac'd too much Weight in the democratic Part of the Constitution; and every Assembly as having allow'd too much to Prerogative. So it was totally rejected.

3. The Stamp Act, 1765

WHEREAS *by an act made in the last session of parliament, several duties were granted, continued, and appropriated, towards defraying the expences of defending, protecting, and securing, the* British *colonies and plantations in* America: *and whereas it is just and necessary, that provision be made for raising a further revenue within your Majesty's dominions in* America, *towards defraying the said expences:* . . . be it enacted. . . , That from and after . . . [November 1, 1765,]. . . there shall be raised, levied, collected, and paid unto his Majesty, his heirs, and successors, throughout the colonies and plantations in *America* which now are, or hereafter may be, under the dominion of his Majesty, his heirs and successors,

For every skin or piece of vellum or parchment, or sheet or piece of paper, on which shall be ingrossed, written or printed, any declaration, plea, replication, rejoinder, demurrer, or other pleading, or any copy thereof, in any court of law within the *British* colonies and plantations in *America,* a stamp duty of three pence. . . .

LIV. And be it further enacted. . . , That all the monies which shall arise by the several rates and duties hereby granted (except the necessary charges of raising, collecting, recovering, answering, paying, and accounting for the same and the necessary charges from time to time incurred in relation to this act, and the execution thereof) shall be paid into the receipt of his Majesty's exchequer, and shall be entered separate and apart from all other monies, and shall be there reserved to be from time to time disposed of by parliament, towards further defraying the necessary expences of defending, protecting, and securing, the said colonies and plantations.

4. The Stamp Act Resolutions, 1765

The members of this Congress, sincerely devoted with the warmest sentiments of affection and duty to His Majesty's person and Government, inviolably attached to the present happy establishment of the Protestant succession, and with minds deeply impressed by a sense of the present and impending misfortunes of the British colonies on this continent; having considered as maturely as time will permit the circumstances of the said colonies, esteem it our indispensable duty to make the following declarations of our humble opinion respecting the most essential rights and liberties of the colonists, and of the grievances under which they labour, by reason of several late Acts of Parliament.

I. That His Majesty's subjects in these colonies owe the same allegiance to the Crown of Great Britain that is owing from his subjects born within the realm, and all due subordination to that august body the Parliament of Great Britain.

II. That His Majesty's liege subjects in these colonies are intitled to all the inherent rights and liberties of his natural born subjects within the kingdom of Great Britain.

III. That it is inseparably essential to the freedom of a people, and the undoubted right of Englishmen, that no taxes be imposed on them but with their own consent, given personally or by their representatives.

IV. That the people of these colonies are not, and from their local circumstances cannot be, represented in the House of Commons in Great Britain.

V. That the only representatives of the people of these colonies are persons chosen therein by themselves, and that no taxes ever have been, or can be constitutionally imposed on them, but by their respective legislatures.

VI. That all supplies to the Crown being free gifts of the people, it is unreasonable and inconsistent with the principles and spirit of the British Constitution, for the people of Great Britain to grant to His Majesty the property of the colonists.

VII. That trial by jury is the inherent and invaluable right of every British subject in these colonies.

VIII. That the late Act of Parliament, entitled *An Act for granting and applying certain stamp duties, and other duties, in the British colonies and plantations in America, etc.,* by imposing taxes on the inhabitants of these colonies; and the said Act, and several other Acts, by extending the jurisdiction of the courts of Admiralty beyond its ancient limits, have a manifest tendency to subvert the rights and liberties of the colonists.

IX. That the duties imposed by several late Acts of Parliament, from the peculiar circumstances of these colonies, will be extremely burthensome and grievous; and from the scarcity of specie, the payment of them absolutely impracticable.

X. That as the profits of the trade of these colonies ultimately center in Great Britain, to pay for the manufactures which they are obliged to take from thence, they eventually contribute very largely to all supplies granted there to the Crown.

XI. That the restrictions imposed by several late Acts of Parliament on the trade of these colonies will render them unable to purchase the manufactures of Great Britain.

XII. That the increase, prosperity, and happiness of these colonies depend on the full and free enjoyments of their rights and liberties, and an intercourse with Great Britain mutually affectionate and advantageous.

XIII. That it is the right of the British subjects in these colonies to petition the King or either House of Parliament.

Lastly, That it is the indispensable duty of these colonies to the best of sovereigns, to the mother country, and to themselves, to endeavour by a loyal and dutiful address to His Majesty, and humble applications to both Houses of Parliament, to procure the repeal of the Act for granting and applying certain stamp duties, of all clauses of any other Acts of Parliament, whereby the jurisdiction of the Admiralty is extended as aforesaid, and of the other late Acts for the restriction of American commerce.

5. The First Continental Congress States Colonial Rights and Grievances, 1774

The good people of the several colonies of New Hampshire, Massachusetts Bay, Rhode Island and Providence Plantations, Connecticut, New York, New Jersey, Pennsylvania, New Castle, Kent and Sussex on Delaware, Maryland, Virginia, North Carolina and South Carolina, justly alarmed at these arbitrary proceedings of Parliament and administration, have severally elected, constituted, and appointed deputies to meet and sit in general congress, in the city of Philadel-phia, in order to obtain such establishment, as that their religion, laws, and liberties may not be subverted.

Whereupon the deputies so appointed being now assembled, in a full and free representation of these colonies, taking into their most serious consideration the best means of attaining the ends aforesaid, do, in the first place, as Englishmen, their ancestors in like cases have usually done, for asserting and vindicating their rights and liberties, declare,

That the inhabitants of the English colonies in North America, by the immutable laws of nature, the principles of the English constitution, and the several charters or compacts, have the following rights:

Resolved, N. C. D. 1. That they are entitled to life, liberty and property, and they have never ceded to any sovereign power whatever, a right to dispose of either without their consent.

Resolved, N. C. D. 2. That our ancestors who first settled these colonies, were at the time of their emigration from the mother country, entitled to all the rights, liberties, and immunities of free and nat-ural-born subjects, within the realm of England.

Resolved, N. C. D. 3. That by such emigration they by no means forfeited, surrendered, or lost any of those rights, but that they were, and their descendants now are, entitled to the exercise and enjoyment of all such of them, as their local and other circumstances enable them to exercise and enjoy.

Resolved, 4. That the foundation of English liberty, and of all free government, is a right in the people to participate in their legislative council: and as the English colonists are not represented, and from their local and other circumstances, cannot properly be represented in the British Parliament, they are entitled to a free and exclusive power of legislation in their several provincial legislatures, where their right of representation can alone be preserved, in all cases of taxation and internal polity, subject only to the negative of their sovereign, in such manner as has been heretofore used and accustomed. But, from the necessity of the case, and a regard to the mutual interest of both countries, we cheerfully consent to the operation of such Acts of the British Parliament, as are *bona fide,* restrained to the regulation of our external commerce, for the purpose of securing the commercial advantages of the whole empire to the mother country, and the commercial benefits of its respective members; excluding every idea of taxation, internal or external, for raising a revenue on the subjects in America, without their consent.

Resolved, N. C. D. 5. That the respective colonies are entitled to the common law of England, and more especially to the great and inestimable privilege of being tried by their peers of the vicinage, according to the course of that law.

Resolved, 6. That they are entitled to the benefit of such of the English statutes as existed at the time of their colonization; and which they have, by experience, respectively found to be applicable to their several local and other circumstances.

Resolved, N. C. D. 7. That these, his Majesty's colonies, are likewise entitled to all the immunities and privileges granted & confirmed to them by royal charters, or secured by their several codes of provincial laws.

Resolved, N. C. D. 8. That they have a right peaceably to assemble, consider of their grievances, and petition the king; and that all prosecutions, prohibitory proclamations and commitments for the same, are illegal.

Resolved, N. C. D. 9. That the keeping a standing army in these colonies, in times of peace, without the consent of the legislature of that colony, in which such army is kept, is against law.

Resolved, N. C. D. 10. It is indispensably necessary to good government, and rendered essential by the English constitution, that the constituent branches of the legislature be independent of each other; that, therefore, the exercise of legislative power in several colonies, by a council appointed, during pleasure, by the Crown, is unconstitutional, dangerous, and destructive to the freedom of American legislation.

All and each of which the aforesaid deputies, in behalf of themselves and their constituents, do claim, demand, and insist on, as their indubitable rights and liberties; which cannot be legally taken from them, altered or abridged by any power whatever, without their own consent, by their representatives in their several provincial legislatures.

In the course of our inquiry, we find many infringements and violations of the foregoing rights, which, from an ardent desire, that harmony and mutual intercourse of affection and interest may be restored, we pass over for the present, and proceed to state such acts and measures as have been adopted since the last war, which demonstrate a system formed to enslave America.

Resolved, N. C. D. That following Acts of Parliament are infringements and violations of the rights of the colonists; and that the repeal of them is essentially necessary in order to restore harmony between Great Britain and the American colonies, viz:

The several Acts of 4 Geo. III, c. 15 and c. 34; 5 Geo. III, c. 25; 6 Geo. III, c. 52; 7 Geo. III, c. 41 and c. 46; 8 Geo. III, c. 22, which impose duties for the purpose of raising a revenue in America, extend the powers of the admiralty courts beyond their ancient limits, deprive the American subject of trial by jury, authorize the judges' certificate to indemnify the prosecutor from damages that he might otherwise be liable to, requiring oppressive security from a claimant of ships and goods seized, before he shall be allowed to defend his property, and are subversive of American rights.

Also the 12 Geo. III, c. 24, entitled "An Act for the better securing his Majesty's dockyards, magazines, ships, ammunition, and stores," which declares a new offence in America, and deprives the American subject of a constitutional trial by a jury of the vicinage, by authorizing the trial of any person charged with the committing any offence described in the said Act, out of the realm, to be indicted and tried for the same in any shire or country within the realm.

Also the three Acts passed in the last session of Parliament, for stopping the port and blocking up the harbour of Boston, for altering the charter and government of the Massachusetts Bay, and that which is entitled "An Act for the better administration of justice," etc.

Also the Act passed in the same session for establishing the Roman Catholic religion in the province of Quebec, abolishing the equitable system of English laws, and erecting a tyranny there, to the great danger, from so total a dissimilarity of religion, law, and government of the neighbouring British colonies, by the assistance of whose blood and treasure the said country was conquered from France.

Also the Act passed in the same session for the better providing suitable quarters for officers and soldiers in his Majesty's service in North America.

Also that the keeping a standing army in several of these colonies, in time of peace, without the consent of the legislature of that colony in which such army is kept, is against law.

To these grievous acts and measures, Americans cannot submit, but in hopes that their fellow subjects in Great Britain will, on a revision of them, restore us to that state in which both countries found happiness and prosperity, we have for the present only resolved to pursue the following peaceable measures:

1. To enter into a non-importation, non-consumption, and non-exportation agreement or association,

2. To prepare an address to the people of Great Britain, and a memorial to the inhabitants of British America, and

3. To prepare a loyal address to his Majesty, agreeable to resolutions already entered into.

6. The First Continental Congress Pledges Resistance, 1774

We, his Majesty's most loyal subjects, the delegates of the several colonies of New Hampshire, Massachusetts Bay, Rhode Island, Connecticut, New York, New Jersey, Pennsylvania, the three lower counties of Newcastle, Kent, and Sussex on Delaware, Maryland, Virginia, North Carolina, and South Carolina, deputed to represent them in a continental congress, held in the city of Philadelphia, on the 5th day of September, 1774, avowing our allegiance to his Majesty, our affection and regard for our fellow-subjects in Great Britain and elsewhere, affected with the deepest anxiety and most alarming apprehensions, at those grievances and distresses, with which his Majesty's American subjects are oppressed; . . . are of opinion that a non-importation, non-consumption, and non-exportation agreement, faithfully adhered to, will prove the most speedy, effectual, and peaceable measure: and therefore, we do, for ourselves, and the inhabitants of the several colonies whom we represent, firmly agree and associate, under the sacred ties of virtue, honour and love of our country. . . .

And we do solemnly bind ourselves and our constituents, under the ties aforesaid, to adhere to this Association, until such parts of the several Acts of Parliament passed since the close of the last war, . . . are repealed. . . . And we recommend it to the provincial conventions, and to the committees in the respective colonies, to establish such farther regulations as they may think proper, for carrying into execution this Association.

The foregoing Association being determined upon by the Congress, was ordered to be subscribed by the several members thereof; and thereupon, we have hereunto set our respective names accordingly.

7. Benjamin Franklin Promotes the Concept of Union, 1754

Chapter 5:
Document Set 1 References

1. The Albany Plan of Union, 1754
Benjamin Franklin, "Albany Plan of Union," Albert Henry Smyth, ed., *The Writings of Benjamin Franklin* (New York, 1905–1907), Vol. 3, pp. 207, 212, 213–215, 220–221, 223–224, 226.

2. Benjamin Franklin's Recollection of the Albany Plan's Potential, 1789
Benjamin Franklin, "Memorandum," February 9, 1789, Leonard W. Labaree, ed., *The Papers of Benjamin Franklin* (New Haven: Yale University Press, 1962), Vol. 5, p. 417.

3. The Stamp Act, 1765
"The Stamp Act," March 22, 1765, in Danby Pickering, ed., *The Statutes at Large,* Vol. 26, pp. 179–204.

4. The Stamp Act Resolutions, 1765
"Resolutions," October 19, 1765, in John Almon, ed., *Collection of Interesting, Authentic Papers Relative to the Dispute between Great Britain and North America* (London, 1777), p. 27.

5. The First Continental Congress States Colonial Rights and Grievances, 1774
"Declaration of Colonial Rights and Grievances," October 1, 1774, in Worthington C. Ford *et al.*, eds., *Journals of the Continental Congress, 1774–1779* (Washington, 1904–1937), Vol. 1, pp. 66–73.

6. The First Continental Congress Pledges Resistance, 1774
"The Association of the First Continental Congress," October 20, 1774, in *Journals of the Continental Congress,* Vol. 1, pp. 75–80.

7. Benjamin Franklin Promotes the Concept of Union, 1754
Benjamin Franklin, "Join or Die," 1754. Library of Congress.

Chapter 5:
Document Set 1 Credits

7. Stock Montage

CHAPTER 5

DOCUMENT SET 2
The People's Rebellion: Popular Protest and Revolutionary Potential

The documents in Set 1 stress ideology and principle, but there was another factor important to revolutionary ferment: the role played by nonelite activists who supported the initiatives of popular party leaders. In recent years historians have explored not only the well-known activities of merchants and upper-class radicals but also the importance of the lower classes and urban mobs as the shock troops of the Revolution. The following documents provide a sample of mob action in the 1760s and the 1770s. As you weigh the evidence, try to assess the extent to which lower-class rebels were autonomous and independent.

Your textbook's description of the Stamp Act riots clearly establishes the importance of mob violence in the successful resistance against the hated revenue measure. In his history of Massachusetts Bay, Lieutenant Governor Thomas Hutchinson described the impact that lower-class elements had on colonial stamp agents. Examine his remarks for evidence of the mob's goals and the connection between the popular party and enforcement groups such as the Sons of Liberty. Compare Hutchinson's account with printer John Holt's description of the Sons' activities in New York colony. Note the extent to which the urban crowds acted independently.

Several documents contain clues to the social and economic makeup of the patriot organizations. Review the Charleston, South Carolina, Sons of Liberty membership list with an eye to its class composition. Com-

pare the Charleston data with evidence from the other documents to determine what social groups dominated the Sons' activities. How did such organizations interact with mob leaders?

The next two documents deal with the controversial events surrounding the Boston Massacre. As you review the conflicting accounts provided by the *Boston Gazette* and Captain Thomas Preston, arrive at your own conclusion about responsibility for the violence that occurred. Explain the differences in interpretation, especially the disagreement over the spontaneity of the clash. What was the significance of autonomous crowd behavior in provoking the incident?

The mob actions described in this document set raised an important question for colonial elite groups. Examine Gouverneur Morris's reaction to the events of the period 1765–1774 in light of other evidence of popular activism found in the remaining documents. Account for the fears of the aristocratic Morris as you reflect on the democratic implications of lower-class initiative.

In assessing the importance of popular initiative and crowd activity, consider the process of mob formation and explain the appearance of mobs on the political scene. Think about the reasons for the authorities' failure to quell the violence and assess the meaning of mob action for the future. Finally, be aware of the link between urban violence during the Revolution and the purposes of elite group patriots.

Questions for Analysis

1. What do the documents reveal about the extent of popular involvement in revolutionary activity? What was the significance of crowd action in the pursuit of radical goals? How were urban crowds mobilized for political action? What evidence do the documents contain of purposeful mob action? Relate your response to the broader issue of the crowd's role in history.

2. What was the social and economic composition of the Sons of Liberty? What was the significance of such organizations in the movement toward rebellion? How did they relate to the urban crowds?

3. Compare your textbook's description of the Boston Massacre with the two divergent accounts in the documents. What is your interpretation of the events that led to violence? What do the documents suggest about the spontaneity of the mob's behavior? Use evidence from the documents to support your position.

4. What were the social implications of the popular activities described in the documents? What were the concerns of elite group commentators on pre-Revolutionary

violence? How do these actions by the urban masses contribute to an analysis of the Revolution? What was the relationship between internal social conflicts and external political relations?

1. Thomas Hutchinson Recounts the Mob Reaction to the Stamp Act in Boston, 1765

The distributor of stamps for the colony of Connecticut arrived in Boston from London; and, having been agent for that colony, and in other respect of a very reputable character, received from many gentlemen of the town such civilities as were due to him. When he set out for Connecticut, Mr. Oliver, the distributor for Massachusetts Bay, accompanied him out of town. This occasioned murmuring among the people, and an inflammatory piece in the next Boston Gazette. A few days after, early in the morning, a stuffed image was hung upon a tree, called the great tree of the south part of Boston [subsequently called Liberty Tree]. Labels affixed denoted it to be designed for the distributor of stamps. . . .

Before night, the image was taken down, and carried through the townhouse, in the chamber whereof the governor and council were sitting. Forty or fifty tradesmen, decently dressed, preceded; and some thousands of the mob followed down King street to Oliver's dock, near which Mr. Oliver had lately erected a building, which, it was conjectured, he designed for a stamp office. This was laid flat to the ground in a few minutes. From thence the mob proceeded for Fort Hill, but Mr. Oliver's house being in the way, they endeavoured to force themselves into it, and being opposed, broke the windows, beat down the doors, entered, and destroyed part of his furniture, and continued in riot until midnight, before they separated. . . .

Several of the council gave it as their opinion, Mr. Oliver being present, that the people, not only of the town of Boston, but of the country in general, would never submit to the execution of the stamp act, let the consequence of an opposition to it be what it would. It was also reported, that the people of Connecticut had threatened to hang their

distributor on the first tree after he entered the colony; and that, to avoid it, he had turned aside to Rhode-Island.

Despairing of protection, and finding his family in terror and great distress, Mr. Oliver came to a sudden resolution to resign his office before another night. . . .

The next evening, the mob surrounded the house of the lieutenant-governor and chief justice [Hutchinson]. He was at Mr. Oliver's house when it was assaulted, and had excited the sheriff, and the colonel of the regiment, to attempt to suppress the mob. A report was soon spread, that he was a favourer of the stamp act, and had encouraged it by letters to the ministry. Upon notice of the approach of the people, he caused the doors and windows to be barred; and remained in the house. . . .

Certain depositions had been taken, many months before these transactions, by order of the governor, concerning the illicit trade carrying on; and one of them, made by the judge of the admiralty, at the special desire of the governor, had been sworn to before the lieutenant-governor, as chief justice. They had been shewn, at one of the offices in England, to a person who arrived in Boston just at this time, and he had acquainted several merchants, whose names were in some of the depositions as smugglers, with the contents. This brought, though without reason, the resentment of the merchants against the persons who, by their office, were obliged to administer the oaths, as well as against the officers of the customs and admiralty, who had made the depositions; and the leaders of the mob contrived a riot, which, after some small efforts against such officers, was to spend its principal force upon the lieutenant-governor. And, in the evening of the 26th of

August, such a mob was collected in King street, drawn there by a bonfire, and well supplied with strong drink. After some annoyance to the house of the registrar of the admiralty, and somewhat greater to that of the comptroller of the customs, whose cellars they plundered of the wine and spirits in them, they came, with intoxicated rage, upon the house of the lieutenant-governor. The doors were immediately split to pieces with broad axes, and a way made there, and at the windows, for the entry of the mob; which poured in, and filled, in an instant, every room in the house.

The lieutenant-governor had very short notice of the approach of the mob. He directed his children, and the rest of his family, to leave the house immediately, determining to keep possession himself. His eldest daughter, after going a little way from the house, returned, and refused to quit it, unless her father would do the like.

This caused him to depart from his resolutions, a few minutes before the mob entered. They continued their possession until day-light; destroyed, carried away, or cast into the street, every thing that was in the house; demolished every part of it, except the walls, as far as lay in their power; and had begun to break away the brickwork.

The damage was estimated at about twenty-five hundred pounds sterling, without any regard to a great collection of publick as well as private papers, in the possession and custody of the lieutenant-governor.

This town was, the whole night, under the awe of this mob; many of the magistrates, with the field officers of the militia, standing by as spectators; and no body daring to oppose, or contradict.

2. John Holt's Account of the Stamp Act Riots in New York, 1766

The Matter was intended to be done privately, but it got wind, and by ten o Clock I suppose 2000 people attended at the Coffee House, among them most of the principal men in Town—The Culprits apologies did not satisfy the people, they were highly blamed and the Sons of Liberty found it necessary to use their Influence to moderate the Resentments of the People. Two Men were dispatch'd to the Collector for the Stamp'd Bonds of which he had 30 in all, he desired Liberty to confer with the Governor, which was granted. The Governor sent Word, if the Stamps were deliver'd to him, he would give his Word and Honour they should not be used; but that if the people were not satisfied with this, they might do as they pleased with them—The message being returned to the gathering Multitude, they would not agree to the Governors Proposal, but insisted upon the Stamps being deliver'd and burnt, one or two men attended by about a thousand others were then sent for the Stamps, which were brought to the Coffee House, and the Merchant who had used them was order'd himself to kindle the Fire and consume them, those filled in and all, this was accordingly done amidst the Huzza's of the people who were by this Time swell'd to the Number I suppose of about 5000, and in another hour I suppose would have been 10,000—The people pretty quietly dispersed soon After, but their Resentment was not allay'd, Toward the Evening . . . tho' the Sons of Liberty exerted themselves to the utmost, they could not prevent the gathering of the Multitude, who went to Mr. Williams's house, broke open the Door and destroyed some of the Furniture. . . .

The people were generally satisfied and soon dispersed—but many of those of inferior Sort, who delight in mischief merely for its own sake, or for plunder, seem yet to be in such a turbulent Disposition that the two mortified Gentlemen are still in some Danger, but the Sons of Liberty intend to Exert themselves in their Defense.

3. Charleston, South Carolina, Sons of Liberty, 1766

1. Christopher Gadsden, merchant.
2. William Johnson, blacksmith.
3. Joseph Veree, carpenter.
4. John Fullerton, carpenter.
5. James Brown, carpenter.
6. Nath[anie]l Libby, ship carpenter.
7. George Flagg, painter and glazier.
8. Tho[ma]s Coleman, upholsterer.
9. John Hall, coachmaker.
10. W[illia]m Field, carver.
11. Robert Jones, sadler.
12. John Loughton, coachmaker.
13. "W." Rogers, wheelwright.
14. John Calvert, "Clerk in some office."
15. H[enry] Y. Bookless, wheelwright.
16. J. Barlow, sadler.
17. Tunis Teabout, blacksmith.
18. Peter Munclean, clerk.
19. W[illia]m Trusler, butcher.
20. Robert Howard, carpenter.
21. Alexander Alexander, schoolmaster.
22. Ed[ward] Weyman, clerk of St. Philip's Church, and glass grinder.
23. Tho[ma]s Swarle, painter.
24. W[illia]m Laughton, tailor.
25. Daniel Cannon, carpenter.
26. Benjamin Hawes, painter.

4. The *Boston Gazette* Describes the Boston Massacre, 1770

On the evening of Monday, being the fifth current, several soldiers of the 29th Regiment were seen parading the streets with their drawn cutlasses and bayonets, abusing and wounding numbers of the inhabitants.

A few minutes after nine o'clock four youths, named Edward Archbald, William Merchant, Francis Archbald, and John Leech, jun., came down Cornhill together, and separating at Doctor Loring's corner, the two former were passing the narrow alley leading to Murray's barrack in which was a soldier brandishing a broad sword of an uncommon size against the walls, out of which he struck fire plentifully. A person of mean countenance armed with a large cudgel bore him company. Edward Archbald admonished Mr. Merchant to take care of the sword, on which the soldier turned round and struck Archbald on the arm, then pushed at Merchant and pierced through his clothes inside the arm close to the armpit and grazed the skin. Merchant then struck the soldier with a short stick he had; and the other person ran to the barrack and brought with him two soldiers, one armed with a pair of tongs, the other with a shovel. He with the tongs pursued Archbald back through the alley, collared and laid him over the head with the tongs. The noise brought people together; and John Hicks, a young lad, coming up, knocked the soldier down but let him get up again; and more lads gathering, drove them back to the barrack where the boys stood some time as it were to keep them in. In less than a minute ten or twelve of them came out with drawn cutlasses, clubs, and bayonets and set upon the unarmed boys and young folk who stood them a little while but, finding the inequality of their equipment, dispersed. On hearing the noise, one Samuel Atwood came up to see what was the matter; and entering the alley from dock square, heard the latter part of the combat; and when the boys had dispersed he met the ten or twelve soldiers aforesaid rushing down the alley towards the square and asked them if they intended to murder people? They answered Yes, by G-d, root and branch! With that one of them struck Mr. Atwood with a club which was repeated by another; and being unarmed, he turned to go off and received a wound on the left shoulder which reached the bone and gave him much pain. Retreating a few steps, Mr. Atwood met two officers and said, gentlemen, what is the matter? They answered, you'll see by and by. Immediately after, those heroes appeared in the square, asking where were the boogers? where were the cowards? But notwithstanding their fierceness to naked men, one of them advanced towards a youth who had a split of a raw stave in his hand and said, damn them, here is one of them. But the young man seeing a person near him with a drawn sword and good cane ready to support him, held up his stave in defiance; and they quietly passed by him up the little alley by Mr. Silsby's to King Street where they attacked single and unarmed persons till they raised much clamour, and then turned down Cornhill Street, insulting all they met in like manner and pursuing some to their very doors. Thirty or forty persons, mostly lads, being by this means gathered in King Street, Capt. Preston with a party of men with charged bayonets, came from the main guard to the commissioner's house, the soldiers pushing their bayonets, crying, make way! They took place by the custom house and, continuing to push to drive the people off, pricked some in several places, on which they were clamorous and, it is said, threw snow balls. On this, the Captain commanded them to fire; and more snow balls coming, he again said, damn you, fire, be the consequence what it will! One soldier then fired, and a townsman with a cudgel struck him over the hands with such force that he dropped his firelock; and, rushing forward, aimed a blow at the Captain's head which grazed his hat and fell pretty heavy upon his arm. However, the soldiers continued the fire successively till seven or eight or, as some say, eleven guns were discharged.

5. Captain Thomas Preston's Defense of Military Action in Boston, 1770

It is [a] matter of too great notoriety of need any proofs that the arrival of his Majesty's troops in Boston was extremely obnoxious to its inhabitants. . . .

On Monday night about 8 o'clock two soldiers were attacked and beat. But the party of townspeople in order to carry matters to the utmost length, broke into two meeting houses and rang the alarm bells, which I supposed was for fire as usual, but was soon undeceived. About 9 some of the guard come to and informed me the town inhabitants were assembling to attack the troops, and that the bells were ringing as the signal for that purpose and not for fire, and the beacon intended to be fired to bring in the distant people of the country. This, as I was captain of the day, occasioned my repairing immediately to the main guard. In my way there I saw the people in great commotion, and heard them use the most cruel and horrid threats against the troops. In a few minutes after I reached the guard, about 100 people passed it and went towards the custom house where the king's money is lodged. They immediately surrounded the sentry posted there, and with clubs and other weapons threatened to execute their vengeance on him. I was soon informed by a townsman their intention was to carry off the soldier from his post and probably murder him. On which I desired him to return for further intelligence, and he soon came back and assured me he heard the mob declare they would murder him. This I feared might be a prelude to their plundering the king's chest. I immediately sent a noncommissioned officer and 12 men to protect both the sentry and the king's money, and very soon followed myself to prevent, if possible, all disorder, fearing lest the officer and soldiers, by the insults and provocations of the rioters, should be thrown off their guard and commit some rash act. They soon rushed through the people, and by charging their bayonets in half circles, kept them at a little distance. Nay, so far was I from intending the death of any person that I suffered the troops to go to the spot where the unhappy affair took place without any loading in their pieces; nor did I ever give orders for loading them. This remiss conduct in me perhaps merits censure; yet it is evidence, resulting from the nature of things, which is the best and surest that can be offered, that my intention was not to act offensively, but the contrary part, and that not without compulsion. The mob still increased and were more outrageous, striking their clubs or bludgeons one against another, and calling out, come on you rascals, you bloody backs, you lobster scoundrels, fire if you dare, G-d damn you, fire and be damned, we know you dare not, and much more such language was used. At this time I was between the soldiers and the mob, parleying with, and endeavouring all in my power to persuade them to retire peaceably, but to no purpose. They advanced to the points of the bayonets, struck some of them and even the muzzles of the pieces, and seemed to be endeavouring to close with the soldiers. On which some well behaved persons asked me if the guns were charged. I replied yes. They then asked me if I intended to order the men to fire. I answered no. . . . While I was thus speaking, one of the soldiers having received a severe blow with a stick, stepped a little on one side and instantly fired, on which turning to and asking him why he fired without orders, I was struck with a club on my arm, which for some time deprived me of the use of it, which blow had it been placed on my head, most probably would have destroyed me. On this a general attack was made on the men by a great number of heavy clubs and snowballs being thrown at them, by which all our lives were in imminent danger, some persons at the same time from behind calling out, damn your bloods—why don't you fire. Instantly three or four of the soldiers fired, one after another, and directly after three more in the same confusion and hurry. . . . On my asking the soldiers why they fired without orders, they said they heard the word fire and supposed it came from me. This might be the case as many of the mob called out fire, fire, but I assured the men that I gave no such order; that my words were, don't fire, stop your firing. In short, it was scarcely possible for the soldiers to know who said fire, or don't fire, or stop your firing.

6. Gouverneur Morris Warns Against Democratic Revolution, 1774

These sheep, simple as they are, cannot be gulled as heretofore. In short, there is no ruling them; and now, to leave the metaphor, the heads of the mobility [the mob] grow dangerous to the gentry, and how to keep them down is the question. While they correspond with the other colonies, call and dismiss popular assemblies, make resolves to bind the consciences of the rest of mankind, bully poor printers, and exert with full force all their other tribunitial powers, it is impossible to curb them. . . .

I stood in the balcony, and on my right hand were ranged all the people of property, with some few poor dependents, and on the other all the tradesmen, etc., who thought it worth their while to leave daily labor for the good of the country. This spirit of the English constitution has yet a little influence left, and but a little. The remains of it, however, will give the wealthy people a superiority this time, but would they secure it they must banish all schoolmasters and confine all knowledge to themselves. This cannot be. The mob begin to think and to reason. Poor reptiles! it is with them a vernal morning; they are struggling to cast off their winter's slough, they bask in the sunshine, and ere noon they will bite, depend upon it.

The gentry begin to fear this. Their committee will be appointed; they will deceive the people and again forfeit a share of their confidence. And if these instances of what with one side is policy, with the other perfidy, shall continue to increase and become more frequent, farewell aristocracy. I see, and I see it with fear and trembling, that if the disputes with Great Britain continue, we shall be under the worst of all possible dominions; we shall be under the domination of a riotous mob.

Chapter 5:
Document Set 2 References

1. Thomas Hutchinson Recounts the Mob Reaction to the Stamp Act in Boston, 1765
   Thomas Hutchinson, *The History of the Colony and Province of Massachusetts Bay*, 3 vols. (Boston, 1764–1828), ed. Lawrence Shaw Mayo, III (Cambridge: Harvard University Press, 1936), Vol. 3, pp. 86–88.

2. John Holt's Account of the Stamp Act Riots in New York, 1766
   "John Holt to Mrs. Deborah Franklin," February 15, 1766, in *Papers of Benjamin Franklin*, ed. I. Minis Hays (Philadelphia: American Philosophical Society, 1908), Vol. 48, p. 92.

3. Charleston, South Carolina, Sons of Liberty, 1766 Charleston, S.C., Sons of Liberty, Membership List, 1766, in Robert W. Gibbes, ed., *Documentary History of the American Revolution, South Carolina, 1764–1776* (New York, 1855), pp. 10–11.

4. The *Boston Gazette* Describes the Boston Massacre, 1770
   Boston Gazette and Country Journal, March 12, 1770.

5. Captain Thomas Preston's Defense of Military Action in Boston, 1770
   British Public Records Office, C.O. 5/759, in Merrill Jensen, ed., *English Historical Documents: American Colonial Documents to 1776* (New York: Oxford University Press, 1962), pp. 750–752.

6. Gouverneur Morris Warns Against Democratic Revolution, 1774
Gouverneur Morris to John Penn, May 20, 1774, *American Archives: Fourth Series Containing a Documentary History of the English Colonies in North America from the King's Message to Parliament of March 7, 1774 to the Declaration of Independence by the United States,* ed. Peter Force (Washington, 1837–1846). Vol. 1, pp. 342–343.

Chapter 5:
Document Set 2 Credits

CHAPTER 5

DOCUMENTS SET 3
Women's Patriotism: The Revolutionary Experience

The central problem in Chapter 5 is the escalation of the bitter Anglo-American quarrel that led to open resistance to imperial authority in 1775 and 1776. Your textbook notes that women's activism constituted one important component of the developing revolutionary crisis. This document set examines several expressions of women's patriotism both before and after the Declaration of Independence, including active support for the war.

Your task is to analyze the evidence for clues to the meaning of revolutionary rhetoric to those women who openly aligned themselves with the patriot cause. Watch for indications of the relationship between revolutionary sentiments and the deeper social assumptions of the time concerning women's sphere of activity. How did women's participation in the events leading up to the Revolution influence their concept of acceptable social and political behavior? In considering the impact of a revolutionary environment on female self-image, ask yourself whether a radical break with past tradition actually occurred.

As you search the documents for evidence of changing political roles, try to determine if the new concept of female participation in public affairs had an impact on nonpolitical spheres of activity. Think about the implications of revolutionary rhetoric for the future of gender relations in American society.

Finally, assess the range of nontraditional activity explored by women in Revolutionary America. In what ways did the actions of female patriots challenge the accepted value system? As you review the documents originating after the break with England, identify the new directions charted by women whose consciousness had been raised during the period of nonviolent resistance. Consider the implications of patriotic sentiments for historians' assumptions concerning female political awareness in the 1770s and 1780s.

Questions for Analysis

1. What do the documents reveal about the contributions made by women to the success of the Revolution? In what ways did women's activities reflect or depart from traditional social assumptions?

2. What were the implications of women's revolutionary activities for relationships between men and women? In what unanticipated directions did revolutionary actions lead?

3. Using the documents as evidence, develop an argument for or against the radicalizing potential of revolution. In what directions did women's participation in economic resistance to imperial authority lead?

4. Assess the results of the Revolution, with emphasis on women's place in American society. What was the impact of the Revolution on the status of American women?

1. The Women of Edenton, North Carolina, Embrace Nonimportation, 1774

As we cannot be indifferent on any occasion that appears nearly to affect the peace and happiness of our country, and as it has been thought necessary for the public good, to enter into several particular resolves by a meeting of members deputed from the whole Province, it is a duty which we owe, not only to our near and dear relations and connections . . . but to ourselves, who are essentially interested in their welfare, to do everything as far as lies in our power, to testify our sincere adherence to the same; and we do therefore accordingly subscribe this paper, as a witness of our fixed intention and solemn determination to do so.

2. The British Perception of the Edenton Patriots, ca. 1774

A SOCIETY of PATRIOTIC LADIES,

3. Abigail Adams Describes an Attack on a Profiteering Merchant, 1777

July 31, 1777

I have nothing new to entertain you with, unless it is an account of a New Set of Mobility which have lately taken the Lead in B[osto]n. You must know that there is a great Scarcity of Sugar and Coffe, articles which the Female part of the State are very loth to give up, especially whilst they consider the Scarcity occasiond by the merchants having secreted a large Quantity. There has been much rout and Noise in the Town for several weeks. Some Stores had been opend by a number of people and the Coffe and Sugar carried into the Market and dealt out by pounds. It was rumourd that an eminent, wealthy, stingy Merchant (who is a Batchelor) had a Hogshead of Coffe in his Store which he refused to sell to the committee under 6 shillings per pound. A Number of Females some say a hundred, some say more assembled with a cart and trucks, marchd down to the Ware House and demanded the keys, which he refused to deliver, upon which one of them seazd him by his Neck and tossd him into the cart. Upon his finding no Quarter he deliverd the keys, when they tipd up the cart and dischargd him, then opend the Warehouse, Hoisted out the Coffe themselves, put it into the trucks and drove off.

It was reported that he had a Spanking among them, but this I believe was not true. A large concourse of Men stood amazd silent Spectators of the whole transaction.

4. Philadelphia Women Raise Funds to Support the Revolution, 1780

On the commencement of actual war, the Women of America manifested a firm resolution to contribute . . . to the deliverance of their country. Animated by the purest patriotism, they are sensible of sorrow at this day, in not offering more than barren wishes for the success of so glorious a Revolution. They aspire to render themselves more really useful; and this sentiment is universal from the north to the south of the Thirteen United States. Our ambition is kindled by the fame of those heroines of antiquity, who have rendered their sex illustrious, and have proved to the universe, that, if the weakness of our Constitution, if opinion and manners did not forbid us to march to glory by the same paths as the Men, we should at least equal, and sometimes surpass them in our love for the public good. I glory in all that which my sex has done great and commendable. I call to mind with enthusiasm and with admiration, all those acts of courage, of constancy and patriotism, which history has transmitted to us: The people favoured by Heaven, preserved from destruction by the virtues, the zeal and the resolution of Deborah, of Judith, of Esther! The fortitude of the mother of the Macchabees, in giving up her sons to die before her eyes: Rome saved from the fury of a victorious enemy by the efforts of Volumnia, and other Roman Ladies: So many famous sieges where the Women have been seen forgetting the weakness of their sex, building new walls, digging trenches with their feeble hands, furnishing arms to their defenders, they themselves darting the missile weapons on the enemy, resigning the ornaments of their apparel, and their fortune, to fill the public treasury, and to hasten the deliverance of their country; burying themselves under its ruins; throwing themselves into the flames rather than submit to the disgrace of humiliation before a proud enemy.

Born for liberty, disdaining to bear the irons of a tyrannic Government, we associate ourselves to the grandeur of those Sovereigns, cherished and revered, who have held with so much splendour the scepter of the greatest States, The Batildas, the Elizabeths, the Maries, the Catharines, who have extended the empire of liberty, and contented to reign by sweetness and justice, have broken the chains of slavery, forged by tyrants in times of ignorance and barbarity. . . .

We know that at a distance from the theatre of war, if we enjoy any tranquility, it is the fruit of your watchings, your labours, your dangers. . . . Who, amongst us, will not renounce with the highest pleasure, those vain ornaments, when she shall consider that the valiant defenders of America will be able to draw some advantage from the money which she may have laid out in these. . . . The time is arrived to display the same sentiments which animated us at the beginning of the Revolution, when we renounced the use of teas, however agreeable to our taste, rather than receive them from our persecutors; when we made it appear to them that we placed former necessaries in the rank of superfluities, when our liberty was interested; when our republican and laborious hands spun the flax, prepared the linen intended for the use of our soldiers; when [as] exiles and fugitives we supported with courage all the evils which are the concomitants of war.

5. Deborah Sampson Gannett Recalls Service in the Continental Army, 1782–1783

Know then, that my juvenile mind early became inquisitive to understand—not merely whether the principles, or rather the seeds of war are analogous to the genuine nature of man—not merely to know why he should forego every trait of humanity and assume the character of a brute; or, in plainer language, why he should march out tranquilly, or in a paroxysm of rage against his fellow man to butcher, or be butchered? For these, alas! were too soon horribly verified by the massacres in our streets, in the very streets which encompass this edifice—in yonder adjacent villas [Lexington and adjacent towns], on yonder memorable eminence [Breed's Hill], where now stand living monuments of the atrocious, heart distracting, momentous scenes that followed in rapid succession! . . .

But most of all, my mind became agitated with the enquiry—why a nation, separated from us by an ocean more than three thousand miles in extent, should endeavor to enforce on us plans of subjugation, the most unnatural in themselves, unjust, inhuman in their operations, and unpractised even by the uncivilized savages of the wilderness? Perhaps nothing but the critical juncture of the times could have excused such a philosophical disquisition of politics in woman, notwithstanding it was a theme of universal speculation and concern to man. We indeed originated from her [England], as from a parent, and perhaps would have continued to this period in subjection to her mandates, had we not discovered that her romantic, avaricious and cruel disposition extended to murder, after having bound the slave!

Confirmed by this time in the justness of a defensive war on the one side, from the most aggravated one on the other, my mind ripened with my strength. While our beds and our roses were sprinkled with the blood of indiscriminate youth, beauty, innocence and decrepit old age, I only seemed to want the license to become one of the severest avengers of the wrong.

For several years I looked on these scenes of havoc, rapacity and devastation, as one looks on a drowning man, on the conflagration of a city—where are not only centered his coffers of gold, but with them his choicest hopes, friends, companions, his all—without being able to extend the rescuing hand to either.

Wrought upon at length by an enthusiasm and frenzy that could brook no control, I burst the tyrant bonds which held my sex in awe, and clandestinely, or by stealth, grasped an opportunity, which custom and the world seemed to deny, as a natural privilege. And whilst poverty, hunger, nakedness, cold and disease had dwindled the American armies to a handful—whilst universal terror and dismay ran through our camps, ran through our country—while even Washington himself, at their head, though like a god, stood, as it were, on a pinnacle tottering over the abyss of destruction, the last prelude to our falling a wretched prey to the yawning jaws of the monster aiming to devour—I threw off the soft habiliment of my sex, and assumed those of the warrior, already prepared for battle.

Thus I became an actor in that important drama, with an inflexible resolution to persevere through the last scene; when we might be permitted and acknowledged to enjoy what we had so nobly declared we would possess, or lose with our lives—freedom and independence! . . .

You may have heard the thunderings of a volcano; you may have contemplated, with astonishment and wonder, the burial of a city by its eruption. Your ears then are yet deafened from the thunderings of the invasion of York Town—your eyes dazzled, your imaginations awfully sublimed, by the fire which belched from its environs, and towered, like that from an eruption of Etna, to the clouds! Your hearts yet bleed, from every principle of humanity, at the recollection of the havoc, carnage and death that reigned there!

Three successive weeks, after a long and rapid march, found me amidst this storm. But, happily for America, happily for Europe, perhaps for the world, when, on the delivery of Cornwallis's sword to the illustrious, immortal Washington, that sun of liberty and independence burst through a sable cloud, and his benign influence was, almost instantaneously, felt in our remotest corners! The phalanx of war was thus broken through, and the palladium of peace blossomed on its ruins. . . .

Such is my experience—not that I ever mourned the loss of a child, but that I considered myself as lost! For, on the one hand, if I fell not a victim to the infuriating rabble of a mob, or of a war not yet fully terminated—the disclosure of my peculiar situation seemed infinitely worse than either. And if from stratagem and perseverance, I may acquire as great knowledge in every respect as I have of myself in this, then my knowledge, at least of human nature, will be as complete as it is useful.

But we will now hasten from the field, from the embattled entrenchments built for the destruction of man, from a long, desolating war, to contemplate more desirable and delightful scenes. And notwithstanding curiosity may prompt any to retrace the climax of our revolution, the means, under a smiling, superintending providence, by which we have outrode the storms of danger and distress. What heart will forget to expand with joy and gratitude, to beat in unison, at the propitious recollection? And I enquire, what infant tongue can ever forget or cease being taught to lisp the praises of Washington, and those of that bright constellation of worthies who swell the list of Colombian fame—those, by whose martial skill and philanthropic labours, we were first led to behold, after a long and stormy night, the smiling sun of peace burst on our benighted world! And while we may drop a tear over the flowery turf of those patriots and sages, may she unrivaled enjoy and increase her present bright sunshine of happiness! May agriculture and commerce, industry and manufactures, arts and sciences, virture and decorum, union and harmony—those richest sources of our worth, and strongest pillars of our strength—become stationary, like fixed stars in the firmament, to flourish in her clime!

But the question again returns: "What particular inducement could she have thus to elope from the soft sphere of her own sex, to perform a deed of val-our by way of sacrilege on unhallowed ground—voluntarily to face the storms both of elements and war, in the character of him, who is more fitly made to brave and endure all danger?"

And dost thou ask what fairy hand inspired
A nymph to be with martial glory fired?
Or, what from art, or yet from nature's laws,
Has joined a female to her country's cause?
Why on great Mars's theatre she drew
Her female portrait, though in soldier's hue?
Then ask—why Cincinnatus left his farm?
Why science did old Plato's bosom warm?
Why Hector in the Trojan war should dare?
Or why should Homer trace his actions there?
Why Newton in philosophy has shown?
Or Charles, for solitude, has left his throne?
Why Locke in metaphysics should delight—
Precisian sage, to set false reason right?
Why Albion's sons should kindle up a war?
Why Jove or Vulcan hurried on the car?
Perhaps the same propensity you use,
Has prompted her a martial course to choose.
Perhaps to gain refinements where she could,
This rare achievement for her country's good.
Or was some hapless lover from her torn—
As Emma did her valiant Hammon mourn?
Else he must tell, who would this truth attain,
Why one is formed for pleasure—one for pain:
Or, boldly, why our maker made us such—
Why here he gives too little—there too much!

. . . Yet if even this be deemed too much of an extenuation of a breach in the modesty of the female world, humbled and contented will I sit down, inglorious for having unfortunately performed an important part assigned for another—like a bewildered star traversing out of its accustomed orbit, whose twinkling beauty at most has become totally obscured in the presence of the sun.

But as the rays of the sun strike the eye with the greatest lustre when emerging from a thick fog, and as those actions which have for their objects the extended hand of charity to the indigent and wretched—to restore a bewildered traveller to light—and, to reform in ourselves any irregular and forlorn course of life; so, allowing myself to be one of the greatest of these, do I still hope for some claim on the indulgence and patronage of the public; as in such case I might be conscious of the approbation of my God.

I cannot contentedly quit this subject or this place without expressing, more emphatically, my high respect and veneration for my own sex. The indulgence of this respectable circle supersedes my merit, as well as my most sanguine expectations. You receive, at least, in return, my warmest gratitude. And though you can neither have, nor perhaps need, from me the instructions of a sage, or the advice of the counsellor, you surely will not be wholly indifferent to my most sincere declaration of friendship for that sex, for which this checkered flight of my life may have rendered me the least ornamental example; but which, neither adversity or prosperity, could I ever learn to forget or degrade. . . .

. . . But in whatever I may be thought to have been unnatural, unwise and indelicate, it is now my most fervent desire that it may have a suitable impression on you—and on me, a penitent for every wrong thought and step. The rank you hold in the scale of beings is, in many respects, superior to that of man. Nurses of his growth, and invariable models of his habits, he becomes a suppliant at your shrine, emulous to please, assiduous to cherish and support, to live and to die for you! Blossoms from your very birth, you become his admiration, his joy, his Eden companions in this world. How important then is it, that these blossoms bring forth such fruit as will best secure your own delights and felicity, and those of him, whose every enjoyment, and even his very existence, is so peculiarly interwoven with your own!

6. Deborah Sampson Gannett Recounts Her Wartime Experience, 1802

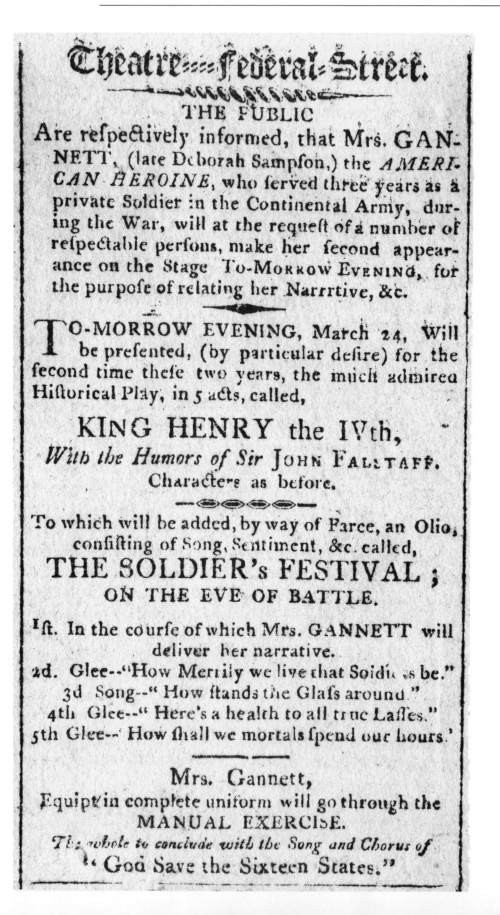

Chapter 5:
Document Set 3 References

1. The Women of Edenton, North Carolina, Embrace Nonimportation, 1774
   Richard T. H. Halsey, *The Boston Port Bill as Pictured by a Contemporary London Cartoonist* (New York, 1904), pp. 314–315.

2. The British Perception of the Edenton Patriots, ca. 1774
   "A Society of Patriotic Ladies," ca. 1774, Library of Congress, in Mary Beth Norton, *Liberty's Daughters: The Revolutionary Experience of American Women* (Boston: Little Brown and Company, 1980), p. 162.

3. Abigail Adams Describes an Attack on a Profiteering Merchant, 1777
   Abigail Adams to John Adams, July 31, 1777, *Adams Family Correspondence,* ed. L. H. Butterfield, Vol. 2 (Cambridge: Belknap Press of Harvard University Press, 1963), p. 295.

4. Philadelphia Women Raise Funds to Support the Revolution, 1780
   The Sentiments of an American Woman (Philadelphia: John Dunlap, 1780), in *Women's America: Refocusing the Past,* eds. Linda Kerber and Jane DeHart Mathews (New York: Oxford University Press, 1987), pp. 80–81.

5. Deborah Sampson Gannett Recalls Service in the Continental Army, 1782–1783
   "Deborah Sampson Gannett," in Elizabeth Evans, *Weathering the Storm: Women of the Revolution* (New York: Paragon House, 1989), pp. 321–322, 325–327, 328.

6. Deborah Sampson Gannett Recounts Her Wartime Experience, 1802
   The Mercury, 1802, in Evans, p. 319.

Chapter 5:
Document Set 3 Credits

2. Stock Montage
6. The Boston Athenaeum

CHAPTER 6

DOCUMENT SET 1

Republican Womanhood: Citizenship in a New Nation

The textbook notes that the Revolution did not affect the legal status of white women in most respects, nor did it enhance their political position. Review the text section on "Women in the New Republic" as background for your analysis of the following documents. Then examine the primary sources for evidence of both the subordination of women and resistance to the traditional sphere allotted to them.

The documents examined in Chapter 5, Set 3, focus on revolutionary sentiments and activities, but the materials that follow extend the analysis beyond the context of colonial rebellion. Your task is to assess the residual impact of revolutionary aspirations and ideology on women's status and gender relations. Search the documents for evidence of the Revolution's influence beyond the strictly political sphere. As you explore the claims made by late-eighteenth-century white women, think about the identities and background of the witnesses. What clues does your investigation provide with regard to the general acceptance of their ideas?

The Confederation period witnessed a tremendous spurt of political creativity, most clearly expressed in the new institutions crafted by the founders. One of the critical issues addressed by these new governmental forms was the definition of citizenship and the qualifications for political participation. Restrictions on the voting franchise and office-holding meant that white women's citizenship was to be exercised in nontraditional ways. As you dissect the documents, look for evidence of alternative modes of influence exploited by those women who sought to fulfill political roles.

Despite the ideology of the Revolution, women's lives, both private and political, continued to be defined by dependence and deference. The lingering concept of hierarchy clashed with the principles of egalitarianism that flowed from the successful Revolution. As men moved to create a politically democratic society, the female equivalent of full citizenship appeared in the form of "Republican Motherhood," an idea that emphasized the role played by white women within the confines of the domestic sphere in educating their children for citizenship. Examine the documents for hints of the ways in which this restricted form of citizenship was practiced. Do the sources suggest that Republican Motherhood was a satisfying political outlet for women of the early Republic? Think about the options available and the alternatives advanced by white women as the new nation took shape.

Questions for Analysis

1. Define "Republican Motherhood." How do the documents reflect the advantages and limitations inherent in this type of female citizenship in the post-Revolutionary era? In what ways did this concept imply improvement and/or decline in women's position in society in comparison to the colonial era?

2. What do the documents reveal about the organization, structure, and practice of education in the post-Revolutionary era? What were the impact and social significance of female education?

3. In what ways do the documents shed light on women's conceptions of their potential political and social roles in the early Republic? How did educated white women react to the domestication of their citizenship function? Assess their arguments.

4. How do the documents reflect the connection between the ideology of Revolution and the status of women? What is the relationship between the documents in Chapter 5, Set 3, and Chapter 6, Set 1? Explain.

1. Abigail and John Adams Exchange Sentiments on Women's Rights, 1776

Abigail Adams to John Adams:

Braintree March 31 1776

I long to hear that you have declared an independency—and by the way in the new Code of Laws which I suppose it will be necessary for you to make I desire you would Remember the Ladies, and be more generous and favorable to them than your ancestors. Do not put such unlimited power into the hands of the Husbands. Remember all Men would be tyrants if they could. If particular care and attention is not paid to the Ladies we are determined to foment a Rebellion, and will not hold ourselves bound by any Laws in which we have no voice, or Representation.

That your Sex are Naturally Tyrannical is a Truth so thoroughly established as to admit of no dispute, but such of you as wish to be happy willingly give up the harsh title of Master for the more tender and endearing one of Friend. Why then, not put it out of the power of the vicious and the Lawless to use us with cruelty and indignity with impunity. Men of Sense in all Ages abhor those customs which treat us only as the vassals of your Sex. Regard us then as Beings placed by providence under your protection and in imitation of the Supreme Being make use of that power only for our happiness.

John to Abigail:

Ap. 14. 1776

As to Declarations of Independency, be patient. Read our Privateering Laws, and our Commercial Laws. What signifies a Word.

As to your extraordinary Code of Laws, I cannot but laugh. We have been told that our Struggle has loosened the bands of Government every where. That Children and Apprentices were disobedient—that schools and Colleges were grown turbulent—that Indians slighted their Guardians and Negroes grew insolent to their Masters. But your Letter was the first Intimation that another Tribe more numerous and powerful than all the rest were grown discontented.—This is rather too coarse a Compliment but you are so saucy, I wont blot it out.

Depend upon it, We know better than to repeal our Masculine systems. Although they are in full Force, you know they are little more than Theory. We dare not exert our Power in its full Latitude. We are obliged to go fair, and softly, and in Practice you know We are the subjects. We have only the Name of Masters, and rather than give up this, which would completely subject Us to the Despotism of the Petticoat, I hope General Washington, and all our brave Heroes would fight. I am sure every good Politician would plot, as long as he would against Despotism, Empire, Monarchy, Aristocracy, Oligarchy, or Ochlocracy,—A fine Story indeed. I begin to think the Ministry as deep as they are wicked. After stirring up Tories, Landjobbers, Trimmers, Bigots, Canadians, Indians, Negroes, Hanoverians, Hessians, Russians, Irish Roman Catholics, Scots Renegades, at last they have stimulated them to demand new Privileges and threaten to rebel.

Abigail to John:

B[raintre]e May 7 1776

I can not say that I think you very generous to the Ladies, for whilst you are proclaiming peace and good will to Men, Emancipating all Nations, you insist upon retaining an absolute power over Wives. But you must remember that Arbitrary power is like most other things which are very hard, very liable to be broken—and notwithstanding all your wise Laws and Maxims we have it in our power not only to free our selves but to subdue our Masters, and without violence throw both your natural and legal authority at our feet—

*"Charm by accepting, by submitting sway
Yet have our Humor most when we obey."*

2. Eliza Wilkinson Argues for an Expansion of the Feminine Sphere, 1782

After various discourses, the conversation took a turn on the subject of the present war. I was proud to hear my friends express themselves in a manner not unworthy of their country. Maj. Moore made a comparison, which, as I perfectly remember, I will give you. Your opinion is also required of the same.

"Suppose," said he, "I had a field of wheat, upon these conditions, that out of that field I was to give so much to a certain person yearly; well, I think nothing of it, I give it cheerfully, and am very punctual; it goes on thus for some years; at length the person sends me word I must let him have so much more, for he wants it; still I comply with cheerfulness. The next year he requires a still larger supply, and tells me he cannot do without it. This startles me! I find him encroaching, by little and little, on my property. I make some difficulty in complying; however, as he says 'he cannot do without it,' I let him have it, though I see it hurts me; but it puts me on my guard. Well, things go on so for some time; at length he begins again, and at last seems to have a design of taking my whole field. Then what am I to do?—Why, if I give it up, I am ruined. I must lie at his mercy. Is not this slavery? For my part," continued he, "I would rather explore unknown regions, blessed with liberty, than remain in my native country if to be cursed with slavery."

The land of Liberty! how sweet the sound! enough to inspire cowardice itself with a resolution to confirm the glorious title, "the land of Liberty." Let me again repeat it—how enchanting! It carries every idea of happiness in it, and raises a generous warmth in every bosom capable of discerning its blessings. O! Americans—Americans! strive to retain the glorious privilege which your virtuous ancestors left you; "it is the price of blood"; and let not the blood of your brave countrymen, who have so lately (in all the States) died to defend it, be split in vain. Pardon this digression, my dear Mary—my pen is inspired with sympathetic ardor, and has run away with my thoughts before I was aware. I do not love to meddle with political matters; the men say we have no business with them, it is not in our sphere! and Homer (did you ever read Homer, child?) gives us two or three broad hints to mind our domestic concerns, spinning, weaving, &c. and leave affairs of higher nature to the men; but I must beg his pardon—I won't have it thought, that because we are the weaker sex as to *bodily* strength, my dear, we are capable of nothing more than minding the dairy, visiting the poultry-house, and all such domestic concerns; our thoughts can soar aloft, we can form conceptions of things of higher nature; and have as just a sense of honor, glory, and great actions, as these "Lords of the Creation." What contemptible *earth worms* these authors make us! They won't even allow us the liberty of thought, and that is all I want. I would not wish that we should meddle in what is unbecoming female delicacy, but surely we may have sense enough to give our opinions to commend or discommend such actions as we may approve or disapprove; without being reminded of our spinning and household affairs as the only matters we are capable of thinking or speaking of with justness or propriety. I won't allow it, positively won't.

3. Abigail Adams Instructs Her Son on Republican Virtue, 1783

Braintree, 26 December, 1783

The early age at which you went abroad gave you not an opportunity of becoming acquainted with your own country. Yet the revolution, in which we were engaged, held it up in so striking and important a light, that you could not avoid being in some measure irradiated with the view. The characters with which you were connected, and the conversation you continually heard, must have impressed your mind with a sense of the laws, the liberties, and the glorious privileges, which distinguish the free, sovereign, independent States of America.

Compare them with the vassalage of the Russian government you have described, and say, were this highly favored land barren as the mountains of Switzerland, and covered ten months in the year with snow, would she not have the advantage even of Italy, with her orange groves, her breathing statues, and her melting strains of music? or of Spain, with her treasures from Mexico and Peru? not one of which can boast that first of blessings, the glory of human nature, the inestimable privilege of sitting down under their vines and fig-trees, enjoying in peace and security whatever Heaven has lent them, having none to make them afraid.

Let your observations and comparisons produce in your mind an abhorrence of domination and power, the parent of slavery, ignorance, and barbarism, which places man upon a level with his fellow tenants of the woods;

A day, an hour, of virtuous liberty
Is worth a whole eternity of bondage.

You have seen power in its various forms—a benign deity, when exercised in the suppression of fraud, injustice, and tyranny, but a demon, when united with unbounded ambition—a wide-wasting fury, who has destroyed her thousands. Not an age of the world but has produced characters, to which whole human hecatombs have been sacrificed. . . .

The history of your own country and the late revolution are striking and recent instances of the mighty things achieved by a brave, enlightened, and hardy people, determined to be free; the very yeomanry of which, in many instances, have shown themselves superior to corruption, as Britain well knows, on more occasions than the loss of her André. Glory, my son, in a country which has given birth to characters, both in the civil and military departments, which may lie with the wisdom and valor of antiquity. As an immediate descendant of one of those characters, may you be led to an imitation of that disinterested patriotism and that noble love of your country, which will teach you to despise wealth, titles, pomp, and equipage, as mere external advantages, which cannot add to the internal excellence of your mind, or compensate for the want of integrity and virtue.

May your mind be thoroughly impressed with the absolute necessity of universal virtue and goodness, as the only sure road to happiness, and may you walk therein with undeviating steps—is the sincere and most affectionate wish of

Your mother,

A. ADAMS

4. Priscilla Mason Calls for Sexual Equality, 1793

Venerable Trustees of this Seminary, Patrons of the improvement of the female mind; suffer us to present the first fruits of your labours as an offering to you. . . .

A female, young and inexperienced, addressing a promiscuous assembly, is a novelty which requires an apology, as some may suppose. I therefore, with submission, beg leave to offer a few thoughts in vindication of female eloquence.

I mean not at this early day, to become an advocate for that species of female eloquence, of which husbands so much, and so justly, stand in awe,—a species of which the famous Grecian orator, Xantippe, was an illustrious example. Although the free exercise of this natural talent, is a part of the rights of woman, and must be allowed by the courtesy of Europe and America too; yet it is rather to be *tolerated* than *established;* and should rest like the sword in the scabbard, to be used only when occasion requires.—Leaving my sex in full possession of this prerogative, I claim for them the further right of being heard on more proper occasions—of addressing the reason as well as the fears of the other sex.

Our right to instruct and persuade cannot be disputed, if it shall appear, that we possess the talents of the orator—and have opportunities for the exercise of those talents. Is a power of speech, and volubility of expression, one of the talents of the orator? Our sex possess it in an eminent degree.

Do personal attractions give charms to eloquence, and force to the orator's arguments? There is some truth mixed with the flattery we receive on this head. Do tender passions enable the orator to speak in a moving and forcible manner? This talent of the orator is confessedly ours. In all these respects the female orator stands on equal,—nay, on *superior* ground.

If therefore she should fail in the capacity for mathematical studies, or metaphysical profoundities, she has, on the whole, equal pretensions to the palm of eloquence. Granted it is, that a perfect knowledge of the subject is essential to the accomplish'd Orator. But seldom does it happen, that the abstruse sciences, become the subject of eloquence. And, as to that knowledge which is popular and practical,—that knowledge which alone is useful to the orator; who will say that the female mind is incapable?

Our high and mighty Lords (thanks to their arbitrary constitutions) have denied us the means of knowledge, and then reproached us for the want of it. Being the stronger party, they early seized the sceptre and the sword; with these they gave laws to society; they denied women the advantage of a liberal education; forbid them to exercise their talents on those great occasions, which would serve to improve them. They doom'd the sex to servile or frivolous employments, on purpose to degrade their minds, that they themselves might hold unrivall'd, the power and pre-eminence they had usurped. Happily, a more liberal way of thinking begins to prevail. The sources of knowledge are gradually opening to our sex. Some have already availed themselves of the privilege so far, . . .

But supposing now that we posses'd all the talents of the orator, in the highest perfection; where shall we find a theatre for the display of them? The Church, the Bar, and the Senate are shut against us. Who shut them? *Man;* despotic man, first made us incapable of the duty, and then forbid us the exercise. Let us by suitable education, qualify ourselves for those high departments—they will open before us. They *will,* did I say? They have done it already. Besides several Churches of less importance, a most numerous and respectable Society, has display'd its impartiality.—I had almost said gallantry in this respect. With *others,* women forsooth, are complimented with the wall, the right hand, the head of the table,—with a kind of mock pre-eminence in small matters: but on great occasions the sycophant changes his tune, and says, "Sit down at my feet and learn." Not so the members of the enlightened and liberal Church. They regard not the anatomical formation of the body. They look to the soul, and allow all to teach who are capable of it, be they male or female.

But Paul forbids it! Contemptible little body! The girls laughed at the deformed creature. To be revenged, he declares war against the whole sex: advises men not to marry them; and has the insolence to order them to keep silence in the Church—: afraid, I suppose, that they would say something against celibacy, or ridicule the old bachelor.

With respect to the bar, citizens of either sex have an undoubted right to plead their own cause there. Instances could be given of females being admitted to plead the cause of a friend, a husband, a son; and they have done it with energy and effect. I am assured that there is nothing in our laws or constitution, to prohibit the licensure of female Attornies; and sure our judges have too much gallantry, to urge *prescription* in bar on their claim. In regard to the senate, prescription is clearly in our favour. We have one or two cases exactly in point.

Heliogabalus, the Roman Emperor, the blessed memory, made his grandmother a Senator of Rome. He also established a senate of women; appointed his mother President; and committed to them the important business of regulating dress and fashions. And truly methinks the dress of our country, at this day, would admit of some regulation, for it is subject to no rules at all—It would be worthy the wisdom of Congress, to consider whether a similar institution, established at the seat of our Federal Government, would not be a public benefit. We cannot be independent, while we receive our fashions from other countries, nor act properly, while we imitate the manners of governments not congenial to our own. Such a Senate, composed of women most noted for wisdom, learning and taste, delegated from every part of the Union, would give dignity, and independence to our manners; uniformity, and even authority to our fashions.

It would fire the female breast with the most generous ambition, prompting to illustrious actions. It would furnish the most noble Theatre for the display, the exercise and improvement of every faculty. It would call forth all that is human—all that is *divine* in the soul of woman; and having proved them equally capable with the other sex, would lead to their equal participation of honor and office.

Chapter 6:
Document Set 1 References

1. Abigail and John Adams Exchange Sentiments on Women's Rights, 1776
   Abigail Adams to John Adams, March 31, 1776, and May 7, 1776; John Adams to Abigail Adams, April 14, 1776, in L. H. Butterfield *et al.*, eds., *The Book of Abigail and John* (Cambridge: Harvard University Press, 1975), pp. 120–122, 127.

2. Eliza Wilkinson Argues for an Expansion of the Feminine Sphere, 1782

Letter 6, 1782, Caroline Gilman, ed., *Letters of Eliza Wilkinson* (New York: Samuel Colman, 1839), pp. 59–62.

3. Abigail Adams Instructs Her Son on Republican Virtue, 1783
Abigail Adams to John Quincy Adams, December 26, 1783, Charles Francis Adams, ed., *Letters of Mrs. Adams, the Wife of John Adams,* 4th ed. (Boston: Wilkins, Carter, and Co., 1848), pp. 152–155.

4. Priscilla Mason Calls for Sexual Equality, 1793
Priscilla Mason, *Salutatory Oration,* May 15, 1793, *The Rise and Progress of the Young Ladies' Academy of Philadelphia . . .* (Philadelphia: Stewart and Cochran, 1794), pp. 90–95.

CHAPTER 6

DOCUMENT SET 2

The Origins of American Political Institutions: The Constitution and the War Powers

The delegates who gathered at Philadelphia's Independence Hall in May of 1787 to revise the Articles of Confederation embarked on a more important project than anyone at the time could have realized. They created a new constitution and a new nation and made innumerable political decisions of profound historical significance. Problems recognized as important at the Constitutional Convention received much attention; other issues deemed unimportant or noncontroversial received little, although they were important in their implications.

One matter of substantial consensus was the power to declare war, an essential function of government. The war powers necessarily came to reside in the national government, not the states; yet the locus of authority in the national government was a debatable issue. Should they reside in Congress, the presidency, or both? In later years this issue was to become ambiguous and cause controversy, particularly during undeclared wars. At the convention, however, it caused little disagreement. The report of the Committee of Detail, charged to systematize the work of the convention, assigned Congress the power to make war, although the full convention had not formally made that decision. There were minor disagreements over the precise wording of the committee's war power clause (Art. VII,

Sec. I, Clause 14), and some delegates proposed fundamental changes, one placing the power in the presidency. Extended debate was unnecessary, however, because there was broad agreement in the convention on the Committee of Detail's recommendation.

The Constitutional Convention was closed to the public. The only records were notes taken by participants and the official journal kept by the convention's secretary, James Madison. Of these sources, Madison's record is the most enlightening. Another document of interest is *The Federalist,* a collection of essays defending and explaining the proposed Constitution. Written during the struggle for ratification by Alexander Hamilton, James Madison, and John Jay, the essays were originally targeted for New York but were distributed widely. The following documents include selections from Madison's record and Hamilton's essays. As primary sources relating to the power to declare war and grant letters of marque and reprisal, they provide insight into the intent of the delegates at the convention. As you review the evidence, trace the origins of the ongoing debate over presidential and congressional war powers. Relate the deliberations of the founders to the exercise of executive authority in foreign and military affairs since 1945. Try to account for the controversy that has developed in recent years.

Questions for Analysis

1. The Committee of Detail recommended to the convention delegates that Congress have the power to make war and that the president be the commander-in-chief of the army, navy, and state militia. What was the intent of the committee? What prompted its recommendations?

2. Although the convention in broad consensus accepted the Committee of Detail's recommendation on who should have the power to declare war, some members rejected it and proposed alternative views. Who were these members? What did they propose? Why? Do the documents reveal their reasoning?

3. What are letters of marque and reprisal? Which department of the national government was given authority to issue such letters? What implications, if any, does this have for later controversy over the power of the president to engage the armed forces in undeclared war?

4. What is the thesis of Alexander Hamilton's *Federalist* No. 34? What relevance, if any, do his comments have for understanding the Constitutional Convention's view of the war powers?

5. In *Federalist* No. 69, Hamilton discussed his view of the proposed presidency. His purpose was to expose "the unfairness of the representations which have been made in regard to" the presidency. What "unfairness" did he seek to expose? Was he successful in his effort? What evidence from the essay bears on the debate over presidential and congressional war powers?

1. James Madison's Convention Notes on the Power to Declare War, 1787

Monday August 6th.

Mr. Rutledge (delivered in) the Report of the Committee of detail as follows; (a printed copy being at the same time furnished to each member.)

"We the people of the States of New Hampshire, Massachusetts, Rhode-Island and Providence Plantations, Connecticut, New-York, New-Jersey, Pennsylvania, Delaware, Maryland, Virginia, North-Carolina, South-Carolina, and Georgia, do ordain, declare, and establish the following Constitution for the Government of Ourselves and our Posterity.

Article I

The stile of the [this] Government shall be. "The United States of America"

II

The Government shall consist of supreme legislative, executive, and judicial powers.

III

The legislative power shall be vested in a Congress, to consist of two separate and distinct bodies of men, a House of Representatives and a Senate; each of which shall [,] in all cases [,] have a negative on the other. . . .

VII [VI]

Sect. I. The Legislature of the United States shall have the power to lay and collect taxes, duties, imposts and excises; . . .

To make war;

To raise armies;

To build and equip fleets;

To call forth the aid of the militia, in order to execute the laws of the Union, enforce treaties, suppress insurrections, and repel invasions;

And to make all laws that shall be necessary and proper for carrying into execution the foregoing powers, and all other powers vested, by this Constitution, in the government of the United States, or in any department or officer thereof; . . . .

X [IX]

Sect. I. The Executive Power of the United States shall be vested in a single person. . . .

He shall be commander in chief of the Army and Navy of the United States, and of the Militia of the Several States. . . .

Friday August 17th.

"To make war"

Mr. Pinkney opposed the vesting this power in the Legislature. Its proceedings were too slow. It wd. meet but once a year. The Hs. of Reps. would be too numerous for such deliberations. The Senate would be the best depositary, being more acquainted with foreign affairs, and most capable of proper resolutions. If the States are equally represented in Senate, so as to give no advantage to large States, the power will notwithstanding be safe, as the small have their all at stake in such cases as well as the large States. It would be singular for one—authority to make war, and another peace.

Mr. Butler. The Objections agst the Legislature lie in a great degree agst the Senate. He was for vesting the power in the President, who will have all the requisite qualities, and will not make war but when the Nation will support it.

Mr. M(adison) and Mr. Gerry moved to insert *"declare,"* striking out *"make"* war; leaving to the Executive the power to repel sudden attacks.

Mr. Sharman thought it stood very well. The Executive shd. be able to repel and not to commence war. "Make" better than "declare" the latter narrowing the power too much.

Mr. Gerry never expected to hear in a republic a motion to empower the Executive alone to declare war.

Mr. Elseworth. there is a material difference between the cases of making *war*, and making *peace*. It shd. be more easy to get out of war, than into it. War also is a simple and overt declaration, peace attended with intricate & secret negociations.

Mr. Mason was agst giving the power of war to the Executive, because not (safely) to be trusted with it; or to the Senate, because not so constructed as to be entitled to it. He was for clogging rather than facilitating war; but for facilitating peace. He preferred "*declare*" to "*make*".

On the Motion to insert *declare*—in place of *Make*, (it was agreed to.)

N. H. no. Mas. abst. Cont. no.* Pa ay. Del. ay. Md. ay. Va. ay. N. C. ay. S. C. ay. Geo—ay. [Ayes—7; noes—2; absent—1.]

Mr. Pinkney's motion to strike out whole clause, disagd. to without call of States.

Mr Butler moved to give the Legislature power of peace, as they were to have that of war.

Mr Gerry 2ds. him. 8 Senators may possibly exercise the power if vested in that body, and 14 if all should be present; and may consequently give up part of the U. States. The Senate are move liable to be corrupted by an Enemy than the whole Legislature.

On the motion for adding "and peace" after "war"

N. H. no. Mas. no. Ct. no. Pa. no. Del. no. Md. no. Va. no. N. C. (no) S. C. no. Geo. no. [Ayes—0; noes—10.]

Adjourned

Saturday August 18.

These propositions were referred to the Committee of detail which had prepared the Report and at the same time the following which were moved by Mr. Pinkney:—in both cases unanimously.

"To fix and permanently establish the seat of Government of the U. S. in which they shall possess the exclusive right of soil & jurisdiction"

"To establish seminaries for the promotion of literature and the arts & sciences"

"To grant charters of incorporation"

"To grant patents for useful inventions"

"To secure to Authors exclusive rights for a certain time"

"To establish public institutions, rewards and immunities for the promotion of agriculture, commerce, trades and manufactures"

"That funds which shall be appropriated for the payment of public Creditors, shall not during the time of such appropriation, be diverted or applied to any other purpose—and that the Committee prepare a clause or clauses for restraining the Legislature of the U. S. from establishing a perpetual revenue"

"To secure the payment of the public debt"

"To secure all creditors under the New Constitution from a violation of the public faith when pledged by the authority of the Legislature"

"To grant letters of mark and reprisal"

"To regulate Stages on the post roads"

Mr Mason introduced the subject of regulating the militia. He thought such a power necessary to be given to the Genl. Government. He hoped there would be no standing army in time of peace, unless it might be for a few garrisons. The Militia ought therefore to be the more effectually prepared for the public defence. Thirteen States will never concur in any one system, if the disciplining of the Militia be left in their hands. If they will not give up the power over the whole, they probably will over a part as a select militia. He moved as an addition to the propositions just referred to the Committee of detail, & to be referred in like manner, "a power to regulate the militia".

Mr. Gerry remarked that some provision ought to be made in favor of public Securities, and something inserted concerning letters of marque, which he thought not included in the power of war. He proposed that these subjects should also go to a Committee.

Wednesday Sepr. 5. 1787

Mr. Brearley from the Committee of Eleven made a farther report as follows,

(1) To add to the clause "to declare war" the words "and grant letters of marque and reprisal" . . .

This report being taken up.—The (1) clause was agreed to.

---

*On the remark by Mr. King that "*make*" war might be understood to "conduct" it which was an Executive function, Mr. Elseworth gave up his objection (and the vote of Cont was changed to—ay.)

2. Alexander Hamilton on Raising Revenue for Defense, 1788

The Federalist No. 34

January 5, 1788

To the People of the State of New York.

I flatter myself it has been clearly shewn in my last number, that the particular States, under the proposed Constitution, would have co-equal authority with the Union in the article of revenue, except as to duties on imports. As this leaves open to the States far the greatest part of the resources of the community, there can be no color for the assertion, that they would not possess means, as abundant as could be desired, for the supply of their own wants, independent of all external control. . . .

To form a more precise judgment of the true merits of this question, it will be well to advert to the proportion between the objects that will require a Federal provision in respect to revenue; and those which will require a State provision. We shall discover that the former are altogether unlimited; and, that the latter are circumscribed within very moderate bounds. In pursuing this enquiry, we must bear in mind, that we are not to confine our view to the present period, but to look forward to remote futurity. . . . The support of a navy, and of naval wars must baffle all the efforts of political arithmetic admitting that we ought to try the novel and absurd experiment in politics, of tying up the hands of Government from offensive war, founded upon reasons of state: Yet, certainly we ought not to disable it from guarding the community against the ambition or enmity of other Nations. A cloud has been for some time hanging over the European world. If it should break forth into a storm, who can insure us, that in its progress, a part of its fury would not be spent upon us? No reasonable man would hastily pronounce that we are entirely out of its reach. Or if the combustible materials that now seem to be collecting, should be dissipated without coming to maturity; or, if a flame should be kindled, without extending to us, what security can we have, that our tranquility will long remain undisturbed from some other cause, or from some other quarter? Let us recollect, that peace or war, will not always be left to our option; that however moderate or unambitious we may be, we cannot count upon the moderation, or hope to extinguish the ambition of others. . . .

What are the chief sources of expence in every Government? What has occasioned that enormous accumulation of debts with which several of the European Nations are oppressed? The answer, plainly is, wars and rebellions—the support of those institutions which are necessary to guard the body politic, against these two most mortal diseases of society. The expences arising from those institutions, which are relative to the mere domestic police of a State—to the support of its Legislative, Executive and Judicial departments, with their different appendages, and to the internal encouragement of agriculture and manufactures, (which will comprehend almost all the objects of State expenditure) are insignificant, in comparison with those which relate to the National defence. . . .

But let us advert to the large debt which we have ourselves contracted in a single war, and let us only calculate on a common share of the events which disturb the peace of nations, and we shall instantly perceive without the aid of any elaborate illustration, that there must always be an immense disproportion between the objects of Federal and State expenditures. It is true that several of the States separately are incumbered with considerable debts, which are an excrescence of the late war. But when these are discharged, the only call for revenue of any consequence, which the State Governments will continue to experience, will be for the mere support of their respective civil lists; to which, if we add all contingencies, the total amount in every State, ought not to exceed two hundred thousand pounds. . . .

The preceeding train of observations will justify the position which has been elsewhere laid down, that, "A concurrent jurisdiction in the article of taxation, was the only admissible substitute for an entire subordination, in respect to this branch of power, of the State authority to that of the Union." Any separation of the objects of revenue, that could have been fallen upon, would have amounted to a sacrifice of the great interests of the Union to the power of the individual States. The Convention thought the concurrent jurisdiction preferable to that subordination; and it is evident that it has at least the merit of reconciling an indefinite constitutional power of taxation in the Federal Government, with an adequate and independent power in the States to provide for their own necessities. . . .

Publius

3. Alexander Hamilton on the Powers of the Presidency, 1788

The Federalist No. 69
[68]

March 14, 1788

To the People of the State of New York.

I proceed now to trace the real characters of the proposed executive as they are marked out in the plan of the Convention. This will serve to place in a strong light the unfairness of the representations which have been made in regard to it.

The first thing which strikes our attention is that the executive authority, with few exceptions, is to be vested in a single magistrate. This will scarcely however be considered as a point upon which any comparison can be grounded; for if in this particular there be a resemblance to the King of Great-Britain, there is not less a resemblance to the Grand Signior, to the Khan of Tartary, to the man of the seven mountains, or to the Governor of New-York. . . . The President is to be the "Commander in Chief of the army and navy of the United States, and of the militia of the several States, when called into the actual service of the United States. He is to have power to grant reprieves and pardons for offences against the United States, *except in cases of impeachment;* to recommend to the consideration of Congress such measures as he shall judge necessary and expedient; to convene on extraordinary occasions both houses of the Legislature, or either of them, and in case of disagreement between them *with respect to the time of adjournment,* to adjourn them to such time as he shall think proper; to take care that the laws be faithfully executed; and to commission all officers of the United States." In most of these particulars the power of the President will resemble equally that of the King of Great-Britain and of the Governor of New-York. The most material points of difference are these—First; the President will have only the occasional command of such part of the militia of the nation, as by legislative provision may be called into the actual service of the Union. The King of Great-Britain and the Governor of New-York have at all times the entire command of all the militia within their several jurisdictions. In this article therefore the power of the President would be inferior to that of either the Monarch or the Governor. Secondly; the President is to be Commander in Chief of the army and navy of the United States. In this respect his authority would be nominally the same with that of the King of Great-Britain, but in substance much inferior to it. It would amount to nothing more than the supreme command and direction of the military and naval forces, as first General and Admiral of the confederacy; while that of the British King extends to the *declaring* of war and to the *raising* and *regulating* of fleets and armies; all which by the Constitution under consideration would appertain to the Legislature. The Governor of New-York on the other hand, is by the Constitution of the State vested only with the command of its militia and navy. . . .

Hence it appears, that except as to the concurrent authority of the President in the article of treaties, it would be difficult to determine whether that Magistrate would in the aggregate, possess more or less power than the Governor of New-York. And it appears yet more unequivocally that there is no pretence for the parallel which has been attempted between him and the King of Great-Britain. But to render the contrast, in this respect, still more striking, it may be of use to throw the principal circumstances of dissimilitude into a closer groupe.

The President of the United States would be an officer elected by the people for *four* years. The King of Great-Britain is a perpetual and *hereditary* prince. The one would be amenable to personal punishment and disgrace: The person of the other is sacred and inviolable. The one would have a *qualified* negative upon the acts of the legislative body: The other has an *absolute* negative. The one would have a right to command the military and naval forces of the nation: The other in addition to this right, possesses that of *declaring* war, and of *raising* and *regulating* fleets and armies by his own authority. The one would have a concurrent power with a branch of the Legislature in the formation of treaties: The other is the *sole possessor* of the power of making treaties. The one would have a like concurrent authority in appointing to offices: The other is the sole author of all appointments. The one can infer no privileges whatever: The other can make denizens of aliens, noblemen of commoners, can erect corporations with all the rights incident to corporate bodies. The one can prescribe no rules concerning the commerce or currency of the nation: The other is in several respects the arbiter of commerce, and in this capacity can establish markets and fairs, can regulate weights and measures, can lay embargoes for a limited time, can coin money, can authorise or prohibit the circulation of foreign coin. The one has no particle of spiritual jurisdiction: The other is the supreme head and Governor of the national church! What answer shall we give to those who would persuade us that things so unlike resemble each other? The same that ought to be given to those who tell us, that a government, the whole power of which would be in the hands of the elective and periodical servants of the people, is an aristocracy, a monarchy, and a despotism.

Publius

Chapter 6:
Document Set 2 References

1. James Madison's Convention Notes on the Power to Declare War, 1787
   James Madison, "Journal," August 6, 17, 18; September 5, 1787, Max Farrand, ed., *The Records of the Federal Convention of 1787* (New Haven: Yale University Press, 1911), Vol. 2, pp. 177, 181–182, 185, 314, 318–319, 324–326, 508–509.

2. Alexander Hamilton on Raising Revenue for Defense, 1788
   Alexander Hamilton, "The Federalist No. 34," January 5, 1788, in Jacob E. Cooke, ed., *The Federalist* (Middleton, Conn.: Wesleyan University Press, rep. 1961), pp. 209–215.

3. Alexander Hamilton on the Powers of the Presidency, 1788
   Alexander Hamilton, "The Federalist No. 69," March 14, 1788, in Cooke, pp. 462, 464–466, 469–470.

CHAPTER 6

DOCUMENT SET 3
The Fate of the Loyalists: The Other Americans

Your textbook refers to the Revolution as "America's First Civil War." This phrase underscores the divisive internal conflict that separated the inhabitants of British North America from one another between 1775 and 1783. In an extended discussion of the loyalists, the text emphasizes a sometimes forgotten reality of Revolutionary America: the fact that the colonial population was deeply divided on the issue of a complete break with England. By focusing on the impact of the Revolution on the crown's loyal subjects in America, these documents serve as a reminder that revolutions are not and never have been polite disagreements among friends. Weigh the arguments for and against loyalty, and assess the impact of the Revolution on those who chose not to support the patriot cause.

As a first step, try to arrive at a satisfactory definition of the term *loyalty.* Be sure to place the word within the context of the Revolutionary era. Consider the reasons and motivations behind Tory social and political activity and determine whether colonial supporters of the crown were loyal or disloyal. Given the revolutionary situation, what government was the legitimate object of loyalty?

As you search the documents for clues to Tory attitudes, be aware of the socioeconomic backgrounds of the loyalists. Think about their positions in the social structure of Revolutionary America and the implications of class status for political behavior. As you examine the Tory social profile, watch for sectional patterns and geographic areas that appear to have been more receptive to the loyalist argument. Finally, try to gain insight into the self-images of those who sided with Britain.

Once you have analyzed Tory motivation, turn to the ideas of the militant patriots who opposed the loyalists with such vigor. What factors induced American radicals to be so extreme in their vilification of the Tories? Think about the reasons that lay behind patriot attitudes, and ask yourself whether revolutionary activists were justified in their behavior. Review the textbook's treatment of the "civil war" for information that will help explain the militancy of the Revolution's backers.

As you examine the documents, explore the consequences of loyalty to the crown for those who refused to become revolutionaries. What did a loyalist stand mean for Tories and their families? Pay particular attention to legislative activity, official harassment, and mob actions that reinforced the patriot position. Search for a deeper explanation of this quasi-legal activity. Think about the social and economic dimensions of crowd behavior, and explore Tory values and actions as you develop a fuller, more sophisticated interpretation of the conflicts that broke out among Americans under the stress of revolution.

Finally, examine the results of the internal social upheaval that shook the American colonies, noting the new social order that emerged from the cauldron of rebellion. Focus on the winners and losers in this struggle, and trace the fate of Tories who were forced from positions of social prominence, economic influence, and political power. Try to decide if the loyalists, whether exiles or American citizens, received justice at the hands of their governments, either American or British. In the final analysis, whose interests were served by the Revolution?

Questions for Analysis

1. Compare and contrast the socioeconomic profiles of revolutionaries and loyalists. What was the relationship among social class, economic standing, and Toryism? To what extent is generalization possible on the question? What precautions are necessary in analyzing the available social and economic data?
2. Since political and military activity was largely in the male domain, is it fair to say that women were less affected than men by the social conflict stemming from the debate between Tories and patriots? What were the gender implications of the internal revolution? In what ways do the documents shed light on the Revolution's impact on women and families?
3. Define the term *loyalty* as it was used by both patriots and Tories. Which colonial Americans were "loyal" between 1775 and 1783? If, as one classical scholar writes, "loyalty is the holiest good in the human breast," why were the American loyalists vilified and regarded with contempt? To what extent were the patriots justified in their behavior?

4. What was the responsibility of England to those loyal subjects who supported the crown during the Revolution? To what extent did the British government accept that obligation? What were the consequences for the Tories?
5. Women in colonial America had come to enjoy clearly defined property rights through marriage (see Document Set 3-3.) What does the evidence on the disposition of Tory property reveal about the security women enjoyed in the exercise of those rights?

1. A Maryland Preacher Resists the Patriots, 1775

In the usual and regular course of preaching, I happened one Sunday to recommend peaceableness; on which a Mr. Lee and sundry others, supposing my sermon to be what they called a stroke at the times, rose up and left the church. This was a signal to the people to consider every sermon of mine as hostile to the views and interests of America; and accordingly I never after went into a pulpit without something very disagreeable happening. I received sundry messages and letters threatening me with the most fatal consequences if I did not (not desist from preaching at all, but) preach what should be agreeable to the friends of America.

All the answer I gave to these threats was in my sermons, in which I uniformly and resolutely declared that I never could suffer any merely human authority to intimidate me from performing what in my conscience I believed and knew to be my duty to God and his Church. And for more than six months I preached, when I did preach, with a pair of loaded pistols lying on the cushion; having given notice that if any man, or body of men, could possibly be so lost to all sense of decency and propriety as to attempt really to do what had been long threatened, that is, to drag me out of my own pulpit, I should think myself justified before God and man in repelling violence by violence.

2. A New Jersey Artisan Is Tarred and Feathered, 1775

From the Records of the Committee of Safety

New York, December 28, 1775
The 6th of December, at Quibbletown, Middlesex County, Piscataway Township, New-Jersey, Thomas Randolph, cooper, who had publickly proved himself an enemy to his country, by reviling and using

his utmost endeavours to oppose the proceedings of the Continental and Provincial Conventions and Committees, in defence of their rights and liberties; and he, being judged a person of not consequence enough for a severer punishment, was ordered to be stripped naked, well coated with tar and feathers, and carried in a wagon publickly round the town; which punishment was accordingly inflicted. And as he soon became duly sensible of his offence, for which he earnestly begged pardon, and promised to atone, as far as he was able, by a contrary behaviour for the future, he was released, and suffered to return to his house in less than half an hour. The whole was conducted with that regularity and decorum that ought to be observed in all publick punishments.

3. The Legislative Attack on the Loyalists, 1777–1782

Laws Amercing [Fining], Taxing or Confiscating the Estates of Loyalists or Anticipating such Action

New Hampshire

November 29, 1777.
An act to prevent the transfer or conveyance of the estates and property of all such persons who have been or shall be apprehended upon suspicion of being guilty of treason, misprision of treason, or other inimical practices respecting this State, the United States, any or either of them, and also for securing all lands within this State as well of such persons as have traitorously deserted, or may hereafter desert the common cause of America, and have gone over to, or in any way or manner joined our enemies, as of those who belong to, or reside in Great Britain. . . .

December 26, 1778.
An act to make void all attachments which have been or hereafter shall be laid or made on the estates of persons who have left this State or any of the United States, and have gone over to the enemies of the said States since the commencement of hostilities by Great Britain; or on the estates of any inhabitant or subjects of Great Britain. . . .

Rhode Island

October, 1775.
Act to confiscate and sequester estates and banish persons of a certain description. [Special acts confiscating special estates are to be found in the Rhode Island records from this date to October of 1783.]

October, 1779.
An act for confiscating the estates of certain persons therein described. [See "Records of Rhode Island," Vol. IX., p. 461.]

New York

October 22, 1779.
Act for forfeiture and sales of the estates of persons who have adhered to the enemies of this State. . . .
March 10, 1780.
Act for the immediate sale of part of the confiscated estates. (Amended October 7, 1780.)

New Jersey

April 18, 1778.
An act for taking charge of and leasing real estates and for forfeiting personal estates of certain fugitives and offenders. . . .
December 11, 1778.
Act for forfeiting to and vesting in the State the real estates of certain fugitives and offenders. . . . (June 26, 1781, an act to suspend the sales, and December 16, 1783, an act to continue the sales.) (Supplemented, December 23, 1783.)

Pennsylvania

March 18, 1779.
(Provides for the disposition of Joseph Galloway's house.)

North Carolina

November, 1777.
An act for confiscating the property of all such persons as are inimical to the United States, and of such persons as shall not within a certain time therein

mentioned, appear and submit to the State whether they shall be received as citizens thereof and of such persons as shall so appear and shall not be admitted as citizens. . . .

Georgia

March 1, 1778.

An act for attainting such persons as are herein mentioned, of high treason and for confiscating their estates . . . for establishing boards of commissioners

for the sales of such estates. . . . (Amended October 30, 1778.)
November 15, 1778.

An act to compel non-residents to return within a certain time, or in a default . . . their estates to be confiscated. . . .
January 11, 1782.

An act for the confiscating of the estates of certain persons . . . and for providing funds for defraying the contingent expenses of this State.

4.   Grace Growden Galloway Defies the Radicals in Philadelphia, 1778, 1779

[*July 22, 1778*] Sent for Mr Dickison last Night & he told Me he would look over the law to see if I could recover My own estate & this evening he came & told Me I could Not recover dower & he fear'd my income in My estate was forfeited likewise & yet no trial wou'd be of service: but advised Me to draw up a petition to the Chief Justice Mccean for the recovery of my estate & refused a fee in the Politest Manner. . . . So I find I am beggar indeed I expect every hour to be turned out of doors & where to go I know not. No one will take me in & all the Men keeps from Me. Was I assured that My husband & child was happy nothing could make me very wretched but I am fled from as a Pestilence. Mrs Jones here in the morn: sent nurse to Parson Combs to desire him to [tell] Mr G of my unhappy situation.

[*August 10, 1778*] Peggy Johns & Becky Redman came in the Morn, Lewis sent Me word Smith had gave his honour not to Molest Me till the Opinion of the executive council was known but in a short time after came Peel, Will, & Shriner with a Spanish Merchant & his attendants & took Possession of My house. I was taken very ill & obliged to Lay down & sent them word I could not see them; they went every where below stairs & the Spaniard offer'd to let Me choose My own bed chamber; but I sent them no Message but was very ill Upstairs. But between 2 & 3 o'clock the last went away. Peel told Nurse now they had given the Spanish Gentleman possession they had nothing more to do with it. But they took the key out of the front parlor door & locked Me out. . . .

[*August 16, 1778*] . . . As I have No friends they [patriot Quakers] treat me as they please. So much

for Mr G [Galloway's] great friends. He has not one who will go out of the way to serve him. I am in hopes they will let me have my estate but that will be on my own account. No favor shown to J G [Joseph Galloway] or his Child: Nor has he a friend that will say one word in his favor. I am tired with sending after a set of men that always keeps from me when I most need them. Am vexed.

[*August 20, 1778*] Mrs Erwin & Sidney Howell & Peggy Johns came in the morn: but could get no man to bear evidence. Lewise sent me word that I must shut my doors & windows & if they would come to let them Make a forcible Entry. Accordingly I did so & a little after 10 o'clock they knocked violently at the door three times. The third time I sent Nurse & called out myself to tell them I was in possession of my own House & would keep so & that they should gain no admittance hereupon which they went round in the yard & Tried every door but could none open. Then they went to the kitchen door & with a scrubbing brush which they broke to pieces they forced that open, we women standing in the Entry in the Dark. They made repeated strokes at the door & I think was 8 or 10 Minutes before they got it open. When they came in I had the windows opened they looked very mad. There was Peel, Smith, the Hatter, & a Col Will, a pewterer in second street. I spoke first & told them I was used ill: & showed them the Opinion of the Lawyers. Peel read it; but they all despised it & Peel said he had studied the Law & knew they did right. I told them nothing but force should get me out of my house. Smith said they knew how to manage that & that they would throw my clothes in the street. . . . Peel said the chariot was ready but he would not hasten me. I told him I was at home & in my own house & nothing but force should drive me out of it. He said it was not the first time he had taken a lady by the hand an insolent wretch. This speech was made some time in the room; at last he beckoned for the chariot for the General would not let it come till I wanted it & as the chariot drew up Peel fetched my bonnets & gave one to me the other to Mrs Craig: then with greatest air said come Mrs Galloway give me your hand. I answered indeed I will not nor will I go out of my house but by force. He then took hold of my arm & I rose & he took me to the door. I then took hold one side & look round & said pray take notice I do not leave my house of my own accord or with my own inclination but by force & nothing but force should have made me give up possession. Peel said with a sneer very well Madam & when he led me down the step I said now Mr Peel let go my arm I want not your assistance. He said he could help me to the Carriage. I told him I could go without & you

Mr Peel are the last man on earth I would wish to be obliged to. Mrs Craig then stepped into the Carriage & we drove to her house where we dined. . . . Distressed in the afternoon when I reflected on the occurences of the day & that I was drove out of my house destitute & without any maintenance. . . . Sent for Mr. Chew. He came & told me I must sue them for a forcible entry. I am just distracted but glad it is over.

[*April 20, 1779*] Went to Billy Turners. The two Mrs Bonds there. The Widow & I very sociable but Mrs Bond rather shy but did not mind her but got my spirits at command & laughed at the whole wig party. I told them I was the happiest woman in town for I had been stripped & turned out of doors yet I was still the same & must be Joseph Galloways wife & Lawrence Growdens daughter & that it was not in their power to humble me for I should be Grace Growden Galloway to the last & as I had now suffer'd all that they can inflict upon me.

5. Pennsylvania Radicals Attack Loyalism, 1778, 1779

A. A Patriot Demand for the Banishment of Tories, 1779

Who were the occasion of this war? The Tories! Who persuaded the tyrant of Britain to prosecute it in a manner before unknown to civilized nations, and shocking even to barbarians? The Tories! Who prevailed on the savages of the wilderness to join the standard of the enemy? The Tories! Who have assisted the Indians in taking the scalp from the aged matron, the blooming fair one, the helpless infant, and the dying hero? The Tories! Who advised and who assisted in burning your towns, ravaging your country, and violating the chastity of your women? The Tories! Who are the occasion that thousands of you now mourn the loss of your dearest connections? The Tories! Who have always counteracted the endeavors of Congress to secure the liberties of this country? The Tories!

Who refused their money when as good as specie, though stamped with the image of his most sacred Majesty? The Tories! Who continue to refuse it? The Tories! Who do all in their power to depreciate it?

The Tories! Who propagate lies among us to discourage the Whigs? The Tories! Who corrupt the minds of the good people of these States by every species of insidious counsel? The Tories! Who hold a traitorous correspondence with the enemy? The Tories! Who daily send them intelligence? The Tories! Who take the oaths of allegiance to the States one day, and break them the next? The Tories! Who prevent your battalions from being filled? The Tories! Who dissuade men from entering the army? The Tories! Who persuade those who have enlisted to desert? The Tories! Who harbor those who do desert? . . .

Awake, Americans, to a sense of your danger. No time to be lost. Instantly banish every Tory from among you. Let America be sacred alone to freemen.

Drive far from you every baneful wretch who wishes to see you fettered with the chains of tyranny. Send them where they may enjoy their beloved slavery to perfection—send them to the island of Britain; there let them drink the cup of slavery and eat the bread of bitterness all the days of their existence—there let them drag out a painful life, despised and accursed by those very men whose cause they have had the wickedness to espouse. Never let them return to this happy land—never let them taste the sweets of that independence which they strove to prevent. Banishment, perpetual banishment, should be their lot.

B. The Hanging of Loyalist Joseph Wilson, ca. 1778

Whilst in this painful suspension [hanging by toes and thumbs] he [Wilson] attested his innocence with all the energy he was master of. By this time his wife, who had been informed of the tragical scene, came from her house, with tears gushing in streams, and with a countenance of terror. . . .

The bitter cries of the poor woman, the solemn asseverations of her husband, seemed for a few moments to lull the violence of their [the patriots'] rage. . . . But all of a sudden one of the company arose, more vindictive than the rest. He painted to them their conflagrated houses and barns, the murder of their relations and friends. The sudden recollection of these dreadful images wrought them up to a pitch of fury fiercer than before. Conscious as they were that he was the person who had harbored the destroyers of their country, they resolved finally to hang him by the neck.

. . . What was he then to do? Behold here innocence pregnant with as much danger as guilt itself, a situation which is very common and is characteristic

of these times. You may be punished tomorrow for thoughts and sentiments for which you were highly commended the preceding day, and alternately.

On hearing of his doom, he flung himself at the feet of the first man. He solemnly appealed to God, the searcher of hearts, for the truth of his assertions. He frankly owned that he was attached to the King's cause from ancient respect and by the force of custom; that he had no idea of any other government, but that at the same time he had never forcibly opposed the measures of the country. . . .

The passive character of this man, though otherwise perfectly inoffensive, had long before been the cause of his having been suspected. Their hearts were hardened and their minds prepossessed; they refused his request and justified the sentence of death they had passed. They, however, promised him his life if he would confess who were those traitors that came to his house. . . . The poor culprit denied his having the least knowledge whatever of these persons, but, seeing that it was all in vain, he peaceably submitted to his fate, and gave himself up to those who were preparing the fatal cord. It was soon tied round the limb of a tree to which they hanged him.

[Some of the executioners, Crèvecoeur relates, experienced a change of heart, and cut Wilson down in time to revive him with water. He was subsequently given an impartial trial and acquitted.]

6. A Loyalist Widow Decries the Fate of Tory Exiles in Canada, 1787

Kingston, New Brunswick
Nov^{br} 17.87

Dear Billy

I have received your two letters and the trunk, and I feel the good effects of the clothes you sent me and my children, and I value them to be worth more than I should have valued a thousand Pounds sterling in the year 1774. Alas, my brother, that Providence should permit so many evils to fall on me and my fatherless children—I know the sensibility of your heart—therefore will not exaggerate in my story, lest I should contribute towards your infelicity on my account—Since I wrote you, I have been twice burnt out, and left destitute of food and raiment; and in this dreary country I know not where to find relief— for poverty has expelled friendship and charity from

the human heart, and planted in its stead the law of self-preservation—which scarcely can preserve alive the rustic hero in this frozen climate and barren wilderness—

You say "that you have received accounts of the great sufferings of the Loyalists for want of provisions, and I hope that you and your children have not had the fate to live on potatoes alone—" I assure you, my dear Billy, that many have been the days since my arrival in this inhospitable country, that I should have thought myself and family truly happy could we have "had potatoes alone—" but this mighty boon was denied us—! I could have borne these burdens of loyalty with fortitude had not my poor children in doleful accents cried, Mama, why don't you help me and give me bread?

O gracious God, that I should live to see such times under the protection of a British Government for whose sake we have done and suffered every thing but that of dying—

May you never experience such heart piercing troubles as I have and still labor under—you may depend on it that the sufferings of the poor Loyalists are beyond all possible description.... The British rulers value loyal subjects less than the refuse of the Gaols of England and America in former days—inhumane Treatment I suffered under the power of American mobs and rebels for that loyalty, which is now thought handsomely compensated for, by neglect and starvation—I dare not let my friends at Stamford know of my calamatous situation lest it should bring down the grey hairs of my mother to the grave; and besides they could not relieve me without distressing themselves should I apply—as they have been ruined by the rebels during the war—therefore I have no other ground to hope, but, on your goodness and bounty— ...

I have only to add—that by your brother Dibblee's death—my miseries were rendered complete in this world but as God is just and merciful my prospects in a future world are substantial and pleasing—I will therefore endeavour to live on hopes till I hear again from you—I remain in possession of a grateful heart,

> Dear Billy
> your affectionate sister,
> Polly Dibblee

7. A Socioeconomic Profile of Loyalist Claimants, ca. 1780s

Occupations of Loyalists Submitting Claims to the British Government

Occupation	No. of Claimants	% of Claimants
Farmers	1,368	49.1
Commerce		
(a) Artisans	274	9.8
(b) Merchants and shopkeepers	517	18.6
(c) Miscellaneous inn-keepers, seamen, etc.	92	3.3
Combined commerce	883	31.7
Professions		
(a) Lawyers	55	
(b) Teachers and professors	21	
(c) Doctors	81	
(d) Anglican clerics	63	
(e) Other clerics	7	
(f) Miscellaneous	26	
Combined professions	253	9.1
Officeholders	282	10.1

Chapter 6:
Document Set 3 References

1. A Maryland Preacher Resists the Patriots, 1775
   Jonathan Boucher, ed., *Reminiscences of an American Loyalist* (Boston: Houghton Mifflin Company, 1925), p. 113.

2. A New Jersey Artisan Is Tarred and Feathered, 1775
   "From the Records of the Committee of Safety," New York, December 28, 1775, in Peter Force, ed., *American Archives: Fourth Series* (Washington, D.C.: St. Clair Clarke and Peter Force, 1837–1846), Vol. 4, p. 203.

3. The Legislative Attack on the Loyalists, 1777–1782
   Claude Halstead Van Tyne, *The Loyalists in the American Revolution* (Gloucester, Mass.: Peter Smith, 1959), Appendix C, pp. 335–340.

4. Grace Growden Galloway Defies the Radicals in Philadelphia, 1778, 1779
   Raymond C. Warner, ed., "Diary of Grace Growden Galloway, Kept at Philadelphia," *Pennsylvania Magazine of History and Biography,* 55 (1931), pp. 41, 47–48, 50–53, 75–76.

5. Pennsylvania Radicals Attack Loyalism, 1778, 1779
   A. A Patriot Demand for the Banishment of Tories, 1779. *Pennsylvania Packet,* August 5, 1779, in Frank Moore, *Diary of the American Revolution* (1859), Vol. 2, pp. 166–168.
   B. The Hanging of Loyalist Joseph Wilson, ca. 1778
      M. G. J. de Crévecoeur, *Sketches of Eighteenth Century America,* ca. 1778 (New Haven: Yale University Press, 1925), pp. 183–185.

6. A Loyalist Widow Decries the Fate of Tory Exiles in Canada, 1787
   Polly Dibblee to Billy, November 17, 1787, Audit Office Papers, Public Record Office, London, in Wallace Brown, *The Good Americans: The Loyalists in the American Revolution* (New York: William Morrow and Company, 1969), pp. 206–207.

7. A Socioeconomic Profile of Loyalist Claimants, ca. 1780s
   Brown, p. 240.

CHAPTER 7

DOCUMENT SET 1
Economic Conflict: Alexander Hamilton's Financial Program and Thomas Jefferson's Opposition

The 1790s were important years in the development of the United States. During this time the young republic faced a myriad of problems, including diplomatic differences with Spain, Great Britain, and France; Indian threats on the frontier; internal political dissension; and nagging economic difficulties. None of these problems, however, was more challenging than that of launching successfully the new national government under the guidance and restraints of a new constitution, and no one played a more important role in this process than Alexander Hamilton, President Washington's close friend and treasury secretary.

Hamilton had a vision of what the national government could become. He attempted to implement it through a sweeping financial program, proposed to Congress in three reports. The first, Hamilton's Report on Public Credit, was submitted to Congress in January 1790; the second, his Report on a National Bank, was submitted in December 1790; and the third, a Report on Manufacturing, in December 1791. Congress enacted into law nearly all of Hamilton's financial program, which helped create a strong central government, establish a sound fiscal system, and improve the economic potential of the United States. But the financial program also produced bitter controversy and stimulated the development of political parties.

The following documents include excerpts from Hamilton's Report on Public Credit, stressing those aspects of his proposal known as "funding and assumption." The funding program called for the national government to fund the old confederation debt at par and in full, while the assumption program provided that the national government would assume the debts of the individual states. The immediate aim of these proposals, although not the only one intended by Hamilton, was to establish a good credit rating for the United States. The documents also include passages from Thomas Jefferson's *Anas* that reveal his reasons for opposing funding and assumption and illustrate rising factionalism.

The documents offer a glimpse of statesmen grappling with national problems at a critical point in American history. As you review these readings, identify the key elements of Hamilton's funding and assumption programs and evaluate the reasoning that led him to propose them. Account for Jefferson's opposition to Hamilton's plan, and search the evidence for fallacies in Hamilton's and Jefferson's arguments.

Questions for Analysis

1. Hamilton thought that the United States would need to borrow money. Why? Since debt was inevitable, he also held that it was important for the new country to establish a good credit rating. Why? How, then, should a good credit rating be established?

2. A critical issue raised by Hamilton's proposal to fund the existing confederation debt was whether a distinction should be made between the original holders of the debt and the current holders, particularly speculators who purchased the public securities at a bargain price from original holders. What position did Hamilton take on this controversial issue? Why?

3. What views of Hamilton's political philosophy are presupposed by Jefferson in his interpretation of the objectives of Hamilton's financial program? Did Jefferson provide adequate evidence to support these views? Explain.

4. Together with funding, Hamilton proposed that the national government assume the state debts. Why? Why did Jefferson oppose the assumption program? Given strong opposition, why did the assumption program pass?

1. Hamilton's Funding and Assumption Programs, 1790

In the opinion of the Secretary, the wisdom of the House, in giving their explicit sanction to the proposition which has been stated, cannot but be applauded by all who will seriously consider and trace, through their obvious consequences, these plain and undeniable truths:

That exigencies are to be expected to occur, in the affairs of nations, in which there will be a necessity for borrowing;

That loans in times of public danger, especially from foreign war, are found an indispensable resource, even to the wealthiest of them;

And that, in a country which, like this, is possessed of little active wealth, or, in other words, little moneyed capital, the necessity for that resource must in such emergencies, be proportionably urgent.

And as, on the one hand, the necessity for borrowing, in particular emergencies, cannot be doubted; so, on the other, it is equally evident, that, to be able to borrow upon good terms, it is essential that the credit of a nation should be well established.

For, when the credit of a country is in any degree questionable, it never fails to give an extravagant premium, in one shape or another, upon all the loans it has occasion to make. Nor does the evil end here; the same disadvantage must be sustained on whatever is to be bought on terms of future payment. . . .

If the maintenance of public credit, then, be truly so important, the next inquiry which suggests itself is, By what means it is to be effected? The ready answer to which question, is by good faith: by a punctual performance of contracts. States, like individuals, who observe their engagements, are respected and trusted, while the reverse is the fate of those who pursue an opposite conduct. . . .

To justify and preserve their confidence; to promote the increasing respectability of the American name; to answer the calls of justice; to restore landed property to its due value; to furnish new resources, both to agriculture and commerce; to cement more closely the union of the States, to add to their security against foreign attack; to establish public order on the basis of an upright and liberal policy;—these are the great and invaluable ends to be secured by a proper and adequate provision at the present period, for the support of public credit. . . .

While the observance of that good faith, which is the basis of public credit, is recommended by the strongest inducements of political expediency, it is enforced by considerations of still greater authority. There are arguments for it which rest on the immutable principles of moral obligation. . . .

This reflection derives additional strength from the nature of the debt of the United States. It was the price of liberty. The faith of America has been repeatedly pledged for it, and with solemnities that give peculiar force to the obligation. There is, indeed, reason to regret that it has not hitherto been kept; that the necessities of the war, conspiring with inexperience, in the subjects of finance, produced direct infractions; and that the subsequent period has been a continued scene of negative violation, or noncompliance. But a diminution of this regret arises from the reflection, that the last seven years have exhibited an earnest and uniform effort, on the part of the Government of the Union, to retrieve the national credit, by doing justice to the creditors of the nation; and that the embarrassments of a defective constitution, which defeated this laudable effort, have ceased.

From this evidence of a favorable disposition given by the former Government, the institution of a new one, clothed with powers competent to calling forth the resources of the community, has excited correspondent expectations. A general belief accordingly prevails, that the credit of the United States will quickly be established on the firm foundation of an effectual provision for the existing debt. The influence which this has had at home, is witnessed by the rapid increase that has taken place in the market value of the public securities. . . .

But there is a consequence of this, less obvious, though not less true, in which every other citizen is interested. It is a well known fact, that, in countries in which the national debt is properly funded, and an object of established confidence, it answers most of the purposes of money. Transfers of stock or public debt, are there equivalent to payments in specie; or, in other words, stock, in the principal transactions of business, passes current as specie. The same thing would, in all probability, happen here under the like circumstances. . . .

Having now taken a concise view of the inducements to a proper provision for the public debt, the next inquiry which presents itself is, What ought to be the nature of such a provision? This requires some preliminary discussions.

It is agreed on all hands, that that part of the debt which has been contracted abroad, and is denominated the foreign debt, ought to be provided for according to the precise terms of the contracts relating to it. The discussions which can arise, therefore, will have reference essentially to the domestic part of it, or to that which has been contracted at home. It is to be regretted that there is not the same unanimity of sentiment on this part as on the other.

The Secretary has too much deference for the opinions of every part of the community, not to have observed one, which has more than once made its appearance in the public prints, and which is occasionally to be met with in conversation. It involves this question: Whether a discrimination ought not to be made between original holders of the public securities, and present possessors, by purchase? Those who advocate a discrimination, are for making a full provision for the securities of the former at their nominal value; but contend that the latter ought to receive no more than the cost to them, and the interest. And the idea is sometimes suggested, of making good the difference to the primitive possessor.

In favor of this scheme, it is alleged, that it would be unreasonable to pay twenty shillings in the pound, to one who had not given more for it than three or four. And it is added, that it would be hard to aggravate the misfortune of the first owner, who, probably, through necessity, parted with his property at so great a loss, by obliging him to contribute to the profit of the person who had speculated on his distresses.

The Secretary, after the most mature reflection on the force of this argument, is induced to reject the doctrine it contains, as equally unjust and impolitic; as highly injurious, even to the original holders of public securities; as ruinous to public credit.

It is inconsistent with justice, because, in the first place, it is a breach of contract—a violation of the right of a fair purchaser.

The nature of the contract, in its origin, is, that the public will pay the sum expressed in the security, to the first holder or his assignee. The intent in making the security assignable, is, that the proprietor may be able to make use of his property, by selling it for as much as it may be worth in the market, and that the buyer may be safe in the purchase.

Every buyer, therefore, stands exactly in the place of the seller; has the same right with him to the identical sum expressed in the security; and, having acquired that right, by fair purchase, and in conformity to the original agreement and intention of the Government, his claim cannot be disputed, without manifest injustice. . . .

The impolicy of a discrimination results from two considerations: One, that it proceeds upon a principle destructive of that quality of the public debt, or the stock of the nation, which is essential to its capacity for answering the purposes of money, that is, the security of transfer; the other, that, as well on this account as because it includes a breach of faith, it renders property, in the funds, less valuable, consequently, induces lenders to demand a high premium for what they lend, and produces every other inconvenience of a bad state of public credit.

It will be perceived, at first sight, that the transferable quality of stock is essential to its operation as money, and that this depends on the idea of complete security to the transferee, and a firm persuasion, that no distinction can, in any circumstances, be made between him and the original proprietor.

The precedent of an invasion of this fundamental principle, would, of course, tend to deprive the community of an advantage with which no temporary saving could bear the least comparison. . . .

But there is still a point in view, in which it will appear perhaps even more exceptionable then in either of the former. It would be repugnant to an express provision of the constitution of the United States. This provision is, that "all debts contracted, and engagements entered into, before the adoption of that constitution, shall be as valid against the United States under it, as under the Confederation"; which amounts to a constitutional ratification of the contracts respecting the debt, in the state in which they existed under the confederation. And, resorting to that standard, there can be no doubt that the right of assignees and original holders must be considered as equal. . . .

The Secretary, concluding that a discrimination between the different classes of creditors of the United States cannot, with propriety, be made, proceeds to examine whether a difference ought to be permitted to remain between them and another description of public creditors—those of the States, individually. The Secretary, after mature reflection on this point, entertains a full conviction, that an assumption of the debts of the particular States by the Union, and a like provision for them, as for those of the Union, will be a measure of sound policy and substantial justice. . . .

There are several reasons, which render it probable that the situation of the State creditors would be worse than that of the creditors of the Union, if there be not a national assumption of the State debts. Of these it will be sufficient to mention two: one, that a principle branch of revenue is exclusively vested in the Union; the other, that a State must always be checked in the imposition of taxes on articles of consumption, from the want of power to extend the same regulation to the other States, and from the tendency of partial duties to injure its industry and commerce. . . .

The result of the foregoing discussion is this: That there ought to be no discrimination between the original holders of the debt, and present possessors by purchase. That it is expedient there should be an assumption of the State debts by the Union, and that the arrears of interest should be provided for on an equal footing with the principal.

2. Jefferson's Rejection of the Funding Program, 1790

Hamilton's financial system had two objects. 1st as a puzzle, to exclude popular understanding and inquire. 2dly, as a machine for the corruption of the legislature; for he avowed the opinion that man could be governed by one of two motives only, force or interest: force he observed, in this country, was out of the question; and the interests therefore of the members must be laid hold of, to keep the legislature in unison with the Executive. And with grief and shame it must be acknowledged that his machine was not without effect. That even this, the birth of our government, some members were found sordid enough to bend their duty to their interests, and to look after personal, rather than public good. It is well known that, during the war, the greatest difficulty we encountered was the want of money or means, to pay our soldiers who fought, or our farmers, manufacturers & merchants who furnished the necessary supplies of food & clothing for them. After the expedient of paper money had exhausted itself, certificates of debt were given to the individual creditors with assurance of payment, so soon as the U.S. should be able. But the distresses of these people often obliged them to part with these for the half, the fifth, and even a tenth of their value; and Speculators had made a trade of cozening them from the holders, by the most fraudulent practices and persuasions that they would never be paid. In the bill for funding & paying these, Hamilton made no difference between the original holders, & the fraudulent purchasers of this paper. Great & just repugnance arose at putting these two classes of creditors on the same footing, and great exertions were used to pay to the former the full value, and to the latter the price only which he had paid, with interest. But this would have prevented the game which was to be played, & for which the minds of greedy members were already tutored and prepared. When the trial of strength on these several efforts had indicated the form in which the bill would finally pass, this being known within doors sooner than without, and especially than to those who were in distant parts of the Union, the base scramble began. Couriers & relay horses by land, and swift sailing pilot boats by sea, were flying in all directions. Active part(n)ers & agents were associated & employed in every state, town and country, neighborhood and this paper was brought up at 5/ and even as low as 2/ in the pound, before the holder knew that Congress had already provided for its redemption at par. Immense sums were thus filched from the poor & ignorant, and fortunes accumulated by those who had themselves been poor enough before. Men thus enriched by the dexterity of a leader, would follow of course the chief who was leading them to fortune, and become the zealous instruments of all his enterprises. This game was over, and another was on the carpet at the moment of my arrival and to this I was most ignorantly & innocently made to hold the candle. This fiscal maneuvre is well known by the name of the Assumption. Independently of the debts of Congress, the states, had, during the war, contracted separate and heavy debts; and Massachusetts particularly in an absurd attempt, absurdly conducted, on the British post of Penobscot: and the more debt Hamilton could rake up, the more plunder for his mercenaries. This money, whether wisely or foolishly spent, was pretended to have been spent for general purposes, and ought therefore to be paid from the general purse. But it was objected that nobody knew what these debts were, what their amount, or what their proofs. No matter; we will guess them to be 20. millions. But of these 20. millions we do not know how much should be reimbursed to one state, nor how much to another. No matter; we will guess. And so another scramble was set on foot among the several states, and some got much, some little, some nothing. But the main object was obtained, the phalanx of the treasury was reinforced by additional recruits. This measure produced the most bitter and angry contests ever known in Congress, before or since the union of the states. But it was finally agreed that, whatever importance had been attached to the rejection of this proposition, the preservation of the union, & of concord among the states was more important, and that therefore it would be better that the vote of rejection should be rescinded, to effect which some members should change their votes. But it was observed that this pill would be peculiarly bitter to the Southern States, and that some concomitant measure should be adopted to sweeten it a little to them. There had before been propositions to fix the seat of government either at Philadelphia, or at Georgetown on the Potomac; and it was thought that by giving it to Philadelphia for ten years, and to Georgetown permanently afterwards, this might, as an anodyne, calm in some degree the ferment which might be excited by the other measure alone. So two of the Potomac members White & Lee, but White (with a revulsion of stomach almost convulsive) agreed to change their votes, & Hamilton undertook to carry the other point. In doing this the influence he had established

over the Eastern members, with the agency of Robert Morris with those of the middle states, effected his side of the engagement, and so the assumption was passed, and 20. millions of stock divided among favored states, and thrown in as pablum to the stockjobbing herd. This added to the number of votaries to the treasury and made its Chief the master of every vote in the legislature which might give to the government the direction suited to his political views. I know well, and so must be understood, that nothing like a majority in Congress had yielded to this corruption. Far from it. But a division, not very unequal, had already taken place in the honest part of that body, between the parties styled republican and federal. The latter being monarchists in principle, adhered to Hamilton of course, as their leader in that principle, and mercenary phalanx added to them ensured him always a majority in both houses: so that the whole action of the legislature was now under the direction of the treasury. Still the machine was not compleat. The effect of the funding system, & of the assumption, would be temporary. It would be lost with the loss of the individual members whom it had enriched, and some engine of influence more permanent must be contrived, while these myrmidons [loyal followers] were yet in place to carry it thro' all opposition. This engine was the Bank of the U.S.

Chapter 7:
Document Set 1 References

1. Hamilton's Funding and Assumption Programs, 1790 Alexander Hamilton, *First Report on Public Credit,* January 9, 1790, communicated to the House of Representatives, January 14, 1790, in Henry Cabot Lodge, ed., *The Works of Alexander Hamilton* (New York: G. P. Putnam's Sons, 1904), pp. 227–291.

2. Jefferson's Rejection of the Funding Program, 1790 Thomas Jefferson, *Anas,* 1818 (New York: The Round Table Press, rep. 1903), pp. 30–35.

CHAPTER 7

Political Conflict: The Alien and Sedition Acts and the Virginia and Kentucky Resolutions

Hamilton's financial proposals sparked sharp political conflict in the developing nation of the 1790s. So, too, did the French crisis. In the wake of French espionage, seizures of American ships, impressment of American citizens, and the infamous XYZ affair, the Federalists strengthened their hold on the federal government in the late 1790s and, despite President Adams's desire for peace, prepared for war. The size of the military was significantly increased, and American vessels confronted the French in a quasi-naval war in the Caribbean. In June and July 1798, Congress passed the Alien and Sedition acts, defended by their supporters as essential to national security in the face of the French threat. The legislation, signed into law by President Adams, consisted of four specific measures: the Naturalization Act, the Alien Act, the Alien Enemies Act, and the Sedition Act. Excerpts from the last three appear in the following documents.

Opposition to the Alien and Sedition acts was immediate and intense, particularly in Virginia and Kentucky, where the state legislatures in late 1798 passed resolutions denouncing them. Jefferson and Madison, authors of the resolutions, were alarmed and embittered, viewing the Federalist laws as a serious threat to freedom of expression, the Constitution, and the Democratic-Republican conception of the nature of the newly created union. The following excerpts from the Virginia and Kentucky resolutions reveal both the emotional reaction and the detailed rationale of those who opposed the Alien and Sedition acts.

The documents examine one aspect of the momentous political struggle between Federalists and Democratic-Republicans for power to shape the future of the United States. Reread the textbook sections on "The French Crisis" and "The Alien and Sedition Acts" for background on this confrontation. As you review the evidence, note the specific provisions of the laws, reasons for their enactment, their sponsors' motivations, the way in which they were used, and the reasons Jefferson and Madison so decisively rejected them. You may identify in this controversy early evidence of an enduring theme in American political history.

Questions for Analysis

1. The Alien and Sedition acts were passed by a Federalist Congress and signed into law by Federalist President John Adams. What reasons did the Federalists have for passing the acts? What political end did some Federalists hope to achieve by implementing these laws? In the world of power politics, does the end justify the means?

2. Jefferson, Madison, and a growing number of their Democratic-Republican supporters opposed the Alien and Sedition acts. They expressed their opposition in the Virginia and Kentucky resolutions, drafted respectively by Madison and Jefferson and adopted by the Virginia and Kentucky legislatures. According to the resolutions, why did Jefferson, Madison, and their supporters oppose the Alien and Sedition acts? Assess their reasoning.

3. The Virginia and Kentucky resolutions presuppose a compact theory of the federal union. Analyze the compact theory and its implications for the decision of the South to secede from the Union in 1861.

4. One well-known general interpretation of United States history, called the *consensus theory*, asserts that the American past has been characterized primarily by agreement and that real conflict between classes, sections, and interest groups has been minimal in the American experience. What implication does the controversy surrounding the Alien and Sedition acts, as revealed in these documents, have for the consensus theory? Is the evidence sufficient to sustain or refute the theory? Why or why not?

1. Alien Act, 1798

SECTION I. *Be it enacted . . .* , That it shall be lawful for the President of the United States at any time during the continuance of this act, to *order* all such *aliens* as he shall judge dangerous to the peace and safety of the United States, or shall have reasonable grounds to suspect are concerned in any treasonable or secret machinations against the government thereof, to depart out of the territory of the United States, within such time as shall be expressed in such order, which order shall be served on such alien by delivering him a copy thereof, or leaving the same at his usual abode, and returned to the office of the Secretary of State, by the marshal or other person to whom the same shall be directed. And in case any alien, so ordered to depart, shall be found at large within the United States after the time limited in such order for his departure, and not having obtained a *license* from the President to reside therein, or having obtained such *license* shall not have conformed thereto, every such alien shall, on conviction thereof,

be imprisoned for a term not exceeding three years, and shall never after be admitted to become a citizen of the United States. . . .

SEC. 2. *And be it further enacted,* That it shall be lawful for the President of the United States, whenever he may deem it necessary for the public safety, to order to be removed out of the territory thereof, any alien who may or shall be in prison in pursuance of this act; and to cause to be arrested and sent out of the United States such of those aliens as shall have been ordered to depart therefrom and shall not have obtained a license as aforesaid, in all cases where, in the opinion of the President, the public safety requires a speedy removal. And if any alien so removed or sent out of the United States by the President shall voluntarily return thereto, unless by permission of the President of the United States, such alien on conviction thereof, shall be imprisoned so long as, in the opinion of the President, the public safety may require.

2. Alien Enemies Act, 1798

SECTION I. *Be it enacted . . . ,* That whenever there shall be a declared war between the United States and any foreign nation or government, or any invasion or predatory incursion shall be perpetrated, attempted, or threatened against the territory of the United States, by any foreign nation or government, and the President of the United States shall make public proclamation of the event, all natives, citizens, denizens, or subjects of the hostile nation or government, being males of the age of fourteen years and upwards, who shall be within the United States, and not actually naturalized, shall be liable to be apprehended, restrained, secured and removed, as alien enemies. And the President of

the United States shall be, and he is hereby authorized, in any event, as aforesaid, by his proclamation thereof, or other public act, to direct the conduct to be observed, on the part of the United States, towards the aliens who shall become liable, as aforesaid; the manner and degree of the restraint to which they shall be subject, and in what cases, and upon what security their residence shall be permitted, and to provide for the removal of those, who, not being permitted to reside within the United States, shall refuse or neglect to depart therefrom; and to establish any other regulations which shall be found necessary in the premises and for the public safety.

3. Sedition Act, 1798

SECTION I. *Be it enacted . . . ,* That if any persons shall unlawfully combine or conspire together, with intent to oppose any measure or measures of the government of the United States, which are or shall be directed by proper authority, or to impede the opera-

tion of any law of the United States, or to intimidate or prevent any person holding a place or office in or under the government of the United States, from undertaking, performing or executing his trust or duty; and if any person or persons, with intent as aforesaid, shall counsel, advise or attempt to procure any insurrection, riot, unlawful assembly, or combination, whether such conspiracy, threatening, counsel, advice, or attempt shall have the proposed effect or not, he or they shall be deemed guilty of a high misdemeanor, and on conviction, before any court of the United States having jurisdiction thereof, shall be punished by a fine not exceeding five thousand dollars, and by imprisonment during a term not less than six months nor exceeding five years; and further, at the discretion of the court may be holden to find sureties for his good behaviour in such sum, and for such time, as the said court may direct.

SEC. 2. *And be it further enacted,* That if any person shall write, print, utter or publish, or shall cause or procure to be written, printed, uttered or published, or shall knowingly and willingly assist or aid in writing, printing, uttering or publishing any false, scandalous and malicious writing or writings against the government of the United States, or either house of the Congress of the United States, or the President of the United States, with intent to defame the said government, or either house of the said Congress, or the said President, or to bring them, or either of them, into contempt or disrepute; or to excite against them, or either or any of them, the hatred of the good people of the United States, or to stir up sedition within the United States, or to excite any unlawful combinations therein, for opposing or resisting any law of the United States, or any act of the President of the United States, done in pursuance of any such law, or of the powers in him vested by the constitution of the United States, or to resist, oppose, or defeat any such law or act, or to aid, encourage or abet any hostile designs of any foreign nation against the United States, their people or government, then such person, being thereof convicted before any court of the United States having jurisdiction thereof, shall be punished by a fine not exceeding two thousand dollars, and by imprisonment not exceeding two years.

4. Kentucky Resolutions, 1798

I. *Resolved,* that the several States composing the United States of America, are not united on the principle of unlimited submission to their general government; but that by compact under the style and title of a Constitution for the United States and of amendments thereto, they constituted a general government for special purposes, delegated to that government certain definite powers, reserving each State to itself, the residuary mass of right to their own self-government; and that whensoever the general government assumes undelegated powers, its acts are unauthoritative, void, and of no force: That to this compact each State acceded as a State, and is an integral party, its co-States forming, as to itself, the other party: That the government created by this compact was not made the exclusive or final judge of the extent of the powers delegated to itself; since that would have made its discretion, and not the Constitution, the measure of its powers; but that as in all other cases of compact among parties having no common Judge, each party has an equal right to judge for itself, as well of infractions as of the mode and measure of redress.

II. *Resolved,* that the Constitution of the United States having delegated to Congress a power to punish treason, counterfeiting the securities and current coin of the United States, piracies and felonies committed on the high seas, and offenses against the laws of nations, and no other crimes whatever, and it being true as a general principle, and one of the amendments to the Constitution having also declared "that the powers not delegated to the United States by the Constitution, nor prohibited by it to the States, are reserved to the States respectively, or to the people," therefore also . . . [the Sedition Act of July 14, 1798] . . . ; as also the act passed by them on the 27th day of June, 1798, entitled "An act to punish frauds committed on the Bank of the United States" (and all other their acts which assume to create, define, or punish crimes other than those enumerated in the Constitution), are altogether void and of no force, and that the power to create, define, and punish such other crimes is reserved and of right appertains solely and exclusively to respective States, each within its own Territory.

III. *Resolved,* that it is true as a general principle, and is also expressly declared by one of the amendments to the Constitution that "the powers not delegated to the United States by the Constitution, nor prohibited by it to the States, are reserved to the States respectively or to the people"; and that no power over the freedom of religion, freedom of speech, or freedom of the press being delegated to the United States by the Constitution, nor prohibited by it to the States, all lawful powers respecting the same did of right remain, and were reserved to the States, or to the people: That thus was manifested their determination to retain to themselves the right of judging how far the licentiousness of speech and of the press may be abridged without lessening their useful freedom, and how far those abuses which cannot be separated from their use should be tolerated rather than the use be destroyed; and thus also they guarded against all abridgment by the United States of the freedom of religious opinions and exercises, and retained to themselves the right of protecting the same, as this State, by a law passed on the general demand of its citizens, had already protected them from all human restraint or interference: And that in addition to this general principle and express declaration, another and more special provision has been made by one of the amendments to the Constitution which expressly declares, that "Congress shall make no law respecting an establishment of religion, or prohibiting the free exercise thereof, or abridging the freedom of speech, or of the press," thereby guarding in the same sentence, and under the same words, the freedom of religion, of speech, and of the press, insomuch, that whatever violates either, throws down the sanctuary which covers the others, and that libels, falsehoods, defamation equally with heresy and false religion, are withheld from the cognizance of Federal tribunals. That therefore . . . [the Sedition Act] . . . , which does abridge the freedom of the press, is not law, but is altogether void and of no effect.

IV. *Resolved,* that alien friends are under the jurisdiction and protection of the laws of the State wherein they are; that no power over them has been delegated to the United States, nor prohibited to the individual States distinct from their power over citizens; and it being true as a general principle, and one of the amendments to the Constitution having also declared that "the powers not delegated to the United States by the Constitution, nor prohibited by it to the States, are reserved to the States respectively, or to the people," the . . . [Alien Act of June 22, 1798] . . . , which assumes power over alien friends not delegated by the Constitution, is not law, but is altogether void and of no force.

V. *Resolved,* that in addition to the general principle as well as the express declaration, that powers not delegated are reserved, another and more special provision inserted in the Constitution from abundant caution has declared, "that the migration or importation of such persons as any of the States now existing shall think proper to admit, shall not be prohibited by the Congress prior to the year 1808." That this Commonwealth does admit the migration of alien friends described as the subject of the said act concerning aliens; that a provision against prohibiting their migration is a provision against all acts equivalent thereto, or it would be nugatory; that to remove them when migrated is equivalent to a prohibition of their migration, and is therefore contrary to the said provision of the Constitution, and void.

VI. *Resolved,* that the imprisonment of a person under the protection of the laws of this Commonwealth on his failure to obey the simple order of the President to depart out of the United States, as is undertaken by the said act entitled "An act concerning aliens," is contrary to the Constitution, one amendment to which has provided, that "no person shall be deprived of liberty without due process of law," and that another having provided "that in all criminal prosecutions, the accused shall enjoy the right to a public trial by an impartial jury, to be informed of the nature and cause of the accusation, to be confronted with the witnesses against him, to have compulsory process for obtaining witnesses in his favour, and to have the assistance of counsel for his defense," the same act undertaking to authorize the President to remove a person out of the United States who is under the protection of the law, on his own suspicion, without accusation, without jury, without public trial, without confrontation of the witnesses against him, without having witnesses in his favour, without defense, without counsel, is contrary to these provisions also of the Constitution, is therefore not law, but utterly void and of no force. That transferring the power of judging any person who is under the protection of the laws, from the courts to the President of the United States, as is undertaken by the same act concerning aliens, is against the article of the Constitution which provides, that "the judicial power of the United States shall be vested in courts, the judges of which shall hold their offices during good behavior," and that the said act is void for that reason also; and it is further to be noted, that this transfer of judiciary power is to that magistrate of the general government who already possesses all the executive, and a qualified negative in all the legislative powers. . . .

[T]his Commonwealth does therefore call on its co-States for an expression of their sentiments on the acts concerning aliens, and for the punishment of certain crimes herein before specified, plainly declaring whether these acts are or are not authorized by the Federal Compact. And it doubts not that their sense will be so announced as to prove their attachment unaltered to limited government, whether general or particular, and that the rights and liberties of their co-States will be exposed to no dangers by remaining embarked on a common bottom with their own: That they will concur with this Commonwealth in considering the said acts so palpably against the Constitution as to amount to an undisguised declaration, that the compact is not meant to be the measure of the powers of the general government, but that it will proceed in the exercise over these States of all powers whatsoever: That they will view this as seizing the rights of the States and consolidating them in the hands of the general government with a power assumed to bind the States (not merely in cases made Federal) but in all cases whatsoever, by laws made, not with their consent, but by others against their consent: That this would be to surrender the form of government we have chosen, and to live under one deriving its powers from its own will, and not from our authority; and that the co-States, recurring to their natural right in cases not made Federal, will concur in declaring these acts void and of no force, and will each unite with this Commonwealth in requesting their repeal at the next session of Congress.

5. Virginia Resolutions, 1798

Resolved, . . . That the General Assembly doth particularly protest against the palpable and alarming infractions of the Constitution in the two late cases of the "Alien and Sedition Acts," passed at the last session of Congress; the first of which exercises a power nowhere delegated to the Federal Government, and which, by uniting legislative and judicial powers to those of [the] executive, subvert the general principles of free government, as well as the particular organization and positive provisions of the Federal Constitution: and the other of which acts exercises, in like manner, a power not delegated by the Constitution, but, on the contrary, expressly and positively forbidden by one of the amendments thereto,—a power which, more than any other, ought to produce universal alarm, because it is levelled against the right of freely examining public characters and measures, and of free communication among the people thereon, which has ever been justly deemed the only effectual guardian of every other right.

That this State having by its Convention which ratified the Federal Constitution expressly declared that, among other essential rights, "the liberty of conscience and of the press cannot be cancelled, abridged, restrained or modified by any authority of the United States,". . . . [T]he General Assembly doth solemnly appeal to the like dispositions of the other States, in confidence that they will concur with this Commonwealth in declaring, as it does hereby declare, that the acts aforesaid are unconstitutional; and that the necessary and proper measures will be taken by each for co-operating with this State, in maintaining unimpaired the authorities, rights, and liberties reserved to the States respectively, or to the people.

Chapter 7:
Document Set 2 References

1. Alien Act, 1798
   "An Act Concerning Enemy Aliens," June 25, 1798, *U. S. Statutes at Large,* Vol. 1, pp. 570–572.

2. Alien Enemies Act, 1798
   "An Act Respecting Alien Enemies," July 6, 1798, *U.S. Statutes at Large,* Vol. 1, pp. 577–578.

3. Sedition Act, 1798
   "An Act in Addition to the Act, Entitled 'An Act for the Punishment of Certain Crimes Against the United States,'" July 14, 1798, in *U.S. Statutes at Large,* Vol. 1, pp. 596–597.

4. Kentucky Resolutions, 1798
   "Kentucky Resolutions," November 16, 1798, Nathaniel Southgate Shaler, *Kentucky: A Pioneer Commonwealth* (Boston: Houghton, Mifflin and Co., 1888), pp. 409–416.

5. Virginia Resolutions, 1798
   "Virginia Resolutions," December 24, 1798, James Madison, *Letters and Other Writings of James Madison, Fourth President of the United States* (Philadelphia: J. B. Lippincott Co., 1865), Vol. 4, pp. 506–507.

CHAPTER 8

Aaron Burr's Imperial Dream: A Test for the Young Republic

An important feature of American life in the Jeffersonian Era was the absence of communications in a large and expanding republic. Natural geographic barriers effectively separated the cosmopolitan seaboard area from the more undeveloped and isolated areas of the Ohio and Mississippi valleys. Not surprisingly, physical isolation accentuated the perception of westerners that their economic and political interests were distinct from those of the East. Conscious of eastern domination, inhabitants of the new western empire grew restless and sometimes flirted with separatist ideas.

Despite these rising tensions, Jefferson persisted in a foreign policy of westward expansion. In one bold stroke, the Louisiana Purchase of 1803 dramatically expanded the "empire of liberty." While he pragmatically departed from his earlier strict construction of the Constitution, Jefferson remained sympathetic to Republican ideology of political decentralization, which, as noted in your text, reserved local and undelegated powers to the sovereign states.

Adherence to this philosophy, though consistent with democratic principle, entailed serious risks. As the American empire expanded, the threat of western separatism became more serious. Robust expansionism, frontier alienation, and a charged political environment combined to produce one of the most bizarre incidents in the history of the American West—the Burr conspiracy to establish an independent empire in the Mississippi Valley.

Your textbook's account of Aaron Burr's activities reveals that the roots of intrigue were present in the unconventional political career of the flamboyant New Yorker and in the intense Republican factionalism of the Jefferson years. As early as 1804, the spurned vice president was embroiled in separatist plots with the High Federalists of New England, and in the wake of his ill-fated duel with Alexander Hamilton, Burr launched a bold scheme to detach the Southwest from the United States and establish his own empire.

In league with the eccentric Harmon Blennerhasset and the duplicitous General James Wilkinson, Burr moved in 1806 to implement his plans. It was his misfortune, however, to be allied with the pragmatic Wilkinson who, when confronted with Jefferson's awareness of the plot, manifested renewed (and convenient) patriotism in deserting his co-conspirators. Though the scheme never reached fruition and its perpetrators were acquitted in dramatic treason trials, its existence bore stark testimony to separatist sentiment on the frontier.

The following documents explore the involvement of Burr, Blennerhassett, and Wilkinson in what Jefferson called treasonous activity. As you review the evidence, try to determine what the goals of the conspiracy were. Look for reasons the plot found sympathetic supporters in the West. Explore the relationship between Burr's machinations and the Hartford Convention of 1815. Try to gain insight into both the domestic and foreign-policy problems of the young republic.

Questions for Analysis

1. What do the documents revel about the foreign-policy challenges confronting the United States in its formative years? How did Burr's goals mesh with the national interests of Spain and England on the American continent? How did Burr's activities relate to foreign involvement in American hemispheric affairs?

2. What do the documents reveal about the imperial ideology of the postrevolutionary generation? What were the most pressing problems confronted by the United States as its leadership attempted to design a western policy? Do you find evidence of western reaction to policies originating in the seaboard states?

3. What was the relationship between domestic politics and the Burr conspiracy? Where do you find the origins of Burr's intrigue? What was the previous relationship between Jefferson and Burr, and how did it affect the progress of events in the West?

4. Can you determine from the documents what Jefferson's goals were in the Burr prosecution? How did the president perceive Burr's activities, and how did he cope with them? How would you account for the views expressed by Jefferson and the prosecutor?

5. What is the definition of the word *treason?* In view of your textbook reading and examination of the documentary evidence, do you believe that Burr, Blennerhassett, and their followers were guilty? Were they equally culpable? How would you support your position, using evidence from the documents? Why did the prosecution fail?

1. Jefferson Exposes the Conspiracy, 1807

Some time in the latter part of September I received intimations that designs were in agitation in the Western country unlawful and unfriendly to the peace of the Union, and that the prime mover in these was Aaron Burr, heretofore distinguished by the favor of his country. The grounds of these intimations being inconclusive, the objects uncertain, and the fidelity of that country known to be firm, the only measure taken was to urge the informants to use their best endeavors to get further insight into the designs and proceedings of the suspected persons and to communicate them to me.

It was not till the latter part of October that the objects of the conspiracy began to be perceived, but still so blended and involved in mystery that nothing distinct could be singled out for pursuit.... By this time it was known that many boats were under preparation, stores of provisions collecting, and an unusual number of suspicious characters in motion on the Ohio and its waters. Besides dispatching the confidential agent to that quarter, orders were at the same time sent to the governors of the Orleans and Mississippi Territories and to the commanders of the land and naval forces there to be on their guard against surprise and in constant readiness to resist any enterprise which might be attempted on the vessels, posts, or other objects under their care; and on the 8th of November instructions were forwarded to General Wilkinson to hasten an accommodation with the Spanish commandant on the Sabine, and as soon as that was effected to fall back with his principal force to the hither bank of the Mississippi for the defense of the interesting points on that river. By a letter received from that officer on the 25th of November, but dated October 21, we learnt that a confidential agent of Aaron Burr had been deputed to him with communications, partly written in cipher and partly oral, ex-

plaining his designs, exaggerating his resources, and making such offers of emolument and command to engage him and the army in his unlawful enterprise as he had flattered himself would be successful. The General, with the honor of a soldier and fidelity of a good citizen, immediately dispatched a trusty officer to me with information of what had passed, proceeding to establish such an understanding with the Spanish commandant on the Sabine as permitted him to withdraw his force across the Mississippi and to enter on measures for opposing the projected enterprise....

Burr's general designs ... contemplated two distinct objects, which might be carried on either jointly or separately, and either the one or the other first, as circumstances should direct. One of these was the severance of the Union of these States by the Allegheny Mountains; the other an attack on Mexico. A third object was provided, merely ostensible, to wit, the settlement of a pretended purchase of a tract of country on the Washita claimed by a Baron Bastrop....

He found at once that the attachment of the Western country to the present Union was not to be shaken; that its dissolution could not be effected with the consent of its inhabitants, and that his resources were inadequate as yet to effect it by force. He took his course then at once, determined to seize on New Orleans, plunder the bank there, possess himself of the military and naval stores, and proceed on his expedition to Mexico, and to this object all his means and preparations were now directed.... He seduced good and well-meaning citizens, some by assurances that he possessed the confidence of the Government and was acting under its secret patronage, a pretense which procured some credit from the state of our differences with Spain, and others by offers of land in Bastrop's claim on the Washita....

[O]rders were sent to the governors of Orleans and Mississippi, supplementary to those which had been given on the 25th of November, to hold the militia of their Territories in readiness to cooperate for their defense with the regular troops and armed vessels then under command of General Wilkinson. Great alarm, indeed, was excited at New Orleans by the exaggerated accounts of Mr. Burr, disseminated through his emissaries, of the armies and navies he was to assemble there. General Wilkinson had arrived there himself on the 24th of November, and had immediately put into activity the resources of the place for the purpose of its defense, and on the 10th of December he was joined by his troops from the Sabine. Great zeal was shewn by the inhabitants generally, the merchants of the place readily agreeing to the most laudable exertions and sacrifices for manning the armed vessels with their seamen, and the other citizens manifesting unequivocal fidelity to the Union and a spirit of determined resistance to their expected assailants.

Surmises have been hazarded that this enterprise is to receive aid from certain foreign powers; but these surmises are without proof or probability. The wisdom of the measures sanctioned by Congress at its last session has placed us in the paths of peace and justice with the only powers with whom we had any differences, and nothing has happened since which makes it either their interest or ours to pursue another course.

2. Prosecutor George Hay States the Government's Case, 1807

It is incumbent on those who prosecute to show: (1) that there was a treasonable design; and (2) that there was an assemblage of men for the purpose of effectuating that design. It will be proved to you, gentlemen of the jury, that the design of the prisoner was not only to wage war against the Spanish provinces but to take possessions of the city of New Orleans as preparatory to that design; to detach the people of that country from this and establish an independent government there; and to dismember the Union, separate the Western from the Eastern states, making the Allegheny Mountains the boundary line. You will perceive from the evidence that he intended to take possession of New Orleans to excite the people there to insurrection, and to take advantage of the hostile sentiments which prevailed to the west of the Allegheny against the Spaniards.

If either of these be proved; if it be established that his design was to separate the states; or, after seizing New Orleans, to invade the Spanish provinces, he is guilty of treason. If, in fact, it be proved that he intended to take New Orleans at all, he is completely guilty of treason; whether he designed to take possession of the whole or of a part, he is equally guilty of treason. . . .

For the purpose of accomplishing these great designs—of establishing an empire in the West, of which New Orleans was to be the capital and the accused was to be the chief—he made two long visits to the Western country. He went to Ohio, Tennessee, and Kentucky, in fact to all the Western world, and traveled in various directions, till he went finally to New Orleans. Wherever he went, he spoke disrespectfully of the government of his country, with a view to facilitate the consummation of his own designs. He represented it as destitute of energy to support or defend our national rights against foreign enemies, and of spirit to maintain our national character. He uniformly said that we had no character, either at home or abroad. To those in whom he confided, he asserted that all the men of property and influence were dissatisfied with its arrangements, because they were not in the proper situation to which they were entitled; that with 500 men he could effect a revolution by which he could send the President to Monticello, intimidate Congress, and take the government of the United States into his own hands; that the people of the United States had so little knowledge of their rights, and so little disposition to maintain them, that they would meanly and tamely acquiesce in this shameful usurpation.

3. The Indictment, 1807

VIRGINIA DISTRICT:

In the Circuit Court of the United States of America in and for the fifth circuit and Virginia district.

The grand inquest of the United States of America, for the Virginia district, upon their oath, do present, that AARON BURR, . . . on the tenth day of December, in the year of Christ one thousand eight hundred and six, at a certain place called and known by the name of Blennerhassett's island, in the county of Wood, and district of Virginia aforesaid, and within the jurisdiction of this court, with force and arms, unlawfully, falsely, maliciously and traitorously did compass, imagine and intend to raise and levy war, insurrection and rebellion against the said United States, and in order to fulfil and bring to effect the said traitorous compassings, imaginations and intentions of him the said Aaron Burr, he, the said Aaron Burr, afterwards, to wit, on the said tenth day of December, in the year one thousand eight hundred and six aforesaid, at the said island called Blennerhassett's island as aforesaid, in the county of Wood aforesaid, in the district of Virginia aforesaid, and within the jurisdiction of this court, with a great multitude of persons whose names at present are unknown to the grand inquest aforesaid, to a great number, to wit: To the number of thirty persons and upwards, armed and arrayed in a warlike manner, that is to say, with guns, swords and dirks, and other warlike weapons, as well offensive as defensive, being then and there unlawfully, maliciously and traitorously assembled and gathered together, did falsely and traitorously assemble and join themselves together against the said United States, and then and there with force and arms did falsely and traitorously, and in a warlike and hostile manner, array and dispose themselves against the said United States, . . . did array themselves in a warlike manner, with guns and other weapons, offensive and defensive, and did proceed from the said island down the river Ohio in the county aforesaid, within the Virginia district and within the jurisdiction of this court, on the . . . eleventh day of December, in the year one thousand eight hundred and six aforesaid, with the wicked and traitorous intention to descend the said river and the river Mississippi, and by force and arms traitorously to take possession of a city commonly called New Orleans, in the territory of Orleans, belonging to the United States, contrary to the duty of their said allegiance and fidelity, against the constitution, peace and dignity of the said United States, and against the form of the act of the Congress of the United States in such case made and provided.

HAY, Attorney of the United States,
for the Virginia district.

4. Harmon Blennerhassett Accepts Burr's Invitation, 1805

Estimating the value of your reflections on the view you have taken of the western country, and particularly of Louisiana, I have thought it of great importance to obtain your sentiments to confirm or correct the irresistible attraction my friend, Mr. James Brown, assures me I should follow, to settle in his vicinity, if I would but visit that country. His words are, my "removal would be inevitable"—an expression, truly, strong enough, when viewed through my regard for his friendship, and my confidence in his judgment, to endanger my repose on this island, where for eight years I have dreamed and hoped I should rest my bones forever. . . .

If I could sell or leave the place, I would move forward with a firmer confidence in any undertaking which your sagacity might open to profit and fame.

Having thus advised you of my desire and motives to pursue a change of life, to engage in any thing which may suit my circumstances, I hope, sir, you will not regard it indelicate in me to observe to you how highly I should be honored in being associated with you, in any contemplated enterprise you would permit me to participate in. The amount of means I could at first come forward with would be small. You might command my services as a lawyer, or in any other way you should suggest as being most useful. I could, I have no doubt, unite the talents and energy of two of my particular friends, who would share in any fortune which might follow you. . . .

Not presuming to know or guess at the intercourse, if any, subsisting between you and the present Government, but viewing the probability of a rupture with Spain, the claim for action the country will make upon your talents, in the event of an engagement against, or subjugation of, any of the Spanish Territories, I am disposed in the confidential spirit of this letter to offer you my friends, and my own services to co-operate in any contemplated measures in which you may embark.

5. Blennerhassett's Defense, 1807

5. From such opportunities, . . . as the prisoner derived during all the private interviews afforded him, at this time, and the disclosures therein made to him with rapidity, but also with reserve, he was led to conclude, that the sentiments of a respectable majority of the people in the Orleans and Mississippi Territories were disaffected to the present government, to a degree that, in Aaron Burr's opinion, would, at no very distant period, produce a revolt which would probably call in the aid of some foreign succour to support it.

That, in such an event, the States and Territories west of the Mountains would be placed in a dilemma, out of which they [must] withdraw, as they might be governed by an Eastern or Western ascendency of interests: that it was the colonel's opinion the discontents, particularly in the Territory of Orleans, would induce the Western country to examine the grounds and interests of its present connection with the Atlantic States, and probably induce a separation; that he, A.B., had no further concern with these things than in a speculative way; but that he thought, as well as the prisoner, that the people should be informed on the subject before they might be drawn unawares to a crisis for which they might not be prepared.

That a separation of the Western from the Eastern States was an event spoken of and apprehended, at the seat of government, by some of the heads of Department, which the maladministration of the country might bring about much sooner than was desired or expected; and finally, the people of New Orleans were so much disgusted with the conduct of government towards themselves, and on Spanish affairs, that he should not be surprised to hear of their beginning a revolt by seizing the Bank and Customhouse there.

He spoke of a society of young men of that city, openly denominated the Mexican Society, seizing and shipping some French cannon lying there, for an expedition against Mexico [,which when] at Orleans they had solicited him to lead, but he had declined to be concerned in.

6. In the course of such private conversation as opportunity offered the prisoner to have with Aaron Burr, whilst on the island and at Marietta in the month of August, 1806, prisoner naturally endeavoured to elicit from him a disclosure of some specific project, by referring to the letter of the prisoner whereof the substance is set forth in the second paragraph. But from a reserve and conciseness observable on the part of Col: Burr on such solicitation, and from entire confidence in the honour and judgment of the Ex-Vice-President, the prisoner forbore to urge particular inquiries, that seemed to be displeasing to him, from their tendency to a development of the details of his objects and his means of effecting them.

7. Your client, however, did not take leave of Col: Burr without matter of some satisfaction of his curiosity and interest, sufficient to engage his serious reflections on the expediency of adopting or avoiding that concern, which now seemed to be proffered to the election of the prisoner in his interests. For, after having made the prisoner the general remarks set forth in the fifth article, with the contingency of which Col: Burr declared he had no concern, but which would not be adverse to his own particular views whether they should precede or follow them, he then signified to your client, "that the expulsion of the Spaniards from the American territory then violated by them, or even an invasion of Mexico, would be very pleasing to the administration, if either or both could be effected without a war being declared against Spain, which would be avoided as long as possible, from parsimonious motives on the one hand, and dread of France on the other; although the then existing circumstances would, to a probable certainty, occasion its commencement before he should engage in any operation."

Chapter 8:
Document Set 1 References

1. Jefferson Exposes the Conspiracy, 1807
"To the Senate and House of Representatives," January 22, 1807, in James D. Richardson, ed., *A Compilation of the Messages and Papers of the Presidents, 1789–1908* (Washington, D.C.: Bureau of National Literature and Art, 1909), Vol. 1, pp. 412–416.

2. Prosecutor George Hay States the Government's Case, 1807
Reports of the Trials of Aaron Burr, etc., etc., 1808, pp. 433–451.

3. The Indictment, 1807
J. J. Coombs, *The Trial of Aaron Burr for High Treason* (Washington, D.C.: W. H. & O. H. Morrison, 1864), pp. 140–143.

4. Harmon Blennerhassett Accepts Burr's Invitation, 1805
"Harmon Blennerhassett to Aaron Burr," December 21, 1805, in William H. Safford, *The Blennerhassett Papers* (Cincinnati: Moore, Wilstach & Baldwin, 1864), pp. 117–119.

5. Blennerhassett's Defense, 1807
"Brief on Behalf of Harmon Blennerhassett," 1807, in Raymond E. Fitch, *Breaking with Burr: Harmon Blennerhassett's Journal, 1807* (Athens, Ohio: Ohio University Press, 1988), pp. 190–194.

CHAPTER 8

A Second War for Independence: Understanding the Role of the West

Historians have often disagreed over the motives behind the American decision for war with England in 1812. Particularly troublesome has been the role of young western congressmen who spoke vigorously for a war program that would vindicate the national honor then under attack. Though geographically removed from the states most directly involved in the shipping trade, western farmers had a clear interest in overseas markets and hence in the rights of the United States as a neutral nation. Some scholars, therefore, have seen a relationship between the economic concerns of the West and the belligerence of the war hawks in Congress.

Yet even if frontier interests led to western assertiveness, was the West influential enough to force war? Recent interpretations have acknowledged that support for war was not confined to the West. Historians have noted the significance of Republican political ideology and party conflict in the decision for war. Nonetheless, the leadership of frontier politicians in the prewar debate was important as a catalyst for the prowar sentiment that congealed in 1811–1812. After detailed treatment of the struggle over neutral rights, your textbook emphasizes the war hawks and western concerns as factors in the drive for war.

The following documents provide a sampling from the debate over war, as well as the words of President James Madison. Your objective is to examine the political rhetoric for clues to the primary goals of the American leaders who led the nation to war in 1812. As you review these readings, try to assess and account for the role of the West in the decision-making process.

One focal point for your analysis should be the concept of pride or "honor" in the nineteenth-century context. The speeches cited refer to British violations of national honor in the prewar era. Look for documentary evidence to substantiate this charge. Try also to determine why French offenses against American neutral rights failed to produce the same intensity of response.

Finally, examine the tables in the documents to gain insight into the significance of the West and the war hawks in the decision for war. If, as the text indicates, they were not decisive in bringing about hostilities, then other areas, interests, and motivating forces must have been responsible for the war. Identify concrete factors that add content to the abstract idea of national honor. Try to determine what was to be gained through the war. As you analyze the documents, be aware of the distinction between causes and precipitating events. In addition, note the importance of Republican principles, such as free commercial relations and economic independence.

Questions for Analysis

1. What do the tables included in the document set reveal about the geographic bases of support for war in 1812? How do they support the idea that sectional interests were important in the decision to declare war in 1812? What is your assessment of western influence on Madison's policies and on the congressional decision in 1812? What evidence in the documents supports your conclusion?

2. Define the term *national honor* as used in the documents. To what extent do you view pride as a factor in the decision for war in 1812? How was national honor related to the political and diplomatic environment of the period 1801–1812? How would you account for the prominence of this theme in the prowar argument?

3. Try to identify the causes of the War of 1812, recognizing that there were many and that a definitive explanation may not be possible. Reviewing the conflicting personal backgrounds, economic interests, political orientations, and sectional biases in the documents, develop a hypothesis to explain the origins of the War of 1812. Read between the lines to identify common concerns among western proponents of war. Which pieces of evidence are the most significant indicators of sectional or national sentiment? Why?

4. What do the documents reveal about Republican political ideology? How important were party interests in determining the views and actions of important figures such as Madison and Clay? In what way did partisanship influence national policy?

1. Congressional Voting on the Declaration of War, by States, 1812

	House of Representatives		Senate	
	For	*Against*	*For*	*Against*
New Hampshire	3	2	1	1
Vermont	3	1	1	0
Massachusetts (including Maine)	6	8	1	1
Rhode Island	0	2	0	2
Connecticut	0	7	0	2
New York	3	11	1	1
New Jersey	2	4	1	1
Delaware	0	1	0	2
Pennsylvania	16	2	2	0
Maryland	6	3	1	1
Virginia	14	5	2	0
North Carolina	6	3	2	0
South Carolina	8	0	2	0
Georgia	3	0	2	0
Ohio	1	0	0	1
Kentucky	5	0	1	1
Tennessee	3	0	2	0
	79	49	19	13

2. Geographic Support for the Declaration of War, 1812

▲ Residence of congressmen voting for war
● Residence of congressmen voting against war
(Congressmen absent and not voting are omitted.)

3. State Populations, 1790–1870

Series No.	State	1870	1860	1850	1840	1830	1820	1810	1800	1790
123	New England	3,487,924	3,135,283	2,728,116	2,234,822	1,954,717	1,660,071	1,471,973	1,233,011	1,009,408
124	Maine	626,915	628,279	583,169	501,793	399,455	298,335	228,705	151,719	96,540
125	New Hampshire	318,300	326,073	317,976	284,574	269,328	244,161	214,460	183,858	141,885
126	Vermont	330,551	315,098	314,120	291,948	280,652	235,981	217,895	154,465	85,425
127	Massachusetts	1,457,351	1,231,066	994,514	737,699	610,408	523,287	472,040	422,845	378,787
128	Rhode Island	217,353	174,620	147,545	108,830	97,199	83,059	76,931	69,122	68,825
129	Connecticut	537,454	460,147	370,792	309,978	297,675	275,248	261,942	251,002	237,946
130	Middle Atlantic	8,810,806	7,458,985	5,898,735	4,526,260	3,587,664	2,699,845	2,014,702	1,402,565	958,632
131	New York	4,382,759	3,880,735	3,097,394	2,428,921	1,918,608	1,372,812	959,049	589,051	340,120

Series No.	State	1870	1860	1850	1840	1830	1820	1810	1800	1790
132	New Jersey	906,096	672,035	489,555	373,306	320,823	277,575	245,562	211,149	184,139
133	Pennsylvania	3,521,951	2,906,215	2,311,786	1,724,033	1,348,233	1,049,458	810,091	602,365	434,373
134	East North Central	9,124,517	6,926,884	4,523,260	2,924,728	1,470,018	792,719	272,324	51,006	
135	Ohio	2,665,260	2,339,511	1,980,329	1,519,467	937,903	581,434	230,760	45,365	
136	Indiana	1,680,637	1,350,428	988,416	685,866	343,031	147,178	24,520	5,641	
137	Illinois	2,539,891	1,711,951	851,470	476,183	157,415	55,211	12,282		
138	Michigan	1,184,059	749,113	397,654	212,267	31,639	8,896	4,762		
139	Wisconsin	1,054,670	775,881	305,391	30,945					
140	West North Central	3,856,594	2,169,832	880,335	426,814	140,455	66,586	19,783		
141	Minnesota	439,706	172,023	6,077						
142	Iowa	1,194,020	674,913	192,214	43,112					
143	Missouri	1,721,295	1,182,012	682,044	383,702	140,455	66,586	19,783		
144	North Dakota	2,405	4,837							
145	South Dakota	11,776								
146	Nebraska	122,993	28,841							
147	Kansas	364,399	107,206							
148	South Atlantic	5,853,610	5,364,703	4,679,090	3,925,299	3,645,752	3,061,063	2,674,891	2,286,494	1,851,806
149	Delaware	125,015	112,216	91,532	78,085	76,748	72,749	72,674	64,273	59,096
150	Maryland	780,894	687,049	583,034	470,019	447,040	407,350	380,546	341,548	319,728
151	Dist. of Columbia	131,700	75,080	51,687	33,745	30,261	23,336	15,471	8,144	
152	Virginia	1,225,163	1,219,630	1,119,348	1,025,227	1,044,054	938,261	877,683	807,557	691,737
153	West Virginia	442,014	376,688	302,313	224,537	176,924	136,808	105,469	78,592	55,873
154	North Carolina	1,071,361	992,622	869,039	753,419	737,987	638,829	555,500	478,103	393,751
155	South Carolina	705,606	703,708	668,507	594,398	581,185	502,741	415,115	345,591	249,073
156	Georgia	1,184,109	1,057,286	906,185	691,392	516,823	340,989	252,433	162,686	82,548
157	Florida	187,748	140,424	87,445	54,477	34,730				
158	East South Central	4,404,445	4,020,991	3,363,271	2,575,445	1,815,969	1,190,489	708,590	335,407	109,368
159	Kentucky	1,321,011	1,155,684	982,405	779,828	687,917	564,317	406,511	220,955	73,677
160	Tennessee	1,258,520	1,109,801	1,002,717	829,210	681,904	422,823	261,727	105,602	35,691
161	Alabama	996,992	964,201	771,623	590,756	309,527	127,901	9,046	1,250	
162	Mississippi	827,922	791,305	606,526	375,651	136,621	75,448	31,306	7,600	
163	West South Central	2,029,965	1,747,667	940,251	449,985	246,127	167,680	77,618		
164	Arkansas	484,471	435,450	209,897	97,574	30,388	14,273	1,062		
165	Louisiana	726,915	708,002	517,762	352,411	215,739	153,407	76,556		
166	Oklahoma									
167	Texas	818,579	604,215	212,592						
168	Mountain	315,385	174,923	72,927						
169	Montana	20,595								
170	Idaho	14,999								
171	Wyoming	9,118								
172	Colorado	39,864	34,277							
173	New Mexico	91,874	93,516	61,547						
174	Arizona	9,658								
175	Utah	86,786	40,273	11,380						
176	Nevada	42,491	6,857							
177	Pacific	675,125	444,053	105,891						
178	Washington	23,955	11,594	1,201						
179	Oregon	90,923	52,465	12,093						
180	California	560,247	379,994	92,597						

4. The Kentucky Legislature Calls for Action, 1811

The people of this state, though not immediately exposed to those piratical depredations, which vex, and destroy the commerce of their eastern brethren on the ocean, cannot be less deeply interested in their effects. They look to the sufferings and wrongs of a single member as intimately affecting the whole body. But when an evil becomes so general and inveterate in its deleterious effects, as to threaten dissolution, unless a proper and forcible remedy is applied— The state of Kentucky, yielding to none in patriotism; in its deep rooted attachment to the sacred bond of the union; in its faithful remembrance of the price of our freedom, and in the heartfelt conviction that our posterity have a sacred claim upon us, to transmit to them unimpaired, this God-like inheritance, cannot fail to be penetrated, with any event which threatens even to impair it; much less then, can she be insensible to those daring wrongs of a foreign power, which lead to its immediate destruction. . . .

But when we have discovered a systematic course of injury from her towards our country, evidencing too strongly to be mistaken, an utter disregard of almost every principle of acknowledged rights between independent nations, endeavoring by almost every act of violence on the high seas—on the coasts of foreign powers with whom we were in amity—and even in sight of our own harbours by capturing and destroying our vessels: confiscating our property: forcibly imprisoning and torturing our fellow-citizens: condemning some to death: slaughtering others, by attacking our ships of war: impressing all she can lay her hand upon, to man her vessels: bidding defiance to our seaports: insulting our national honour by every means that lawless force and brutality can devise: inciting the savages to murder the inhabitants on our defenceless frontiers: furnishing them with arms and ammunition lately, to attack our forces: to the loss of a number of brave men: and by every art of power and intrigue, seeking to dispose of our whole strength and resources, as may suit her unrestrained ambition or interest—and when her very offers of redress, go only to sanction her wrongs, and seek merely a removal of those obstacles interposed by our government, to the full enjoyment of her iniquitous benefits; we can be at no loss what course should be pursued. . . .

1. Resolved, by the general assembly for the state of Kentucky, that this state feel deeply sensibly, of the continued, wanton, and flagrant violations by Great Britain and France, of the dearest rights of the people of the United States, as a free and independent nation: that those violations if not discontinued, and ample compensation made for them, ought to be resisted with the whole power of our country.

2. Resolved, that as war seems probable so far as we have any existing evidence of a sense of justice on the part of the government of Great Britain, that the state of Kentucky, to the last mite of her strength and resources, will contribute them to maintain the contest and support the right of their country against such lawless violations; and that the citizens of Kentucky, are prepared to take the field when called on.

5. Henry Clay Endorses War, 1811

What are we to gain by war, has been emphatically asked? In reply, he would ask, what are we not to lose by peace?—commerce, character, a nation's best treasure, honor! If pecuniary considerations alone are to govern, there is sufficient motive for the war. Our revenue is reduced, by the operation of the belligerent edicts, to about six million of dollars, according to the Secretary of the Treasury's report. The year preceding the embargo, it was sixteen. Take away the Orders in Council it will again mount up to sixteen millions. By continuing, therefore, in peace, if the mongrel state in which we are deserve that denomination, we lose annually, in revenue only, ten millions of dollars. . . .

Not content with seizing all our property, which falls within her rapacious grasp, the personal rights of our countrymen—rights which forever ought to be sacred, are trampled upon and violated. The Orders in Council were pretended to have been reluctantly adopted as a measure of retaliation. The French decrees, their alleged basis, are revoked. England resorts to the expedient of denying the fact of the revocation . . . . We are invited, conjured to drink the potion of British poison actually presented to our lips, that we may avoid the imperial dose prepared by perturbed imaginations. We are called upon to submit to debasement, dishonor, and disgrace—to bow the neck to royal insolence, as a course of preparation for manly resistance to Gallic invasion! . . . We were but yesterday contending for the indirect trade—the right to export to Europe the coffee and sugar of the West Indies. To-day we are asserting our claim to the direct trade—the right to export our cotton, tobacco, and other domestic produce to market. Yield this point, and to-morrow intercourse between New Orleans and New York—between the planters on James river and Richmond, will be interdicted. For, sir, the career of encroachment is never arrested by submission. It will advance while there remains a single privilege on which it can operate. Gentlemen say that this Government is unfit for any war, but a war of invasion. What, is it not equivalent to invasion, if the mouths of our harbors and outlets are blocked up, and we are denied egress from our own waters? Or, when the burglar is at our door, shall we bravely sally forth and repel his felonious entrance, or meanly skulk within the cells of the castle? . . .

[Y]ou must look for an explanation of [England's] conduct in the jealousies of a rival. She sickens at your prosperity, and beholds in your growth—your sails spread on every ocean, and your numerous seamen—the foundations of a Power which, at no very distant day, is to make her tremble for naval superiority. . . .

What! shall it be said that our *amor patriæ* is located at these desks—that we pusillanimously cling to our seats here, rather than boldly vindicate the most inestimable rights of the country? Whilst the heroic Daviess and his gallant associates, exposed to all the perils of treacherous savage warfare, are sacrificing themselves for the good of their country, shall we shrink from our duty?

6. John C. Calhoun Insists on Free Trade, 1811

Although Mr. Speaker, I believe, under existing circumstances, a war attitude necessary, or at least preparatory steps calculated to meet that event; and although situated as we are, I am for the whole of our legitimate rights; yet sir, I would not be willing to involve the country in war, in defence of the extensive and circuitous carrying trade, separate from the other causes; that is, that we should become carriers for the whole world; as Government receives no benefit from this circuitous carrying trade, only as it is calculated to aggrandize a few individuals engaged in it. I should be for holding fast the claim to the circuitous carrying trade, and would be willing to operate on our enemies by adopting countervailing restrictive systems. But, sir, I would not be willing, that the good of the States, the good of the people, the agriculturists and mechanics, should be put at hazard to gratify the avarice and cupidity of a small class of men, who in fact may be called citizens of the world, attached to no particular country; any country is their country where they can make the most money. But, sir, for what is an inherent right, for what I deem the legitimate, or necessary carrying trade, the liberty of carrying our productions to foreign markets, and with the return cargo, in which agriculture is particularly interested, I would fight in defence of.

7. A Southerner Urges Continental Expansion, 1811

The true question in controversy . . . involves the interest of the whole nation. It is the right of exporting the productions of our own soil and industry to foreign markets. . . .

What, Mr. Speaker, are we now called on to decide? It is whether we will resist by force the attempt made by that government to subject our maritime rights to the arbitrary and capricious rule of her will; for my part I am not prepared to say that this country shall submit to have her commerce interdicted or regulated by any foreign nation. Sir, I prefer war to submission.

Over and above these unjust pretensions of the British government, for many years past they have been in the practice of impressing our seamen from merchant vessels; this unjust and lawless invasion of personal liberty calls loudly for the interposition of this government. . . .

This war, if carried on successfully, will have its advantages. We shall drive the British from our continent—they will no longer have an opportunity of intriguing with our Indian neighbors, and setting on the ruthless savage to tomahawk our women and children. That nation will lose her Canadian trade, and, by having no resting place in this country, her means of annoying us will be diminished. The idea I am now about to advance is at war, I know, with sentiments of the gentleman from Virginia. I am willing to receive the Canadians as adopted brethren; it will have beneficial political effects; it will preserve the equilibrium of the government. When Louisiana shall be fully peopled, the Northern states will lose their power; they will be at the discretion of others; they can be depressed at pleasure; and then this Union might be endangered. I therefore feel anxious not only to add the Floridas to the South, but the Canadas to the North of this empire.

8. President Madison States the Case for War, 1812

British cruisers have been in the continued practice of violating the American flag on the great highway of nations, and of seizing and carrying off persons sailing under it, not in the exercise of a belligerent right founded on the law of nations against an enemy, but of a municipal prerogative over British subjects. British jurisdiction is thus extended to neutral vessels in a situation where no laws can operate but the law of nations and the laws of the country to which the vessels belong, and a self-redress is assumed which, if British subjects were wrongfully detained and alone concerned, is that substitutions of force for a resort to the responsible sovereign which falls within the definition of war. Could the seizure of British subjects in such cases be regarded as within the exercise of a belligerent right, the acknowledged laws of war, which forbid an article of captured property to be adjudged without a regular investigation before a competent tribunal, would imperiously demand the fairest trial where the sacred rights of persons were at issue. In place of such a trial these rights are subjected to the will of every petty commander. . . .

British cruisers have been in the practice also of violating the rights and the peace of our coasts. They hover over and harass our entering and departing commerce. To the most insulting pretensions they

have added the most lawless proceedings in our very harbors, and have wantonly spilt American blood within the sanctuary of our territorial jurisdiction. . . .

Not content with these occasional expedients for laying waste our neutral trade, the cabinet of Britain resorted at length to the sweeping system of blockades, under the name of orders in council, which has been molded and managed as might best suit its political views, its commercial jealousies, or the avidity of British cruisers. . . .

In reviewing the conduct of Great Britain toward the United States our attention is necessarily drawn to the warfare just renewed by the savages on one of our extensive frontiers—a warfare which is known to spare neither age nor sex and to be distinguished by features peculiarly shocking to humanity. It is difficult to account for the activity and combinations which have for some time been developing themselves among tribes in constant intercourse with British traders and garrisons without connecting their hostility with that influence and without recollecting the authenticated examples of such interpositions heretofore furnished by the officers and agents of that Government. . . .

Our moderation and conciliation have had no other effect than to encourage perseverance and to enlarge pretensions. We behold our seafaring citizens still the daily victims of lawless violence, committed on the great common and highway of nations, even within sight of the country which owes them protection. We behold our vessels, freighted with the products of our soil and industry, or returning with the honest proceeds of them, wrested from their lawful destinations, confiscated by prize courts no longer the organs of public law but the instruments of arbitrary edicts, and their unfortunate crews dispersed and lost, or forced or inveigled in British ports into British fleets, whilst arguments are employed in support of these aggressions which have no foundation but in a principle equally supporting a claim to regulate our external commerce in all cases whatsoever.

We behold, in fine, on the side of Great Britain a state of war against the United States, and on the side of the United States a state of peace toward Great Britain.

Whether the United States shall continue passive under these progressive usurpations and these accumulating wrongs, or, opposing force to force in defense of their national rights, shall commit a just cause into the hands of the Almighty Disposer of Events, avoiding all connections which might entangle it in the contest or views of other powers, and preserving a constant readiness to concur in an honorable reestablishment of peace and friendship, is a solemn question which the Constitution wisely confides to the legislative department of the Government. In recommending it to their early deliberations I am happy in the assurance that the decision will be worthy [of] the enlightened and patriotic councils of a virtuous, a free, and a powerful nation.

Chapter 8: Document Set 2 references

1. Congressional Voting on the Declaration of War, by States, 1812
   Bradford Perkins, *The Causes of the War of 1812: National Honor or National Interest?* (New York: Holt, Rinehart and Winston, 1962), frontispiece.

2. Geographic Support for the Declaration of War, 1812
   Bradford Perkins, *Prologue to War: England and the United States, 1805–1812* (Berkeley: University of California Press, 1961), p. 409.

3. State Populations, 1790–1870
   The Statistical History of the United States from Colonial Times to the Present (Stamford, Conn.: Fairfield Publishers, Inc., 1965), p. 13.

4. The Kentucky Legislature Calls for Action, 1811
   Resolution, Kentucky Legislature, December 16, 1811, in *Niles' Weekly Register,* I (January 11, 1812).

5. Henry Clay Endorses War, 1811
   Henry Clay, Speech, in *Annals of Congress,* 12th Cong., 1st Sess., pp. 599–602.

6. John C. Calhoun Insists on Free Trade, 1811
   John C. Calhoun, Speech, in *Annals of Congress,* 12th Cong., 1st Sess., pp. 482–483, 487.

7. A Southerner Urges Continental Expansion, 1811
   Felix Grundy, Speech, in *Annals of Congress,* 12th Cong., 1st Sess., pp. 422–427.

8. President Madison States the Case for War, 1812
   "To the Senate and House of Representatives of the United States, June 1, 1812," in James D. Richardson, *A Compilation of the Messages and Papers of the Presidents, 1789–1908* (Washington: Bureau of National Literature and Art, 1909), Vol. I, pp. 500–505.

Chapter 8: Document Set 2 Credits

DOCUMENT SET 3
Virgin Land: The Trans-Mississippi West Through the Eyes of Lewis and Clark

After the American acquisition of Louisiana in 1803, President Thomas Jefferson moved quickly to gain a firmer understanding of the resources, opportunities, geographic dimensions, and physical characteristics of the new territory. For a variety of economic, scientific, and diplomatic reasons, Jefferson had determined that an exploratory expedition was essential to the national interest. As a result, he commissioned Meriwether Lewis and William Clark to conduct a thorough investigation of the Missouri River Valley and the Pacific Northwest.

Jefferson's request for congressional authorization of an expedition to the Northwest actually predated the formal acquisition of the vast new territory. For many years, Jefferson had dreamed and written of an "empire of liberty" to be occupied by enterprising Americans who would expand republicanism into the trans-Mississippi West. The Louisiana Purchase therefore fulfilled the president's goal of acquiring a new arena for American expansion. The documents that follow explore Jefferson's objectives and the implementation of his goals, with emphasis on the president's intellectual curiosity and scientific purposes. In addition, they record the process by which the outlines of the western environment became clearer to Americans living in the seaboard states.

As you review the documents relating to the expedition's planning stages, examine the president's motives for authorizing the mission. Your textbook suggests that scientific knowledge was Jefferson's highest priority, but the evidence presents a more complex picture of the reasons for undertaking the expedition. Evaluate the various factors that influenced

the president's thinking, and develop your own hypothesis about the primary motivation behind the decision to explore the Pacific Northwest.

Because Jefferson emphasized science and the expansion of knowledge, these documents have been selected and arranged to stress that aspect of the expedition's work. The excerpts from the Lewis and Clark journals contain evidence of a consistent preoccupation with natural phenomena and the wonders of nature. Note the explorers' first impressions of the physical and geographic features of the western environment, and consider the impact of the new images on their thinking. Try to assess their objectives as they recorded their observations.

Finally, use the sketches, maps, and logs to evaluate the expedition's commitment to scientific inquiry and the advancement of knowledge. As the textbook indicates, Lewis had been sent to Philadelphia in 1803 for scientific training that would prepare him for his responsibilities. Reflect on the documents as evidence of his seriousness with regard to this aspect of his mission. To what extent does he seem to have been faithful to the spirit of scientific research? Look for indications that the expedition succeeded in fulfilling Jefferson's expectations.

A review of Lewis's report will provide some evidence of the expedition's outcomes. Review his own analysis of the results, including the explorers' most important findings. As you examine the Lewis report, think about the practical consequences of the expedition's achievements. Compare the original goals and unanticipated discoveries as you evaluate the long-term results of Jefferson's initiative.

Questions for Analysis

1. Examine Jefferson's instructions to Meriwether Lewis. What were the president's highest priorities for the expedition? How did his instructions compare with the justification for the trip given to Congress? How would you account for disparities between the two documents?

2. Compare Jefferson's instructions with Lewis's final report on the expedition. How do they relate to each other in terms of focal issues and problems? What findings seemed most significant to Lewis? Why?

3. What were the expedition's implications for the future of American economic development and foreign policy? What evidence do you find in the documents to clarify these relationships?

4. To what extent were the Native Americans viewed as a part of the natural environment? How do the documents clarify the explorers' view of the human element in

the ecology of the West? How effective were Lewis and Clark as representatives of the United States government to the native population? How did they attempt to ensure the achievement of this goal?

5. Describe the impressions of Lewis and Clark when confronting new data or experiencing new vistas. What new knowledge of the physical world became available as a result of the expedition? To what extent did Lewis and Clark remain faithful to scientific method in their approach to their task?

1. Jefferson Seeks Congressional Funding for Exploration of the Louisiana Territory, 1803

An intelligent officer, with ten or twelve chosen men, fit for the enterprise and willing to undertake it, taken from our posts, where they may be spared without inconvenience, might explore the whole line, even to the western ocean; have conferences with the natives on the subject of commercial intercourse; get admission among them for our traders; as others are admitted, agree on convenient deposits for an interchange of articles; and return with the information acquired, in the course of two summers.... While other civilized nations have encountered great expense to enlarge the boundaries of knowledge by undertaking voyages of discovery and for other literary purposes, in various parts and directions, our nation seems to owe to the same object, as well as to its own interests, to explore this, the only line of easy communication across the continent, and so directly traversing our own part of it.

The interests of commerce place the principal object within the constitutional powers and care of Congress, and that it should incidentally advance the geographical knowledge of our own continent cannot be but an additional gratification. The nation claiming the territory, regarding this as a literary pursuit, which is in the habit of permitting within its dominions, would not be disposed to view it with jealousy, even if the expiring state of its interests there did not render it a matter of indifference. The appropriation of $2,500, "for the purpose of extending the external commerce of the United States," while understood and considered by the executive as giving the legislative sanction, would cover the undertaking from notice, and prevent the obstructions which interested individuals might otherwise previously prepare in its way.

2. The President's Instructions to Meriwether Lewis, 1803

The object of your mission is to explore the Missouri river, & such principal stream of it, as, by its course & communication with the waters of the Pacific Ocean, may offer the most direct & practicable water communication across this continent, for the purposes of commerce.

Beginning at the mouth of the Missouri, you will take observations of latitude & longitude, at all remarkable points on the river, & especially at the mouths of rivers, at rapids, at islands & other places & objects distinguished by such natural marks &

characters of a durable kind, as that they may with certainty be recognized hereafter. The courses of the river between these points of observation may be supplied by the compass, the log-line & by time, corrected by the observations themselves. The variations of the compass too, in different places, should be noticed.

The interesting points of portage between the heads of the Missouri & the water offering the best communication with the Pacific Ocean should also be fixed by observation, & the course of that water to the ocean, in the same manner as that of the Missouri.

Your observations are to be taken with great pains & accuracy, to be entered distinctly, & intelligently for others as well as yourself, to comprehend all the elements necessary, with the aid to the usual tables, to fix the latitude and longitude of the places at which they were taken, & are to be rendered to the war office, for the purpose of having the calculations made concurrently by proper persons within the U.S. Several copies of these, as well as your other notes, should be made at leisure times & put into the care of the most trustworthy of your attendants, to guard by multiplying them, against the accidental losses to which they will be exposed. A further guard would be that one of these copies be written on the paper of the birch, as less liable to injury from damp than common paper.

The commerce which may be carried on with the people inhabiting the line you will pursue, renders a knolege of these people important. . . .

Other object worthy of notice will be

the soil & face of the country, its growth & vegetable productions; especially those not of the U.S.

the animals of the country generally, & especially those not known in the U.S.

the remains and accounts of any which may [be] deemed rare or extinct;

the mineral productions of every kind; but more particularly metals, limestone, pit coal &

salpetre; salines & mineral waters, noting the temperature of the last, & such circumstances as may indicate their character.

Volcanic appearances.

climate as characterized by the thermometer, by the proportion of rainy, cloudy & clear days, by lightening, hail, snow, ice, by the access & recess of frost, by the winds prevailing at different seasons, the dates at which particular plants put forth or lose their flowers, or leaf, times of appearance of particular birds, reptiles or insects.

Altho' your route will be along the channel of the Missouri, yet you will endeavor to inform yourself, by inquiry, of the character & extent of the country watered by its branches, & especially on its southern side. The North river or Rio Bravo which runs into the gulph of Mexico, and the North river, or Rio colorado, which runs into the gulph of California, are understood to be the principal streams heading opposite to the waters of the Missouri, and running Southwardly. . . . But if you can learn anything certain of the most Northern source of the Mississippi, & of its position relative to the lake of the woods, it will be interesting to us. Some account too of the path of the Canadian traders from the Mississippi, at the mouth of the Ouisconsin river, to where it strikes the Missouri and of the soil & rivers in its course, is desireable.

3. The Expedition Pursues Its Interest in the Native American Population, 1805

[Lewis]   MONDAY JULY 22D 1805.

The river being divided into such a number of channels by both large and small Island[s] that I found it impossible to lay it down [the courses] correctly following one channel only in a canoe and therefore walked on shore. . . .

The Indian woman [Sacajawea] recognizes the country and assures us that this is the river on which her relations live, and that the three forks are at no great distance. this peice of information has cheered the sperits of the party who now begin to console themselves with the anticipation of shortly seeing the head of the missouri yet unknown to the civilized world. . . .

[Lewis]   THURSDAY AUGUST 8TH 1805.

[T]he Indian woman recognized the point of a high plain to our right which she informed us was not very distant from the summer retreat of her nation on a river beyond the mountains which runs to the west. this hill she says her nation calls the beaver's head from a conceived re[se]mblance of it's figure to the head of that animal. she assures us that we shall either find her people on this river or on the river immediately west of it's source; which from it's present size cannot be distant. as it is now all important with us to meet with those people as soon as possible I determined to proceed tomorrow with a small party to the source of the principal stream of this river and pass the mountains to the Columbia; and down that river until I found the Indians; in short it is my resolution to find them or some others, who have horses if it should cause me a trip of one month. for without horses we shall be obliged to leave a great part of our stores, of which, it appears to me that we have a stock already sufficiently small for the length of the voyage before us.

[Biddle]   SATURDAY, AUGUST 17TH, 1805. On setting out at seven o'clock, Captain Clarke with Chaboneau and his wife walked on shore, but they had not gone more than a mile before Clarke saw Sacajawea, who was with her husband 100 yards ahead, began to dance and show every mark of the most extravagant joy, turning round him and pointing to several Indians, whom he now saw advancing on horseback, sucking her fingers at the same time to indicate that they were of her native tribe. As they advanced, Captain Clarke discovered among them Drewyer dressed like an Indian, from whom he learnt the situation of the party. While the boats were performing the circuit, he went towards the forks with the Indians, who as they went along, sang aloud with the greatest appearance of delight.

We soon drew near to the camp, and just as we approached it a woman made her way through the croud towards Sacajawea, and recognising each other, they embraced with the most tender affection. The meeting of these two young women had in it something peculiarly touching, not only in the ardent manner in which their feelings were expressed, but from the real interest of their situation. They had been companions in childhood, in the war with the Minnetarees they had both been taken prisoners in the same battle, they had shared and softened the rigours of their captivity, till one of them had escaped from the Minnetarees, with scarce a hope of ever seeing her friend relieved from the hands of her enemies. While Sacajawea was renewing among the women the friendships of former days, Captain Clark went on, and was received by Captain Lewis and the chief, who after the first embraces and salutations were over, conducted him to a sort of circular tent or shade of willows. Here he was seated on a white robe; and the chief immediately tied in his hair six small shells resembling pearls, an ornament highly valued by these people, who procure them in the course of trade from the sea-coast. The moccasins of the whole party were then taken off, and after much ceremony the smoking began. After this the confer-

ence was to be opened, and glad of an opportunity of being able to converse more intelligibly, Sacajawea was sent for; she came into the tent, sat down, and was beginning to interpret, when in the person of Cameahwait she recognised her brother: She instantly jummped up, and ran and embraced him, throwing over him her blanket and weeping profusely: The chief was himself moved, though not in the same degree. After some conversation between them she resumed her seat, and attempted to interpret for us, but her new situation seemed to overpower her, and she was frequently interrupted by her tears. After the council was finished the unfortunate woman learnt that all her family were dead except two brothers, one of whom was absent, and a son of her eldest sister, a small boy, who was immediately adopted by her.

[Lewis]   MONDAY AUGUST 19TH 1805. They seldom correct their children particularly the boys who soon become masters of their own acts. they give as a reason that it cows and breaks the sperit of the boy to whip him, and that he never recovers his independence of mind after he is grown. They treat their women but with little rispect, and compel them to perform every species of drudgery. they collect the wild fruits and roots, attend to the horses or assist in that duty, cook, dress the skins and make all their apparel, collect wood and make their fires, arrange and form their lodges, and when they travel pack the horses and take charge of all the baggage; in short the man dose little else except attend his horses hunt and fish. the man considers himself degraded if he is compelled to walk any distance; and if he is so unfortunately poor as only to possess two horses he rides the best himself and leavs the woman or women if he has more than one, to transport their baggage and children on the other, and to walk if the horse is unable to carry the additional weight of their persons. the chastity of their women is not held in high estimation, and the husband will for a trifle barter the companion of his bead for a night or longer if he conceives the reward adiquate; tho' they are not so importunate that we should caress their women as the sioux were, and some of their women appear to be held more sacred than in any nation we have seen. I have requested the men to give them no cause of jealousy by having connection with their women without their knowledge, which with them, strange as it may seem is considered as disgracefull to the husband as clandestine connections of a similar kind are among civilized nations. to prevent this mutual exchange of good offices altogether I know it impossible to effect, particularly on the part of our young men whom some months abstance have made very polite to those tawney damsels. no evil has yet resulted and I hope will not from these connections. . . .

I was anxious to learn whether these people had the venerial, and made the enquiry through the interpreter and his wife; the information was that they sometimes had it but I could not learn their remedy; they most usually die with it's effects. this seems a strong proof that these disorders bothe ganaraehah and Louis Venerae [syphilis] are native disorders of America. tho' these people have suffered much by the small pox which is known to be imported and perhaps those other disorders might have been contracted from other indian tribes who by a round of communications might have obtained from the Europeans since it was introduced into that quarter of the globe. but so much detached on the other ha[n]d from all communication with the whites that I think it most probable that those disorders are original with them.

4. Lewis and Clark as Pioneer Naturalists, 1805–1806

[Lewis]   SUNDAY MAY 26TH 1805.
Capt. Clark walked on shore this morning and ascended to the summit of the river hills he informed me on his return that he had seen mountains on both sides of the river runing nearly parrallel with it and at no great distance; also an irregular range of mountains on lard. about 50 Mls. distant; the extremities of which boar W. and N.W. from his station. . . .

In the after part of the day I also walked out and ascended the river hills which I found sufficiently fortiegueing. on arriving to the summit [of] one of the highest points in the neighbourhood I thought myself well repaid for my labour; as from this point I beheld the Rocky Mountains for the first time,* I could only discover a few of the most elivated points above the horizon, the most remarkable of which by my pocket compass I found bore N. 65° W. being a little to the N. of the N.W. extremity of the range of broken mountains seen this morning by Capt. C. these points of the Rocky Mountains were covered with snow and the sun shone on it in such manner as to give me the most plain and satisfactory view. while I viewed these mountains I felt a secret pleasure in finding myself so near the head of the heretofore conceived boundless Missouri; but when I reflected on the difficulties which this snowey barrier would most probably throw in my way to the Pacific, and the sufferings and hardships of myself and party in thim, it in some measure counterballanced the joy I had felt in the first moments in which I gazed on them; but as I have always held it a crime to anticipate evils I will believe it a good comfortable road until I am compelled to believe differently.

[Clark]   JUNE 20TH THURSDAY 1805
[T]he Mountains to the N.W. and West of us are still entirely covered are white and glitter with the reflection of the sun. I do not believe that the clouds that pervale at this season of the year reach the summits of those lofty mountains; and if they do the probability is that they deposit snow only for there has been no proceptable diminution of the snow which they contain since we first saw them. I have thought it probable that these mountains might have derived their appellation of *Shineing Mountains*, from their glittering appearance when the sun shines in certain directions on the snow which cover them.

Dureing the time of my being on the Plains and above the falls I as also all my party repeatedly heard a nois which proceeded from a Direction a little to the N. of West, a loud [noise] and resembling precisely the discharge of a piece of ordinance of 6 pounds at the distance of 5 or six miles. I was informed of it several times by the men J: Fields particularly before I

---

*Actually the Little Rocky Mountains of northern Montana.

paid any attention to it, thinking it was thunder most probably which they had mistaken. at length walking in the plains yesterday near the most extreem S. E. bend of the River above the falls I heard this *nois* very distinctly, it was perfectly calm clear and not a cloud to be seen, I halted and listened attentively about two hour[s]. . . . I am at a great loss to account for this Phenomenon. I well recollect hereing the Minitarees say that those Rocky mountains make a great noise, but they could not tell me the cause, neither could they inform me of any remarkable substance or situation in these mountains which would autherise a conjecture of a probable cause of this noise. . . .

[Clark]   OCTOBER 24TH THURSDAY 1805
The first pitch of this falls is 20 feet perpendecular, then passing thro' a narrow chanel for 1 mile to rapid of about 8 feet fall below which the water has no perceptable fall but verry rapid Capt. Lewis and three men crossed the river [the Columbia] and on the opposit Side to view the falls which he had not yet taken a full view of. At 9 oClock a. m. I Set out with the party and proceeded on down a rapid Stream of about 400 yards wide at 2-½ miles the river widened into a large bason to the stard. Side on which there is five Lodges of Indians. here a tremendious black rock Presented itself high and Steep appearing to choke up the river; nor could I See where the water passed further than the current was drawn with great velocity to the Lard. Side of this rock at which place I heard a great roreing. I landed at the Lodges and the natives went with me to the top of this rock which makes from the Stard. Side, from the top of which I could See the dificuelties we had to pass for Several miles below; at this place the water of this great river is compressed into a chanel between two rocks not exceeding *forty five* yards wide and continues for a ¼ of a mile when it again widens to 200 yards and continues this width for about 2 miles when it is again intersepted by rocks. The whole of the Current of this great river must at all Stages pass thro' this narrow chanel of 45 yards wide.

    . . . I deturmined to pass through this place notwithstanding the horrid appearance of this agitated gut swelling, boiling & whorling in every direction, which from the top of the rock did not appear as bad as when I was in it; however we passed Safe to the astonishment of all the Inds.

[Lewis]   TUESDAY FEBRUARY 4TH 1806.
There are s[e]veral species of fir in this neighbourhood which I shall discribe as well as my slender botanical skil wil enable me and for the convenience of comparison with each other shal number them. (No. 1.) a species which grows to immence size; very commonly 27 feet in the girth six feet above the surface of the earth, and in several instances we have found them as much as 36 feet in the girth or 12 feet diameter perfectly solid and entire. they frequently rise to the hight of 230 feet, and one hundred and twenty or 30 of that hight without a limb. this timber is white and soft throughout and rives better than any other species we have tryed. the bark shales off in irregula[r] rounded flakes and is of a redish brown colour particularly of the younger growth. the stem of this tree is simple branching, ascending, not very defuse, and proliferous. the leaf of this tree is acerose, ⅒th of an Inh in width, and ¾ of an Inch in length; is firm, stif and accuminate; they are triangular, a little declining, thickly scattered on all sides of the bough, but rispect the three uppersides only and are also sessile growing from little triangular pedestals of soft spungy elastic bark. at the junction of the boughs, the bud-scales continued to incircle their rispective twigs for several yea[r]s; at least three year[s] is common and I have counted as many as the growth of four years beyond these scales. this tree [the Sitka spruce, *Picea sitchensis*] affords but little rosin. it's cone I have not yet had an opportunity to discover altho' I have sought it frequently; the trees of this kind which we have felled have had no cones on them. . . .

[Lewis]   SATURDAY FEBRUARY 15TH 1806.
The quadrupeds of this country from the Rocky Mountains to the pacific Ocean are 1st the *domestic animals,* consisting of the horse and the dog only; 2edly the *native wild animals,* consisting of the Brown white or grizly bear, (which I beleive to be the same family with a mearly accedental difference in point of colour) the black bear, the common red deer, the black tailed fallow deer, the Mule deer, Elk, the large brown wolf, the small woolf of the plains, the large wolf of the plains, the tiger cat, the common red fox, black fox or fisher, silver fox, large red fox of the plains, small fox of the plains or kit fox, Antelope, sheep, beaver, common otter, sea Otter, mink, spuck, seal, racoon, large grey squirrel, small brown squirrel, small grey squirrel, ground squirrel, *sewelel,* Braro, rat, mouse, mole, Panther, hare, rabbit, and polecat or skunk. all of which shall be severally noticed in the order in which they occur as well as shuch others as I learn do exist and which [have] not been here recapitulated.

5. Charting the Columbia River, 1805–1806

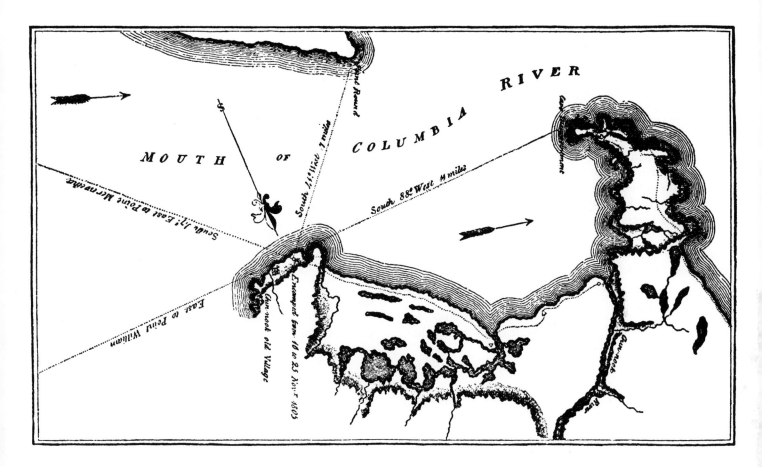

6. Specimens and Artifacts Sent to Jefferson, 1805

Itemized List of Specimens and Artifacts Sent to Jefferson from Fort Mandan

Box No. 1, contains the following articles i. e.

In package No. 3 & 4 Male & female antelope, with their Skelitons.

No. 7 & 9 the horns of two mule or Black tailed deer. a Mandan bow an quiver of arrows—with some Recara's tobacco seed.

No. 11. a Martin Skin, Containing the tail of a Mule Deer, a weasel and three Squirels from the Rockey mountains.

No. 12. The bones & Skeleton of a Small burrowing wolf of the Praries the Skin being lost by accedent.

No. 99. The Skeliton of the white and Grey *hare*.

Box No. 2, Contains 4 Buffalow *Robes,* and a ear of Mandan Corn.

The large Trunk Contains a male & female *Braro* or burrowing dog of the Praire and the female's *Skeliton.*

a carrote of Ricaras *Tobacco*

a red fox Skin Containing a *Magpie*

No. 14 Minitarras Buffalow robe Containing Some articles of Indian dress.

No. 15 a mandan *robe* containing two burrowing Squirels, a white *weasel* and the Skin of a Loucirvia, also

13 red fox Skins.

1 white Hare Skin &c.

4 horns of the mountain ram

1 Robe representing a battle between the Sioux & Ricaras against the Minetares and Mandans.

In Box No. 3.

Nos. 1 & 2 the Skins of the Male & female Antelope with their Skeletons. & the Skin of a Yellow *Bear* which I obtained from the *Sieoux*

No. 4 Box. Specimens of plants numbered from 1. to 67.

Specimens of Plants numbered from 1 to 60.

1 Earthen pot Such as the Mandans manufacture and use for culinary purposes.

1 Tin box containing insects mice &c.

a Specimine of the fur of the antilope.

a Specimon of a plant, and a parcel of its roots higly prized by the natives as an efficatious remidy in cases of the bite of the rattle Snake or Mad Dog.

In a large Trunk

Skins of a male and female Braro, or burrowing Dog of the Prarie, with the Skeleton of the female.

1 Skin of the red fox Containing a Magpie

2 Cased Skins of the white hare.

1 Minitarra Buffalow robe Containing Some articles of Indian Dress.

1 Mandan Buffalow robe Containing a dressed Lousirva Skin, and 2 cased Skins of the Burrowing Squirel of the Praries.

13 red fox Skins

4 Horns of the Mountain Ram, or *big horn*.

1 Buffalow robe painted by a mandan man representing a battle fought 8 years Since by the Sioux & Recaras against the mandans, me ni tarras & Ah wah har ways. (Mandans &c. on horseback

Cage No. 6.

Contains a liveing burrowing Squirel of the praries

Cage No. 7.

Contains 4 liveing Magpies

Cage No. 9.

Containing a liveing hen of the Prairie a large par of Elks horns containing by the frontal bone.

7. Clark's Sketch of the Heathcock, 1805

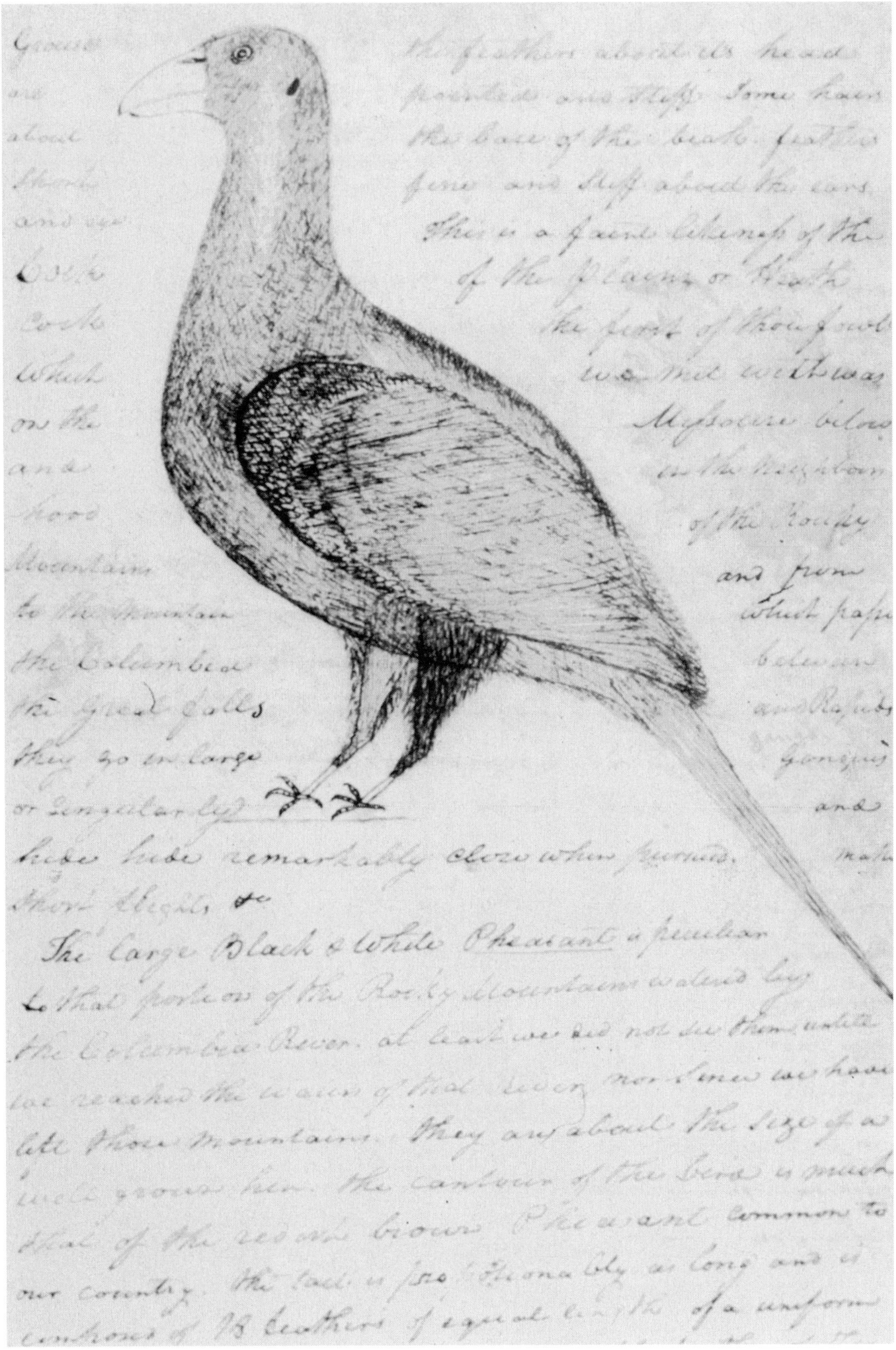

8. The Scientfic Observation of Climate, 1805

Thermometrical observations, showing also the rise and fall of the Mississippi (Missouri); appearances of weather, winds, &c. commencing at the mouth of the river.

Duboes in latitude 38°55' 19" $\frac{6}{10}$ north, and longitude 89° 57' 45" west, January 1, 1804.

Thermometer on the north side of a tree in the woods.

Explanations of the Notations of the Weather

f means fair weather.
r means rain.
h means hail.
l means lightning.

c means cloudy.
s means snow.
t means thunder.
a after, as f a r means

c a s means cloudy after snow intervening.
c a r s means cloudy after rain and snow.

fair after rain, which has intervened since the last observation.

Notations of the River

r means risen in the last 24 hours, ending at sunrise.

f means fallen in the last 24 hours, ending at sunrise.

Notations of Thermometer

a means above naught.

b means below naught.

Day of the Month	Therm. at Sunrise	Weather	Wind	Therm. at four o'clock	Weather	Wind	River		
							r. and f.	Feet	Inches
1805.	Deg.			Deg.					
Ap. 18	52 a.	f.	N.E.	64 a.	c.	N.			
19	54 a.	c.	N.W.	56 a.	c.	N.W.			
20	40 a.	c.	N.W.	42 a.	c. a. s.	N.W.			
21	28 a.	f.	N.W.	40 a.	c.	N.W.	f		$\frac{1}{2}$
22	34 a.	f. a. c.	W.	40 a.	f.	N.W.	r.		2
23	34 a.	f.	W.	52 a.	c.	N.W.	r.		2
24	40 a.	f.	N.	56 a.	f.	N.	r.		1
25	36 a.	f.	N.	52 a.	f.	N.W.	r.		2
26	32 a.	f.	S.	63 a.	f.	S.E.	r.		3
27	36 a.	f.	S.W.	64 a.	f.	N.W.	f.		2
28	44 a.	f.	S.E.	63 a.	f.	S.E.	f.		$1\frac{1}{2}$
29	42 a.	f.	N.E.	64 a.	f.	E.	f.		$1\frac{1}{2}$
30	50 a.	f.	N.W.	58 a.	f.	S.E.	f.		$\frac{1}{2}$
May 1	36 a.	c.	E.	46 a.	c. a. f.	N.E.	f.		$1\frac{1}{2}$
2	28 a.	s.	N.E.	34 a.	c. a. s.	N.W.	f.		1
3	26 a.	f.	W.	46 a.	c.	W.	f.		$\frac{1}{4}$
4	38 a.	c.	W.	48 a.	f. a. c.	W.			
5	38 a.	f.	N.W.	62 a.	f. a. r.	S.E.	r.		1
6	48 a.	f.	E.	61 a.	c. a. r.	S.E.	r.		2
7	42 a.	c.	S.	60 a.	f.	N.E.	r.		$1\frac{1}{2}$
8	41 a.	c.	E.	52 a.	c. a. r.	E.	f.		$\frac{1}{4}$

Day of the Month	Therm. at Sunrise	Weather	Wind	Therm. at four o'clock	Weather	Wind	River r. and f.	River Feet	River Inches
9	38 a.	f.	E.	58 a.	f.	W.	r.		$\frac{3}{4}$
10	38 a.	f. a. c.	W.N.W.	62 a.	c. a. r.	N.W.	f.		$\frac{3}{4}$
11	44 a.	f.	N.E.	60 a.	c.	S.W.			
12	52 a.	f.	S.E.	54 a.	c. a. r.	N.W.	r.		2
13	52 a.	c. a. r.	N.W.	54 a.	f. a. c.	N.W.	f.		$2\frac{1}{4}$
14	32 a.	f.	S.W.	52 a.	c.	S.W.	f.		$1\frac{3}{4}$
15	48 a.	c. a. r.	S.W.	54 a.	c.	N.W.	f.		$\frac{3}{4}$
16	48 a.	c.	S.W.	67 a.	f.	S.W.			

9. Lewis's Initial Report to the President, 1806

It is with pleasure that I announce to you the safe arrival of myself and party at 12 o'clock today at this place with our papers and baggage. In obedience to your orders we have penetrated the continent of North America to the Pacific Ocean, and sufficiently explored the interior of the country to affirm with confidence that we have discovered the most practicable route which does exist across the continent by means of the navigable branches of the Missouri and Columbia Rivers. . . .

We view this passage across the continent as affording immense advantages to the fur trade, but fear that the advantages which it offers as a communication for the productions of the East Indies to the United States and thence to Europe will never be found equal on an extensive scale to that by way of the Cape of Good Hope; still we believe that many articles not bulky, brittle nor of a very perishable nature may be conveyed to the United States by this route with more facility and at less expense than by that at present practiced.

The Missouri and all its branches from the Cheyenne upwards abound more in beaver and common otter, than any other streams on earth, particularly that proportion of them lying within the Rocky Mountains. The furs of all this immense tract of country including such as may be collected on the upper portion of the River St. Peters, Red River, and the Assinniboin with the immense country watered by the Columbia, may be conveyed to the mouth of the Columbia by the 1st of August in each year and from thence be shipped to, and arrive in Canton [China] earlier than the furs at present shipped from Montreal annually arrive in London. . . .

If the government will only aid, even in a very limited manner, the enterprise of her citizens I am fully convinced that we shall shortly derive the benefits of a most lucrative trade from this source, and that in the course of ten to twelve years a tour across the continent by the route mentioned will be undertaken by individuals with as little concern as a voyage across the Atlantic is at present. . . .

I have brought with me several skins of the sea otter, two skins of the native sheep of America, five skins and skeletons complete of the Bighorn or mountain ram, and a skin of the mule deer besides the skins of several other quadrapeds and birds native of the countries through which we have passed. I have also preserved a pretty extensive collection of plants, and collected nine other vocabularies [of Indian tribes].

I have prevailed on the great chief of the Mandan nation to accompany me to Washington; he is now with my friend and colleague Capt. Clark at this place, in good health and spirits, and very anxious to proceed.

Chapter 8:
Document Set 3 References

1. Jefferson Seeks Congressional Funding for Exploration of the Louisiana Territory, 1803
   Thomas Jefferson, Message to Congress, January 18, 1803, in Paul L. Ford, ed., *The Writings of Thomas Jefferson* (New York: G. P. Putnam's Sons, 1897), Vol. 8, pp. 198–203.

2. The President's Instructions to Meriwether Lewis, 1803
   Jefferson to Meriwether Lewis, June 20, 1803, in Ford, Vol. 8, pp. 194–199.

3. The Expedition Pursues Its Interest in the Native American Population, 1805
   Bernard DeVoto, ed., *The Journals of Lewis and Clark* (Boston: Houghton Mifflin & Co., 1953), pp. 163, 181–182, 202–203, 207–209.

4. Lewis and Clark as Pioneer Naturalists, 1805–1806
   DeVoto, pp. 117–118, 144–146, 263–264, 307–318, 322–323.

5. Charting the Columbia River, 1805–1806
   The Mouth of the Columbia, ca. 1806, in *History of the Expedition Under the Command of Captains Lewis and Clark to the Sources of the Missouri and Thence Across the Rocky Mountains and Down the River Columbia to the Pacific Ocean* (Philadelphia: Bradford and Inskeep, 1814), Vol. 2, p. 71.

6. Specimens and Artifacts Sent to Jefferson, 1805
   DeVoto, Appendix 3, pp. 493–494.

7. Clark's Sketch of the Heathcock, 1805
   Paul Russell Cutright, *Lewis and Clark: Pioneering Naturalists* (Urbana, Ill.: University of Illinois Press, 1969), photo inset.

8. The Scientific Observation of Climate, 1805
   History of the Expedition, Vol. 2, pp. 476, 485.

9. Lewis's Initial Report to the President, 1806
   Reuben Gold Thwaites, ed., *Original Journals of the Lewis and Clark Expedition* (New York, 1904–1905), Vol. 7, pp. 334–337.

Chapter 8:
Document Set 3 Credits

7. Photo courtesy of the Missouri Historical Society

CHAPTER 9

DOCUMENT SET 1
The Women of Lowell: Enslavement or Liberation?

Significant changes in the social and ethnic composition of the work force accompanied the rise of manufacturing after the War of 1812. A key feature of that transformation was the entry of large numbers of women into the labor force, particularly in northern New England, where young, single females increasingly found employment outside the home. Promising a "home away from home" in a controlled environment, the Lowell textile mills successfully recruited the daughters of moderately prosperous farmers to serve as workers in the new factories of the Merrimack River Valley. Widely regarded as an exemplary labor force, the Lowell "girls" constituted an important, if temporary, segment of an evolving working-class community.

The Lowell system reflected management's hope that the social problems of industrialism could be avoided and class warfare averted. As the experiment matured, however, optimism faded. With the tightening of industrial discipline, the model work force itself changed significantly. Labor strife increased, and New England farm girls were replaced by Irish and French-Canadian immigrant workers who toiled in a transformed workplace. The Lowell experiment had been eclipsed by harsh industrial reality.

The following set of documents provides several perspectives on the worker experience at Lowell. As you analyze the evidence, look at the source and think about intent. Consider who the author is, to whom the document is addressed, and what the primary argument is. Decide what the evidence reveals about the impact of the Lowell system on workers. Note the disagreement that is evident and try to explain it. All the documents included bear on the work environment, the social and cultural context in which operatives functioned, and the impact of the work experience on employees. As you examine the evidence, consider the relationship between economic modernization and social change.

Questions for Analysis

1. What do the documents reveal about the impact of industrialization on the worker and the transformation of the workplace in the mid-nineteenth century? How do the authors' backgrounds, motives, and goals influence their reactions to the Lowell system?

2. What assumptions are made in these documents with regard to the place of women in a changing society? How was women's "sphere" being defined by the authors of these documents?

3. What evidence of shifting class relations can be found in this set of documents? In what ways did the experiences of working-class and middle-class women differ? What were the implications of this divergence?

4. What was the impact of the Lowell social environment on relationships among the "girls"? What was the significance of the Labor Reform Association?

5. What do the documents reveal about changing perceptions of labor and the self-images of nineteenth-century workers? In what way was the "dignity of labor" a central issue at Lowell? What do these concerns reflect about the development of the work process at Lowell?

6. How did the social and ethnic composition of the labor force in the 1850s differ from that of the 1830s? What were the implications of this change for the Lowell system as a model of paternalistic capitalism? Where does the Lowell model fit into the history of the modernization process?

1. Harriet Robinson Remembers Preindustrial Lowell, ca. 1836

Before 1836 the era of mechanical industry in New England had hardly begun, the industrial life of its people was yet in its infancy, and nearly every article in domestic use that is now made by the help of machinery was then "done by hand." It was, with few exceptions, a rural population, and the material for clothing was grown on the home-farm, and spun and woven by the women. . . .

Their lives had kept pace for so many years with the stage-coach and the canal that they thought, no doubt, if they thought about it at all, that they should crawl along in this way forever. But into this life there came an element that was to open a new era in the activities of the country.

This was the genius of mechanical industry, which would build the cotton-factory, set in motion the loom and the spinning-frame, call together an army of useful people, open wider fields of industry for men and (which was quite as important at that time) for women also. For hitherto woman had always been a money-*saving,* rather than a money-earning, member of the community, and her labor could command but small return. If she worked out as servant, or "help," her wages were from fifty cents

to one dollar a week; if she went from house to house by the day to spin and weave, or as tailoress, she could get but seventy-five cents a week and her meals. As teacher her services were not in demand, and nearly all the arts, the professions, and even the trades and industries, were closed to her, there being, as late as 1840, only seven vocations, outside the home, into which the women of New England had entered. . . .

Before 1840, the foreign element in the factory population was almost an unknown quantity. The first immigrants to come to Lowell were from England. The Irishman soon followed; but not for many years did the Frenchman, Italian, and German come to take possession of the cotton-mills. The English were of the artisan class, but the Irish came as "hewers of wood and drawers of water." The first Irish-women to work in the Lowell mills were usually scrubbers and waste-pickers. . . . They were not intemperate, nor "bitterly poor." They earned good wages, and they and their children, especially their children, very soon adapted themselves to their changed conditions of life, and became as "good as anybody."

2. The Lowell Work Force Described, ca. 1840s

When I look back into the factory life of fifty or sixty years ago, I do not see what is called "a class" of young men and women going to and from their daily work, like so many ants that cannot be distinguished one from another; I see them as individuals, with personalities of their own. This one has about her the atmosphere of her early home. That one is impelled by a strong and noble purpose. The other,—what she is, has been an influence for good to me and to all womankind.

Yet they were a class of factory operatives, and were spoken of (as the same class is spoken of now) as a set of persons who earned their daily bread, whose condition was fixed, and who must continue to spin and to weave to the end of their natural existence. Nothing but this was expected of them, and they were not supposed to be capable of social or mental improvement. That they could be educated and developed into something more than mere work-

people, was an idea that had not yet entered the public mind. So little does one class of persons really know about the thoughts and aspirations of another! It was the good fortune of these early mill-girls to teach the people of that time that this sort of labor is not degrading; that the operative is not only "capable of virtue," but also capable of self-cultivation.

At the time the Lowell cotton-mills were started, the factory girl was the lowest among women. In England, and in France particularly, great injustice had been done to her real character; she was represented as subjected to influences that could not fail to destroy her purity and self-respect. . . .

But in a short time the prejudice against factory labor wore away, and the Lowell mills became filled with blooming and energetic New England women. They were naturally intelligent, had mother-wit, and fell easily into the ways of their new life. They soon began to associate with those who formed the community in which they had come to live, and were invited to their houses. They went to the same church, and sometimes married into some of the best families. Or if they returned to their secluded homes again, instead of being looked down upon as "factory girls" by the squire's or the lawyer's family, they were more often welcomed as coming from the metropolis, bringing new fashions, new books, and new ideas with them. . . .

The life in the boarding-houses was very agreeable. These houses belonged to the corporation, and were usually kept by widows (mothers of mill-girls), who were often the friends and advisers of their boarders. . . .

Each house was a village or community of itself. There fifty or sixty young women from different parts of New England met and lived together. When not at their work, by natural selection they sat in groups in their chambers, or in a corner of the large dining-room, busy at some agreeable employment; or they wrote letters, read, studied, or sewed, for, as a rule, they were their own seamstresses and dressmakers. . . .

The boarding-houses were considered so attractive that strangers, by invitation, often came to look in upon them, and see for themselves how the mill-girls lived. . . . There was a feeling of *esprit de corps* among these households; any advantage secured to one of the number was usually shared by others belonging to her set or group. Books were exchanged, letters from home were read, and "pieces," intended for the Improvement Circle, were presented for friendly criticism.

3. A Lowell Workers' Petition and the Legislative Response, 1845

The First Official Investigation into Labor Conditions by the Massachusetts Legislature in 1845

Massachusetts House Document, *no. 50, March 1845*

. . . The first petition which was referred to your committee, came from the city of Lowell, and was signed by Mr. John Quincy Adams Thayer, and eight hundred and fifty others, "peaceable, industrious, hard working men and women of Lowell." The Petitioners declare that they are confined "from thirteen to fourteen hours per day in unhealthy apartments," and are thereby "hastening through pain, disease and privation, down to a premature grave." They therefore ask the Legislature "to pass a law providing that ten hours shall constitute a day's work," and that no corporation or private citizen "shall be allowed, except in cases of emergency, to employ one set of hands more than ten hours per day.". . .

The first petitioner who testified was Eliza R. Hemmingway. She had worked two years and nine months in the Lowell Factories; two years in the Middlesex, and nine months in the Hamilton Corporations. Her employment is weaving—works by the piece. The Hamilton Mill manufactures cotton fabrics. The Middlesex, woolen fabrics. She is now at work in the Middlesex Mills, and she attends one loom. Her wages average from $16 to $23 a month exclusive of board. She complained of the hours for labor being too many, and the time for meals too limited. In the summer season the work is commenced at 5 o'clock, a.m. and continued till 7 o'clock, p.m., with half an hour for breakfast and three quarters of an hour for dinner. During eight months of the year, but half an hour is allowed for dinner. The air in the room she considered not to be wholesome. There were 293 small lamps and 61 large lamps lighted in the room in which she worked, when evening work is required. These lamps are also lighted sometimes in the morning. About 130 females, 11 men and 12 children (between the ages of 11 and 14) work in the room with her. She thought the children enjoyed about as good health as children usually do. The children work but nine months out of twelve. The other three months they must attend school. Thinks there is no day when there are less than six females out of the mill from sickness. Has known as many as thirty. She, herself, is out quite often, on account of sickness. There was more sickness in the summer than in the winter months; though in the summer, lamps were not lighted. She thought there was a general desire among females to work but ten hours, regardless of pay. . . .

Miss Sarah G. Bagley said she had worked in the Lowell Mills eight and a half years, six years and a half on the Hamilton Corporation, and two years on the Middlesex. She is a weaver and works by the piece. She worked in the mills three years before her health began to fail. She is native of New Hampshire and went home six weeks during the summer. Last year she was out of the mill a third of the time. She thinks the health of the operatives is not as good as the health of the females who do house-work or the millinery business. The chief evil, as far as health is concerned, is the shortness of the time allowed for meals. The next evil the length of time employed—not giving them time to cultivate their minds.... She thought that girls were generally favorable to the ten hour system. She had presented a petition, same as the one before the Committee, to 132 girls, most of whom said that they would prefer to work but ten hours. In a pecuniary point of view, it would be better as their health would be improved. They would have more time for sewing. Their intellectual, moral and religious habits would be benefited by the change....

Your Committee have not been able to give the petitions from the other towns in this state a hearing. We believe that the whole case was covered by the petition from Lowell, and to the consideration of that petition we have given our undivided attention, and we have come to the conclusion unanimously, that legislation is not necessary at the present time and for the following reasons:

1st. That a law limiting the hours of labor, if enacted at all, should be of a general nature. That it should apply to individuals or copartnerships as well as corporations. Because, if it is wrong to labor more than ten hours in a corporation it is also wrong when applied to individual employers, and your Committee are not aware that more complaint can justly be made against incorporated companies in regard to hours of labor than can be against individuals or co-partnerships....

2d. Your Committee believe that the factory system as it is called, is not more injurious to health than other kinds of indoor labor. That a law which would compel all of the factories in Massachusetts to run their machinery but ten hours out of the 24, while those in Maine, New Hampshire, Rhode Island and other States in the Union, were not restricted at all, the effect would be to close the gate of every mill in the State....

3d. It would be impossible to legislate to restrict the hours of labor, without affecting very materially the question of wages; and that is a matter which experience has taught us can be much better regulated by parties themselves than by the Legislature. Labor in Massachusetts is a very different commodity from what it is in foreign countries. Here labor is on an equality with capital, and indeed controls it, and so it ever will be while free education and free constitutions exist.... Labor is intelligent enough to make its own bargains, and look out for its own interest without any interference from us....

4th. The Committee do not wish to be understood as conveying the impression, that there are no abuses in the present system of labor; we think there are abuses; we think that many improvements may be made, and we believe will be made, by which labor will not be so severely tasked as it now is. We think that it would be better if the hours for labor would be less, if more time was allowed for meals, if more attention were paid to ventilation and pure air in our manufactories, and workshops, and many other matters. We acknowledge all this, but we say, the remedy is not with us.

4. Orestes Brownson Questions the Lowell System, 1840

The operatives are well dressed, and we are told, well paid. They are said to be healthy, content and happy. This is the fair side of the picture; the side exhibited to distinguished visitors. There is a dark side moral, as well as physical. Of the common operatives, few, if any, by their wages acquire a competence. A few of what Carlyle terms not inaptly the *body-servants*, and now and then an agent or an overseer rides in his coach. But the great mass wear out their health, spirits and morals, without becoming one whit better off than when they commenced labor. The bills of mortality in their factory villages are not striking, we admit, for the poor girls when they can toil no longer go home to die. The average life, working life we mean, of the girls that come to Lowell ... we have been assured is only about three years. What becomes of them then? Few of them ever marry, fewer still return to their native places with their reputations unimpaired. "She has worked in a factory" is almost enough to damn to infamy the most worthy and virtuous girl. We know no sadder sight on earth than one of our factory villages presents; when the bell at the break of day, or breakfast or dinner, calls out its hundreds or thousands of operatives. We stand and look at these hard working men and women hurrying in all directions and ask ourselves where go the proceeds of their labor? The man who employs them and for whom they are toiling as so many slaves is one of our city nabobs, revelling in luxury . . . or in these times is shedding crocodile tears over the deplorable conditions of the poor laborer while he docks his wages 25%. . . . And this man would fain pass for a Christian . . . and is horrified at a Southern planter who keeps slaves.

5. A Lowell Worker Defends the System, 1841

And whom has Mr. Brownson slandered? A class of girls who in this city alone are numbered by thousands, and who collect in many of our smaller (towns) by hundreds, girls who generally come from quiet country homes, where their minds and manners have been formed under the eyes of the worthy sons of the Pilgrims, and their virtuous partners, and who return again to become the wives of the free intelligent yeomanary of New England, and the mothers of quite a proportion of our future republicans. Think, for a moment, how many of the next generation are to spring from mothers doomed to infamy! "Ah" it may be replied, "Mr. Brownson acknowledges that you may still be worthy and virtuous." There we must be a set of worthy and virtuous idiots, for no virtuous girl of common sense would choose for an occupation one that would consign her to infamy. . . .

That there has been prejudice against us, we know; but [it] is wearing away and has never been so deep or universal as Mr. B's statement would lead us to believe. Even now it would be that "mushroom aristocracy" and "would-be fashionables" of Boston, turn up their eyes in horror at the sound of those vulgar words, *factory girls;* but *they* form but a small part of the community, and theirs are not the opinions which Mr. Brownson intended to represent. . . .

There are among us all sorts of girls. I believe that there are few occupations which can exhibit so many gradations of piety and intelligence; but the majority may at least lay claim to as much of the former as females in other stations in life. . . . The Improvement Circle, the Lyceum and Institute, the social religious meetings, the circulating and other libraries, can bear testimony that the little time they have is spent in a better manner. Our well filled churches and lecture halls, and the high character of our clergymen and lecturers, will testify that the state of morals and intelligence is not low.

6. A Worker's Memories of the Mills, ca. 1840s

There were compensations for being shut in to daily toil so early. The mill itself had its lessons for us. But it was not, and could not be, the right sort of life for a child, and we were happy in the knowledge that, at the longest, our employment was only to be temporary.

When I took my next three months at the grammar school, everything there was changed, and I too was changed. The teachers were kind, and thorough in their instruction; and my mind seemed to have been ploughed up during that year of work, so that knowledge took root in it easily. It was a great delight to me to study, and at the end of the three months the master told me that I was prepared for high school.

But alas! I could not go. The little money I could earn—one dollar a week, besides the price of my bread—was needed in the family, and I must return to the mill. . . .

In the older times it was seldom said to little girls, as it always has been said to boys, that they ought to have some definite plan, while they were children, what to be and do when they were grown up. There was usually but one path open before them, to become good wives and housekeepers. And the ambition of most girls was to follow their mothers' footsteps in this direction; a natural and laudable ambition. But girls, as well as boys, must often have been conscious of their own peculiar capabilities,— must have desired to cultivate and make use of their individual powers. When I was growing up, they had already begun to be encouraged to do so. . . .

My grandfather came to see my mother once at about this time and visited the mills. When he had entered the room, and looked around for a moment, he took off his hat and made a low bow to the girls, first toward the right, and then toward the left. We were familiar with his courteous habits, partly due to his French descent; but we had never seen anybody bow to a room full of mill girls in that polite way, and some one of the family afterwards asked him why he did so. He looked a little surprised at the question, but answered promptly and with dignity, "I always take off my hat to ladies."

His courtesy was genuine. Still, we did not call ourselves ladies. We did not forget that we were working-girls, wearing coarse aprons suitable to our work, and that there was some danger of our becoming drudges. I know that sometimes the confinement of the mill became very wearisome to me. In the sweet June weather I would lean far out of the window, and try not to hear the unceasing clash of sound inside. Looking away to the hills, my whole stifled being would cry out

"Oh, that I had wings!"
Still I was there from choice, and
"The prison unto which we doom ourselves,
No prison is."

7. The *Lowell Offering* Emphasizes the Dignity of Labor, 1842

From whence originated the idea, that it was derogatory to a lady's dignity, or a blot upon the female character, to labor? and who was the first to say, sneeringly, "Oh, she *works* for a living"? Surely, such ideas and expressions ought not to grow on republican soil. The time has been, when ladies of the first rank were accustomed to busy themselves in domestic employment. . . .

Few American fortunes will support a woman who is above the calls of her family; and a man of sense, in choosing a companion to jog with him through all the up-hills and down-hills of life, would sooner choose one who *had* to work for a living, than one who thought it beneath her to soil her pretty hands with manual labor, although she possessed her thousands. To be able to earn one's own living by laboring with the hands, should be reckoned among female accomplishments; and I hope the time is not far distant when none of my country-women will be ashamed to have it known that they are better versed in useful, than they are in ornamental accomplishments.

Chapter 9:
Document Set 1 References

1. Harriet Robinson Remembers Preindustrial Lowell, ca. 1836
   "Lowell Sixty Years Ago," in Harriet H. Robinson, *Loom and Spindle,* 1898 (Reprint edition, Kailua: Press Pacifica, 1976), pp. 1–3, 7–8.

2. The Lowell Work Force Described, ca. 1840s
   "The Characteristics of the Early Factory Girls," in Robinson, pp. 37–38, 54–55.

3. A Lowell Workers' Petition and the Legislative Response, 1845
   "The First Official Investigation into Labor Conditions by the Massachusetts Legislature," Massachusetts House Document 50 (March 1845).

4. Orestes Brownson Questions the Lowell System, 1840

   Orestes Brownson, "The Laboring Classes," *Boston Quarterly Review,* Vol. 3 (June 1840).

5. A Lowell Worker Defends the System, 1841
   "Factory Girls," *Lowell Offering,* Series 1 (December 1841).

6. A Worker's Memories of the Mills, ca. 1840s
   Lucy Larcom, *A New England Girlhood* (Boston: Houghton Mifflin and Co., 1889), pp. 155–156, 157, 182.

7. The *Lowell Offering* Emphasizes the Dignity of Labor, 1842
   Lowell Offering, Series 2, Vol. 3 (1842), pp. 69–70.

CHAPTER 9

DOCUMENT SET 2
End of the Trail: Andrew Jackson and the Rationale for Indian Removal

Just as industrialization transformed the society and economy of urban America, an advancing frontier forced dramatic social adjustments in the Old Northwest and in the Southwest. Perhaps the most striking confrontation was the cultural clash between Native Americans and land-hungry speculators and frontier people, who escalated pressure on tribes that retained title to their ancestral lands. Rapid economic and political development in the West resulted in the subordination of the Indians east of the Mississippi River by 1840. Their misery increased in direct proportion to the strength of an increasingly powerful national government.

While Americans had long grappled with the problem of Indian resistance, rapid population movement following the War of 1812 lent urgency to the search for a solution. A further complication lay in the absence of consensus on an acceptable philosophy of Indian relations. Federal government policy initially reflected an assimilationist approach, which assumed that the Indians would willingly adopt the ways of white American society. But white settlers rarely shared this vision of the future. Their relentless drive into tribal lands had precipitated sharp conflicts by the time Andrew Jackson assumed the presidency.

Since overt extermination was not acceptable to most Americans, and the federal government seemed unable to protect tribal enclaves against aggressive settlers and uncooperative state governments, politicians sought an alternative policy. The result was increasing support in Washington for Indian removal to the trans-Mississippi West. There, it was argued, the segregated Indian could move gradually toward the white man's concept of civilization.

The following documents examine the ways in which the removal policy was carried out. Examine the sources in light of the "trail of tears" described in the textbook's "Place in Time" essay on Cherokee removal. These events must be placed in the context of a government approach to the Indians that evolved from the presidency of James Monroe through that of Martin Van Buren. The main focus of this unit, however, is on the crucial innovations of the Jacksonian period.

As you explore the evidence, be especially conscious of white cultural assumptions. Notice how the term *civilization* was used in these documents. Identify the long-term goal of the federal Indian policy. Try to determine what legal, constitutional, and moral problems the removal issue raised. A careful review of these documents will reveal how the ethnocentrism of white people influenced their relations with Indians on the advancing frontier.

Questions for Analysis

1. As you work with these documents, what do you identify as the central theme of American thinking concerning Native American cultural traditions and practices? Define *ethnocentrism*. How are ethnocentric ideas expressed? Why did the Five Civilized Tribes constitute a serious practical and moral problem for the political figures responsible for developing and implementing Indian policy?

2. What does the evidence reveal about the psychological and physical impact of the removal policy on the tribes affected? What factors prevented the tribal leadership from successfully resisting government policy? Were these problems internal or external to the tribes themselves?

3. Reviewing the documents before you, compare the arguments presented for and against removal by government officials, chief executives, and "friends" of the American Indian. In what ways did their fundamental assumptions about the Indian and the long-term interests of the tribes differ? What light does the evidence shed on the reasons for those differences? How do the documents help you to account for similarities in outlook?

4. What do the documents reveal about the constitutional relationship of the executive and judicial branches of government? How did the debate over the legal

rights and prerogatives of state and federal governments relate to the evolution of American federalism? What were the future implications of these disagreements?

5. In what ways did the removal policy reflect Andrew Jackson's overall political and social philosophy? How did it clarify his convictions concerning the role of the federal government in securing the general welfare and serving the public interest?

1. John C. Calhoun Outlines the War Department's Indian Policy, 1825

Of the four southern tribes, two of them (the Cherokees and Choctaws) have already allotted to them a tract of country west of the Mississippi. That which has been allotted to the latter is believed to be sufficiently ample for the whole nation, should they emigrate; and if an arrangement, which is believed not to be impracticable, could be made between them and the Chickasaws, who are their neighbors, and of similar habits and dispositions, it would be sufficient for the accommodation of both. A sufficient country should be reserved to the west of the Cherokees on the Arkansas, as a means of exchange with those who remain on the east. To the Creeks might be allotted a country between the Arkansas and the Canadian river, which limits the northern boundary of the Choctaw possessions in that quarter. There is now pending with the Creeks a negotiation, under the appropriation of the last session, with a prospect that the portion of that nation which resides within the limits of Georgia may be induced, with the consent of the nation, to cede the country which they now occupy for a portion of the one which it is proposed to allot for the Creek nation on the west of the Mississippi. Should the treaty prove successful, its stipulations will provide for the means of carrying it into effect, which will render any additional provision, at present, unnecessary. . . .

Almost all of the tribes proposed to be affected by the arrangement are more or less advanced in the arts of civilized life, and there is scarcely one of them which has not the establishments of schools in the nation, affording, at once, the means of moral, religious, and intellectual improvement. These schools have been established, for the most part, by religious societies, with the countenance and aid of the Government; and, on every principle of humanity, the continuance of similar advantages of education ought to be extended to them in their new residence. There is another point which appears to be indispensable to be guarded, in order to render the condition of this race less afflicting. One of the greatest evils to which they are subject is that incessant pressure of our population, which forces them from seat to seat, without allowing time for that moral and intellectual improvement, for which they appear to be naturally eminently susceptible. To guard against this evil, so fatal to the race, there ought to be the strongest and the most solemn assurance that the country given them should be theirs, as a permanent home for themselves and their posterity, without being disturbed by the encroachments of our citizens. To such assurance, if there should be added a system, by which the Government, without destroying their independence, would gradually unite the several tribes under a simple but enlightened system of government and laws formed on the principles of our own, and to which, as their own people would partake in it, they would, under the influence of the contemplated improvement, at no distant day, become prepared, the arrangements which have been proposed would prove to the Indians and their posterity a permanent blessing.

2. The Cherokees Resist Removal, 1830

We are aware, that some persons suppose it will be for our advantage to remove beyond the Mississippi. We think otherwise. Our people universally think otherwise. Thinking that it would be fatal to their interests, they have almost to a man sent their memorial to congress, deprecating the necessity of a removal. This question was distinctly before their minds when they signed their memorial. Not an adult person can be found, who has not an opinion on the subject, and if the people were to understand distinctly, that they could be protected against the laws of the neighboring states, there is probably not an adult person in the nation, who would think it best to remove; though possibly a few might emigrate individually. There are doubtless many, who would flee to an unknown country, however beset with dangers, privations and sufferings, rather than be sentenced to spend six years in a Georgia prison for advising one of their neighbors not to betray his country. And there are others who could not think of living as outlaws in their native land, exposed to numberless vexations, and excluded from being parties or witnesses in a court of justice. It is incredible that Georgia should ever have enacted the oppressive laws to which reference is here made, unless she had supposed that something extremely terrific in its character was necessary in order to make the Cherokees willing to remove. We are not willing to remove; and if we could be brought to this extremity, it would be not by argument, not because our judgment was satisfied, not because our condition will be improved; but only because we cannot endure to be deprived of our national and individual rights and subjected to a process of intolerable oppression.

We wish to remain on the land of our fathers. We have a perfect and original right to remain without interruption or molestation. The treaties with us, and laws of the United States made in pursuance of treaties, guarantee our residence and our privileges, and secure us against intruders. Our only request is, that these treaties may be fulfilled, and these laws executed. . . .

The removal of families to a new country, even under the most favorable auspices, and when the spirits are sustained by pleasing visions of the future, is attended with much depression of mind and sinking of heart. This is the case, when the removal is a matter of decided preference, and when the persons concerned are in early youth or vigorous manhood. Judge, then, what must be the circumstances of a removal, when a whole community, embracing persons of all classes and every description, from the infant to the man of extreme old age, the sick, the blind, the lame, the improvident, the reckless, the desperate, as well as the prudent, the considerate, the industrious, are compelled to remove by odious and intolerable vexations and persecutions, brought upon them in the forms of law, when all will agree only in this, that they have been cruelly robbed of their country, in violation of the most solemn compacts, which it is possible for communities to form with each other; and that, if they should make themselves comfortable in their new residence, they have nothing to expect hereafter but to be the victims of a future legalized robbery!

Such we deem, and are absolutely certain, will be the feeling of the whole Cherokee people, if they are forcibly compelled, by the laws of Georgia, to remove; and with these feelings, how is it possible that we should pursue our present course of improvement, or avoid sinking into utter despondency? We have been called a poor, ignorant, and degraded people. We certainly are not rich; nor have we ever boasted of our knowledge, or our moral or intellectual elevation. But there is not a man within our limits so ignorant as not to know that he has a right to live on the land of his fathers, in the possession of his immemorial privileges, and that this right has been acknowledged and guaranteed by the United States; nor is there a man so degraded as not to feel a keen sense of injury, on being deprived of this right and driven into exile.

3. Andrew Jackson's Second Annual Message to Congress, 1830

It gives me pleasure to announce to Congress that the benevolent policy of the Government, steadily pursued for nearly thirty years, in relation to the removal of the Indians beyond the white settlements is approaching . . . a happy consummation. Two important tribes, [the Choctaws and the Chickasaws], have accepted the provision made for their removal at the last session of Congress, and it [is] believed that their example will induce the remaining tribes also to seek the same obvious advantages.

The consequences of a speedy removal will be important to the United States, to individual States, and to the Indians themselves. The pecuniary advantages which it promises to the Government are the least of its recommendations. It puts an end to all possible danger of collision between the authorities of the General and State Governments on account of the Indians. It will place a dense and civilized population in large tracts of country now occupied by a few savage hunters. By opening the whole territory between Tennessee on the north and Louisiana on the south to the settlement of the whites it will incalculably strengthen the southwestern frontier and render the adjacent States strong enough to repel future invasions without remote aid. It will relieve the whole State of Mississippi and the western part of Alabama of Indian occupancy, and enable those States to advance rapidly in population, wealth, and power. It will separate the Indians from immediate contact with settlements of whites; free them from the power of the States; enable them to pursue happiness in their own way and under their own rude institutions; will retard the progress of decay, which is lessening their numbers, and perhaps cause them gradually, under the protection of the Government and through the influence of good counsels, to cast off their savage habits and become an interesting, civilized, and Christian community. . . .

It is . . . a duty which this Government owes to the new States to extinguish as soon as possible the Indian title to all lands which Congress themselves have included within their limits. When this is done the duties of the General Government in relation to the States and the Indians within their limits are at an end. The Indians may leave the State or not, as they choose. The purchase of their lands does not alter in the least their personal relations with the State government. No act of the General Government has ever been deemed necessary to give the States jurisdiction over the persons of the Indians. That they possess by virtue of their sovereign power within their own limits in as full a manner before as after the purchase of the Indian lands; nor can this Government add to or diminish it.

4. Christian Missionaries Oppose Removal, 1830

At present many of the Cherokees are dressed as well as the whites around them, and of most of them the manner of dress is *substantially* the same. A part of the old men, perhaps nearly half, retain, not indeed the original Indian dress, but that, nearly, which prevailed a dozen years since. Almost all the younger men have laid it aside. A very few aged women are seen with only a petticoat and short gown, meeting each other at the waist, which, twenty years ago, was the general style of female dress. Except these very few, no woman appears without at least a decent gown, extending from the neck to the feet. . . . If the present course continues, when those who are now in the decline of life shall have passed away, the dress of the Cherokees will scarcely distinguish them from their white neighbors. . . .

Thirty years ago a plough was scarcely seen in the nation. Twenty years ago there were nearly 500. Still the ground was cultivated chiefly by the hoe only. Six years ago the number of ploughs, as enumerated, was 2,923. Among us all, we scarcely know a field which is now cultivated without ploughing. Consequently the quantity of land under cultivation is increased several fold. Habits of industry are much increased, and still increasing. . . .

The diffusion of property among the people is becoming more general.

In no respect, perhaps, is the approach to civilization more evident than in regard to the station assigned to women. Though in this respect there is still room for improvement, yet in general they are allowed to hold their proper place.

Polygamy, which has prevailed to some extent, is becoming rare. It is forbidden by law, but the law being as yet without a penalty annexed, has probably much less influence than public opinion, which makes the practice highly disreputable. A few are still living in a state of polygamy, but at present almost no one enters the state. . . .

In regard to intemperance there is much to deplore, but it is, we believe, an undisputed fact, that its prevalence has greatly diminished, and is still diminishing. Indeed we are confident that, at present, the Cherokees would not suffer in this respect by a comparison with the white population around. . . .

In education we do not know that the progress of the Cherokees should be called rapid. Certainly it is far less so than is desirable. The following facts, however, will serve to correct some misstatements on this subject. We have before us the names of 200 Cherokee men and youths who are believed to have obtained an English education sufficient for the transaction of ordinary business. . . .

Of the number who are able to read their own language in Guess's alphabet we should vary somewhat in our individual estimates. None of us, however, supposes that less than a majority of those who are between childhood and middle age can read with greater or less facility. . . .

In regard to the state of religion we deem it sufficient to state, as nearly as we are able, the number of members of the several religious societies. To the Presbyterian churches belong 219 members, of whom 167 are Cherokees. In the United Brethren's churches are 45 Cherokee members. In the Baptist churches probably about 90; we know not the exact number. The official statement of the Methodist missionaries made a little more than a year ago gave 736 as the number of members in their societies, including those who are denominated seekers. . . .

The [Cherokee] legislature consists of two branches, styled the National Committee and Council, the former numbering 16 members and the latter 24. The presiding officers of both these branches are full Cherokees. . . . No measure can be adopted without the concurrence of both houses, and consequently every public measure has the sanction of a body of which two thirds of the members are of unmixed Indian blood. . . .

One sentiment manifestly pervades the whole nation—that the extension of the laws of the states over them, without their consent, would be a most oppressive and flagrant violation of their natural and conventional rights; and the sufferance of it by the United States, as flagrant a violation of those treaties on which alone they have relied for security. . . .

To us it appears that the Cherokees are in a course of improvement, which promises, if uninterrupted, to place them, at no distant period, nearly on a level with their white brethren. Laboring, as we are, to aid them in their progress, we cannot do otherwise than earnestly deprecate any measure which threatens to arrest it. In this light we view the attempt to remove them from their inheritance, or subject them, against their will, to the dominion of others. Our sympathies are with them.

5. The Supreme Court's Assertion of National Sovereignty, 1832

WORCESTER v. GEORGIA, 1832

The Indian nations had always been considered as distinct, independent political communities, retaining their original natural rights, as the undisputed possessors of the soil, from time immemorial, with the single exception of that imposed by irresistible power, which excluded them from intercourse with any other European potentate than the first discoverer of the coast of the particular region claimed; and this was a restriction which those European potentates imposed on themselves, as well as on the Indians. The very term "nation," so generally applied to them, means "a people distinct from others." The Constitution, by declaring treaties already made, as well as those to be made, to be the supreme law of the land, has adopted and sanctioned the previous treaties with the Indian nations, and consequently admits their rank among those powers who are capable of making treaties. The words "treaty" and "nation" are words of our own language, selected in our diplomatic and legislative proceedings, by ourselves, having each a definite and well understood meaning. We have applied them to Indians, as we have applied them to the other nations of the earth. . . .

The settled doctrine of the law of nations is, that a weaker power does not surrender its independence—its right to self-government, by associating with a stronger, and taking its protection. A weak state, in order to provide for its safety, may place itself under the protection of one more powerful, without stripping itself of the right of government, and ceasing to be a state. Examples of this kind are not wanting in Europe. . . .

The Cherokee nation, then, is a distinct community, occupying its own territory, with boundaries accurately described, in which laws of Georgia can have no force, and which the citizens of Georgia have no right to enter, but with the assent of the Cherokees themselves, or in conformity with treaties, and with the acts of Congress. The whole intercourse between the United States and this nation, is, by our Constitution and laws, vested in the government of the United States.

6. Alexis de Tocqueville Observes Legalism in American Indian Relations, 1864

The development of European habits has been much accelerated among these Indians by the mixed race which has sprung up. Deriving intelligence from the father's side, without entirely losing the savage customs of the mother, the half-blood forms the natural link between civilization and barbarism. Wherever this race has multiplied, the savage state has become modified, and a great change has taken place in the manners of the people.

The success of the Cherokees proves that the Indians are capable of civilization, but it does not prove that they will succeed in it. . . .

From whichever side we consider the destinies of the aborigines of North America, their calamities appear irremediable: if they continue barbarous, they are forced to retire; if they attempt to civilize themselves, the contact of a more civilized community subjects them to oppression and destitution. . . .

The conduct of the Americans of the United States towards the aborigines is characterized, on the other hand, by a singular attachment to the formalities of law. Provided that the Indians retain their barbarous condition, the Americans take no part in their affairs; they treat them as independent nations, and do not possess themselves of their hunting-grounds without a treaty of purchase; and if an Indian nation happen to be so encroached upon as to be unable to subsist upon their territory, they kindly take them by the hand and transport them to a grave far from the land of their fathers.

The Spaniards were unable to exterminate the Indian race by those unparalleled atrocities which brand them with indelible shame, nor did they even succeed in wholly depriving it of its rights; but the Americans of the United States have accomplished this twofold purpose with singular felicity, tranquilly, legally, philanthropically, without shedding blood, and without violating a single great principle of morality in the eyes of the world. It is impossible to destroy men with more respect for the laws of humanity.

Chapter 9:
Document Set 2 References

1. John C. Calhoun Outlines the War Department's Indian Policy, 1825
   "Report of John C. Calhoun to President James Monroe," January 25, 1825, *American State Papers, Indian Affairs* (Washington, D.C., 1834), Vol. 2, pp. 543–544.

2. The Cherokees Resist Removal, 1830
   "Memorial of the Cherokee Nation," *Niles Weekly Register,* Vol. 38 (August 21, 1830), pp. 454–457.

3. Andrew Jackson's Second Annual Message to Congress, 1830
   Andrew Jackson, Second Annual Message, December 6, 1830, in James D. Richardson, ed., A *Compilation of the Messages and Papers of the Presidents, 1789–1897* (Washington, D.C.: Government Printing Office, 1896), Vol. 2, pp. 519–523.

4. Christian Missionaries Oppose Removal, 1830
   The Missionary Herald, Vol. 27 (March 1830), pp. 80–84.

5. The Supreme Court's Assertion of National Sovereignty, 1832
   "Worcester v. Georgia," 1832, Richard Peters, Jr., *Reports of Cases Argued and Adjudged in the Supreme Court, 1828–1824,* Vol. 6, pp. 515–517.

6. Alexis de Tocqueville Observes Legalism in American Indian Relations, 1864
   Alexis de Tocqueville, *Democracy in America,* Reeve-Bowen trans. (Cambridge: Sever and Francis, 1864), Vol. 1, pp. 345–355.

DOCUMENT SET 1
The New Politics of Popular Sovereignty: Andrew Jackson and the "Language of Democracy"

A key theme in Chapter 10 is the rise of popular partici-pation in politics and government after the War of 1812. One important result of the democratization of American life was what many Americans perceived as a trend to-ward economic and social equality that matched the new political atmosphere. As white male suffrage be-came broader and the Democratic-Republican party fragmented into sectional wings, new political figures emerged to compete for national leadership. None was more significant or successful than the western favorite, war hero Andrew Jackson, whose presidential victory in 1828 was the climax of the new popular sovereignty in politics. As your textbook notes, Jackson's election was widely interpreted as a class triumph of democratic forces over entrenched economic aristocracy.

Despite the fact that Jackson was a slaveholder, landowner, and wealthy man, his supporters regarded him as the living embodiment of the American dream. A self-made man, his economic and political successes seemed to confirm the reality of open economic oppor-tunity in a fluid frontier society. To bolster this percep-tion, Jackson and his followers practiced an early ver-sion of "the politics of symbolism." Emphasizing Jackson's popular image as a simple, natural, rough-hewn westerner, they successfully appealed to the common citizen. As historian Marvin Myers has ob-served, Jacksonian strategists succeeded in develop-ing a "language of democracy" that was instrumental in strengthening and maintaining the president's popular appeal throughout a stormy political career.

The following documents emphasize the symbolic language that aided Jackson and the emerging Democratic party during the turbulent 1830s. Perhaps the clearest illustration of the Jacksonian attack on privilege can be found in his bold veto of the recharter of the Bank of the United States. As you analyze the evidence, note the prominent position of the bank issue in the rhetoric of democracy. Link the textbook coverage of the bank war to the evolving democratic ideology evident in the documents. In a wider sense, consider the relationship between economic equality and political freedom in the other statements of dem-ocratic thought in this set of documents, such as the republicanism of *The Democratic Review* and the earthy conversation between U.S. senators reported by foreign observer Francis Grund.

Finally, notice that by 1840, the Whigs had learned to employ the "language of democracy" in their own campaign materials. The pen advertisement for William Henry Harrison explicitly focuses attention on the Whig candidate's allegedly humble origins, while a political cartoon portrays a newly elected Harrison preparing to clear the kitchen of special interests identified with the vanquished Martin Van Buren's administration.

As you review these materials, be aware of the re-lationship between rhetoric and political success. Your goal should be to gain a clearer understanding of the often used but infrequently analyzed term *Jacksonian democracy.*

Questions for Analysis

1. What do the veto message and Jackson's farewell address reveal about the eco-nomic, social, and political assumptions of Jacksonian Democrats? How did Jackson's opponents regard the president's economic decisions? How would you account for these differences?

2. As you review the evidence, what reasons do you see for Jackson's popularity? What is meant by the phrase "language of democracy," and how does it help to explain Jackson's political strength?

3. Examine the documents for indications of Jackson's understanding of the exec-utive-legislative relationship. What distinguished the Jackson presidency with re-gard to the exercise of executive authority?

4. Using your textbook as a resource, analyze the changes in the American politi-cal party system that occurred between 1824 and 1840. What do the documents reveal about Jackson's role in those alterations? How do party politics them-selves change in this period? Why?

5. A term used frequently in the documents is *republicanism.* What was the meaning of this term to Americans of the 1830s? What does the emphasis on this concept reveal about the values and goals of politicians and the voters to whom they appealed? How did the social and economic background of each writer in the document set affect the way the term *republicanism* was used?

6. What was the Whig response to Jacksonian democracy? What was the Whig model for effective government? How did Whigs and Democrats differ in their political philosophies? Compare their campaign appeals.

1. "The Hunters of Kentucky" and the Jackson Image, ca. 1820s

1. Ye gentlemen and ladies fair,
   Who grace this famous city,
   Just listen if you've time to spare,
   While I rehearse a ditty;
   And for the opportunity
   Conceive yourselves quite lucky,
   For 'tis not often that you see
   A hunter from Kentucky
   O Kentucky, the hunters of Kentucky!
   O Kentucky, the hunters of Kentucky!

2. We are a hardy, free-born race,
   Each man to fear a stranger;
   Whate'er the game we join in chase,
   Despising toil and danger,
   And if a daring foe annoys,
   Whate'er his strength and forces,
   We'll show him that Kentucky boys
   Are alligator horses.
   Oh Kentucky, &c.

3. I s'pose you've read it in the prints,
   How Packenham attempted
   To make old Hickory Jackson wince,
   But soon his scheme repented;
   For we with rifles ready cock'd,
   Thought such occasion lucky,
   And soon around the gen'ral flock'd
   The Hunters of Kentucky.
   Oh Kentucky, &c.

4. You've heard, I s'pose how New-Orleans
   Is fam'd for wealth and beauty,
   There's girls of ev'ry hue it seems,
   From snowy white to sooty.
   So Packenham he made his brags,
   If he in fight was lucky,
   He'd have their girls and cotton bags,
   In spite of old Kentucky.
   Oh Kentucky, &c.

5. But Jackson he was wide awake,
   And was not scar'd at trifles,
   For well he knew what aim we take
   With our Kentucky rifles.
   So he led us down to Cypress swamp,
   The ground was low and mucky,
   There stood John Bull in martial pomp
   And here was old Kentucky.
   Oh Kentucky, &c.

6. A bank was rais'd to hide our breasts,
   Not that we thought of dying,
   But that we always like to rest,
   Unless the game is flying.
   Behind it stood our little force,
   None wished it to be greater,
   For ev'ry man was half a horse,
   And half an alligator.
   Oh Kentucky, &c.

7. They did not let our patience tire,
   Before they showed their faces;
   We did not choose to waste our fire,
   So snugly kept our places.
   But when so near we saw them wink,
   We thought it time to stop 'em,
   And 'twould have done you good I think,
   To see Kentuckians drop 'em.
   Oh Kentucky, &c.

8. They found, at last, 'twas vain to fight,
   Where *lead* was all the *booty,*
   And so they wisely took to flight,
   And left *us* all our *beauty.*
   And now if danger e'er annoys,
   Remember what our trade is,
   Just send for us Kentucky boys,
   And we'll protect ye, ladies.
   Oh Kentucky, &c.

2. The Downfall of Mother Bank, 1833

President Jackson removes federal deposits from the national bank as Whig politicians, including bank president Nicholas Biddle, are crushed beneath the bank pillars. Newspapers supported by the bank are caught in the confusion.
By "Zek Downing"

3. Jackson's Bank Veto: A Campaign Document, 1832

The bill "to modify and continue" the act entitled "An act to incorporate the subscribers to the Bank of the United States" was presented to me on the 4th July instant. Having considered it with that solemn regard to the principles of the Constitution which the day was calculated to inspire, and come to the conclusion that it ought not to become a law, I herewith return it to the Senate, in which it originated, with my objections. . . .

But this act does not permit competition in the purchase of this monopoly [the bank]. It seems to be predicated on the erroneous idea that the present stockholders have a prescriptive right not only to the favor but to the bounty of Government. It appears that more than a fourth part of the stock is held by foreigners and the residue is held by a few hundred of our own citizens, chiefly of the richest class. For their benefit does this act exclude the whole American people from competition in the purchase of this monopoly and dispose of it for many millions less than it is worth. This seems the less excusable because some of our citizens not now stockholders petitioned that the door of competition might be opened, and offered to take a charter on terms much more favorable to the Government and country. . . .

It is to be regretted that the rich and powerful too often bend the acts of government to their selfish purposes. Distinctions in society will always exist under every just government. Equality of talents, of education, or of wealth can not be produced by human institutions. In the full enjoyment of the gifts of Heaven and the fruits of superior industry, economy, and virtue, every man is equally entitled to protection by law; but when the laws undertake to add to these natural and just advantages artificial distinctions, to grant titles, gratuities, and exclusive privileges, to make the rich richer and the potent more powerful, the humble members of society—the farmers, mechanics, and laborers—who have neither the time nor the means of securing like favors to themselves, have a right to complain of the injustice of their Government. There are no necessary evils in government. Its evils exist only in its abuses. If it would confine itself to equal protection, and, as Heaven does its rains, shower its favors alike on the high and the low, the rich and the poor, it would be an unqualified blessing. In the act before me there

seems to be a wide and unnecessary departure from these just principles. . . .

Many of our rich men have not been content with equal protection and equal benefits, but have besought us to make them richer by act of Congress. By attempting to gratify their desires we have in the results of our legislation arrayed section against section, interest against interest, and man against man, in a fearful commotion which threatens to shake the foundations of our Union. It is time to pause in our career to review our principles, and if possible revive that devoted patriotism and spirit of compromise which distinguished the sages of the Revolution and the fathers of our Union. If we can not at once, in justice to interests vested under improvident legislation, make our Government what it ought to be, we can at least take a stand against all new grants of monopolies and exclusive privileges, against any prostitution of our Government to the advancement of the few at the expense of the many, and in favor of compromise and gradual reform in our code of laws and system of political economy.

4. Jackson's Farewell Address, 1837

We are not left to conjecture how the moneyed power, thus organized and with such a weapon in its hands, would be likely to use it. The distress and alarm which pervaded and agitated the whole country when the Bank of the United States waged war upon the people in order to compel them to submit to its demands cannot yet be forgotten. The ruthless and unsparing temper with which whole cities and communities were oppressed, individuals impoverished and ruined, and a scene of cheerful prosperity suddenly changed into one of gloom and despondency ought to be indelibly impressed on the memory of the people of the United States.

If such was its power in a time of peace, what would it not have been in a season of war with an enemy at your doors? No nation but the freemen of the United States could have come out victorious from such a contest; yet, if you had not conquered, the government would have passed from the hands of the many to the hands of the few; and this organized money power, from its secret conclave, would have dictated the choice of your highest officers and com-

pelled you to make peace or war as best suited their own wishes. The forms of your government might, for a time, have remained; but its living spirit would have departed from it. . . .

Defeated in the general government, the same class of intriguers and politicians will now resort to the states and endeavor to obtain there the same organization which they failed to perpetuate in the Union; and with specious and deceitful plans of public advantages and state interests and state pride they will endeavor to establish, in the different states, one moneyed institution with overgrown capital and exclusive privileges sufficient to enable it to control the operations of the other banks.

Such an institution will be pregnant with the same evils produced by the Bank of the United States, although its sphere of action is more confined; and in the state in which it is chartered the money power will be able to embody its whole strength and to move together with undivided force to accomplish any object it may wish to attain. You have already had abundant evidence of its power to inflict injury upon the agricultural, mechanical, and laboring classes of society, and over those whose engagements in trade or speculation render them dependent on bank facilities, the dominion of the state monopoly will be absolute, and their obedience unlimited. With such a bank and a paper currency, the money power would, in a few years, govern the state and control its measures; and if a sufficient number of states can be induced to create such establishments, the time will soon come when it will again take the field against the United States and succeed in perfecting and perpetuating its organization by a charter from Congress.

It is one of the serious evils of our present system of banking that it enables one class of society, and that by no means a numerous one, by its control over the currency to act injuriously upon the interests of all the others and to exercise more than its just proportion of influence in political affairs. The agricultural, the mechanical, and the laboring classes have little or no share in the direction of the great moneyed corporations; and from their habits and the nature of their pursuits, they are incapable of forming extensive combinations to act together with united force. . . .

The planter, the farmer, the mechanic, and the laborer all know that their success depends upon their own industry and economy and that they must not expect to become suddenly rich by the fruits of their toil. Yet these classes of society form the great body of the people of the United States; they are the bone and sinew of the country; men who love liberty and desire nothing but equal rights and equal laws and who, moreover, hold the great mass of our national wealth.

5. Two Senators Explain Why They Support Jackson, 1839

"General Jackson," said one of the senators, "understands the people of the United States twenty times better than his antagonists; and, if his successor have but half the same tact, the Whigs may give up the hope of governing the country for the next half century."

"You ought not to say '*tact*,'" interrupted the other senator, "for that alone will not do it; he must have the same manners as our present President. General Jackson has a peculiar way of addressing himself to the feelings of every man with whom he comes in contact. His simple unostentatious manners carry into every heart the conviction of his honesty; while the firmness of his character inspires his friends with the hope of success. . . . "

"Precisely so," ejaculated the [first] member. "General Jackson is popular, just because he is General Jackson; so much so, that if a man were to say a word against him in the Western States, he would be '*knocked into eternal smash.*'"

". . . The appearance of General Jackson was a phenomenon, and would at the present time have been one in every country. He called himself 'the people's friend,' and gave proofs of his sincerity and firmness in *adhering* to his friends, and of his power to protect them. The people believed in General Jackson as much as the Turks in their prophet, and would have followed him wherever he chose to lead them. . . .

"In the same manner it has been said of General Jackson that he is incapable of writing a good English sentence, as if this were the standard by which to measure the capacity of a political chief, especially in America, where, out of a hundred senators and representatives, scarcely one has received what in Europe would be called a literary education. . . . General Jackson understood the people of the United States better than, perhaps, any President before him, and developed as much energy in his administration as any American statesman. . . . "

"You have spoken my very heart," cried the other senator. "I Like *Old Hickory*, because he is just the man for the people, and as immovable as a rock. One always knows where to find him."

"He is just the man our party wanted," rejoined the first senator, "in order to take the lead."

"And I like Old Ironhead," said the member, "because he is a man after my own sort. When he once says he is your friend, he *is* your friend; but once your enemy, then *look out for breakers.*"

6. John L. O'Sullivan Defines Republicanism, 1837

We believe, then, in the principle of *democratic republicanism,* in its strongest and purest sense. We have an abiding confidence in the virtue, intelligence, and full capacity for self-government of the great mass of our people—our industrious, honest, manly, intelligent millions of freemen.

We are opposed to all self-styled "wholesome restraints" on the free action of the popular opinion and will, other than those which have for their sole object the prevention of precipitate legislation. This latter object is to be attained by the expedient of the division of power, and by causing all legislation to pass through the ordeal of successive forms; to be sifted through the discussions of coordinate legislative branches, with mutual suspensive veto powers. Yet all should be dependent with equal directness and promptness on the influence of public opinion; the popular will should be equally the animating and moving spirit of them all. . . .

In the first place, the greatest number are *more likely,* at least as a general rule, to understand and follow their own greatest good than is the minority.

In the second, a minority is much more likely to abuse power for the promotion of its own selfish interests, at the expense of the majority of numbers—the substantial and producing mass of the nation—than the latter is to oppress unjustly the former. The social evil is also, in that case, proportionately greater. This is abundantly proved by the history of all aristocratic interests that have existed, in various degrees and modifications, in the world. A majority cannot subsist upon a minority; while the natural, and in fact uniform, tendency of a minority entrusted with governmental authority is to surround itself with wealth, splendor, and power, at the expense of the producing mass, creating and perpetuating those artificial social distinctions which violate the natural equality of rights of the human race, and at the same time offend and degrade the true dignity of human nature.

In the third place, there does not naturally exist any such original superiority of a minority class above the great mass of a community in intelligence and competence for the duties of government. . . .

We are willing to make every reform in our institutions that may be commanded by the test of the democratic principle—to *democratize* them—but only so rapidly as shall appear, to the most cautious wisdom, consistent with a due regard to the existing development of public opinion and to the permanence of the progress made. . . .

For democracy is the cause of humanity. It has faith in human nature. It believes in its essential equality and fundamental goodness. It respects, with a solemn reverence to which the proudest artificial institutions and distinctions of society have no claim, the human soul. It is the cause of philanthropy. Its object is to emancipate the mind of the mass of men from the degrading and disheartening fetters of social distinctions and advantages; to bid it walk abroad through the free creation "in its own majesty"; to war against all fraud, oppression, and violence; by striking at their root, to reform all the infinitely varied human misery which has grown out of the old and false ideas by which the world has been so long misgoverned.

7. John Pendleton Kennedy Outlines Whig Political Philosophy, 1844

The calm and philosophic temper of Mr. Madison, the purity of his character, the sincerity of his patriotism, and the sagacity of his intellect had inspired universal trust—except, perhaps, in a few Federalists, in whose minds an ancient grudge yet rankled. With this exception, a balmy peace reigned throughout our political world. The extremes of Federalism had been tempered with an infusion of democratic flavor; the extremes of Democracy had been melted in an amalgam of Federalism. Both were the better for it. Above all, the Constitution was settled; its Whig basis strengthened; and many men thought that, from that day, it was a book interpreted and certain. Truly, I think that the Constitution of the United States, as expounded and practised by Marshall and Madison, is the very Constitution of our forefathers! I desire no farther commentary: from that day forth it has been to me an article of faith: my creed therein is written.

This was the glory of Mr. Madison's administration, that it made peace between parties; that it established the true import of our fundamental law; and that it marked out the administrative policy of this people, both in their outward relations and in their domestic affairs. The Madisonian basis of the American government and policy may be regarded as one established by the almost universal consent of the country. It was wise, being the product of careful thought and just consideration of the temper and aims of our people: it was likely to be permanent, because it grew out of a calm and dispassionate state of public feeling, auspicious to durable settlements. An experience of twelve years, from 1816 to 1829, has proved it to be eminently calculated to advance the comfort, the prosperity, and the strength of the people.

First. It settled the construction and practice of the Constitution on the foundation of the Whig doctrines: this construction and practice was chiefly manifested in the high respect and confidence of the nation in the Legislative Power, and the scrupulous adherence of the executive to its orbit.

Second. It settled the policy of the Government. Witness these measures:

It regulated the Currency by the control of a National Bank, and, through this instrumentality, checked and finally removed the mischief of excessive State Banking.

It protected the Domestic Industry of our people, by the establishment of a Tariff of Duties specially directed to that object.

It promoted Internal Improvements in the nation, by giving the aid of government to useful enterprises which were beyond the capacity of individual States; a policy which, if it had not been since abandoned, would have saved the country that load of State debt which has become of late almost equally our misfortune and our disgrace.

It enlarged the sphere of our Commerce and Navigation, by tendering to foreign nations reciprocal privileges of trade restricted within certain limits defined in the legislation of 1815, and in the Convention of London of that year.

It devised the plan for paying off the public debt.

It placed the public expenditures upon the footing of a strict economy.

It discountenanced and subdued all attempts to connect office with the means of political influence; and left the public servant free from that odious inquisition into his opinions which has since made him either the victim or the confederate of spies and informers.

In short, its whole scheme of administration was national, American, liberal and honorable. It infused that sentiment into the mind of the people, and rendered them, everywhere, throughout all classes, honorable, high-minded, and patriotic.

This was the inheritance to which Mr. Monroe, and, in due succession, Mr. Adams succeeded. They conscientiously adhered to this truly republican, equal and beneficent system of administration. The consequence was a progressive increase in every element of national happiness. Under the working of this system the nation gradually arose to a state of unexampled vigor. The havoc of the war was slowly but surely repaired. The currency, from a state of extraordinary derangement, was brought into singular purity. Manufactures and the mechanic arts were rapidly trained from a feeble infancy to a robustness almost incredible. Commerce and navigation were increased; the war debt was paid; and that series of internal improvements begun which, however they may have involved those who constructed them in debt, are worth more to this Union than ten times the cost expended upon them. They are works from which the National Treasury should never have been withheld: they are works which now belong more to the people of the United States than to the States in whose borders they lie, and for which the People of the Union are equitably and honorably the true debtors: they are works which, by a policy as cruel as it was unstatesmanlike, were ever committed to the unassisted enterprise of the States.

This is the outline of the Whig doctrine in reference to the fundamental characteristics of our government, and also of its policy.

The Whigs stand emphatically upon the Madisonian platform.

8. The Whigs Learn the "Language of Democracy," 1840

A. The Log Cabin Image

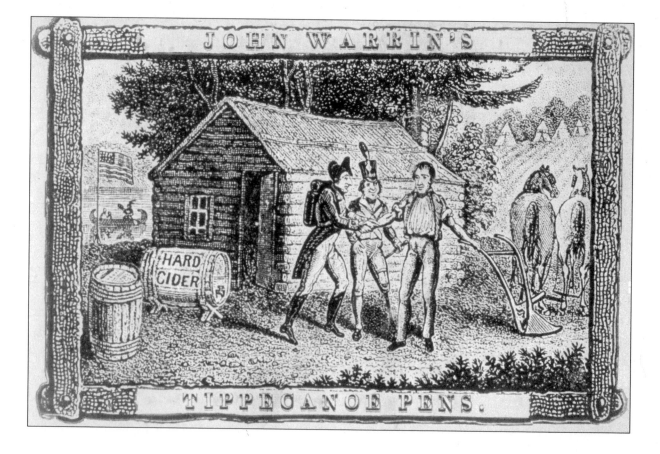

B. The Whig Vision of Martin Van Buren as Aristocrat

A BEAUTIFUL GOBLET OF WHITE HOUSE CHAMPAGNE

AN UGLY MUG OF LOG-CABIN HARD CIDER

C. President-Elect William Henry Harrison
Prepares to Rout Democratic Special
Interests

Chapter 10:
Document Set 1 References

1. "The Hunters of Kentucky" and the Jackson Image, ca. 1820s
   "The Hunters of Kentucky," ca. 1820s, John William Ward, *Andrew Jackson: Symbol for an Age* (New York: Oxford University Press, 1962), pp. 217–218.

2. The Downfall of Mother Bank, 1833
   Cartoon published by H. R. Robinson, in Allan Nevins and Frank Weitenkampf, *A Century of Political Cartoons* (1944), p. 39.

3. Jackson's Bank Veto: A Campaign Document, 1832
   Andrew Jackson, Veto Message, in James D. Richardson, ed., *A Compilation of the Messages and Papers of the Presidents, 1789–1897* (Washington, D.C.: Government Printing Office, 1896), Vol. 2, pp. 576–577, 590–591.

4. Jackson's Farewell Address, 1837
   Andrew Jackson, *Farewell Address of Andrew Jackson to the People of the United States and the Inaugural Address of Martin Van Buren, President of the United States* (1837), pp. 3–16, in *The Annals of America* (Chicago: Encyclopaedia Britannica, 1968), Vol. 6, pp. 307–308.

5. Two Senators Explain Why They Support Jackson, 1839
   Francis J. Grund. *Aristocracy in America* (London: 1839), Vol. 2, pp. 239–246.

6. John L. O'Sullivan Defines Republicanism, 1837
   John L. O'Sullivan, "The Democratic Principle," *United States Magazine and Democratic Review* (October 1837).

7. John Pendleton Kennedy Outlines Whig Political Philosophy, 1844
   John Pendleton Kennedy, *Defense of the Whigs, by a Member of the Twenty-Seventh Congress* (New York, 1844), pp. 12–24.

8. The Whigs Learn the "Language of Democracy," 1840
   A. The Log Cabin Image
   "John Warren's Tippecanoe Pens," 1840, in Keith Melder, *Hail to the Candidate: Presidential Campaigns from Banners to Broadcasts* (Washington, D.C.: Smithsonian Institution Press, 1992), p. 35.
   B. The Whig Vision of Martin Van Buren as Aristocrat
   "A Beautiful Collet of White House Champagne" and "An Ugly Mug of Log Cabin Hard Cider," 1840, in Melder, p. 86.
   C. President-Elect William Henry Harrison Prepares to Rout Democratic Special Interests
   "Clar De Kitchen," 1840, Cartoon Published by H. R. Robinson, in Nevins and Weitenkampf, p. 55.

Chapter 10:
Document Set 1 Credits

2. Courtesy, American Antiquarian Society
8. A. Division of Political History, Smithsonian Institution Photo No. S64-77
   B. *(both)* Division of Political History, National Museum of American History, Smithsonian Institution Photos Nos. S80-3968 and S80-3967
   C. The Granger Collection

CHAPTER 10

Revivalism and Social Activism: The Roots of Reform

The democratization of American politics was matched by the rise of popular religion, discussed in Chapter 10 of your textbook. Just as political participation had increased by the 1830s, large numbers of common people also had become engaged in participatory religious experience. As a result of the revivalism associated with the Second Great Awakening, legions of Christian converts broke with the formalism of elite religion to rededicate themselves to a higher morality that seemed to lead toward a democratic hereafter.

The key figure in the new revivalism was the charismatic Presbyterian minister Charles Grandison Finney, whose revivals throughout New York's "burned over district" shook the foundations of establishment religion in the 1820s and 1830s. Finney was a controversial figure whose ideas and successes made him the leading evangelical of his generation.

Not only does your text emphasize religious experimentalism in the age of Jackson, but it also links the evangelical movement with the trend toward social reform. Mass participation in religious revivals, especially by women, guaranteed dedicated recruits for the struggle to rid a suffering society of numerous social evils. The "perfectionist" doctrine that men and women could live without sin gave a powerful impetus to social reforms, and revivalism clearly contributed to the reformers' intense moralism.

The varieties of reform experience are evident in your textbook's description of the "age of reform." Similarly, the following documents mirror the richness of antebellum social reform. As you examine them, focus on the link between religious revivalism and the drive to purify the nation's social institutions. In addition, identify characteristics of revivalism unique to frontier religion, including those aspects of revivalism which drew the attention of the critics. Examine the relationship between social reform and the character of frontier society and culture, and try to account for the multiplicity of proposed solutions to the nation's social problems. At all times, be aware of the writer's background and purposes as you interpret a document's social meaning.

Questions for Analysis

1. Are there unifying themes in the writings of the social reformers? What broad goals did they share? What insight do the documents provide about American culture in the 1830s, 1840s, and 1850s?

2. As you examine the writings of religious revivalists, can you identify ideas that challenged the accepted social values of antebellum America? Why were frontier dwellers so attracted to revivals, such as the meeting described by German-born scholar Francis Lieber? Was there anything uniquely American about frontier religion? What were the underlying concerns behind the writings of the critics?

3. What was the relationship between religion and American democracy? What is the link between the evidence presented in Document Sets 1 and 2? Do you see any relationship between frontier revivalism and modern evangelical religion?

4. Several documents reveal that women were activists in the revivals and reform movements of the 1830s, 1840s, and 1850s. How would you account for this enlarged social and political role? Do the documents contain clues to the prominence of women in these movements?

5. The documents reveal a strong interest among revivalists and reformers in the problem of alcohol. Temperance advocate Timothy Shays Arthur's novel, *Ten Nights in a Bar-Room and What I Saw There,* reveals problems similar to those warned against by an Episcopal bishop, Charles P. McIlvaine of Ohio. What is the solution advanced by each? What problems regarding personal liberties did their solutions raise? What justified the radical prescription proposed? What link do these documents suggest between revivalism and reform?

1. Charles G. Finney Defines Revivalism, 1834

Religion is the work of man. It is something for man to do. It consists in obeying God with and from the heart. It is man's duty. It is true; God induces him to do it. He influences him by His Spirit, because of his great wickedness and reluctance to obey. If it were not necessary for God to influence men, if men were disposed to obey God, there would be no occasion to pray, "O Lord, revive thy work." The ground of necessity for such a prayer is that men are wholly indisposed to obey; and unless God interpose the influence of His Spirit, not a man on earth will ever obey the commands of God. . . .

It is the renewal of the first love of Christians, resulting in the awakening and conversion of sinners to God. In the popular sense, a revival of religion in a community is the arousing, quickening, and reclaiming of the more or less backslidden church and the more or less general awakening of all classes and insuring attention to the claims of God.

It presupposes that the church is sunk down in a backslidden state, and a revival consists in the return of the church from her backslidings and in the conversion of sinners.

1. A revival always includes conviction of sin on the part of the church. Backslidden professors cannot wake up and begin right away in the service of God without deep searchings of heart. The fountains of sin need to be broken up. In a true revival, Christians are always brought under such convictions; they see their sins in such a light that often they find it impossible to maintain a hope of their acceptance with God. . . .

2. Backslidden Christians will be brought to repentance. A revival is nothing else than a new beginning of obedience to God. Just as in the case of a converted sinner, the first step is a deep repentance, a breaking down of heart, a getting down into the dust before God, with deep humility and forsaking of sin.

3. Christians will have their faith renewed. While they are in their backslidden state they are blind to the state of sinners. Their hearts are as hard as marble. The truths of the Bible only appear like a dream. . . . But when they enter into a revival, they no longer see men as trees walking, but they see things in that strong light which will renew the love of God in their hearts. . . . And they will set themselves feelingly to persuade their neighbors to give Him their hearts. So their love to men will be renewed. They will be filled with a tender and burning love for souls. They will have a longing desire for the salvation of the whole world. They will be in agony for individuals whom they want to have saved: their friends, relations, enemies. . . .

4. A revival breaks the power of the world and of sin over Christians. It brings them to such vantage ground that they get a fresh impulse toward heaven. They have a new foretaste of heaven and new desires after union to God; and the charm of the world is broken and the power of sin overcome.

5. When the churches are thus awakened and reformed, the reformation and salvation of sinners will follow, going through the same stages of conviction, repentance, and reformation. Their hearts will be broken down and changed. Very often the most abandoned profligates are among the subjects. Harlots, and drunkards, and infidels, and all sorts of abandoned characters, are awakened and converted. The worst part of human society is softened and reclaimed, and made to appear as a lovely specimen of the beauty of holiness. . . .

What sinners do is to submit to the truth or to resist it. It is a mistake of sinners to think they are using means for their own conversion. The whole drift of a revival, and everything about it, is designed to present the truth to your mind for your obedience or resistance.

2. Francis Lieber Reacts to Religious Enthusiasm, 1835

After having listened to their singing, exhorting, praying and violent preaching, we entered one of the tents, which distinguished itself by a greater noise, and wilder devotional exercise, at nearly two o'clock in the morning. The air was pestilential; the dust

from pulverized straw and particles of dried earth very thick; the general appearance of the whole was similar to that of a room in an insane hospital, but even more frightful; the same motions of the limbs, expressions of faces, and fearful noise. Some were seen rubbing their hands, apparently in great agony, others clapping them together, others stretching them out toward heaven, and distorting their eyes, some stamping with the feet, some rubbing their knees, some moving the upper part of the body forward and backward, others screaming, and weeping, surrounded by a number of friends, who prevented the small current of air, which yet existed, from reaching them, and sung and spoke into their ears; some leaping up and down, with staring eyes, their hair dishevelled, others, lying on the ground, distended as if in a swoon, some sitting in a state of perfect exhaustion and inanity, with pale cheeks and vacant eyes, which bore traces of many tears. One before all, was lying on his knees, apparently in a state of great agony, and uttering the expressions of a desponding soul, addressed to a wrathful God. . . .

At nine o'clock on Saturday morning, a procession was formed, when each member shook hands with each minister. We had then a sight of every individual, and I was horror-struck at the dire expression of many countenances among those who came up.

Some continued their distortions and frightful movements even in this procession, some looked down, many girls cried, and looked shockingly worn out. Beware, beware ye who promote this fanaticism, what you are enacting—literally the most revolting physical and mental mischief, to the advancement of ignorance and the depriving your fellow-beings of the choicest blessing—peace of spirit, and an enlightened mind.

There are many reasons, physical, moral and political, by which we must explain the great religious excitement now prevailing in the United States. . . .

The American is an independent being; his government is founded upon an appeal to the reason of every individual, and as there is nothing in human life—no principle of action, no disposition or custom which forms an isolated part of his being, but must necessarily send its ramifications in every direction through his whole character, so also this spirit of independence, although productive of much good in many respects, induces the American sometimes to act for himself, in circumstances where he cannot have sufficient knowledge or experience to guide him.

3. Bishop McIlvaine Decries the Curse of Intemperance, 1830s

It cannot be denied that our country is most horribly scourged by intemperance. In the strong language of Scripture: "it groaneth and travaileth in pain, to be delivered from the bondage of this corruption." . . . [I]t cannot be denied that our country is enslaved [by intemperance]. Yes, we are groaning under a most desolating bondage. The land is trodden down under its polluting foot. Our families are continually dishonored, ravaged, and bereaved; thousands annually slain and hundreds of thousands carried away into a loathsome slavery, to be ground to powder under its burdens or broken upon the wheel of its tortures. . . .

Another assertion is equally unquestionable. *The time has come when a great effort must be made to exterminate this unequaled destroyer.* It was high time this was done when the first drunkard entered eternity to receive the award of Him who has declared that no drunkard shall enter the kingdom of God. The demand for this effort has been growing in the peremptory tone of its call, as "the overflowing scourge" has passed with constantly extending sweep through the land. But a strange apathy has prevailed among us. As if the whole nation had been drinking the cup of delu-

sion, we saw the enemy coming in like a flood and we lifted up scarcely a straw against him. . . .

There is but one possible answer. *Persuade people to use none at all. Total abstinence* is the only plan on which reformation can be hoped for. We are shut up to this. We have tried the consequences of encouraging people to venture but moderately into the atmosphere of infection; and we are now convinced that it was the very plan to feed its strength and extend its ravages. We are forced to the conclusion that to arrest the pestilence we must starve it. All the healthy must abstain from its neighborhood. All those who are now temperate must give up the use of the means of intemperance. The deliverance of this land from its present degradation and from the increasing woes attendant on this vice depends altogether upon the extent to which the principle of total abstinence shall be adopted by our citizens. . . .

In order to exert ourselves with the best effect in the promotion of the several objects in this great cause to which young men should apply themselves, let us associate ourselves into *temperance societies.*

We know the importance of associated exertions. We have often seen how a few instruments, severally weak, have become mighty when united. Every work, whether for evil or benevolent purposes, has felt the life, and spur, and power of cooperation. The whole progress of the temperance reformation, thus far, is owing to the influence of *societies;* to the coming together of the temperate and the union of their resolutions, examples, and exertions under the articles of temperance societies.

4. Ten Nights in a Bar-Room, 1854

On taking the chair, Mr. Hargrove made a brief address, something to this effect.

"Ten years ago," said he, his voice evincing a light unsteadiness as he began, but growing firmer as he proceeded, "there was not a happier spot in Bolton county than Cedarville. Now, the marks of ruin are everywhere. Ten years ago, there was a kindhearted, industrious miller in Cedarville, liked by every one, and as harmless as a little child. Now, his bloated, disfigured body lies in that room. His death was violent, and by the hand of his own son!" . . .

"Shall I go on? Shall I call up and pass in review before you, one after another, all the wretched victims who have fallen in Cedarville during the last ten years? Time does not permit. It would take hours for the enumeration! No: I will not throw additional darkness into the picture. Heaven knows it is black enough already! But what is the root of this great evil? Where lies the fearful secret? Who understands the disease? A direful pestilence is in the air—it walketh in darkness, and wasteth at noonday. It is slaying the firstborn in our houses, and the cry of anguish is swelling on every gale. Is there no remedy?"

"Yes! yes! There is a remedy!" was the spontaneous answer from many voices.

"Be it our task, then, to find and apply it this night," answered the chairman as he took his seat.

"And there is but one remedy," said Morgan, as Mr. Hargrove sat down. "The accursed traffic must cease among us. You must cut off the fountain, if you would dry up the stream. If you would save the young, the weak, and the innocent—on you God has laid the solemn duty of their protection—you must cover them from the tempter. . . .

"Be it resolved by the inhabitants of Cedarville, That from this day henceforth, no more intoxicating drink shall be sold within the limits of the corporation.

"Resolved, further, That all the liquors in the 'Sickle and Sheath' be forthwith destroyed, and that a fund be raised to pay the creditors of Simon Slade, therefor, should they demand compensation.

"Resolved, That in closing up all other places where liquor is sold, regard shall be had to the right of property which the law secures to every man.

"Resolved, That with the consent of the legal authorities, all the liquor for sale in Cedarville be destroyed; provided the owners thereof be paid its full value out of a fund specially raised for that purpose." . . .

[G]ood sense and reason prevailed. Somewhat modified, the resolution passed, and the more ultra-inclined contented themselves with carrying out the second resolution, to destroy forthwith all liquor to be found on the premises; which was immediately done. After which the people dispersed to their homes, each with a lighter heart, and better hopes for the future of their village.

5. William Lloyd Garrison Justifies Organization Against Slavery, 1833

Whereas the Most High God "hath made of one blood all nations of men to dwell on all the face of the earth," and hath commanded them to love their neighbors as themselves;

and whereas, our National Existence is based upon this principle, as recognized in the Declaration of Independence, "that all mankind are created equal, and that they are endowed by their Creator with certain inalienable rights, among which are life, liberty, and the pursuit of happiness";

and whereas, after the lapse of nearly sixty years, since the faith and honor of the American people were pledged to this avowal, before Almighty God and the World, nearly one-sixth part of the nation are held in bondage by their fellow-citizens;

and whereas, Slavery is contrary to the principles of natural justice, of our republican form of government, and of the Christian religion, and is destructive of the prosperity of the country, while it is endangering the peace, union, and liberties of the States;

and whereas, we believe it the duty and interest of the masters immediately to emancipate their slaves, and that no scheme of expatriation, either voluntary or by compulsion, can remove this great and increasing evil;

and whereas, we believe that it is practicable, by appeals to the consciences, hearts, and interests of the people, to awaken a public sentiment throughout the nation that will be opposed to the continuance of Slavery in any part of the Republic, and by effecting the speedy abolition of Slavery, prevent a general convulsion;

and whereas, we believe we owe it to the oppressed, to our fellow-citizens who hold slaves, to our whole country, to posterity, and to God, to do all that is lawfully in our power to bring about the extinction of Slavery, we do hereby agree, with a prayerful reliance on the Divine aid, to form ourselves into a society, to be governed by the following Constitution:—

ART. I.—This Society shall be called the AMERICAN ANTI-SLAVERY SOCIETY.

6. Garrison Renounces War, 1838

We register our testimony, not only against all wars, whether offensive or defensive, but all preparations for war; against every naval ship, every arsenal, every fortification; against the militia system and a standing army; against all military chieftains and soldiers; . . . .

We believe that the penal code of the old covenant, *an eye for an eye, and a tooth for a tooth*, has been abrogated by Jesus Christ; and that, under the new covenant, the forgiveness instead of the punishment of enemies has been enjoined upon all His disciples, in all cases whatsoever. . . .

The history of mankind is crowded with evidences proving that physical coercion is not adapted to moral regeneration; that the sinful dispositions of men can be subdued only by love; that evil can be exterminated from the earth only by goodness; that it is not safe to rely upon an arm of flesh, upon man whose breath is in his nostrils, to preserve us from harm; that there is great security in being gentle, harmless, long-suffering, and abundant in mercy; that it is only the meek who shall inherit the earth, for the violent who resort to the sword are destined to perish with the sword.

Hence, as a measure of sound policy; of safety to property, life, and liberty; of public quietude and private enjoyment, as well as on the ground of allegiance to Him who is King of kings and Lord of lords, we cordially adopt the nonresistance principle; being confident that it provides for all possible consequences, will ensure all things needful to us, is armed with omnipotent power, and must ultimately triumph over every assailing force.

7. Angelina Grimké Urges Northern Women to Fight Racial Prejudice, 1838

[In] a country where women are degraded and brutalized, and where their exposed persons bleed under the lash—where they are sold in the shambles of "negro brokers"—robbed of their hard earnings—torn from their husbands, and forcibly plundered of their virtue and their offspring; surely in *such* a country, it is very natural that *women* should wish to know "the reason *why*"—especially when these outrages of blood and nameless horror are practiced in violation of the principles of our national Bill of Rights and the Preamble of our Constitution. We do not, then, and cannot concede the position, that because this is a *political subject* women ought to fold their hands in idleness, and close their eyes and ears to the "horrible things" that are practiced in our land. The denial of our duty to act, is a bold denial of our right to act; . . .

We have hitherto addressed you more as moral and responsible beings, than in the distinctive character of women; we have appealed to you on the broad ground of *human rights* and human responsibilities, rather than on that of your peculiar duties as women. We have pursued this course of argument designedly, because, in order to prove that you have any duties to perform, it is necessary first to establish the principle of moral being—for all our rights and all our duties grow out of this principle. *All moral beings have essentially the same rights and the same duties,* whether they be male or female. . . .

Women are Slaveholders

Multitudes of the Southern women hold men, women and children as *property. They* are pampered in luxury, and nursed in the school of tyranny; *they* sway the iron rod of power, and *they* rob the laborer of his hire. Immortal beings tremble at *their* nod, and bow in abject submission at *their* word, and under the cowskin too often wielded by *their* own delicate hands. Women at the South hold *their own sisters* and brothers in bondage. Start not at this dreadful assertion—we speak that which some of us do know—we testify that which some of us have seen. Such facts ought to be known, that the women of the North may understand *their* duties, and be incited to perform *them.* . . .

[T]here are *female tyrants* too, who are prompt to lay their complaints of misconduct before their husbands, brothers and sons, and to urge them to commit acts of violence against their helpless slaves. Others still more cruel, place the lash in the hands of some trusty domestic, and stand by whilst he lays the heavy strokes upon the unresisting victim, deaf to the cries for mercy which rend the air, or rather the more enraged at such appeals, which are only answered by the Southern lady with the prompt command of "give her more for that." This work of chastisement is often performed by a brother, or other relative of the poor sufferer, which circumstance stings like an adder the very heart of the slave while her body writhes under the lash. Other mistresses who cannot bear that their delicate ears should be pained by the screams of the poor sufferers, write an order to the master of the Charleston workhouse, or the New Orleans calaboose, where they are most cruelly stretched in order to render the stroke of the whip or the blow of the paddle more certain to produce cuts and wounds which cause the blood to flow at every stroke. And let it be remembered that these poor creatures are often *women* who are most indecently divested of their clothing and exposed to the gaze of the executioner of a *woman's* command.

What then, our beloved sisters, must be the effects of such a system upon the domestic character of the white females? Can a corrupt tree bring forth good fruit? Can such despotism mould the character of the Southern woman to gentleness and love? or may we not fairly conclude that all that suavity, for which slaveholding ladies are so conspicuous, is in many instances the paint and the varnish of hypocrisy, the fashionable polish of a heartless superficiality? . . .

The Colored Women of the North are Oppressed

[Another] reason we would urge for the interference of northern women with the system of slavery is, that in consequence of the odium which the degradation of slavery has attached to *color* even in the free States, our *colored sisters* are dreadfully oppressed here. Our seminaries of learning are closed to them, they are almost entirely banished from our lecture rooms, and even in the house of God they are separated from their white brethren and sisters. . . .

Here, then, are some of the bitter fruits of that inveterate prejudice which the vast proportion of northern women are cherishing towards their colored sisters; and let us remember that every one of us who denies the sinfulness of this prejudice, . . . is awfully guilty in the sight of Him who is no respecter of persons. . . .

But our colored sisters are oppressed in other ways. As they walk the streets of our cities, they are continually liable to be insulted with the vulgar epithet of "nigger"; no matter how respectable or wealthy, they cannot visit the Zoological Institute of New-York except in the capacity of nurses or servants—no matter how worthy, they cannot gain admittance into or receive assistance from any of the charities of this city. In Philadelphia, they are cast out of our Widow's Asylum, and their children are refused admittance to the House of Refuge, the Orphan's House and the Infant School connected with the Alms-House, though into these are gathered the very offscouring of our population. These are only specimens of that soul-crushing influence from which the colored women of the north are daily suffering. . . .

Much may be done, too, by sympathizing with our oppressed colored sisters, who are suffering in our very midst. Extend to them the right hand of fellowship on the broad principles of humanity and Christianity, treat them as *equals,* visit them as *equals,* invite them to co-operate with you in Anti-Slavery and Temperance and Moral Reform

Societies—in Maternal Associations and Prayer meetings and Reading Companies. . . .

Multitudes of instances will continually occur in which you will have the opportunity of *identifying yourselves with this injured class* of our fellow-beings: embrace these opportunities at all times and in all places, in the true nobility of our great Exemplar, who was ever found among the *poor and the despised,* elevating and blessing them with his counsels and presence. In this way, and this alone, will you be enabled to subdue that deep-rooted prejudice which is doing the work of oppression in the free States to a most dreadful extent.

When this demon has been cast out of your own hearts, when *you* can recognize the colored woman as a WOMAN—*then* will you be prepared to send out an appeal to our Southern sisters, entreating them to "go and do likewise."

Chapter 10:
Document Set 2 References

1. Charles G. Finney Defines Revivalism, 1834
   Charles G. Finney, "What a Revival of Religion Is," *Lectures on Revivals of Religion* (New York: 1838).

2. Francis Lieber Reacts to Religious Enthusiasm, 1835
   Francis Lieber, *The Stranger in America* (1835), pp. 310–317, 324.

3. Bishop McIlvaine Decries the Curse of Intemperance, 1830s
   Charles P. McIlvaine, *Tracts of the American Tract Society,* General Series (n.d.), Vol. 7, No. 244, pp. 1–23.

4. Ten Nights in a Bar-Room, 1854
   Timothy Shays Arthur, *Ten Nights in a Bar-Room and What I Saw There* (1854; Philadelphia: J. W. Bradley, 1860 ed.), pp. 68–81.

5. William Lloyd Garrison Justifies Organization Against Slavery, 1833
   William Lloyd Garrison, *Platform of the American Anti-Slavery Society and Its Auxiliaries,* 1833 (New York: 1860 ed.), p. 3.

6. Garrison Renounces War, 1838
   William Lloyd Garrison, *Declaration of Sentiments* (1838), and *William Lloyd Garrison, The Story of His Life Told by His Children* (1885–1889), Vol. 2, pp. 230–232.

7. Angelina Grimké Urges Northern Women to Fight Racial Prejudice, 1838
   Angelina Grimké, *An Appeal to the Women of the Nominally Free States,* Issued by an Anti-slavery Convention of American Women, 2d ed. (Boston: Isaac Knapp, 1838), in Nancy F. Cott, ed., *Root of Bitterness: Documents of the Social History of American Women* (New York: E. P. Dutton, 1972), pp. 194–199.

CHAPTER 10

The Search for Community: Social Experimentation in a Reform Era

Among the most fascinating of antebellum reform efforts were the numerous utopian experiments launched by social innovators of all varieties. Common to these ventures was a communitarian ethic and a search for alternatives to harsh economic competition. Driven by an intense sense of mission, utopian visionaries hoped to reshape competitive society through force of example.

Your textbook devotes extensive attention to the diverse utopian communities founded during the reform era. As you prepare to examine the following documents, review the text's analysis of utopianism, giving special attention to the Place in Time essay on the Oneida community. In your initial reading of the documents, search for common themes that link these social experiments with one another.

The documents have been arranged to emphasize the ways in which collectivists saw reformed gender relations as central to the new social order that they were building. Note that the various communities expressed a wide range of attitudes toward women's economic and social roles. As you review the sources, watch for evidence of emphasis on women's potential for growth and leadership as well as indications that communal life could perpetuate traditional values and attitudes.

The document set includes the voices of both men and women who thought deeply about the search for the good life. For both, correct sexual and domestic relationships were essential to the creation of model communities. As you examine the documents, try to determine how gender relations and sexual relationships were defined by the various groups examined. Rely on the textbook to provide the necessary context for your analysis of the primary sources. Be especially aware of nuances of disagreement and agreement among male and female utopians. Account for these similarities and differences. As you probe the sources, watch for evidence that utopian ventures like Brook Farm and Oneida had an impact on the drive for equality and an enlarged sphere for women in wider American society.

Communitarian sects operated on both secular and religious models. Study the documents with an eye to the variety of attitudes toward traditional Christianity expressed in the utopian communities of antebellum America. Think about the relative importance of religion in shaping the development of the communitarian ideal.

Finally, search the documents for explanations to account for the early collapse of most utopian experiments. What kind of men and women were attracted to the communal life? How did their social and intellectual backgrounds influence the fortunes and longevity of the model communities? Try to place these communities in the context of a nineteenth-century value system that celebrated the ethic of individualism and competition.

Questions for Analysis

1. In what ways did life in utopian communities encourage or discourage the exploration of new and enlarged roles for women? How did these roles differ from community to community? Can you identify common themes in gender relations, as expressed at Brook Farm, Oneida, the Shaker villages, and other communities?

2. Why did some utopian communities provoke negative reactions from inhabitants of nearby communities? Do the documents shed light on the reasons for hostility toward the adherents of the communal life? Explain.

3. How would you account for the short life of most utopian communities? How do the documents help clarify the reasons for their failure?

4. How was it possible for some Americans to both endorse individualism and support communal experimentation? In what ways do the documents help resolve this paradox?

5. To what extent was religious commitment a factor in the origin and growth of nineteenth-century utopian communities? How did the proponents of the communitarian ideal define religion? How did religious values shape their goals?

6. How did sexual relationships become a factor in the growth and development of utopian communities? What did the Oneida reformers mean by "free love"? How did their views on sexual relations influence gender equity in the Oneida community?

1. A *Lowell Offering* Correspondent Describes a Shaker Community, 1841

Sometime in the summer of 18—, I paid a visit to one of the Shaker villages in the State of New York. Previously to this, many times and oft had I (when tired of the noise and contention of the world, its erroneous opinions, and its wrong practices) longed for some retreat, where, with a few chosen friends, I could enjoy the present, forget the past, and be free from all anxiety respecting any future portion of time. And often had I pictured, in imagination, a state of happy society, where one common interest prevailed—where kindness and brotherly love were manifested in all of the every-day affairs of life—where liberty and equality would live, not in name, but in very deed—where idleness in no shape whatever would be tolerated—and where vice of every description would be banished, and neatness, with order, would be manifested in all things.

Actually to witness such a state of society, was a happiness which I never expected. I thought it to be only a thing among the airy castles which it has ever been my delight to build. But with this unostentatious and truly kind-hearted people, the Shakers, I found it; and the reality, in beauty and harmony, exceeded even the picturings of imagination. . . .

1st. The domestic arrangements of the Shakers. However strange the remark may seem, it is nevertheless true, that our factory population work fewer hours out of every twenty-four, than are required by the Shakers, whose bell to call them from their slumbers, and also to warn them that it is time to commence the labors of the day, rings much earlier than our factory bells; and its calls were obeyed, in the family where I was entertained, with more punctuality than I ever knew the greatest "workey" among my numerous acquaintances (during the fourteen years in which I have been employed in different manufacturing establishments) to obey the calls of the factory-bell. And not until nine o'clock in the evening were the labors of the day closed, and the people assembled at their religious meetings. . . .

2d. With all deference, I beg leave to introduce some of the religious views and ceremonies of the Shakers.

From the conversation of the elders, I learned that they considered it doing God service, to sever the sacred ties of husband and wife, parent and child—the relationship existing between them being contrary to their religious views—views which they believe were revealed from heaven to "Mother Ann Lee," the founder of their sect, and through whom they profess to have frequent revelations from the spiritual world. . . .

Apart from their religious meetings, the Shakers have what they call "union meetings." These are for social converse, and for the purpose of making the people acquainted with each other. During the day, the elders tell who may visit such and such chambers. A few minutes past nine, work is laid aside; the females change, or adjust, as best suits their fancy, their caps, handkerchiefs, and pinners, with a precision which indicates that they are not *altogether* free from vanity. The chairs, perhaps to the number of a dozen, are set in two rows, in such a manner that those who occupy them may face each other. At the ringing of a bell, each one goes to the chamber where either he or she has been directed by the elders, or remains at home to receive company, as the case may be. . . . But beyond their own little world, they do not appear to extend scarcely a thought. And why should they? Having so few sources of information, they know not what is passing beyond them. They however make the most of their own affairs, and seem to regret that they can converse no longer, when, after sitting together from half to three-quarters of an hour, the bell warns them that it is time to separate, which they do by rising up, locking their hands across their breasts, and bowing. Each one then goes silently to his own chamber.

2. Orestes Brownson Views Brook Farm as an Expression of American Egalitarianism, 1842

With respect to the labor, which is the material wealth of the establishment, and the body of its life, they intend to have all trades and occupations which contribute to necessities and healthy elegancies, within their own borders, so as not to buy them from without, which is too expensive; but at present their labor is agriculture, and the simplest housekeeping. . . .

Every one prescribes his own hours of labor, controlled only by his conscience, and the spirit of place, which tends to great industry, and almost to too much exertion. A drone would soon find himself isolated and neglected, and could not live there. The new comers, especially if they come from the city, have to begin gradually, but soon learn to increase the labor of one hour a day in the field, to six or seven hours, and some work all day long; but there can be no drudgery where there is no constraint. As all eat together, they change their dress for their meals; and so after tea they are all ready for grouping, in the parlors of the ladies, or in the library, or in the music-room, or they can go to their private rooms, or into the woods, or anywhere. They visit a good deal; and when they have business out of the community, nothing seems more easy than for them to arrange with others of their own number, to take their work or teaching for the time being; so that while they may work more than people out of the community, none seem such prisoners of their duties. The association of labor makes distribution according to taste and ability easy, and this takes the sting out of fatigue. . . .

For the women, there is, besides many branches of teaching, washing and ironing, housekeeping, sewing for the other sex, and for the children, and conducting all the social life. They have to hire one washerwoman now, but hope, bye and bye, to do all the washing within themselves. By the wide distribution of these labors, no one has any great weight of any one thing. They iron every forenoon but one; but they take turns, and each irons as long as she thinks right. The care of the houses is also distributed among those who are most active, in a way mutually satisfactory. . . .

. . . It is truly a most religious life, and does it not realize in miniature that identity of church and state which you think is the deepest idea of our American government? It seems to me that this community, point by point, corresponds with the great community of the Republic, whose divine lineaments are so much obscured by the rubbish of reported abuses (that, however, only lie on the surface, and may be shaken off, "like dewdrops from the lion's mane";) and whose divine proportions are now lost to our sight by the majestic grandeur with which they tower beyond the apprehension of our time-bound senses. For the theory of our government also proposes education (the freest development of the individual, according to the law of God) as its main end; an equal distribution of the results of labor among the laborers, as its means; and a mutual respect of each man by his neighbor as the basis. Only in America, I think, could such a community have so succeeded as I have described, composed of persons coming by chance, as it were, from all circumstances of life, and united only by a common idea and plan of life. They have succeeded, because they are the children of a government the ideal of which is the same as their own, although, as a mass, we are unconscious of it; so little do we understand our high vocation, and act up to it. But these miniatures of the great original shall educate us to the apprehension and realization of it, as a nation.

3. Marianne Dwight's Reflections on the Promise and Failure of Brook Farm Association, 1844, 1845

Mr. Ripley told Fanny and me in a very amusing way, how "pleasant it was to him to see *Christian people* about (alluding to us) and *proper, grown up*, well *behaved* young women, free from all the vices of the *world*, and *filled with all the virtues of association*." In the afternoon came the rest of our furniture (except what didn't) and the piano-forte, and about tea time came father. He said the supper reminded him of college commons, except that there were ladies present. Father is pleased with the place, and we are all thus far pleased and happy. I must own to one little *twinge of heart*.

. . . You speak of a crisis,—this is one of the things I can't write fully about, and whatever I may say will be confidential. We have reached, I believe, our severest crisis. If we survive it, we shall probably go on safely and not be obliged to struggle thro' another. I think here lies the difficulty,—we have not had business men to conduct our affairs—we have had *no* strictly business transactions from the beginning, and those among us who have some business talents, see this error, and feel that we cannot go on as we have done. They are ready to give up if matters cannot be otherwise managed, for they have no hope of success here under the past and present government. All important matters have been done up in council of one or two or three individuals, and everybody else kept in the dark (perhaps I exaggerate somewhat) and now it must be so no longer;—our young men have started "enquiry meetings," and it must be a sad state of things that calls for such measures. We are perplexed by debts, by want of capital to carry on any business to advantage,—by want of our Phalanstery or the

means to finish it. From want of wisdom we have failed to profit by some advantages we have had. And then Brisbane is vague and unsteady; the help he promised us from his efforts comes not—but on the contrary, he and other friends to the cause in New York, instead of trying to concentrate all efforts upon Brook Farm as they promised, have wandered off,—have taken up a vast plan of getting $100,000 and starting anew, so they are for disposing of us in the shortest manner,—would set their foot upon us, as it were, and divert what capital might come to us. What then remains for us, and where are our hopes? . . .

. . . My hopes are here; our council seems to be awake and ready for action; if we get the money, we will finish the building,—then we will enlarge our school, which should bring us in a handsome income. Our sash and blind business is very profitable, and may be greatly enlarged in the spring, the tailor's business is good, the tin block, and why do I forget the printing, and the Farm? Also we shall have together a better set of people than ever before. Heaven help us, and make us wise, for the failure of Brook Farm must defer the cause a long time. This place as it is (take it all in all) is the best place under the sky; why can't people see this, and look upon it hopefully and encouragingly?

4. An Ohio Associationist Sees Women's Activism as the Key to Social Harmony, 1847

Tupperford, near Marietta, O.,
June 23, 1847

I have read, in "The Harbinger" of the 12th of July, the Circular letter of our sister Associationists. Allow me to answer them through your means.

Dear Sisters:—Your letter through the Harbinger has conferred on me a deep, an intense blessing! How long have I not prayed with the most earnest fervor of the heart, to the Almighty Power who rules us all, to inspire my sisters who were so situated, to *unite together* in their own behalf and that of the human family! At last, my ardent wish is accomplished. Dear sisters, you come out with broad and noble views, in search of undisguised truth! in search of the means to redeem our unfortunate Race from the chaotic discordance and misery into which it has fallen for so long! Then, Dear Sisters, behold a new era opening before us, as never was one before! Women (made by the laws of Nature the ministering angels for their

Race) no longer shy or cringing, confined in obscurity, where they do isolatedly, the little good they can, in impotence, ignorance, and feebleness; but coming forward with the noble determination to unite their energies with those of their brothers in the work of restoring human society to harmony and happiness! Oh Sisters, persevere and it will be done, for you will possess among you all the necessary materials to accomplish it. From the moment that hideous, brutal War grasped unfortunate females, and made them slaves and victims wherever it reigned, the responsibility of social order devolved entirely on men. What have we had since? War! war! war! discord, confusion, wranglings, all sorts of miseries, and sufferings. Not because men are naturally bad; but because they are only one half of the social body, and they can act but that half. The *moral* and intellectual powers of the Mothers of our Race are as necessary to create social harmony, as their physical power for the creation and suckling of their offspring.

Whatever power I have, pecuniary or mental, whatever exertion I am capable of, I will cheerfully lend it to assist you in your movements; only let me know them and what I can do. We should command a Press. No doubt there are some among you, who could undertake the management of it. I would wish to see some females among your lecturers. Does the sincerity of moral persuasion lose all its power in coming from a woman's lips, that I see so very few of them

undertake the task? By all means establish a reciprocal guarantee among you. Ask some of our kind brothers who sympathize with us to put you in the way of it. But act for yourselves. It is high time that the *Mother of Mankind* should cease to play the *child!*

May the Almighty bless your efforts in the most holy cause that woman ever undertook!

Your devoted sister

5. John Humphrey Noyes Outlines Free Love, as Practiced at Oneida, 1865

The obvious and essential difference between marriage and whoredom may be stated thus:

Marriage is a permanent union. Whoredom is a temporary flirtation.

In Marriage, communism of property goes with communism of persons. In Whoredom, love is paid for by the job.

Marriage makes the man responsible for the consequences of his acts of love to a woman. In whoredom a man imposes on a woman the heavy burdens of maternity, ruining perhaps her reputation and her health, and then goes his way without responsibility.

Marriage provides for the maintenance and education of children. Whoredom ignores children as nuisances, and leaves them to chance.

Now in respect to every one of these points of difference between marriage and whoredom, *we stand with marriage*. Free love with us does not mean freedom of love today and leave tomorrow; or freedom to take a woman's person and keep our property to ourselves; or freedom to freight a woman with

our offspring and send her downstream without care or help; or freedom to beget children and leave them to the street and the poorhouse.

Our Communities are *families*, as distinctly bounded and separated from promiscuous society as ordinary households. The tie that binds us together is as permanent and sacred, to say the least, as that of marriage, for it is our religion. We receive no members (except by deception and mistake), who do not give heart and hand to the family interest for life and forever. Community of property extends just as far as freedom of love. Every man's care and every dollar of the common property is pledged for the maintenance and protection of the women and the education of the children of the Community. Bastardy, in any disastrous sense of the word, is simply impossible in such a social state. Whoever will take the trouble to follow our track from the beginning will find no forsaken women or children by the way. In this respect we claim to be a little ahead of marriage in common civilization.

6. The Oneida Sisters Comment on Love and Labor in the Association, 1853, 1855, 1858

[July 23, 1853]

Our women had a meeting a few days since, to inquire into the experience about labor, and make all free to express the choice if they had any. It was very wonderful to see the unanimity there was in expressing contentment and good appetite in all

the departments of labor; not more than two wanted a change because there were drags; but on the contrary most testified to increasing enjoyment in it. We surmised that there might be some discontent but were pleased with the result of our inquiry. We know there is a great deal more work done here than there used to be; but it is done easier; and the resurrectional-life working more and more makes what work is done sport, and a positive means of health and energy. The sewing-room women spoke of the ease with which they executed the orders for the sister Communes; the work was done before they knew it, and with fewer mistakes than common.

[April 26, 1855]

Some conversation this evening on woman's education, and the new course she has entered upon here. It was resolved that our women ought not to let a day pass without engaging in some *manly* work. A lesson in manly work every day would do more for their education than ever so much playing on the piano, or sewing and sweeping. We calculated that every woman in the Association could give as many as two hours a day to outdoor manly industry, and a proposal to this effect was well received.

[January 23, 1858]

Mrs. F. said I will not detain the ladies long, but would like to say a word. I am a woman's rights advocate but my ideas of her rights are peculiar perhaps. The grand right I ask for women is to love the men and be loved by them. That I imagine would adjust all other claims. It is but a cold, dismal right, in my opinion, to be allowed to vote, or to acquire and hold property. I want the right of the most intimate partnership with man, not in politics particularly but in business, in his studies and pleasures, and in the occupation of his whole time. I would rather be tyrannized over by him, than to be *independent* of him, and I would rather have no *rights* than be separate.

7. Noyes Acknowledges the Associationist Debt to the Shakers, 1869

France also had heard of Shakerism, before St. Simon or Fourier began to meditate and write Socialism. These men were nearly contemporaneous with Owen, and all three evidently obeyed a common impulse. That impulse was the sequel and certainly in part the effect of Shakerism. Thus it is no more than bare justice to say, that we are indebted to the Shakers more than to any or all other social architects of modern times. Their success has been the 'specie basis' that has upheld all the paper theories, and counteracted the failures, of the French and English schools. It is very doubtful whether Owenism or Fourierism would have ever existed, or if they had, whether they would have ever moved the practical American nation, if the facts of Shakerism had not existed before them and gone along with them. But to do complete justice we must go a step further. While we say that the Rappites, the Zoarites, the Ebenezers, the Owenites, and even the Fourierists are all echoes of the Shakers, we must also say that the Shakers are the far-off echoes of the PRIMITIVE CHRISTIAN CHURCH.

Chapter 10:
Document Set 3 References

1. A *Lowell Offering* Correspondent Describes a Shaker Community, 1841
   "Visit to the Shakers," *Lowell Offering* (1841), and "A Second Visit to the Shakers," *Lowell Offering* (1841).

2. Orestes Brownson Views Brook Farm as an Expression of American Egalitarianism, 1842
   O. E. Brownson, "Brook Farm" *United States Magazine and Democratic Review*, 11 (November 1842).

3. Marianne Dwight's Reflections on the Promise and Failure of Brook Farm Association, 1844, 1845
   Marianne Dwight to Anna Parsons, Spring 1844 and December 7, 1845, reprinted from Marianne Dwight, *Letters from Brook Farm*, ed. Amy L. Reed (Poughkeepsie, N.Y.: Vassar College, 1928), pp. 1–4, 136–139.

4. An Ohio Associationist Sees Women's Activism as the Key to Social Harmony, 1847
   Harbinger, 9 (August 7, 1847).

5. John Humphrey Noyes Outlines Free Love, as Practiced at Oneida, 1865
   Circular, February 6, 1865.

6. The Oneida Sisters Comment on Love and Labor in the Association, 1853, 1855, 1858

Circular, July 23, 1853; April 26, 1855; and January 23, 1858.

7. Noyes Acknowledges the Associationist Debt to the Shakers, 1869

John Humphrey Noyes, *Strange Cults and Utopias of 19th Century America*, 1869 (New York: Dover, rep. 1966), p. 670.

CHAPTER 11

Modernization and Social Change in the Antebellum Era

One of the crucial changes evident in the antebellum years involved the widespread introduction of what came to be called technology. Modern scientific principles were being applied to agricultural and manufacturing problems around the world. As your textbook indicates, however, the striking feature of technical innovation in the United States was the unbounded enthusiasm with which so many Americans embraced novel manufacturing techniques and processes. There was a clear element of optimism in this early endorsement of efficiency, invention, and entrepreneurial activity. The result was the beginning of a long American romance with science and technology that has not yet run its course.

With some justification, Americans first greeted technological innovation as progressive, a source of the good life. Your textbook recounts many achievements that flowed from the spirit of invention, including greater productivity in agriculture and industry, lower prices, improved transportation, and national prosperity. While scientific agriculture boosted production, the industrial sector experienced even more revolutionary advances with the improvement of machine tools and the rapid development of a national railroad network. At first imitative of European inventions, American technology soon emerged as independently innovative.

Technology was viewed by many observers as a positive force. A common view stressed the role of technical invention in extending benefits to all classes. As your textbook notes, there was considerable validity to the argument that the railroad, telegraph, and other developments brought goods and services to an expanding population. In this sense, technology was itself democratic.

Yet it is clear from the following documents that technological change was a mixed blessing. Although the excerpts from scientific and agricultural journals emphasize limitless opportunity, some analysts saw problems on the horizon. Scottish industrialist Robert Owen caught a glimpse of the future, and the vision was bleak. Not only was the exploitation of wage labor ahead, but craft workers were destined to be separated from both their tools and the finished product. The sense of loss was to be deep.

As you examine the evidence, be aware of the source person's background and try to account for the views expressed. The problems and opportunities perceived by observers of the technological revolution raised new and conflicting questions. Your goal should be to develop an understanding of the ambivalence evident in these early responses to economic modernization.

Questions for Analysis

1. It has been asserted that by the 1850s the American economy had entered the "take-off period" of sustained industrial growth. What evidence do you find in the documents and statistics to support or refute such an argument? Focus on the necessary components of an industrial base.

2. Basing your analysis on textbook reading and the documents, assess the role of individuals, government, and natural resources in the growth of technology and in economic expansion. How would you account for the great economic explosion and technological advance between 1830 and 1865?

3. What was the impact of technological innovation on American workers and the work process by 1865? What questions were raised by the acceleration of the manufacturing pace?

4. As you review the evidence, be aware of conflicting perceptions of technology's impact on American society and culture. Do you agree with the assertion that technological change was a democratizing influence? What evidence in the documents confirms or refutes the concept of technology as a progressive force?

1. Manufactures Summary: 1849–1954

Year	Persons engaged in manufacturing				Salaries and wages (1,000)			Value added by manufacture² ($1,000)	Horsepower (1,000)	
	Number of establishments	Proprietors and firm members	Nonproduction employees¹	Production and related workers (average for year)	Total	Salaries	Wages		Prime movers	Motors run by purchased energy
	1	2	3	4	5	6	7	8	9	10
FACTORIES, EXCLUDING HAND AND NEIGHBORHOOD INDUSTRIES										
1954	286,817	197,850	³3,278,264	12,373,030	62,993,321	18,397,864	44,595,457	116,912,526	35,579	72,783
1947	240,807	188,948	2,376,079	11,917,884	39,695,558	9,451,587	30,243,971	74,290,475	21,077	28,816
1939⁴	173,802	⁵123,655	⁶1,719,101	7,808,205	⁶12,706,102	⁶3,708,587	8,997,515	24,487,304	.....	.....
1937	166,794	99,268	1,217,171	8,569,231	12,829,749	2,716,866	10,112,883	25,173,539	.....	.....
1935	167,916	81,521	1,058,501	7,203,794	9,564,754	2,253,425	7,311,329	18,552,553	.....	.....
1933	139,325	72,267	⁷770,314	5,787,611	⁷6,237,800	⁷1,297,654	4,940,146	14,007,540	.....	.....
1931	171,450	.....	.....	6,163,144	.....	.....	6,688,541	18,600,532	.....	.....
1929	206,663	132,686	1,290,037	8,369,705	14,284,282	3,399,363	10,884,919	30,591,435	19,328	21,794
1927	187,629	132,151	1,223,982	7,848,070	13,123,135	3,023,670	10,099,465	26,325,394	.....	.....
1925	183,877	132,971	1,271,008	7,871,409	12,957,707	2,978,058	9,979,649	25,667,624	19,243	15,116
1923	192,096	147,958	1,280,488	8,194,170	12,996,460	2,847,836	10,148,624	24,569,487	.....	.....
1921	192,059	172,291	1,081,890	6,475,476	9,870,199	2,418,900	7,451,299	17,252,775	.....	.....
1919	270,231	249,865	1,371,885	8,464,916	12,426,902	2,762,893	9,664,009	23,841,624	19,432	8,966
1914	268,436	258,560	911,899	6,602,287	5,015,977	1,233,655	3,782,322	9,385,622	17,858	3,707
1909	264,810	272,421	750,330	6,261,736	4,105,470	900,257	3,205,213	8,160,075	16,393	1,668
1904	213,444	225,115	493,297	5,181,660	2,990,937	550,086	2,440,851	6,019,171	12,605	428
1899	204,754	.....	348,100	4,501,919	2,258,654	366,080	1,892,574	4,646,981	9,633	178
FACTORIES AND HAND AND NEIGHBORHOOD INDUSTRIES										
1899	509,490	.....	380,739	5,097,562	2,595,566	389,019	2,206,547	5,474,892	10,805	183
1889	353,864	.....	457,139	4,129,355	2,209,058	388,204	1,820,854	4,102,301	5,939	.....
1879	253,852	.....	.....	2,732,595	.....	.....	947,954	1,972,756	3,411	.....
1869	252,148	.....	.....	2,053,996	.....	.....	620,467	1,395,119	2,346	.....
1859	140,433	.....	.....	1,311,246	.....	.....	378,879	854,257	.....	.....
1849	123,025	.....	.....	957,059	.....	.....	236,755	463,983	.....	.....

[1] 1954 figure is an average based on reported employment totals for payroll periods nearest the 15th March, May, August, and November except for seasonal industries in 1954 when a 12-month average was used. For 1947, figure represents the average of 12 monthly figures; for 1939 and earlier years, figures represent nonproduction workers reported for 1 payroll period (usually in October).

[2] For 1849–1933, cost of contract work was not subtracted from value of products in calculating value added by manufacture.

[3] Revised.

[4] Figures for 1939, but not for earlier years, represent figures which have been revised by retabulation of returns to exclude data for establishments classified as manufacturing in 1939 and prior years, but classified as nonmanufacturing beginning with 1947. Value added by manufacture for 1939, prior to revision and on a basis comparable with 1937 and previous years, was $24.7 billion.

[5] Not revised to exclude data for establishments classified as manufacturing in 1939 and prior years but classified as nonmanufacturing beginning with 1947.

[6] 1939 figures for "Nonproduction employees" revised on basis of estimates rather than by retabulation of 1939 reports. Estimates were made in the following manner. For nonproduction employees, by multiplying the retabulated figure for number of production and related workers by the ratio of all employees to production and related workers computed from unrevised 1939 statistics; for salaries and wages, by multiplying the retabulated wage figure by the ratio for salaries and wages also derived from the unrevised 1939 statistics.

[7] Excludes data for salaried officers of corporations and their salaries and, therefore, not strictly comparable with figures for other years.

2. Railroad Mileage and Equipment: 1830–1890

| Year | Mileage | | | Equipment[2] | | | | |
| | Road operated (Dec. 31) 15 | Road owned[1] 16 | All track (Dec. 31) 17 | Loco-motives 18 | Revenue cars | | | |
					Total 19	Passenger 20	Freight 21	Baggage, mail, express 22
1890	166,703	163,359	208,152	31,812	1,090,869	21,664	1,061,952	7,253
1889	161,276	159,934	202,088	30,566	1,080,665	21,471	1,051,141	7,053
1888	156,114	154,222	191,376	29,006	1,032,182	20,247	1,005,108	6,827
1887	149,214	147,953	184,935	27,275	[3]976,772	19,339	950,889	6,554
1886	136,338	133,565	167,952	26,108	870,602	18,365	845,912	6,325
1885	128,320	127,689	160,506	25,662	828,058	16,497	805,517	6,044
1884	125,345	125,119	156,414	24,353	820,954	16,644	798,399	5,911
1883	121,422	120,519	149,101	23,405	800,741	16,230	778,663	5,848
1882	114,677	114,428	140,878	21,889	750,933	14,934	730,435	5,564
1881	103,108	103,530	130,455	19,911	667,218	13,947	648,295	4,976
1880	93,262	92,147	115,647	17,949	[3]556,930	12,789	539,255	4,786
1879	86,556	84,393	104,756	17,084	496,718	12,009	480,190	4,519
1878	81,747	80,832	103,649	16,445	439,109	11,683	428,013	4,413
1877	79,082	79,208	97,308	15,911	408,082	12,053	392,175	3,854
1876	76,808	76,305	94,665	15,618	399,524	[4]414,621	384,903	....
1875	74,096	74,096	....	....	....	....	....	....
1874	72,385	72,623	....	....	....	....	....	....
1873	70,268	70,651	....	....	....	....	....	....
1872	66,171	57,823	....	....	....	....	....	....
1871	60,301	51,455	....	....	....	....	....	....

Year	Miles of road operated (Dec. 31) 15	Year	Miles of road operated (Dec. 31) 15
1870	52,922	1850	9,021
1869	46,844	1849	7,365
1868	42,229	1848	5,996
1867	39,050	1847	5,598
1866	36,801	1846	4,930
1865	35,085	1845	4,633
1864	33,908	1844	4,377
1863	33,170	1843	4,185
1862	32,120	1842	4,026
1861	31,286	1841	3,535
1860	30,626	1840	2,818
1859	28,789	1839	2,302
1858	26,968	1838	1,913
1857	24,503	1837	1,497
1856	22,076	1836	1,273
1855	18,374	1835	1,098
1854	16,720	1834	633
1853	15,360	1833	380
1852	12,908	1832	229
1851	10,982	1831	95
		1830	23

[1]Prior to 1882, includes elevated railways.
[2]Prior to 1881, includes elevated railways.
[3]Agrees with source; however, figures for components do not add to total shown.
[4]Includes baggage, mail, and express.

3. Patent Applications Filed and Patents Issued, by Type and by Patentee: 1790–1879

Year	Inventions, patent applications filed[1]	Patents issued			Year	Inventions, patent applications filed[1]	Patents issued		
		Inventions	Designs	To residents of foreign countries			Inventions	Designs	To residents of foreign countries
	66	69	74	76		66	69	74	76
1879	20,059	12,125	591	648	1857	4,771	2,674	113	45
1878	20,260	12,345	590	581	1856	4,960	2,302	107	31
1877	20,308	12,920	699	590					
1876	21,425	14,169	802	787	1855	4,435	1,881	70	41
					1854	3,328	1,755	57	35
1875	21,638	13,291	915	563	1853	2,673	844	86	26
1874	21,602	12,230	886	547	1852	2,639	885	109	20
1873	20,414	11,616	747	493	1851	2,258	752	90	17
1872	18,246	12,180	884	581					
1871	19,472	11,659	903	522	1850	2,193	883	83	20
					1849	1,955	984	49	17
1870	19,171	12,137	737	644	1848	1,628	583	46	14
1869	19,271	12,931	506	377	1847	1,531	495	60	21
1868	20,420	12,526	445	337	1846	1,272	566	59	19
1867	21,276	12,277	325	275					
1866	15,269	8,863	294	244	1845	1,246	473	17	12
					1844	1,045	478	12	20
1865	10,664	6,088	221	181	1843	819	493	14	8
1864	6,932	4,630	139	181	1842	761	488	1	11
1863	6,014	3,773	176	125	1841	847	490	....	21
1862	5,038	3,214	196	80					
1861	4,643	3,020	142	83	1840	765	458	....	19
					1839	[2]800	404	....	10
1860	7,653	4,357	183	49	1838	[2]900	514	....	17
1859	6,225	4,160	107	47	1837	[2]650	426	....	7
1858	5,364	3,455	102	28	1836	[2][3]400	[3]103	....	8

Year	Inventions, patents issued 69	Year	Inventions, patents issued 69	Year	Inventions, patents issued 69	Year	Inventions, patents issued 69	Year	Inventions, patents issued 69
1836	[4]599	1825	304	1815	173	1805	57	1795	12
		1824	228	1814	210	1804	84	1794	22
1835	752	1823	173	1813	181	1803	97	1793	20
1834	630	1822	200	1812	238	1802	65	1792	11
1833	586	1821	168	1811	215	1801	44	1791	33
1832	474								
1831	573	1820	155	1810	223	1800	41	1790	3
		1819	156	1809	203	1799	44		
1830	544	1818	222	1808	158	1798	28		
1829	447	1817	174	1807	99	1797	51		
1828	368	1816	206	1806	63	1796	44		
1827	331								
1826	323								

[1]Applications for reissue included with inventions 1836–1876; design applications included with inventions 1836–1879.

[2]Estimate.

[3]From July 4 to end of year.

[4]To July 4.

4. An Anonymous Endorsement of Scientific Agriculture, 1858

We have a numerous, increasing, and industrious farming population; we rejoice in a comparatively rich soil; our agricultural machinery and implements are eminently practical, time- and laborsaving ones. Let us add theoretical knowledge, science, system to skill, experience, and inventive mood, and we shall not only be safe but may reach the climax. . . .

But wherein does consist the gain, if the annexation of a new agricultural district is analogous to the exhaustion and partial desertion of another? What have Virginia, Massachusetts, New York, etc., gained by the access and development of new territories and states? Has the process of exhaustion been retarded or checked in consequence; the population, the fertility, produce, wealth, and general prosperity increased in the ratio of her original capability? Not at all. The acquisition and occupation of new territory have only tempted and enabled people to be the more regardless of the mother state, and to quit it at the first signs of its receding prosperity, or its slower progress. . . .

That our great Confederacy cannot, without serious, vital injury to its imposing and still growing agricultural, industrial, and commercial interests, long remain behind other countries in nursing that branch of the natural sciences which is the teacher, guide, and benefactor of almost every trade and craft requires no argumentation in this place; nor do we think to have failed to make it manifest that no species of human pursuit is more depending and more indebted to chemistry than the agriculture. . . .

It is, therefore, much to be regretted that the most useful and most practical feature of the National Agricultural Bureau has not been worked out in the shape that had been wisely suggested in the original Senate bill of 1850. The establishment of *agricultural laboratories* is the great desideratum for any successful initial step toward material improvements in the state of our agriculture. Single, solitary investigations of soil and ashes and subsequent devices to turn them to account will benefit locally or individually and should be more frequently resorted to as heretofore; but the whole object, the national aim, cannot be attained by this means. To accomplish that desirable and great end, a perfect chemical survey is wanting. . . .

In Ohio a very practical plan was once suggested to that end, but unfortunately has never been carried out. The plan was this: At an expense of but a few thousand dollars, a chemical laboratory would have been erected in the capital of the state; next, an assessment of $50 levied upon the agricultural society of each county, and then, with the funds furnished by the state legislature and those of the just-named societies, a sufficient number of chemical analyses and other researches instituted to furnish such a chemical survey of the whole arable area of the state, upon which a more uniform, advantageous, and less exhausting method of cultivation could have been based.

If, with such an arrangement, a "state farm," "muster farm," or "farmers' high school," upon the principle as one is about being founded in Pennsylvania, would be connected, every desirable end could not only be achieved but the practical results and benefits to the farming community at large would be such as to warrant and secure for any future task the cooperation and assistance of every well-wisher of this country.

5. American Technology as an Influence Abroad, 1859

The value of labor and its productions is daily becoming more felt and hourly receiving a wider acknowledgment. Though we have few conquests of arms to boast of and no graves of mighty dead to revere—save one, and that we have too little patriotism to buy at once—though we have no long line of ancestral greatness to look back to; yet we have educated labor to be proud of, and skilled work that is winning for America a name among the nations of the world of more value to real progress than conquest, shrines, or ancestry. Americans, by their mechanical skill, are contesting in the glorious field of the liberal arts and are gaining peaceful victories on the continent of Europe of more importance to the world than Austerlitz or Waterloo. Reaping machines are greater civilizers than swords and Yankee unpickable locks greater securities to property than jails or gallows. We are led to these observations by the number of patents which our countrymen are continually securing in foreign countries—a number which is daily on the increase; and a few important ones recently secured in England through the Scientific American Patent Agency, we will now proceed to notice. . . .

Such inventions as these, useful and new, are the best means we can adopt to keep our place in the ranks of the nations; and we hope that our citizens will ever be sending their improvements across the sea.

6. A Senate Report Measures the Railroads' Economic Significance, 1852

[R]ailroads in this country actually add to the immediate means of our people by the saving effected in the expenses of transportation, to a much greater extent than cost. We are, therefore, in no danger from embarrassment on account of the construction of lines called for by the business wants of the community, as these add much more to our active capital than they absorb. Only a very few years are required to enable a railroad to repay its cost of construction in the manner stated.

Railroads in the United States exert a much greater influence upon the value of property than in other countries. . . . The actual increase in the value of lands due to the construction of railroads is controlled by so many circumstances that an accurate estimate can only be approximated and must, in most cases, fall far short of the fact. Not only are cultivated lands and city and village lots lying immediately upon the route affected but the real estate in cities hundreds and thousands of miles distant. The railroads of Ohio exert as much influence in advancing the prices of real property in the city of New York as do the roads lying within that state. This fact will show how very imperfect every estimate must be. But taking only the farming lands of the particular district traversed by a railroad, where the influence of such a work can be more directly seen, there is no doubt that in such case the increased value is many times greater than the cost of the road. . . .

We have considered the effect of railroads in increasing the value of property in reference only to lands devoted to agriculture; but such results do not by any means give the most forcible illustration of their use. An acre of farming land can at most be made to yield only a small annual income. An acre of coal or iron lands, on the other hand, may produce a thousandfold more in value than the former. These deposits may be entirely valueless without a railroad. With one, every ton of ore they contain is worth $1, $2, $3, or $4, as the case may be.

Take, for example, the coalfields of Pennsylvania. The value of the coal sent yearly from them, in all the agencies it is called upon to perform, is beyond all calculation. Upon this article are based our manufacturing establishments, and our government and merchant steamships, representing values, in their various relations and ramifications, equal to thousands of millions of dollars. Without coal it is impossible to conceive the spectacle that we should have presented as a people, so entirely different would it have been from our present condition. Neither our commercial nor our manufacturing, nor, consequently, our agricultural interests, could have borne any relation whatever to their present enormous magnitude. Yet all this result has been achieved by a few railroads and canals in Pennsylvania, which have not cost over $50 million. With these works, coal can be brought into the New York market for about $3.50 per ton; without them, it could not have been made available either for ordinary fuel or as a motive power. So small, comparatively, are the agencies by which such immense results have been effected that the former are completely lost sight of in the magnitude of the latter.

What is true of the Pennsylvania coalfields is equally true of all others to a greater or lesser extent.

7. A Trade Journal Outlines Technology's Impact on the Work Process in the Shoe Industry, 1864

Comparatively few people are aware of the quiet, steady revolution that is going on in the business of shoemaking, and particularly as that business is conducted in Lynn. Previous to the introduction of the original sewing machines, which are now universally used for the binding and stitching of the uppers, but little or no improvement or even change had been made in the manufacture of shoes. The awl, the bristle and thread, the lapstone and hammer, with plenty of "elbow grease" were, as they had been for years, the main appliances of the shoemakers, and little was known or thought of laborsaving machinery. After a time, women's nimble fingers were found inadequate to the demand, and sewing machines soon transformed the old-fashioned "shoe-binder" into a new and more expensive class of "machine girls" whose capacity for labor was only limited by the capabilities of the machines over which they presided. Iron and steel came to the aid of wearied fingers and weakened eyes. This was the beginning of the new era, which is destined to produce results big with lasting benefits to our flourishing city.

It is scarcely ten years since the first introduction of machinery of any kind into the manufacture of shoes in this city. Everything was done by hand, even to the cutting out of the soles, which was a slow process, and required the expenditure of a large amount of physical force. The introduction of sole-cutting and stripping machines, although used sparingly, was the first indication that a change was to take place in the business of shoemaking; but no one, even ten years ago, would have dared to prophesy that the change was to be so immediate and so great. The rapid progress that has been made during that time, and *especially within the past year or two*, in the introduction of machinery in shoemaking, has been beyond all previous calculation. It may almost be said that handwork has already become the exception, and machinery the rule. The little shoemaker's shop and the shoemaker's bench are passing rapidly away, soon to be known no more among us; and the immense factory, with its laboring steam engine and its busy hum of whirling wheels, is rising up in their place to change the whole face of things in this ancient and honored metropolis of the "workers in the gentle craft of leather."

The problem as to how best to bring in and concentrate the vast army of men and women employed in the shoe manufacture of Lynn is one that has attracted the attention of many thinking minds among our businessmen, but it has never been satisfactorily solved until now. Machinery, and particularly the sewing machine, has done in a few short months what years of theorizing and speculation could not do. It has demonstrated that the factory system can be successfully and profitably introduced into the shoe business; in fact, that, with the rapid strides which the business has made within a few years, it is the only system that can be made available for its successful application in the future. Of course, the new system is yet in its infancy—the business is yet in a transition state; but the wheels of revolution are moving rapidly, and they never move backward. Operatives are pouring in as fast as room can be made for them; buildings for "shoe factories" are going up in every direction; the hum of machinery is heard on every hand; old things are passing away, and all things are becoming new.

8. Robert Owen's Alternative to Industrial Degradation, 1845

Had the capitalists and men of business in extensive operations been trained to understand their own interests and the interests of their country and of society generally, the late disasters which produced such overwhelming distress throughout the commercial world, arising solely from artificial causes, could never have occurred.

You desire to be independent of pecuniary circumstances, and to enjoy the advantages of wealth to the greatest extent when wisely expended. . . .

The mode to accomplish these most desirable objects will be to form joint stock companies with unlimited amount of capital—for any amount may be immediately advantageously employed—to form new superior establishments for producing and distributing wealth, for educating the children of the persons to be employed so that they shall acquire from their infancy a sound, practical, and active character, both physical and mental, under a new combination of greatly improved external circumstances, by which these establishments will, after paying a liberal interest for the capital during the intermediate time, always repay the capital by a sinking fund annually appropriated for that purpose, and will be easily governed on such principles as will be highly beneficial to the capitalists and operatives.

These establishments will enable the capitalists and men of extensive practical experience to solve without difficulty the great problem of the age, that is, how to apply the enormous and ever growing new scientific powers for producing wealth beneficially for the entire population, instead of allowing them to continue, as heretofore, most injuriously to create enormous riches for the few and to impoverish the many, driving them toward a desperation that will ultimately, if not untimely prevented by this measure, involve the overwealthy in utter destruction? . . .

My great desire is, without regard to class, party, sect, or present condition, permanently to benefit all.

Chapter 11:
Document Set 1 References

1. "Manufactures Summary: 1849–1954"
   Statistical History of the United States (Stamford: Fairfield Publishers, Inc., 1965), p. 409.

2. "Railroad Mileage and Equipment, 1830–1890"
   Statistical History of the United States, p. 427.

3. "Patent Applications Filed and Patents Issued, by Type and by Patentee: 1790–1879"
   Statistical History of the United States, p. 608.

4. An Anonymous Endorsement of Scientific Agriculture, 1858
   DeBow's Review, August 1858.

5. American Technology as an Influence Abroad, 1859
   Scientific American, March 5, 1859.

6. A Senate Report Measures the Railroads' Economic Significance, 1852
   U.S. Senate, Senate Document No. 112, 32nd Cong., 1st Sess., pp. 379–384.

7. A Trade Journal Outlines Technology's Impact on the Work Process in the Shoe Industry, 1864
   Fincher's Trade Review, March 26, 1864.

8. Robert Owen's Alternative to Industrial Degradation, 1845
   New York Daily Tribune, April 2, 1845.

CHAPTER 11

DOCUMENT SET 2
Health Issues as Social Concern: Physical Well-Being and the Quality of Life, 1840–1860

Side by side with the antebellum technological revolution there were more modest changes in everyday life as Americans learned to cope with a new social and economic environment. Your textbook demonstrates that, in countless ways, material conditions changed in response to the problems and opportunities inherent in a nation undergoing dramatic economic change. Related to the growth of cities was an increased concern for personal and social well-being that took the form of an emphasis on health-related issues. The following documents provide a sample of the new concern for physical health in the antebellum period.

As your textbook indicates, most Americans saw little improvement in the quality of their lives, although a rising middle class began to enjoy new physical comforts. More typical were the dangers of disease associated with the congestion of overcrowded urban communities. Consistent with the trend toward standardization and professionalization in an age of technology, reformers began to see health standards as a legitimate public concern. This interest is mirrored in the report of the Massachusetts public-health commission, which advanced a plan to safeguard the wellness of the state's population.

Related concerns were expressed in an appeal for physical fitness that appeared in the *Atlantic Monthly.*

Although it emphasized personal responsibility, its objectives were in some ways comparable to those contained in the Massachusetts report. Examine the two documents for evidence of shared goals.

One theme that emerges in these documents is the perception of personal and public health as reform issues. Note that social reformer Dorothea Dix addresses the welfare of mental patients as a humanitarian matter. Be aware of the connection between the search for social improvement and the concern for physical and mental well-being (see Chapter 10).

The prominence of health issues in this period also reflected a rising interest in scientific explanations for human maladies. Your textbook notes that several important medical breakthroughs raised hopes for healthier lives and greater longevity. The penchant for science reached its peak in the popularity of phrenology as the key to understanding human character and behavior. The excerpts from a phrenological journal reveal both the nature of this pseudoscience and a popular fascination with its study.

As you review the evidence, try to establish the relationships among the documents. Look for a common denominator. The documents reveal a great deal about the hopes and fears of Americans as a new society took shape.

Questions for Analysis

1. What was the relationship between personal/public-health issues and the social currents evident in the antebellum United States? What evidence can be found in the documents to clarify the link between physical health and social improvement?

2. How do the documents reflect changes in the American economic system between 1840 and 1860? What problems resulted from the new economic realities?

3. What do the excerpts from the *American Journal of Phrenology* reveal about popular interests in the antebellum years? How are these ideas consistent with the social and scientific developments described in the textbook? Does the phrenology craze provide insight into the future of American social attitudes?

4. What is the meaning of *professionalization,* as applied to the evolution of medicine and law in nineteenth-century America? What assumptions and attitudes were associated with the trend toward professionalization? How does the evidence reflect the influence of middle-class thought and professional values?

5. What light do the documents shed on the objectives of their authors? What goals were shared by the reformers who concerned themselves with the health issues of the 1840s and 1850s? Why were they promoting their respective causes?

1. A Commission Plan for Public Health in Massachusetts, 1850

I. *We recommend that the laws of the state relating to public health be thoroughly revised, and that a new and improved act be passed in their stead.*

We suppose that it will be generally conceded that no plan for a sanitary survey of the state, however good or desirable, can be carried into operation unless established by law. The legislative authority is necessary to give it efficiency and usefulness. The efforts, both of associations and individuals, have failed in these matters. We have shown that the present health laws of the state are exceedingly imperfect, even for the general object for which they were designed; that it is difficult, and perhaps impracticable, to ascertain what precise powers they confer and what duties they require; and that they are not adapted, in any way, to the purposes of a sanitary survey. . . .

II. *We recommend that a General Board of Health be established, which shall be charged with the general execution of the laws of the state, relating to the enumeration, the vital statistics, and the public health of the inhabitants. . . .*

The cause of public health needs a . . . central agency to give to the whole sanitary movement a uniform, wise, efficient, economical, and useful direction. If different local authorities, or individuals—not always possessed of the best means of information—are left to originate plans for their own guidance, and anything is done, they will be more likely to make unintentional mistakes and create unnecessary expense than if wise and able minds were devoted to the subject, and suggested what ought to be done, and the best and most economical mode of doing it. . . .

III. *We recommend that the Board, as far as practicable, be composed of two physicians, one counselor at law, one chemist or natural philosopher, one civil engineer, and two persons of other professions or occupations; all properly qualified for the office by their talents, their education, their experience, and their wisdom. . . .*

XV. *We recommend that provision be made for obtaining observations of the atmospheric phenomena, on a systematic and uniform plan, in different stations in the commonwealth.*

The atmosphere of air which surrounds the earth is essential to all living beings. Life and health depend upon it; and neither could exist without it. Its character is modified in various ways; but especially by temperature, weight, and composition; and each of these modifications has an important sanitary influence. . . .

XVIII. *We recommend that, in erecting schoolhouses, churches, and other public buildings, health should be regarded in their site, structure, heating apparatus, and ventilation.*

To provide for all public buildings where large numbers of people congregate, an abundant and constant supply of air in its pure, natural state and of a proper temperature is a very important though difficult matter. It is so, too, in regard to private dwellings. . . .

XIX. *We recommend that, before erecting any new dwelling house, manufactory, or other building, for personal accommodation, either as a lodging house or place of business, the owner or builder be required to give notice to the local Board of Health of his intention and of the sanitary arrangements he proposes to adopt.*

XX. *We recommend that local Boards of Health endeavor to prevent or mitigate the sanitary evils arising from overcrowded lodging houses and cellar dwellings.*

Such places are universally acknowledged to be incompatible with health. The hints already given have shown the destructive influence of corrupted air. . . .

XXI. *We recommend that open spaces be reserved in cities and villages for public walks; that wide streets be laid out; and that both be ornamented with trees. . . .*

XXV. *We recommend that measures be taken to ascertain the amount of sickness suffered in different localities; and among persons of different classes, professions, and occupations. . . .*

XXVII. *We recommend that every city and town in the state be required to provide means for the periodical vaccination of the inhabitants. . . .*

XXX. *We recommend that measures be taken to prevent or mitigate the sanitary evils arising from the use of intoxicating drinks and from haunts of dissipation.*

That intemperance is an enormous evil is universally acknowledged. That it is the cause of a vast amount of direct sanitary suffering—of unnecessary sickness and of unnecessary death—to those who indulge in it; and of a still greater amount of indirect sanitary suffering and death to their associates, relatives, and dependents is equally true. . . .

XXXII. *We recommend that the authority now vested in justices of the peace relating to insane and idiotic persons not arrested or indicted for crime be transferred to the local Boards of Health.*

By the present laws of the state, no insane or idiotic person other than paupers can be committed to any hospital or place of confinement except on complaint, in writing, before two justices of the peace, or some police court. Paupers may be committed by the overseers of the poor. By these proceedings, this unfortunate class of persons appear on the records as criminals while they are guilty of no crime, unless the possession of an unsound mind be considered one. A sanitary question, merely, is often the only one presented in such cases, and it has occurred to us that the local Boards of Health would be the proper tribunals before whom they should be brought and by whom they should be disposed of. . . .

XXXVI. *We recommend that measures be adopted for preventing or mitigating the sanitary evils arising from foreign emigration.* . . .

The state should pass suitable laws on the subject, and the general and local Boards of Health should carefully observe these evils in all their sanitary bearings and relations. We would, however, suggest:

1. That emigration, especially of paupers, invalids, and criminals, should, by all proper means, be discouraged; and that misrepresentation and falsehood, to induce persons to embark in passenger ships, should be discountenanced and counteracted.

2. That ship owners and others should be held to strict accountability for all expenses of pauper emigrants, and that existing bonds for their support should be strictly enforced.

3. That a system be devised by which all emigrants, or those who introduce them, by water or by land, should be required to pay a sufficient sum to create a general sinking fund for the support of all who may require aid in the state, at least within five years after their arrival.

2. A Plea for Physical Fitness, 1858

Physical health is a necessary condition of all permanent success. To the American people it has a stupendous importance, because it is the only attribute of power in which they are losing ground. Guarantee us against physical degeneracy, and we can risk all other perils—financial crisis, slavery, Romanism, Mormonism, border ruffians, and New York assassins; "domestic malice, foreign levy, nothing" can daunt us. Guarantee us health, and Mrs. Stowe cannot frighten us with all the prophecies of Dred; but when her sister Catherine informs us that in all the vast female acquaintance of the Beecher family there are not a dozen healthy women, we confess ourselves a little tempted to despair of the republic. . . .

A great physician has said, "I know not which is most indispensable for the support of the frame, food or exercise." But who in this community really takes exercise? Even the mechanic commonly confines himself to one set of muscles; the blacksmith acquires strength in his right arm and the dancing master in his left leg. But the professional or businessman, what muscles has he at all? . . .

Let any man test his physical condition, we will not say by sawing his own cord of wood, but by an hour in the gymnasium or at cricket, and his enfeebled muscular apparatus will groan with rheumatism for a week. Or let him test the strength of his arms and chest by raising and lowering himself a few times upon a horizontal bar, or hanging by the arms to a rope, and he will probably agree with Galen in pronouncing it *robustum validumque laborem* [firm and strong effort]. Yet so manifestly are these things within the reach of common constitutions that a few weeks or months of judicious practice will renovate his whole system, and the most vigorous exercise will refresh him like a cold bath. . . .

We have shown that, in one way or another, American schoolboys obtain active exercise. The same is true, in a very limited degree, even of girls. They are occasionally, in our larger cities, sent to gymnasiums, the more the better. Dancing schools are better than nothing, though all the attendant circumstances are usually unfavorable. A fashionable young lady is estimated to traverse her 300 miles a season on foot; and this needs training. But outdoor exercise for girls is terribly restricted—first, by their costume, and second, by the remarks of Mrs. Grundy. All young female animals unquestionably require as much motion as their brothers, and naturally make as much noise; but what mother would not be shocked, in the case of her girl of twelve, at one-tenth part the activity and uproar which are recognized as being the breath of life to her twin brother? Still, there is a change going on, which is tantamount to an admission that there is an evil to be remedied. . . .

But even among American men, how few carry athletic habits into manhood! The great hindrance, no doubt, is absorption in business; and we observe that this winter's hard times and consequent leisure have given a great stimulus to outdoor sports. But in most places there is the further obstacle, that a certain stigma of boyishness goes with them.

3. Dorothea Dix Calls for Humane Treatment of the Mentally Ill, 1843

Gentlemen,—I respectfully ask to present this Memorial [report], believing that the *cause,* which actuates to and sanctions so unusual a movement, presents no equivocal claim to public consideration and sympathy. Surrendering to calm and deep convictions of duty my habitual views of what is womanly and becoming, I proceed briefly to explain what has conducted me before you unsolicited and unsustained, trusting, while I do so, that the memorialist will be speedily forgotten in the memorial. . . .

I come to present the strong claims of suffering humanity. I come to place before the Legislature of Massachusetts the condition of the miserable, the desolate, the outcast. I come as the advocate of helpless, forgotten, insane, and idiotic men and women; of beings sunk to a condition from which the most unconcerned would start with real horror; of beings wretched in our prisons, and more wretched in our almshouses. And I cannot suppose it needful to employ earnest persuasion, or stubborn argument, in order to arrest and fix attention upon a subject only the more strongly pressing in its claims because it is revolting and disgusting in its details.

I must confine myself to few examples, but am ready to furnish other and more complete details, if required. If my pictures are displeasing, coarse, and severe, my subjects, it must be recollected, offer no tranquil, refined, or composing features. The condition of human beings, reduced to the extremest states of degradation and misery, cannot be exhibited in softened language, or adorn a polished page.

I proceed, gentlemen, briefly to call your attention to the *present* state of insane persons confined within this Commonwealth, in *cages, closets, cellars, stalls, pens! Chained, naked, beaten with rods,* and *lashed* into obedience.

As I state cold, severe *facts,* I feel obliged to refer to persons, and definitely to indicate localities. But it is upon my subject, not upon localities or individuals, I desire to fix attention; and I would speak as kindly as possible of all wardens, keepers, and other responsible officers, believing that *most* of these have erred not through hardness of heart and wilful cruelty so much as want of skill and knowledge, and want of consideration. Familiarity with suffering, it is said, blunts the sensibilities, and where neglect once finds a footing other injuries are multiplied. This is not all, for it may justly and strongly be added that, from the deficiency of adequate means to meet the wants of these cases, it has been an absolute impossibility to do justice in this matter. Prisons are not constructed in view of being converted into county hospitals, and almshouses are not founded as receptacles for the insane. And yet, in the face of justice and common sense, wardens are by law compelled to receive, and the masters of almshouses not to refuse, insane and idiotic subjects in all stages of mental disease and privation.

It is the Commonwealth, not its integral parts, that is accountable for most of the abuses which have lately and do still exist. I repeat it, it is defective legislation which perpetuates and multiplies these abuses.

4. The Wonders of Phrenology Revealed, 1841

Between eminently intellectual individuals and idiots the difference is similar to that which obtains between man and mammalia. Men of large heads, according to Magendie, have capacious minds; whereas in idiots, as in the quadrumana, the brain is small, the convolutions few and shallow, and the anterior lobes but little developed. If, indeed, we extend the comparison through all the intermediate gradations of intellect, we shall be astonished to find a corresponding agreement. "The mind of the negro and the Hottentot, of the Calmuck and Carib, is inferior to that of the European, and their organization is less perfect,"—"the intellectual characters are reduced, the animal features enlarged and exaggerated." Even hatters have ascertained that servants and negroes have smaller heads than others. Women are as unlike men in the form of their heads as in the qualities of their minds. In men of commanding talents the greater quantity of cerebral matter is anterior to the ear; but in heads which are truncated before, and largely developed in the opposite direction, the passions will be found to be stronger than the understanding. The higher sentiments elevate the *calvaria* or top of the head; it is accordingly observed, that from men whose heads are flattened, as in quadrupeds,

"Conscience, virtue, honor, are exiled."

Pope Alexander the Second is an illustrious example. Other differences might be enumerated; but to extend our observations farther would be to trench upon the discoveries of Messrs. Gall and Spurzheim, whose conclusions, indeed, are but an extension of this comparison founded on *observation* and confirmed by *experiment*.

5. Phrenology Draws an Enthusiastic Endorsement, 1840

Mr. Combe's Lectures in Albany, N.Y.—The Albany Argus, of February 10, contained the following account of Mr. Combe's recent course of lectures in that city:—

"*Chapel of the Albany Female Academy, February 7, 1840.*

"At the close of Mr. Combe's course of lectures on phrenology, a meeting of the class was called, and on motion, Thomas W. Olcott, Esq., was appointed chairman, and the Rev. Dr. Buillions, secretary.

"Mr. Olcott stated the object of the meeting in a brief address, as follows:—

" 'Ladies and Gentlemen: We have listened to the exposition of the principles of phrenology, be decidedly the most gifted and distinguished advocate and teacher of that science now living, and the object of the meeting now called, is to convey to Mr. Combe, on bidding him farewell, the assurance of the pleasure with which we have attended his class, and heard his lectures. The importance of phrenology, as a guide to health and physical education, most of competent judges will freely admit. The respected senior trustee of the institution in which we are now assembled, has long been an able and faithful champion of this branch of the subject; and Combe of Phrenology has been adopted as a text-book in this academy. If the science has not attained the accuracy of precision in details, yet its general principles are beginning to be acknowledged, and to occupy the attention of the most profound and cultivated minds. The proof of this fact, I have in the character of the audience before me. If the gentlemen have any remarks or resolutions to offer, they will now be entertained.'

"The following resolutions were offered by Rufus W. Peckham, Esq., and unanimously adopted:—

" '*Resolved,* That we have listened with deep and increasing interest to the lectures delivered by George Combe, Esq., of Edinburgh, on the subject of phrenology and its application.

" '*Resolved,* That we feel gratified, and in the highest degree instructed, by the clear and able manner in which the principles of that science have been explained, and that the facts and numerous illustrations with which Mr. Combe has fortified and enforced his principal positions, entitle them, in our view, to great weight and consideration.

" '*Resolved,* That the application made by Mr. Combe, of the science of phrenology to the explaining of life's complicated phenomena, and to the unfolding of the great principles upon which the physical education and the intellectual and moral culture of the young should be conducted, invest it with an interest, which, we believe, has not hitherto been properly appreciated; and we hope the day is not far distant, when every parent in this country shall be familiar with those principles.

" 'Resolved, That, in our estimation, the American people are greatly indebted to Mr. Combe for his eminently successful efforts in promulgating doctrines so vitally essential to the proper development of the physical and mental powers of man, and the increasing consequences of which can be realised in a manner adequate to their importance, only by coming generations.' . . . "

Chapter 11:
Document Set 2 References

1. A Commission Plan for Public Health in Massachusetts, 1850
   Report of a General Plan for the Promotion of Public and Personal Health (Boston: 1850), pp. 109–206.

2. A Plea for Physical Fitness, 1858
   Atlantic Monthly (March 1858).

3. Dorothea Dix Calls for Humane Treatment of the Mentally Ill, 1843
   Dorothea Dix, "Memorial to the Legislature of Massachusetts," in *Old South Leaflets* (Boston: Directors of the Old South Work, 1902), Vol. 6, No. 148, pp. 1–3.

4. The Wonders of Phrenology Revealed, 1841
   American Phrenological Journal, Vol. 3 (July 1841).

5. Phrenology Draws an Enthusiastic Endorsement, 1840
   American Phrenological Journal, Vol. 2 (March 1840).

CHAPTER 12

DOCUMENT SET 1
Life in Bondage: Voices from Below

Essential to an understanding of the Civil War is a familiarity with the antebellum South's central social and economic institution, chattel slavery. Recognizing its importance, your textbook emphasizes slave life and African American culture in its treatment of the Old South. However, any attempt to assess the impact of enslavement on the slaves themselves is complicated by serious methodological difficulties, most of them rooted in the scarcity and unreliability of evidence. One problem is the potential bias in the elite sources often used in historical research and writing. Since most slaves were illiterate, leaving few letters, diaries, or memoirs, later generations interpreted their lives through the eyes of the master class or contemporary outside observers.

In recent years, however, scholars have turned increasingly to social history and the examination of the past "from the bottom up." This trend has led to an increased emphasis on the story of the underclass in America, including a strong focus on black history. The result has been a heightened awareness of the research problems encountered in interpreting slavery and its impact on those who struggled within its confines.

Among the most important sources of documentation in this effort are slave narratives and the memoirs of escaped slaves. While both are valuable, they present significant challenges to students and scholars seeking to form a balanced view of the "peculiar institution." Modern scholars understand the special value of oral tradition in preserving black culture and depicting black experience, but they also recognize the limitations of relying on memory as well as the possible influence of an interviewer. Significant as slave memoirs are, the purposes of black abolitionists also must be considered when evaluating their recollections as accounts of enslavement.

The primary problem addressed in the following documents is slavery's impact on the enslaved as seen from the slave's perspective. As you review the evidence, be aware of the factors that influenced the authors' accounts. Ask whether the source persons were educated and whether they remained slaves until after the war. Determine what their goals were in providing the accounts. Compare these accounts with your textbook's treatment of slave discipline, family life, black music, and the nature of resistance.

Questions for Analysis

1. What do the documents reveal about the relationships between slaves and their masters and mistresses? Was the experience of bondage different for men and women? How? Why?

2. How was slave culture influenced by enslavement? What were the respective roles of religion, musical expression, and the family in slave life? What do the documents reveal about the black and the white perspectives on these institutions?

3. What was the impact of enslavement on slave personality? What light do the documents shed on the self-images developed by slaves? What was the impact of bondage on the slave's view of the world and response to slavery?

4. Compare the recollections of escaped slaves who fled north with the memories of those who remained entrapped in the "peculiar institution." How would you account for the differences? What is the significance of disagreements revealed by the available evidence?

5. What precautions should scholars take in evaluating slave music, narratives, and memoirs? What are the limitations of the evidence? What unique opportunities does it offer?

1. Frederick Douglass Comments on the Pain of Enslavement, 1845

I have met many religious colored people, at the south, who are under the delusion that God requires them to submit to slavery, and to wear their chains with meekness and humility. I could entertain no such nonsense as this; and I almost lost my patience when I found any colored man weak enough to believe such stuff. Nevertheless, the increase of knowledge was attended with bitter, as well as sweet results. The more I read, the more I was led to abhor and detest slavery, and my enslavers. . . . Knowledge had come; light had penetrated the moral dungeon where I dwelt; and, behold! there lay the bloody whip, for my back, and here was the iron chain; and my good, *kind master,* he was the author of my situation. The revelation haunted me, stung me, and made me gloomy and miserable. As I writhed under the sting and torment of this knowledge, I almost envied my fellow slaves their stupid contentment. . . . It was this everlasting thinking which distressed and tormented me; and yet there was no getting rid of the subject of my thoughts. All nature was redolent of it. Once awakened by the silver trump of knowledge, my spirit was roused to eternal wakefulness. Liberty! the inestimable birthright of every man, had, for me, converted every object into an asserter of this great right. . . .

My feelings were not the result of any marked cruelty in the treatment I received; they sprung from the consideration of my being a slave at all. It was *slavery*—not its mere *incidents*—that I hated. I had been cheated. I saw through the attempt to keep me in ignorance; I saw that slaveholders would have gladly made me believe that they were merely acting under the authority of God, in making a slave of me, and in making slaves of others; and I treated them as robbers and deceivers. The feeding and clothing me well, could not atone for taking my liberty from me. . . . [P]ious as Mr. Covey was, he proved himself to be as unscrupulous and base as the worst of his neighbors. In the beginning, he was only able—as he said—"to buy one slave"; and, scandalous and shocking as is the fact, he boasted that he bought her simply *"as a breeder."* But the worst is not told in this naked statement. This young woman (Caroline was her name) was virtually compelled by Mr. Covey to abandon herself to the object for which he had purchased her; and the result was, the birth of twins at the end of the year. At this addition to his human stock, both Edward Covey and his wife, Susan, were ecstatic with joy. No one dreamed of reproaching the woman, or of finding fault with the hired man—Bill Smith—the father of the two children, for Mr. Covey himself had locked the two up together every night, thus inviting the result.

But I will pursue this revolting subject no further. No better illustration of the unchaste and demoralizing character of slavery can be found, than is furnished in the fact that this professedly Christian slaveholder, amidst all his prayers and hymns, was shamelessly and boastfully encouraging, and actually compelling, in his own house, undisguised and unmitigated fornication, as a means of increasing his human stock. I may remark here, that, while this fact will be read with disgust and shame at the north, it will be *laughed at,* as smart and praiseworthy in Mr. Covey, at the south; for a man is no more condemned there for buying a woman and devoting her to this life of dishonor, than for buying a cow, and raising stock from her. The same rules are observed, with a view to increasing the number and quality of the former, as of the latter. . . .

[A]s I now look back, I can see that we [slaves] did many silly things, very well calculated to awaken suspicion. We were, at times, remarkably buoyant, singing hymns and making joyous exclamations, almost as triumphant in their tone as if we had reached a land of freedom and safety. A keen observer might have detected in our repeated singing of

"O Canaan, sweet Canaan,
I am bound for the land of Canaan,"

something more than a hope of reaching heaven. We meant to reach the *north*—and the north was our Canaan.

2. Slave Music and the Desire for Liberation

Go Down, Moses

Go down, Moses,
’Way down in Egypt land,
Tell ole Pharaoh,
To let my people go.

Go down, Moses,
’Way down in Egypt land,
Tell ole Pharaoh,
To let my people go.

When Israel was in Egypt land,
Let my people go,
Oppressed so hard they could not stand,
Let my people go,
Thus spoke the Lord, bold Moses said,
Let my people go,
If not I’ll smite your first-born dead,
Let my people go.

Go down, Moses,
’Way down in Egypt land,
Tell ole Pharaoh,
To let my people go.

I Thank God I’m Free at Last

Free at last, free at last,
I thank God I’m free at last.
Free at last, free at last,
I thank God I’m free at last.

Way down yonder in the graveyard walk,
I thank God I’m free at last,
Me and my Jesus gonna meet an’ talk,
I thank God I’m free at last.

On-a my knees when the light pass by,
I thank God I’m free at last,
Thought my soul would rise an’ fly,
I thank God I’m free at last.

One o’ these mornin’s bright an’ fair,
I thank God I’m free at last,
Gonna meet my Jesus in the middle o’ the air,
I thank God I’m free at last.

Free at last, free at last,
I thank God I’m free at last,
Free at last, free at last,
I thank God I’m free at last.

3. A Slave Perspective on Family Ties

Once Massa goes to Baton Rouge and brung back a yaller gal dressed in fine style. She was a seamster nigger. He builds her a house ’way from the quarters, and she done fine sewing for the whites. Us niggers knowed the doctor took a black woman quick as he did a white and took any on his place he wanted, and he took them often. But mostly the children born on the place looked like niggers. Aunt Cheyney always says four of hers was Massa’s, but he didn’t give them no mind. But this yaller gal breeds so fast and gits a mess of white young-uns. She larnt them fine manners and combs out they hair.

Oncet two of them goes down the hill to the doll-house, where the Missy’s children am playing. They wants to go in the dollhouse and one the Missy’s boys say, “That’s for white children.” They say, “We ain’t no niggers, ’cause we got the same daddy you has, and he comes to see us near every day and fotches us clothes and things from town.” They is fussing, and Missy is listening out her chamber window. She heard them white niggers say, “He is our daddy and we call him daddy when he comes to our house to see our mama.”

When Massa come home that evening, his wife hardly say nothing to him, and he ask her what the matter, and she tells him, "Since you asks me, I'm studying in my mind 'bout them white young-uns of that yaller nigger wench from Baton Rouge." He say, "Now, honey, I fotches that gal just for you, 'cause she a fine seamster." She say, "It look kind of funny they got the same kind of hair and eyes as my children, and they got a nose look like yours." He say, "Honey, you just paying 'tention to talk of little children that ain't got no mind to what they say." She say, "Over in Mississippi I got a home and plenty with my daddy, and I got that in my mind."

Well, she didn't never leave, and Massa bought her a fine, new span of surrey hosses. But she don't never have no more children, and she ain't so cordial with the Massa. That yaller gal has more white young-uns, but they don't never go down the hill no more to the big house.

4. Religion as Social Control: A Catechism for Slaves, 1854

Q. Who keeps the snakes and all bad things from hurting you?
A. God does.
Q. Who gave you a master and a mistress?
A. God gave them to me.
Q. Who says that you must obey them?
A. God says that I must.
Q. What book tells you these things?
A. The Bible.
Q. How does God do all his work?
A. He always does it right.
Q. Does God love to work?
A. Yes, God is always at work.
Q. Do the angels work?
A. Yes, they do what God tells them.
Q. Do they love to work?
A. Yes, they love to please God.

Q. What does God say about your work?
A. He that will not work shall not eat.
Q. Did Adam and Eve have to work?
A. Yes, they had to keep the garden.
Q. Was it hard to keep that garden?
A. No, it was very easy.
Q. What makes the crops so hard to grow now?
A. Sin makes it.
Q. What makes you lazy?
A. My wicked heart.
Q. How do you know your heart is wicked?
A. I feel it every day.
Q. Who teaches you so many wicked things?
A. The Devil.
Q. Must you let the Devil teach you?
A. No, I must not.

5. A Slave Recollection of Insecurity

Weren't none o' de slaves offen our plantation ever sold, but de ones on de other plantation of Marse William were. Oh, dat was a terrible time! All de slaves be in de field, plowin', hoein', and singin' in de boilin' sun. Ole Marse, he come through de field with a man call de speculator. Dey walked round just lookin', just lookin'. All de darkies know what dis mean. Dey didn't dare look up, just work right on. Den de speculator he see who he want. He talk to Ole Marse, den dey slaps de handcuffs on him and take him away to de cotton country.

Oh, dem was awful times! When de speculator was ready to go with de slaves, if dere was anyone who didn't want to go, he thrash 'em, den tie 'em behind de wagon and make 'em run till dey fall on de ground, den he thrash 'em till dey say dey go without no trouble. Sometime some of dem run away and come back to de plantation, den it was harder on dem dan before. When de darkies went to dinner de ole nigger mammy she ask where am such and such. None of de others want to tell her. But when she see dem look down to de ground she just say: "De speculator, de speculator." Den de tears roll down her cheeks, cause maybe it her son or husband and she know she never see 'em again. Maybe dey leaves babies to home, may be just pappy and mammy. Oh, my lordy, my ole boss was mean, but he never sent us to de cotton country.

Dey was very few schools back in dat day and time, very few. We darkies didn't dare look at no book, not even to pick it up. Ole Missie, dat is, my first ole missie, she was a good ole woman. She read to de niggers and to de white chillun. She come from 'cross de water. She weren't like de smart white folks livin' here now. When she come over here she brung darky boy with her. He was her personal servant. 'Course, dey got different names for dem now, but in dat day dey calls 'em "Guinea niggers." She was good ole woman, not like other white folks. Niggers like Ole Missie.

6. Memories of a Brutal Institution

Me and my husband couldn't live together till after freedom 'cause we had different marsters. When freedom come, Marster wanted all us niggers to sign up to stay till Christmas. After dat we worked on shares on de Hart plantation; den we farmed four-five years with Mr. Bill Johnson.

I'm goin' to tell you de truth. I don't tell no lies. Dese has been better times to me. I think it's better to work for yourself and have what you make dan to work for somebody else and don't get nothin' out of it. Slavery days was mighty hard. My marster was good to us (I mean he didn't beat us much, and he give us plenty plain food), but some slaves suffered awful. My aunt was beat cruel once, and lots de other slaves. When dey got ready to beat you, dey'd strip you stark mother naked and dey'd say, "Come here to me, God damn you! Come to me clean! Walk up to dat tree, and damn you, hug dat tree!" Den dey tie your hands round de tree, den tie your feets; den dey'd lay de rawhide on you and cut your buttocks open. Sometimes dey'd rub turpentine and salt in de raw places, and den beat you some more. Oh, it was awful! And what could you do? Dey had all de advantage of you. I never did get no beatin' like dat, but I got whippin's—plenty o' 'em. I had plenty o' devilment in me, but I quit all my devilment when I was married. I used to fight—fight with anything I could get my hands on.

You had to have passes to go from one plantation to another. Some de niggers would slip off sometime and go without a pass, or maybe Marster was busy and dey didn't bother him for a pass, so dey go without one. In every district dey had about twelve men dey call patterrollers. Dey ride up and down and round looking for niggers without passes. If dey ever caught you off your plantation with no pass, dey beat you all over.

7. Josiah Henson Recalls Broken Families and Personal Opportunity

Common as are slave-auctions in the southern states, and naturally as a slave may look forward to the time when he will be put upon the block, still the full misery of the event—of the scenes which precede and succeed it—is never understood till the actual experience comes. . . . Young as I was then, the iron entered into my soul. The remembrance of the breaking up of McPherson's estate is photographed in its minutest features in my mind. The crowd collected round the stand, the huddling group of negroes, the examination of muscle, teeth, the exhibition of agility, the look of the auctioneer, the agony of my mother—I can shut my eyes and see them all.

My brothers and sisters were bid off first, and one by one, while my mother, paralyzed by grief, held me by the hand. Her turn came, and she was bought by Isaac Riley of Montgomery county. Then I was offered to the assembled purchasers. My mother, half distracted with the thought of parting forever from all her children, pushed through the crowd while the bidding for me was going on, to the spot where Riley was standing. She fell at his feet, and clung to his knees, entreating him in tones that a mother only could command, to buy her *baby* as well as herself, and spare to her one, at least, of her little ones. Will it, can it be believed that this man, thus appealed to, was capable not merely of turning a deaf ear to her supplication, but of disengaging himself from her with such violent blows and kicks, as to reduce her to the necessity of creeping out of his reach, and mingling the groan of bodily suffering with the sob of a breaking heart? As she crawled away from the brutal man I heard her sob out, "Oh, Lord Jesus, how long, how long shall I suffer this way!" I must have been then between five and six years old. I seem to see and hear my poor weeping mother now. . . .

The character of Riley, the master whom I faithfully served for many years, is by no means an uncommon one in any part of the world; the evil is, that a domestic institution should anywhere put it in the power of such a one to tyrannize over his fellow beings, and inflict so much needless misery as is sure to be inflicted by such a man in such a position. . . . The natural tendency of slavery is to convert the master into a tyrant, and the slave into the cringing, treacherous, false, and thieving victim of tyranny. Riley and his slaves were no exception to the general rule, but might be cited as apt illustrations of the nature of the relation. . . .

My situation as overseer I retained, together with the especial favor of my master, who was not displeased either with saving the expense of a large salary for a white superintendent, or with the superior crops I was able to raise for him. I will not deny that I used his property more freely than he would have done himself, in supplying his people with better food; but if I cheated him in this way, in small matters, it was unequivocally for his own benefit in more important ones; and I accounted, with the strictest honesty, for every dollar I received in the sale of the property entrusted to me. . . . For many years I was his factotum, and supplied him with all his means for all his purposes, whether they were good or bad. I had no reason to think highly of his moral character; but it was my duty to be faithful to him in the position in which he placed me; and I can boldly declare, before God and man, that I was so. I forgave him the causeless blows and injuries he had inflicted on me in childhood and youth, and was proud of the favor he now showed me, and of the character and reputation I had earned by strenuous and persevering efforts.

8. Slaves as Property

A. Slave Branding Irons, Early Nineteenth Century

B. An Abolitionist View of Slave Discipline

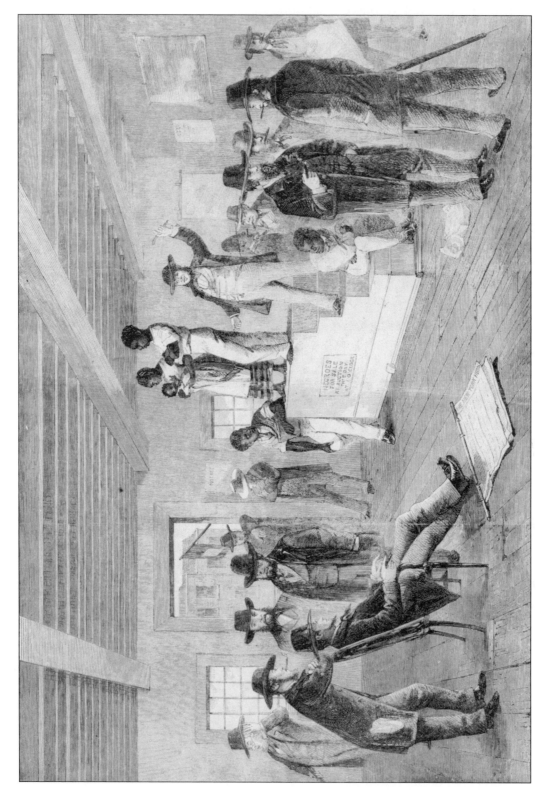

C. Slave Auction in Virginia, ca. 1850s

D. Routine Transfer of Property, 1858

ESTATE SALE.

124 RICE FIELD NEGROES,

Belonging to the Estate of the late Dr. G. W. MORRIS,

By JACOB COHEN & SON.

Will be Sold, in the Chalmers Street Mart,

ON TUESDAY, JANUARY 12, 1858, AT 11 O'CLOCK,

TERMS:

One-third CASH; balance in three equal annual instalments, interest payable annually, secured by bond and mortgage, with approved personal security.

☞ Purchasers to pay us for papers.

Chapter 12:
Document Set 1 References

1. Frederick Douglass Comments on the Pain of Enslavement, 1845
   Frederick Douglass, *My Bondage and My Freedom* (New York: Miller, Orton and Co., 1857), pp. 159–161, 218–219, 278–279.

2. Slave Music and the Desire for Liberation
   "Go Down, Moses," "I Thank God I'm Free at Last," in Thomas R. Frazier, ed., *Afro-American History: Primary Sources* (New York: Harcourt, Brace, & World, Inc., 1970), pp. 92, 95.

3. A Slave Perspective on Family Ties
   Mary Reynolds/A Narrative, from B. A. Botkin, ed., *Lay My Burden Down: A Folk History of Slavery* (Chicago: University of Chicago Press, 1945), pp. 122–123.

4. Religion as Social Control: A Catechism for Slaves, 1854
   "Frederick Douglass' Paper," June 2, 1854, from *The Southern Episcopalian* (Charleston, S.C., April 1854).

5. A Slave Recollection of Insecurity
   Sara Gudger/A Narrative, from Federal Writers' Project, Slave Narratives, "A Folk History of Slavery in the United States from Interviews with Former Slaves" (Washington, D.C.: Typewritten Records Prepared by the Federal Writers' Project, 1941), in Norman R. Yetman, *Life Under the "Peculiar Institution"* (New York: Holt, Rinehart and Winston, Inc., 1970), p. 152.

6. Memories of a Brutal Institution
   Ferebe Rodgers/A Narrative, in Yetman, pp. 257–258.

7. Josiah Henson Recalls Broken Families and Personal Opportunity
   Josiah Henson, "My First Great Trial," in Harvey Wish, ed., *Slavery in the South* (New York: Noonday Press; Farrar, Straus, & Giroux, 1968), pp. 25–26, 36.

8. Slaves as Property
   A. Slave Branding Irons, Early Nineteenth Century. Branding irons belonging to George Hyde Clarke, 1768–1835, who operated large plantations in Jamaica, Hull Museums.
   B. An Abolitionist View of Slave Discipline. *American Anti-Slavery Almanac* (Boston: American Anti-Slavery Society, 1838). American Antiquarian Society.
   C. Slave Auction in Virginia, ca. 1850s. *London Illustrated News*, Vol. 38, p. 139, ca. 1857. New York Public Library.
   D. Routine Transfer of Property, 1858. American Antiquarian Society.

Chapter 12:
Document Set 1 Credits

DOCUMENT SET 2
The Economy of the Old South: King Cotton and the Dissenters

Chapter 12 examines the economy of the Old South, with emphasis on the cotton culture that was central to the region's growth. As your text notes, the lure of cotton cast an irresistible spell over white southerners, who exploited both soil and slave in the quest for prosperity. The result was the rapid expansion of the cotton belt into the trans-Mississippi Southwest by the 1850s, accompanied by consolidation of the slave system.

However, the extension of the "Cotton Kingdom" did not occur without economic penalties. Not only did cotton cultivation place a strain on the soil, but it also required a significant capital investment that sometimes led planters into heavy debt. Equally significant was an increasing divergence between the economies of North and South. While staple crop agriculture proved profitable and brought money into the South, there was also a semicolonial aspect to a southern economy that relied increasingly on external sources for manufactured goods.

Despite the influence of "King Cotton's" supporters, there was another line of southern economic thought. As your textbook indicates, the region was not without its proponents of commercial and industrial activity. In fact, there were several striking examples of successful southern manufacturing establishments, especially in the older, eastern South. Yet in the final analysis, the profitability and social endorsement of a slave-based system undermined any hopes for significant economic diversification.

Beneath the surface of southern cultural consensus lay a lively controversy over the South's economic future. The following documents provide samples of the divergent views expressed in the 1850s. Although the northern position is represented in the excerpts from New York and Cincinnati journalists Frederick Law Olmsted and David Christy, most of the documents are the work of southern commentators on the cotton economy. James D. B. De Bow was a southern journalist and editor. James Henry Hammond was a South Carolina politician who served at various times as U.S. congressman, governor of his state, and U.S. senator. Hinton Rowan Helper was a middle-class nonslaveholder from North Carolina who moved north to pursue a writing career.

As you review the evidence, be sensitive to the authors' economic assumptions and long-term goals. Be aware of their purposes in arguing for or against southern social and economic institutions. Watch for the influence of personal beliefs on the various arguments. Try to assess the writers' success in defending their positions.

Your analysis of the evidence will reveal the wide variety of political and economic opinions in the antebellum South. Moreover, the documents contain conflicting definitions of social and economic progress that belie easy generalization about southern thought prior to the Civil War. Try to determine why the argument for a cotton-based economy was ultimately accepted by the majority of southerners.

Questions for Analysis

1. Analyze the arguments for southern industrialization and commercial growth. What fears were evident in the writings of southern journalists, including the well-known census official and publisher, James D. B. De Bow? How did the ideas of transplanted southerner Hinton Rowan Helper compare with those of commercial journalists?

2. How did social assumptions affect the reasoning of the writers with regard to the future of the southern economy? What role did the institution of slavery play in the arguments of Helper, Olmsted, John Hays Hammond, and others? What was the relationship between social belief and economic conviction?

3. Why did Helper and De Bow emphasize urbanization? What was the relationship between urban development and the entrepreneurial spirit? What factors slowed the process of southern urbanization?

4. Beginning with the statistical evidence from Helper, compare the divergent patterns in the southern and northern economies in the 1840s and 1850s. What factors discouraged industrialization in the South? Why did the South undergo little significant socioeconomic change, while the North underwent a major transformation?

1. David Christy on the Cotton Economy, 1855

Slavery is not an isolated system, but is so mingled with the business of the world, that it derives facilities from the most innocent transactions. Capital and labor, in Europe and America, are largely employed in the manufacture of cotton. These goods, to a great extent, may be seen freighting every vessel, from Christian nations, that traverses the seas of the globe; and filling the warehouses and shelves of the merchants, over two-thirds of the world. By the industry, skill, and enterprise, employed in the manufacture of cotton, mankind are better clothed; their comfort better promoted; general industry more highly stimulated; commerce more widely extended; and civilization more rapidly advanced, than in any preceding age. . . .

KING COTTON cares not whether he employs slaves or freemen. It is the *cotton,* not the *slaves,* upon which his throne is based. Let freemen do his work as well, and he will not object to the change. Thus far the experiments in this respect have failed, and they will not soon be renewed. The efforts of his most powerful ally, Great Britain, to promote that object, have already cost her people many hundreds of millions of dollars: with total failure as a reward for her zeal. . . .

KING COTTON is a profound statesman, and knows what measures will best sustain his throne. He is an acute mental philosopher, acquainted with the secret springs of human action, and accurately perceives who will best promote his aims. He has no evidence that colored men can grow his cotton, but in the capacity of slaves. It is his policy, therefore, to defeat all schemes of emancipation. . . .

In speaking of the economical connections of Slavery with the other material interests of the world, we have called it a *tri-partite alliance.* It is more than this. It is *quadruple.* Its structure includes four parties, arranged thus: The Western Agriculturists; the Southern Planters; the English Manufacturers; and the American Abolitionists! By this arrangement, the Abolitionists do not stand in direct contact with Slavery:—they imagine, therefore, that they have clean hands and pure hearts, so far as sustaining the system is concerned. But they, no less than their allies, aid in promoting the interests of Slavery. Their sympathies are with England on the Slavery question, and they very naturally incline to agree with her on other points. She advocates *Free Trade,* as essential to her manufactures and commerce; and they do the same, ... England, we were about to say, is in alliance with the cotton planter, to whose prosperity Free Trade is indispensable. Abolitionism is in alliance with England. All three of these parties, then, agree in their support of the Free Trade policy. It needed but the aid of the Western Farmer, therefore, to give permanency to this principle. His adhesion has been given, the *quadruple alliance* has been perfected, and Slavery and Free Trade *nationalized!*

2. James D. B. DeBow Calls for Economic Diversification, 1847

No mind can look back upon the history of this region for the last twenty years, and not feel convinced that the labor bestowed in cotton growing during that period has been a total loss to this part of the country. . . .

No country has ever acquired permanent wealth by exporting its unmanufactured products. And if any such case could be found in history the experience of the southwest would furnish satisfactory testimony that the exportation of the commodities produced here, tends rather to impoverish than to enrich the country. With the experience and the lights of the past before them it would seem to be madness to persevere in a course so detrimental to their interest. If when the prices of the leading staples were much better than they are likely to be for the future, and when the lands were more fertile and productive than now, this system proved unprofitable and ruinous, what hope is there that the result of the future will be better? Nay, is it not quite certain that each succeeding year will accelerate the progressive deterioration until a state of irredeemable ruin will ensue? . . .

This is the great evil under which the southwest labors. She is yearly wearing out her soil in the production of one great staple, which has become ruinously low in price by reason of its great supply: she parts with this staple at prime cost, and purchases almost all her necessary appliances of comfort from abroad, not at prime cost, but burthened with the profits of merchants, the costs of transportation, duties, commissions, exchange, and numerous other charges, all of which go to support and enrich others at her expense. This is the true reason that she is growing poorer while the rest of the world is growing rich, for it is easy for the world to enrich itself from such a customer on such terms.

If she were wise she would cease to carry on a traffic in which she always has been and always must be a loser; she will set up for herself, and instead of parting with the products of all her labor to support the balance of the world, she will manufacture her own clothing, and not stopping at this, proceed to manufacture the whole of her crop, and thereby draw upon the world for a portion of her former losses. . . .

I have endeavored to show, that the agricultural system hitherto pursued in the south and southwest, has proved ruinous to the country by exhausting the soil, and thereby rendering it every year, less and less capable of producing the appliances of human want and of human comfort; and that it has a tendency to divide the population into two classes, widely differing from each other in many important respects; that to these and other causes, must be assigned the reason of the small increase of the population of the older southern states for the ten years preceding the year 1840; and the great want of education among the poorer classes. On the other hand, I have endeavored to show some of the effects which may be expected from the introduction of manufactures into the southwest; among which I have supposed that the moral condition of the people would be improved, and that by diversifying the employments of the country, the means of human comfort would be greatly increased, and that all classes of the population would share in these benefits; that the value of the exports would be greatly enlarged by the process of manufacturing, and that instead of a constant drain from the country of the products of all its labor and soil, that wealth would flow into it from every part of the world. I have called the attention of the south and southwest to the rapid increase of labor in this region, and the necessity of finding profitable employment for it; and have taken the liberty of suggesting a plan of introducing manufactures by degrees as well for the purpose of preventing a shock to the established pursuits of the country, as to avoid the creation of a state of indebtedness. These with various other topics I have desired to impress upon the mind of the people of the southwest.

3. James Henry Hammond Acknowledges Slavery's Disadvantages, 1852

In an economical point of view—which I will not omit—Slavery presents some difficulties. As a general rule, I agree it must be admitted, that free labor is cheaper than slave labor. It is a fallacy to suppose that ours is *unpaid labor*. The slave himself must be paid for, and thus his labor is all purchased at once, and for no trifling sum. . . . But besides the first cost of the slave, he must be fed and clothed, well fed and

well clothed, if not for humanity's sake, that he may do good work, retain health and life, and rear a family to supply his place. When old or sick, he is a clear expense, and so is the helpless portion of his family. No poor law provides for him when unable to work, or brings up his children for our service when we need them. These are all heavy charges on slave labor. Hence, in all countries where the denseness of the population has reduced it to a matter of perfect certainty, that labor can be obtained, whenever wanted, and the laborer be forced, by sheer necessity, to hire for the smallest pittance that will keep soul and body together, and rags upon his back while in actual employment—dependent at all other times on alms or poor rates—in all such countries it is found cheaper to pay this pittance, than to clothe, feed, nurse, support through childhood, and pension in old age, a race of slaves. Indeed, the advantage is so great as speedily to compensate for the loss of the value of the slave.... But the question is, whether free or slave labor is cheapest to us in this country, at this time, situated as we are. And it is decided at once by the fact that we cannot avail ourselves of any other than slave labor. We neither have, nor can we procure, other labor to any extent, or on anything like the terms mentioned. We must therefore, content ourselves with our dear labor, under the consoling reflection that what is lost to us, is gained to humanity; and that, inasmuch as our slave costs us more than your free man costs you, by so much is he better off.

4. Hinton Rowan Helper Urges Southern Commercial Development, 1857

Product of Manufactures in the Free States—1850

States	Val. of annual products	Capital invested	Hands employed
California	$ 12,862,522	$ 1,006,197	3,964
Connecticut	45,110,102	23,890,348	47,770
Illinois	17,236,073	6,385,387	12,065
Indiana	18,922,651	7,941,602	14,342
Iowa	3,551,783	1,292,875	1,707
Maine	24,664,135	14,700,452	28,078
Massachusetts	151,137,145	83,357,642	165,938
Michigan	10,976,894	6,534,250	9,290
New Hampshire	23,164,503	18,242,114	27,092
New Jersey	39,713,586	22,184,730	37,311
New York	237,597,249	99,904,405	199,349
Ohio	62,647,259	29,019,538	51,489
Pennsylvania	155,044,910	94,473,810	146,766
Rhode Island	22,093,258	12,923,176	20,881
Vermont	8,570,920	5,001,377	8,445
Wisconsin	9,293,068	3,382,148	6,089
	$842,586,058	$430,240,051	780,576

Product of Manufactures in the Slave States—1850

States	Val. of annual products	Capital invested	Hands employed
Alabama	$ 4,538,878	$ 3,450,606	4,936
Arkansas	607,436	324,065	903
Delaware	4,649,296	2,978,945	3,888

Product of Manufactures in the Slave States—1850 *(Continued)*

States	Val. of annual products	Capital invested	Hands employed
Florida	668,338	547,060	991
Georgia	7,086,525	5,460,483	8,378
Kentucky	24,588,483	12,350,734	24,385
Louisiana	7,320,948	5,318,074	6,437
Maryland	32,477,702	14,753,143	30,124
Mississippi	2,972,038	1,833,420	3,173
Missouri	23,749,265	9,079,695	16,850
North Carolina	9,111,245	7,252,225	12,444
South Carolina	7,063,513	6,056,865	7,009
Tennessee	9,728,438	6,975,279	12,032
Texas	1,165,538	539,290	1,066
Virginia	29,705,387	18,109,993	29,109
	$165,433,030	$95,029,877	161,725

Whether Southern merchants ever think of the numerous ways in which they contribute to the aggrandizement of the North, while, at the same time, they enervate and dishonor the South, has, for many years, with us, been a matter of more than ordinary conjecture.... Let them scrutinize the workings of Southern money after it passes north of Mason and Dixon's line. Let them consider how much they pay to Northern railroads and hotels, how much to Northern merchants and shop-keepers, how much to Northern shippers and insurers, how much to Northern theatres, newspapers, and periodicals. Let them also consider what disposition is made of it after it is lodged in the hands of the North. Is not the greater part of it paid out to Northern manufacturers, mechanics, and laborers, for the very articles which are purchased at the North—and to the extent that this is done, are not Northern manufacturers, mechanics, and laborers directly countenanced and encouraged, while, at the same time, Southern manufacturers, mechanics, and laborers, are indirectly abased, depressed, and disabled?... And yet, our cousins of the North are not, by any means, blameworthy for availing themselves of the advantages which we have voluntarily yielded to them. They have shown their wisdom in growing great at our expense, and we have shown our folly in allowing them to do so. Southern merchants, slaveholders, and slave-breeders,

should be the objects of our censure; they have desolated and impoverished the South; they are now making merchandize of the vitals of their country;....

What about Southern Commerce? Is it not almost entirely tributary to the commerce of the North? Are we not dependent on New York, Philadelphia, Boston, and Cincinnati, for nearly every article of merchandise, whether foreign or domestic? Where are our ships, our mariners, our naval architects? Alas! echo answers, where? ...

True it is that the South has wonderful powers of endurance and recuperation; but she cannot forever support the reckless prodigality of her sons. We are all spendthrifts; some of us should become financiers. We must learn to take care of our money; we should withhold it from the North, and open avenues for its circulation at home. We should not run to New York, to Philadelphia, to Boston, to Cincinnati, or to any other Northern city, every time we want a shoe-string or a bedstead, a fish-hook or a handsaw, a tooth-pick or a cotton-gin. In ease and luxury we have been lolling long enough; we should now bestir ourselves, and keep pace with the progress of the age. We must expand our energies, and acquire habits of enterprise and industry; we should arouse ourselves from the couch of lassitude, and inure our minds to thought and our bodies to action.

5. Frederick Law Olmsted Critiques the Slave Economy, 1861

The interests of the owners of all soil in the Slave States which is not adapted to cotton culture, and of all capital not engaged in cotton culture, or in supplying slaves for it, are thus injured by the demand for cotton, they being, in fact, forced to be co-partners in an association in which they do not share the profits.

And as to what are commonly called the Cotton States, if we assume that cotton cultivation is profitable only where the production is equal to two bales for each slave employed, it will be seen that wherever the land will not yield as much as this, the owner of it suffers all the disadvantages of the difficulty of getting good labourers as much as the owner of the land which produces seven or ten bales to the hand, although none of the profits of supplying the cotton demand, which gives this extraordinary price to labour, come to him.

According to the Census, the whole crop of cotton is produced on 5,000,000 acres. It could be produced, at the rate common on good South-western plantations, on less than half that area. The rest of the land of the Slave States, which amounts to over 500,000,000 acres, is condemned, so far as the tendencies I have indicated are not overweighed here and there by some special advantages, to non-cultivation, except for the hand-to-mouth supply of its people. And this is true not only of its agricultural but of all other of its resources.

That for all practical purposes this is not an exaggerated statement is clearly enough shown by the difference in the market value of land, which as officially given by De Bow, as, notwithstanding the extraordinary demand of the world upon the cotton land, between four and five hundred per cent. higher in the Free than in the Slave States, the frontier and unsettled districts, Texas, California and the territories not being considered.

One of the grand errors out of which this rebellion has grown came from supposing that whatever nourishes wealth and gives power to an ordinary civilized community must command as much for a slaveholding community. The truth has been overlooked that the accumulation of wealth and the power of a nation are contingent not merely upon the primary value of the surplus of productions of which it has to dispose, but very largely also upon the way in which the income from its surplus is distributed and reinvested. Let a man be absent from almost any part of the North twenty years, and he is struck, on his return, by what we call the "improvements" which have been made: better buildings, churches, schoolhouses, mills, railroads, etc. In New York city alone, for instance, at least two hundred millions of dollars have been reinvested merely in an improved housing of the people; in labour-saving machinery, waterworks, gasworks, etc., and much more. It is not difficult to see where the profits of our manufacturers and merchants are. Again, go into the country, and there is no end of substantial proof of twenty years of agricultural prosperity, not alone in roads, canals, bridges, dwellings, barns and fences, but in books and furniture, and gardens, and pictures, and in the better dress and evidently higher education of the people. But where will the returning traveller see the accumulated cotton profits of twenty years in Mississippi? Ask the cotton-planter for them, and he will point in reply, not to dwellings, libraries, churches, schoolhouses, mills, railroads, or anything of the kind; he will point to his negroes—to almost nothing else. Negroes such as stood for five hundred dollars once, now represent a thousand dollars. We must look then in Virginia and those Northern Slave States which have the monopoly of supplying negroes for the real wealth which the sale of cotton has brought to the South. But where is the evidence of it? where anything to compare with the evidence of accumulated profits to be seen in any Free State? If certain portions of Virginia have been a little improving, others unquestionably have been deteriorating, growing shabbier, more comfortless, less convenient. The total increase in wealth of the population during the last twenty years shows for almost nothing. One year's improvements of a Free State exceed it all.

6. A Southern Plea for Southern Commerce, 1858

Let our citizens feel the truth of this statement now and act as they should in relationship to the mechanics of Atlanta. Let them foster, encourage, and support those worthy members of our community who are engaged in these avocations. Heretofore there has been a habit among many of our people of sending off to some other place, to some Northern town or to some smaller other Southern town, for articles which they could easily obtain at home. We know this to be the fact of several merchants in Atlanta, as well as others. Such a policy, let us tell them, is not only directly opposed to the interests of the city but to their own interests, and the man who upon reflection will not abandon such a course doesn't deserve to receive the patronage of his fellow citizens.

If you will build up a substantial community, you will gradually increase in wealth and thus be better able to indulge in all comforts and luxuries, support and sustain your domestic manufacturers and mechanics. Whatever you can buy from your neighbor in your own town, don't send off somewhere else for it because you can obtain it a fraction cheaper. What will be gained in that way will be lost tenfold in the long run. The merchant who doesn't sustain the home mechanic should not receive in turn for his goods the hard-earned money of the mechanical population.

Chapter 12:
Document Set 2 References

1. David Christy on the Cotton Economy, 1855
   David Christy, *Cotton Is King: On the Culture of Cotton, and Its Relation to Agriculture, Manufactures, and Commerce; to the Free Colored People; and to Those Who Hold That Slavery Is in Itself Sinful* (Cincinnati: Moore, Wilstach, Keys & Co., 1856), pp. 45–46, 263–267.

2. James D. B. De Bow Calls for Economic Diversification, 1847
   J. D. B. De Bow, "Domestic Manufactures in the South and West," *The Commercial Review of the South and West,* Vol. 3, No. 3 (March 1847).

3. James Henry Hammond Acknowledges Slavery's Disadvantages, 1852
   James Henry Hammond, "Letters on Slavery," *The Pro-Slavery Argument* (Charleston: Walker, Richards, and Company, 1852), pp. 121–122.

4. Hinton Rowan Helper Urges Southern Commercial Development, 1857
   Hinton Rowan Helper, *The Impending Crisis of the South: How to Meet It* (New York: Burdick Brothers, 1857), pp. 284, 331, 334–335, 355, 357.

5. Frederick Law Olmsted Critiques the Slave Economy, 1861
   Frederick Law Olmsted, *The Cotton Kingdom: A Traveller's Observations on Cotton and Slavery in the American Slave States* (New York: Mason Brothers, 1861), Vol. 1, pp. 24–26.

6. A Southern Plea for Southern Commerce, 1858
   Editorial, *Atlanta Daily Intelligencer,* October 8, 1858.

CHAPTER 12

DOCUMENT SET 3

Free But Contained: The Free Black Population
of the Antebellum South

While the plight of the South's slave population is well known, the experience of free persons of color has drawn less scholarly attention, at least until recent years. Your textbook describes the "life on the margin" led by the minority of African-Americans who gained their freedom before 1863. The following documents provide evidence of the varieties of free black experience in the South during the two generations preceding the Civil War.

A central point raised by the textbook is that the position of free blacks in the Old South was complicated and filled with contradictions. Review the documents for clues to the paradoxes of living free in the midst of enslavement. Look for evidence that free people of color were torn between conflicting interests and objectives. Try to understand why they acted as they did and how they resolved the tensions inherent in their anomalous position in an increasingly closed society.

As you observe the details of everyday life among free blacks, examine the institutions, communities, and class structures created by free people of color. Be aware of the challenges they confronted and the strategies they employed to establish a measure of liberty within an essentially unfree system. Search the documents for evidence of their attempts to bring stability to families and communities that constantly hovered on the edge of legitimacy.

Even as free people of color strove to strengthen their communities and preserve their culture, they also struggled to find their place in the white world and the southern economy. The documents contain numerous reminders that free black life was filled with interaction, accommodation, and tension between white and black. As you study the sources, try to identify the ways in which free blacks were integrated into the economy of the antebellum South.

Your review of these documents will also advance your understanding of the white perspective on the presence of free persons of color in southern society. Observe the interaction between the two races, and ask yourself how whites were able to reconcile themselves to the presence of free African-Americans in their midst. As you think about white perceptions and attitudes, determine why some whites viewed the free black community with suspicion or alarm. Your analysis will reveal that while white southerners saw freemen as slaves without masters, African-Americans were intent on carving out their own independent space within a hostile environment.

Your study of the source material also should bring to light the multiplicity of economies, societies, and communities that flourished in the antebellum South. Examine the tables, for example, for clues to regional variations in the patterns and rhythms of black life. Relying on both textbook and documents, determine how race relations and economic life varied from region to region and place to place. As you review the evidence, try to formulate a hypothesis to characterize and explain the ways in which free blacks accommodated themselves to the institution of slavery.

Questions for Analysis

1. What do the documents reveal about southern white attitudes toward free persons of color? What challenges did the free black community present to the social institutions of the antebellum South? In what ways were free blacks a potential threat to social stability?

2. Describe the economic roles assumed by free people of color in the Old South. In what ways and in what occupational roles did they complement the other elements in the developing southern economy? How would you describe the economic status of free blacks in the generation before the Civil War? To what extent is generalization possible?

3. What do the documents reveal about the origins of the free black community? Who were the free people of color, and how did they become numerically significant? In what regions were they most prominent as a component of the population? How would you explain these patterns of population distribution?

4. What was the status of the family in the free black community of the antebellum South? What hazards to family life existed in the southern caste system, and how did free people of color act to protect the integrity of the family unit?

5. What does the textbook mean by "contradictions" in the position of free blacks in southern society? What do the documents reveal about the ways in which those contradictions were resolved?

1. Free People of Color as Conspirators, 1822

A. Denmark Vesey's Complicity in a Slave Conspiracy, 1822

I know Denmark Vesey. On one occasion he asked me, "What news"; I told him, "None." He replied, "We are free but the white people here won't let us be so, and the only way is to rise up and fight the whites." I went to his house one night to learn where the meetings were held. I never conversed on this subject with Batteau or Ned—Vesey told me he was the leader in this plot. I never conversed either with Peter or Mingo. Vesey induced me to join; when I went to Vesey's house there was a meeting there, the room was full of people, but none of them white. That night at Vesey's we determined to have arms made, and each man put in twelve and one-half cents toward that purpose. Though Vesey's room was full I did not know one individual there. At this meeting Vesey said we were to take the Guard-House and Magazine to get arms; that we ought to rise up and speak, and he *read to us from the Bible, how the Children of Israel were delivered out of Egypt from bondage.* He said that the rising would take place, last Sunday night week (the 16th June), and that Peter Poras was one.

B. A White Perspective on Vesey's Machinations, 1822

Denmark proved, for 20 years, a most faithful slave. In 1800, Denmark drew a prize of $1500 in the East-Bay-Street Lottery, with which he purchased his freedom from his master, at six hundred dollars, much less than his real value. From that period to day of his apprehension he has been working as a carpenter in this city, distinguished for great strength and activity. Among his colour he was always looked up to with awe and respect. His temper was impetuous and domineering in the extreme, qualifying him for the despotic rule, of which he was ambitious. All his passions were ungovernable and, savage; and to his numerous wives and children, he displayed the haughty and capricious cruelty of an Eastern Bashaw. He had nearly effected his escape, after information had been lodged against him. For three days the town was searched for him without success. As early as Monday, the 17th, he had concealed himself. It was not until the night of the 22nd of June, during a perfect tempest, that he was found secreted in the house of one of his wives. It is to the uncommon efforts and vigilance of Mr. Wesner, and Capt. Dove, of the City Guard, (the latter of whom seized him) that public justice received its necessary tribute, in the execution of this man. If the party had been one moment later, he would, in all probability, have effected his escape the next day in some outward bound vessel.

2. Free Blacks Attempt to Preserve Family Unity, 1811, 1825

A. A Free Woman of Color Acts to Protect Her Family, 1811

Petition Number, 5870,
Southampton County, Dec. 9, 1811.

To the Honorable, the Speaker & house of Delegates of . . . Virginia.

The Petition of Jemima Hunt (a free woman of color) of the County of Southampton, humbly sheweth—that sometime in the month of November, in the Year 1805—Your petitioner entered into a contract with a certain Benj Barrett of said County for the purchase of Stephen a Negro man Slave, the property of said Barrett, & husband to your petitioner. . . . Your petitioner farther states that she has paid the full amount of the purchase money and has obtained a bill of sale for the said negro Stephen; who (being her husband) she intended to emancipate after she had complied with her contract,—but in some short time after as your petitioner has been informed an act of Assembly was passed, prohibiting slaves, being emancipated after the law went into operation, from residing in the state—Your petitioner farther states that she has a numerous family of Children by the said Stephen, who are dependent upon the daily labor of herself & husband for a support, & without the assistance of her husband Stephen they must suffer or become burthensome to their county.

Therefore your petitioner humbly prays that the legislature would take her case into consideration & pass a law to permit the said negro Stephen to reside in the State after emancipation, and to enjoy all the privileges that other free people of colour are entitled to.

B. A Family of Color Fights to Reside in Virginia, 1825

Your petitioner, John Dungee, and Lucy Ann, his wife, who are free persons of colour residing in King William County ask permission most respectfully to represent to the legislature of Virginia. That your petitioner John Dungee (who is descended from the aborigines of this dominion) was born free and 'tis his birth-right to reside therein. That having many relations and connections in this section of the county in which he was raised, all his feelings and attachments have bound him to Virginia. . . . Your petitioner Lucy Ann is the illegitimate daughter of the late Edmund Littlepage Esq., a highly respected and wealthy citizen, who by his last will and testament and as an act of justice and atonement for an error of an unguarded moment bequeathed to his innocent offspring the boon of freedom and a pecuniary legacy. . . . During the last year your petitioners urged by the strongest and purest attachment to each other were lawfully united to each other in matrimony and fondly flattered themselves that they had the prospect of passing through life with a portion of happiness that is decreed to but few. Only a few months had passed away, however, before your petitioners were aroused from their halcyon state by being informed that by the laws of the land it was necessary that your petitioner Lucy Ann should remove from the Commonwealth or be sold into slavery. The intelligent and humane can at once imagine how appalling the information was to your petitioners, how frightful the consequence of a rigid and unbending enforcement of the law, how totally destructive of the right, the interest, and happiness, of your petitioners. . . . If they are compelled to leave this land your petitioner John in a moment loses the labor of his life in acquiring an accurate knowledge of the Chesapeake Bay and of the rivers which disembark themselves therein by which knowledge he is rendered useful to himself and others and the legacy bequeathed to your petitioner Lucy Ann be lost or of little value to them. They will be torn from their parents, relatives, and friends, and driven in a state of destitution to migrate to a foreign land.

3. A Free Man of Color Is Warned Against Returning to North Carolina, 1830

It seems very plain to me that you are now going to make one of the worst mistakes that you ever made, in many ways. The first is that you are taking your children to an old country that is worn out and to slave on, where they are in between two fires as I may call them, for it is well known to me that where there is slavery it is not a good place for us to live, for they are the most of them very disagreeable and think themselves above free people of color.

We are always in danger of them doing us injury by some way or other. We are now away from them and I think it the best for me when I am out of such a country to stay away. I want you as a friend to look at these things and remember how times have altered since you could remember. To think that you are a going to take your small children to that place and can't tell how soon you may be taken away from them and they may come under the hands of some cruel slave holder, and you know that if they can get a colored child they will use them as bad again as they will one of their own slaves, it is right that parents should think of this, most especially if they are going to the very place and know it at the same time.

I would not this night, if I had children, take them to such a place and there to stay for the best five farms in three miles around where we came from, for I think I should be going to do something to bring them to see trouble and not enjoy themselves as free men but be in a place where they are not able to speak for their rights, the master takes his servant and makes them come to and do what he will. We dare not say you did so and so or made Negro do so without we can prove it by a white man and many of them will turn their backs when they think they would be witness for us.

I cannot do myself justice to think of living in such a country. When I think of it I can't tell how any man of color can think of going there with small children. It has been my intention ever since I had notice of such if I lived to be a man and God was willing I would leave such a place.

I wish you well and all your family and I hope that you all may do well, as much so as any people I ever saw or ever shall see, and I hope that you may see what you are going to do before it is too late.

4. The Diary of a Free Black, 1835–1837

Nov. 3, 1835. Mr. Hough Leaves this place for New Orleans on S. B. Chester, I sent a Dayly paper & a Letter to Jas Miller—He Directs me to Collect the money that he Owes me from his partner Mr Skeggs—Mr Bledsoe Orders a wig to be made very Light Hair—Finds William at Mr Parkers Kitchen with his Girls Struck him with the whip 1st and then with the stick He ran home and I followed him there and whiped him well for it, having often told him about going Down there—He then Comes Out on Bill Nix and Seys that he Bought five finger Rings & c. . . .

7   Col Bingaman & Mr Chambers gives a Dinner at Mr Parkers. Underwood & John Mason fights. Underwood whiped him very Easy—I paid Mr S.

Cotten $27.00 the amount Due to Dr Hunt, Deceased. I Loaned Mr Whiting $8.00 pd Mr Harrison Black mare runs a mile against Sorril mare Called the Sumpter Filly—Black M. won the Race very Easy, by 30 yards—Cryzers horse ran against the one Eyed Sorrel mare The mare won the race by Eleven feet. They ran 750 yards. . . .

9   I Commenced to pull Down the part of the Stable to Rebuild it up again—Paid $10.00 for 2000 Shingles—The Jone Left here at Night taking 4 or 5 more of the Fencibles to Vicksburg Mr Massy Came to buy my Land for Mr Flecheo—Mr Newman pays me $5.00 that he Borrowed Tuesday 27th day of October I Loaned Dr Benbrook $2.00.

10 Mrs. Merricks House on Main street Sold at Auction and was Bought by Abby for five thousand & Eighty Dollars—Hyred———To Drive for me—1.50 per Day—Receid a Letter by Greenburg Wade for [from] Orleans. Mrs Miller wishes me to purchase a house & Lot Down there at $3500. Mr F. Rowland pays me $50.00 the ballance of the money Due me from Mr Robert for house Rent. I stoped Stephen in to work for Mr Rowes from 9 Oclock untill Night, tho he did not work any. . . .

12 Mc & myself went out to Parson Connelly Sale to Look at his Cows. They were all Dry—Stephen & John went to Rayley place for my mule Came home with him at 11 A. M. Oclock Mr M. Williams sends his sick Boy to Bourd until he returns from Red River I made Maj Dunbar a present of 2 guinea pigs.

13 Bought a Sorrel Horse—Rob. Roy—at Auction for $106 cash—I thought Mc would take him when I Bought him and when he came up I asked him if he wanted to buy a Horse and he told no, that the food was too high. . . .

24 I Loaned Dr Hubbard One hundred and 75 dollars—Mr Baynton arrives here. . . .

June 3, [*1836.*] I Bot Moses from a man by the name of William Good, at Least I Bot him at auction under the Hammer for four Hundred Dollars cash—I Bot also 2 Boxes of wine at 2.871/2 per Box and 5 small Boxes of shaving soap, 43 cents per Box Mr Samuel Davis sells his Family Residence to Mr Gildart for twenty thousand Dollars. No Sail I Bot of Mr Chew all the Birds that Mr Grayson Left here and their Cages also for ten Dollars Cash. . . .

22 Business only Tolerably Brisk, Mr McGetrick makes a Bet with Mr Cobler to day of $25 that his Brown Horse would beat Mr Mardices Little Bay mare a 1/2 mile Race They gave me the $50 to hold as there stakes The winner was to have the fifty Dollars—I Loaned Dr Hubbard $400 to be paid on Monday; Some Talk about town of Lynching—————————the Painter for taking off Dr——s Daughter. . . .

29 To Day I went up to the Agricultural Bank and Received in cash Seventeen Hundred and Fifty Dollars being the amount of a note that I Received from Flecheaux given him by Mr R. Bledsoe for Land that I sold to Flecheaux which Said Flecheaux Sold to Mr R. Bledsoe—I went to day around to Dr Hubbards office to shave young Mr Stewarts head, he was quite ill—I then went on up to Mrs Rowans to Shave Dr Dalhgreens Beard off—he was very Comfortably Situated and in a thriving condition. . . .

March 6, 1837. Col A L. Bingaman Received a challenge from Col Osburn Claibourne To fight. The Col. Came in very Early this morning and got shaved He seemed to be wraped up in thought, he had nothing to say—The Roumer Says that they are to fight with Riffles—I am very Sorry to heare that they are agoing to fight—I only wish that they may be preventd from fighting for I Like them Both.

5. A Mississippi Opinion of Free People of Color, 1858

As we have before remarked, a *free* negro is an anomaly—a violation of the unerring laws of nature—a stigma upon the wise and benevolent system of Southern labor—a contradiction of the Bible. The status of slavery is the only one for which the African is adapted; and a great wrong is done him when he is removed to a higher and more responsible sphere.

6. A Demographic Snapshot of the Free Black Population, 1820–1860

Free Negro Population, 1820–1860

	1820	1830	1840	1850	1860
United States	233,504	319,599	386,303	434,449	488,070
North	99,281	137,529	170,728	196,262	226,152
South	134,223	182,070	215,575	238,187	261,918
Upper South	114,070	151,877	174,357	203,702	224,963
Lower South	20,153	30,193	41,218	34,485	36,955
Delaware	12,958	15,855	16,919	18,073	19,829
D.C.	4,048	6,152	8,361	10,059	11,131
Kentucky	2,759	4,917	7,317	10,011	10,684
Maryland	39,730	52,938	62,078	74,723	83,942
Missouri	347	569	1,574	2,618	3,572
North Carolina	14,612	19,543	22,732	27,463	30,463
Tennessee	2,727	4,555	5,524	6,422	7,300
Virginia	36,889	47,348	49,852	54,333	58,042
Alabama	571	1,572	2,039	2,265	2,690
Arkansas	59	141	465	608	144
Florida	—	844	817	932	932
Georgia	1,763	2,486	2,753	2,931	3,500
Louisiana	10,476	16,710	25,502	17,462	18,647
Mississippi	458	519	1,366	930	773
South Carolina	6,826	7,921	8,276	8,960	9,914
Texas	—	—	—	397	355

Proportion of Negroes Free, 1820–1860

	1820	1840	1860
United States	13.2%	13.4%	11.0%
North	83.9	99.3	100.0
South	8.1	8.0	6.2
Upper South	10.6	12.5	12.8
Lower South	3.5	3.1	1.5
Delaware	74.1	86.7	91.7
D.C.	38.8	64.0	77.8
Kentucky	2.1	3.9	4.5
Maryland	27.0	40.9	49.1
Missouri	3.3	2.6	3.0
North Carolina	6.7	8.5	8.4
Tennessee	3.3	2.9	2.6
Virginia	8.0	10.0	10.6
Alabama	1.3	.8	.6
Arkansas	3.5	2.3	.1
Florida	—	3.1	1.5
Georgia	1.2	1.0	.8
Louisiana	13.2	13.1	5.3
Mississippi	1.4	.7	.2
South Carolina	2.6	2.5	2.4
Texas	—	—	.2

Chapter 12:
Document Set 3 References

1. Free People of Color as Conspirators, 1822
   A. Denmark Vesey's Complicity in a Slave Conspiracy, 1822. *An Official Report of the Trials of Sundry Negroes, Charged with an Attempt to Raise an Insurrection in the State of South Carolina*, prep., Lionel H. Kennedy and Thomas Parker (Charleston, 1822), pp. 66–67.
   B. A White Perspective on Vesey's Machinations, 1822. James Hamilton, Jr., *Negro Plot, An Account of the Late Intended Insurrections Among a Portion of the Blacks of the City of Charleston, South Carolina* (Boston, 1822), in Patricia W. Romero, comp. and ed., *I Too Am America: Documents from 1619 to the Present* (New York: Publishers Company, Inc., 1970), pp. 57–58.

2. Free Blacks Attempt to Preserve Family Unity, 1811, 1825
   A. A Free Woman of Color Acts to Protect Her Family, 1811. Petition Number 5870, Southhampton County, Va., December 9, 1811, in Romero, p. 40.

   B. A Family of Color Fights to Reside in Virginia, 1825. James Hugo Johnston, "Documentary Evidence of the Relations of Indians and Negroes," *Journal of Negro History*, Vol. 14 (January 1929), pp. 30–31.

3. A Free Man of Color Is Warned Against Returning to North Carolina, 1830
   James Roberts to Willis Roberts, n.d., ca. 1830, Jonathan Roberts and Family Papers (Washington, D.C., Library of Congress), in Romero, p. 42.

4. The Diary of a Free Black, 1835–1837
   William R. Hogan and Edwin A. Davis, eds., *William Johnson's Natchez: The Ante-Bellum Diary of a Free Negro* (Baton Rouge, 1951), pp. 73, 74, 75, 78, 123, 125, 150, 167.

5. A Mississippi Opinion of Free People of Color, 1858
   Jackson *Semi-Weekly Mississippian*, May 21, 1858.

6. A Demographic Snapshot of the Free Black Population, 1820–1860
   Population of the United States in 1860 (Washington, D.C., 1864), pp. 598–604.

CHAPTER 13

DOCUMENT SET 1
Manifest Destiny and Mission: The Mexican War and the Extension of Freedom

Chapter 13 focuses on the extensive territorial expansion of the United States during the 1840s and the sociopolitical consequences of national growth. The central event of the decade was the controversial Mexican War, which resulted in a dramatic enlargement of the American republic at the expense of its weaker Mexican neighbor. The war produced sharp internal debate over first the origins of the struggle and then the distribution of the spoils. For President James K. Polk, the course of American foreign policy was never in doubt. Driven by a conviction of racial superiority and the assumption that it was the country's Manifest Destiny to occupy the continent, expansionists found adequate justification for war. Yet the flavor of aggressive warfare was unpalatable to the American public, which required a defensive rationale for the administration's decision. Polk accordingly cast the conflict as "war by the act of Mexico."

Despite the president's indictment of the adversary, the roots of conflict were complex. Historical causation is rarely a simple matter, and the origins of international disagreements are not easily understood. Manifest Destiny ideology, detailed in your textbook, provides vital background for the study of American expansion into Texas, California, and Oregon. The explosion of the 1840s was the result of an often belligerent continentalism that had originated in the imperial outlook of the Revolutionary generation fifty years earlier.

Beyond imperial thinking, however, lay economic and political forces associated with the westward movement. Both agricultural and commercial expansion provided strong motivation for continental thinkers and political doers. And never far from the relentless American advance was the divisive issue of slavery and its extension into the new territories. This issue threatened to destroy all harmony between the different sections of the country.

The forces simmering beneath the surface of national politics are revealed in the following documents that explore Manifest Destiny, together with conflicting interpretations of the Mexican War's origins and purposes. As you approach the evidence, you will be engaged in analysis of a complicated historical problem: the assessment of human motivation, cause and effect, and responsibility for the outbreak of war. Try to subject the documents to the cold eye of the scholar, always skeptical of the written word and aware of historical context. Determine whether the author was in a position to observe the events in question. Note when the document appeared and to whom it was addressed. See how personal beliefs, values, or assumptions influenced each account. Assess long-term foreign-policy developments in conjunction with the immediate events of the 1840s and evaluate Polk's rationale for the war.

Questions for Analysis

1. As you analyze each document, be aware of the potential for nationalist bias in dealing with the sensitive issue of war and peace. How does the Mexican scholars' account help you analyze the problem of responsibility for the war? What is your conclusion with regard to predominant causes and the burden of responsibility?

2. Define the term *Manifest Destiny.* As you review the evidence, identify American assumptions about the role of the United States on the North American continent. What benefits were assumed to be conferred on a territory acquired by the United States? What racial attitudes were evident in the rationale for Manifest Destiny?

3. Turning to "the great man" thesis of historical interpretation, evaluate Polk's role in bringing about war with Mexico. Examine the sequence of events preceding the declaration of war, as recorded in his diary entries. What does the diary reveal about his decision for war? What were the constitutional implications of Polk's executive decisions?

4. What do the documents reveal about war aims? What was the significance of John Slidell's mission to Mexico? How did Polk, the Whig critics, and the Mexican scholars interpret the Slidell mission?

5. Using a map of the Texas-Mexico frontier in 1846, examine the locations of the Nueces River and the Rio del Norte. According to your textbook, what was the status of this territory? What was Lincoln's purpose in stressing the spot where "the first blood of the war was shed"? Why did Lincoln disapprove of Polk's policy? What is the distinction between an underlying cause and a short-term problem?

1. Expressions of American Destiny, 1839

[O]ur national birth was the beginning of a new history, the formation and progress of an untried political system, which separates us from the past and connects us with the future only; and so far as regards the entire development of the natural rights of man, in moral, political, and national life, we may confidently assume that our country is destined to be *the great nation* of futurity. . . .

It is our unparalleled glory that we have no reminiscences of battlefields, but in defense of humanity, of the oppressed of all nations, of the rights of conscience, the rights of personal enfranchisement. . . .

Yes, we are the nation of progress, of individual freedom, of universal enfranchisement. Equality of rights is the cynosure of our Union of states, the grand exemplar of the correlative equality of individuals; and while truth sheds its effulgence, we cannot retrograde without dissolving the one and subverting the other. We must onward to the fulfillment of our mission, to the entire development of the principle of our organization—freedom of conscience, freedom of person, freedom of trade and business pursuits, universality of freedom and equality. This is our high destiny, and in nature's eternal, inevitable decree of cause and effect we must accomplish it.

All this will be our future history, to establish on earth the moral dignity and salvation of man—the immutable truth and beneficence of God. For this blessed mission to the nations of the world which are shut out from the life-giving light of truth has America been chosen; and her high example shall smite unto death the tyranny of kings, hierarchs, and oligarchs, and carry the glad tidings of peace and good-will where myriads now endure an existence scarcely more enviable than that of beasts of the field. Who, then, can doubt that our country is destined to be *the great nation* of futurity?

2. Senator Benton Justifies White Supremacy, 1846

It would seem that the White race alone received the divine command, to subdue and replenish the earth! for it is the only race that has obeyed it—the only one that hunts out new and distant lands, and even a New World, to subdue and replenish. Starting from western Asia, taking Europe for their field, and the Sun for their guide, and leaving the Mongolians behind, they arrived, after many ages, on the shores of the Atlantic, which they lit up with the lights of science and religion, and adorned with the useful and the elegant arts. Three and a half centuries ago, this race, in obedience to the great command, arrived in the New World, and found new lands to subdue and replenish. . . . The van of the Caucasian race now top the Rocky mountains, and spread down to the shores of the Pacific. In a few years a great population will grow up there, luminous with the accumulated lights of European and American civilization. Their presence in such a position cannot be without its influence upon eastern Asia. . . . Civilization, or extinction, has been the fate of all people who have found themselves in the track of the advancing Whites, and civilization, always the preference of the Whites, has been pressed as an object, while extinction has followed as a consequence of its resistance. The Black and the Red races have often felt their ameliorating influence.

3. President Polk Takes the Nation to War, 1846

Saturday, 9th May, 1846.—The Cabinet held a regular meeting today; all the members present. I brought up the Mexican question, and the question of what was the duty of the administration in the present state of our relations with that country. The subject was very fully discussed. All agreed that if the Mexican forces at Matamoras committed any act of hostility on General Taylor's forces I should immediately send a message to Congress recommending an immediate declaration of war. I stated to the Cabinet that up to this time, as we knew, we had heard of no open act of aggression by the Mexican army, but that the danger was imminent that such acts would be committed. I said that in my opinion we had ample cause of war, and that it was impossible that we could stand in *statu quo,* or that I could remain silent much longer; that I thought it was my duty to send a message to Congress very soon and recommend definite measures. I told them that I thought I ought to make such a message by Tuesday next, that the country was excited and impatient on the subject, and if I failed to do so I would not be doing my duty. I then propounded the distinct question to the Cabinet, and took their opinions individually, whether I should make a message to Congress on Tuesday, and whether in that message I should recommend a declaration of war against Mexico. All except the Secretary of the Navy gave their advice in the affirmative.... Mr. Buchanan said he would feel better satisfied in his course if the Mexican forces had or should commit any act of hostility, but that as matters stood we had ample cause of war against Mexico, and he gave his assent to the measure. It was agreed that the message should be prepared and submitted to the Cabinet in their meeting on Tuesday....

About six o'clock P.M. General R. Jones, the Adjutant-General of the army, called and handed to me despatches received from General Taylor by the Southern mail which had just arrived, giving information that a part of the Mexican army had crossed the Del Norte and attacked and killed and captured two companies of dragoons of General Taylor's army consisting of 63 officers and men.... I immediately summoned the Cabinet to meet at half past seven o'clock this evening. The Cabinet accordingly assembled at that hour; all the members present. The subject of the despatch received this evening from General Taylor, as well as the state of our relations with Mexico, were fully considered. The Cabinet

were unanimously of opinion, and it was so agreed, that a message should be sent to Congress on Monday laying all the information in my possession before them and recommending vigorous and prompt measures to enable the executive to prosecute the war....

Sunday, 10th May, 1846.—As the public excitement in and out of Congress was very naturally very great, and as there was a great public necessity to have the prompt action of Congress on the Mexican question, and therefore an absolute necessity for sending my message to Congress on tomorrow, I resumed this morning the preparation of my message....

Monday, 11th May, 1846.—I refused to see company generally this morning. I carefully revised my message on the Mexican question, but had no time to read the copies of the correspondence furnished by the War and State Departments which was to accompany it....

The Secretaries of War and State called a few minutes before eight o'clock but before I had consulted the former in relation to Col. Benton's note, Col. Benton came in.... Col. Benton said that the House of Representatives had passed a bill today declaring war in two hours, and that one and a half hours of that time had been occupied in reading the documents which accompanied my message, and that in his opinion in the nineteenth century war should not be declared without full discussion and much more consideration than had been given to it in the House of Representatives. Mr. Buchanan then remarked that war already existed by the act of Mexico herself and therefore it did not require much deliberation to satisfy all that we ought promptly and vigorously to meet it....

Wednesday, 13th May, 1846.— ... Among other things Mr. Buchanan had stated that our object was not to dismember Mexico or to make conquests, and that the Del Norte was the boundary to which we claimed; or rather that in going to war we did not do so with a view to acquire either California or New Mexico or any other portion of the Mexican territory. I told Mr. Buchanan that I thought such a declaration to foreign governments unnecessary and improper; that the causes of the war as set forth in my message to Congress and the accompanying documents were altogether satisfactory. I told him that though we had not gone to war for conquest, yet it was clear that in making peace we would if practicable obtain California and such other portion of the Mexican territory as would be sufficient to indemnify our claimants on Mexico, and to defray the expense of the war which that power by her long continued wrongs and injuries had forced us to wage. I told him it was well known that the Mexican Government had no other means of indemnifying us.

4. President Polk's Message to Congress, 1846

An envoy of the United States repaired to Mexico, with full powers to adjust every existing difference. But though present on the Mexican soil, by agreement between the two governments, invested with full powers, and bearing evidence of the most friendly dispositions, his mission has been unavailing. The Mexican government not only refused to receive him, or listen to his propositions, but, after a long continued series of menaces, have at last invaded our territory, and shed the blood of our fellow-citizens on our own soil. . . .

In my message at the commencement of the present session, I informed you that, upon the earnest appeal both of the congress and convention of Texas, I had ordered an efficient military force to take a position "between the Nueces and the Del Norte." This had become necessary, to meet a threatened invasion of Texas by the Mexican forces, for which extensive military preparations had been made. The invasion was threatened solely because Texas had determined, in accordance with a solemn resolution of the Congress of the United States, to annex herself to our Union; and, under these circumstances, it was plainly our duty to extend our protection over her citizens and soil.

This force was concentrated at Corpus Christi, and remained there until after I had received such information from Mexico as rendered it probable, if not certain, that the Mexican government would refuse to receive our envoy.

Meantime Texas, by the final action of our Congress, had become an integral part of our Union. The Congress of Texas, by its act of December 19, 1836, had declared the Rio del Norte to be the boundary of that republic. Its jurisdiction had been extended and exercised beyond the Nueces. The country between that river and the Del Norte had been represented in the congress and in the convention of Texas; had thus taken part in the act of annexation itself; and is now included within one of our congressional districts. . . . It became, therefore, of urgent necessity to provide for the defence of that portion of our country. Accordingly, on the 13th of January last, instructions were issued to the general in command of these troops to occupy the left bank of the Del Norte. This river, which is the southwestern boundary of the State of Texas, is an exposed frontier; from this quarter invasion was threatened; upon it, and in its immediate vicinity, in the judgment of high military experience, are the proper stations for the protecting forces of the government. . . .

The Mexican forces at Matamoras assumed a belligerent attitude, and, on the twelfth of April, General Ampudia, then in command, notified General Taylor to break up his camp within twenty-four hours, and to retire beyond the Nueces river, and, in the event of his failure to comply with these demands, announced that arms, and arms alone, must decide the question. . . . A party of dragoons, of sixty-three men and officers, were on the same day despatched from the American camp up the Rio del Norte, on its left bank, to ascertain whether the Mexican troops had crossed, or were preparing to cross, the river, "became engaged with a large body of these troops, and, after a short affair, in which some sixteen were killed and wounded, appear to have been surrounded and compelled to surrender." . . .

In the meantime, we have tried every effort at reconciliation. The cup of forebearance had been exhausted, even before the recent information from the frontier of the Del Norte. But now, after reiterated menaces, Mexico has passed the boundary of the United States, has invaded our territory, and shed American blood upon the American soil. She has proclaimed that hostilities have commenced, and that the two nations are now at war.

As war exists, and, notwithstanding all our efforts to avoid it, exists by the act of Mexico herself, we are called upon by every consideration of duty and patriotism to vindicate with decision and honor, the rights, and the interests of our country.

5. Abraham Lincoln Calls Polk to Account, 1848

The President, in his first war message of May, 1846, declares that the soil was ours on which hostilities were commenced by Mexico, and he repeats that declaration almost in the same language in each successive annual message, thus showing that he deems that point a highly essential one. In the importance of that point I entirely agree with the President. To my judgment it is the very point upon which he should be justified, or condemned. . . .

Now, admitting for the present that the Rio Grande was the boundary of Louisiana, what, under heaven, had that to do with the present boundary between us and Mexico? How, Mr. Chairman, the line that once divided your land from mine can still be the boundary between us after I have sold my land to you is to me beyond all comprehension. . . . His next piece of evidence is that "the Republic of Texas always claimed this river (Rio Grande) as her western boundary." That is not true, in fact. Texas has claimed it, but she has not always claimed it. There is at least one distinguished exception. Her State constitution—the republic's most solemn and well-considered act; that which may, without impropriety, be called her last will and testament, revoking all others—makes no such claim. But suppose she had always claimed it. Has not Mexico always claimed the contrary? . . . Now all of this is but naked claim; and what I have already said about claim is strictly ap-

plicable to this. If I should claim your land by word of mouth, that certainly would not make it mine; . . .

But next the President tells us the Congress of the United States understood the State of Texas they admitted into the Union to extend beyond the Nueces. Well, I suppose they did. I certainly so understood it. But how far beyond? That Congress did not understand it to extend clear to the Rio Grande is quite certain, by the fact of their joint resolutions for admission expressly leaving all questions of boundary to future adjustment. . . .

[L]et the President answer the interrogatories I proposed, as before mentioned, or some other similar ones. Let him answer fully, fairly, and candidly. Let him answer with facts and not with arguments. . . . And, if, so answering, he can show that the soil was ours where the first blood of the war was shed,—that it was not within an inhabited country, or, if within such, that the inhabitants had submitted themselves to the civil authority of Texas or of the United States, and that the same is true of the site of Fort Brown,—then I am with him for his justification. . . . But if he can not or will not do this,—if on any pretense or no pretense he shall refuse or omit it—then I shall be fully convinced of what I more than suspect already— that he is deeply conscious of being in the wrong; that he feels the blood of this war, like the blood of Abel, is crying to Heaven against him.

6. A Mexican View of the War, 1850

Thus began anew the negotiations in December, 1845, and the Minister, Mr. John Slidell, presented himself in Mexico. But immediately this difficulty arose, that his government desired him to be received as a Minister Plenipotentiary, ordinary or general, and ours would only admit him as a Commissioner *ad hoc* for the question of Texas. . . . By admitting Mr. Slidell as he wished, it resulted also that, without Mexico receiving the satisfaction due to her, diplomatic negotiations would become re-established between both powers; that the business of annexation would be complicated with the pecuniary reclamations; that Mexico would withdraw her hand from making war, and the United States would follow up all the consequent advantages to her commerce and interests.

This opinion, concluded upon in a cabinet council, was that the agreement to admit a Plenipotentiary of the United States, with special powers to treat upon the subject of Texas, did not oblige Mexico to receive an Envoy Extraordinary and Minister Plenipotentiary, charged to reside near the government; and in which character Mr. Slidell came, according to his credentials. In conformity with these principles, the administration of General Herrera made them known to the envoy, and refused to receive him. Mr. Slidell insisted on being received on the terms which his government offered, but ours returned a decided negative. . . .

To explain the occupation of the Mexican territory by the troops of General Taylor, the strange idea occurred to the United States that the limits of Texas extended to the Rio Bravo del Norte [Rio Grande]. This opinion was predicated upon two distinct principles: one, that the Congress of Texas had so declared it in December, in 1836; and another, that the river mentioned had been the natural line of Louisiana. To state these reasons is equivalent at once to deciding the matter; for no one could defend such palpable absurdities. The first, which this government prizing its intelligence and civilization, supported with refined malice, would have been ridiculous in the mouth of a child. Whom could it convince that the declaration of the Texas Congress bore a legal title for the acquisition of the lands which it appropriated to itself with so little hesitation? If such a principle were recognised, we ought to be very grateful to these gentlemen senators who had the kindness to be satisfied with so little. Why not declare the limits of the rebel state extended to San Luis, to the capital, to our frontier with Guatemala?

The question is so clear in itself that it would only obscure by delaying to examine it further. We pass then to the other less nonsensical than the former. In the first place to pretend that the limits of Louisiana came to the Rio Bravo, it was essential to confound this province with Texas, which never can be tolerated. In the beginning of this article we have already shown the ancient and peaceable possession of Spain over the lands of the latter. Again, this same province, and afterwards State of Texas, never had extended its territory to the Rio Bravo, being only to the Nueces, in which always had been established the boundary. Lastly, a large part of the territory situated on the other side of the Bravo, belonged, without dispute or doubt, to other states of the Republic—to New Mexico, Tamaulipas, Coahuila, and Chihuahua.

Then, after so many and such plain proceedings, is there one impartial man who would not consider the forcible occupation of our territory by the North American arms a shameful usurpation? . . . The Secretary of State, Mr. Buchanan, on the 27th of July, 1846, proposed anew, the admission of an Envoy to open negotiations which might lead to the concluding of an honorable peace. The national government answered that it could not decide, and left it to Congress to express its opinion of the subject. Soon to follow up closely the same system of policy, they ordered a commissioner with the army, which invaded us from the east, to cause it to be understood that peace would be made when our opposition ceased. Whom did they hope to deceive with such false appearances? Does not the series of acts which we have mentioned speak louder than this hypocritical language? By that test then, as a question of justice, no one who examines it in good faith can deny our indisputable rights.

Chapter 13:
Document Set 1 References

1. Expressions of American Destiny, 1839
   Editorial, *United States Magazine and Democratic Review,* November 1839.

2. Senator Benton Justifies White Supremacy, 1846
   Thomas Hart Benton, speech before the U.S. Senate, *Congressional Globe,* May 28, 1846.

3. President Polk Takes the Nation to War, 1846
   Allen Nevins, ed., *Polk: The Diary of a President, 1845–1849* (New York: Capricorn, 1968), pp. 80–91.

4. President Polk's Message to Congress, 1846
   James K. Polk, "War Message," May 11, 1846, James D. Richardson, ed., *A Compilation of the Messages and Papers of the Presidents, 1789–1897* (New York: Bureau of National Literature and Art, 1909), Vol. 5, pp. 2287–2293.

5. Abraham Lincoln Calls Polk to Account, 1848
   Abraham Lincoln, speech before the U.S. House of Representatives, *Congressional Globe,* January 12, 1848, 30th Cong., 1st Sess., pp. 154–156.

6. A Mexican View of the War, 1850
   Apuntas para la historia de querra entre Mexico y los Estados Unidos, A. C. Ramsey, ed. and trans. (New York, 1850), pp. 19–32.

CHAPTER 13

The Clash of Cultures: Nativism in Antebellum America

By the 1830s dramatic social and economic changes were transforming American life. One of the most significant developments involved the altered ethnic composition of the population. Your textbook notes a sharp acceleration in immigration after 1820 that encouraged the growth of cultural pluralism in America. The adjustment did not occur without ethnocultural conflict, and the pain of transition is evident in your textbook's account of the reaction to diversity.

Crucial to an understanding of the social disruption produced by these changes are the ethnic backgrounds and cultural traditions of the transplanted Europeans. Irish and German immigrants flocked to eastern and midwestern cities, where their presence gave rise to a virulent nativism that threatened to destroy the harmony of American social and political life. Immigration statistics reveal the ethnocultural character of antebellum immigration and provide substantial insight into the effect of the new immigrants on American society.

Several of the documents reveal the religious dimension of nativist reaction to the newcomers. Most dramatic, perhaps, were the assertions of Samuel F. B. Morse, who developed an elaborate conspiracy theory to account for the acceleration of immigration in the 1830s. Morse's emphasis on an external plot to undermine American institutions and the spurious "disclosures" of Maria Monk reflect the deep anti-Catholicism stressed in your text.

Although these accounts were the work of educated middle-class/upper-class Americans, prejudice was not confined to these groups. Working-class concerns are evident in the editorial from *Voice of Industry,* a labor journal that spoke for native-born workers fearful of heavy immigration for economic reasons. Using your textbook's account of labor and its protests against immigrants, you should be able to develop an explanation for such views.

Ethnic, religious, and political tensions also colored American politics in the 1840s and 1850s. As immigrants flocked to the Democratic party, the concerns of the Whig party escalated. Even more dramatic was the rise in the 1840s of the Native American party with its explicit anti-immigrant program. The documents reveal the political controversy generated by a proposal to revise the naturalization laws. As you review the nativist argument, try to determine the primary purpose of the proposed legislation.

In analyzing these documents, focus on the legitimacy of the nativist concerns. Try to assess the validity of the nationalist analysis. Be aware of the complex of motivations that underlay the nativism of the 1840s.

Questions for Analysis

1. To what extent does the evidence reveal a class or occupational factor as an explanation for the rise of nativism? How would you account for your findings? Consider the "cultural baggage" inherent in the sources.

2. How did nativists define the term *Americanism*? What did the widespread emphasis on patriotism and flag worship reveal about their thinking? How was the reaction to immigrants reconciled with the American ideology of egalitarianism?

3. How does the cultural conflict of this era relate to ethnic and religious patterns established during the colonial and early national periods in American history? Do the documents clarify the sources of conflict? How do you account for the social approval given to anti-Catholicism?

4. What is the meaning of the term *conspiracy theory?* When have such theories gained public support, and which elements in American society have adopted them? What insight do the documents provide on the reasons behind the acceptance of a conspiracy theory in the 1840s?

5. What is the relationship between the influx of immigrants after 1830 and the growth of the American economy? Relate the changing ethnic character of the population to the intensification of labor-management conflict in the 1840s. What were the social results (see Chapter 9)?

1. Immigration Statistics by Country and Occupation Group, 1820–1898

Immigrants, by Country: 1820 to 1885

Year	All countries[1] (88)	Total (89)	Northwestern Europe — Great Britain (90)	Ireland[2] (91)	Scandinavia[3] (92)	Other Northwestern[4] (93)	Central Europe — Germany[5] (94)	Poland[6] (95)	Other Central[7] (96)	Eastern Europe — U.S.S.R. and Baltic States[8] (97)	Other Eastern[9] (98)	Southern Europe — Italy (99)	Other Southern[10] (100)
1885	395,346	353,083	57,713	51,795	40,704	13,732	124,443	3,085	27,309	17,158	941	13,642	2,561
1884	518,592	453,686	65,950	63,344	52,728	18,768	179,676	4,536	36,571	12,689	388	16,510	2,526
1883	603,322	522,587	76,606	81,486	71,994	24,271	194,786	2,011	27,625	9,909	163	31,792	1,944
1882	788,992	648,186	102,991	76,432	105,326	27,796	250,630	4,672	29,150	16,918	134	32,159	1,978
1881	669,431	528,545	81,376	72,342	81,582	26,883	210,485	5,614	27,935	5,041	102	15,401	1,784
1880	457,257	348,691	73,273	71,603	65,657	15,042	84,638	2,177	17,267	5,014	35	12,354	1,631
1879	177,826	134,259	29,955	20,013	21,820	9,081	34,602	489	5,963	4,453	29	5,791	2,063
1878	138,469	101,612	22,150	15,932	12,254	6,929	29,313	547	5,150	3,048	29	4,344	1,916
1877	141,857	106,195	23,581	14,569	11,274	8,621	29,298	533	5,396	6,599	32	3,195	3,097
1876	169,986	120,920	29,291	19,575	12,323	10,923	31,937	925	6,276	4,775	38	3,015	1,842
1875	227,498	182,961	47,905	37,957	14,322	11,987	47,769	984	7,658	7,997	27	3,631	2,724
1874	313,339	262,783	62,021	53,707	19,178	15,998	87,291	1,795	8,850	4,073	62	7,666	2,142
1873	459,803	397,541	89,500	77,344	35,481	22,892	149,671	3,338	7,112	1,634	53	8,757	1,759
1872	404,806	352,155	84,912	68,732	28,575	15,614	141,109	1,647	4,410	1,018	20	4,190	1,928
1871	321,350	265,145	85,455	57,439	22,132	7,174	82,554	535	4,887	673	23	2,816	1,457
1870	387,203	328,626	103,677	56,996	30,742	9,152	118,225	223	4,425	907	6	2,891	1,382
1869	352,768	315,963	84,438	40,786	43,941	10,585	131,042	184	1,499	343	18	1,489	1,638
1868	138,840	130,090	24,127	32,068	11,985	4,293	55,831	....	192	141	4	891	558
1867	315,722	283,751	52,641	72,879	8,491	12,417	133,426	310	692	205	26	1,624	1,040
1866	318,568	278,916	94,924	36,690	14,495	13,648	115,892	412	93	287	18	1,382	1,075
1865	248,120	214,048	82,465	29,772	7,258	7,992	83,424	528	422	183	14	924	1,066
1864	193,418	185,233	53,428	63,523	2,961	5,621	57,276	165	230	256	11	600	1,162
1863	176,282	163,733	66,882	55,916	3,119	3,245	33,162	94	85	77	16	547	590
1862	91,985	83,710	24,639	23,351	2,550	4,386	27,529	63	111	79	11	566	425
1861	91,918	81,200	19,675	23,797	850	3,769	31,661	48	51	34	5	811	499
1860	153,640	141,209	29,737	48,637	840	5,278	54,491	82	....	65	4	1,019	1,056
1859	121,282	110,949	26,163	35,216	1,590	3,727	41,784	106	....	91	10	932	1,330
1858	123,126	111,354	28,956	26,873	2,662	4,580	45,310	9	....	246	17	1,240	1,461
1857	251,306	216,224	58,479	54,361	2,747	6,879	91,781	124	....	25	11	1,007	810
1856	200,436	186,083	44,658	54,349	1,330	12,403	71,028	20	....	9	5	1,365	916
1855	200,877	187,729	47,572	49,627	1,349	14,571	71,918	462	....	13	9	1,052	1,156
1854	427,833	405,542	58,647	101,606	4,222	23,070	215,009	208	....	2	7	1,263	1,508

Year	(1)	(2)	(3)	(4)	(5)	(6)	(7)	(8)	(9)	(10)	(11)	(12)	(13)
1853	368,645	361,576	37,576	162,649	3,396	14,205	141,946	33	—	3	15	555	1,198
1852	371,603	362,484	40,699	159,548	4,106	11,278	145,918	110	—	2	3	351	469
1851	379,466	369,510	51,487	221,253	2,438	20,905	72,482	10	—	1	2	447	485
1850	369,980	308,323	51,085	164,004	1,589	11,470	78,896	5	—	31	15	431	797
1849	297,024	286,501	55,132	159,398	3,481	7,634	60,235	4	—	44	9	209	355
1848	226,527	218,025	35,159	112,934	1,113	9,877	58,465	—	—	1	3	241	232
1847	234,968	229,117	23,302	105,536	1,320	24,336	74,281	8	—	5	2	164	163
1846	154,416	146,315	22,180	51,752	2,030	12,303	57,561	4	—	248	4	151	82
1845	114,371	109,301	19,210	44,821	982	9,466	34,355	6	—	1	3	137	320
1844	78,615	74,745	14,353	33,490	1,336	4,343	20,731	36	—	13	10	141	292
1843	52,496	49,013	8,430	19,670	1,777	4,364	14,441	17	—	6	5	117	186
1842	104,565	99,945	22,005	51,342	588	5,361	20,370	10	—	28	2	100	139
1841	80,289	76,216	16,188	37,772	226	6,077	15,291	15	—	174	6	179	288
1840	84,066	80,126	2,613	39,430	207	7,978	29,704	5	—	—	1	37	151
1839	68,069	64,148	10,271	23,963	380	7,891	21,028	46	—	7	1	84	477
1838	38,914	34,070	5,420	12,645	112	3,839	11,683	41	—	13	—	86	231
1837	79,340	71,039	12,218	28,508	399	5,769	23,740	81	—	19	3	36	269
1836	76,242	70,465	13,106	30,578	473	5,189	20,707	53	—	2	—	115	239
1835	45,374	41,987	8,970	20,927	68	3,369	8,311	54	—	9	1	60	219
1834	65,365	57,510	10,490	24,474	66	4,468	17,686	54	—	15	1	105	151
1833	58,640	29,111	4,916	8,648	189	5,355	6,988	1	—	159	1	1,699	1,155
1832	60,482	34,193	5,331	12,436	334	5,695	10,194	34	—	52	—	3	114
1831	22,633	13,039	2,475	5,772	36	2,277	2,413	—	—	1	—	28	37
1830	23,322	7,217	1,153	2,721	19	1,305	1,976	2	—	3	2	9	27
1829	22,520	12,523	3,179	7,415	30	1,065	597	—	—	1	1	23	212
1828	27,382	24,729	5,352	12,488	60	4,700	1,851	1	—	7	6	34	230
1827	18,875	16,719	4,186	9,766	28	1,829	432	1	—	19	1	35	422
1826	10,837	9,751	2,319	5,408	26	968	511	—	—	4	2	57	456
1825	10,199	8,543	2,095	4,888	18	719	450	1	—	10	2	75	287
1824	7,912	4,965	1,264	2,345	20	671	230	4	—	7	2	45	377
1823	6,354	4,016	1,100	1,908	7	528	183	3	—	7	—	33	245
1822	6,911	4,418	1,221	2,267	28	522	148	3	—	10	4	35	180
1821	9,127	5,936	3,210	1,518	24	521	383	1	—	7	—	63	209
1820	8,385	7,691	2,410	3,614	23	452	968	5	—	14	1	30	174

[1] For 1820–1867 excludes returning citizens; therefore for those years, does not agree with series C 115 and C 133.

[2] Comprises Eire and Northern Ireland.

[3] Comprises Norway, Sweden, Denmark, and Iceland.

[4] Comprises Netherlands, Belgium, Luxembourg, Switzerland, and France.

[5] Includes Austria, 1938 to 1945.

[6] Between 1899 and 1919, included with Austria-Hungary, Germany, and Russia.

[7] Comprises Czechoslovakia (since 1920), Yugoslavia (since 1861), and Austria (since 1861, except for the years 1938–1945, when Austria was included with Germany).

[8] Comprises U.S.S.R. in Europe, Latvia, Estonia, Lithuania, and Finland.

[9] Comprises Rumania, Bulgaria, and Turkey in Europe.

[10] Comprises Spain, Portugal, Greece, and other Europe, not elsewhere classified.

Immigrants, by Country: 1820 to 1885

Year	Asia Total (101)	Turkey in Asia[1] (102)	China (103)	Japan[2] (104)	Other Asia[3] (105)	America Total (106)	Canada and Newfoundland[4] (107)	Mexico (108)	Other America (109)	Africa, total (110)	Australasia Total (111)	Australia and New Zealand (112)	Other Pacific Islands[3] (113)	All other countries[3] (114)
1885	198	......	22	49	127	41,203	38,336	323	2,544	112	679	449	230	71
1884	510	......	279	20	211	63,339	60,626	430	2,283	59	900	502	398	98
1883	8,113	......	8,031	27	55	71,729	70,274	469	986	67	747	554	193	79
1882	39,629	......	39,579	5	45	100,129	98,366	366	1,397	60	889	878	11	99
1881	11,982	5	11,890	11	76	127,577	125,450	325	1,802	33	1,191	1,188	3	103
1880	5,839	4	5,802	4	29	101,692	99,744	492	1,456	18	954	953	1	63
1879	9,660	31	9,604	4	21	33,043	31,286	556	1,201	12	816	813	3	36
1878	9,014	7	8,992	2	13	27,204	25,592	465	1,147	18	606	606	......	15
1877	10,640	3	10,594	7	36	24,065	22,137	445	1,483	16	914	912	2	27
1876	22,943	8	22,781	4	150	24,686	22,505	631	1,550	89	1,312	1,205	107	36
1875	16,499	1	16,437	3	58	26,640	24,097	610	1,933	54	1,268	1,104	164	76
1874	13,838	6	13,776	21	35	35,339	33,020	386	1,933	58	1,193	960	233	128
1873	20,325	3	20,292	9	21	40,335	37,891	606	1,838	28	1,414	1,135	279	160
1872	7,825	......	7,788	17	20	42,205	40,204	569	1,432	41	2,416	2,180	236	164
1871	7,240	4	7,135	78	23	48,835	47,164	402	1,269	24	21	18	3	85
1870	15,825	......	15,740	48	37	42,658	40,414	463	1,781	31	36	36	......	27
1869	12,949	2	12,874	63	10	23,767	21,120	320	2,327	72	......	......	......	17
1868	5,171	......	5,157	......	14	3,415	2,785	129	501	3	......	......	......	161
1867	3,961	......	3,863	67	31	24,715	23,379	292	1,044	25	......	......	......	3,270
1866	2,411	......	2,385	7	19	33,582	32,150	239	1,193	33	......	......	......	3,626
1865	2,947	......	2,942	......	5	22,778	21,586	193	999	49	......	......	......	8,298
1864	2,982	......	2,975	......	7	4,607	3,636	99	872	37	......	......	......	559
1863	7,216	......	7,214	......	2	4,147	3,464	96	587	3	......	......	......	1,183
1862	3,640	......	3,633	......	7	4,175	3,275	142	758	12	......	......	......	448
1861	7,528	......	7,518	1	9	2,763	2,069	218	476	47	......	......	......	380
1860	5,476	......	5,467	......	9	6,343	4,514	229	1,600	126	......	......	......	486
1859	3,461	......	3,457	......	4	5,466	4,163	265	1,038	11	......	......	......	1,395
1858	5,133	......	5,128	......	5	5,821	4,603	429	789	17	......	......	......	801
1857	5,945	......	5,944	......	1	6,811	5,670	133	1,008	25	......	......	......	22,301
1856	4,747	......	4,733	......	14	9,058	6,493	741	1,824	6	......	......	......	542
1855	3,540	......	3,526	......	14	9,260	7,761	420	1,079	14	......	......	......	334
1854	13,100	......	13,100	......	......	8,533	6,891	446	1,196	......	......	......	......	658
1853	47	......	42	......	5	6,030	5,424	162	444	8	......	......	......	984
1852	4	......	......	......	4	7,695	6,352	72	1,271	......	......	......	......	1,420
1851	2	......	......	......	2	9,703	7,438	181	2,084	3	......	......	......	248

Year										
1850	7	……	……	……	4	15,768	9,376	597	5,795	……	45,882
1849	11	……	3	……	8	8,904	6,890	518	1,496	3	1,605
1848	8	……	3	……	8	7,989	6,473	24	1,492	10	495
1847	12	……	4	……	8	5,231	3,827	62	1,342	……	608
1846	11	……	7	……	4	5,525	3,855	222	1,448	1	2,564
1845	6	……	6	……	……	5,035	3,195	498	1,342	4	25
1844	6	……	3	……	3	3,740	2,711	197	832	14	110
1843	11	……	3	……	8	2,854	1,502	398	954	6	612
1842	7	……	4	……	3	3,994	2,078	403	1,513	3	616
1841	3	……	2	……	1	3,429	1,816	352	1,261	14	627
1840	1	……	……	……	1	3,815	1,938	395	1,482	6	118
1839	……	……	……	……	……	3,617	1,926	353	1,338	10	294
1838	1	……	……	……	1	2,990	1,476	211	1,303	10	1,843
1837	11	……	……	……	11	3,628	1,279	627	1,722	2	4,660
1836	4	……	……	……	4	4,936	2,814	798	1,324	6	831
1835	17	……	8	……	9	3,312	1,193	1,032	1,087	14	44
1834	6	……	……	……	6	2,779	1,020	885	874	1	5,069
1833	3	……	……	……	3	3,282	1,194	779	1,309	1	26,243
1832	4	……	……	……	4	2,871	608	827	1,436	2	23,412
1831	1	……	……	……	1	2,194	176	692	1,326	2	7,397
1830	……	……	……	……	……	2,296	189	983	1,124	2	13,807
1829	2	……	1	……	1	3,299	409	2,290	600	1	6,695
1828	3	……	……	……	3	2,090	267	1,089	734	6	554
1827	1	……	……	……	1	580	165	127	288	4	1,571
1826	1	……	……	……	1	831	223	106	502	……	254
1825	1	……	1	……	……	846	314	68	464	1	808
1824	1	……	……	……	1	559	155	110	294	……	2,387
1823	……	……	……	……	……	382	167	35	180	……	1,956
1822	1	……	1	……	1	378	204	5	169	2	2,114
1821	……	……	……	……	……	303	184	4	115	……	2,886
1820	5	……	1	……	4	387	209	1	177	1	301

[1] No record of immigration from Turkey in Asia until 1869.

[2] No record of immigration from Japan until 1861.

[3] Philippine Islands are included in "Other Asia" in 1952 (1,179), 1953 (1,074), 1954 (1,234), 1955 (1,598), 1956 (1,792), and 1957 (1,874). From 1934 to 1951, inclusive, they are included in "All other countries."

[4] Prior to 1920 Canada and Newfoundland were recorded as British North America. From 1820 to 1898 the figures include all British North American possessions.

Immigrants, by Major Occupation Group: 1820 to 1898

Year	Total[1]	No occupation	Professional	Commercial	Skilled	Farmers	Servants	Laborers	Miscel-laneous
	115	125	126	127	128	129	130	131	132
1898	229,299	90,569	1,347	5,959	33,145	16,243	23,656	52,531	5,849
1897	230,832	91,624	1,732	7,159	33,161	22,560	23,739	46,198	4,659
1896	343,267	123,196	2,324	6,174	46,807	29,251	38,926	91,262	5,327
1895	258,536	92,193	2,029	5,314	43,844	13,055	35,960	61,430	4,711
1894	285,631	113,247	1,791	6,033	49,736	21,762	29,653	56,732	6,677
1893	439,730	209,767	2,362	837	51,145	34,070	(²)	114,295	²27,254
1892	579,663	255,832	2,932	2,683	63,128	51,630	(²)	171,483	²31,975
1891	560,319	248,635	3,431	11,340	54,951	36,398	32,596	167,290	5,678
1890	455,302	195,770	3,236	7,802	44,540	29,296	28,625	139,365	6,668
1889	444,427	208,761	2,815	7,359	50,457	28,962	30,220	111,809	4,044
1888	546,889	243,900	3,360	7,597	59,985	29,335	27,310	170,273	5,129
1887	490,109	224,073	2,882	8,032	52,403	30,932	27,510	140,938	3,339
1886	334,203	157,952	2,078	6,237	36,522	20,600	20,198	86,853	3,763
1885	395,346	211,730	2,097	6,707	39,817	27,585	20,213	83,068	4,129
1884	518,592	277,052	2,284	7,691	55,061	42,050	24,249	106,478	3,727
1883	603,322	322,318	2,450	8,280	62,505	39,048	27,988	136,071	4,662
1882	788,992	402,835	2,992	10,102	72,664	61,888	23,010	209,605	5,896
1881	669,431	355,670	2,812	9,371	66,457	58,028	19,342	147,816	9,935
1880	457,257	217,446	1,773	7,916	49,929	47,204	18,580	105,012	9,397
1879	177,826	81,772	1,639	5,202	21,362	19,907	6,804	36,897	4,243
1878	138,469	62,622	1,510	4,475	16,531	14,843	6,157	26,656	5,675
1877	141,857	63,316	1,885	4,667	21,006	13,188	5,158	25,482	7,155
1876	169,986	71,111	2,400	4,963	24,200	14,536	6,493	38,847	7,436
1875	227,498	106,723	2,426	5,029	33,803	16,447	10,579	46,877	5,614
1874	313,339	155,122	2,476	5,641	38,700	28,775	12,427	65,895	4,303
1873	459,803	239,307	2,980	7,593	48,792	36,983	16,259	104,423	3,466
1872	404,806	213,959	1,905	7,156	44,967	38,159	11,108	85,934	1,618
1871	321,350	172,215	2,247	5,553	33,577	27,042	13,814	65,936	966
1870	387,203	207,174	1,831	7,139	35,698	35,656	14,261	84,577	867
1869	352,768	181,453	1,700	8,837	33,345	28,102	10,265	88,649	417
1868	282,189	150,983	1,398	8,556	32,197	23,046	6,561	59,151	297
1867	342,162	182,794	2,288	14,706	44,097	32,626	7,715	57,419	517
1866	359,957	202,456	2,242	15,827	41,091	30,302	8,883	58,629	527
1865	287,399	161,580	1,743	12,700	36,522	20,012	9,231	45,247	364
1864	221,535	106,656	1,120	9,473	26,542	13,837	15,623	48,041	243
1863	199,811	99,039	1,173	7,590	24,155	12,348	9,103	46,198	205
1862	114,463	62,860	788	7,774	11,986	9,265	3,683	17,752	355
1861	112,702	60,760	668	7,683	11,601	11,668	739	19,413	170
1860	179,691	93,925	792	11,207	19,342	21,742	1,415	31,268	....
1859	155,509	78,228	858	12,495	24,628	16,323	1,281	21,696	....
1858	144,906	71,320	662	10,217	18,742	20,506	1,142	22,317	....

Immigrants, by Major Occupation Group: 1820 to 1898 (*Continued*)

Year	Total[1]	No occupation	Professional	Commercial	Skilled	Farmers	Servants	Laborers	Miscellaneous
	115	125	126	127	128	129	130	131	132
1857	271,982	153,963	570	12,114	26,062	34,702	1,322	43,249	....
1856	224,496	130,647	462	11,101	18,797	24,722	1,748	37,019	....
1855	230,476	117,603	780	14,759	17,463	34,693	2,598	42,580	....
1854	460,474	235,216	699	15,173	36,468	87,188	3,357	82,373	....
1853	400,982	223,390	722	12,782	20,806	56,322	3,938	83,022	....
1852	397,343	223,861	572	11,502	27,176	58,023	942	75,267	....
1851	474,398	257,376	938	14,983	36,297	59,095	3,733	101,976	....
1850	315,334	188,931	918	6,400	26,369	42,873	3,203	46,640	....
1849	299,683	157,657	972	3,508	32,021	39,675	3,671	62,179	....
1848	229,483	118,528	517	3,407	24,705	31,670	4,433	46,223	....
1847	239,482	126,005	703	4,218	25,895	43,594	3,198	35,869	....
1846	158,649	91,132	592	4,189	13,250	27,944	3,349	18,193	....
1845	119,896	65,055	542	5,049	10,857	19,349	2,492	16,552	....
1844	84,764	49,843	755	3,960	9,476	9,831	1,174	9,725	....
1843	56,529	32,842	578	3,226	6,093	8,031	413	5,346	....
1842	110,980	60,526	744	4,976	14,553	12,966	1,264	15,951	....
1841	87,805	46,197	541	5,267	11,111	12,343	923	11,423	....
1840	92,207	47,305	481	5,311	10,811	18,476	183	9,640	....
1839	74,666	37,985	584	5,692	10,026	12,410	99	7,870	....
1838	45,159	24,627	459	4,005	5,675	6,667	42	3,684	....
1837	84,959	52,011	522	3,893	8,483	10,835	120	9,095	....
1836	80,972	50,684	472	3,379	8,879	8,770	39	8,749	....
1835	48,716	28,736	487	3,875	6,005	6,117	599	2,897	....
1834	67,948	45,906	561	3,021	7,190	7,160	1,236	2,874	....
1833	59,925	30,944	459	4,913	12,800	6,618	82	4,109	....
1832	61,654	33,840	176	5,424	10,333	8,502	56	3,323	....
1831	23,880	15,218	183	2,368	2,383	2,685	115	928	....
1830	24,837	19,363	136	1,427	1,745	1,424	22	720	....
1829	24,513	15,535	252	2,661	2,579	1,264	337	1,885	....
1828	30,184	18,066	331	2,328	3,868	2,542	421	2,628	....
1827	21,777	12,415	262	2,076	3,056	2,071	136	1,761	....
1826	13,908	7,478	190	1,943	2,129	1,382	70	716	....
1825	12,858	7,031	204	1,841	1,416	1,647	69	650	....
1824	9,627	4,965	187	1,926	1,237	918	13	381	....
1823	8,265	4,247	179	1,427	1,268	800	6	338	....
1822	8,549	4,302	151	1,431	1,397	834	20	414	....
1821	11,644	6,670	204	1,441	1,533	1,249	94	453	....
1820	10,311	6,836	105	933	1,090	874	139	334	....

[1]For 1820–1867 includes returning citizens.
[2]Servants included with "miscellaneous" (series C 132).

2. Samuel F. B. Morse Expresses Anti-Catholicism, 1835

I have set forth in a very brief and imperfect manner the evil the great and increasing evil that threatens our free institutions from *foreign interference.* Have I not shown that there is real cause for alarm? Let me recapitulate the facts in the case, and see if any one of them can be denied; and if not, I submit it to the calm decision of every American whether he can still sleep in fancied security while incendiaries are at work; and whether he is ready quietly to surrender his liberty, civil and religious, into the hands of foreign powers.

1. It is a fact that in this age the subject of civil and religious liberty agitates in the most intense manner the various European governments.

2. It is a fact that the influence of American free institutions in subverting European despotic institutions is greater now than it has ever been, from the fact of the greater maturity and long-tried character of the American form of government.

3. It is a fact that popery is opposed in its very nature to democratic republicanism; and it is, therefore, as a political system, as well as religious, opposed to civil and religious liberty, and consequently to our form of government.

4. It is a fact that this truth, respecting the intrinsic character of popery, had lately been clearly and demonstratively proved in public lectures by one of the Austrian cabinet, a devoted Roman Catholic, and with the evident design (as subsequent events show) of exciting the Austrian government to a great enterprise in support of absolute power.

5. It is a fact that this member of the Austrian cabinet, in his lectures, designated and proscribed this country by name, as the "great nursery of destructive principles; as the revolutionary school for France and the rest of Europe," whose contagious example of democratic liberty had given, and would still give, trouble to the rest of the world unless the evil were abated.

6. It is a fact that very shortly after the delivery of these lectures, a society was organized in the Austrian capital, called the St. Leopold Foundation, for the purpose "of promoting the greater activity of Catholic missions in America."

7. It is a fact that this society is under the patronage of the emperor of Austria; has its central direction at Vienna; is under the supervision of Prince Metternich; that it is an extensive combination, embodying the civil as well as the ecclesiastical *officers,* not only of the whole Austrian Empire, but of the neighboring despotic states; that it is actively at work collecting moneys and sending agents to this country to carry out into effect its designs.

8. It is a fact that the agents of these foreign despots are, for the most part, Jesuits.

9. It is a fact that the effects of this society are already apparent in the otherwise unaccountable increase of Roman Catholic cathedrals, churches, colleges, convents, nunneries, etc., in every part of the country; in the sudden increase of Catholic emigration; in the increased clannishness of the Roman Catholics, and the boldness with which their leaders are experimenting on the character of the American people.

10. It is a fact that an unaccountable disposition to riotous conduct has manifested itself within a few years, when exciting topics are publicly discussed wholly at variance with the former peaceful, deliberative character of our people.

11. It is a fact that a species of police, unknown to our laws, has repeatedly been put in requisition to keep the peace among a certain class of foreigners who are Roman Catholics, viz., priest-police.

12. It is a fact that Roman Catholic priests have interfered to influence our elections.

13. It is a fact that politicians on both sides have propitiated these priests to obtain the votes of their people.

14. It is a fact that numerous societies of Roman Catholics, particularly among the Irish foreigners, are organized in various parts of the country, under various names and ostensibly for certain benevolent objects; that these societies are united together by correspondence, all which may be innocent and praiseworthy, but viewed in connection with the recent aspect of affairs are at least suspicious.

15. It is a fact that an attempt has been made to organize a military corps of Irishmen in New York, to be called the O'Connel Guards; thus commencing a military organization of foreigners.

16. It is a fact that the greater part of the foreigners in our population is composed of Roman Catholics. . . .

It may be, Americans, that you still doubt the *existence* of a conspiracy, and the reality of danger from foreign combination; or, if the attempt is made, you yet doubt the power of any such secret intrigue in your society. Do you wish to test its existence and its power? . . .

Again, I say, let the proposition be that the law of the land be so changed, that NO FOREIGNER WHO COMES INTO THE COUNTRY AFTER THE LAW IS PASSED SHALL EVER BE ENTITLED TO THE RIGHT OF SUFFRAGE. This is just ground; it is practicable ground; it is defensible ground, and it is safe and prudent ground; and I cannot better close than in the words of Mr. Jefferson: "The time to guard against corruption and tyranny is *before* they shall have gotten hold on us; IT IS BETTER TO KEEP THE WOLF OUT OF THE FOLD THAN TO TRUST TO DRAWING HIS TEETH AND TALONS AFTER HE HAS ENTERED."

3. A Fictitious Account of Life in a Convent, 1836

The Superior now informed me, that having taken the black veil, it only remained that I should swear the three oaths customary on becoming a nun; and that some explanations would be necessary from her. I was now, she told me, to have access to every part of the edifice, even to the cellar, where two of the sisters were imprisoned for causes which she did not mention. I must be informed, that one of my great duties was, to obey the priests in all things; and this I soon learnt, to my utter astonishment and horror, was to live in the practice of criminal intercourse with them. . . .

She gave me another piece of information which excited other feelings in me, scarcely less dreadful. Infants were sometimes born in the convent: but they were always baptized and immediately strangled! This secured their everlasting happiness; for the baptism purified them from all sinfulness, and being sent out of the world before they had time to do any thing wrong, they were at once admitted into heaven. How happy, she exclaimed, are those who secure immortal happiness to such little beings! Their little souls would thank those who kill their bodies, if they had it in their power!

Into what a place and among what society had I been admitted! How differently did a Convent now appear from what I had supposed it to be! The holy women I had always fancied the nuns to be, the venerable Lady Superior, what were they? And the priests of the Seminary adjoining, some of whom indeed I had had reason to think were base and profligate men, what were they all? I now learnt they were often admitted into the nunnery, and allowed to indulge in the greatest crimes, which they and others called virtues.

4. A Workers' Newspaper Warns Against the Native American Party, 1844

The Native American Party. What has given rise to the new party now organized in this city and two or three other places under the above name? Evidently, an influx of foreign labor into a market already overstocked. The existence of this conspicuous evil is clearly the motive of those who form the body, the rank and file, of the Native American Party. The officers and leaders of the party, who are chiefly composed of the disappointed office seekers of the other parties, are incensed against the foreign population for the very disinterested reason that their occupation of office seeking has been encroached upon by adopted citizens. Another truth connected with this subject is that both of the old parties have, to curry favor with the foreign-born interest, freely dealt out to them the bribe of petty offices in order to secure their influence and votes for offices of more importance.

This state of things has very naturally led to the formation of the Native American Party. The body of the party, the suffering working classes, smarting under the effects to competition and justly incensed to see foreigners promoted to office merely because they are foreigners, are led on by men to expect a distribution of the city offices as a reward of victory. . . . Let no workingman be deluded with the idea that, even could the measures of the Native American Party, the exclusion of foreigners from the polls and from office, be accomplished, one cent would be added to their daily pittance.

5. A Protest Against Oppressive Capitalism, 1845

This talk about the continued prosperity, happy condition, and future independence of the producing class of this country, as a class, is all fiction, moonshine. There is at this very moment a great strife between capital and labor, and capital is fast gaining the mastery—the gradual abasement of the working-men and women of this country abundantly sustain this position—the various "strikes" among the operatives and workingmen in New England and other sections of the country, which have almost invariably proved abortive and ineffectual, evidently show that combined, incorporated, and protected capital can "starve out" and dismay the disorganized, competing, and dependent laborers, whose daily toil provides the scanty portion to satisfy the pinching necessities of those dependent upon them. . . .

Now the capitalists of the Danville Iron Works wish to protect themselves against these "disorderly strikes" by importing a surplus of help; the Lowell capitalists entertain the same republican idea of self-protection, the Pittsburgh and Allegheny city capitalists, whose sympathies (if they have any) have been recently appealed to, wish to secure themselves against "turnouts" by creating a numerous poor and dependent populace. Isolated capital everywhere and in all ages protects itself by the poverty, ignorance, and servility of a surplus population who will submit to its base requirements.

Hence the Democratic or Whig capital of the United States is striving to fill the country with foreign workmen—English workmen, whose abject condition in their own country has made them tame, submissive, and "peaceable, orderly citizens"; that is, work *fourteen* and *sixteen* hours per day for what capital sees fit to give them; and if it is not enough to provide them a comfortable house to shelter their wives and children and furnish them with decent food and clothes, why, they must live in cellars, go hungry and ragged! And for this state of things, capitalists are not answerable. O! no—"they (the laborers) ain't obliged to take it—they are free to go when they please!". . .

Let the American laborers recollect that the same grasping system which has driven thousands from the Old World in utter destitution to this country, for refuge, is here being nourished; and should they suffer it to go on, their children will look in vain for an asylum for their ills and oppressions; and, perchance, in their wild breathing after that rational freedom which God gave to *all* and which brings peace, plenty, and happiness, curse the day that gave them existence and the beautiful heavens and earth that mock and aggravate their misery.

6. Daniel Webster Argues for Revision of the Naturalization Laws, 1844

The result of the recent elections in several states has impressed my mind with one deep and strong conviction: that is, that there is an imperative necessity for reforming the naturalization laws of the United States. The preservation of the government, and consequently the interest of all parties, in my opinion, clearly and strongly demand this.

All are willing and desirous, of course, that America should continue to be the safe asylum for the oppressed of all nations. All are willing and desirous that the blessings of a free government should be open to the enjoyment of the worthy and industrious from all countries who may come hither for the purpose of bettering their circumstances by the successful employment of their own capital, enterprise, or labor. But it is not unreasonable that the elective franchise should not be exercised by a person of a foreign birth until after such a length of residence among us as that he may be supposed to have become, in some good measure, acquainted with our Constitution and laws, our social institutions, and the general interest of the country; and to have become an American in feeling, principle, character, and sympathy, as well as by having established his domicile among us. . . .

Now it seems to me impossible that every honest man and every good citizen, every true lover of liberty and the Constitution, every real friend of the country, would not desire to see an end put to these enormous abuses. I avow it, therefore, as my opinion that it is the duty of us all to endeavor to bring about an efficient reformation of the naturalization laws of the United States. . . .

Gentlemen, there is not a solitary doubt that if the elections have gone against us it has been through false and fraudulent votes. Pennsylvania, if, as they say, she has given 6,000 for our adversaries, has done so through the basest fraud. Is it not so? And look at New York. In the city there were thrown 60,000 votes, or one vote to every five inhabitants. You know that, fairly and honestly, there can be no such thing on earth. [*Cheers.*] And the great remedy is for us to go directly to the source of true popular power and to purify the elections. [*Twenty-six cheers.*]. . .

A foreign demagogue addresses a political missive to a certain body of so-called American citizens, banded together as a distinct political organization, and tells them, *"Where you have the elective franchise, give your votes to none but those who will assist you in carrying out the intentions"*—of what? The American Constitution? Oh, no! Of what? American freedom? Oh, no! But poll your votes to carry out the intentions of a foreign despot who aims at the overthrow of American institutions. Was it a crime, sir, for native Americans to repel this aggression, and proclaim to the world that no foreign potentate, or agent, or demagogue, should invade the constitutional rights of any portion of our American population? . . .

Will the House permit us to place before the nation such records, drawn from the proper departments, as will show that, unless some remedy be applied to this great and growing evil, THE DAY IS NOT FAR DISTANT WHEN THE AMERICAN-BORN VOTER WILL FIND HIMSELF IN A MINORITY IN HIS OWN LAND! . . .

Sir, I disclaim all pretensions to "liberality" on this question, in which lies coiled up the future happiness or misery of millions of unborn American citizens. We are now struggling for national character and national identity, and not for the meed of courtesy, or the extent of a generous disposition. We stand now on the very verge of overthrow by the impetuous force of invading foreigners. Europe can no longer contain the growing population that is swelling her to bursting. She must disgorge it at any price, no matter what. . . .

If the heart of the alien is in his native land—if all his dearest thoughts and fondest affections cluster around the altar of his native gods—let us not disturb his enjoyments by placing this burden of new affections on his bosom, through the moral force of an oath of allegiance, and the onerous obligation of political duties that jar against his sympathies, and call on him to renounce feelings that he can never expel from his bosom. Let us secure him the privilege at least of mourning for his native land, by withholding obligations that he cannot discharge either with fidelity, ability, or pleasure. Give him time, sir, to wean himself from his early love. Why should he not, like our own sons, enjoy twenty-one years of infant freedom from political cares, to look around him, grow familiar with the new scene in which he finds himself placed—become acquainted with all the new and intricate relations by which man is made a sovereign by the voice of his fellowman and yet still retains all the responsibilities of the citizen, even while he exercises all the power of a monarch.

Chapter 13:
Document Set 2 References

1. Immigration Statistics by Country and Occupation Group, 1820–1898
U.S. Bureau of the Census, "Immigrants, by Country: 1820 to 1885," "Immigrants, by Major Occupational Group: 1820 to 1898," in *Statistical History of the United States from Colonial Times to the Present* (Stamford: Fairfield Publishers, Inc., 1965), pp. 57–61.

2. Samuel F. B. Morse Expresses Anti-Catholicism, 1835
An American (Samuel F. B. Morse), *Imminent Dangers to the Free Institutions of the United States Through Foreign Immigration, and the Present State of Naturalization Laws* (New York, 1835), Numbers 6, 11.

3. A Fictitious Account of Life in a Convent, 1836
Maria Monk, *Awful Disclosures of the Hotel Dieu Nunnery* (New York: 1836; facsimile of 1836 edition, Archon Books, 1962), pp. 56–58.

4. A Workers' Newspaper Warns Against the Native American Party, 1844
Workingman's Advocate, March 23, 1844.

5. A Protest Against Oppressive Capitalism, 1845
Voice of Industry (Fitchburg, Mass.), October 9, 1845.

6. Daniel Webster Argues for Revision of the Naturalization Laws, 1844
Daniel Webster, Remarks to Boston Whigs, November 1844, in John P. Sanderson, *Republican Landmarks: The Views and Opinions of American Statesmen* (Philadelphia: J. B. Lippincott and Co., 1856), pp. 323–324.

CHAPTER 13

DOCUMENT SET 3
The Overland Trail: Sharing the Burden

In the expanding republic of the 1840s, the American population demonstrated extensive geographic mobility. One of the most attractive destinations for people on the move was the widely publicized Oregon country in the Pacific Northwest. As the result of an aggressive promotional effort, thousands of easterners and midwesterners were stricken by what came to be known as the "Oregon fever" and chose to relocate in hopes of finding economic success in this agricultural paradise. However, to reach their new home, it was necessary to endure a grueling journey over plains and mountains, a trek that tested their commitment to a better future. The following documents reveal some of the hardships and changes encountered by emigrant families on the trail and in the promised land.

As your textbook and documents indicate, the trip west was typically a family enterprise. It was inevitable, therefore, that women would become full partners in the undertaking, which meant that traditional sex roles were often abandoned under the pressures of the frontier experience. Your review of the sources should begin with an analysis of existing gender relations at that time and the migrants' initial expectations concerning the roles to be occupied by men and women. Be aware of the assumptions that prevailed in the communities and societies from which the emigrants had come.

Once you have determined how men and women thought about their respective roles and responsibilities, turn to the diaries for an account of the harsh realities of life on the overland trail. Consider the traumatic effect of harsh weather, physical obstacles, isolation, illness, and contact with the Native American population. Be especially aware of the contrast between initial expectations and the realities of trail life, as the amenities of more settled communities receded into memory.

Because the journey took months to complete, emigrant parties witnessed all the events normally associated with the traditional life cycle. Observe the responses of these hardy travelers to such occurrences as birth, marriage, illness, and death. Since the wagon train functioned as an organic community, it became necessary to develop some means of maintaining order and providing the rudiments of governance. Note the institutions created by the emigrants to ensure civic harmony.

Equally important was the urgent need for families to function as integrated units. The necessity of intrafamily cooperation raised the question of sexual spheres and the division of labor on the trail and in the new country. Search the documents for insights into changes in male and female self-images that occurred as a result of the demands imposed on men and women by the frontier environment. Relate the adjustment of gender roles to the nineteenth-century cult of domesticity that had flourished in the settled areas of the East or Midwest. Be aware of the ways in which men's and women's experiences as emigrants contributed to a new form of sexual equality.

Finally, speculate with regard to the permanence of the new relationships and the gender equity thrust on frontier men and women. Search the documents for evidence of the economic roles assumed by women in the Oregon country. Consider the origins of the predominant social assumptions of the era, and decide whether the experience of overland migration was sufficiently traumatic to produce a permanent alteration in values.

Questions for Analysis

1. Compare the emigrants' prior expectations with the realities encountered during the overland migration and the establishment of new homes on the Oregon frontier. What were the sources of contradiction? How did these disparities influence traditional gender roles?

2. What do the documents reveal about male and female self-images before and after the emigration experience? To what extent were their assumptions altered by life on the overland trail?

3. As you review the diary excerpts and promotional articles, do you identify any distinctions between the experiences and attitudes of their authors? Did men and women perceive the frontier experience differently? How would you account for these differences?

4. To what extent did life on the frontier produce sexual equality? What *kind* of equality developed on the trail and on the Oregon frontier? What evidence of equality may be found in the diaries?

5. What was the lasting impact of the overland journey on the concept of "separate spheres"? To what extent were the changes in sex-role definition that had occurred on the trail permanent in their influence?

1. The Lure of the Northwest Spawns "Oregon Fever," 1843

Just now Oregon is the pioneer's land of promise. Hundreds are already prepared to start thither with the spring, while hundreds of others are anxiously awaiting the action of congress in reference to that country, as the signal for their departure. Some have already been to view the country, and have returned with a flattering tale of the inducements it holds out. They have painted it to their neighbors in the brightest colors; these have told it to others; the Oregon fever has broke out, and is now raging like any other contagion. . . . "Wilson," said I a few days since to an old settler, "so you are going to Oregon." "Well, I is, horse. Tice Pitt was out looking at it last season, and he says it is a leetle the greatest country on the face of the earth. So I'm bound to go." "How do the old woman and the girls like the idea of such a long journey?" "They feel mighty peert about it, and Suke says she shan't be easy till we start."

2. An Idealized Description of the Trek West, 1845

Even while we write, we see a long train of wagons coming through our busy streets; they are hailed with shouts of welcome by their fellow voyagers, and, to judge from the pleased expression on every face, it "all goes merry as a marriage bell." On looking out at the passing train, we see among the foremost a very comfortably covered wagon, one of the sheets drawn aside, and an extremely nice looking lady seated inside very quietly sewing; the bottom of the wagon is carpeted; there are two or three chairs, and at one end there is a bureau, surmounted by a mirror; various articles of ornament and convenience hang around the sides—a perfect prairie boudoir. Blessed be woman! Shedding light and happiness where'er she goes; with her the wild prairie will be a paradise! Blessed be him who gave us this connecting link between heaven and man to win us from our wilder ways. Hold on there; this is getting entirely too sentimental; but we don't care who laughs, we felt better and happier when we looked on this picture than we may express. That fine manly fellow riding along by the side of the wagon, and looking in so pleasantly, is doubtless the lady's husband; we almost envy him. But they are past, and now comes team after team, each drawn by six or eight stout oxen, and such drivers! positively sons of Anak! not one of them less than six feet two in his stockings. Whoo ha! Go it boys! We're in perfect *Oregon fever*.

3. An Oregon Emigrant Describes Civil Government on the Trail, 1844

Linnton, Oregon Territory
January 18, 1844

James G. Bennett, Esq.—

Dear Sir: Having arrived safely in this beautiful country, and having seen, at least, its main features, I propose to give you some concise description of the same, as well as a short history of our trip. I reached the rendezvous, twenty miles from Independence, on the seventeenth of May, and found a large body of emigrants there, waiting for the company to start. On the 18th we held a meeting, and appointed a committee to see Doctor Whitman, for the purpose of obtaining information in regard to the practicability of the trip. Other committees were also appointed, and the meeting adjourned to meet again, at the Big Spring, on the 20th. On the 20th, all the emigrants, with few exceptions, were there, as well as several from the western part of Missouri. The object of the meeting was to organize, by adopting some rules for our government. . . .

The following are the rules and regulations for the government of the Oregon Emigrating Company:

Resolved, Whereas we deem it necessary for the government of all societies, either civil or military, to adopt certain rules and regulations for their government, for the purpose of keeping good order and promoting civil and military discipline. In order to insure union and safety, we deem it necessary to adopt the following rules and regulations for the government of the said company:—

Rule 1. Every male person of the age of sixteen, or upward, shall be considered a legal voter in all affairs relating to the company.

Rule 2. There shall be nine men elected by a majority of the company, who shall form a council, whose duty it shall be to settle all disputes arising between individuals, and to try and pass sentence on all persons for any act for which they may be guilty, which is subversive of good order and military discipline. They shall take especial cognizance of all sentinels and members of the guard, who may be guilty of neglect of duty, or sleeping on post. Such persons shall be tried, and sentence passed upon them at the discretion of the council. A majority of two thirds of the council shall decide all questions that may come before them, subject to the approval or disapproval of the captain. If the captain disapprove of the decision of the council, he shall state to them his reasons, when they shall again pass upon the question, and if the same decision is again made by the same majority, it shall be final.

4. A Pioneer Woman Copes with Personal Tragedy, 1847–1850

April 21, 1847—Commenced our journey from La Porte, Indiana, to Oregon; made fourteen miles. . . .

[After six months of overland travel the party has reached the Columbia River.]

November 9—Finds us still in trouble. Waves dashing over our raft and we already stinting ourselves in provisions. My husband started this morning to hunt provisions. Left no man with us except our oldest boy. It is very cold. The icicles are hanging from our wagon beds to the water. Tonight about dusk Adam Polk expired. No one with him but his wife and myself. We sat up all night with him while the waves was dashing below. . . .

November 12—Ferried our cattle over the river and buried Mr. Polk. Rain all day. We are living entirely on beef.

November 18—My husband is sick. It rains and snows. We start this morning around the falls with our wagons. We have 5 miles to go. I carry my babe and lead, or rather carry, another through snow, mud and water, almost to my knees. It is the worst road that a team could possibly travel. I went ahead with my children and I was afraid to look behind me for fear of seeing the wagons turn over into the mud and water with everything in them. My children gave out with cold and fatigue and could not travel, and the boys had to unhitch the oxen and bring them and carry the children on to camp. I was so cold and numb that I could not tell by the feeling that I had any feet at all. We started this morning at sunrise and did not get to camp until after dark, and there was not one dry thread on one of us—not even my babe. I had carried my babe and I was so fatigued that I could scarcely speak or step. When I got here I found my husband lying in Welch's wagon, very sick. He had brought Mrs. Polk down the day before and was taken sick here. We had to stay up all night tonight for our wagons are left half-way back. I have not told half we suffered. I am not adequate to the task. Here was some hundreds camped, waiting for boats to come and take them down the Columbia to Vancouver or Portland or Oregon City.

November 19—My husband is sick and can have but little care. Rain all day.

November 20—Rain all day. It is almost an impossibility to cook, and quite so to keep warm or dry. I froze or chilled my feet so that I cannot wear a shoe, so I have to go around in the cold water barefooted.

November 21—Rain all day. The whole care of everything falls upon my shoulders. I cannot write any more at present.

November 27—Embarked once more on the Columbia on a flatboat. Ran all day, though the waves threatened hard to sink us. Passed Fort Vancouver in the night. Landed a mile below. My husband never has left his bed since he was taken sick.

November 28—Still moving on the water.

November 29—Landed at Portland on the Willamette, 12 miles above the mouth, at 11 o'clock at night.

November 30—Raining. This morning I ran about trying to get a house to get into with my sick husband. At last I found a small, leaky concern, with two families already in it. . . . My children and I carried up a bed. The distance was nearly a quarter of a mile. Made it down on the floor in the mud. I got some men to carry my husband up through the rain and lay him on it, and he never was out of that shed until he was carried out in his coffin. Here lay five of us bedfast at one time. . . .

January 15, [1848]—My husband is still alive, but very sick. There is no medicine here except at Fort Vancouver, and the people there will not sell one bit—not even a bottle of wine. . . .

January 31—Rain all day. If I could tell you how we suffer you would not believe it. Our house, or rather a shed joined to a house, leaks all over. The roof descends in such a manner as to make the rain run right down into the fire. I have dipped as much as six pails of water off of our dirt hearth in one night. Here I sit up, night after night, with my poor sick husband, all alone, and expecting him every day to die. I neglected to tell you that Welch's and all the rest moved off and left us. Mr. Smith has not been moved off his bed for six weeks only by lifting him by each corner of the sheet, and I had hard work to get help enough for that, let alone getting watchers. I

have not undressed to lie down for six weeks. Besides all our sickness, I had a cross little babe to take care of. Indeed, I cannot tell you half.

February 1—Rain all day. This day my dear husband, my last remaining friend, died.

February 2—Today we buried my earthly companion. Now I know what none but widows know; that is, how comfortless is that of a widow's life, especially when left in a strange land, without money or friends, and the care of seven children. Cloudy. . . .

[September 2, 1850—] Well, after the boys were gone, it is true I had plenty of cows and hogs and plenty of wheat to feed them on and to make my bread. Indeed, I was well off if I had only known it; but I lived in a remote place where my strength was of little use to me. I could get nothing to do, and you know I could not live without work. I employed myself in teaching my children: yet that did not fully occupy my mind. I became as poor as a snake, yet I was in good health, and never was so nimble since I was a child. I could run a half a mile without stopping to breathe. Well, I thought perhaps I had better try my fortune again; so on the 24th of June, 1849, I was married to a Mr. Joseph Geer, a man 14 years older than myself, though young enough for me. He is the father of ten children. They are all married, but two boys and two girls. He is a Yankee from Connecticut and he is a Yankee in every sense of the word, as I told you he would be if it ever proved my lot to marry again. . . .

[W]e are all well but Perley. I cannot answer for him; he has gone to the Umpqua for some money due him. The other two are working for four dollars a day. The two oldest boys have got three town lots in quite a stirring place called Lafayette in Yamhill County. Perley has four horses. A good Indian horse is worth one hundred dollars. A good American cow is worth sixty dollars. My boys live about 25 miles from me, so that I cannot act in the capacity of a mother to them; so you will guess it is not all sunshine with me, for you know my boys are not old enough to do without a mother. Russell Welch done very well in the mines. He made about twenty hundred dollars. He lives 30 miles below me in a little town called Portland on the Willamette River. Sarah has got her third son. It has been one year since I saw her. Adam Polk's two youngest boys live about wherever they see fit. The oldest, if he is alive, is in California. There is some ague in this country this season, but neither I nor my children, except those that went to California, have had a day's sickness since we came to Oregon.

5. An Oregon Pioneer Records the Journey West to Start a New Life, 1853

Saturday, April 9th, 1853—Started from home about 11 o'clock and traveled 8 miles and camped in an old house; night cold and frosty.

Sunday, April 10th—Cool and pleasant, road hard and dusty. Evening—Came 18 ½ miles and camped close to the Fulkerson's house.

Monday, April 11th—Morn. Cloudy and signs of rain, about 10 o'clock it began to rain. At noon it rains so hard we turn out and camp in a school house after traveling 11 ½ miles; rains all the afternoon and all night, very unpleasant. Jefferson and Lucy have the mumps. Poor cattle bawled all night. . . .

Saturday, April 16th—Camped last night three miles east of Chariton Point in the prairie. Made our beds down in the tent in the wet and mud. Bed clothes nearly spoiled. Cold and cloudy this morning, and every body out of humour. Seneca is half sick. Plutarch has broke his saddle girth. Husband is scolding and hurrying all hands (and the cook), and Almira says she wished she was home, and I say ditto. "Home, Sweet Home." . . .

Tuesday, May 17th—We had a dreadful storm of rain and hail last night and very sharp lightning. It killed two oxen for one man. We have just encamped on a large flat prairie, when the storm commenced in all its fury and in two minutes after the cattle were taken from the wagons every brute was gone out of sight, cows, calves, horses, all gone before the storm like so many wild beasts. I never saw such a storm. The wind was so high I thought it would tear the wagons to pieces. Nothing but the stoutest covers could stand it. The rain beat into the wagons so that everything was wet, in less than 2 hours the water was a foot deep all over our camp grounds. As we could have no tents pitched, all had to crowd into the wagons and sleep in wet beds, with their wet clothes on, without supper. The wind blew hard all night, and this morning presents a dreary prospect surrounded by water, and our saddles have been soaking in it all night and are almost spoiled. . . .

Wednesday, June 1st—It has been raining all day long and we have been traveling in it so as to be able to keep ahead of the large droves. The men and boys are all soaking wet and look sad and comfortless. The little ones and myself are shut up in the wagons from the rain. Still it will find its way in and many things are wet; and take us all together we are poor looking set, and all this for Oregon. I am thinking while I write, "Oh, Oregon, you must be wonderful country." . . .

Tuesday, June 7th—Rained some last night; quite warm today. Just passed Fort Laramie, situated on the opposite side of the river. This afternoon we passed a large village of Sioux Indians. Numbers of them came around our wagons. Some of the women had moccasins and beads, which they wanted to trade for bread. I gave the women and children all the cakes I had baked. Husband traded a big Indian a lot of hard crackers for a pair of moccasins and after we had started on he came up with us again, making a great fuss, and wanted them back (they had eaten part of the crackers). He did not seem to be satisfied, or else he wished to cause us some trouble, or perhaps get into a fight. However, we handed the moccasins to him in a hurry and drove away from them as soon as possible. Several lingered along watching our horses that were tied behind the wagons, no doubt with the view of stealing them, but our folks kept a sharp lookout till they left. We had a thunderstorm of rain and hail and a hard blow this afternoon. . . .

Monday, June 27th—Cold, cloudy and very windy—more like November than June. I am not well enough to get out of the wagon this morning. The men have just got their breakfast over and drove up the stock. It is all hurry and bustle to get things in order. It's children milk the cows, all hands help yoke these cattle, the d——l's in them. Plutarch answers, "I can't, I must hold the tent up, it is blowing away." Hurrah boys. Who tied these horses? "Seneca, don't stand there with your hands in your pocket. Get your saddles and be ready." Evening—Traveled 18 miles today and have camped on the bank of Green River and must wait our turn to cross on a ferry boat. No grass for the poor cattle. All hands discouraged. . . .

Wednesday, August 31st—Still in camp. It was too stormy to start out last evening, as intended. The wind was very high all the afternoon, and the dust and sand so bad we could hardly see. Thundered and rained a little in the evening. It rained and blew very hard all night. Is still raining this morning, the air cold and chilly. It blew so hard last night as to blow our buckets and pans from under the wagons, and this morning we found them (and other things which were not secured) scattered all over the valley. One or two pans came up missing. Everything is packed up ready for a start. The men folks are out hunting the cattle. The children and myself are out shivering around in the wagons, nothing for fires in these parts, and the weather is very disagreeable. . . .

Tuesday, September 6th—Still in camp, washing and overhauling the wagons to make them as light as possible to cross the mountains. Evening—After throwing away a good many things and burning up most of the deck boards of our wagons so as to lighten them, got my washing and cooking done and started on again. Crossed two branches, traveled 3 miles and have camped near the gate or foot of the Cascade Mountains (here I was sick all night caused by my washing and working too hard). . . .

Saturday, September 17th—In camp yet. Still raining. Noon—It has cleared off and we are all ready for a start again, for some place we don't know where. Evening—Came 6 miles and have encamped in a fence corner by a Mr. Lambert's, about 7 miles from Milwaukie. Turn our stock out to tolerably good feed.

A few days later my eighth child was born. After this we picked up and ferried across the Columbia River, utilizing skiff, canoes and flatboat to get across, taking three days to complete. Here husband traded two yoke of oxen for a half section of land with one-half acre planted to potatoes and a small log cabin and lean-to with no windows. This is the journey's end.

6. Images of Life and Death on the Oregon Trail

A. Oregon: The Promised Land, 1841

B. Crossing the Platte River, ca. 1850

C. Death on the Trail, ca. 1840s

Chapter 13:
Document Set 3 References

1. The Lure of the Northwest Spawns "Oregon Fever," 1843
   National Intelligencer, April 18, 1843, reprinted in *Oregon Historical Quarterly,* Vol. 3 (September 1902), pp. 311–312.

2. An Idealized Description of the Trek West, 1845
   Niles National Register, May 21, 1845, quoting the *Missouri Expositor,* May 3, 1845, p. 203.

3. An Oregon Emigrant Describes Civil Government on the Trail, 1844
   "Letters of Peter H. Burnett," *Oregon Historical Quarterly,* Vol. 3 (December 1902), pp. 405–407.

4. A Pioneer Woman Copes with Personal Tragedy, 1847–1850
   "Diary of Mrs. Elizabeth Dixon Smith Geer," April 21, 1847–September 2, 1850, in *35th Transactions of the Oregon Pioneer Association* (1907), pp. 153, 171–178.

5. An Oregon Pioneer Records the Journey West to Start a New Life, 1853
   "Diary of Mrs. Amelia Stewart Knight, an Oregon Pioneer of 1853," April 9–September 17, 1853, in *Transactions of the Fifty-Sixth Annual Reunion of the Oregon Pioneer Association,* 1928 (Portland: F. W. Bates & Co., 1933), pp. 38–53.

6. Images of Life and Death on the Oregon Trail
   A. Oregon: The Promised Land, 1841. Astoria in 1841, from Charles Wilkes, U.S.N., *Narrative of the U.S. Exploring Expedition, 1838–1842,* Vol. 5, p. 112. Oregon Historical Society.
   B. Crossing the Platte River, ca. 1850. Huntington Library, San Marino, California.
   C. Death on the Trail, ca. 1840s. The Bancroft Library, University of California at Berkeley.

Chapter 13:
Document Set 3 Credits

6. A. Oregon Historical Society neg. no. CN 000535
   B. This item is reproduced by permission of the *Huntington Library, San Marino, California,* HM 8044#50
   C. Courtesy of the Bancroft Library, University of California, Berkeley

CHAPTER 14

DOCUMENT SET 1
Prelude to War: The Destruction of Sectional Comity

The disruption of sectional harmony in the divisive 1850s set the stage for the central national experience of the nineteenth century—a bitter civil war. Your textbook's treatment of these dramatic events stresses the decline of compromise in the American political process between 1850 and 1861. As the moral aspects of slavery came to dominate the political and social debate, the adjustment of differences became more difficult. Throughout Chapter 14 we see evidence of an increasing tendency to resist authority in the name of "higher law." In the end, defiance of the law and challenge to the government played crucial roles in the breakdown of relations between North and South as the nation veered toward war.

The following documents focus on the reasons for the collapse of the national consensus, with emphasis on resistance to what many northerners perceived as the moral evil of slavery. As you review the evidence, be particularly aware of moral considerations as the driving force in abolitionist activities. Assess the extent of antislavery opinion as you try to understand the absence of compromise.

Your text emphasizes the uncertainty generated by the patchwork Compromise of 1850, which left extremists in both sections dissatisfied. Although concessions were made by both sides, it is clear that southern gains were limited. In the last analysis, the strengthened fugitive slave law constituted the major advantage for the South. As your text notes, however, the law's enforcement did much to damage the delicate intersectional comity previously observed.

Your analysis of the evidence should begin with northern response to the new fugitive slave law, which is revealed in Senator Charles Sumner's impassioned attack on the law in the Senate and in the underground railroad's activities. It can also be seen in the resistance of northern state governments. In Wisconsin, for example, abolitionist Sherman Booth engineered the rescue of an imprisoned slave in defiance of the law. Consider what these varied actions reveal about the impact of the Compromise of 1850. Search the documents for clues to the motives and forces behind these activities. Identify the root issues in the controversy, and relate them to the rise of symbolic politics dominated by commitment to principles.

As you review these materials, note the relationship between the fundamental constitutional issue and the problem introduced with the Alien and Sedition Laws (see Chapter 7). The basic constitutional position of the South Carolina "Declaration of Causes" may also be traced through a series of important historical clashes considered earlier in the course.

Your task is to use the documents to enhance understanding of intersectional relations in 1860. As you work with the sources, focus especially on the role of activists in American politics and the reasons for the escalation of sectional tensions. Look for signs of continuity between the 1850s and earlier periods of tension. Try to understand why political leaders were able to adjust their differences in 1850 but not in 1861.

Questions for Analysis

1. Using evidence drawn from the documents, explain why the fugitive slave law, strengthened in the Compromise of 1850, aggravated sectional tensions. What were the consequences of this abortive attempt at compromise? What was the relationship of this issue to previous governmental efforts to deal with the problem of escaped slaves?

2. Both Charles Sumner and Abraham Lincoln were members of the same political party. Review their reactions to the fugitive slave law. How would you account for their divergent responses?

3. After reading the excerpt from the South Carolina "Declaration of Causes," work backward through previous debates over the nature of the federal union. To what extent was South Carolina's reasoning consistent with historical precedent? Relate the secessionist argument in 1861 to the issues raised in the other documents. Does the evidence provide any clues to the success of the secessionists?

4. By now you have engaged in several analyses of historical causation. Basing your argument on both documentary evidence and your textbook's treatment of Civil War origins, develop your own hypothesis to explain the outbreak of war. What were the deep, underlying causes of the war? Be sure to distinguish between fundamental causes and precipitating events.

1. Charles Sumner Pledges Disobedience, 1852

I have occupied much time; but the great subject still stretches before us. One other point yet remains, which I must not leave untouched, and which justly belongs to the close. The Slave Act violates the Constitution, and shocks the Public Conscience. With modesty, and yet with firmness, let me add, Sir, it offends against the Divine Law. No such enactment is entitled to support. As the throne of God is above every earthly throne, so are his laws and statutes above all the laws and statutes of man. . . .

And now, Sir, the rule is commended to us. The good citizen, who sees before him the shivering fugitive, guilty of no crime, pursued, hunted down like a beast, while praying for Christian help and deliverance, and then reads the requirements of this Act, is filled with horror. Here is a despotic mandate "to aid and assist in the prompt and efficient execution of this law." And let me speak frankly. Not rashly would I set myself against any requirement of law. This grave responsibility I would not lightly assume. But here the path of duty is clear. By the Supreme Law, which commands me to do no injustice, by the comprehensive Christian Law of Brotherhood, *by the Constitution, which I have sworn to support,* I AM BOUND TO DISOBEY THIS ACT. Never, in any capacity, can I render voluntary aid in its execution. Pains and penalties I will endure, but this great wrong I will not do. "Where I cannot obey actively, there I am willing to lie down and to suffer what they shall do unto me": such was the exclamation of him to whom we are indebted for the "Pilgrim's Progress," while in prison for disobedience to an earthly statute. Better suffer injustice than do it. Better victim than instrument of wrong. Better even the poor slave returned to bondage than the wretched Commissioner.

2. Levi Coffin Remembers the Underground Railroad, ca. 1850s

I was personally acquainted with all the active and reliable workers on the Underground Railroad in the city, both colored and white. There were a few wise and careful managers among the colored people, but it was not safe to trust all of them with the affairs of our work. Most of them were too careless, and a few were unworthy—they could be bribed by the slave hunters to betray the hiding places of the fugitives. We soon found it to be the best policy to confine our affairs to a few persons and to let the whereabouts of the slaves be known to as few people as possible.

When slave hunters were prowling around the city we found it necessary to use every precaution. We were soon fully initiated into the management of Underground Railroad matters in Cincinnati, and did not lack for work. Our willingness to aid the slaves was soon known, and hardly a fugitive came to the city without applying to us for assistance. There seemed to be a continual increase of runaways, and such was the vigilance of the pursuers that I was obliged to devote a large share of time from my business to making arrangements for their concealment and safe conveyance of the fugitives.

They sometimes came to our door frightened and panting and in a destitute condition, having fled in such haste and fear that they had no time to bring any clothing except what they had on, and that was often very scant. The expense of providing suitable clothing for them when it was necessary for them to go on immediately, or of feeding them when they were obliged to be concealed for days or weeks, was very heavy. . . .

Our house was large and well adapted for secreting fugitives. Very often slaves would lie concealed in upper chambers for weeks without the boarders or frequent visitors at the house knowing anything about it. My wife had a quiet unconcerned way of going about her work as if nothing unusual was on hand, which was calculated to lull every suspicion of those who might be watching, and who would have been at once aroused by any sign of secrecy or mystery. Even the intimate friends of the family did not know when there were slaves hidden in the house. . . .

The fugitives generally arrived in the night and were secreted among the friendly colored people or hidden in the upper room of our house. They came alone or in companies, and in a few instances had a white guide to direct them.

3. Sherman Booth Flouts the Fugitive Slave Law, 1854

The Fugitive Slave Law Repealed*

We send greetings to the Free States of the Union, that, in Wisconsin, the Fugitive Slave Law is repealed! The first attempt to enforce the law, in this State, has signally, gloriously failed! No Slave-catcher can hereafter tread our soil but at his peril. The Slave Power may repeal the Compromises in favor of Freedom. We will repeal those in favor of Slavery. The Slave Power may pass its Nebraska bills extending Slavery over Free territory, and exclude all foreign-born inhabitants from voting and holding office, even though they have declared their intentions to become citizens. Our foreign-born citizens send back the indignant answer—NO MORE COMPROMISES WITH SLAVERY! FREEDOM MUST AND SHALL BE PRESERVED! PERISH ALL ENACTMENTS ESTABLISHING SLAVERY ON FREE SOIL!

---

*After fugitive slave Joshua Glover was liberated from a Milwaukee jail, abolitionist Sherman Booth published this defiant assertion of Wisconsin's attitude toward the Fugitive Slave Law.

4. The Wisconsin Legislature Defies the Supreme Court, 1859

Joint resolution relative to the decision of the United States Supreme Court, reversing decision of the Supreme Court of Wisconsin.

Whereas, the Supreme Court of the United States has assumed appellate jurisdiction in the matter of the petition of Sherman M. Booth for a writ of habeas corpus, presented and prosecuted to final judgment in the Supreme Court of this state, and has, without process or any of the forms recognized by law, assumed the power to reverse that judgment in a matter involving the personal liberty of the citizen. . . .

Resolved, the Senate concurring, that we regard the action of the Supreme Court of the United States, in assuming jurisdiction in the case before mentioned, as an arbitrary act of power, unauthorized by the Constitution, and virtually superseding the benefit of the writ of habeas corpus, and prostrating the rights and liberties of the people at the foot of unlimited power.

Resolved, that this assumption of jurisdiction by the federal judiciary in the said case, and without process, is an act of undelegated power, and therefore without authority, void, and of no force.

Resolved, that the government formed by the Constitution of the United States was not made the exclusive or final judge of the extent of the powers delegated to itself; but that, as in all other cases of compact among parties having no common judge, each party has an equal right to judge for itself, as well of infractions as of the mode and measure of redress.

Resolved, that the principle and construction contended for by the party, which now rules in the councils of the nation, that the general government is the exclusive judge of the extent of the powers delegated to it, stop nothing short of despotism, since the *discretion* of those who administer the government and not the *Constitution* would be the measure of their powers; that the several states which formed that instrument, being sovereign and independent, have the unquestionable right to judge of its infraction; and that a *positive defiance* of those sovereignties, of all unauthorized acts done or attempted to be done under color of that instrument, is the rightful remedy.

5. Lincoln the Pragmatist Responds to Civil Disorder, 1858

Second Debate with Stephen A. Douglas at Freeport, Illinois

August 27, 1858

[I]n regard to the Fugitive Slave Law, I have never hesitated to say, and I do not now hesitate to say, that I think, under the Constitution of the United States, the people of the Southern States are entitled to a Congressional Fugitive Slave Law. Having said that, I have had nothing to say in regard to the existing Fugitive Slave Law further than that I think it should have been framed so as to be free from some of the objections that pertain to it, without lessening its efficiency. And inasmuch as we are not now in an agitation in regard to an alteration or modification of that law, I would not be the man to introduce it as a new subject of agitation upon the general question of slavery.

6. South Carolina Defines the Causes of Secession, 1860

We assert that fourteen of the states have deliberately refused for years past to fulfill their constitutional obligations, and we refer to their own statutes for the proof.

The Constitution of the United States, in its 4th Article, provides as follows: "No person held to service or labor in one state, under the laws thereof, escaping into another shall, in consequence of any law or regulation therein, be discharged from such service or labor, but shall be delivered up, on claim of the party to whom such service or labor may be due."

This stipulation was so material to the compact that without it that compact would not have been made. The greater number of the contracting parties held slaves, and they had previously evinced their estimate of the value of such a stipulation by making it a condition in the ordinance for the government of the territory ceded by Virginia, which obligations, and the laws of the general government, have ceased to effect the objects of the Constitution. The states of Maine, New Hampshire, Vermont, Massachusetts, Connecticut, Rhode Island, New York, Pennsylvania, Illinois, Indiana, Michigan, Wisconsin, and Iowa have enacted laws which either nullify the acts of Congress or render useless any attempt to execute them. In many of these states the fugitive is discharged from the service of labor claimed, and in none of them has the state government complied with the stipulation made in the Constitution. . . .

Those states have assumed the right of deciding upon the propriety of our domestic institutions; and have denied the rights of property established in fifteen of the states and recognized by the Constitution. They have denounced as sinful the institution of slavery; they have permitted the open establishment among them of societies, whose avowed object is to disturb the peace of and eloign the prop erty of the citizens of other states. They have encouraged and assisted thousands of our slaves to leave their homes; and, those who remain, have been incited by emissaries, books, and pictures to servile insurrection. . . .

On the 4th of March next this party [the Republican party] will take possession of the government. It has announced that the South shall be excluded from the common territory, that the judicial tribunal shall be made sectional, and that a war must be waged against slavery until it shall cease throughout the United States.

The guarantees of the Constitution will then no longer exist; the equal rights of the states will be lost. The slaveholding states will no longer have the power of self-government or self-protection, and the federal government will have become their enemy.

Sectional interest and animosity will deepen the irritation; and all hope of remedy is rendered vain by the fact that the public opinion at the North has invested a great political error with the sanctions of a more erroneous religious belief.

We, therefore, the people of South Carolina, by our delegates in convention assembled, appealing to the Supreme Judge of the world for the rectitude of our intentions, have solemnly declared that the Union heretofore existing between this state and the other states of North America is dissolved; and that the state of South Carolina has resumed her position among the nations of the world, as [a] separate and independent state, with full power to levy war, conclude peace, contract alliances, establish commerce, and to do all other acts and things which independent states may of right do.

Chapter 14:
Document Set 1 References

1. Charles Sumner Pledges Disobedience, 1852
   "Freedom National, Slavery Sectional," August 26, 1852, *The Works of Charles Sumner* (Boston: Lee and Shepard, 1875), Vol. III, pp. 191–195.

2. Levi Coffin Remembers the Underground Railroad, ca. 1850s
   Levi Coffin, *Reminiscences,* 2d ed., 1880, pp. 298–311; reprint edition (New York: Arno Press, 1968), pp. 298–299, 301, 304.

3. Sherman Booth Flouts the Fugitive Slave Law, 1854
   Milwaukee *Daily Free Democrat,* March 13, 1854.

4. The Wisconsin Legislature Defies the Supreme Court, 1859

General Laws Passed by the Legislature of Wisconsin in the Year 1859 (Madison: State of Wisconsin, 1859), pp. 247–248.

5. Lincoln the Pragmatist Responds to Civil Disorder, 1858
   Debate, Freeport, August 27, 1858, in Roy P. Basler, ed., *The Collected Works of Abraham Lincoln* (New Brunswick: Rutgers University Press, 1953), Vol. 3, p. 41.

6. South Carolina Defines the Causes of Secession, 1860
   "South Carolina Declaration of the Causes of Secession," December 24, 1860, Frank Moore, ed., *The Rebellion Record,* Vol. 1, Document 3, pp. 3–4.

Chapter 14:
Document Set 1 Credits

CHAPTER 14

Women and the Attack on Slavery: The "Little Lady Who Began a Big War"

Your textbook has underscored the quickening of the reform impulse in the thirty years preceding the Civil War (see Chapter 10). Of all antebellum moral crusades, none matched abolition in intensity and scope; it is also true that abolitionism intersected with several other reforms, including the drive for women's rights. Not only were women deeply involved in antislavery activity, but the debate over their full participation played an important role in the split in the national movement in 1839–1840. Despite the disagreement, women supplied much of the volunteer support that had energized abolitionism by the 1850s.

Since women were nonvoters, they exploited other channels of influence to bring about emancipation. Women sometimes appeared on the lecture circuit, and they played a crucial role in the petition drives of the 1830s and 1840s. Equally significant was female activism in the creation and production of propaganda tracts designed to persuade the public to embrace the cause of abolition.

The focal point of these documents is the work of Harriet Beecher Stowe, whose writings bear striking witness to the political power of the written word. As your textbook notes, her novel, *Uncle Tom's Cabin* (1852), was a profound influence on northern public opinion. Originally written as sentimental women's fiction for a female audience, the book reached a much wider readership and played an important role in shaping northern attitudes toward the South's "peculiar institution." Asserting that slavery corrupted human relationships and destroyed the domestic values it theoretically endorsed, Stowe struck a blow later noted in Lincoln's assessment that she had "begun a big war."

As you review Stowe's *Uncle Tom's Cabin* and *Altar of Liberty*, examine style, argument, and impact. Try to identify what southern critics, such as George Frederick Holmes, found unpalatable in her work. Note how she defended her position. Moreover, be aware of the link between racial equality and sexual equality, as implied by the rhetoric of abolition. Projecting your analysis forward into the future, try to evaluate the impact of abolitionism on the thinking of its female adherents. This unit will remind you of the intellectual cross-fertilization that characterized the social reform movement in antebellum America.

Questions for Analysis

1. Relying on textbook coverage of *Uncle Tom's Cabin,* as well as the documents, account for the popularity of Stowe's writings. What factors might help explain the book's appeal and its impact on the northern audience?

2. What was the relationship between abolitionism and feminism? In what way did the image of womanhood shape reform? How did the objectives of female abolitionists evolve between 1840 and 1860? What new goals were destined to surface once emancipation was achieved?

3. What was the relationship between the fugitive slave law provision of the Compromise of 1850 and the appearance of *Uncle Tom's Cabin?* Do you find evidence of a connection in the documents? Explain.

4. In *A Key to Uncle Tom's Cabin,* Stowe responds to widespread nineteenth-century assumptions with regard to black native intelligence. Summarize her position and assess her reasoning. What is the heart of Stowe's analysis? What is your evaluation of her argument?

5. In a modern context, what is the meaning of the phrase *Uncle Tom?* What insight on this definition do the documents provide?

6. What light does the evidence shed on the causes of the Civil War? What was the significance of the conflicting arguments of Stowe and George Frederick Holmes? What did Holmes's analysis reveal about the character of intellectual, social, and political discourse in the 1850s?

1. Harriet Beecher Stowe Portrays Slavery's Brutality, 1852

"And now," said Legree, "come here, you Tom. You see I telled ye I didn't buy ye jest for the common work; I mean to promote ye and make a driver of ye; and tonight ye may jest as well begin to get yer hand in. Now, ye jest take this yer gal and flog her; ye've seen enough on't to know how."

"I beg Mas'r's pardon," said Tom, "hopes Mas'r won't set me at that. It's what I an't used to—never did—and can't do, no way possible."

"Ye'll larn a pretty smart chance of things ye never did know before I've done with ye!" said Legree, taking up a cowhide and striking Tom a heavy blow across the cheek, and following up the infliction by a shower of blows.

"There!" he said, as he stopped to rest, "now will ye tell me ye can't do it?"

"Yes, Mas'r," said Tom, putting up his hand to wipe the blood that trickled down his face. "I'm willin' to work night and day, and work while there's life and breath in me, but this yer thing I can't feel it right to do; and, Mas'r, I *never* shall do it—*never!*"

Tom had a remarkably smooth, soft voice, and a habitually respectful manner that had given Legree an idea that he would be cowardly and easily subdued. When he spoke these last words, a thrill of amazement went through everyone; the poor woman clasped her hands and said, "O Lord!" and everyone involuntarily looked at each other and drew in their breath, as if to prepare for the storm that was about to burst.

Legree looked stupefied and confounded; but at last burst forth—

"What! ye blasted black beast! tell *me* ye don't think it *right* to do what I tell ye! What have any of you cussed cattle to do with thinking what's right? I'll put a stop to it! Why, what do ye think ye are? May be ye think ye're a gentleman, master Tom, to be a telling your master what's right and what an't! So you pretend it's wrong to flog the gal!"

"I think so, Mas'r," said Tom, "the poor crittur's sick and feeble; 't would be downright cruel, and it's what I never will do, not begin to. Mas'r, if you mean to kill me, kill me; but as to my raising my hand agin anyone here, I never shall—I'll die first!"

Tom spoke in a mild voice but with a decision that could not be mistaken. Legree shook with anger; his greenish eyes glared fiercely and his very whiskers seemed to curl with passion; but, like some ferocious beast that plays with its victim before he devours it, he kept back his strong impulse to proceed to immediate violence and broke out into bitter raillery.

"Well, here's a pious dog, at last, let down among us sinners!—a saint, a gentleman, and no less, to talk to us sinners about our sins! Powerful, holy crittur, he must be! Here, you rascal, you make believe to be so pious—didn't you never hear out of yer Bible, 'Servants, obey yer masters'? An't I yer master? Didn't I pay down $1,200 cash for all there is inside yer old cussed black shell? An't yer mine, now, body and soul?" he said, giving Tom a violent kick with his heavy boot. "Tell me!"

In the very depth of physical suffering, bowed by brutal oppression, this question shot a gleam of joy and triumph through Tom's soul. He suddenly stretched himself up, and, looking earnestly to heaven, while the tears and blood that flowed down his face mingled, he exclaimed—

"No! no! no! my soul an't yours, Mas'r! You haven't bought it—ye can't buy it! It's been bought and paid for by one that is able to keep it—no matter, no matter, you can't harm me!"

"I can't!" said Legree, with a sneer, "we'll see—we'll see! Here, Sambo, Quimbo, give this dog such a breakin' in as he won't get over this month!"

The two gigantic Negroes that now laid hold of Tom, with fiendish exultation in their faces, might have formed no unapt personification of the powers of darkness. The poor woman screamed with apprehension and all arose as by a general impulse while they dragged him unresisting from the place. . . .

2. A Southern Woman's Response to Slavery and the Abolitionist Attack, 1861

On one side Mrs. Stowe, Greeley, Thoreau, Emerson, Sumner. They live in nice New England homes, clean, sweet-smelling, shut up in libraries, writing books which ease their hearts of their bitterness against us. What self-denial they do practice is to tell John Brown to come down here and cut our throats in Christ's name. . . .

The Mrs. Stowes have the plaudits of crowned heads; we take our chances, doing our duty as best we may among the woolly heads. My husband supported his plantation by his law practice. Now it is running him in debt. Our people have never earned their own bread. Take this estate, what does it do, actually? It all goes back in some shape to what are called slaves here, called operatives, or tenants, or peasantry elsewhere. I doubt if ten thousand in money ever comes to this old gentleman's hands. When Mrs. Chesnut married South, her husband was as wealthy as her brothers-in-law. How is it now? Their money had accumulated for their children. This old man's goes to support a horde of idle dirty Africans, while he is abused as a cruel slave owner. I say we are no better than our judges in the North, and no worse. We are human beings of the nineteenth century and slavery has to go, of course. All that has been gained by it goes to the North and to Negroes. The slave owners, when they are good men and women, are the martyrs. I hate slavery. I even hate the harsh authority I see parents think it their duty to exercise toward their children.

3. A Southern Critique of *Uncle Tom's Cabin*, 1852

This is a fiction—professedly a fiction; but, unlike other works of the same type, its purpose is not amusement, but proselytism. The romance was formerly employed to divert the leisure, recreate the fancy, and quicken the sympathies of successive generations, changing its complexion and enlarging the compass of its aims with the expanding tastes of different periods; but never forgetting that its main object was to kindle and purify the imagination, while fanning into a livelier flame the slumbering charities of the human heart. But, in these late and evil days, the novel, notwithstanding those earlier associations, has descended from its graceful and airy home, and assumed to itself a more vulgar mission, incompatible with its essence and alien to its original design. Engaging in the coarse conflicts of life, and mingling in the fumes and gross odours of political or polemical dissension, it has attained and tainted the robe of ideal purity. . . .

It should be observed that the whole tenor of this pathetic tale derives most of its significance and colouring from a distorted representation or a false conception of the sentiments and feelings of the slave. It presupposes an identity of sensibilities between the races of the free and the negroes, whose cause it pretends to advocate. It takes advantage of this presumption, so suspiciously credited where slavery is unknown, to arouse sympathies for what might be grievous misery to the white man, but is none to the differently tempered black. Every man adapts himself and his feelings more or less to the circumstances of his condition: without this wise provision of nature life would be intolerable to most of us. . . . The joys and the sorrows of the slave are in harmony with his position, and are entirely dissimilar from what would make the happiness, or misery, of another class. It is therefore an entire fallacy, or a criminal perversion of truth, according to the motive of the writer, to attempt to test all situations by the same inflexible rules, and to bring to the judgment of the justice of slavery the prejudices and opinions which have been formed when all the characteristics of slavery are not known but imagined. . . .

We maintain that the distinguishing characteristic of slavery is its tendency to produce effects exactly opposite to those laid to its charge; to diminish the amount of individual misery in the servile classes; to mitigate and alleviate all the ordinary sorrows of life; to protect the slaves against want as well as against material and mental suffering; to prevent the separation and dispersion of families; and to shield them from the frauds, the crimes, and the casualties of others, whether masters or fellow-slaves, in a more eminent degree than is attainable under any other organization of society, where slavery does not prevail. This is but a small portion of the peculiar advantages to the slaves themselves resulting from the institution of slavery, but these suffice for the present, and furnish a most overwhelming refutation of the philanthropic twaddle of this and similar publications. . . .

It is needless to repeat the evidence that the average condition of the slave at the South is infinitely superior, morally and materially, in all respects, to that of the labouring class under any other circumstances in any other part of the world. . . .

We dismiss Uncle Tom's Cabin with the conviction and declaration that every holier purpose of our nature is misguided, every charitable sympathy betrayed, every loftier sentiment polluted, every moral purpose wrenched to wrong, and every patriotic feeling outraged, by its criminal prostitution of the high functions of the imagination to the pernicious intrigues of sectional animosity, and to the petty calumnies of willful slander.

4. Stowe as Antislavery Propagandist, 1852

"Well," said George, "we both work hard for our money, and we don't owe anybody a cent; and why shouldn't we have our treats, now and then, as well as rich folks?"

And gayly passed the supper hour; the tea-kettle sung, the baby crowed, and all chatted and laughed abundantly.

"I'll tell you," said George, wiping his mouth, "wife, these times are quite another thing from what it used to be down in Georgia. I remember then old Mas'r used to hire me out by the year; and one time, I remember, I came and paid him in two hundred dollars,—every cent I'd taken. He just looked it over, counted it, and put it in his pocket-book, and said, 'You are a good boy, George,'—and he gave me *half-a-dollar!*"

"I want to know, now!" said his wife.

"Yes, he did, and that was every cent I ever got of it; and, I tell you, I was mighty bad off for clothes, them times."

"Well, well, the Lord be praised, they're over, and you are in a free country now!" said the wife, as she rose thoughtfully from the table, and brought her husband the great Bible. The little circle were ranged around the stove for evening prayers.

"Henry, my boy, you must read,—you are a better reader than your father,—thank God, that let you learn early!"

The boy, with a cheerful readiness, read, "The Lord is my shepherd," and the mother gently stilled the noisy baby, to listen to the holy words. Then all kneeled, while the father, with simple earnestness, poured out his soul to God.

They had but just risen,—the words of Christian hope and trust scarce died on their lips,—when lo! the door was burst open, and two men entered; and one of them, advancing, laid his hand on the father's shoulder. "This is the fellow," said he.

"You are arrested in the name of the United States!" said the other.

"Gentlemen, what is this?" said the poor man, trembling.

"Are you not the property of *Mr. B.*, of Georgia?" said the officer.

"Gentlemen, I've been a free, hard-working man, these ten years."

"Yes, but you are arrested, on suit of Mr. B., as his slave."

Shall we describe the leave-taking?—the sorrowing wife, the dismayed children, the tears, the anguish,—that simple, honest, kindly home, in a moment so desolated! Ah, ye who defend this because it is law, think, for one hour, what if this that happens to your poor brother should happen to you! . . .

It was a crowded court-room, and the man stood there to be tried—for life?—no; but for the life of life—for liberty!

Lawyers hurried to and fro, buzzing, consulting, bringing authorities,—all anxious, zealous, engaged,—for what?—to save a fellow-man from bondage?—no; anxious and zealous lest he might escape,—full of zeal to deliver him over to slavery. The poor man's anxious eyes follow vainly the busy course of affairs, from which he dimly learns that he is to be sacrificed—on the altar of the Union; and that his heart-break and anguish, and the tears of his wife, and the desolation of his children, are, in the eyes of these well-informed men, only the bleat of a sacrifice, bound to the horns of the glorious American altar!

5. Black Potential and the *Key to Uncle Tom's Cabin*, 1853

In conducting the education of negro, mulatto, and quadroon children, the writer has often observed this fact:—that for a certain time, and up to a certain age, they kept equal pace with, and were often superior to, the white children with whom they were associated; but that there came a time when they became indifferent to learning, and made no further progress. This was invariably at the age when they were old enough to reflect upon life, and to perceive that society had no place to offer them for which anything more would be requisite than the rudest and most elementary knowledge. . . .

Does not every one know that, without the stimulus which teachers and parents thus continually present, multitudes of children would never gain a tolerable education? And is it not the absence of all such stimulus which has prevented the negro child from an equal advance?

It is often objected to the negro race that they are frivolous and vain, passionately fond of show, and are interested only in trifles. And who is to blame for all this? Take away all high aims, all noble ambition, from any class, and what is left for them to be interested in *but* trifles?

The present Attorney-general of Liberia, Mr. Lewis, is a man who commands the highest respect for talent and ability in his position; yet, while he was in America, it is said that, like many other young coloured men, he was distinguished only for foppery and frivolity. What made the change in Lewis after he went to Liberia? Who does not see the answer? Does any one wish to know what is inscribed on the seal which keeps the great stone over the sepulchre of African mind? It is this,—which was so truly said by poor Topsy,—"NOTHING BUT A NIGGER."

It is this, burnt into the soul by the branding-iron of cruel and unchristian scorn, that is a sorer and deeper wound than all the physical evils of slavery together.

There never was a slave who did not feel it. Deep, deep down in the dark, still waters of his soul is the conviction, heavier, bitterer than all others, that he is *not regarded as a man.*

6. Promoting *Uncle Tom's Cabin*, ca. 1854

Chapter 14:
Document Set 2 References

1. Harriet Beecher Stowe Portrays Slavery's Brutality, 1852
   Harriet Beecher Stowe, *Uncle Tom's Cabin* (Boston: J. P. Jewett and Co., 1852), pp. 419–423.

2. A Southern Woman's Response to Slavery and the Abolitionist Attack, 1861
   Mary Boykin Chesnut, November 27, 1861, *A Diary from Dixie* (Boston: Houghton Mifflin and Co., 1949), pp. 21–22, 122, 163–164.

3. A Southern Critique of *Uncle Tom's Cabin*, 1852
   George Frederick Holmes, "Uncle Tom's Cabin," *Southern Literary Messenger*, XVIII (December 1852).

4. Stowe as Antislavery Propagandist, 1852
   Harriet Beecher Stowe, *The Two Altars; or, Two Pictures in One*, Liberty Tracts—No. 1 (Boston: 1852), Part II.

5. Black Potential and the *Key to Uncle Tom's Cabin*, 1853
   Harriet Beecher Stowe, *A Key to Uncle Tom's Cabin, Presenting the Original Facts and Documents Upon Which the Story Is Founded, Together with Corroborative Statements Verifying the Truth of the Work* (London: Thomas Bosworth, 1853), pp. 107–109.

6. Promoting *Uncle Tom's Cabin*, ca. 1854
   "Uncle Tom's Cabin," in David Burner *et al.*, *An American Portrait: A History of the United States*, 2d ed., Vol. 1 (New York: Charles Scribner's Sons, 1985), p. 326.

Chapter 14:
Document Set 2 Credits

6. The Granger Collection

CHAPTER 14

Terrorism and Freedom: Abolition by All Means Necessary

A key theme in the textbook's treatment of the 1850s is the polarization of American politics once the issue of slavery had taken on an irrevocably moral tone. As Americans divided over the question, extremists on both sides raised the stakes in a debate cast increasingly in terms of good and evil. Once morality came to dominate political discourse, the prospects for compromise receded.

Perhaps the most prominent example of this rigidity was the controversy ignited by John Brown's raid in 1859 on the federal arsenal at Harpers Ferry, Virginia—an attack intended to spark a slave rebellion that would end in the destruction of involuntary servitude in America. Brown's sensational actions raised southern paranoia over a suspected northern conspiracy to end slavery by violence.

A religious zealot, Brown acted in the confidence that his was a divinely inspired mission to remove the cancer of bondage from the American body politic. His self-assurance, combined with intense religious fervor, persuaded many Americans that he was a deluded lunatic. Yet his testimony caused others to wonder if he was a rational plotter in league with those in the abolitionist movement who were known to favor an immediate end to slavery. Whether lunatic, self-deluded martyr, or abolitionist activist, Brown was perceived as an incendiary bent on working dramatic and violent change.

The following documents address both the motivations and consequences of Brown's actions. As you review the evidence, try to determine if his activities were the work of a sane and calculating revolutionary. As you proceed with this analysis, consider also the question of ends and means. Think about the factors lying beneath acts of terrorism and violence in a political context. What causes do you feel are sufficiently urgent to produce violence as a weapon to promote social change? Can violence ever be justified?

As you attempt to account for John Brown's behavior, consider the way in which images are constructed. Compare the two illustrations found in your textbook in terms of the impressions conveyed through the visual media. Consider the impression created by John Steuart Curry in his 1930s portrayal of Brown. Similarly, think about the explanations for the writings of Brown's critics and supporters, several of which appear in the document set. As you attempt to interpret the meaning of John Brown's life and death, try to uncover the motivations, agenda, and assumptions of those who commented on the events at Harpers Ferry. Try to establish the relationship between the more bizarre aspects of his exploits and the instability of a generation of Americans drifting toward mortal combat.

Questions for Analysis

1. What do the documents reveal about the difficulties of John Brown's generation in agreeing on the reasons for his actions? How did the disagreement among Brown's contemporaries concerning Harpers Ferry reflect the political and social dilemmas of the 1850s?

2. Compare the positions of Brown, Garrison, and Thoreau on the slavery question in 1860 with those of Lincoln and the Republican party. Which was more representative of northern opinion? In what ways?

3. What separated the actions of John Brown from other links in the chain of events that led to war? In what way was Brown's raid unique? What did it indicate about the politics of compromise as the election of 1860 neared?

4. Use the documents to develop your own assessment of Brown's motivation and objectives at Harpers Ferry. How would you employ the available evidence to support your position?

5. To what extent do the documents shed light on the contemporary and subsequent allegations of Brown's insanity? What is your assessment of his state of mind in 1859? Was John Brown more or less sane than others of his generation?

1. John Brown States His Case, 1859

John Brown:

I have, may it please the Court, a few words to say. In the first place, I deny everything but what I have all along admitted, of a design on my part to free slaves. I intended certainly to have made a clean thing of that matter, as I did last winter when I went into Missouri, and there took slaves without the snapping of a gun on either side, moving them through the country, and finally leaving them in Canada. I designed to have done the same thing again on a larger scale. That was all I intended to do. I never did intend murder or treason, or the destruction of property, or to excite or incite the slaves to rebellion, or to make insurrection. I have another objection, and that is that it is unjust that I should suffer such a penalty. Had I interfered in the manner, which I admit, and which I admit has been fairly proved—for I admire the truthfulness and candor of the greater portion of the witnesses who have testified in this case—had I so interfered in behalf of any of the rich, the powerful, the intelligent, the so-called great, or in behalf of any of their friends, either father, mother, brother, sister, wife, or children, or any of that class, and suffered and sacrificed what I have in this interference, it would have been all right, and every man in this court would have deemed it an act worthy of reward rather than punishment. This Court acknowledges, too, as I suppose, the validity of the law of God. I see a book kissed, which I suppose to be the Bible, or at least the New Testament, which teaches me that all things whatsoever I would that men should do to me, I should do even so to them. It teaches me further to remember them that are in bonds, as bound with them. I endeavored to act up to that instruction. I say I am yet too young to understand that God is any respecter of persons. I believe that to have interfered as I have done, as I have always freely admitted I have done in behalf of His despised poor, is no wrong, but right. Now, if it is deemed necessary that I should forfeit my life for the furtherance of the ends of justice, and mingle my blood further with the blood of my children and with the blood of millions in this slave country whose rights are disregarded by wicked, cruel, and unjust enactments, I say let it be done.

2. William Lloyd Garrison Justifies John Brown's Actions, 1859

As to his trial, I affirm that it was an awful mockery, before heaven and earth! He was not tried in a court of JUSTICE. Mark how they crowded the counts together in one indictment—MURDER, TREASON, and INSURRECTION! Of what was John Brown convicted? Who knows? Perhaps some of the jury convicted him of treason; others of murder; and others, again, of insurrection. Who can tell? There was no trial on any specific point. John Brown has been judicially assassinated. . . .

Was John Brown justified in his attempt? Yes, if Washington was in his; if Warren and Hancock were in theirs. If men are justified in striking a blow for freedom, when the question is one of a threepenny tax on tea, then, I say, they are a thousand times more justified, when it is to save fathers, mothers, wives and children from the slave-coffle and the auction-block, and to restore to them their God-given rights. (Loud applause.) Was John Brown justified in interfering in behalf of the slave population of Virginia, to secure their freedom and independence? Yes, if LaFayette was justified in interfering to help our revolutionary fathers. If Kosciusko, if Pulaski, if Steuben, if De Kalb, if all who joined them from abroad were justified in that act, then John Brown was incomparably more so. If you believe in the right of assisting men to fight for freedom who are of your own color—(God knows nothing of color or complexion—human rights know nothing of these distinctions)—then you must cover, not only with a mantle of charity, but with the admiration of your hearts, the effort of John Brown at Harper's Ferry. . . .

I am a non-resistant and I not only desire, but have labored unremittingly to effect, the peaceful abolition of slavery, by an appeal to the reason and conscience of the slaveholder; yet, as a peace man—an "ultra" peace man—I am prepared to say, "Success to every slave insurrection at the South, and in every slave country." (Enthusiastic applause.) And I do not see how I compromise or stain my peace profession in making that declaration. Whenever there is a contest between the oppressed and the oppressor,—the weapons being equal between the parties,—God knows my heart must be with the oppressed, and always against the oppressor. Therefore, whenever commenced, I cannot but wish success to all slave insurrections. (Loud applause.) I thank God when men who believe in the right and duty of wielding carnal weapons are so far advanced that they will take those weapons out of the scale of despotism, and throw them into the scale of freedom. It is an indication of progress, and a positive moral growth; it is one way to get up to the sublime platform of non-resistance; and it is God's method of dealing retribution upon the head of the tyrant. Rather than see men wear their chains in a cowardly and servile spirit, I would, as an advocate of peace, much rather see them breaking the head of the tyrant with their chains. Give me, as a non-resistant, Bunker Hill, and Lexington, and Concord, rather than the cowardice and servility of a Southern slave plantation.

3. Owen Lovejoy Refuses to Denounce Brown, 1859

This raid confronts us with slavery, and makes us ask, is slaveholding right? and if so, what rights has it? When the curtain rose and startled the nation with this tragedy, John Brown lay there like a wounded lion with his head upon his paws, a saber cut on his brow, bayonet gashes in his side, the blood oozing out, and life itself apparently ebbing fast; around were certain little specimens of the canine species, snuffing and smelling, and finally one of them yelped out: "Mr. Lion, was the old war-horse that pastured on the Western Reserve with you on this expedition?" The lion slowly raised his head, cast a disdainful side glance upon the inquirer, growled out a contemptuous negative, and reposed his head as before.

In regard to John Brown, you want me to curse him. I will not curse John Brown. You want me to pour out execrations upon the head of old Ossawatomie. Though all the slaveholding Balaks in the country fill their houses with silver and proffer it, I will not curse John Brown. I do honestly condemn what he did, from my standpoint, and with my convictions I disapprove of his action, that is true; but I believe that his purpose was a good one; that so far as his own motives before God were concerned, they were honest and truthful; and no one can deny that he stands head and shoulders above any other character that appeared on the stage in that tragedy from beginning to end; from the time he entered the armory there to the time when he was strangled by Governor "Fussation." [General laughter.]

He was not guilty of murder or treason. He did unquestionably violate the statute against aiding slaves to escape; but no blood was shed, except by the panic-stricken multitude, till Stevens was fired upon while waving a flag of truce. The only murder was that of Thompson, who was snatched from the heroic protection of a woman, and riddled with balls at the railroad bridge. Despotism has seldom sacrificed three nobler victims than Brown, Stevens, and Hazlitt.

4. A Black Perspective on John Brown, 1859

I am not terrified by the gallows, which I see staring me in the face and upon which I am soon to stand and suffer death for doing what George Washington was made a hero for doing. . . . For having lent my aid to a general no less brave and engaged in a cause no less honorable and glorious, I am to suffer death. Washington entered the field to fight for the freedom of the American people—not for the white man alone, but for both black and white. Nor were they white men alone who fought for the freedom of this country. The blood of black men flowed as freely as that of white men. . . . And some of the very last blood shed was that of black men. . . . It was a sense of the wrongs which we have suffered that prompted the noble but unfortunate Captain Brown and his associates to attempt to give freedom to a small number, at least, of those who are now held by cruel and unjust laws, and by no less cruel and unjust men. . . . And now, dear brother, could I die in a more noble cause? Could I die in a manner and for a cause which would induce true and honest men more to honor me, and the angels more ready to receive me to their happy home of everlasting joy above? I imagine that I hear you, and all of you—mother, father, sisters, and brothers—say—"No, there is not a cause for which we, with less sorrow, could see you die." Believe me when I tell you that, though shut up in prison and under sentence of death, I have spent many very happy hours here, and were it not that I know that the hearts of those to whom I am attached . . . will be filled with sorrow, I would almost as lief die now as at any time, for I feel that I am now prepared to meet my Maker.

5. William Gilmore Simms Offers a Southern Reaction to the Breakdown of Order, 1860

Why, my dear deluded friend, do you still desire to save the Union? Of what sort of value, to a Christian man, is that sort of union which persists in keeping men in the same household, who hate and blaspheme each other? And can you be really a friend to the South—a wise one you certainly are not—when you desire us, the minority States, to submit to the uncontrolled legislation of a majority, which has not only proved faithless to all its pledges, but which has declared its determined purpose to subdue, rule and destroy the minority, and abrogate all its rights and securities? . . .

I look in vain, my excellent friend, among all your excellent letters to me, to find one single expression of your horror at the John Brown raid in Virginia! Your indignation, I suppose, was so intense as to keep you dumb! I cannot, of course, suppose that you were indifferent! Oh! no; your expressions of love forbid that idea! So, too, I see not a word of your wrath and indignation, in any of these letters, at the burnings of our towns, and the poisoning of our fountains, in Texas, by creatures of the same kidney with the vulture Brown! And when Brown is made a martyr of in the North, and his day made a sacred record in the Northern calendar, I do not perceive that you covered your head with sackcloth and ashes, and wrote to me lamenting!

6. Henry David Thoreau Endorses Brown's Moral Character, 1859

A man does a brave and humane deed, and at once, on all sides, we hear people and parties declaring, "I didn't do it, nor countenance *him* to do it, in any conceivable way. It can't be fairly inferred from my past career." I, for one, am not interested to hear you define your position. I don't know that I ever was or ever shall be. I think it is mere egotism, or impertinent at this time. Ye needn't take so much pains to wash your skirts of him. No intelligent man will ever be convinced that he was any creature of yours. He went and came, as he informs us, "under the auspices of John Brown and nobody else." The Republican party does not perceive how many his *failure* will make to vote more correctly than they would have them. They have counted the votes of Pennsylvania & Co., but they have not correctly counted Captain Brown's vote. . . .

Insane! A father and six sons, and one son-in-law, and several more men beside,—as many at least as twelve disciples,—all struck with insanity at once; while the same tyrant holds with a firmer grip than ever his four millions of slaves, and a thousand sane editors, his abettors, are saving the country and their bacon! Just as insane were his efforts in Kansas. Ask the tyrant who is his most dangerous foe, the sane man or the insane? Do the thousands who know him best, who have rejoiced at his deeds in Kansas, and have afforded him material aid there, think him insane? Such a use of this word is a mere trope with most who persist in using it, and I have no doubt that many of the rest have already in silence retracted their words.

Read his admirable answers to Mason and others. How they are dwarfed and defeated by the contrast! On the one side, half-brutish, half-timid questioning; on the other, truth, clear as lightning, crashing into their obscene temples. They are made to stand with Pilate, and Gessler, and the Inquisition. How ineffectual their speech and action! . . .

"All is quiet at Harper's Ferry," say the journals. What is the character of that calm which follows when the law and the slaveholder prevail? I regard this event as a touchstone designed to bring out, with glaring distinctness, the character of this government. We needed to be thus assisted to see it by the light of history. It needed to see itself. When a government puts forth its strength on the side of injustice, as ours to maintain slavery and kill the liberators of the slave, it reveals itself a merely brutal force, or worse, a demoniacal force. . . .

The only government that I recognize—and it matters not how few are at the head of it, or how small its army—is that power that establishes justice in the land, never that which establishes injustice. What shall we think of a government to which all the truly brave and just men in the land are enemies, standing between it and those whom it oppresses? A government that pretends to be Christian and crucifies a million Christs every day!

Treason! Where does such treason take its rise? I cannot help thinking of you as you deserve, ye governments. Can you dry up the fountains of thought?

High treason, when it is resistance to tyranny here below, has its origin in, and is first committed by, the power that makes and forever recreates man. . . .

It was his peculiar doctrine that a man has a perfect right to interfere by force with the slaveholder, in order to rescue the slave. I agree with him. They who are continually shocked by slavery have some right to be shocked by the violent death of the slaveholder, but no others. Such will be more shocked by his life than by his death. I shall not be forward to think him mistaken in his method who quickest succeeds to liberate the slave. I speak for the slave when I say that I prefer the philanthropy of Captain Brown to that philanthropy which neither shoots me nor liberates me. . . .

I am here to plead his cause with you. I plead not for his life, but for his character,—his immortal life; and so it becomes your cause wholly, and is not his in the least. Some eighteen hundred years ago Christ was crucified; this morning, perchance, Captain Brown was hung. These are the two ends of a chain which is not without its links. He is not Old Brown any longer; he is an angel of light.

7. The Republican Lincoln Dismisses Brown's Raid, 1860

Address at Cooper Institute, New York City

February 27, 1860

And now, if they would listen—as I suppose they will not—I would address a few words to the Southern people. . . .

You charge that we stir up insurrections among your slaves. We deny it; and what is your proof? Harper's Ferry! John Brown!! John Brown was no Republican; and you have failed to implicate a single Republican in his Harper's Ferry enterprise. If any member of our party is guilty in that matter, you know it or you do not know it. If you do know it, you are inexcusable for not designating the man and proving the fact. If you do not know it, you are inexcusable for asserting it, and especially for persisting in the assertion after you have tried and failed to make the proof. You need not be told that persisting in a charge which one does not know to be true, is simply malicious slander.

Some of you admit that no Republican designedly aided or encouraged the Harper's Ferry affair; but still insist that our doctrines and declarations necessarily lead to such results. We do not

believe it. We know we hold to no doctrine, and make no declaration, which were not held to and made by "our fathers who framed the Government under which we live." You never dealt fairly by us in relation to this affair. When it occurred, some important State elections were near at hand, and you were in evident glee with the belief that, by charging the blame upon us, you could get an advantage of us in those elections. The elections came, and your expectations were not quite fulfilled. Every Republican man knew that, as to himself at least, your charge was a slander, and he was not much inclined by it to cast his vote in your favor. Republican doctrines and declarations are accompanied with a continual protest against any interference whatever with your slaves, or with you about your slaves. Surely, this does not encourage them to revolt. . . .

John Brown's effort was peculiar. It was not a slave insurrection. It was an attempt by white men to get up a revolt among slaves, in which the slaves refused to participate. In fact, it was so absurd that the slaves, with all their ignorance, saw plainly enough it could not succeed. That affair, in its philosophy, corresponds with the many attempts, related in history, at the assassination of kings and emperors. An enthusiast broods over the oppression of a people till he fancies himself commissioned by Heaven to liberate them. He ventures the attempt, which ends in little else than his own execution.

Chapter 14:
Document Set 3 References

1. John Brown States His Case, 1859
   6 Am. State Trials 700, 800 (1859).

2. William Lloyd Garrison Justifies John Brown's Actions, 1859
   Liberator, December 16, 1859.

3. Owen Lovejoy Refuses to Denounce Brown, 1859
   Congressional Globe, 1859–1860, Part IV (appendix), pp. 205–206 abridged.

4. A Black Perspective on John Brown, 1859
   John A. Copeland, quoted in Richard J. Hinton, *John Brown and His Men* (New York, 1968), p. 509.

5. William Gilmore Simms Offers a Southern Reaction to the Breakdown of Order, 1860
   William Gilmore Simms to John J. Bockee, September 12, 1860, in Mary C. Simms Oliphant *et al.,* eds., *The Letters of William Gilmore Simms* (Columbia: University of South Carolina Press, 1952–1956), Vol. 4, pp. 287–306.

6. Henry David Thoreau Endorses Brown's Moral Character, 1859
   Henry David Thoreau, "A Plea for Captain John Brown," *The Writings of Henry David Thoreau* (Boston: Riverside Edition, 1893), 11 Vols., X, pp. 197–236.

7. The Republican Lincoln Dismisses Brown's Raid, 1860
   Address, Cooper Institute, New York, NY, February 27, 1860, in Roy P. Basler, ed., *The Collected Works of Abraham Lincoln* (New Brunswick: Rutgers University Press, 1953), Vol. 3, pp. 535, 538–539, 541.

CHAPTER 15

DOCUMENT SET 1
The Road to Emancipation: Freedom as a War Aim

From the Confederate attack on Fort Sumter in 1861 to the issuance of the final Emancipation Proclamation in 1863, President Lincoln's overriding war aim was the preservation of the Union. Emphasis on the integrity of the nation-state and preoccupation with holding the border states produced a conservative executive policy. That policy did not call for the destruction of slavery. As your textbook indicates, however, Radicals within Lincoln's own party had a different vision of the war's purpose, and it was these Republicans who ultimately forced the president's hand on this sensitive issue.

Because of his reputation as the "Great Emancipator" and the tragic circumstances surrounding his death, Lincoln's stature has assumed heroic proportions. Due to the widespread acceptance of the legend since his death, Lincoln's views on slavery and his reluctance to move aggressively toward emancipation have not been well understood. Yet his administration was evasive on confiscation of property and cautious on emancipation of the slaves.

Behind Lincoln's conservatism lay a deep personal hatred of slavery, expressed as early as the 1850s. Nonetheless, he shared the predominant social views of his age, which made him question the inherent capabilities of the African American population. If his views were complicated or even contradictory, they reflected the depth and complexity of the race issue in the 1860s.

Your textbook shows that war aims escalated after combat intensified. As the Union victories mounted, the Radicals increased pressure for revolutionary social change. Despite concern over the border states and the social ramifications of emancipation, Lincoln's revulsion against bondage gradually led him toward the Radical position. Equally significant were urgent manpower needs, which made freed slaves potentially valuable in the war effort. Failing in an attempt at compensated emancipation for the loyal slave states, President Lincoln edged closer to freedom with the Preliminary Emancipation Proclamation of 1862. In January 1863 the final proclamation freed slaves in unsecured territory, elevating the war in one bold stroke to a new moral plane.

The following documents reveal the social and political pressures operating as Lincoln moved to embrace freedom as a war aim. They include the views of free African Americans, abolitionists, and religious leaders. Excerpts from Lincoln's own correspondence provide insight into the president's objectives and opinions. As you review these materials, analyze the motivations and goals of those who urged emancipation. Define the arguments in favor of immediate action. Identify Lincoln's strategies and expectations. Compare his ideas with African American hopes for the future. Examine the documents for evidence of emancipation's impact on the course of the war.

Questions for Analysis

1. Describe Lincoln's attitude toward the institution of slavery when the war began. What were his solutions to the problem, and how would you account for them? What was the relationship between his views on this question and his primary war aim?

2. What objectives did African American leaders support as the desired outcome of the war? What arguments did African Americans and other proponents of emancipation use to advance their cause? How did their long-term goals mesh with the intentions of Lincoln and the Radicals?

3. Analyze the evolution of Lincoln's views with regard to emancipation. Why did he eventually change his mind on the question in 1862? What does the emergence of the emancipation question reveal about the consequences of total warfare?

4. Describe the goals and scope of the Emancipation Proclamation itself. What were its limitations, and what did they reveal about the war aims of the Union leadership? How did the statement reflect social and racial attitudes in the North?

5. Examine the documents for evidence of the political pressures with which Lincoln was forced to cope. In what ways was the president's freedom of action limited? How were the pressures of politics related to the timing and execution of Lincoln's decisions on slavery, black participation in combat, and emancipation?

1. The Meaning of Civil War: An African American View, 1862

Slavery is treason against God, man, and the nation. The master has no right to be a partner in a conspiracy which has shaken the very foundation of the government. Even to apologize for it, while in open rebellion, is to aid and abet in treason. The master's right to his property in human flesh cannot be equal to the slave's right to his liberty. . . .

Today, when it is a military necessity, and when the safety of the country is dependent upon emancipation, our humane political philosophers are puzzled to know what would become of the slaves if they were emancipated! The idea seems to prevail that the poor things would suffer if robbed of the glorious privileges that they now enjoy! If they could not be flogged, half starved, and work to support in ease and luxury those who have never waived an opportunity to outrage and wrong them, they would pine away and die! Do you imagine that the Negro can live outside of slavery? Of course, now, they can take care of themselves and their masters too; but if you give them their liberty, must they not suffer?. . .

Can the slaves take care of themselves? What do you suppose becomes of the thousands who fly, ragged and penniless, from the South every year, and scatter themselves throughout the free states of the North? Do they take care of themselves? I am neither ashamed nor afraid to meet this question. Assertions like this, long uncontradicted, seem to be admitted as established facts. I ask your attention for one moment to the fact that colored men at the North are shut out of almost every avenue to wealth, and, yet, strange to say, the proportion of paupers is much less among us than among you! . . .

This rebellion for slavery means something! Out of it emancipation must spring. I do not agree with those men who see no hope in this war. There is nothing in it but hope. Our cause is onward. As it is with the sun, the clouds often obstruct his vision, but in the end we find there has been no standing still. It is true the government is but little more antislavery now than it was at the commencement of the war; but while fighting for its own existence, it has been obliged to take slavery by the throat and, sooner or later, *must* choke her to death.

2. Frederick Douglass Demands Emancipation, 1862

If I were asked to describe the most painful and mortifying feature presented in the prosecution and management of the present war on the part of the United States Government, against the slaveholding rebels now marshalled against it, I should not point to Ball's Bluff, Big Bethel, Bull Run, or any of the many blunders and disasters on flood or field; but I should point to the vacillation, doubt, uncertainty and hesitation, which have thus far distinguished our government in regard to the true method of dealing with the vital cause of the rebellion. We are without any declared and settled policy—and our policy seems to be, to have no policy. . . .

By why, O why should we not abolish slavery now? All admit that it must be abolished at some time. What better time than now can be assigned for

that great work—Why should it longer live? What good thing has it done that it should be given further lease of life? What evil thing has it left undone? Behold its dreadful history! Saying nothing of the rivers of tears and streams of blood poured out by its 4,000,000 victims—saying nothing of the leprous poison it has diffused through the life blood of our morals and our religion—saying nothing of the many humiliating concessions already made to it—saying nothing of the deep and scandalous reproach it has brought upon our national good name—saying nothing of all this, and more the simple fact that this monster Slavery has eaten up and devoured the patriotism of the whole South, kindled the lurid flames of a bloody rebellion in our midst, invited the armies of hostile nations to desolate our soil, and break down our Government, is good and all-sufficient cause of smiting it as with a bolt from heaven. . . .

But to return. What shall be done with the four million slaves, if emancipated? I answer, deal justly with them; pay them honest wages for honest work; dispense with the biting lash, and pay them the ready cash; awaken a new class of motives in them; remove those old motives of shriveling fear of punishment which benumb and degrade the soul, and supplant them by the higher and better motives of hope, of self-respect, of honor, and of personal responsibility. Reverse the whole current of feeling in regard to them. They have been compelled hitherto to regard the white man as a cruel, selfish, and remorseless tyrant, thirsting for wealth, greedy of gain, and caring nothing as to the means by which he obtains it. Now, let him see that the white man has a nobler and better side to his character, and he will love, honor, esteem the white man.

But it is said that the black man is naturally indolent, and that he will not work without a master. I know that this is a part of his bad reputation; but I also know that he is indebted for this bad reputation to the most indolent and lazy of all the American people, the slaveholders—men who live in absolute idleness, and eat their daily bread in the briny sweat of other men's faces. That the black man in Slavery shirks labor—aims to do as little as he can, and to do that little in the most slovenly manner—only proves that he is a man. . . .

Again, it is affirmed that the Negro, if emancipated, could not take care of himself. My answer to this is, let him have a fair chance to try it. For 200 years he has taken care of himself and his master in the bargain. I see no reason to believe that he could not take care, and very excellent care, of himself when having only himself to support. . . .

We are asked if we would turn the slaves all loose. I answer, Yes. Why not? They are not wolves nor tigers, but men. They are endowed with reason—can decide upon questions of right and wrong, good and evil, benefits and injuries—and are therefore subjects of government precisely as other men are.

3. Christian Leaders Urge Emancipation, 1862

We observed, further, that we freely admitted the probability, and even the certainty, that God would reveal the path of duty to the President. . . .

That it was true he could not now enforce the Constitution at the South; but we could see in that fact no reason whatever for not proclaiming emancipation, but rather the contrary. . . .

That to proclaim emancipation would secure the sympathy of Europe and the whole civilized world, which now saw no other reason for the strife than national pride and ambition, an unwillingness to abridge our domain and power. No other step would be so potent to prevent foreign intervention.

Furthermore, it would send a thrill through the entire North, firing every patriotic heart, giving the people a glorious principle for which to suffer and to fight, and assuring them that the work was to be so thoroughly done as to leave our country free forever from danger and disgrace in this quarter.

We added, that when the proclamation should become widely known (as the law of Congress has *not* been) it would withdraw the slaves from the rebels, leaving them without laborers, and giving us *both laborers and soldiers.* . . .

We answered that, being fresh from the people, we were naturally more hopeful than himself [Lincoln] as to the necessity and probable effect of such a proclamation. The value of constitutional government is indeed a grand idea for which to contend; but the people know that *nothing else has put constitutional government in danger but slavery*; that the toleration of that aristocratic and despotic element among our free institutions was the inconsistency that had nearly wrought our ruin and caused free government to appear a failure before the world, and therefore the people demand emancipation to preserve and perpetuate constitutional government. . . . [A] proclamation of general emancipation, "giving Liberty and Union" as the national watch-word, would rouse the people and rally them to his support beyond any thing yet witnessed—appealing alike to conscience, sentiment, and hope. He must remember, too that present manifestations are no index of what would then take place. If the leader will but utter a trumpet call the nation will respond with patriotic ardor. No one can tell the power of the right word from the right man to develop the latent fire and enthusiasm of the masses. . . .

The struggle has gone too far, and cost too much treasure and blood, to allow of a partial settlement. Let the line be drawn at the same time between freedom and slavery, and between loyalty and treason. The sooner we know who are our enemies the better.

4. Horace Greeley Expresses Disappointment in Lincoln's Leadership, 1862

The Prayer of Twenty Millions

To Abraham Lincoln, President of the United States:

Dear Sir: I do not intrude to tell you—for you must know already—that a great proportion of those who triumphed in your election, and of all who desire the unqualified suppression of the rebellion now desolating our country, are sorely disappointed and deeply pained by the policy you seem to be pursuing with regard to the slaves of rebels. I write only to set succinctly and unmistakably before you what we require, what we think we have a right to expect, and of what we complain. . . .

II. We think you are strangely and disastrously remiss in the discharge of your official and imperative duty with regard to the emancipating provisions of the new Confiscation Act. Those provisions were designed to fight Slavery with Liberty. They prescribe that men loyal to the Union, and willing to shed their blood in her behalf, shall no longer be held, with the nation's consent, in bondage to persistent, malignant traitors, who for twenty years have been plotting and for sixteen months have been fighting to divide and destroy our country. Why these traitors should be treated with tenderness by you, to the prejudice of the dearest rights of loyal men, we cannot conceive.

III. We think you are unduly influenced by the councils, the representations, the menaces, of certain fossil politicians hailing from the Border Slave States. . . . It seems to us the most obvious truth, that whatever strengthens or fortifies Slavery in the Border States strengthens also treason, and drives home the wedge intended to divide the Union. . . .

V. We complain that the Union cause has suffered, and is now suffering immensely, from mistaken deference to rebel Slavery. Had you, sir, in your Inaugural Address, unmistakably given notice that, in case the rebellion already commenced, were persisted in, and your efforts to preserve the Union and enforce the laws should be resisted by armed force, *you would recognize no loyal person as rightfully held in Slavery by a traitor,* we believe the rebellion would therein have received a staggering if not fatal blow. . . .

VI. We complain that the Confiscation Act which you approved is habitually disregarded by your Generals, and that no word of rebuke for them from you has yet reached the public ear. Frémont's Proclamation and Hunter's Order favoring Emancipation were promptly annulled by you; . . . . [W]e complain that you, Mr. President, elected as a Republican, knowing well what an abomination Slavery is, and how emphatically it is the core and essence of this atrocious rebellion, seem never to interfere with these atrocities, and never give a direction to your military subordinates, ...

VIII. On the face of this wide earth, Mr. President, there is not one disinterested, determined, intelligent champion of the Union cause who does not feel that all attempts to put down the rebellion and at the same time uphold its inciting cause are preposterous and futile—that the rebellion, if crushed out tomorrow, would be renewed within a year if Slavery were left in full vigor. . . .

IX. I close as I began with the statement that what an immense majority of the loyal millions of your countrymen require of you is a frank, declared, unqualified, ungrudging execution of the laws of the land, more especially of the Confiscation Act. That act gives freedom to the slaves of rebels coming within our lines, or whom those lines may at any time inclose—we ask you to render it due obedience by publicly requiring all your subordinates to recognize and obey it.

5. Abraham Lincoln on Emancipation, 1862

Hon. Horace Greeley: Executive Mansion, Washington, August 22, 1862.

Dear Sir

I have just read yours of the 19th. addressed to myself through the New-York Tribune. If there be in it any statements, or assumptions of fact, which I may know to be erroneous, I do not, now and here, controvert them. . . .

I would save the Union. I would save it the shortest way under the Constitution. The sooner the national authority can be restored, the nearer the Union will be "the Union as it was." If there be those who would not save the Union, unless they could at the same time *save* slavery, I do not agree with them. If there be those who would not save the Union unless they could at the same time *destroy* slavery, I do not agree with them. My paramount object in this struggle *is* to save the Union, and is *not* either to save or to destroy slavery. If I could save the Union without freeing *any* slave I would do it, and if I could save it by freeing *all* the slaves I would do it; and if I could save it by freeing some and leaving others alone I would also do that. What I do about slavery, and the colored race, I do because I believe it helps to save the Union; and what I forbear, I forbear because I do *not* believe it would help to save the Union. I shall do *less* when-

ever I shall believe what I am doing hurts the cause, and I shall do *more* whenever I shall believe doing more will help the cause. I shall try to correct errors when shown to be errors; and I shall adopt new views so fast as they shall appear to be true views.

I have here stated my purpose according to my view of *official* duty; and I intend no modification of my oft-expressed *personal* wish that all men every where could be free. Yours,

A. Lincoln

6. The Emancipation Proclamation, 1863

By the President of the United States of America A Proclamation

Whereas on the 22d day of September, A.D. 1862, a proclamation was issued by the President of the United States, containing, among other things, the following to wit:

That on the 1st day of January, A.D. 1863, all persons held as slaves within any State or designated part of a State the people whereof shall then be in rebellion against the United States shall be then, thenceforward, and forever free; and the executive government of the United States, including the military and naval authority thereof, will recognize and maintain the freedom of such persons and will do no act or acts to repress such persons, or any of them, in any efforts they may make for their actual freedom.

That the Executive will on the 1st day of January aforesaid, by proclamation, designate the States and parts of States, if any, in which the people thereof, respectively, shall then be in rebellion against the United States;. . . .

Now [January 1, 1863], therefore, I, Abraham Lincoln, President of the United States, by virtue of the power in me vested as Commander in Chief of the Army and Navy of the United States in time of actual armed rebellion against the authority and Government of the United States, and as a fit and necessary war measure for suppressing said rebellion, . . . do order and declare that all persons held

as slaves within said designated States and parts of States are and henceforward shall be free, and that the executive government of the United States, including the military and naval authorities thereof, will recognize and maintain the freedom of said persons.

And I hereby enjoin upon the people so declared to be free to abstain from all violence, unless in necessary self-defense; and I recommend to them that in all cases when allowed they labor faithfully for reasonable wages.

And I further declare and make known that such persons of suitable condition will be received into the armed service of the United States to garrison forts, positions, stations, and other places and to man vessels of all sorts in said service.

And upon this act, sincerely believed to be an act of justice, warranted by the Constitution upon military necessity, I invoke the considerate judgment of mankind and the gracious favor of Almighty God. . . .

Done at the city of Washington, this 1st day of January, A.D. 1863, and of the [SEAL.] Independence of the United States of America the eighty-seventh.

ABRAHAM LINCOLN.

7. Lincoln Reviews His Policy, 1864

I am naturally anti-slavery. If slavery is not wrong, nothing is wrong. I can not remember when I did not so think, and feel. And yet I have never understood that the Presidency conferred upon me an unrestricted right to act officially upon this judgment and feeling. It was in the oath I took that I would, to the best of my ability, preserve, protect, and defend the Constitution of the United States. I could not take the office without taking the oath. Nor was it my view that I might take an oath to get power, and break the oath in using the power. I understood, too, that in ordinary civil administration this oath even forbade me to practically indulge my primary abstract judgment on the moral question of slavery. . . . I could not feel that, to the best of my ability, I have even tried to preserve the Constitution, if, to save slavery, or any minor matter, I should permit the wreck of government, country, and Constitution all together. When, early in the war, Gen. Fremont attempted military emancipation, I forbade it, because I did not then think it an indispensable necessity. When a little later, Gen. Cameron, then Secretary of War, suggested the arming of the blacks, I objected, because I did not yet think it an indispensable necessity. When, still later, Gen. Hunter attempted military emancipation, I again forbade it, because I did not yet think the indispensable necessity had come. When, in March, and May, and July 1862 I made earnest, and successive appeals to the border states to favor compensated emancipation, I believed the indispensable necessity for military emancipation, and arming the blacks would come, unless averted by that measure. They declined the proposition; and I was, in my best judgment, driven to the alternative of either surrendering the Union, and with it, the Constitution, or of laying strong hand upon the colored element. I chose the latter. In choosing it, I hoped for greater gain than loss; but of this, I was not entirely confident. More than a year of trial now shows no loss by it in our foreign relations, none in our home popular sentiment, none in our white military force,—no loss by it any how or any where. On the contrary, it shows a gain of quite a hundred and thirty thousand soldiers, seamen, and laborers. These are palpable facts, about which, as facts, there can be no cavilling. We have the men; and we could not have had them without the measure. . . .

I claim not to have controlled events, but confess plainly that events have controlled me. Now, at the end of three years' struggle the nation's condition is not what either party, or any man devised, or expected. God alone can claim it. Whither it is tending seems plain. If God now wills the removal of a great wrong, and wills also that we of the North as well as you of the South, shall pay fairly for our complicity in that wrong, impartial history will find therein new cause to attest and revere the justice and goodness of God.

Chapter 15:
Document Set 1 References

1. The Meaning of Civil War: An African American View, 1862
   John S. Rock, speech, January 23, 1862, *Liberator*, February 14, 1862.

2. Frederick Douglass Demands Emancipation, 1862
   Frederick Douglass, "The Future of the Negro People of the Slave States," *Douglass' Monthly* (March 1862).

3. Christian Leaders Urge Emancipation, 1862
   "Reply to Emancipation Memorial Presented by Chicago Christians of All Denominations," September 13, 1862, in Roy P. Basler, ed., *The Collected Works of Abraham Lincoln* (New Brunswick: Rutgers University Press, 1953), Vol. 5, pp. 422–424.

4. Horace Greeley Expresses Disappointment in Lincoln's Leadership, 1862
   New York Tribune, August 19, 1862.

5. Abraham Lincoln on Emancipation, 1862
   Abraham Lincoln to Horace Greeley, August 22, 1862, in Basler, Vol. 5, pp. 388–389.

6. The Emancipation Proclamation, 1863
   "Proclamation," January 1, 1863, in James D. Richardson, *A Compilation of the Messages and Papers of the Presidents* (Washington, D.C.: Bureau of National Literature and Art, 1909), Vol. 6, pp. 157–159.

7. Lincoln Reviews His Policy, 1864
   Abraham Lincoln to Albert G. Hodges, April 4, 1864, in Basler, Vol. 7, pp. 281–282.

CHAPTER 15

The Impact of Total War: War Powers Under the Constitution

The Emancipation Proclamation was one of several dramatic measures that transformed American society between 1861 and 1865. Chapter 15 emphasizes the sweeping social and political influence of the Civil War on both northern and southern institutions. In the North, civil liberties were subject to heavy pressure as a result of Lincoln's adoption of effective emergency policies, yet he consistently maintained that his exercise of crisis powers was carried out within a constitutional framework. His response to the threat of internal disunity reveals much about the social consequences of total warfare.

Your textbook stresses Lincoln's political isolation, which took the form of strained relations with Republican Radicals and the Democratic opposition, most notably the antiwar Copperheads. Democratic fears grew with the president's early decision to suspend the writ of habeas corpus in Maryland. Lincoln was firm in his conviction that the Constitution authorized the executive to determine when rebellion existed and thus when the writ might be suspended. So decisive was the administration on this point that arrest of civilians soon loomed as a key constitutional issue.

Presidential firmness in restricting civil liberties failed to quash dissent. Moreover, Democrats moved to revive their sagging fortunes by claiming guardianship of the Bill of Rights, denouncing Lincoln as a dictator. A leading figure in the Democratic resistance was Clement Vallandigham of Ohio, an ex-congressman who had been convicted of disloyalty. The *Vallandigham* case soon became a symbolic rallying point for peace Democrats, who escalated the attack on Lincoln and his strong leadership.

At the same time that he was expanding his executive authority, Lincoln was careful to cooperate with Congress. Moreover, he developed a constitutional rationale for his actions and remained accountable to the courts. Thus, although bitter disputes broke out over conscription, habeas corpus, emancipation, and other divisive issues, a reign of terror did not materialize. Nonetheless, thirteen thousand civilian arrests and several celebrated civil liberties cases revealed that the social and constitutional fabric was stretched thin by wartime centralization.

The domestic tensions that resulted are reflected in the following documents, which focus on partisan differences stemming from Lincoln's actions to control dissent. As you review the evidence, be aware of disagreement over the power to suspend habeas corpus and the conditions justifying such action. Examining Lincoln's and Vallandigham's words, try to put their basic differences in perspective. Identify their motives and goals. Above all, focus on the issues of war powers, the limits of dissent, and the war's impact on civil liberties.

Questions for Analysis

1. Review the war powers assigned to the president (as described in the document set for Chapter 6). To what extent were Lincoln's actions consistent with the intent of the Constitution's framers? In what ways did the president reinterpret that document?

2. What do the documents reveal about the impact of war on democratic values and institutions? To what extent are wartime presidents justified in expanding governmental restrictions and controls on free speech and expression? Defend your position.

3. Analyze Clement Vallandigham's speech, the resolutions of New York Democrats, and Lincoln's response to their arguments. Why was the Ohio Democrat jailed? Was Lincoln justified in approving Vallandigham's detention? Why or why not?

4. Which groups were the major critics of the Civil War? Who were the Copperheads? What do the documents indicate with regard to their motives and objectives? What can be learned from the evidence about the political and social environment on the northern home front? What does the "Lincoln Catechism" reveal about the political context in which Lincoln operated?

5. Abraham Lincoln has consistently been ranked by historians among the greatest presidents in the history of the United States. Using the documents as your basis for a judgment, evaluate Lincoln's leadership. Was he a successful politician? How would you evaluate his management of dissent? What evidence do you find most persuasive? Why?

1. A Humorist Looks at Lincoln's Opponents, 1863

"Continue this united LEAGUE."—*Richard the Third*, III. 1.

There once was a Copperhead snake   tried to bite Uncle Sam by mistake;
But the Seven League Boot   on old Uncle Sam's foot
Soon crushed this pestiferous snake.

There once was a Copperhead vile,   who attempted to damage a file,
So he tried it in truth,   but soon broke every tooth
On that rusty and crusty Old File.

"One of those who worship dirty gods."—*Cymbeline*, III. 6.

There once was a chap named Vallandigham,
whom the Copperheads chose for commanding 'em;
But a trip to the South   soon silenced his mouth,
And the world as a Tory is branding him.

"O wicked WALL!"—Midsummer Night's Dream, V. 1.

There once was an old party-Wall,   quite cracked and just ready to fall;
The Copperheads came   and completed its shame
By sticking their Bills on this Wall.

2. Lincoln Justifies His Suspension of Habeas Corpus, 1861

Message to Congress in Special Session

July 4, 1861

Soon after the first call for militia, it was considered a duty to authorize the Commanding General, in proper cases, according to his discretion, to suspend the privilege of the writ of habeas corpus; or, in other words, to arrest, and detain, without resort to the ordinary processes and forms of law, such individuals as he might deem dangerous to the public safety. This authority has purposely been exercised but very sparingly. Nevertheless, the legality and propriety of what has been done under it, are questioned; and the attention of the country has been called to the proposition that one who is sworn to "take care that the laws be faithfully executed," should not himself violate them. Of course some consideration was given to the questions of power, and propriety, before this matter was acted upon. The whole of the laws which were required to be

faithfully executed, were being resisted, and failing of execution, in nearly one-third of the States. Must they be allowed to finally fail of execution, even had it been perfectly clear, that by the use of the means necessary to their execution, some single law, made in such extreme tenderness of the citizen's liberty, that practically, it relieves more of the guilty, than of the innocent, should, to a very limited extent, be violated? To state the question more directly, are all the laws, *but one,* to go unexecuted, and the government itself go to pieces, lest that one be violated? Even in such a case, would not the official oath be broken, if the government should be overthrown, when it was believed that disregarding the single law, would tend to preserve it? But it was not believed that this question was presented. It was not believed that any law was violated. The provision of the Constitution that "The privilege of the writ of habeas corpus, shall not be suspended unless when, in cases of rebellion or invasion, the public safety may require it," is equivalent to a provision—is a provision—that such privilege may be suspended when, in cases of rebellion, or invasion, the public safety *does* require it. It was decided that we have a case of rebellion, and that the public safety does require the qualified suspension of the privilege of the writ which was authorized to be made.

3. Clement Vallandigham's Copperhead Dissent, 1863

The men who are in power at Washington, extending their agencies out through the cities and states of the Union and threatening to reinaugurate a reign of terror, may as well know that we comprehend precisely their purpose. I beg leave to assure you that it cannot and will not be permitted to succeed. The people of this country endorsed it once because they were told that it was essential to "the speedy suppression or crushing out of the rebellion" and the restoration of the Union; and they so loved the Union of these states that they would consent, even for a little while, under the false and now broken promises of the men in power, to surrender those liberties in order that the great object might, as was promised, be accomplished speedily.

They have been deceived; instead of crushing out the rebellion, the effort has been to crush out the spirit of liberty. The conspiracy of those in power is not so much for a vigorous prosecution of the war against rebels in the South as against the democracy in peace at home. . . .

Thus, so far as it is possible, by an enactment having the form of law, the Congress of the United States have surrendered, absolutely, the entire military power of the country to the President. Now, if in possession of the purse and the sword absolutely and unqualifiedly, for two years, there be anything else wanting which describes a dictatorship, I beg to know what it is. Why did they not imitate the manhood of the old Roman senators when the exigency of the Republic, in their judgment, demanded it, and declare Mr. Lincoln a dictator in terms?. . .

As originally proposed, the bill not only would have but the 3 or 4 million males between twenty and forty-five under the military control of the President, as commander in chief, but would also have placed every man, woman, and child, by virtue of the two provisions that were stricken out, also in his power. Our civil rights would have been gone, and our judiciary undermined, and he would have been an absolute and uncontrolled dictator, with the power of Cincinnatus, but without one particle of his virtues.

Yet, unfortunately, while this much was accomplished on that bill, the same tyrannical power was conferred by another bill which passed both houses, and is now, so far as forms are concerned, a law of the land—at least an act of the Thirty-seventh Congress. It authorizes the President, whom the people made, whom the people had chosen by the ballot box under the Constitution and laws, to suspend the writ of habeas corpus all over the United States; . . . .

I will not consent to put the entire purse of the country and the sword of the country into the hands of the executive, giving him despotic and dictatorial power to carry out an object which I avow before my countrymen is the destruction of their liberties and the overthrow of the Union of these states. I do not comprehend the honesty of such declarations or of the men who make them. I know that the charge is brought against myself, personally, and against many of us. I have not spent a moment in replying to it—the people will take care of all that.

The charge has been made against us—all who are opposed to the policy of this administration and opposed to this war—that we are for "peace on any terms." It is false. I am not, but I am for an immediate stopping of the war and for honorable peace. I am for peace for the sake of the Union of these states. . . .

I am for peace, because it is the first step toward conciliation and compromise. You cannot move until you have first taken that indispensable preliminary—a cessation of hostilities. But it is said that the South has refused to accept or listen to any terms whatever. How do you know that? Has it been tried?. . .

Take the theory [advocating conciliation and compromise] for what it is worth, and let men of intelligence judge; let history attest it hereafter. My theory upon that subject, then, is this—stop this war.

4. New York Democrats Demand a Rule of Law, 1863

Resolved, That the Democrats of New York point to their uniform course of action during the two years of civil war through which we have passed, to the alacrity which they have evinced in filling the ranks of the army, to their contributions and sacrifices, as the evidence of their patriotism and devotion to the cause of our imperilled country. . . .

Resolved, That as Democrats we are determined to maintain this patriotic attitude, and, despite of adverse and disheartening circumstances, to devote all our energies to sustain the cause of the Union. . . .

Resolved, That while we will not consent to be misapprehended upon these points, we are determined not to be misunderstood in regard to others not less essential. We demand that the Administration shall be true to the Constitution; shall recognize and maintain the rights of the States and the liberties of the citizen; shall everywhere, outside of the lines of necessary military occupation and the scenes of insurrection, exert all its powers to maintain the supremacy of the civil over military law. . . .

Resolved, That in view of these principles we denounce the recent assumption of a military commander to seize and try a citizen of Ohio, Clement L. Vallandigham. . . .

Resolved, That this assumption of power by a military tribunal, if successfully asserted, not only abrogates the right of the people to assemble and discuss the affairs of government, the liberty of speech and of the press, the right of trial by jury, the law of evidence, and the privilege of habeas corpus, but it strikes a fatal blow at the supremacy of law, and the authority of the State and federal constitutions. . . .

Resolved, That these safeguards of the rights of the citizen against the pretensions of arbitrary power were intended more especially for his protection in times of civil commotion. . . . They have stood the test of seventy-six years of trial, under our republican system, under circumstances which show that, while they constitute the foundation of all free government, they are the elements of the enduring stability of the republic.

5. Lincoln's Defense of Executive Action, 1863

The resolutions promise to support me in every constitutional and lawful measure to suppress the rebellion; and I have not knowingly employed, nor shall knowingly employ, any other. But the meeting, by their resolutions, assert and argue, that certain military arrests and proceedings following them for which I am ultimately responsible, are unconstitutional. I think they are not. . . .

Prior to my instalation here it had been inculcated that any State had a lawful right to secede from the national Union; and that it would be expedient to exercise the right, whenever the devotees of the doctrine should fail to elect a President to their own liking. I was elected contrary to their liking; and accordingly, so far as it was legally possible, they had taken seven states out of the Union, had seized many of the United States Forts, and had fired upon the United States' Flag, all before I was inaugurated; and, of course, before I had done any official act whatever. . . . It undoubtedly was a well pondered reliance with them that in their own unrestricted effort to destroy Union,

constitution, and law, all together, the government would, in great degree, be restrained by the same constitution and law, from arresting their progress. Their sympathizers pervaded all departments of the government, and nearly all communities of the people. From this material, under cover of "Liberty of speech" "Liberty of the press" and "*Habeas corpus*" they hoped to keep on foot amongst us a most efficient corps of spies, informers, supplyers, and aiders and abettors of their cause in a thousand ways. They knew that in times such as they were inaugurating, by the constitution itself, the "Habeas corpus" might be suspended; but they also knew they had friends who would make a question as to *who* was to suspend it; . . . .

[T]he provision of the constitution that "The previlege of the writ of Habeas Corpus shall not be suspended, unless when in cases of Rebellion or Invasion, the public Safety may require it" is *the* provision which specially applies to our present case. This provision plainly attests the understanding of those who made the constitution that ordinary courts of justice are inadequate to "cases of Rebellion"—attests their purpose that in such cases, men may be held in custody whom the courts acting on ordinary rules, would discharge. Habeas Corpus, does not discharge men who are proved to be guilty of defined crime, and its suspension is allowed by the constitution on purpose that, men may be arrested and held, who can not be proved to be guilty of defined crime, "when in cases of Rebellion or Invasion the public Safety may require it." This is precisely our present case—a case of Rebellion, wherein the public Safety does require the suspension. . . .

If I be wrong on this question of constitutional power, my error lies in believing that certain proceedings are constitutional when, if cases of rebellion or Invasion, the public Safety requires them, which would not be constitutional when, in absence of rebellion or invasion, the public Safety does not require them. . . . [A]nd I can no more be persuaded that the government can constitutionally take no strong measure in time of rebellion, because it can be shown that the same could not be lawfully taken in time of peace, than I can be persuaded that a particular drug is not good medicine for a sick man, because it can be shown to not be good food for a well one. Nor am I able to appreciate the danger, apprehended by the meeting, that the American people will, by means of military arrests during the rebellion, lose the right of public discussion, the liberty of speech and the press, the law of evidence, trial by jury, and Habeas corpus, throughout the indefinite peaceful future which I trust lies before them, ...

One of the resolutions expresses the opinion of the meeting that arbitrary arrests will have the effect to divide and distract those who should be united in suppressing the rebellion; and I am specifically called on to discharge Mr. Vallandigham. I regard this as, at least, a fair appeal to me, on the expediency of exercising a constitutional power which I think exists. . . . [I]t will afford me great pleasure to discharge him so soon as I can, by any means, believe the public safety will not suffer by it. I further say, that as the war progresses, it appears to me, opinion, and action, which were in great confusion at first, take shape, and fall into more regular channels; so that the necessity for arbitrary dealing with them gradually decreases. I have every reason to desire that it would cease altogether; and far from the least is my regard for the opinions and wishes of those who, like the meeting at Albany, declare their purpose to sustain the government in every constitutional and lawful measure to suppress the rebellion. Still, I must continue to do so much as may seem to be required by the public safety.

A. LINCOLN.

6. An Attack on Lincoln's Leadership, 1864

Lesson the First

I.

What is the Constitution?
A compact with hell—now obsolete.

II.

By whom hath the Constitution been made obsolete?
By Abraham Africanus the First.

III.

To what end?
That his days may be long in office—and that he may make himself and his people the equal of the negroes.

IV.

What is a President?
A general agent for negroes.

V.

What is Congress?
A body organized for the purpose of taxing the people to buy negroes, and to make laws to protect the President from being punished for his crimes. . . .

XVI.

What is the meaning of the word "traitor"?
One who is a stickler for the Constitution and the laws.

XVII.

What is the meaning of the word "Copperhead"?
A man who believes in the Union as it was, the Constitution as it is, and who cannot be bribed with greenbacks, nor frightened by a bastile. . . .

XIX.

What is the meaning of the word "law"?
The will of the President. . . .

XX.

How were the States formed?
By the United States. . . .

XXII.

Have the States any rights?
None whatever, except when the President allows.

XXIII.

Have the people any rights?
None but such as the President gives. . . .

Lesson the Second

I.

What is the *"habeas corpus"*?
The power of the President to imprison whom he pleases, as long as he pleases.

II.

What is Trial by Jury?
Trial by military commission.

III.

What is "security from unreasonable searches and seizures"?
The liability of a man's house to be entered by any Provost Marshal who pleases.

IV.

What is the meaning of the promise that, "no person shall be held to answer for any crime unless on a presentment or indictment of a Grand Jury"?
That any person may be arrested whenever the President or any of his officers please.

V.

What is the meaning of the promise that, "no person shall be deprived of life, liberty or property, without due process of law"?
That any person may be deprived of life, liberty and property, whom the President orders to be so stripped.

VI.

What is the meaning of "the right to a speedy and public trial by an impartial jury"?
A remote secret inquisition conducted by a man's enemies.

VII.

What is the meaning of the promise that the accused shall be tried "in the State and district wherein the crime shall have been committed"?
That he shall be sent away from the State and beyond the jurisdiction of the district where the offence is said to be committed. . . .

XIII.

What is the meaning of the declaration that "the judicial Power of the United States shall be vested in the Supreme Court," etc.?
That it shall be vested in the President and his provost marshals. . . .

Lesson the Ninth

I.

Is the United States a consolidated government?
It is.

II.

Who consolidated it?
Abraham Lincoln.

III.

Does consolidation mean to annihilate the States?
Yes—to a great extent.

IV.

Had he a right to do this?
Yes—under the war power.

V.

Who invented the war power?
Abraham Lincoln.

VI.

For what purpose did he invent the war power?
That he might not have to return to the business of splitting rails.

Chapter 15:
Document Set 2 References

1. A Humorist Looks at Lincoln's Opponents, 1863
   Charles Godfrey Leland and Henry P. Leland, *Ye Book of Copperheads* (Philadelphia: Frederick Leypoldt, 1863), in Frank Freidel, ed., *Union Pamphlets of the Civil War* (Cambridge: Harvard University Press, 1967), Vol. 2, pp. 859, 861–862, 869.

2. Lincoln Justifies His Suspension of Habeas Corpus, 1861
   Abraham Lincoln, "Message to Congress in Special Session," July 4, 1861, in Roy P. Basler, ed., *The Collected Works of Abraham Lincoln* (New Brunswick: Rutgers University Press, 1953), Vol. 4, pp. 429–430.

3. Clement Vallandigham's Copperhead Dissent, 1863
   Clement L. Vallandigham, *Speeches, Arguments, Addresses, and Letters of Clement L. Vallandigham* (New York: J. Walter & Co., 1864), pp. 479–502.

4. New York Democrats Demand a Rule of Law, 1863
   "Resolutions," May 16, 1863, in Frank Moore, ed., *The Rebellion Record: A Diary of American Events* (New York: 1864), Vol. 7, pp. 298–299.

5. Lincoln's Defense of Executive Action, 1863
   "Lincoln to Erastus Corning and Others," June 12, 1863, in Basler, Vol. 6, pp. 262–264, 267, 269.

6. An Attack on Lincoln's Leadership, 1864
   The Lincoln Catechism, Wherein the Eccentricities and Beauties of Despotism Are Fully Set Forth: A Guide to the Presidential Election of 1864 (New York: J. F. Feeks, 1864).

Chapter 15:
Document Set 2 Credit

1. By permission of the Houghton Library, Harvard University

CHAPTER 15

The Crucible of War: Life and Death as a Personal Experience

Chapter 15 provides sweeping coverage of the political, economic, and diplomatic aspects of the Civil War. However, any textbook discussion fails to capture the pain, suffering, and tragedy of the battlefield experience and its grim results. The following documents stress the personal experiences of men and women caught up in the drama of mortal combat and the consequences of war.

As you absorb the textbook account of military strategy and tactics, reflect on the impact of command decisions on the thousands of men who carried them out on the field of battle. Examine the letters of combatants to gain insight into the terrible human price extracted by a nation at war. Use the words of soldiers as the key to a deeper understanding of war's meaning to people called on to die in the name of principles and ideas.

Your review of the documents should provide some useful comparisons between the responses of both southerners and northerners to the trauma of battle. Observe common experiences and reactions to combat on both sides of the conflict. Try to understand the impact of widespread death and destruction on those most directly affected by the war.

The textbook notes that the struggle also was waged behind the lines in hospitals and prison camps, where the human residue of war was dealt with. The documents make it clear that the Civil War touched many people who worked to ease the suffering of the wounded and dying. Among those involved were women, who served as nurses and were therefore personally affected by the carnage wrought by modern warfare. Search the documents for evidence of the role played by these women in the great national experience of the 1860s.

The documents also provide insight into the social impact of war. Try to determine how noncombatants were affected by the war. Use the evidence to explore the incidental consequences of war, both physical and social. Relate the social forces unleashed by the Civil War to problems soon to arise as the nation tried to close the wounds the war had inflicted on the people, land, and institutions of the United States.

As you examine the evidence, recall the origins of the war and the enthusiasm that prevailed when it first broke out. Sentimentalism, romanticism, and optimism concerning quick and glorious victory prevailed on both sides in 1861. Note the textbook discussion of war's realities, including the massive casualties that were destined to embitter the nation in the postwar era. As you turn to the documents, compare the expectations of 1861 with the realities of 1864. Who was "patriotic" in the 1860s, and how was *patriotism* defined? Be aware of the leveling effect of combat as you assess attitudes toward war from the perspective of the participants most directly involved.

Questions for Analysis

1. What do the documents reveal about the broad social impact of the Civil War? What evidence of social change can be found in the source material? In what ways can wartime innovations be related to the reconstruction process that followed?

2. How would you describe the initial reaction to the Civil War from soldiers and civilians in both North and South? What expectations prevailed as northerners and southerners prepared for war? How does the mood expressed in the documents compare with the attitude that dominated when the war began? How do you account for any differences?

3. How would you characterize the role played by women in the war? Do the documents shed any light on the strengths, capabilities, and contributions that women were able to bring to a nation at war? Explain.

4. In what ways were Union and Confederate soldiers alike? Do you find similarities or differences in their reactions to the combat experience and its human consequences?

5. What is a *just* war? Do you think it is appropriate for historians to make moral judgments about past military conflicts? Do the documents provide any clues with regard to the justifications that might have been offered for the Civil War? Explain.

6. Discuss the role played by African American troops in the Civil War. How do the documents clarify the reasons African Americans were willing to fight for a government that still discriminated against them? What was the significance of the decision to use them in combat, both short and long term?

1. A Union Soldier's Opinion of the War, 1862

Camp near Fredericksburg
Dec 19th 1862

Dear Sister

It is with pleasure that I seat my self down this morning to write you a few lines to let you know that I am still alive I have been under the weather for some time but I am getting better now. We had a big fight over here, got whipped like thunder. I was not able to be in the fight. Jno McClure could not be found on the battle field I guess he is killed or taken prisoner but I am afraid he is dead. He is the only one missing in our company.

Sis I dont know what you think about the war but I will tell you what I think and that is the north will nevver whip the south as long as there is a man left in the south. They fight like wild devles. Ever man seems determine to loose the last drop of blood before they give up but there is no use of you and I talking about the war because we cant end it, but I dont care how soon it is stopped. Christmas will soon be here I would like to be at [home].

Jno R. McClure

2. An Enlisted Man Describes Life in a Confederate Prison Camp, 1864

[T]hey marched us down to Libby and all who were not wounded were sent upstairs. The rest of us lay down in the hall and staid there until just at dark. They [finally] took a notion to send us to Hospital about 100 rods from Prison, in an old tobacco house. We were the first [instalment] from the Battle. After washing my head and getting a bandage on it I lay down and slept until morning. The next day there was nothing but bringing in wounded and amputating. The Hospital was soon filled up. For about a month I did not [moove] [arround] much. Had a few [fitts], and came pretty near going under, as near as I can find out.... I changed my bed over next to Pacey, and tried to do a little for him, but there was

nothing to take care of sick with. They would acknowledge that they had no medicine. Some of them as it is the world over, were Gentlemen, but the great part were bitter towards us. Our nurses were all our own men but the most of them were men who had been in Prison a long time and [volluntered] in order to get more to eat, they gave the [attendents] a little additional. They kept us on such a small amount of food that a fellow could think of nothing else during the whole time but something to eat, and about the only topic was, what they had eaten during their lifetime, what they would have when they got out of this, and exchange.... After we had been there about two and $\frac{1}{2}$ months they divided the rations into three meals but that was worse than two, as it was not enough to make the *least* impression on a [mans] insides, still we stood it those of us who lived but it killed a great many. Poor Pacey amongst the rest. It was horrible the way and number of men that died and as for [burrying], strip them naked and put them in a coffin and carry them off, sometimes they would lay in the dead house over night, "[especialy] when there was a great many dying, as it was at first", and then the rats would eat into the box and you can imagine what they would do. It was hard to see ones friend carried away in that manner, right in a large city where there was not the least need of it. But such was our Southern [bretheren]. . . .

Joseph R. Ward

3. The Heat of Battle from the Southern Soldier's Perspective, 1862, 1863

Yesterday evening we (the Texas Brigade) was in one of the hardest fought battles ever known . . . I dont think the Regt (4th Tex) could muster this morning over 150 or 200 men & there were 530 yesterday went into the engagement. . . . I got some of the men from the 5th Regt to go and look up our wounded. . . . I never had a clear conception of the horrors of war untill that night and the [next] morning. On going round on that battlefield with a candle searching for my friends I could hear on all sides the dreadful groans of the wounded and their heart piercing cries for water and assistance. Friends and foes all togather. . . . Oh the awful scene witnessed on the battle field. May I never see any more such in life. . . . I am satisfied not to make another such charge. For I hope dear Ann that this big battle will have some influence in terminating this war. I assure you I am heartily sick of soldiering.

—from A. N. Erskine, 1862

Martha . . . I can inform you that I have Seen the Monkey Show at last and I dont Waunt to see it no more I am satsfide with Ware Martha I Cant tell you how many ded men I did see . . . thay ware piled up one one another all over the Battle feel the Battel was a Six days Battel and I was in all off it . . . I did not go all over the Battle feeld I Jest was one one Winge of the Battel feeld But I can tell you that there Was a meney a ded man where I was men Was shot Evey fashinton that you mite Call for Som had there hedes shot of and som ther armes and leges Won was sot in too in the midel I can tell you that I am tirde of Ware I am satsfide if the Ballence is that is one thing Shore I dont waunt to see that site no more I can inform you that West Brown was shot one the head he Was sent off to the horspitel . . . he was not herte very Bad he was struck with a pease of a Bum

—from Thomas Warrick, 1863

4. Thomas Wentworth Higginson Assesses the Black Soldier, 1870

[T]hey were very much like other men. General Saxton, examining with some impatience a long list of questions from some philanthropic Commission at the North, respecting the traits and habits of the freedmen, bade some staff-officer answer them all in two words,—"Intensely human." We all admitted that it was a striking and comprehensive description.

For instance, as to courage. So far as I have seen, the mass of men are naturally courageous up to a cer-tain point. A man seldom runs away from danger which he ought to face, unless others run; each is apt to keep with the mass, and colored soldiers have more than usual of this gregariousness. In almost every regiment, black or white, there are a score or two of men who are naturally daring, who really hunger after dangerous adventures, and are happiest when allowed to seek them. Every commander gradually finds out who these men are, and habitually uses them; certainly I had such, and I remember with delight their bearing, their coolness, and their dash. . . . The mass of the regiment rose to the same level under excitement, and were more excitable, I think, than whites, but neither more nor less courageous.

Perhaps the best proof of a good average of courage among them was in the readiness they always showed for any special enterprise. I do not remember ever to have had the slightest difficulty in obtaining volunteers, but rather in keeping down the number. The previous pages include many illustrations of this, as well as of their endurance of pain and discomfort. . . .

. . . As to the simple general fact of courage and reliability I think no officer in our camp ever thought of there being any difference between black and white. And certainly the opinions of these officers, who for years risked their lives every moment on the fidelity of their men, were worth more than those of all the world beside.

No doubt there were reasons why this particular war was an especially favorable test of the colored soldiers. They had more to fight for than the whites. Besides the flag and the Union, they had home and wife and child. They fought with ropes round their necks, and when orders were issued that the officers of colored troops should be put to death on capture, they took a grim satisfaction. It helped their *esprit de corps* immensely.

5. General Sherman Recalls the March Through Georgia, 1864

The skill and success of the men in collecting forage was one of the features of this march. Each brigade commander had authority to detail a company of foragers, usually about fifty men, with one or two commissioned officers selected for their boldness and enterprise. This party would be dispatched before daylight with a knowledge of the intended day's march and camp; would proceed on foot five or six miles from the route traveled by their brigade, and then visit every plantation and farm within range. They would usually procure a wagon or family carriage, load it with bacon, corn-meal, turkeys, chickens, ducks, and every thing that could be used as food or forage, and would then regain the main road, usually in advance of their train. When this came up, they would deliver to the brigade commissary the supplies thus gathered by the way. . . . No doubt, many acts of pillage, robbery, and violence, were committed by these parties of foragers, usually called "bummers"; for I have since heard of jewelry taken from women, and the plunder of articles that never reached the commissary; but these acts were exceptional and incidental. I never heard of any cases of murder or rape; and no army could have carried along sufficient food and forage for a march of three hundred miles; so that foraging in some shape was necessary. The country was sparsely settled, with no magistrates or civil authorities who could respond to requisitions, as is done in all the wars of Europe; so that this system of foraging was simply indispensable to our success.

6. The Women's War

A. "Mother" Bickerdyke Cuts Red Tape, 1862

The battle of Corinth had raged from early morning till late in the afternoon, and then General Price was checked and forced to retreat. The struggle had been a bloody one, and the ground was covered with the wounded and the dead. . . .

. . . Every available building, and every church but one, was taken for hospital purposes; and long rows of tents were put up on the grounds of the Ladies' College. But there was a lack of supplies. There were no cots or pillows—only the bare ground.

Among the heroic workers there, was Mother Bickerdyke, who could always find supplies if they were within reach. She took some wagons and a squad of men, and went down to the quartermaster's storehouse. "Come on, boys," she said; "we will see if we can find anything to make the wounded comfortable."

The quartermaster was there to receive her, and to say, "We have no hospital supplies; they are all given out."

"Then, I'll have to take what I can get. Boys, roll out some of those bales of hay and cotton! They will make better beds than the ground."

"You must bring me an order, madam."

"I have no time to hunt up officers to get orders."

"But I am responsible for these supplies, and cannot let them go without proper orders."

The wagons were soon loaded up, and the bales of hay and cotton were soon at the hospital tents. An axe cut the hoops, and the hay went flying into the tents in long even rows with the help of ready hands. An armful of cotton made a good pillow. All night long the work went on. Some with lanterns were searching among the dead for the wounded and bringing them in; others dressing the wounds. No one was idle. The utmost of strength and energy must be put forth at such a time.

But the quartermaster must make his accounts all right, and of course had to enter complaint against Mother Bickerdyke. She was summoned to meet the charge, which she did when she found time to go.

"Mrs. Bickerdyke, you are charged with taking quartermaster's stores without proper orders and over his protest."

"Who ordered the tents put up on the college grounds?"

"I did."

"What were they put up for?"

"To shelter the wounded men, of course."

"Did you expect these wounded men to lie on the ground?"

"You should have obtained orders."

"I had no time to go for orders. Why didn't you order in the hay and the cotton?"

"I did not think of it."

"Well, I did, and used all I needed; and now all you have to do is to draw an order for them and give it to the quartermaster."

She bade the officers good-day and returned to her work, and no one thought of arresting her. Indeed, she had the best of the argument.

B. A Surprise Casualty at Chickamauga, 1863

A woman who had served as a private soldier in the ranks was severely wounded and taken prisoner at Chickamauga. She fell in a charge made upon the Confederates; and as the troops immediately fell back she was left with the other wounded on the field, in the enemy's lines. As she was dressed as the other soldiers were, her sex was not discovered till she was under a surgeon's care in the hospital. She was wounded in the thigh. No bones were broken; but it was a deep, ugly flesh wound, as if torn by a fragment of a shell.

A day or two afterwards she was sent with a flag of truce into the Union lines.

The sum and substance of the official message sent with this woman was: "As the Confederates do not use women in war, this woman, wounded in battle, is returned to you." There was great indignation in the regiment to which this woman belonged; and officers and men hastened to protest, that, although she had been with them for more than a year, not one in the regiment suspicioned that she was a woman. She stood the long, hard marches, did full duty on the picket-line and in camp, and had fought well in all the battles in which the regiment took part. She was in the hospital at Chattanooga for some time.

C. Louisa May Alcott Remembers the "Death of John," ca. 1864

The next night, as I went my rounds with Dr. P., I happened to ask which man in the room probably suffered most; and, to my great surprise, he glanced at John:

"Every breath he draws is like a stab; for the ball pierced the left lung, broke a rib, and did no end of damage here and there; so the poor lad can find neither forgetfulness nor ease, because he must lie on his wounded back or suffocate. It will be a hard struggle, and a long one, for he possesses great vitality; but even his temperate life can't save him; I wish it could."

"You don't mean he must die, doctor?"

"Bless you, there's not the slightest hope for him; and you'd better tell him so before long; women have a way of doing such things comfortably, so I leave it to you. He wont last more than a day or two, at furthest." . . .

It was an easy thing for Dr. P. to say: "Tell him he must die," but a cruelly hard thing to do, and by no means as "comfortable" as he politely suggested. I had not the heart to do it then, and privately indulged the hope that some change for the better might take place, in spite of gloomy prophecies, so rendering my task unnecessary. . . . I had forgotten that the strong man might long for the gentler tendance of a woman's hands, the sympathetic magnetism of a woman's presence, as well as the feebler souls about him. The doctor's words caused me to reproach myself with neglect, not of any real duty, perhaps, but of those little cares and kindnesses that solace homesick spirits, and make the heavy hours pass easier. John looked lonely and forsaken just then, as he sat with bent head, hands folded on his knee, and no outward sign of suffering, till, looking nearer, I saw great tears roll down and drop upon the floor. It was a new sight there; for, though I had seen many suffer, some swore, some groaned, most endured silently, but none wept. Yet it did not seem weak, only very touching, and straightway my fear vanished, my heart opened wide and took him in, as gathering the bent head in my arms, as freely as if he had been a little child, I said, "Let me help you bear it, John."

Never, on any human countenance, have I seen so swift and beautiful a look of gratitude, surprise, and comfort, as that which answered me more eloquently than the whispered—

"Thank you, ma'am; this is right good! this is what I wanted!"...

... [N]ow I knew that to him, as to so many, I was the poor substitute for mother, wife, or sister, and in his eyes no stranger, but a friend who hitherto had seemed neglectful; for, in his modesty he had never guessed the truth. . . .

Poor John! it did not matter now, except that a shot in front might have spared the long agony in store for him. He seemed to read the thoughts that troubled me, as he spoke so hopefully when there was no hope, for he suddenly added:

"This is my first battle; do they think it's going to be my last?"

"I'm afraid they do, John."

It was the hardest question I had ever been called upon to answer; doubly hard with those clear eyes fixed on mine, forcing a truthful answer by their own truth. He seemed a little startled at first, pondered over the fateful fact a moment, then shook his head, with a glance at the broad chest and muscular limbs stretched out before him:

"I'm not afraid, but it's difficult to believe all at once. I am so strong it don't seem possible for such a little wound to kill me."...

...The first red streak of dawn was warming the gray east, a herald of the coming sun; John saw it, and with the love of light which lingers in us to the end, seemed to read in it a sign of hope of help, for over his whole face there broke that mysterious expression, brighter than any smile, which often comes to eyes that look their last. He laid himself gently down, and stretching out his strong right arm, as if to grasp and bring the blessed air to his lips in a fuller flow, lapsed into a merciful unconsciousness, which assured us that for him suffering was forever past. He died then; for, though the heavy breaths still tore their way up for a little longer, they were but the waves of an ebbing tide that beat unfelt against the wreck, which an immortal voyager had deserted with a smile. He never spoke again, but to the end held my hand close, so close that when he was asleep at last, I could not draw it away. Dan helped me, warning me, as he did so, that it was unsafe for dead and living flesh to lie so long together; but though my hand was strangely cold and stiff, and four white marks remained across its back, even when warmth and color had returned elsewhere, I could not but be glad that through its touch, the presence of human sympathy, perhaps, had lightened that hard hour.

7. Photographic Images of War, 1863, 1865

A. The Aftermath of Gettysburg, 1863

B. Richmond in Ruins, 1865

Chapter 15:
Document Set 3 References

1. A Union Soldier's Opinion of the War, 1862
   John R. McClure to Sister, December 19, 1862, in Nancy Niblack Baxter, ed., *Hoosier Farm Boy in Lincoln's Army: The Civil War Letters of Private John R. McClure* (privately printed, 1971), p. 42.

2. An Enlisted Man Describes Life in a Confederate Prison Camp, 1864
   Joseph R. Ward to Friend Jo, September 27, 1864, in D. Duane Cummins and Daryl Hohweiler, eds., *An Enlisted Soldier's View of the Civil War: The Wartime Papers of Joseph Richardson Ward, Jr.* (Belle Publications, 1981), pp. 168–169.

3. The Heat of Battle from the Southern Soldier's Perspective, 1862, 1863
   A. N. Erskine to his Wife, June 28, 1862; Thomas Warrick to his Wife, January 11, 1863; University of Texas; Alabama Archives, in Bell Irvin Wiley, *The Life of Johnny Reb: The Common Soldier of the Confederacy* (Indianapolis: Bobbs-Merrill Company, 1943), pp. 32–33.

4. Thomas Wentworth Higginson Assesses the Black Soldier, 1870
   Thomas Wentworth Higginson, *Army Life in a Black Regiment* (Boston: Fields, Osgood, & Co., 1870), pp. 244–245, 250–251.

5. General Sherman Recalls the March Through Georgia, 1864

William T. Sherman, *Memoirs of General William T. Sherman by Himself,* 1875 (Bloomington: Indiana University Press, 1957), pp. 182–183.

6. The Women's War
   A. "Mother" Bickerdyke Cuts Red Tape, 1862.
      Mrs. Annie Wittenmyer, *Under the Guns: A Woman's Reminiscences of the Civil War* (Boston: E. B. Stillings & Co., 1895), pp. 82–85.
   B. A Surprise Casualty at Chickamauga, 1863. Wittenmyer, pp. 17–18.
   C. Louisa May Alcott Remembers the "Death of John," ca. 1864. Dr. L. P. Brockett, *The Camp, the Battlefield, and the Hospital, or Lights and Shadows of the Great Rebellion* (Philadelphia: National Publishing Company, 1866), pp. 306–308, 311, 314.

7. Photographic Images of War, 1863, 1865.
   A. The Aftermath of Gettysburg, 1863.
      "Field Where General Reynolds Fell, Gettysburg, July, 1863," in Alexander Gardner, *Gardner's Photographic Sketchbook of the Civil War* (New York: Dover Publications, Inc., 1959), Plate 37.
   B. Richmond in Ruins, 1865.
      "Ruins of Arsenal, Richmond, Va., April, 1865," in Gardner, Plate 91.

Chapter 15:
Document Set 3 Credits

7. A. Corbis-Bettman
   B. Library of Congress

CHAPTER 16

DOCUMENT SET 1
Ensuring Suffrage: Equal Rights for Whom?

One important theme in Chapter 16 is the drive to expand suffrage as a consequence of the Civil War. Just as emancipation had altered the meaning of the war, southern recalcitrance transformed Reconstruction into a process that held potential for social revolution. Although revolution was not to be, dramatic political and constitutional changes were implemented before radicalism was contained.

The following documents explore the forces operating in the postwar era to encourage the extension of civil rights to the freedmen. Stressing the arguments that framed the debate, these materials place heavy emphasis on the voting franchise, regarded by most observers as the key to black political and social aspirations. As you review the evidence, pay careful attention to the justifications for and criticisms of a constitutional remedy.

African American initiative is evident in the interview granted by President Andrew Johnson to Frederick Douglass and George Downing. Compare their argument with the position taken by Missouri Senator Carl Schurz in his effort to persuade the president to endorse suffrage. Given the politically charged atmosphere that dominated postwar Washington, you should note the partisan backgrounds of the persons involved. The political context is clarified by your textbook's account of debate over the black codes, the civil rights bill, and the Freedmen's Bureau.

An important aspect of the struggle for equal rights was the close link between abolitionism and feminism. Insisting on "natural rights" for all adult citizens, proponents of women's rights moved in 1866 to establish the American Equal Rights Association, which blended the campaigns for both African American and female suffrage. As your text notes, however, Radical Republicans tried to play down the link between their goals for freedmen and feminist insistence on women's enfranchisement. As you compare Elizabeth Cady Stanton's bitter attack on feminism's abolitionist and Radical "friends" with Henry B. Blackwell's baldly practical argument for female suffrage, be conscious of the relationship between the two reform movements.

As partisan strife increased, Johnson became even more uncooperative. Review your textbook's description of his split with the Radical Congress as you examine his annual message of 1867. Consider the grounds on which Johnson based his argument, including the constitutional implications of his views. His annual message establishes the president's position on the hotly debated Fourteenth Amendment.

As you reflect on the documents, focus on a definition of civil liberties and political equality. In the context of the 1860s, which groups in American society could claim title to equal rights?

Questions for Analysis

1. What arguments were used by African Americans and Republicans to support the extension of suffrage to freedmen in 1865–1866? Were there underlying, yet unspoken, reasons for the endorsement of full political equality?

2. On what grounds did President Johnson base his position on suffrage? How would you account for his position on the Fourteenth Amendment? What is the relationship between the president's social/political background and his views on the voting franchise?

3. What was the relationship between abolitionism and the women's rights movement? What do the documents reveal about the obstacles to female suffrage in the 1860s? What were the ultimate consequences of the tension between abolitionism and feminism?

4. Elizabeth Cady Stanton and Henry B. Blackwell both supported female suffrage, yet they took different positions concerning reform priorities in the 1860s. Do the documents reveal anything of the priorities each established? As you examine their respective arguments for women's voting rights, what differences are evident?

5. What was the purpose of the Fourteenth Amendment? What did this constitutional amendment reflect about the Radicals' conception of federalism? In what ways was the constitutional balance in the American political system affected by the amendment?

1. Republican Carl Schurz Urges Black Suffrage, 1865

The Ballot Necessary for the Negro

The interference of the national authority in the home concerns of the southern States would be rendered less necessary, and the whole problem of political and social reconstruction be much simplified, if, while the masses lately arrayed against the government are permitted to vote, the large majority of those who were always loyal . . . were not excluded from all influence upon legislation. In all questions concerning the Union, the national debt, and the future social organization of the south, the feelings of the colored man are naturally in sympathy with the views and aims of the national government. While the southern whites fought against the Union, the negro did all he could to aid it; while the southern white sees in the national government his conqueror, the negro sees in it his protector; while the white owes to the national debt his defeat, the negro owes to it his deliverance; while the white considers himself robbed and ruined by the emancipation of the slaves, the negro finds in it the assurance of future prosperity and happiness. In all the important issues the negro would be led by natural impulse to forward the ends of the government, and by making his influence, as part of the voting body, tell upon the legislation of the States, render the interference of the national authority unnecessary.

As the most difficult of the pending questions are intimately connected with the status of the negro in southern society, it is obvious that a correct solution can be more easily obtained if he has a voice in the matter. In the right to vote we would find the best permanent protection against oppressive class-legislation, as well as against individual persecution. . . . It is a notorious fact that the rights of a man of some political power are far less exposed to violation than those of one who is, in matter of public interest, completely subject to the will of others. A voter is a man of influence; small as the influence may be in the single individual, it becomes larger when the individual belongs to a numerous class of voters. . . . Such an individual is an object of interest to the political parties that desire to have the benefit of his ballot. . . . The first trials ought certainly to be made while the national power is still there to prevent or repress disturbances; but the practice once successfully inaugurated under the protection of that power, it would probably be more apt than anything else to obliterate old antagonisms.

2. George Downing and Frederick Douglass Argue the Case for Enfranchisement, 1866

Our coming is a marked circumstance, noting determined hope that we are not satisfied with an amendment prohibiting slavery, but that we wish it enforced with appropriate legislation. This is our desire. We ask for it intelligently, with the knowledge and conviction that the fathers of the Revolution intended freedom for every American; that they should be protected in their rights as citizens, and be equal before the law. We are Americans, native born Americans. We are citizens; we are glad to have it known to the world that you bear no doubtful record on this point.

On this fact, and with confidence in the triumph of justice, we base our hope. We see no recognition of color or race in the organic law of the land. It knows no privileged class, and therefore we cherish the hope that we may be fully enfranchised, not only here in this District, but throughout the land. We respectfully submit that rendering anything less than this will be rendering to us less than our just due; that granting anything less than our full rights will be a disregard of our just rights and of due respect for our feelings. If the powers that be do so it will be used as a license, as it were, or an apology, for any community, or for individuals thus disposed, to outrage our rights and feelings. It has been shown in the present war that the Government may justly reach its strong arm into States, and demand for them, from those who owe it allegiance, their assistance and support. May it not reach out a like arm to secure and protect its subjects upon whom it has a claim?

Following upon Mr. Downing, Mr. Fred. Douglass advanced and addressed the President, saying:

Mr. President, we are not here to enlighten you, sir, as to your duties as the Chief Magistrate of this Republic, but to show our respect, and to present in brief the claims of our race to your favorable consideration. In the order of Divine Providence you are placed in a position where you have the power to save or destroy us, to bless or blast us—I mean our whole race. Your noble and humane predecessor placed in our hands the sword to assist in saving the nation, and we do hope that you, his able successor, will favorably regard the placing in our hands the ballot with which to save ourselves.

We shall submit no argument on that point. The fact that we are the subjects of Government, and subject to taxation, subject to volunteer in the service of the country, subject to being drafted, subject to bear the burdens of the State, makes it not improper that we should ask to share in the privileges of this condition.

3. Henry B. Blackwell Appeals to Racism in the Cause of Female Suffrage, 1867

To the Legislatures of the Southern States:—I write to you as the intellectual leaders of the Southern people—men who should be able and willing to transcend the prejudices of section—to suggest the only ground of settlement between North and South which, in my judgment, can be successfully adopted.

Let me state the political situation. The radical principles of the North are immovably fixed upon negro suffrage as a condition of Southern State reconstruction. The proposed Constitutional Amendment is not regarded as a finality. It satisfies nobody, not even its authors. In the minds of the Northern people the negroes are now associated with the idea of loyalty to the Union. They are considered citizens. They are respected as "our allies." It is believed in the North that a majority of the white people of the South are at heart the enemies of the Union. The advocates of negro suffrage daily grow stronger and more numerous. . . .

Now the radicalism of the North is actual, organic, and progressive. Recognize the fact. But if "governments derive their just powers from the consent of the governed"—if "taxation without representation is tyranny"—and "on these two commandments hang all the (Republican) law and the prophets"—then these propositions are as applicable to women as to negroes. . . .

The radicals demand suffrage for the black men on the ground named above. Very good. Say to them, as Mr. Cowan said to the advocates of negro male suffrage in the District, "Apply your principle! Give the suffrage to all men and women of mature age and sound mind, and we will accept it as the basis of State and National reconstruction."

Consider the result from the Southern standpoint. Your 4,000,000 of Southern white women will counterbalance your 4,000,000 of negro men and women, and thus the political supremacy of your white race will remain unchanged. . . .

But the propriety of your making the proposal lies deeper than any consideration of sectional expediency. If you must try the Republican experiment, try it fully and fairly. Since you are compelled to union with the North, remove every seed of future controversy. If you are to share the future government of your States with a race you deem naturally and hopelessly inferior, avert the social chaos, which seems to you so imminent, by utilizing the intelligence and patriotism of the wives and daughters of the South. Plant yourselves upon the logical Northern principle. Then no new demands can ever be made upon you. No future inroads of fanaticism can renew sectional discord.

The effect upon the North would be to revolutionize political parties. "Justice satisfies everybody." The negro, thus protected against oppression by possessing the ballot, would cease to be the prominent object of philanthropic interest. Northern distrust, disarmed by Southern magnanimity, would give place to the liveliest sentiments of confidence and regard. The great political desideratum would be attained. The negro question would be forever removed from the political arena. National parties would again crystallize upon legitimate questions of

National interest—questions of tariff, finance, and foreign relations. The disastrous conflict between Federal and State jurisdictions would cease. North and South, no longer hammer and anvil, would forget and forgive the past.

4. Elizabeth Cady Stanton Questions Abolitionist Support for Female Enfranchisement, 1868

Though many of the leading minds of this country have advocated woman's enfranchisement for the last twenty years, it has been more as an intellectual theory than a fact of life, hence none of our many friends were ready to help in the practical work of the last few months, neither in Kansas or the Constitutional Convention of New York. So far from giving us a helping hand, Republicans and Abolitionists, by their false philosophy—that the safety of the nation demands ignorance rather than education at the polls—have paralyzed the women themselves.

To what a depth of degradation must the women of this nation have fallen to be willing to stand aside, silent and indifferent spectators in the reconstruction of the nation, while all the lower stratas of manhood are to legislate in their interests, political, religious, educational, social and sanitary, moulding to their untutored will the institutions of a mighty continent. . . .

While leading Democrats have been thus favorably disposed, what have our best friends said when, for the first time since the agitation of the question [the enfranchisement of women], they have had an opportunity to frame their ideas into statutes to amend the constitutions of two States in the Union.

Charles Sumner, Horace Greeley, Gerrit Smith and Wendell Phillips, with one consent, bid the women of the nation stand aside and behold the salvation of the negro. Wendell Phillips says, "one idea for a generation," to come up in the order of their importance. First negro suffrage, then temperance, then the eight hour movement, then woman's suffrage. In 1958, three generations hence, thirty years to a generation, Phillips and Providence permitting, woman's suffrage will be in order. What an insult to the women who have labored thirty years for the emancipation of the slave, now when he is their political equal, to propose to lift him above their heads. Gerrit Smith, forgetting that our great American idea is "individual rights," in which abolitionists have ever based their strongest arguments for emancipation, says, this is the time to settle the rights of races; unless we do justice to the negro we shall bring down on ourselves another bloody revolution, another four years' war, but we have nothing to fear from woman, she will not revenge herself! . . .

Horace Greeley has advocated this cause for the last twenty years, but to-day it is too new, revolutionary for practical consideration. The enfranchisement of woman, revolutionizing, as it will, our political, religious, and social condition, is not a measure too radical and all-pervading to meet the moral necessities of this day and generation.

Why fear new things; all old things were once new. . . . We live to do new things! When Abraham Lincoln issued the proclamation of emancipation, it was a new thing. When the Republican party gave the ballot to the negro, it was a new thing, startling too, to the people of the South, very revolutionary to their institutions, but Mr. Greeley did not object to all this because it was new. . . .

And now, while men like these have used all their influence for the last four years, to paralyze every effort we have put forth to rouse the women of the nation, to demand their true position in the reconstruction, they triumphantly turn to us, and say the greatest barrier in the way of your demand is that "the women themselves do not wish to vote." What a libel on the intelligence of the women of the nineteenth century. What means the 12,000 petitions presented by John Stuart Mill in the British Parliament from the first women in England, demanding household suffrage? What means the late action in Kansas, 10,000 women petitioned there for the right of suffrage, and 9,000 votes at the last election was the answer. What means the agitation in every State in the Union? In the very hour when Horace Greeley brought in his adverse report in the Constitutional Convention of New York, at least twenty members rose in their places and presented petitions from every part of the State, demanding woman's suffrage. What means that eloquent speech of George W. Curtis in the Convention, but to show that the ablest minds in the State are ready for this onward step?

5. President Johnson Opposes Black Suffrage, 1867

It is manifestly and avowedly the object of these laws to confer upon negroes the privilege of voting and to disfranchise such a number of white citizens as will give the former a clear majority at all elections in the Southern States. This, to the minds of some persons, is so important that a violation of the Constitution is justified as a means of bringing it about. The morality is always false which excuses a wrong because it proposes to accomplish a desirable end. We are not permitted to do evil that good may come. But in this case the end itself is evil, as well as the means. The subjugation of the States to negro domination would be worse than the military despotism under which they are now suffering. It was believed beforehand that the people would endure any amount of military oppression for any length of time rather than degrade themselves by subjection to the negro race. Therefore they have been left without a choice. Negro suffrage was established by act of Congress, and the military officers were commanded to superintend the process of clothing the negro race with the political privileges torn from white men.

The blacks in the South are entitled to be well and humanely governed, and to have the protection of just laws for all their rights of person and property. If it were practicable at this time to give them a Government exclusively their own, under which they might manage their own affairs in their own way, it would become a grave question whether we ought to do so, or whether common humanity would not re-quire us to save them from themselves. But under the circumstances this is only a speculative point. It is not proposed merely that they shall govern themselves, but that they shall rule the white race, make and administer State laws, elect Presidents and members of Congress, and shape to a greater or less extent the future destiny of the whole country. Would such a trust and power be safe in such hands?

The peculiar qualities which should characterize any people who are fit to decide upon the management of public affairs for a great state have seldom been combined. It is the glory of white men to know that they have had these qualities in sufficient measure to build upon this continent a great political fabric and to preserve its stability for more than ninety years, while in every other part of the world all similar experiments have failed. But if anything can be proved by known facts, if all reasoning upon evidence is not abandoned, it must be acknowledged that in the progress of nations negroes have shown less capacity for government than any other race of people. No independent government of any form has ever been successful in their hands. On the contrary, wherever they have been left to their own devices they have shown a constant tendency to relapse into barbarism. In the Southern States, however, Congress has undertaken to confer upon them the privilege of the ballot. Just released from slavery, it may be doubted whether as a class they know more than their ancestors how to organize and regulate civil society.

6. Text of the Fourteenth Amendment, 1868

Section 1. All persons born or naturalized in the United States, and subject to the jurisdiction thereof, are citizens of the United States and of the State wherein they reside. No State shall make or enforce any law which shall abridge the privileges or immunities of citizens of the United States; nor shall any State deprive any person of life, liberty, or property, without due process of law; nor deny to any person within its jurisdiction the equal protection of the laws.

Section 2. Representatives shall be apportioned among the several States according to their respective numbers, counting the whole number of persons in each State, excluding Indians not taxed. But when the right to vote at any election for the choice of electors for President and Vice-President of the United States, Representatives in Congress, the executive and judicial officers of a State, or the members of the legislature thereof, is denied to any of the male inhabitants of such State, being twenty-one years of age, and citizens of the United States, or in any way abridged, except for participation in rebellion, or other crime, the basis of representation therein shall be reduced in the proportion which the number of such male citizens shall bear to the whole number of male citizens twenty-one years of age in such State.

Section 3. No person shall be a Senator or Representative in Congress, or elector of President and Vice-President, or hold any office, civil or military, under the United States or under any State, who, having previously taken an oath as a member of Congress, or as an officer of the United States, or as a member of any State legislature, or as an executive or judicial officer of any State, to support the Constitution of the United States, shall have engaged in insurrection or rebellion against the same, or given aid or comfort to the enemies thereof. But Congress may, by a vote of two-thirds of each house, remove such disability.

Section 4. The validity of the public debt of the United States, authorized by law, including debts incurred for payment of pensions and bounties for services in suppressing insurrection or rebellion, shall not be questioned. But neither the United States nor any State shall assume or pay any debt or obligation incurred in aid of insurrection or rebellion against the United States, or any claim for the loss or emancipation of any slave; but all such debts, obligations, and claims shall be held illegal and void.

Section 5. The Congress shall have power to enforce, by appropriate legislation, the provisions of this article.

Chapter 16: Document Set 1 References

1. Republican Carl Schurz Urges Black Suffrage, 1865
   Carl Schurz to Andrew Johnson, 1865, Senate Executive Document No. 2, 39th Cong., 1st Sess., p. 42.

2. George Downing and Frederick Douglass Argue the Case for Enfranchisement, 1866
   Interview with the President of the United States, Andrew Johnson, by a delegation of Negroes, headed by Frederick Douglass and George Downing, February 7, 1866.

3. Henry B. Blackwell Appeals to Racism in the Cause of Female Suffrage, 1867
   Henry B. Blackwell, "What the South Can Do: How the Southern States Can Make Themselves Masters of the Situation," 1867, from Elizabeth Cady Stanton *et al.*, *History of Women's Suffrage* (New York: Fowler and Wells, 1887), Vol. II, pp. 929–931.

4. Elizabeth Cady Stanton Questions Abolitionist Support for Female Enfranchisement, 1868
   Elizabeth Cady Stanton, "Who Are Our Friends?" *The Revolution*, 15 (January 1868).

5. President Johnson Opposes Black Suffrage, 1867
   Andrew Johnson, "Third Annual Message," December 3, 1867, James D. Richardson, ed., *A Compilation of the Messages and Papers of the Presidents, 1789–1908* (Washington, D.C.: Bureau of National Literature and Art, 1909), Vol. VI, pp. 564–565.

6. Text of the Fourteenth Amendment, 1868
   James Morton Smith and Paul L. Murphy, *Liberty and Justice: A Record of American Constitutional Development* (New York: Alfred A. Knopf, 1963), p. 253.

DOCUMENT SET 2
"Free at Last": The African American Response to Emancipation

As noted in Chapter 11, African American testimony from the Civil War and Reconstruction era presents special interpretive problems for the historian. Despite questions about the reliability of oral accounts, however, the words of freedmen provide a rich resource for the scholar willing to apply careful analytic rigor in their use. In this chapter, oral tradition is combined with contemporary records to provide insight on the black response to emancipation and the social/economic experience of the freedmen.

The central feature of these documents is their clear description of the freedmen's day-to-day social and economic life. Faced with the challenges and opportunities of freedom, blacks struggled to maintain dignity, initiative, and independence. As noted in your textbook, families were reunited, marriages legalized, education sought, and employment obtained as both black and white southerners worked at racial accommodation and economic adjustment. The following documents indicate that the transition was not easy.

As you analyze the evidence, pay special attention to the critical problem of the southern labor system. Using the textbook material as background, review the documents with an eye to the development of an economic system that would satisfy the conflicting goals of planters and freedmen. As you examine these materials, try to make a judgment on African American progress toward economic independence, as well as the implications of the new regime for planter interests.

Be alert to the immediate problems faced by African Americans following emancipation and the enactment of the Thirteenth Amendment. Try to identify the primary concerns of African Americans as they first experienced freedom. Note common responses to the social confusion resulting from the end of enslavement; in doing so, consider connections between white initiatives and the African American adjustment to the new social relationships.

Eventually, the extension of civil rights led to a white counterreaction in the form of vigilante-paramilitary activity after 1867. In interpreting the Ku Klux Klan, determine what the group's primary goals were.

As you reconstruct the African American response to liberation, be aware of the economic challenge and social uncertainty that pervaded the early Reconstruction years. What answers to the new questions surfaced after 1868? With what results?

Questions for Analysis

1. What do the documents suggest about the first reaction to liberation? How was the black family affected? Do you detect any pattern of response in the black and white accounts of the freedmen's initial actions? How would you explain the reaction that occurred?

2. What do the documents reveal about the economic impact of emancipation? How did African American goals and planter needs relate to one another? How would you account for conflicting objectives? What solution to the labor problem emerged? With what economic consequences?

3. What was the purpose of the black codes? What did they reveal about white perceptions of the outcome of the Civil War and emancipation?

4. In what ways do the documents clarify the origins and purposes of the Ku Klux Klan? How were its goals related to the African American response to freedom? What were the future implications of Klan activity? What did the Klan's efforts reveal about the constitutional guarantees discussed in Chapter 16, Document Set 1?

5. What impression do the documents leave with regard to the goals, functions, and results of Freedmen's Bureau activity? How does knowing the identity of the commentators help you understand the views expressed? Comparing the documentary evidence with your textbook's account of the bureau's efforts, how would you assess its work? What is the relationship between the social principle the bureau represented and the modern American social system?

1. The Louisiana Black Code, 1865

Sec. 1. *Be it ordained by the police jury of the parish of St. Landry,* That no negro shall be allowed to pass within the limits of said parish without special permit in writing from his employer. Whoever shall violate this provision shall pay a fine of two dollars and fifty cents, or in default thereof shall be forced to work four days on the public road, or suffer corporeal punishment as provided hereinafter. . . .

Sec. 3. . . . No negro shall be permitted to rent or keep a house within said parish. Any negro violating this provision shall be immediately ejected and compelled to find an employer; and any person who shall rent, or give the use of any house to any negro, in violation of this section, shall pay a fine of five dollars for each offence.

Sec. 4. . . . Every negro is required to be in the regular service of some white person, or former owner, who shall be held responsible for the conduct of said negro. But said employer or former owner may permit said negro to hire his own time by special permission in writing, which permission shall not extend over seven days at any one time. . . .

Sec. 5. . . . No public meeting or congregations of negroes shall be allowed within said parish after sunset; but such public meetings and congregations may be held between the hours of sunrise and sunset, by the special permission in writing of the captain of patrol, within whose beat such meetings shall take place. . . .

Sec. 6. . . . No negro shall be permitted to preach, exhort, or otherwise declaim to congregations of colored people, without a special permission in writing from the president of the police jury. . . .

Sec. 7. . . . No negro who is not in the military service shall be allowed to carry fire-arms, or any kind of weapons, within the parish, without the special written permission of his employers, approved and endorsed by the nearest and most convenient chief of patrol. . . .

Sec. 8. . . . No negro shall sell, barter, or exchange any articles of merchandise or traffic within said parish without the special written permission of his employer, specifying the article of sale, barter or traffic. . . .

Sec. 9. . . . Any negro found drunk within the said parish shall pay a fine of five dollars, or in default thereof work five days on the public road, or suffer corporeal punishment as hereinafter provided.

Sec. 11. . . . It shall be the duty of every citizen to act as a police officer for the detection of offences and the apprehension of offenders, who shall be immediately handed over to the proper captain or chief of patrol.

2. A Planter's Wife Recalls the African American Response to Emancipation, 1865

After Emancipation, Lewis remained with us many years. His home was only a short distance from our home. He cultivated a farm successfully, and soon had acquired not only the necessaries of life, but some luxuries. He had a pair of nice horses, a buggy and wagon, and other things, and lived well; but he had never known freedom entirely without Mars' Henry's supervision. One day he came to the conclusion that he would move away and enjoy freedom to its fullest extent. He came to see Mr. Clayton in the fall to say something about it. He seemed embarrassed when Mr. Clayton addressed him: "Lewis, what is it you want?" "Well, Mars' Henry, I want to move away and feel ontirely free and see whut I cen do by mysef. You has been kind to me and I has done well, but I want to go anyhow." Mr. Clayton said,

"Very well, Lewis, that is all right, move when you please; but when you leave, nail up the door of your house and leave it until you want to come back. No one shall go into it."

Lewis and his brother, Ned, rented a farm some miles beyond Clayton, moved, and we heard no more of them until the next fall, when Lewis made his appearance, very much dejected. Mr. Clayton said, "How are you, Lewis? How are you getting on?" "Bad, Mars' Henry. I have come to ask ef I cen go into my house again."

Lewis and Ned had hired hands, gotten a merchant to furnish them, and lost almost everything they had started out with. Lewis moved back, and has been loth to leave the Claytons since, and is now with us, an old man.

3. African American Testimony on the Aftermath of Enslavement, 1866

Question. Where do you live?

Answer. Hampton, Virginia. . . .

Question. How do the rebels down there, about Hampton, treat the colored people?

Answer. The returned rebels express a desire to get along in peace if they can. There have been a few outrages out upon the roadside there. One of the returned Union colored soldiers was met out there and beaten very much.

Question. By whom was he beaten?

Answer. It was said they were rebels; they had on Union overcoats, but they were not United States soldiers. Occasionally we hear of an outrage of that kind, but there are none in the little village where I live.

Question. What appears to be the feeling generally of the returned rebels towards the freedmen; is it kind or unkind?

Answer. Well, the feeling that they manifest as a general thing is kind, so far as I have heard.

Question. Are they willing to pay the freedmen fair wages for their work?

Answer. No, sir; they are not willing to pay the freedmen more than from five to eight dollars a month.

Question. Do you think that their labor is worth more than that generally?

Answer. I do, sir; because, just at this time, everything is very dear, and I do not see how people can live and support their families on those wages.

Question. State whether the black people down there are anxious to go to school?

Answer. Yes, sir; they are anxious to go to school; we have schools there every day that are very well filled; and we have night schools that are very well attended, both by children and aged people; they manifest a great desire for education. . . .

Question. How do you feel about leaving the State of Virginia and going off and residing as a community somewhere else?

Answer. They do not wish to leave and go anywhere else unless they are certain that the locality where they are going is healthy and that they can get along.

Question. Are they not willing to be sent back to Africa?

Answer. No, sir.

Question. Why not?

Answer. They say that they have lived here all their days, and there were stringent laws made to keep them here; and that if they could live here contented as slaves, they can live here when free.

Question. Do you not think that to be a very absurd notion?

Answer. No, sir; if we can get lands here and can work and support ourselves, I do not see why we should go to any place that we do not want to go to.

Question. If you should stay here, is there not danger that the whites and blacks would intermarry and amalgamate?

Answer. I do not think there is any more danger now than there was when slavery existed. At that time there was a good deal of amalgamation.

4. James D. B. DeBow Expresses Southern Skepticism of the Freedmen's Bureau, 1866

Question. What is your opinion of the necessity or utility of the Freedmen's Bureau, or of any agency of that kind?

Answer. I think if the whole regulation of the negroes, or freedmen, were left to the people of the communities in which they live, it will be administered for the best interest of the negroes as well as of the white men. I think there is a kindly feeling on the part of the planters towards the freedmen. They are not held at all responsible for anything that has happened. They are looked upon as the innocent cause. In talking with a number of planters, I remember some of them telling me they were succeeding very well with their freedmen, having got a preacher to preach to them and a teacher to teach them, believing it was for the interest of the planter to make the negro feel reconciled; for, to lose his services as a laborer for even a few months would be very disastrous. The sentiment prevailing is, that it is for the interest of the employer to teach the negro, to educate his children, to provide a preacher for him, and to attend to his physical wants. And I may say I have not seen any exception to that feeling in the south. Leave the people to themselves, and they will manage very well. The Freedmen's Bureau, or any agency to interfere between the freedman and his former master, is only productive of mischief. There are constant appeals from one to the other and continual annoyances. It has a tendency to create dissatisfaction and disaffection on the part of the laborer, and is in every respect in its result most unfavorable to the system of industry that is now being organized under the new order of things in the south. . . .

Question. What is your opinion as to the relative advantages . . . of the present system of free labor, as compared with that of slavery as it heretofore existed in this country?

Answer. If the negro would work, the present system is much cheaper. If we can get the same amount of labor from the same persons, there is no doubt of the result in respect to *economy*. Whether the same

amount of labor can be obtained, it is too soon yet to decide. We must allow one summer to pass first. They are working now very well on the plantations. That is the general testimony. The negro women are not disposed to field work as they formerly were, and I think there will be less work from them in the future than there has been in the past. The men are rather inclined to get their wives into other employment, and I think that will be the constant tendency, just as it is with the whites. Therefore, the real number of agricultural laborers will be reduced. I have no idea the efficiency of those who work will be increased. If we can only keep up their efficiency to the standard before the war, it will be better for the south, without doubt, upon the mere money question, because it is cheaper to hire the negro than to own him. Now a plantation can be worked without any outlay of capital by hiring the negro and hiring the plantation. . . .

Question. What arrangements are generally made among the landholders and the black laborers in the south?

Answer. I think they generally get wages. A great many persons, however, think it better to give them an interest in the crops. That is getting to be very common.

5. African American Recollections of Freedom's Impact: Mingo White and Charles Davenport

Mingo White

Interviewed at Burleson, Alabama
Interviewed by Levi D. Shelby, Jr.
Age when interviewed: 85–90

De day dat we got news dat we was free, Mr. White called us niggers to the house. He said: "You are all free, just as free as I am. Now go and get yourself somewhere to stick your heads."

Just as soon as he say dat, my mammy hollered out: "Dat's 'nough for a yearlin'." She struck out across de field to Mr. Lee Osborn's to get a place for me and her to stay. He paid us seventy-five cents a day, fifty cents to her and two bits for me. He gave us our dinner along with de wages. After de crop was gathered for that year, me and my mammy cut and hauled wood for Mr. Osborn. Us left Mr. Osborn dat fall and went to Mr. John Rawlins. Us made a sharecrop with him. Us'd pick two rows of cotton and he'd pick two rows. Us'd pull two rows of corn and he'd pull two rows of corn. He furnished us with rations and a place to stay. Us'd sell our cotton and open corn and pay Mr. John

Rawlins for feedin' us. Den we moved with Mr. Hugh Nelson and made a sharecrop with him. We kept movin' and makin' sharecrops till us saved up 'nough money to rent us a place and make a crop for ourselves.

Us did right well at dis until de Ku Klux got so bad, us had to move back with Mr. Nelson for protection. De mens that took us in was Union men. Dey lived here in the South but dey taken us part in de slave business. De Ku Klux threat to whip Mr. Nelson, 'cause he took up for de niggers. Heap of nights we would hear of de Ku Klux comin' and leave home. Sometimes us was scared not to go and scared to go away from home.

One day I borrowed a gun from Ed Davis to go squirrel huntin'. When I taken de gun back I didn't unload it like I always been doin'. Dat night de Ku Klux called on Ed to whip him. When dey told him to open de door, he heard one of 'em say, "Shoot him time he gets de door open." "Well," he says to 'em, "Wait till I can light de lamp." Den he got de gun what I had left loaded, got down on his knees and stuck it through a log and pulld de trigger. He hit Newt Dobbs in de stomach and kilt him.

He couldn't stay round Burleson any more, so he come to Mr. Nelson and got 'nough money to get to Pine Bluff, Arkansas. The Ku Klux got bad sure 'nough den and went to killin' niggers and white folks, too.

Charles Davenport

Interviewed at Natchez, Mississippi
Interviewed by Edith Wyatt Moore
Age at interview: About 100

Like all de fool niggers o' dat time I was right smart bit by de freedom bug for awhile. It sounded powerful nice to be told: "You don't have to chop cotton no more. You can throw dat hoe down and go fishin' whensoever de notion strikes you. And you can roam 'round at night and court gals just as late as you please. Ain't no marster gwine to say to you, "Charlie, you's got to be back when de clock strikes nine."

I was fool 'nough to believe all dat kind o' stuff. But to tell de honest truth, most o' us didn't know ourselfs no better off. Freedom meant us could leave where us'd been born and bred, but it meant, too, dat us had to scratch for us ownselfs. Dem what left de old plantation seemed so all fired glad to get back dat I made up my mind to stay put. I stayed right with my white folks as long as I could.

My white folks talked plain to me. Dey say real sadlike, "Charlie, you's been a dependence, but now you can go if you is so desirous. But if you wants to stay with us you can sharecrop. Dey's a house for you and wood to keep you warm and a mule to work. We ain't got much cash, but dey's de land and you can count on havin' plenty o' victuals. Do just as you please."

When I looked at my marster and knowed he needed me, I pleased to stay. My marster never forced me to do nary thing about it. . . .

Lord! Lord! I knows about de Kloo Kluxes. I knows a-plenty. Dey was sure 'nough devils a-walkin' de earth a-seekin' what dey could devour. Dey larruped de hide off de uppity niggers an' drove de white trash back where dey belonged.

Us niggers didn't have no secret meetin's. All us had was church meetin's in arbors out in de woods. De preachers would exhort us dat us was de chillen o' Israel in de wilderness an' de Lord done sent us to take dis land o' milk and honey. But how us gwine-a take land what's already been took?

I sure ain't never heard about no plantations bein' divided up, neither. I heard a lot o' yaller niggers spoutin' off how dey was gwine-a take over de white folks' land for back wages. Dem bucks just took all dey wages out in talk. 'Cause I ain't never seen no land divided up yet.

In dem days nobody but niggers and "shawl-strap" folks voted. Quality folks didn't have nothin' to do with such truck. If dey hada wanted to de Yankees wouldn'ta let 'em. My old marster didn't vote and if anybody knowed what was what he did. Sense didn't count in dem days. It was powerful ticklish times and I let votin' alone. . . . [O]ne night a bunch o' uppity niggers went to a entertainment in Memorial Hall. Dey dressed deyselfs fit to kill and walked down de aisle and took seats in de very front. But just about time dey got good set down, de curtain dropped and de white folks rose up without a-sayin' a word. Dey marched out de buildin' with dey chins up and left dem niggers a-sittin' in a empty hall.

Dat's de way it happen every time a nigger tried to get too uppity. Dat night after de breakin' up o' dat entertainment, de Kloo Kluxes rode through de land. I heard dey grabbed every nigger what walked down dat aisle, but I ain't heard yet what dey done with 'em.

6. A Freedman Recalls a Visit from the Ku Klux Klan, 1871

They came to my door and they said "Hey!" I was asleep. They called, "Hey, hey!" My wife says, "Lewis, listen." . . ."What are you doing there?" I says; and they said, "By Christ, come out; I will

show you what I am doing." . . . and I got up and sat on the bed, with my legs hanging out, and peeped out. . . . They says, "Lewis, by Christ, arn't you going to get up and open the door?" . . . I spoke and said, "What do you want; do you want to whip me? I have done nothing to be whipped." . . . Says he, "How did you vote?" I says, "I voted the radical ticket." "You has, sir?" he says. I says, "Yes, sir." "Well, by Christ," says he, "Ain't you had no instruction?" I says, "I can't read, and I can't write, and I can't much more than spell." . . . I says, "How can a black man get along without there is some white gentleman or other with them? We go by instructions. We don't know nothing much." "O, by Christ," says he, "you radicals go side by side with one another, and by Christ us democrats go side and side with one another." I says, "I can't help that." . . . He says . . ."Get in the road and march," and in the road I went. They took me up the road pretty near to the edge of the woods. . . . Says he, "Off with your shirt." I says, "What do you all want to whip me for; what have I done?" "By Christ," he says, "Off with your shirt; if you don't

you shall go dead.["] . . . He says, "Now Lewis, by Christ, you get down on your knees." I says, "It is hard to get down on my knees and take a whipping for nothing." Then I dropped down. He says, "By Christ, don't you get up until we get done with you." They set to work on me and hit me ten or fifteen licks pretty keen, and I raised up. "Get down," he says; "if you ever raise up again you'll go dead before we quit you." Down I went again, and I staid down until they got done whipping me. Says he, "Now, by Christ, you must promise you will vote the democratic ticket?" I says, "I don't know how I will vote; it looks hard when a body thinks this way and that way to take a beating." . . . "You must promise to vote the democratic ticket, or you go dead before we leave you," he says. Then I studied and studied. They gathered right close up around me. "Come out with it—come, out with it, by Christ." Then I says, "Yes, sir, I reckon so."

Chapter 16:
Document Set 2 References

1. The Louisiana Black Code, 1865
   Senate Executive Document No. 2, 39th Cong., 1st Sess., p. 93.

2. A Planter's Wife Recalls the African American Response to Emancipation, 1865
   Mrs. Victoria V. Clayton, *White and Black Under the Old Regime* (Milwaukee: Young Churchman Company, 1899), pp. 172–174.

3. African American Testimony on the Aftermath of Enslavement, 1866
   Report of the Joint Committee on Reconstruction (Washington, D.C.: Government Printing Office, 1866), Part II, pp. 55–56.

4. James D. B. DeBow Expresses Southern Skepticism of the Freedmen's Bureau, 1866
   Report of the Joint Committee, Part IV, pp. 132–135.

5. African American Recollections of Freedom's Impact: Mingo White and Charles Davenport
   Federal Writers' Project, Slave Narratives, "A Folk History of Slavery in the United States from Interviews with Former Slaves" (Washington, D.C.: Typewritten Records Prepared by the Federal Writers' Project, 1941).

6. A Freedman Recalls a Visit from the Ku Klux Klan, 1871
   Report to the Joint Select Committee to Inquire into the Condition of Affairs in the Late Insurrectionary States (Washington, D.C.: Government Printing Office, 1872), Vol. I, p. 436.

DOCUMENT SET 3
Redemption and Salvation: The Reconstruction Experiment Abandoned

During President Grant's second term, the Republican hold on southern state governments weakened rapidly. Your textbook notes that the dramatic revival of the Democratic party coincided with an increase in violence, vigilante activity, and outright voter fraud in the South. Through a combination of economic pressure and voter intimidation, Democratic party leaders succeeded in sufficiently suppressing the African American vote to produce a revolution at the ballot box.

The term *Redemption* was commonly used by southern whites to denote the restoration of Democratic control of state governments in the South. As you examine the documents in this set, think about the emotional impact of Democratic rhetoric in these hotly contested political races. Consider the symbolic power of the concepts of redemption and salvation, especially as the foundation stones of southern folklore. As you review the documents, ask yourself what was saved and what was lost in the Reconstruction settlement. Who were the winners and who were the losers in the contest for social control in the South?

The focal point in these documents is the time-worn issue of ends and means. Concentrate on the devices resorted to by southern whites in the drive to reestablish Democratic party control. Evaluate the justifications offered for using extreme means to achieve the desired end. How did southern explanations affect future generations of historians as they interpreted the process of Redemption?

Beyond direct intimidation and vote fraud, deeper long-term social forces and institutional changes were occurring that sealed the fate of African-American citizens for nearly a century. While it seemed a short-run compromise, the crop-lien/sharecrop system was to shackle them to the land and condemn them to a position of long-term dependency. Probe the documents for indications of the economic system's impact on African American prospects for political participation and social equality.

As a complement to economic pressure, other methods of ensuring effective social control were evident in the post-Reconstruction South. Examine the words of the militant Ida B. Wells to gain a clearer understanding of the southern social system of the late nineteenth century. As you reflect upon the words of both Wells and Douglass, determine what the Redemption settlement meant for the future of a biracial society in America.

Questions for Analysis

1. Define the word *redemption.* What do the documents suggest concerning white southerners' reasons for using this term as they did in the 1870s?

2. What do the documents reveal about the formal and informal techniques used to reestablish white social control in the post-Reconstruction South?

3. How do the documents clarify the relationship between economic and political power in the South? In what ways do the documents provide evidence of a readjustment of the regional economy to normal conditions? What was the significance of the economic settlement for the political future of the African-American population?

4. What was the African-American response to Redemption and to the new political conditions and restraints under which they lived? What was the meaning of Ida B. Wells's reference to a "red record"? Why do you think Wells eventually chose to move out of her native South? What do her writings reveal about the unique aspects of the southern social system?

1. The Atlanta *News* Advocates Violence to Redeem the South, 1874

Let there be White Leagues formed in every town, village and hamlet of the South, and let us organize for the great struggle which seems inevitable. If the October elections which are to be held at the North are favorable to the radicals, the time will have arrived for us to prepare for the very worst. The radicalism of the republican party must be met by the radicalism of white men. We have no war to make against the United States Government, but against the republican party our hate must be unquenchable, our war interminable and merciless. Fast fleeting away is the day of wordy protests and idle appeals to the magnanimity of the republican party. By brute force they are endeavoring to force us into acquiescence to their hideous programme. We have submitted long enough to indignities, and it is time to meet brute-force with brute-force. Every Southern State should swarm with White Leagues, and we should stand ready to act the moment Grant signs the civil-rights bill. It will not do to wait till radicalism has fettered us to the car of social equality before we make an effort to resist it. The signing of the bill will be a declaration of war against the southern whites. It is our duty to ourselves, it is our duty to our children, it is our duty to the white race whose prowess subdued the wilderness of this continent, whose civilization filled it with cities and towns and villages, whose mind gave it power and grandeur, and whose labor imparted to it prosperity, and whose love made peace and happiness dwell within its homes, to take the gage of battle the moment it is thrown down. If the white democrats of the North are men, they will not stand idly by and see us borne down by northern radicals and half-barbarous negroes. But no matter what they may do, it is time for us to organize. We have been temporizing long enough. Let northern radicals understand that military supervision of southern elections and the civil-rights bill mean war, that war means bloodshed, and that we are terribly in earnest, and even they, fanatical as they are, may retrace their steps before it is too late.

2. Senator Blanche K. Bruce Alleges Fraud and Violence in Mississippi, 1876

MR. BRUCE: The conduct of the late election in Mississippi affected not merely the fortunes of partisans—as the same were necessarily involved in the defeat or success of the respective parties to the contest—but put in question and jeopardy the sacred rights of the citizen; and the investigation contemplated in the pending resolution has for its object not the determination of the question whether the offices shall be held and the public affairs of that State be administered by democrats or republicans, but the higher and more important end, the protection in all their purity and significance of the political rights of the people and the free institutions of the country. . . .

The truth of the allegations relative to fraud and violence is strongly suggested by the very success claimed by the democracy. In 1873 the republicans carried the State by 20,000 majority; in November last the opposition claimed to have carried it by 30,000; thus a democratic gain of more than 50,000. Now, by what miraculous or extraordinary interposition was this brought about? . . . [S]uch a change of front is unnatural. . . .

3. South Carolina Governor D. H. Chamberlain Attacks President Hayes's Betrayal of Southern Republicans, 1877

What is the President's Southern policy? In point of physical or external fact, it consists in withdrawing the military forces of the United States from the points in South Carolina and Louisiana where they had been previously stationed for the protection and support of the lawful Governments of those States.

In point of immediate, foreseen, and intended consequence, it consists in the overthrow and destruction of those State Governments, and the substitution in their stead of certain other organizations called State Governments.

In point of actual present results, it consists in the abandonment of Southern Republicans, and especially the colored race, to the control and rule not only of the Democratic party, but of that class at the South which regarded slavery as a Divine Institution, which waged four years of destructive war for its perpetuation, which steadily opposed citizenship and suffrage for the negro—in a word, a class whose traditions, principles, and history are opposed to every step and feature of what Republicans call our national progress since 1860.

In point of general political and moral significance it consists in the proclamation to the country and the world that the will of the majority of the voters of a State, lawfully and regularly expressed, is no longer the ruling power in our States, and that the constitutional guaranty to every State in this Union of a republican form of government and of protection against domestic violence, is henceforth ineffectual and worthless.

4. A Texas Shares Contract Creates the Structure for Economic Bondage, ca. 1860s

Said _____ of the first part furthermore agrees to furnish the said Freedmen of the second part with good and sufficient quarters, _____ wholesome food, fuel, and such medical treatment as can be rendered by the person superintending the place. Said *J C Mitchell* of the 1st part in consideration of the faithful discharge of the duties assumed by the parties of the second part, does hereby agree to furnish *the freedmen* the necessary tools and implements for the cultivation of the land, and allow said Freedmen *one third* interest in the crops raised on said *plantation* by their labor. It is also mutually agreed that ten hours shall constitute a day's work, and if any labor in excess of ten hours per day is rendered it shall be paid for as extra labor. Said parties of the second part do furthermore agree to do all necessary work on Sundays or at night when it is for the protection of plantation or crops against destruction by storms, floods, fire or frost, provided always that such service shall be paid for as extra labor; extra labor to be paid for at the rate of one day's labor and one-half rations extra for each six hours work. Provided that our employer failing to comply with any part of this agreement, this contract shall be annulled; also provided, that should any of the parties of the second part leave said *plantation* without proper authority, or engage elsewhere, or neglect or refuse to work as herein agreed, they or any part of them so offending shall be liable to be discharged and forfeit all wages due up to that time.

Also Provided, that this Contract shall constitute the first lien upon all crops raised by the labor of said parties of the Second part.

Said J C Mitchell shall have power to make such rules and regulations necessary to the management of the plantation as are not inconsistent with the term of this contract; all lost time to [be] deducted from the one third interest in crop to the freedmen.

5. Frederick Douglass Assesses the Post-Reconstruction Economic Settlement, 1883

No more crafty and effective device for defrauding the southern laborers could be adopted than the one that substitutes orders upon shopkeepers for currency in payment of wages. It has the merit of a show of honesty, while it puts the laborer completely at the mercy of the land-owner and the shopkeeper. He is between the upper and the nether millstones, and is hence ground to dust. It gives the shopkeeper a customer who can trade with no other storekeeper, and thus leaves the latter no motive for fair dealing except his own moral sense, which is never too strong. While the laborer holding the orders is tempted by their worthlessness, as a circulating medium, to get rid of them at any sacrifice, and hence is led into extravagance and consequent destitution.

The merchant puts him off with his poorest commodities at highest prices, and can say to him take these or nothing. Worse still. By this means the la-borer is brought into debt, and hence is kept always in the power of the land-owner. When this system is not pursued and land is rented to the freedman, he is charged more for the use of an acre of land for a single year than the land would bring in the market if offered for sale. On such a system of fraud and wrong one might well invoke a bolt from heaven—red with uncommon wrath.

It is said if the colored people do not like the conditions upon which their labor is demanded and secured, let them leave and go elsewhere. A more heartless suggestion never emanated from an oppressor. Having for years paid them in shop orders, utterly worthless outside the shop to which they are directed, without a dollar in their pockets, brought by this crafty process into bondage to the land-owners, who can and would arrest them if they should attempt to leave when they are told to go.

6. Ida B. Wells Denounces Southern Social Control, 1895

Emancipation came and the vested interest of the white man in the Negro's body were lost. The white man had no right to scourge the emancipated Negro, still less has he a right to kill him. But the southern white people had been educated so long in that school of practice, in which might makes right, that they disdained to draw strict lines of action in dealing with the Negro. In slave times the Negro was kept subservient and submissive by the frequency and severity of the scourging, but, with freedom, a new system of intimidation came into vogue; the Negro was not only whipped and scourged; he was killed.

Not all nor nearly all of the murders done by white men, during the past thirty years in the South, have come to light, but the statistics as gathered and preserved by white men, and which have not been questioned, show that during these years more than ten thousand Negroes have been killed in cold blood, without the formality of judicial trial and legal execution. . . .

The first excuse given to the civilized world for the murder of unoffending Negroes was the necessity of the white man to repress and stamp out alleged "race riots." . . .

Then came the second excuse, which had its birth during the turbulent times of reconstruction. By an amendment to the Constitution the Negro was given the right of franchise, and, theoretically at least, his ballot became his invaluable emblem of citizenship. In a government "of the people, for the people, and by the people," the Negro's vote became an important factor in all matters of state and national politics. But this did not last long. The southern white man would not consider that the Negro had any right which a white man was bound to respect, and the idea of a republican form of government in the southern states grew into general contempt. It was maintained that "This is a white man's government," and regardless of numbers the white man should rule. "No Negro domination" became the new legend on the sanguinary banner of the sunny South, and under it rode the Ku Klux Klan, the Regulators, and the lawless mobs, which for any cause chose to murder one man or a dozen as suited their purpose best. . . .

But it was a bootless strife for colored people. The government which had made the Negro a citizen found itself unable to protect him. It gave him the right to vote, but denied him the protection which should have maintained that right. Scourged from his home; hunted through the swamps; hung by midnight raiders, and openly murdered in the light of day, the Negro clung to his right of franchise with a heroism which would have wrung admiration from the hearts of savages. He believed that in that small white ballot there was a subtle something which stood for manhood as well as citizenship, and thousands of brave black men went to their graves, exemplifying the one by dying for the other.

The white man's victory soon became complete by fraud, violence, intimidation and murder. The franchise vouchsafed to the Negro grew to be a "barren ideality," and regardless of numbers, the colored people found themselves voiceless in the councils of those whose duty it was to rule. With no longer the fear of "Negro Domination" before their eyes, the white man's second excuse became valueless. With the Southern governments all subverted and the Negro actually eliminated from all participation in state and national elections, there could be no longer an excuse for killing Negroes to prevent "Negro Domination."

Brutality still continued; Negroes were whipped, scourged, exiled, shot and hung whenever and wherever it pleased the white man so to treat them, and as the civilized world with increasing persistency held the white people of the South to account for its outlawry, the murderers invented the third excuse—that Negroes had to be killed to avenge their assaults upon women. There could be framed no possible excuse more harmful to the Negro and more unanswerable if true in its sufficiency for the white man. . . .

A word as to the charge itself. In considering the third reason assigned by the Southern white people for the butchery of blacks, the question must be asked, what the white man means when he charges the black man with rape. Does he mean the crime which the statutes of the civilized states describe as such? Not by any means. With the Southern white man, any mesalliance existing between a white woman and a colored man is a sufficient foundation for the charge of rape. The Southern white man says that it is impossible for a voluntary alliance to exist between a white woman and a colored man, and therefore, the fact of an alliance is a proof of force. In numerous instances where colored men have been lynched on the charge of rape, it was positively known at the time of lynching, and indisputably proven after the victim's death, that the relationship sustained between the man and woman was voluntary and clandestine, and that in no court of law could even the charge of assault have been successfully maintained. . . .

It is his regret, that, in his own defense, [the black] must disclose to the world that degree of dehumanizing brutality which fixes upon America the blot of a national crime. Whatever faults and failings other nations may have in their dealings with their own subjects or with other people, no other civilized nation stands condemned before the world with a series of crimes so peculiarly national. It becomes a painful duty of the Negro to reproduce a record which shows that a large portion of the American people avow anarchy, condone murder and defy the contempt of civilization.

7. The Economic Consequences of Redemption in Statistical Terms, 1880–1900

A. Percentage of Land in Farms Operated by Black Farmers, 1910

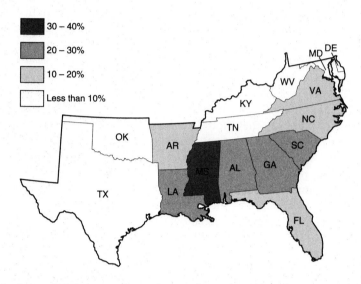

Source: U.S. Census Bureau, Bulletin 129, *Negroes in the U.S.* (Washington, D.C.: Government Printing Office, 1915).

B. Percentage of Farms Operated by Black Farmers, 1910

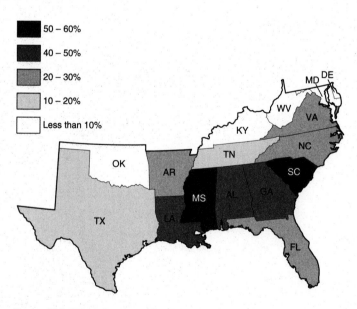

Source: U.S. Census Bureau, Bulletin 129.

C. Farms, by Color and Tenure of Operator, and Acreage and Value, by Tenure of Operator: 1880 to 1900

	Number of Farms		
Color and Tenure of Operator	1900	1890	1880
South	**2,620,391**	**1,836,372**	**1,531,077**
Full Owner	1,237,114		
Part Owner	133,368	1,130,029	977,229
Manager	18,765		
Tenant	1,231,144	706,343	553,848
White	1,879,721		
Full Owner	1,078,635		
Part Owner	105,171		
Manager	17,172		
Tenant	678,743		
Nonwhite	740,670		
Full Owner	158,479		
Part Owner	28,197		
Manager	1,593		
Tenant	552,401		

Source: *Statistical History of the United States* (Stamford, CT: Fairfield Publishers, Inc., 1965), p. 278.

D. Value of Output per Worker and Value of Output per Family Member on Family Farms, by Type of Farm, Tenure, and Race of Farm Operator, Cotton South: 1880

	Value of Output Per Worker($)		Value of Output Per Family Member ($)	
Type of Farm	White	Black	White	Black
Small Family Farms	255.74	159.62	81.35	63.57
Owned	283.70	155.78	88.12	58.11
Tenanted	212.47	160.40	70.87	64.67
Rented	260.19	159.51	88.02	67.63
Sharecropped	200.69	160.81	66.64	63.30
Other Small Farms	262.78	153.79	143.73	127.94
Owned	262.29		149.18	
Tenanted	264.17	147.23	127.93	117.65

Source: Roger L. Ransom and Richard Sutch, *One Kind of Freedom: The Economic Consequences of Emancipation* (Cambridge University Press, 1977), p. 184.

E. Number of Acres of Cropland per Worker on Family Farms, by Race and Tenure, Cotton South: 1880

Form of Tenure	Acres of Crops per Worker	
	White	Black
Owner-Operated Farms	12.5	6.6
Rented Farms	14.5	7.3
Sharecropped Farms	11.7	8.0
All Farms	12.4	7.5

Source: Roger L. Ransom and Richard Sutch, *One Kind of Freedom: The Economic Consequences of Emancipation* (Cambridge University Press, 1977), p. 184.

F. White and Black Proprietorships in Thirty-one Georgian Counties, 1873–1902

Year	White		Black	
	Number	Average Acreage	Number	Average Acreage
1873	17,255	388.6	514	113.9
1880	20,725	339.5	1,865	93.8
1890	24,058	293.7	3,510	71.0
1902	26,957	264.8	5,221	64.3

Source: Enoch Banks, *The Economics of Land Tenure in Georgia* (New York: Columbia University Press, 1905), Appendix, Table B.

Chapter 16:
Document Set 3 References

1. The Atlanta *News* Advocates Violence to Redeem the South, 1874
   Atlanta *News*, September 10, 1874.

2. Senator Blanche K. Bruce Alleges Fraud and Violence in Mississippi, 1876
   Congressional Record, 44th Cong., 1st Sess., March 31, 1876, pp. 2100–2104.

3. South Carolina Governor D. H. Chamberlain Attacks President Hayes's Betrayal of Southern Republicans, 1877
   D. H. Chamberlain, Speech, July 4, 1877, W. A. Allen, *Governor Chamberlain's Administration in South Carolina*, p. 508, in Walter L. Fleming, ed., *Documentary History of Reconstruction*, Vol. 2 (New York: McGraw-Hill, 1966), pp. 387–388.

4. A Texas Shares Contract Creates the Structure for Economic Bondage, ca. 1860s
   "Records of the Assistant Commissioner for the State of Texas," Bureau of Refugees, Freedmen, and Abandoned Lands, Record Group 105, National Archives, Washington, D.C.

5. Frederick Douglass Assesses the Post-Reconstruction Economic Settlement, 1883
   Frederick Douglass, "Address to the People of the United States," delivered at Convention of Colored Men, Louisville, September 24, 1883.

6. Ida B. Wells Denounces Southern Social Control, 1895
   Ida B. Wells, *A Red Record* (Chicago: Privately Published, 1895), pp. 7–8, 9–10, 14–15.

7. The Economic Consequences of Redemption in Statistical Terms, 1880–1900
   A. Percentage of Land in Farms Operated by Black Farmers, 1910, U.S. Census Bureau, Bulletin 129, *Negroes in the U.S.* (Washington, D.C.: Government Printing Office, 1915).
   B. Percentage of Farms Operated by Black Farmers, 1910, U.S. Census Bureau, Bulletin 129.
   C. Farms, by Color and Tenure of Operator, and Acreage and Value, by Tenure of Operator: 1880 to 1900, in *Statistical History of the United States* (Stamford, CT: Fairfield Publishers, Inc., 1965), p. 278.
   D. Value of Output per Worker and Value of Output per Family Member on Family Farms, by Type of Farm, Tenure, and Race of Farm Operator, Cotton South: 1880, Roger L. Ransom and Richard Sutch, *One Kind of Freedom: The Economic Consequences of Emancipation* (Cambridge: Cambridge University Press, 1977), p. 184.
   E. Number of Acres of Cropland per Worker on Family Farms, by Race and Tenure, Cotton South: 1880, in Ransom and Sutch, p. 184.
   F. White and Black Proprietorships in Thirty-one Georgian Counties, 1873–1902, in Enoch Banks, *The Economics of Land Tenure in Georgia* (New York: Columbia University Press, 1905), Appendix, Table B.

Chapter 16:
Document Set 3 Credits